Studies in Adolescence

STUDIES IN ADOLESCENCE

Selected and edited by

ROBERT E. GRINDER
University of Wisconsin

THE MACMILLAN COMPANY, *New York*
COLLIER-MACMILLAN LIMITED, *London*

Library of Congress catalog card number: 63–14190

THE MACMILLAN COMPANY, NEW YORK
COLLIER-MACMILLAN CANADA, LTD., TORONTO, ONTARIO
Divisions of The Crowell-Collier Publishing Company

Printed in the United States of America

Introduction

Studies in Adolescence has been compiled with the aim of introducing students to a series of exploratory investigations concerning the nature of adolescence. The book brings together current, substantive studies, of both a theoretical and empirical nature. On the whole, the hypotheses offered and the findings presented stem from objective, behavioral analyses rather than clinical or case study methods. In addition to contributing to an understanding of adolescence, the selected papers have another significant feature in common: all are highly provocative, stimulating treatises that raise as many questions as they answer. This is as it should be, for the psychology of adolescence while being one of the more ancient domains of psychology is indeed one of its least charted. Therefore, the student of adolescent behavior who searches for definitive conclusions in this volume will eventually forsake its pages in disappointment. If he should seek, however, perspective, insight, and information as bases for his hypotheses and his appraisals, he will swiftly realize his expectations.

Two general assumptions furnish the rationale for the selection of papers that are included in this volume. First, it is assumed that with the advent of adolescence, persons and institutions of society-at-large become increasingly important as agents of socialization while parents and family diminish in status and influence. Second, it is assumed that the adolescent must extinguish many childhood habits and roles as he simultaneously masters several new patterns of behavior, which must be appropriate not only for his sex and age but also for his apprenticeship of the adult positions that he will eventually occupy. Hence, a study of development during adolescence necessitates an analysis of theory and research from several branches of the social sciences, especially psychology, sociology, and anthropology, and a focus upon the specific developmental, sociocultural, familial, peer, and school issues affecting the socialization process.

Social scientists have long affirmed that cultural conditions affect social-

v

ization during adolescence; nonetheless, in the past half-century, viewpoints about the effect of this influence have changed markedly. The papers in Part One, which draw both upon historical precedents and contemporary trends, are presented specifically to acquaint the student with a variety of viewpoints about the ways in which the adolescent and his society interact upon one another. The interdisciplinary approach is attested to by the fact that the section is comprised of the deliberations of an historian and several psychologists, sociologists, and anthropologists.

Parts Two and Three are similarly eclectic. The first selection in Part Two subjects the pronouncements of psychoanalytic theorists to critical analysis; the second paper offers an imaginative new behavioral theory to account for the socialization process. Following these papers, a series of studies demonstrate the relationships of such variables as family background, socioeconomic status, changing interests, delinquency behavior, religious experiences, and ethnic attitudes to development during adolescence. Finally, the last paper in this section comprehensively reviews the empirical research on these theories and variables. Part Three brings together experimental studies of peer and high school influences upon socialization. Popularity, peer-status, and extracurricular activities are given special attention.

Part Four departs from the socialization theme in order to describe the physical and intellectual characteristics that develop during the adolescent period. These growth factors may influence socialization by imposing limitations upon an individual's development. Moreover, even when certain aspects of growth may be functionally insignificant, societal standards place a premium on the attainment of attributes related to athletic prowess, physical attractiveness, and intellectual aptitude. The first papers in this section describe how adolescents grow physically and how this growth is associated with their personality development. Subsequent articles discuss the development of cognitive and intellectual abilities in adolescents and the influence of home and high school variables upon superior scholastic performances.

I am deeply grateful to the authors and publishers who generously granted permission to reprint their materials. I have acknowledged their contribution in appropriate footnotes throughout the volume. I am particularly indebted to those authors who either prepared original papers or revised earlier versions of their papers for inclusion in this collection.

In preparation of the manuscript I was aided immensely by the editorial suggestions of Wendy S. Spotts and by the secretarial assistance and counsel of Dorothy B. Ratcliff. I am very much pleased that I may express my appreciation to them here.

Robert E. Grinder

University of Wisconsin

Contents

INTRODUCTION   v

Part One

SOCIALIZATION: ADOLESCENCE AND SOCIETY

G. Stanley Hall and the Social Significance of Adolescence
Robert E. Grinder and Charles E. Strickland   3

Values and Our Youth
Gordon W. Allport   17

The School Class As a Social System: Some of Its Functions in American Society
Talcott Parsons   28

Work and the Adolescent Transition to Maturity
Dale B. Harris   50

Culture Pattern and Adolescent Behaviour
Francis L. K. Hsu, Blanche G. Watrous, and Edith M. Lord   59

Adolescent Initiation Rites Among Preliterate Peoples
Judith K. Brown   75

Part Two

SOCIALIZATION: THEORY AND PRACTICE

Prepuberty and Adolescence
Gerald S. Blum   89

The Absent Father and Cross-Sex Identity
Roger V. Burton and John W. M. Whiting   107

ix

Some Effects of Paternal Absence on Male Children
Joan McCord, William McCord, and Emily Thurber   118

Family Patterns Correlated with Adolescent Personality
Structure
Robert F. Peck   133

Maternal Behavior and Personality Development Data from the
Berkeley Growth Study
Nancy Bayley and Earl S. Schaefer   141

Stability of Achievement and Recognition Seeking Behaviors from
Early Childhood Through Adulthood
Howard A. Moss and Jerome Kagan   152

Family Structure and Achievement Motivation
Bernard C. Rosen   169

Social Class and Parental Values
Melvin L. Kohn   187

Some Characteristics of High School Pupils from Three
Income Groups
John K. Coster   208

Sex Differences in the Life Problems and Interests of
Adolescents, 1935 and 1957
Dale B. Harris   219

Personality Factors Related to Juvenile Delinquency
Donald R. Peterson, Herbert C. Quay,
and Theodore L. Tiffany   227

Varieties of Religious Experience in Young Adolescents
David Elkind and Sally Elkind   247

The Development of Ethnic Attitudes in Adolescence
W. Cody Wilson   262

Child-Rearing Practices and Moral Development:
Generalizations from Empirical Research
Martin L. Hoffman   275

Part Three

SOCIALIZATION: PEER AND SCHOOL INFLUENCES

Popularity Among Adolescents in Western Australia and
in the United States of America
D. K. Wheeler   297

Status in the Informal Group: Influence and
Influencibility at Differing Age Levels
O. J. Harvey and Jeanne Rutherford   309

The Development of Moral Values in Children—Pre-
Adolescent Gangs and the Moral Development of Children
A. R. Crane   319

Relationships Between Social Need Strivings and the
Development of Heterosexual Affiliations
William J. Meyer   330 √

Predicting Leadership Ratings from High School Activities
John D. Krumboltz, Raymond E. Christal,
and Joe H. Ward, Jr.   341

A Study of Socialization Patterns at the High School Level
Mary Cover Jones   349 √

Residential Segregation of Social Classes and Aspirations
of High School Boys
Alan B. Wilson   374

Psychological Health and Classroom Functioning: A Study of
Dissatisfaction with School Among Adolescents
Philip W. Jackson and Jacob W. Getzels   392

High School Antecedents of Young Adult Achievement
Robert D. Hess   401

Part Four

PHYSICAL AND INTELLECTUAL GROWTH DURING ADOLESCENCE: RELATIONSHIPS BETWEEN MATURATIONAL AND SOCIETAL FACTORS

The Course of Children's Growth
J. M. Tanner   417

Development of Sexual Behavior in Human Beings
Clellan S. Ford and Frank A. Beach   433 √

The Behavior-Inferred Motivations of Late- and Early-
Maturing Boys
Paul Henry Mussen and Mary Cover Jones   446

√ *Self-Conceptions, Motivations, and Interpersonal Attitudes of*
Early- and Late-Maturing Girls
Mary Cover Jones and Paul Henry Mussen   454 √

*Implications of Preadolescent and Early Adolescent Cognitive
Development for Secondary-School Teaching*
David P. Ausubel   466

Quantity Conceptions in Junior and Senior High School Students
David Elkind   474

Factors That Aid and Hinder Creativity
J. P. Guilford   484

Conditions Productive of Superior Children
Robert J. Havighurst   501

Creative and Academic Performance Among Talented Adolescents
John L. Holland   511

Studies in Adolescence

PART ONE

SOCIALIZATION: ADOLESCENCE AND SOCIETY

G. Stanley Hall and the Social Significance of Adolescence*

ROBERT E. GRINDER AND
CHARLES E. STRICKLAND

No other psychologist has written more about adolescence than G. Stanley Hall. His famed two-volume treatise on adolescence was actually an encyclopedia. His interests ranged on the one hand from embryology to education and religion, and on the other, from gynecology to counseling techniques. For all his genius, enthusiasm, and energy, however, his efforts to establish recapitulation theory as the all-explanatory principle of psychological development aborted early in the twentieth century. The anonymity into which he has fallen, as a consequence, has rendered his assumptions about adolescence relatively inaccessible and misunderstood. In the following paper, the authors show how Hall's nineteenth-century Darwinism and his ideas for social reform merge to yield a strikingly unusual interpretation of the adolescent years.

If the influence of historical personages in psychology were to be appraised by contemporary status, the names of Sigmund Freud, William James, Ivan Pavlov, and Edward L. Thorndike would be included in any serious listing. The theoretical formulations of these pioneers have survived rigorous investigations; today they underpin conceptual scaffolds for innumerable systems of learning and personality. But absent from the list would be the name of G. Stanley Hall (1844–1924), the man who earned America's first Ph.D. in psychology, the father of the child study movement in the United States, the founder of the American Psychological Association, and the author of some 350 papers, articles, and books, including an enormously comprehensive two-volume treatise on the psychology of adolescence.[1] Lecturer at Harvard, Professor at Johns Hopkins,

---

[1] G. Stanley Hall, *Adolescence: Its Psychology and Its Relation to Physiology, Anthropology, Sociology, Sex, Crime, Religion and Education* (2 vols.; New York: D. Appleton and Co., 1904).

---

* From *Teachers College Record*, LXIV (February, 1963), pp. 390–399. Reprinted by permission of the authors and the publisher.

and President of Clark University from its inception until his retirement, Hall enjoyed a thoroughly productive professional career. Most of the institutions fathered by him are now nationally prominent, but from its peak at the turn of the century, the influence of his theory and research has ebbed continuously. Even as early as 1928, it was declared in the preface of a highly regarded text on adolescence that "students of Dr. G. Stanley Hall will miss extensive reference to his voluminous pioneer works on adolescence . . . such reference would seem of historic value primarily, rather than of scientific or practical value today."[2]

Although Hall's *magnum opus* on adolescence has been taken as the starting point for discussions of the adolescent phenomena for decades, the majority of psychologists who have worked in this area, except for a small clique of first-generation devotees, have renounced his theoretical formulations unequivocally. Specifically, Hall has been impugned for (a) ignoring the influences of culture and overly emphasizing the importance of physiological functions in the adolescent's development, (b) conceptualizing adolescence as a period of intense storm and stress which arises from instinctual upheavals, and (c) regarding physical growth of adolescents as saltatory rather than as continuous and gradual. These interpretations of Hall's views have had a telling effect upon contemporary thinking in adolescent psychology, and they have caused him to appear, in his historical role, somewhat like an antichrist.

G. Stanley Hall differs from most psychologists, past or present, in the degree to which he attempted to apply Charles Darwin's evolutionary view of man to both psychology and social philosophy. His most important adaptation of Darwinian or evolutionary biology was the theory of recapitulation. He argued that every phase of a person's growth represents one of the different levels at which the human race was once mature; hence, every person recapitulates or repeats the history of the race in his development. Whereas the human fetus reveals a very remote stage of evolution, some adult behaviors are the actual cutting edges of a new stage. Hall reasoned that the phylogeny of the human race could be reconstructed by research not only in human psychology, but also in biology, anthropology, sociology, history, and comparative psychology. On the one hand Hall literally envisaged himself to be the prophet of a new social order. In Hall's opinion, evolution pointed to the development of a super-race, and to this end a collective society should be organized under the control of an elite who could direct mankind toward its goal of evolutionary perfection. On the other hand, Hall enjoyed being honored as a "Darwin of the mind."[3]

[2] Leta S. Hollingworth, *The Psychology of the Adolescent* (New York: D. Appleton and Co., 1928), p. ix.

[3] G. S. Hall, *Life and Confessions of a Psychologist* (New York: D. Appleton and Co., 1923), p. 360.

His ambition was to construct the history of the psyche, from the lowly amoeba to man himself.[4] He believed that possession of this knowledge would reveal the complexities of human development, accelerate evolutionary processes, and unlock even the purpose and destiny of life itself. Primarily, these twin ambitions turned Hall toward the adolescent phenomena.

Although G. Stanley Hall hoped to gain a better understanding of adolescence, and to improve education and psychology, his aims were obviously more grandiose. Interpreting adolescence within the context of his particular Darwinian and utopian premises, Hall made judgments never fully acceptable to many psychologists. His opponents often have attempted to subject his pronouncements to *reductio ad absurdum,* and the resulting misunderstandings doubtless have contributed in part to the decline of his influence in the twentieth century. But even more important, Hall's Darwinian assumptions gave his views of the adolescent phenomena a turn-of-century air that may be strange to many contemporary students of adolescence. Therefore, this paper presents: (a) clarification of his basic assumptions, and (b) in terms of them, the essential features of his views about adolescence.

SOCIAL REFORM[5]

Accustomed as we are to Darwin's evolutionary view of life, it is difficult to imagine the intellectual upheaval occasioned by the theory during Hall's formative years. Within three decades after *The Origin of Species* appeared in 1859, the influence of Darwinism had reached every branch of the social sciences. Although Hall began his career as a divinity student, his interests were also rapidly drawn to Darwinian theory. Toying with this dangerous but fascinating new idea while attending Union Theological Seminary in the 1860's, Hall became disillusioned with theological orthodoxy. The fate of the keen young intellect balanced precariously for a time until Henry Ward Beecher, the famed clergyman, convinced that philosophical studies abroad would do no harm to a young man's piety, secured the funds necessary for Hall's journey to Berlin University.[6] German society fascinated Hall to such an extent that he returned to America only with reluctance, and he later confessed to planning several "unpractical ways" of spending the rest of his life abroad.[7] Events during the Gilded Age convinced Hall that laissez faire individualism would no longer answer the needs of a com-

---

[4] G. S. Hall, "Evolution and Psychology," *Fifty Years of Darwinism,* American Association for the Advancement of Science (New York: Henry Holt and Co., 1909), p. 252.
[5] The authors are greatly indebted to Charles O. Burgess for insight into Hall's social philosophy.
[6] Hall, *Life,* 177–181.
[7] Hall, *Life,* 222.

plex, civilized society, and in his judgment, Germany was leading the civilized world in social reform legislation. As Hall saw it, Germany took seriously the admonitions of her philosopher, Johann Fichte, who early in the century had called for an educational state, governed by an elite and dedicated to the cultural perfection of mankind. The German social order had "actualized the Platonic Republic."[8]

When he condemned laissez faire individualism and materialism, Hall marched in step with a hardy band of nineteenth-century American intellectuals and reformers. But when be began to formulate his own brand of utopia he broke the cadence. To the ideas of Plato and Fichte, he added elements drawn from the thought of Darwin and the German philosopher, Friedrich Nietzsche. The result was a collectivistic utopia based on a profound distrust of reason, individualism, and democratic egalitarianism.

Darwinism provided scientifically respectable support for Hall's pessimism about the intellectual qualities of the average man. Surveying the course of evolutionary development, Hall belittled the rational powers as determinants of behavior. They were a relatively late development in evolution. "Instincts, feelings, emotions and sentiments were vastly older and more all-determining than the intellect," Hall asserted; moreover, they were basically right.[9] Awed by what he perceived to be the perfect social organization of the insect, Hall believed that the "superiority of instinct over reason is that it regulates conduct in the interest of the species at every point."[10] While science in general was affirming that nature could be controlled for service to man's purposes, Hall was contending that man should be controlled in deference to the expressions of nature.[11]

Hall distrusted not only reason but also individualism and democratic forms of government. Here the influence of Nietzsche—as Hall understood him—is apparent. G. Stanley Hall observed that the mediocrity of most men testified to the fact that they lacked the "push" necessary to move them upward on the evolutionary scale,[12] and that democracy "everywhere thus, tends to the dead level of the average man and to the dominance of . . . incompetence and mediocrity."[13] In a paper written for an audience of German educators in 1915, he declared that America was the home of men suffering from "overstimulation." "Our very schoolboys are told that they

8 G. S. Hall, "The Moral and Religious Training of Children," *Princeton Review,* N. S., IX (1882), p. 27.
9 Hall, *Life,* 361–362.
10 G. S. Hall, "A Glance at the Phyletic Background of Genetic Psychology," *American Journal of Psychology,* XIX (April, 1908), p. 211.
11 Charles O. Burgess, "The Educational State in America: Selected Views on Learning as the Key to Utopia, 1800–1924" (unpublished Ph.D. dissertation, Dept. of Education, University of Wisconsin, 1962).
12 G. S. Hall, "The Ideal School Based on Child Study," *Proceedings,* National Education Association (1901), p. 484.
13 Hall, *Life,* 440.

may possibly become presidents or millionaires, that theirs is a land of boundless opportunity."[14] Hall thought "the peril of democracy is that it has aroused so large a body of hopes that are utterly unrealizable. . . ." Inevitably democracy would experience a "gospel of renunciation."[15] Perhaps the most serious evil of democracy, as he saw it, was its encouragement of concern for individuals, and on one occasion he turned the generally accepted definition of pity on its head. Hall argued that "pity" must not be extended to the downtrodden "because by aiding them to survive it interferes with the process of wholesome natural selection by which all that is best has hitherto been developed. . . . Its work is no longer the salvage of the wreckage of humanity. . . . Pity has its highest office then in removing the handicaps from those most able to help man to higher levels— the leaders on more exalted plains who can be of most aid in ushering in the kingdom of superman."[16]

G. Stanley Hall's longing for a superanthropoid utopia bore a significant relation to his view of the adolescent because Hall believed that youth would play an important role in bringing about the new society. Needed were persons who would realize that the destiny of human beings collectively was more important than the welfare of an individual. Needed were persons who would subordinate themselves to the nurture of that "elite youth" who are harbingers of the future.[17] Hall felt that adolescents were well equipped with the collectivistic sentiments necessary to bring about the super-race, and to nourish these sentiments, he called for an educational program that would stress the development of sound body and sound emotions rather than the cultivation of intellectual abilities. He scorned teachers who would "allow or even encourage callow classes to debate, discuss and weigh evidence or regurgitate the matter of the textbook."[18] Early in adolescence, he would have the sexes separated, girls to be prepared for marriage and motherhood, boys to be trained for service and citizenship.[19] For boys, Hall placed particular emphasis on instruction in body culture, patriotism, military discipline, and industrial education.[20] Perhaps the most striking characteristic of Hall's educational plan for adolescents was his belief that intellectual training should be reserved for comparatively few. "Many gather at the foot of the mount, some ascend a

[14] G. S. Hall, "Recreation and Reversion," *Pedagogical Seminary*, XXII (1915), p. 510.

[15] G. S. Hall, "Can the Masses Rule the World?" *Scientific Monthly*, XVIII (May, 1924), p. 466.

[16] G. S. Hall and F. H. Saunders, "Pity," *American Journal of Psychology*, XI (1900), pp. 590–591.

[17] *Ibid.*, 591.

[18] G. S. Hall, "Certain Degenerative Tendencies among Teachers," *Pedagogical Seminary*, XII (1905), p. 459.

[19] Hall, *Adolescence*, II, Chap. 17.

[20] *Ibid.*, I, Chap. 3.

little way, but only a chosen few can scale the summit above the clouds and bring down the tables of the law for those who wait below. . . . The few hundred picked and ripened adolescents who could and would live solely for research and the advancement of the kingdom of man and of truth in the world are too often lost in the growing academic crowds."[21]

RECAPITULATION THEORY

To a democratic nation that was realizing equality in public schooling for all children, the social significance of G. Stanley Hall's concept of adolescent education probably seemed offensive. But Hall believed that his views rested on scientifically respectable grounds, and that the theory of recapitulation provided the psychological justification he needed. Before Hall fully endorsed this new biological interpretation of psychological data, however, he passed through an interlude of enthusiasm for the experimental psychology of Wilhelm Wundt. After completing his doctorate at Harvard in 1878, Hall journeyed to Germany to study at Wundt's newly established laboratory in Leipzig. Convinced that muscle sensations were the bedrock of the psyche, Hall hailed Wundt as the "coming philosopher in Germany,"[22] whose experiments on muscle reactions would settle major epistemological controversies. To Hall the laboratory technique represented an "independent look at nature" that "has opened new impulses and enthusiasm for me such as nothing else has."[23] During the 1880's, however, Hall slowly turned his back on the psychological laboratory. He found it too confining for his ambitions, which were nothing less than to "unlock the past history of the race,"[24] namely, to construct the origin and development of the psyche, not merely the conscious intellect, but the unconscious emotions and instincts as well. Wundt had erred in ignoring Darwin, and G. Stanley Hall resolved not to make the same mistake.[25]

The heart of G. Stanley Hall's grand design was the theory of recapitulation—an imaginative corollary of Darwin's evolutionary theory. By observing species in their natural habitats, Darwin had ordered his data on a scale from lower to higher complexity. But his effort was more than mere description and classification, for in denoting the lower forms as "earlier" and the higher forms as "later," he told a story of the origin and development of life.

---

[21] Hall, *Adolescence*, II, p. 559.

[22] G. S. Hall, "The Philosophy of the Future," *Nation*, XXVII (Nov. 7, 1878), p. 283.

[23] Letter from G. S. Hall to William James, Ralph Barton Perry (ed.), *The Thought and Character of William James* (2 vols.; Boston: Little, Brown, and Co., 1935), II, 20–21.

[24] G. S. Hall, "Evolution and Psychology," *op. cit.*, p. 263.

[25] *Ibid.*, 254.

Nonetheless, how on the basis of observation and hypothesis could Darwin know that simpler forms of life were also earlier? Paleontological evidence was as yet scanty, and archeology and anthropology were still highly speculative; so Darwin and others interested in the validity of his argument turned to the relatively advanced science of embryology. In 1864, a German biologist, Fritz Mueller, published a study showing that in its development the embryo of higher animals recapitulates the forms through which its species had evolved. In 1868 the idea achieved prominence in the popular lectures of Ernst Haeckel, who extended the notion to include postnatal psychic development, and who coined the phrase by which the theory became widely known: "ontogeny is a brief and rapid recapitulation of phylogeny."[26] Haeckel's "bio-genetic law" gave impressive support to Darwin's hypothesis that complex living forms had descended from more simple beginnings. In embryonic development lay the record of evolution for all to see.[27]

Bolstered by Haeckel's biogenetic law, Darwin's view of natural history swept through the field of biology and on into psychology. The great pioneer, Darwin himself, led the way. In *Expression of the Emotions in Man and Animals* Darwin described phenomena such as fear, anger, and joy as inherited remnants of similar expressions in "earlier" forms, e.g., the sneer invoked in human social situations was reminiscent of the canines who bared their teeth in rage. Inspired by Darwin's analyses, Hall praised him as "standing almost alone" in the investigation of emotional expression.[28] Darwin's bold manner of applying to the psyche the methods which he had applied so successfully to physical form and function completely won Hall's admiration. Speaking in 1909 before an assemblage honoring the contributions of Darwin, Hall demonstrated his indebtedness. He assured the group that "psychic rudiments and recapitulatory traces" are "as recognizable as the rudimentary gill-slits in the embryo" for "the child is vastly more ancient than the man." The child is, in fact, "his very venerable and, in his early stages, half-anthropoid ancestor."[29] Impending was a "well-established embryology of the soul," which would provide the necessary basis for a "true mentally, esthetically, and morally orthopedic education."[30]

G. Stanley Hall's enthusiasm for the theory of recapitulation propelled

[26] Ernst Haeckel, *Evolution of Man* (2 vols.; London: C. Kegan Paul and Co., 1879), II, Chap. 26.

[27] See Erik Nordenskiold, *The History of Biology: a Survey* (New York: Tudor Pub. Co., 1935), pp. 516–517; and Loren Eisely, *Darwin's Century: Evolution and the Men Who Discovered It* (Garden City, N.Y.: Doubleday and Co., 1958), p. 5.

[28] G. S. Hall and Theodate Smith, "Curiosity and Interest," *Pedagogical Seminary,* X (September, 1903), p. 315.

[29] G. S. Hall, "Evolution and Psychology," *op. cit.,* pp. 260–262.

[30] *Ibid.,* 263.

him from the laboratory into the leadership of the child study movement in America. After Hall became President of Clark University, men and women flocked there to work under his direction, and the literature about children increased rapidly. From the beginning Hall's interests were less in the development of the child and adolescent per se than in "coordinating childhood and youth with the development of the race . . . and also to establish criteria by which to both diagnose and measure arrest and retardation in the individual and the race."[31] Because Hall argued that study of the history of the race would provide the "true norms" for human development, he held that the psychologist must study the past, not merely traditional history with its concern for war and politics, but also cultural, social, and economic history. Above all, Hall proclaimed the relevance of anthropology, for he believed that some of the more psychologically significant aspects of human nature emerged before the rise of civilization and the advent of written records.[32]

Hall's belief that the psychologist must look to the past for norms of psychological development may appear unorthodox to modern investigators, but it offers an essential key to understanding his view of the adolescent years. The theory of recapitulation gave him confidence that anthropology and other historical data were indeed relevant, and his interpretations of these data provide the broad framework for his evaluations. In anthropology the idea that human culture, like the animal world, evolved from simple beginnings had developed even before Darwin won acceptance for his theory of biological evolution. In America, the most influential representative of the "evolutionary" school of anthropology was Lewis Henry Morgan, whom Hall cited on several occasions. Morgan, in his epoch-making *Ancient Society* (1877) sketched the development of mankind in three broad stages —savagery, barbarism, and civilization. Particularly noteworthy is the fact that Morgan contended the stages exhibited respectively the following patterns of social organization: collectivism, individualism, and collectivism again. On the basis of his findings, Morgan predicted that the individualism characteristic of the nineteenth century would prove only to be a transient stage peculiar to barbarism, and that eventually it would give way to a civilized collectivism.[33] Although Morgan's idea of a collective civilization bore little resemblance to Hall's notion of a totalitarian utopia governed by an elite, nevertheless, the essential pattern—individualism giving way to collectivism—matched Hall's social philosophy. Since Hall believed that every individual retraced the history of the race in his development, he

---

[31] Hall, *Adolescence,* I, viii.

[32] See G. S. Hall, *Educational Problems* (2 vols.; New York: D. Appleton and Company, 1911), II, 292, 306–310.

[33] Carl Resek, *Lewis Henry Morgan:* American Scholar (Chicago: University of Chicago Press. 1960), pp. 139–143.

fully expected everyone to exhibit stages resembling the three that Morgan had outlined.

The parallel between Morgan's evolutionary scheme and Hall's description of the course of human development is striking. Although Hall remained extremely vague about the relation of evolution to early childhood, ignoring infancy and dismissing summarily the "kindergarten" stage as a "sentimental" period, he showed considerable concern for the "juvenile" or "prepubescent" stage, which ranged from eight or nine to twelve or thirteen years of age. The child's entry into this second stage is marked by "a decreased rate of growth, so that the body relatively rests," and the next four years represent "on the recapitulation theory, a long period in some remote age, well above the simian, but mainly before the historic period."[34] The child's eagerness to throw, run, dodge, hit, chase, wrestle, box, fish, and hunt are all lingering vestiges of ancient times when these activities were necessary to survival.

More significant for Hall's total scheme, however, were the social attitudes expressed by the juvenile. The child at this age represents a mature barbarian, who is healthy, vigorous, selfish, and totally unsentimental. While he is responsive to his peers, tending to form "barbaric associations . . . pirates, robbers, soldiers . . . and other savage reversionary combinations,"[35] he is indifferent to the adult, civilized world. "The wisest requirements seem to the child more or less alien, arbitrary, heteronomous, artificial, falsetto."[36] "Reason, true morality, religion, sympathy, love, and esthetic enjoyment are but very slightly developed. Everything, in short, suggests the culmination of one stage of life as if it thus represented what was once, and for a very protracted and relatively stationary period, the age of maturity in some remote, perhaps pigmoid, stage of human evolution."[37] According to Hall, the school should introduce these children into the necessities of learning "as intensively and quickly as possible with a minimal strain and with the least amount of explanation or coquetting for natural interest."[38]

G. Stanley Hall's pessimism about human development gave way to an exhilarating optimism when he saw the individual reach the adolescent years, from fourteen to twenty-four. As early as 1896 Hall observed that, although "the child has been selfish" during a long period of "complete individual development," the adolescence years signal "a second birth." Now one witnesses the "birth of love in the largest Christian sense, psychologi-

[34] G. S. Hall, "The Ideal School," *op. cit.*, p. 477.
[35] G. S. Hall, *Youth: Its Education, Regimen and Hygiene* (New York: D. Appleton and Co., 1904), pp. 226–227.
[36] *Ibid.*, 4.
[37] Hall, *Adolescence*, I, ix–x.
[38] Hall, *Youth*, 5.

cally free from all selfish motives."[39] In *Adolescence,* Hall elaborated this point of view further. As Hall put it, the adolescent "must conquer a higher kingdom of man for himself, break out a new sphere, and evolve a more modern story to his psycho-physical nature."[40] "Adolescence is a new birth, for the higher and more completely human traits are now born."[41] "Individuation is suddenly augmented and begins to sense it limits and its gradual subordination to the race which the Fates prescribe."[42] "In some respects, early adolescence is thus the infancy of man's higher nature, when he receives from the great all-mother his last capital of energy and evolutionary momentum."[43] And in a most significant passage, Hall remarked, "at any rate, for those prophetic souls interested in the future of our race and desirous of advancing it, the field of adolescence is the quarry in which they must seek to find both goals and means. If such a higher stage is ever added to our race, it will not be by increments at any later plateau of adult life, but it will come by increased development of the adolescent stage, which is the bud of promise for the race."[44]

THE ADOLESCENT YEARS

Hall's distrust of democracy and individualism and his aspirations for a utopian super-race merged in his thinking to yield a concept of the adolescent phenomena that other psychologists, from his time onward, have found generally unpalatable. Recapitulation theory persuaded G. Stanley Hall that the outgrowth of plasticity at adolescence was the best hope for mankind's evolutionary progress, and he and his students recognized this period as "the focal point of all psychology."[45] As a result of the controversial nature of his views, and as a consequence of the ensuing confusion, Hall has been misunderstood in this major respect: it has been said that "the work of G. Stanley Hall set the theme for emphasis upon the physiology of adolescence. . . . Hall, and the writers who studied his works, attributed many of the peculiarities of adolescence to the facts of puberty,"[46] and "he ignored the effects of cultural setting."[47] Actually Hall's views

[39] G. S. Hall, "Discussion," *Proceedings,* National Education Association (1896), pp. 193–195. The concept of adolescence as a second birth was first given prominence in modern thought by Jean Jacques Rousseau, *Emile* (originally published in 1762; New York: E. P. Dutton and Co., 1911), pp. 172–173.
[40] Hall, *Adolescence,* II, 71.
[41] *Ibid.,* I, xiii.
[42] *Ibid.,* II, 58.
[43] *Ibid.,* II, 71.
[44] *Ibid.,* I, 50.
[45] E. G. Lancaster, "The Psychology and Pedagogy of Adolescence," *The Pedagogical Seminary,* V (1897), p. 119.
[46] Harold W. Bernard, *Adolescent Development in American Culture* (Yonkers-on-Hudson, N.Y.: World Book Co., 1957), p. 8.
[47] Dorothy Rogers, *The Psychology of Adolescence* (New York: Appleton-Century-Crofts, 1962), p. 26.

were unequivocally and diametrically opposite to these contentions. Although Darwinism committed Hall to an emphasis on the genetic determinants of behavior, he believed firmly that at adolescence the process of recapitulating instincts gave way to the primacy of cultural influences. "No age is so responsive to all the best and wisest adult endeavor. In no psychic soil, too, does seed, bad as well as good, strike such deep root, grow so rankly, or bear fruit so quickly or so surely."[48] To show that phylogenetic recapitulation now abated, he said: "Young children grow despite great hardships, but later adolescence is more dependent upon favoring conditions in the environment, disturbances of which more readily cause arrest and prevent maturity."[49] "The whole future of life depends on how well the new powers now given suddenly and in profusion are husbanded and directed."[50] "There is nothing in the environment to which the adolescent nature does not keenly respond."[51] "The processes last to be attained are least assured by heredity and most dependent upon individual effort, in aid of which nature gives only propulsion, often less defined the later it can be acquired."[52]

To show that *Adolescence* was a product of his concern for cultural influences, he said: "Hence there is need of the most careful study of consummate practical wisdom, in providing the most favorable environment and eliminating every possible cause of arrest or reversion. This is indeed the practical problem of this book."[53] Part of the confusion regarding Hall's views may stem from his attitudes toward the child as opposed to his attitudes toward the adolescent. Hall did disregard the effects of cultural factors upon the former, but he certainly did not do so with respect to the latter. It was, in fact, the very plasticity of adolescence that bolstered Hall's hopes for creating an improved society based on continued evolutionary progress.

Perhaps the most controversial of Hall's views of the adolescent years has been his statement that the period was "suggestive of some ancient period of storm and stress when old moorings were broken and a higher level attained."[54] In physical growth, therefore, Hall observed the presence of instinctual remnants. "Early adolescence brings sudden spring freshets of growth impulse in all directions, and these initial momenta . . . are at first more or less uncoordinated in all."[55] "Different organs and tissues or determinants compete for the available nutritive material in the blood, and

---

[48] Hall, *Adolescence*, I, xviii–xix.
[49] *Ibid.*, I, 47.
[50] *Ibid.*, I, xv.
[51] *Ibid.*, II, 453.
[52] *Ibid.*, II, 94.
[53] *Ibid.*, I, 49.
[54] *Ibid.*, I, xiii.
[55] *Ibid.*, I, 309.

some for a time get ahead of others in this internal struggle for survival."[56]

In the ensuing decades several psychologists and anthropologists, notably Margaret Mead,[57] have attempted to show that instead the adolescent stresses are largely a product of cultural pressures. These investigators have judged Hall correctly in assuming that he conceptualized adolescence as a period of great storm and stress, but in anticipation of contemporary thinking, Hall attributed considerably more influence to cultural factors than he did to instinctual processes. Even in the biological aspects of behavior, Hall noted the permeability of adolescence to the influences of environmental pressures, and he saw that "the great influx of muscular vigor that unfolds during adolescent years . . . seems to be a very plastic quantity."[58] Speaking of the evils of "city life, modern industrialism, and mixture of distinct ethnic stocks," he said "under these provocations, some instincts spring into activity with a suddenness that is almost explosive."[59] "Civilization is so hard on the body that some have called it a disease."[60] "Our vast and complex business organization that has long since outgrown the comprehension of professional economists, absorbs ever more and earlier the best talent and muscle of youth . . . but we are progressively forgetting that . . . youth needs repose."[61]

Within the framework of the social reforms that Hall was seeking, however, storm and stress approached turgid proportions. The adolescent was free of the past and responsive to the present, but above all, he felt the pull of the future. The contemporary student of psychology generally regards adolescence as a period of transition from childhood to adulthood,[62] and the usual criterion marking an individual's successful passage is his achievement of satisfactory physiological and social adjustment in his here and now society, but Hall was much less parochial. Adolescence was a time when "henceforth the race, not the self, must become supreme."[63] Doggedly pursuing a super-race, Hall juxtaposed his concept of what he believed the environment could do for the adolescent with his concept of what it was doing to the adolescent, and the resulting hiatus suggested intensive storm and stress. His notion of adolescent transition extended far beyond the best that he saw in his civilization, and he believed that adolescence, "and not maturity as now defined, is the only point of departure for the superanthropoid

[56] *Ibid.*, I, 241.
[57] Margaret Mead, *Coming of Age in Samoa* (originally published in 1928; New York: Mentor Books, 1949), p. 11.
[58] Hall, *Adolescence*, I, 157.
[59] *Ibid.*, I, 322.
[60] *Ibid.*, I, 169.
[61] *Ibid.*, I, xvi–xvii.
[62] See, for example, Raymond G. Kuhlen, *The Psychology of Adolescent Development* (New York: Harper and Bros., 1952), p. 4; Arthur T. Jersild, *The Psychology of Adolescence* (New York: The Macmillan Co., 1957), p. 4.
[63] Hall, *Adolescence*, II, 303.

that man is to become."[64] To his way of thinking, it was "a colossal assumption that what we call civilization is the end of man, or the best thing in the world."[65] Therefore, Hall not only anticipated recent investigators in attributing primary stress during adolescence to interaction of environmental and genetic factors, but in his zeal to rearrange things and produce a super-anthropoid, he surpassed them.

Another persistent issue facing those who study the adolescent years is whether physical growth is gradual or whether it is saltatory, that is, sudden and abrupt. Impregnated with the theory that every man recapitulates history until at his adolescence the racial instincts exhaust themselves in a new birth of human malleability, Hall perceived adolescent growth to be saltatory.[66] As with most of Hall's views, opinions became differentiated sharply. By the sheer magnitude of their output and prestige, Hall and his students were able to polarize the early balance of scientific opinion in their "cataclysmic" camp.[67] But there were others, namely Edward L. Thorndike and Leta Hollingworth, who disagreed radically. "It is a favorite dictum of superficial psychology and pedagogy that instincts lie entirely dormant and then spring into full strength within a few weeks. At a certain stage, we are told, such and such a tendency has its 'nascent period' or ripening time. . . . These statements are almost certainly misleading . . . what data we have show nothing to justify the doctrine of sudden ripening."[68] Today the preponderance of scientific evidence continues to increase the substance of Thorndike's position. Doubtless Hall's inadequate statistical techniques contributed partly to his analyses; if his studies and those of his students had been more analytical and precise, the saltatory growth phenomena probably would have seemed less apparent. Even so, Hall's saltatory theory retains some of its descriptive merit. For, as was recently observed, "physical growth . . . does *not* occur in a series of jumps, but continuously . . . except in so far as one might consider the rapid change at adolescence as the achievement of a new, and mature, stage."[69]

Stormy in his role as a social prophet and zealous in his exposition of Darwinism, G. Stanley Hall created an image of the adolescent years that always aroused controversy. Convinced by his interpretation of recapitulation theory that the democratic system was little more than barbaric, he sought to achieve social and educational reforms in the face of democratic individualism. On the adolescent he focused his aspirations for a super-race,

[64] *Ibid.*, II, 94.
[65] *Ibid.*, II, 717.
[66] *Ibid.*, I, xiii.
[67] Frederick E. Bolton, *Adolescent Education* (New York: The Macmillan Co., 1931) pp. 76–79.
[68] Edward L. Thorndike, *The Original Nature of Man* (New York: Teachers College Publications, Columbia University, 1930), pp. 260–261.
[69] J. M. Tanner, *Education and Physical Growth* (London: University of London Press Ltd., 1961), p. 63.

and by the force of his ambitions, he neglected the educability of the child, overestimated the potential of the adolescent as an agent of social reform, and consequently, exaggerated the magnitude of storm and stress. Had G. Stanley Hall studied adolescence to test recapitulation theory rather than to justify it, he might never have lost stature in the field he did so much to establish.

Values and Our Youth* [1]

GORDON W. ALLPORT

During adolescence an individual must master a bewildering variety of familial, social, and vocational roles before he is accepted on equal footing by adult citizenry. Today, advances in technology and social systems pre-empt traditional modes of behavior and demand of the adolescent new attitudes and standards for effective citizenship. If youth are to function responsibly in the world of tomorrow, first of all they must perceive and comprehend the critical issues confronting them. In the paper included below, Allport "previews" several of these issues and suggests that many American youth, rather than meeting the challenge, possess "flabby value-fibre," and are quite complacent about their lot. In an articulate presentation, he offers a provocative analysis of the process of educating values.

One aim of education is to make available the wisdom of the past and present so that youth may be equipped to solve the problems of the future. If this is so, then we have good grounds for a feeling of consternation concerning the adequacy of our present educational procedures. The reason is that in the immediate future, the youth of today will have to live in a world very unlike the world of the past from which our store of wisdom has been drawn.

SOME PROSPECTS

Think of the vastly changed nature of life in the future, for which we have little relevant wisdom from the past to call upon:

1. The new generation of students will have to face an ever increasing domination of life by science, by technology, and by automation. (One

[1] Adapted from an address delivered during the 1961 Summer Lecture Series at the Western Washington College of Education, Bellingham, Washington.

* From *Teachers College Record*, LXIII (1961), pp. 211–219. Reprinted by permission of the author and the publisher.

thinks of the story of two cows grazing along the roadside. An immense milk truck passes with the painted legend: Pasteurized, Homogenized, Vitamin B Added. One cow turns to the other and says, "Makes you feel inadequate, doesn't it?")

2. The new generation will have to recognize the impossibility of living any longer in a state of condescension toward the colored peoples of the world (about three-quarters of the world's population). Centuries of comfortable caste discrimination and segregation are from here on impossible to maintain.

3. The coming generation will have to deal with a population explosion whose predicted magnitude staggers our imagination.

4. It will need a more complete understanding of world societies and their marked differences in values. In the past, we could be politely ignorant of such places as Africa, Latin America, and Asia in a way that is no longer possible.

5. It will have to create a world government or, at least, an effective confederation to forestall the threat of thermonuclear war.

6. As if a planetary world view were not difficult enough to achieve, the coming generation may have to develop an interplanetary point of view. (I find this prospect especially alarming because we seem to be solving the problems of outer space before those of the inner space of mind, character, and values.)

It is no wonder that this preview of problems confronting our youth throws us educators into a state of self-scrutiny bordering sometimes on panic. Where can youth find the needed equipment? Are they sound enough in mind and morale?

Sometimes our dismay finds an outlet in gallows humor. They tell of the benevolent lady who saw a depressing specimen of the very young generation sprawled on the curb of a city street, swilling down cans of beer. Greatly shocked, she asked, "Little boy, why aren't you in school?" "Cripes, lady," he replied, "I'm only four years old."

And they tell the story of the London bobby. London police, we know, are well trained for social work, even for psychotherapy. This bobby's beat was Waterloo Bridge. He spotted a man about to jump over and intercepted him. "Come now," he said. "Tell me what is the matter. Is it money?" The man shook his head. "Your wife perhaps?" Another shake of the head. "Well, what is it then?" The would-be suicide replied, "I'm worried about the state of the world." "Oh, come now," said the bobby. "It can't be so bad. Let's walk up and down the bridge here and talk it over." Whereupon they strolled for about an hour discussing the state of the world, and then they *both* jumped over.

Humor helps us put our dilemma into sane perspective, but it does not solve the problem. The vague apprehension we feel has led to certain empirical studies of the values of today's youth, with results, alas, that are not reassuring.

ASSESSING VALUES

Not long ago, Professor Phillip Jacob undertook to survey[2] all available studies concerning the values held by college students. He found a marked uniformity among them. Fully three-quarters of the students were "gloriously contented, both in regard to their present day-to-day activity and their outlook for the future." Their aspirations were primarily for material gratifications for themselves and their families. They "fully accepted the conventions of the contemporary business society as the context within which they will realize their personal desires." While they will not crusade against segregation and racial injustice, they will accept non-discrimination when it comes as a "necessary convention in a homogenized culture." They subscribe to the traditional virtues of sincerity, honesty, and loyalty, but are indulgent concerning laxity in moral standards. They normally express a need for religion, but there is a hollow quality in their beliefs. They do not desire to have an influential voice in public policy or government. Their sense of civic duty stops at the elementary obligation of voting. They predict another major war within a dozen years, but they say that international problems give them little concern and that they spend no time on them. Only a minority value their college education primarily in terms of its intellectual gains. They regard it as good because it gives them vocational preparation, social status, and a good time. Such is the flabby value-fibre that Jacob discovers among college students of today.

The picture becomes more vivid when viewed in cross-national perspective. James Gillespie and I, in a comparative study[3] of the values of college youth in 10 nations, asked students to write their autobiographies of the future ("My life from now until the year 2000") and also gave them an extensive questionnaire. The instrument was translated into nine different languages.

In comparison with youth of other nations, young Americans are delightfully frank and open, unsuspicious and cooperative. Their documents had no literary affectation (and, I may add, little literary quality). But the most important finding was that within these 10 nations, American students were the most self-centered, the most "privatistic" in values. They desired above all else a rich, full life for themselves, and showed little concern for

[2] P. Jacob, *Changing Values in College* (New York: Harper, 1957).
[3] J. Gillespie and G. Allport, *Youth's Outlook on the Future* (New York: Random House, 1955).

national welfare or for the fate of mankind at large. The context of their outlook was private rather than public, passive rather than pioneer. The essential point is made clear by two excerpts, the first drawn from the autobiography of a Mexican girl, 18 years of age, and the second from a Radcliffe student of the same age:

Since I like psychology very much, I wish, on leaving this school, to study it, specializing in it and exercising it as a profession. I shouldn't like to get married right away, although like any woman I am desirous of getting married before realizing all my aspirations. In addition, I should like to do something for my country—as a teacher, as a psychologist, or as a mother. As a teacher, to guide my pupils in the best path, for at the present time they need solid bases in childhood in order in their future lives not to have so many frustrations as the youth of the present. As a psychologist, to make studies which in some way will serve humanity and my beloved country. As a mother, to make my children creatures who are useful to both their country and all humanity.

Now follows the Radcliffe document. Its flavor of privatism is unmistakable:

Our summers will be spent lobster fishing on the Cape. Later we'll take a look at the rest of the country—California, the Southwest, and the Chicago Stockyards. I want the children, when they get past the age of ten, to spend part of the summer away from home, either at camp or as apprentices to whatever profession they may show an interest in. Finally, I hope we will all be able to take a trip to Europe, especially to Russia, to see what can be done about Communism.

Many critics have called attention to the same American value predicament. Our current social pattern, they say, is almost completely geared to one objective alone, namely a profitable, expanding production. To insure expanding production, there must be more and more consumption. Hence comes the expensive glamor of our advertising and its control of our mass media. The sole objective seems to be to stimulate the accretion of goods. Self-respect and status, as well as comfort, are acquired in this way. Someone has called our national disease "galloping consumption." Half a century ago, William James saw the peril and was much worried by what he called "the American terror of poverty." He saw there was truth in the jibes that other countries direct at our "materialism."

HOPE IN UNEASINESS

Now a high standard of living is not in itself an evil thing. All the world wants what we already have. But the singleminded pursuit of production and consumption has brought a dulling of other values. One consequence is symbolized by the scandal of rigged quiz programs. These were in the service of advertising, which in turn was in the service of a profitable expanding economy. Another consequence is the accumulated froth of our TV, radio, and movies. Another is the widely discussed conformity of the organization man, as well as the futile rebellion of the beats. An especially peppery critic, Paul Goodman,[4] has shown that the starved lives of juvenile delinquents and of young people caught in the organizational grind are at bottom much alike. Both are attracted to the cult of easiness and aspire to nothing more than amiable mediocrity. Both styles of living fail to prepare youth for the problems that lie ahead for themselves and for the nation.

A somewhat vulgar story seems to me to summarize all this mordant criticism. Moses, a stalwart leader of the old school, said to the Israelites in Egypt, "Load up your camels, bring along your asses, and I'll lead you to the promised land." By contrast, the modern American prophet seems to urge, "Light up your Camels, sit on your asses, and I'll bring you the promised land."

All this familiar criticism is irritating; yet the fact that it flourishes is a hopeful sign. We suspect it may be too harsh. I am inclined to think so. It is rash indeed to indict a whole generation. At worst, Jacob's gloomy picture held for three-quarters of the college students studied, but not at all for a vital and far from negligible minority. And even though the gloomy generalizations have some truth in them, are the assets given fair attention? I myself have some favorable impressions, although one man's view is not reliable. But youth today appears to enjoy a certain freedom and flexibility that was not common in the more rigid days of our parents and grandparents. I even have the impression that there is less neuroticism among students now than among those of a generation ago. What is more, young people, I find, are not blind to the world changes that are occurring. Their apparent repression of the challenge is due largely to their bewilderment concerning proper paths to take. (And one has the feeling that our own statesmen in Washington are no less bewildered.) All in all, these are hopeful signs that should not be overlooked.

VALUES AND THE SCHOOL

Another hopeful sign is the fact that many teachers are asking, "What can we do to be helpful?" They know, and we all know, that the ability of the school to give training in values is limited. For one thing, the home is vastly more important. A home that infects the child with galloping consumption, that encourages only canned recreation and has no creative out-

[4] P. Goodman, *Growing Up Absurd* (New York: Random House, 1960).

lets, can only with difficulty be offset by the school. Another limitation lies in the fact that the school is ordinarily expected to mirror current social values and to prepare the child to live within the existing frame. It is an unusual school system and an unusual teacher who even *wish* to transcend the current fashions of value.

But assuming that we have an unusual school system and an unusual teacher, what values shall they elect to teach? If they do not choose to follow the prevailing fashions, what standards shall they follow? The ancient Romans were fond of asking, "Who will judge the judges?" and "Who will guard the guardians?" Can the guardians turn perhaps to standard discussions of "the aims of education"? Such discussions are numerous, abstract, and often dull. Their weakness, I feel, is their effort to formulate absolute goals, vistas of abstract perfection. The result is often a series of platitudes or generalizations so broad as to be unhelpful. Of course we want to develop "good citizenship"; we certainly want to "free the child's intellect." These and all other absolutes need to be reduced to concrete, stepwise processes before they can guide us in the strategy of teaching values.

The teacher must start with the situation as he or she finds it and in concrete instances sharpen the value-attributes of the lesson being taught. To a considerable extent, these value-attributes can be drawn from the codified wisdom of our nation. We cannot neglect the value of profitable production and high living standards, for all our vocational and professional education contribute to this end. But the codified wisdom of our unique society extends far beyond the obsession of today. Our values include also such matters as respect for civil liberties. Does the school accent this value? They include approval for individual initiative, for philanthropy, for compassion. And they imply much concerning civic duties that are the reciprocal of civic rights. What must we do to deserve our precious cornucopia of freedom? Vote? Yes. But voting does no good unless the voter is informed above the stereotyped level of the mass media. He must also pay taxes willingly. Do schools and colleges teach the young to pay a glad tax? I wonder. To me the most disturbing finding in *Youth's Outlook on the Future* lay in the elaborate talk about one's right to a rich, full life and in the almost total silence regarding one's duties.

I am saying that in the first instance teachers should choose the values they teach from the whole (not from a part) of our American ethos. Deep in our hearts we know, and most of the world knows, that our national values, derived, of course, from Judeo-Christian ethics, are about the finest mankind has yet formulated. In no sense are these values out of date, nor will they go out of date in the world of tomorrow. Yet many of them are badly rusted. Unless they are revitalized, however, our youth may not have the personal fortitude and moral implements that the future will require.

THE LARGER ANCHOR

Excellent as the American Creed is as a fountainhead of values, it does not contain them all. It says nothing explicitly, for example, about intellectual curiosity. And yet surely schools exist to augment this value. The most severe indictment of our educational procedures I have ever encountered is the discovery that a sizeable percentage of graduates of our colleges after completing their formal education never afterward read a single book.

There are other important values that are not spelled out in our American Creed. I am thinking of those details of human relationships that make all the difference between boorishness and brotherhood in the human family. As our population increases, it becomes more and more important to teach the elements of the new science of human relations which go far toward smoothing the roughness of common life by leading us to respect effectively the integrity of the other fellow. I recall a teacher of English whose class was studying *The Merchant of Venice*. She turned a wave of incipient anti-Semitism in her class to a sound lesson in values. Shylock, she explained, was like the resentful, self-seeking portion of every person's nature. We are all potential Shylocks. But while self-love is prominent in all of us, we are so constructed that it need not be sovereign in our natures.

To return for a moment to the relation between home and school—the former, as I have said, is far more important. Recognizing this fact, some people say, "Well, let's leave the teaching of values to the home and to the church. Schools can't do much of anything about the matter."

This position is untenable. If the school does not teach values, it will have the effect of denying them. If the child at school never hears a mention of honesty, modesty, charity, or reverence, he will be persuaded that, like many of his parents' ideas, they are simply old hat. As they grow toward adolescence, children become critical of the teaching of both parents and the church. They are in a questioning stage. If the school, which to the child represents the larger outside world, is silent on values, the child will repudiate more quickly the lessons learned at home. He will also be thrown onto peer values more completely, with their emphasis on the hedonism of teen-age parties or on the destructiveness of gangs. He will also be more at the mercy of the sensate values peddled by movies, TV, and disk jockeys. What is more, some homes, as we have said, give no fundamental value training. In such a case, it is *only* in the school that the child has any chance at all of finding ethical anchorage.

This brings us to the hardest question: How does the teacher, the instructor, the professor, handle his assignment in the classroom? How is it possible to teach values, including the value of intellectual curiosity?

THE MEANING OF VALUE

Before tackling this question, we must pause to define what we mean by value. You will recognize that I am using the term psychologically, not in its objective philosophical sense. Values, as I use the term, are simply *meanings perceived as related to self.* The child experiences value whenever he knows that a meaning is warm and central to himself. Values, to borrow Whitehead's term, are "matters of importance" as distinct from mere matters of fact.

So much for definition. Now the hard-pressed teacher is given a solid substantive curriculum to teach. The curriculum in its original state consists of mere matters of fact. And on the number of facts absorbed the pupil's standing depends. It takes virtually all of a teacher's time to convey factual information and grade the pupil on his achievement. There is little time left to transmute these matters of fact into matters of importance, let alone teach all of the moral and social values we have thus far been discussing.

The curriculum itself is not, and should not be, a direct aid. Prescribed instruction in values would be laughed out of court. We have recently been bumped by Sputnik headforemost into core subjects. Get on with science, mathematics, language! Away with courses in folk-dancing, personal adjustment, and fudge-making! I agree that value-study has no place in curriculum planning, but not because it is a frivolous subject—rather, because it is a subject too hard and too subtle for curriculum makers.

Education for values occurs only when teachers teach what they themselves stand for, no matter what their subject is. If I were to write a treatise on the teaching of values, I would give most of my emphasis to the moral pedagogy that lies in a teacher's incidental comments, to the *obiter dicta.* The hard core is central, but the hard core has a penumbra of moral significance. I mentioned the teacher of English who made a value-lesson out of Shylock. I recall also my college professor of geology who paused in his lecture on diatom ooze to say to us, "Others would not agree with me, but I confess that whenever I study diatoms, I don't see how anyone can doubt the existence of God because the design and behavior of these protozoa are so marvelous." Is it not interesting how we all recall the *obiter dicta* of our teachers, the penumbra of value they point out to us, surrounding the hard-core data? We remember them better than the subject matter itself.

Why does the student remember them so well? No current theory of learning seems able to tell us. I suspect it is because values, being matters of importance to the self, are always warm and central and ego-involved and therefore claim priority on our attention. The child, being value-ripe, cannot help being impressed when the teacher betrays excitement and enthusiasm for a mode of thought or for the content of the subject being studied. True, the youngster does not, and should not, adopt the teacher's values ready-made; but the teacher's self-disclosure leads the student to self-discovery.

What wouldn't we give if we could develop intellectual ardor in every child for hard core subjects? Why is it that for most pupils arithmetic, spelling, physics, remain forever dull matters of fact and never become a meaning perceived as related to the self? One reason, I think, is that the weary teacher fails to convey his own sense of the importance of the subject to the student. If he did so, he would, as I have said, at least fix attention upon the value-potentiality of the subject.

Another reason perhaps is that not all of a teacher's *obiter dicta* are wholesome. Some, indeed, may be deeply damaging, though the teacher may be innocent of any such intent. Sometimes we hear incidental (but still attitude-forming) remarks like this one: "All right now, children. You have had a good time playing at recess; now settle down to your English lesson." Play is recognized as a matter of joyful importance. English, the teacher is saying in effect, is a mere routine matter of fact.

VALUES AND LEARNING

I think our educational psychology has been mostly wrong about the process of learning—or perhaps not so much wrong as woefully incomplete. At the beginning of his learning career, a young child cannot, of course, be expected to feel adult enthusiasm for the intellectual content of his studies. He does his work in the first instance to avoid a scolding or because he has a habit of obeying instructions. Soon he finds added incentive. The teacher —really in the role of mother—gives praise and love ("Susan, I am proud of you"). There is a great deal of such dependency in the learning situation. Love and social reward (as well as some fear of punishment) sustain the processes of attention and retention. When the child puts forth intellectual effort, he does so in order to obtain a gold star, commendation, or other symbols of love.

All these incentives are extraneous to the subject matter. The youngster does not learn it because it is a matter of importance. When he leaves school or college, he loses these extraneous supports. He finds his love relations directly; they are no longer a reward for intellectual effort. Hence, intellectual apathy sets in, and, distressing to say, no further books are read.

In such a case as this, intellectual curiosity was never tied to independence, only to extraneous supports. At some point in the schooling—and the earlier the better—intellectual activity should become not a secondhand but a first-hand fitting to the sense of self. At the beginning, all learning must be tied, perhaps, to specific reinforcements; but if the dependency is long continued, authentic curiosity fails to develop.

It would be going too far to put the blame for intellectual apathy onto our current teaching of educational psychology. Yet I am inclined to feel somewhat punitive about this matter. Psychology has not yet settled down to the problem of transforming matters of fact—whose acquisition current learning theories explain fairly well—into autonomous matters of importance—which they do not explain at all.

Our emphasis has been on learning by drill and by reinforcement. Such "habit acquisition" receives all the emphasis. But the learning theory involved postulates a continuing dependency relation (extraneous reinforcement). When the relation terminates, the habits of study simply extinguish themselves. I am surprised, therefore, that stimulus-response psychologists do not see this consequence of their own theory. Insofar as teachers employ an educational psychology of this order, they are not likely to break the dependency relation, which belongs properly only to the earlier stages of schooling.

Matters of importance, I strongly believe, are not acquired by drill or by reinforcement. They are transformations of habits and skills from the "opportunistic" layer of personality into the ego-system itself.[5] Once inside the ego-system, these habits and skills turn into true interests and utilize the basic energy, the basic spontaneity, that the organism itself possesses. They are no longer sustained as "operant conditionings" by outside rewards. The interest, now being the very stuff of life itself, needs no outer supports.

FUNCTIONAL AUTONOMY

I have called this process of transforming means into ends, of changing extrinsic values into intrinsic values, *functional autonomy*. Concerning this concept, I am often asked two questions: How do you define "functional autonomy, and how does functional autonomy come about"?

For a definition, I offer the following: Functional autonomy refers to any acquired system of motivation in which the tensions involved are no longer of the same kind as the antecedent tensions from which the acquired system developed.[6] To answer the question of how functional autonomy comes about requires a more extended and technical discussion. I can only hint at the direction of my answer. Neurologists are gradually discovering a basis for what I would call "perseverative functional autonomy." I refer to the "self-sustaining circuits," "feedback mechanisms," and "central motive states" that are now commonly recognized to exist in the nervous system. This line of discovery, I find, provides a partial answer to the question. But

---

[5] G. Allport, *Becoming* (New Haven: Yale University Press, 1955).

[6] If this definition seems too technical to be immediately helpful, see G. Allport, *Pattern and Growth in Personality* (New York: Holt, Rinehart, and Winston, 1961), Chap. 10, for a more extended treatment of functional autonomy.

I believe we have to go further and call on the concept of self. Values, we have said, are meanings perceived as related to the self. Functional autonomy is not a mere perseverative phenomenon; it is, above all, an ego-involved phenomenon. Besides admitting an opportunistic layer to personality, which is the exclusive concern of most current theories of learning, we have no choice but to admit also a "propriate" layer. It is in this layer that all matters of importance reside.

The goal of the educator, then is to shift the content of the subject he teaches from the opportunistic (matter of fact) layer to the propriate. But there is no sure-fire, mechanical strategy to use. The best general rule, one that John Dewey saw clearly, is to strive ceaselessly to integrate routine matters of fact into the growing experience system of the child himself. It would take a long treatise to specify various detailed strategies of teaching that help achieve this goal.

Let me focus on only one aspect of this topic, upon a common mistake that teachers make. I myself am a continual offender. It is to present students with our own carefully thought out conclusions when they themselves lack the raw experience from which these conclusions are fashioned.

This particular error is inherent, for example, in the lecture system. Instead of lecturing on comparative religion, for instance, it would be much better to require all students to attend services of worship that are unfamiliar to them. If raw experience is present, then perhaps a lecture may be effective. Much of the intellectual apathy we complain about is due to our fault of presenting conclusions in lieu of first-hand experience. To us, our well-chiseled conclusion, summing up a long intellectual struggle with a problem of knowledge or of value, seems like a beautiful sonnet. To the student, it may be gibberish.

The fallacy of giving conclusions holds both for subject matter and for values. A lad of 15 cannot profit from the fully fashioned philosophy of life of a man of 50. To register at all, a statement about values must fall precisely on his present growing edge.

Teaching, then, is not the art of offering conclusions, however hard won and valid they may be. No teacher can forcibly enter the students' proprium and plant a functionally autonomous motive. He can at best open channels of experience and, by his *obiter dicta,* sometimes lead the student to see the value-potential in the experience.

The theory of personality that we need to guide a more fully developed educational psychology will teach us something important about our basic verb "to educate." It will show us that only at the outset of learning is it a transitive verb. By drill, by reward, by reinforcement, the teacher does indeed educate the child—in matters of fact. But true maturity comes only when the verb is reflexive. For in matters of importance, where values lie, the growing individual alone can educate himself.

The School Class As a Social System: Some of Its Functions in American Society* [1]

TALCOTT PARSONS

Drawing upon his vast store of sociological data and experience, Parsons, in the paper below, describes how the school class serves as both an agent of socialization for adult roles and for "allocation . . . of the age-cohort which do and do not go to college." The "primary selection process" begins in the elementary school and nears completion when the "seal" is put on the selections in junior high school. Parsons perceives the main process of differentiation as taking place on an axis of achievement. During the elementary years it is the development of a capacity to achieve that counts; during the secondary years it is the type of achievement that is important. A prominent, stratified youth culture aids the socialization and selection functions of the school class, and Parsons' analysis of its patterns will be especially helpful to those who are associated with school systems.

THE PROBLEM: SOCIALIZATION AND SELECTION

Our main interest, then, is in a dual problem: first of how the school class functions to internalize in its pupils both the commitments and capacities for successful performance of their future adult roles, and second of how it functions to allocate these human resources within the role-structure of the adult society. The primary ways in which these two problems are interrelated will provide our main points of reference.

First, from the functional point of view the school class can be treated as an agency of socialization. That is to say, it is an agency through which

[1] I am indebted to Mrs. Carolyn Cooper for research assistance in the relevant literature and for editorial work on the first draft of this paper.

* From *Harvard Educational Review*, XXIX (1959), pp. 297–318. Reprinted by permission of the author and the publisher.

individual personalities are trained to be motivationally and technically adequate to the performance of adult roles. It is not the sole such agency; the family, informal "peer groups," churches, and sundry voluntary organizations all play a part, as does actual on-the-job training. But, in the period extending from entry into first grade until entry into the labor force or marriage, the school class may be regarded as the focal socializing agency.

The socialization function may be summed up as the development in individuals of the commitments and capacities which are essential prerequisites of their future role-performance. Commitments may be broken down in turn into two components: commitment to the implementation of the broad *values* of society, and commitment to the performance of a specific type of role within the *structure* of society. Thus a person in a relatively humble occupation may be a "solid citizen" in the sense of commitment to honest work in that occupation, without an intensive and sophisticated concern with the implementation of society's higher-level values. Or conversely, someone else might object to the anchorage of the feminine role in marriage and the family on the grounds that such anchorage keeps society's total talent resources from being distributed equitably to business, government, and so on. Capacities can also be broken down into two components, the first being competence or the skill to perform the tasks involved in the individual's roles, and the second being "role-responsibility" or the capacity to live up to other people's expectations of the interpersonal behavior appropriate to these roles. Thus a mechanic as well as a doctor needs to have not only the basic "skills of his trade," but also the ability to behave responsibly toward those people with whom he is brought into contact in his work.

While on the one hand, the school class may be regarded as a primary agency by which these different components of commitments and capacities are generated, on the other hand, it is, from the point of view of the society, an agency of "manpower" allocation. It is well known that in American society there is a very high, and probably increasing, correlation between one's status level in the society and one's level of educational attainment. Both social status and educational level are obviously related to the occupational status which is attained. Now, as a result of the general process of both educational and occupational upgrading, completion of high school is increasingly coming to be the norm for minimum satisfactory educational attainment, and the most significant line for future occupational status has come to be drawn between members of an age-cohort who do and do not go to college.

We are interested, then, in what it is about the school class in our society that determines the distinction between the contingents of the age-cohort which do and do not go to college. Because of a tradition of localism and a rather pragmatic pluralism, there is apparently considerable variety among school systems of various cities and states. Although the situation in metropolitan Boston probably represents a more highly structured pattern than in many other parts of the country, it is probably not so extreme as to be misleading in its main features. There, though of course actual entry into college does not come until after graduation from high school, the main dividing line is between those who are and are not enrolled in the college preparatory course in high school; there is only a small amount of shifting either way after about the ninth grade when the decision is normally made. Furthermore, the evidence seems to be that by far the most important criterion of selection is the record of school performance in elementary school. These records are evaluated by teachers and principals, and there are few cases of entering the college preparatory course against their advice. It is therefore not stretching the evidence too far to say broadly that the primary selective process occurs through differential school performance in elementary school, and that the "seal" is put on it in junior high school.[2]

The evidence also is that the selective process is genuinely assortative. As in virtually all comparable processes, ascriptive as well as achieved factors influence the outcome. In this case, the ascriptive factor is the socioeconomic status of the child's family, and the factor underlying his opportunity for achievement is his individual ability. In the study of 3,348 Boston high school boys on which these generalizations are based, each of these factors was quite highly correlated with planning college. For example, the percentages planning college, by father's occupation, were: 12 per cent for semi-skilled and unskilled, 19 per cent for skilled, 26 per cent for minor white collar, 52 per cent for middle white collar, and 80 per cent for major white collar. Likewise, intentions varied by ability (as measured by IQ), namely, 11 per cent for the lowest quintile, 17 per cent for the next, 24 per cent for the middle, 30 per cent for the next to the top, and 52 per cent for the highest. It should be noted also that within any ability quintile, the relationship of plans to father's occupation is seen. For example, within the very important top quintile in ability as measured, the range in college intentions was from 29 per cent for sons of laborers to 89 per cent for sons of major white collar persons.[3]

2 The principal source for these statements is a study of social mobility among boys in ten public high schools in the Boston metropolitan area, conducted by Samuel A. Stouffer, Florence R. Kluckhohn, and the present author. Unfortunately the material is not available in published form.

3 See table from this study in J. A. Kahl, *The American Class Structure* (New York: Rinehart & Co., 1953), p. 283. Data from a nationwide sample of high school students, published by the Educational Testing Service, show similar patterns of relationships. For example, the ETS study shows variation, by father's occupation, in proportion of high school seniors planning college, of from 35 per cent to 80 per cent for boys and 27 per cent to 79 per cent for girls. (From *Background Factors Related to College Plans and College Enrollment among High School Students* [Princeton, N.J.: Educational Testing Service, 1957]).

The essential points here seem to be that there is a relatively uniform criterion of selection operating to differentiate between the college and the non-college contingents, and that for a very important part of the cohort the operation of this criterion is not a "put-up job"—it is not simply a way of affirming a previously determined ascriptive status. To be sure, the high-status, high-ability boy is very likely indeed to go to college, and the low-status, low ability boy is very unlikely to go. But the "cross-pressured" group for whom these two factors do not coincide[4] is of considerable importance.

Considerations like these lead me to conclude that the main process of differentiation (which from another point of view is selection) that occurs during elementary school takes place on a single main axis of *achievement*. Broadly, moreover, the differentiation leads up through high school to a bifurcation into college-goers and non-college-goers.

To assess the significance of this pattern, let us look at its place in the socialization of the individual. Entering the system of formal education is the child's first major step out of primary involvement in his family of orientation. Within the family certain foundations of his motivational system have been laid down. But the only characteristic fundamental to later roles which has clearly been "determined" and psychologically stamped in by that time is sex role. The postoedipal child enters the system of formal education clearly categorized as boy or girl, but beyond that his *role* is not yet differentiated. The process of selection, by which persons will select and be selected for categories of roles, is yet to take place.

On grounds which cannot be gone into here, it may be said that the most important single predispositional factor with which the child enters the school is his level of *independence*. By this is meant his level of self-sufficiency relative to guidance by adults, his capacity to take responsibility and to make his own decisions in coping with new and varying situations. This, like his sex role, he has as a function of his experience in the family.

The family is a collectivity within which the basic status-structure is ascribed in terms of biological position, that is, by generation, sex, and age. There are inevitably differences of performance relative to these, and they are rewarded and punished in ways that contribute to differential character formation. But these differences are not given the sanction of institutionalized social status. The school is the first socializing agency in the child's

---

[4] There seem to be two main reasons why the high-status, low-ability group is not so important as its obverse. The first is that in a society of expanding educational and occupational opportunity the general trend is one of upgrading, and the social pressures to downward mobility are not as great as they would otherwise be. The second is that there are cushioning mechanisms which tend to protect the high status boy who has difficulty "making the grade." He may be sent to a college with low academic standards, he may go to schools where the line between ability levels is not rigorously drawn, etc.

experience which institutionalizes a differentiation of status on nonbiological bases. Moreover, this is not an ascribed but an achieved status; it is the status "earned" by differential performance of the tasks set by the teacher, who is acting as an agent of the community's school system. Let us look at the structure of this situation.

THE STRUCTURE OF THE ELEMENTARY SCHOOL CLASS

In accord with the generally wide variability of American institutions, and of course the basically local control of school systems, there is considerable variability of school situations, but broadly they have a single relatively well-marked framework.[5] Particularly in the primary part of the elementary grades, i.e., the first three grades, the basic pattern includes one main teacher for the class, who teaches all subjects and who is in charge of the class generally. Sometimes this early, and frequently in later grades, other teachers are brought in for a few special subjects, particularly gym, music, and art, but this does not alter the central position of the main teacher. This teacher is usually a woman.[6] The class is with this one teacher for the school year, but usually no longer.

The class, then, is composed of about 25 age-peers of both sexes drawn from a relatively small geographical area—the neighborhood. Except for sex in certain respects, there is initially no formal basis for differentiation of status within the school class. The main structural differentiation develops gradually, on the single main axis indicated above as achievement. That the differentiation should occur on a single main axis is insured by four primary features of the situation. The first is the initial equalization of the "contestants' " status by age and by "family background," the neighborhood being typically much more homogeneous than is the whole society. The second circumstance is the imposition of a common set of tasks which is, compared to most other task-areas, strikingly undifferentiated. The school situation is far more like a race in this respect than most role-performance situations. Third, there is the sharp polarization between the pupils in their initial equality and the *single* teacher who is an adult and "represents" the adult world. And fourth, there is a relatively systematic process of evaluation of the pupils' performances. From the point of view of a pupil, this evaluation, particularly (though not exclusively) in the form of

---

[5] This discussion refers to public schools. Only about 13 per cent of all elementary and secondary school pupils attend non-public schools, with this proportion ranging from about 22 per cent in the Northeast to about 6 per cent in the South. U.S. Office of Education, *Biennial Survey of Education in the United States, 1954–56* (Washington: U.S. Government Printing Office, 1959), chap. ii, "Statistics of State School Systems, 1955–56," Table 44, p. 114.

[6] In 1955–56, 13 per cent of the public elementary school instructional staff in the United States were men. *Ibid.*, p. 7.

report card marks, constitutes reward and/or punishment for past performance; from the viewpoint of the school system acting as an allocating agency,
it is a basis of *selection* for future status in society.

Two important sets of qualifications need to be kept in mind in interpreting this structural pattern, but I think these do not destroy the significance of its main outline. The first qualification is for variations in the
formal organization and procedures of the school class itself. Here the most
important kind of variation is that between relatively "traditional" schools
and relatively "progressive" schools. The more traditional schools put more
emphasis on discrete units of subject-matter, whereas the progressive type
allows more "indirect" teaching through "projects" and broader topical
interests where more than one bird can be killed with a stone. In progressive schools there is more emphasis on groups of pupils working together,
compared to the traditional direct relation of the individual pupil to the
teacher. This is related to the progressive emphasis on co-operation among
the pupils rather than direct competition, to greater permissiveness as opposed to strictness of discipline, and to a de-emphasis on formal marking.[7]
In some schools one of these components will be more prominent, and in
others, another. That it is, however, an important range of variation is
clear. It has to do, I think, very largely with the independence-dependence
training which is so important to early socialization in the family. My
broad interpretation is that those people who emphasize independence
training will tend to be those who favor relatively progressive education.
The relation of support for progressive education to relatively high socio-
economic status and to "intellectual" interests and the like is well known.
There is no contradiction between these emphases both on independence
and on co-operation and group solidarity among pupils. In the first instance this is because the main focus of the independence problem at these
ages is vis-à-vis adults. However, it can also be said that the peer group,
which here is built into the school class, is an indirect field of expression of
dependency needs, displaced from adults.

The second set of qualifications concerns the "informal" aspects of the
school class, which are always somewhat at variance with the formal expectations. For instance, the formal pattern of nondifferentiation between
the sexes may be modified informally, for the very salience of the one-sex
peer group at this age period means that there is bound to be considerable
implicit recognition of it—for example, in the form of teachers' encouraging group competition between boys and girls. Still, the fact of coeducation
and the attempt to treat both sexes alike in all the crucial formal respects

[7] This summary of some contrasts between traditional and progressive patterns is
derived from general reading in the literature rather than any single authoritative
account.

remain the most important. Another problem raised by informal organization is the question of how far teachers can and do treat pupils particularistically in violation of the universalistic expectations of the school. When compared with other types of formal organizations, however, I think the extent of this discrepancy in elementary schools is seen to be not unusual. The school class is structured so that opportunity for particularistic treatment is severely limited. Because there are so many more children in a school class than in a family and they are concentrated in a much narrower age range, the teacher has much less chance than does a parent to grant particularistic favors.

Bearing in mind these two sets of qualifications, it is still fair, I think, to conclude that the major characteristics of the elementary school class in this country are such as have been outlined. It should be especially emphasized that more or less progressive schools, even with their relative lack of emphasis on formal marking, do not constitute a separate pattern, but rather a variant tendency within the same pattern. A progressive teacher, like any other, will form opinions about the different merits of her pupils relative to the values and goals of the class and will communicate these evaluations to them, informally if not formally. It is my impression that the extremer cases of playing down relative evaluation are confined to those upper-status schools where going to a "good" college is so fully taken for granted that for practical purposes it is an ascribed status. In other words, in interpreting these facts the selective function of the school class should be kept continually in the forefront of attention. Quite clearly its importance has not been decreasing; rather the contrary.

THE NATURE OF SCHOOL ACHIEVEMENT

What, now, of the content of the "achievement" expected of elementary school children? Perhaps the best broad characterization which can be given is that it involves the types of performance which are, on the one hand, appropriate to the school situation and, on the other hand, are felt by adults to be important in themselves. This vague and somewhat circular characterization may, as was mentioned earlier, be broken down into two main components. One of these is the more purely "cognitive" learning of information, skills, and frames of reference associated with empirical knowledge and technological mastery. The *written* language and the early phases of mathematical thinking are clearly vital; they involve cognitive skills at altogether new levels of generality and abstraction compared to those commanded by the pre-school child. With these basic skills goes assimilation of much factual information about the world.

The second main component is what may broadly be called a "moral" one. In earlier generations of schooling this was known as "deportment." Somewhat more generally it might be called responsible citizenship in the school community. Such things as respect for the teacher, consideration and co-operativeness in relation to fellow-pupils, and good "work-habits" are the fundamentals, leading on to capacity for "leadership" and "initiative."

The striking fact about this achievement content is that in the elementary grades these two primary components are not clearly differentiated from each other. Rather, the pupil is evaluated in diffusely general terms; a *good* pupil is defined in terms of a fusion of the cognitive and the moral components, in which varying weight is given to one or the other. Broadly speaking, then, we may say that the "high achievers" of the elementary school are both the "bright" pupils, who catch on easily to their more strictly intellectual tasks, and the more "responsible" pupils, who "behave well" and on whom the teacher can "count" in her difficult problems of managing the class. One indication that this is the case is the fact that in elementary school the purely intellectual tasks are relatively easy for the pupil of high intellectual ability. In many such cases, it can be presumed that the primary challenge to the pupil is not to his intellectual, but to his "moral," capacities. On the whole, the progressive movement seems to have leaned in the direction of giving enhanced emphasis to this component, suggesting that of the two, it has tended to become the more problematical.[8]

The essential point, then, seems to be that the elementary school, regarded in the light of its socialization function, is an agency which differentiates the school class broadly along a single continuum of achievement, the content of which is relative excellence in living up to the expectations imposed by the teacher as an agent of the adult society. The criteria of this achievement are, generally speaking, undifferentiated into the cognitive or technical component and the moral or "social" component. But with respect to its bearing on societal values, it is broadly a differentiation of *levels* of capacity to act in accord with these values. Though the relation is far from neatly uniform, this differentiation underlies the processes of selection for levels of status and role in the adult society.

Next, a few words should be said about the out-of-school context in which this process goes on. Besides the school class, there are clearly two primary social structures in which the child participates: the family and the child's informal "peer group."

---

[8] This account of the two components of elementary school achievement and their relation summarizes impressions gained from the literature, rather than being based on the opinions of particular authorities. I have the impression that achievement in this sense corresponds closely to what is meant by the term as used by McClelland and his associates. Cf. D. C. McClelland *et al., The Achievement Motive* (New York: Appleton-Century-Crofts, Inc., 1953).

FAMILY AND PEER GROUP IN RELATION TO THE SCHOOL CLASS

The school age child, of course, continues to live in the parental household and to be highly dependent, emotionally as well as instrumentally, on his parents. But he is now spending several hours a day away from home, subject to a discipline and a reward system which are essentially independent of that administered by the parents. Moreover, the range of this independence gradually increases. As he grows older, he is permitted to range further territorially with neither parental nor school supervision, and to do an increasing range of things. He often gets an allowance for personal spending and begins to earn some money of his own. Generally, however, the emotional problem of dependence-independence continues to be a very salient one through this period, frequently with manifestations by the child of compulsive independence.

Concomitantly with this, the area for association with age-peers without detailed adult supervision expands. These associations are tied to the family, on the one hand, in that the home and yards of children who are neighbors and the adjacent streets serve as locations for their activities; and to the school, on the other hand, in that play periods and going to and from school provide occasions for informal association, even though organized extracurricular activities are introduced only later. Ways of bringing some of this activity under another sort of adult supervision are found in such organizations as the boy and girl scouts.

Two sociological characteristics of peer groups at this age are particularly striking. One is the fluidity of their boundaries, with individual children drifting into and out of associations. This element of "voluntary association" contrasts strikingly with the child's ascribed membership in the family and the school class, over which he has no control. The second characteristic is the peer group's sharp segregation by sex. To a striking degree this is enforced by the children themselves rather than by adults.

The psychological functions of peer association are suggested by these two characteristics. On the one hand, the peer group may be regarded as a field for the exercise of independence from adult control; hence it is not surprising that it is often a focus of behavior which goes beyond independence from adults to the range of adult-*disapproved* behavior; when this happens, it is the seed bed from which the extremists go over into delinquency. But another very important function is to provide the child a source of non-adult approval and acceptance. These depend on "technical" and "moral" criteria as diffuse as those required in the school situation. On the one hand, the peer group is a field for acquiring and displaying various types of "prowess"; for boys this is especially the physical prowess which may later ripen into athletic achievement. On the other hand, it is a matter of gaining acceptance from desirable peers as "belonging" in the group, which later ripens into the conception of the popular teen-ager, the "right guy." Thus the adult parents are augmented by age-peers as a source of rewards for performance and of security in acceptance.

The importance of the peer group for socialization in our type of society should be clear. The motivational foundations of character are inevitably first laid down through identification with parents, who are generation-superiors, and the generation difference is a type example of a hierarchical status difference. But an immense part of the individual's adult role performance will have to be in association with status-equals or near-equals. In this situation it is important to have a reorganization of the motivational structure so that the original dominance of the hierarchical axis is modified to strengthen the egalitarian components. The peer group plays a prominent part in this process.

Sex segregation of latency period peer groups may be regarded as a process of reinforcement of sex-role identification. Through intensive association with sex-peers and involvement in sex-typed activities, they strongly reinforce belongingness with other members of the same sex and contrast with the opposite sex. This is the more important because in the coeducational school a set of forces operates which specifically plays down sex-role differentiation.

It is notable that the latency period sex-role pattern, instead of institutionalizing relations to members of the opposite sex, is characterized by an avoidance of such relations, which only in adolescence gives way to dating. This avoidance is clearly associated with the process of reorganization of the erotic components of motivational structure. The pre-oedipal objects of erotic attachment were both intra-familial and generation-superior. In both respects there must be a fundamental shift by the time the child reaches adulthood. I would suggest that one of the main functions of the avoidance pattern is to help cope with the psychological difficulty of overcoming the earlier incestuous attachments, and hence to prepare the child for assuming an attachment to an age-mate of opposite sex later.

Seen in this perspective, the socialization function of the school class assumes a particular significance. The socialization functions of the family by this time are relatively residual, though their importance should not be underestimated. But the school remains adult-controlled and, moreover, induces basically the same kind of identification as was induced by the family in the child's pre-oedipal stage. This is to say that the learning of achievement-motivation is, psychologically speaking, a process of identification with the teacher, of doing well in school in order to please the teacher (often backed by the parents) in the same sense in which a pre-oedipal child learns new skills in order to please his mother.

In this connection I maintain that what is internalized through the process of identification is a reciprocal pattern of role-relationships.[9] Unless there is a drastic failure of internalization altogether, not just one, but both sides of the interaction will be internalized. There will, however, be an emphasis on one or the other, so that some children will more nearly identify with the socializing agent, and others will more nearly identify with the opposite role. Thus, in the pre-oedipal stage, the "independent" child has identified more with the parent, and the "dependent" one with the child-role vis-à-vis the parent.

In school the teacher is institutionally defined as superior to any pupil in knowledge of curriculum subject-matter and in responsibility as a good citizen of the school. In so far as the school class tends to be bifurcated (and of course the dichotomization is far from absolute), it will broadly be on the basis, on the one hand, of identification with the teacher, or acceptance of her role as a model; and, on the other hand, of identification with the pupil peer group. This bifurcation of the class on the basis of identification with teacher or with peer group so strikingly corresponds with the bifurcation into college-goers and non-college-goers that it would be hard to avoid the hypothesis that this structural dichotomization in the school system is the primary source of the selective dichotomization. Of course in detail the relationship is blurred, but certainly not more so than in a great many other fields of comparable analytical complexity.

These considerations suggest an interpretation of some features of the elementary teacher role in American society. The first major step in socialization, beyond that in the family, takes place in the elementary school, so it seems reasonable to expect that the teacher-figure should be characterized by a combination of similarities to and differences from parental figures. The teacher, then, is an adult, characterized by the generalized superiority, which a parent also has, of adult status relative to children. She is not, however, ascriptively related to her pupils, but is performing an occupational role—a role, however, in which the recipients of her services are tightly bound in solidarity to her and to each other. Furthermore, compared to a parent's, her responsibility to them is much more universalistic, this being reinforced, as we saw, by the size of the class; it is also much more oriented to performance rather than to solicitude for the emotional "needs" of the children. She is not entitled to suppress the distinction between high and low achievers, just because not being able to be included among the high group would be too hard on little Johnny—however much tendencies in this direction appear as deviant patterns. A mother, on the other hand, must give *first* priority to the needs of her child, regardless of his capacities to achieve.

It is also significant for the parallel of the elementary school class with

[9] On the identification process in the family see my paper, "Social Structure and the Development of Personality," *Psychiatry*, XXI (November, 1958), pp. 321–40.

the family that the teacher is normally a woman. As background it should be noted that in most European systems until recently, and often today in our private parochial and non-sectarian schools, the sexes have been segregated and each sex group has been taught by teachers of their own sex. Given coeducation, however, the woman teacher represents continuity with the role of the mother. Precisely the lack of differentiation in the elementary school "curriculum" between the components of subject-matter competence and social responsibility fits in with the greater diffuseness of the feminine role.

But at the same time, it is essential that the teacher is not a mother to her pupils, but must insist on universalistic norms and the differential reward of achievement. Above all she must be the agent of bringing about and legitimizing a differentiation of the school class on an achievement axis. This aspect of her role is furthered by the fact that in American society the feminine role is less confined to the familial context than in most other societies, but joins the masculine in occupational and associational concerns, though still with a greater relative emphasis on the family. Through identification with their teacher, children of both sexes learn that the category "woman" is not co-extensive with "mother" (and future wife), but that the feminine role-personality is more complex than that.

In this connection it may well be that there is a relation to the once-controversial issue of the marriage of women teachers. If the differentiation between what may be called the maternal and the occupational components of the feminine role is incomplete and insecure, confusion between them may be avoided by insuring that both are not performed by the same persons. The "old maid" teacher of American tradition may thus be thought of as having renounced the maternal role in favor of the occupational.[10] Recently, however, the highly affective concern over the issue of married women's teaching has conspicuously abated, and their actual participation has greatly increased. It may be suggested that this change is associated with a change in the feminine role, the most conspicuous feature of which is the general social sanctioning of participation of women in the labor force, not only prior to marriage, but also after marriage. This I should interpret as a process of structural differentiation in that the same category of persons is permitted and even expected to engage in a more complex set of role-functions than before.

The process of identification with the teacher which has been postulated here is furthered by the fact that in the elementary grades the child typically has one teacher, just as in the pre-oedipal period he had one parent, the

[10] It is worth noting that the Catholic parochial school system is in line with the more general older American tradition, in that the typical teacher is a nun. The only difference in this respect is the sharp religious symbolization of the difference between mother and teacher.

mother, who was the focus of his object-relations. The continuity between the two phases is also favored by the fact that the teacher, like the mother, is a woman. But, if she acted only like a mother, there would be no genuine reorganization of the pupil's personality system. This reorganization is furthered by the features of the teacher role which differentiate it from the maternal. One further point is that while a child has one main teacher in each grade, he will usually have a new teacher when he progresses to the next higher grade. He is thus accustomed to the fact that teachers are, unlike mothers, "interchangeable" in a certain sense. The school year is long enough to form an important relationship to a particular teacher, but not long enough for a highly particularistic attachment to crystallize. More than in the parent-child relationship, in school the child must internalize his relation to the teacher's *role* rather than her particular personality; this is a major step in the internalization of universalistic patterns.

SOCIALIZATION AND SELECTION IN THE ELEMENTARY SCHOOL

To conclude this discussion of the elementary school class, something should be said about the fundamental conditions underlying the process which is, as we have seen, simultaneously (1) an emancipation of the child from primary emotional attachment to his family, (2) an internalization of a level of societal values and norms that is a step higher than those he can learn in his family alone, (3) a differentiation of the school class in terms both of actual achievement and of differential *valuation* of achievement, and (4) from society's point of view, a selection and allocation of its human resources relative to the adult role system.[11]

Probably the most fundamental condition underlying this process is the sharing of common values by the two adult agencies involved—the family and the school. In this case the core is the shared valuation of *achievement*. It includes, above all, recognition that it is fair to give differential rewards for different levels of achievement, so long as there has been fair access to opportunity, and fair that these rewards lead on to higher-order opportunities for the successful. There is thus a basic sense in which the elementary school class is an embodiment of the fundamental American value of equality of opportunity, in that it places value *both* on initial equality and on differential achievement.

As a second condition, however, the rigor of this valuational pattern must be tempered by allowance for the difficulties and needs of the young child. Here the quasi-motherliness of the woman teacher plays an important

---

[11] The following summary is adapted from T. Parsons, R. F. Bales *et al.*, *Family, Socialization and Interaction Process* (Glencoe, Ill.: The Free Press, 1955), esp. chap. iv.

part. Through her the school system, assisted by other agencies, attempts to minimize the insecurity resulting from the pressures to learn, by providing a certain amount of emotional support defined in terms of what is due to a child of a given age level. In this respect, however, the role of the school is relatively small. The underlying foundation of support is given in the home, and as we have seen, an important supplement to it can be provided by the informal peer associations of the child. It may be suggested that the development of extreme patterns of alienation from the school is often related to inadequate support in these respects.

Third, there must be a process of selective rewarding of value performance. Here the teacher is clearly the primary agent, though the more progressive modes of education attempt to enlist classmates more systematically than in the traditional pattern. This is the process that is the direct source of intra-class differentiation along the achievement axis.

The final condition is that this initial differentiation tends to bring about a status system in the class, in which not only the immediate results of school work, but a whole series of influences, converge to consolidate different expectations which may be thought of as the children's "levels of aspiration." Generally some differentiation of friendship groups along this line occurs, though it is important that it is by no means complete, and that children are sensitive to the attitudes not only of their own friends, but of others.

Within this general discussion of processes and conditions, it is important to distinguish, as I have attempted to do all along, the socialization of the individual from the selective allocation of contingents to future roles. For the individual, the old familial identification is broken up (the family of orientation becomes, in Freudian terms, a "lost object") and a new identification is gradually built up, providing the first-order structure of the child's identity apart from his originally ascribed identity as son or daughter of the "Joneses." He both transcends his familial identification in favor of a more independent one and comes to occupy a differentiated status within the new system. His personal status is inevitably a direct function of the position he achieves, primarily in the formal school class and secondarily in the informal peer group structure. In spite of the sense in which achievement-ranking takes place along a continuum, I have put forward reasons to suggest that, with respect to this status, there is an important differentiation into two broad, relatively distinct levels, and that his position on one or the other enters into the individual's definition of his own identity. To an important degree this process of differentiation is independent of the socio-economic status of his family in the community, which to the child is a prior ascribed status.

When we look at the same system as a selective mechanism from the societal point of view, some further considerations become important. First, it may be noted that the valuation of achievement and its sharing by family and school not only provides the appropriate values for internalization by individuals, but also performs a crucial integrative function for the system. Differentiation of the class along the achievement axis is inevitably a source of strain, because it confers higher rewards and privileges on one contingent than on another within the same system. This common valuation helps make possible the acceptance of the crucial differentiation, especially by the losers in the competition. Here it is an essential point that this *common* value on achievement is shared by units with different statuses in the system. It cuts across the differentiation of families by socioeconomic status. It is necessary that there be realistic opportunity and that the teacher can be relied on to implement it by being "fair" and rewarding achievement by whoever shows capacity for it. The fact is crucial that the distribution of abilities, though correlated with family status, clearly does not coincide with it. There can then be a genuine selective process within a set of "rules of the game."

This commitment to common values is not, however, the sole integrative mechanism counteracting the strain imposed by differentiation. Not only does the individual pupil enjoy familial support, but teachers also like and indeed "respect" pupils on bases independent of achievement-status, and peer-group friendship lines, though correlated with position on the achievement scale, again by no means coincide with it, but cross-cut it. Thus there are cross-cutting lines of solidarity which mitigate the strains generated by rewarding achievement differentially.[12]

It is only *within* this framework of institutionalized solidarity that the crucial selective process goes on through selective rewarding and the consolidation of its results into a status-differentiation within the school class. We have called special attention to the impact of the selective process on the children of relatively high ability but low family status. Precisely in this group, but pervading school classes generally, is another parallel to

[12] In this, as in several other respects, there is a parallel to other important allocative processes in the society. A striking example is the voting process by which political support is allocated between party candidates. Here, the strain arises from the fact that one candidate and his party will come to enjoy all the perquisites—above all the power—of office, while the other will be excluded for the time being from these. This strain is mitigated, on the one hand, by the common commitment to constitutional procedure, and, on the other hand, by the fact that the nonpolitical bases of social solidarity, which figure so prominently as determinants of voting behavior, still cut across party lines. The average person is, in various of his roles, associated with people whose political preference is different from his own; he therefore could not regard the opposite party as composed of unmitigated scoundrels without introducing a rift within the groups to which he is attached. This feature of the electorate's structure is brought out strongly in B. R. Berelson, P. F. Lazarsfeld and W. N. McPhee, *Voting* (Chicago: University of Chicago Press, 1954). The conceptual analysis of it is developed in my own paper, " 'Voting' and the Equilibrium of the American Political System" in E. Burdick and A. J. Brodbeck (eds.), *American Voting Behavior* (Glencoe, Ill.: The Free Press, 1959).

what was found in the studies of voting behavior.[13] In the voting studies it was found that the "shifters"—those voters who were transferring their allegiance from one major party to the other—tended, on the one hand, to be the "cross-pressured" people, who had multiple status characteristics and group allegiances which predisposed them simultaneously to vote in opposite directions. The analogy in the school class is clearly to the children for whom ability and family status do not coincide. On the other hand, it was precisely in this group of cross-pressured voters that political "indifference" was most conspicuous. Non-voting was particularly prevalent in this group, as was a generally cool emotional tone toward a campaign. The suggestion is that some of the pupil "indifference" to school performance may have a similar origin. This is clearly a complex phenomenon and cannot be further analyzed here. But rather than suggesting, as is usual on common sense grounds, that indifference to school work represents an "alienation" from cultural and intellectual values, I would suggest exactly the opposite: that an important component of such indifference, including in extreme cases overt revolt against school discipline, is connected with the fact that the stakes, as in politics, are very high indeed. Those pupils who are exposed to contradictory pressures are likely to be ambivalent; at the same time, the personal stakes for them are higher than for the others, because what happens in school may make much more of a difference for their futures than for the others, in whom ability and family status point to the same expectations for the future. In particular for the upwardly mobile pupils, too much emphasis on school success would pointedly suggest "burning their bridges" of association with their families and status peers. This phenomenon seems to operate even in elementary school, although it grows somewhat more conspicuous later. In general I think that an important part of the anti-intellectualism in American youth culture stems from the *importance* of the selective process through the educational system rather than the opposite.

One further major point should be made in this analysis. As we have noted, the general trend of American society has been toward a rapid upgrading in the educational status of the population. This means that, relative to past expectations, with each generation there is increased pressure to educational achievement, often associated with parents' occupational ambitions for their children.[14] To a sociologist this is a more or less classical situation of anomic strain, and the youth-culture ideology which plays down intellectual interests and school performance seems to fit in this context. The orientation of the youth culture is, in the nature of the case, ambivalent, but for the reasons suggested, the anti-intellectual side of the ambivalence tends to be overtly stressed. One of the reasons for the domi-

13 *Ibid.*
14 J. A. Kahl, "Educational and Occupational Aspirations of 'Common Man' Boys," *Harvard Educational Review,* XXIII (Summer, 1953), pp. 186–203.

nance of the anti-school side of the ideology is that it provides a means of protest against adults, who are at the opposite pole in the socialization situation. In certain respects one would expect that the trend toward greater emphasis on independence, which we have associated with progressive education, would accentuate the strain in this area and hence the tendency to decry adult expectations. The whole problem should be subjected to a thorough analysis in the light of what we know about ideologies more generally.

The same general considerations are relevant to the much-discussed problem of juvenile delinquency. Both the general upgrading process and the pressure to enhanced independence should be expected to increase strain on the lower, most marginal groups. The analysis of this paper has been concerned with the line between college and non-college contingents; there is, however, another line between those who achieve solid non-college educational status and those for whom adaptation to educational expectations at *any* level is difficult. As the acceptable minimum of educational qualification rises, persons near and below the margin will tend to be pushed into an attitude of repudiation of these expectations. Truancy and delinquency are ways of expressing this repudiation. Thus the very *improvement* of educational standards in the society at large may well be a major factor in the failure of the educational process for a growing number at the lower end of the status and ability distribution. It should therefore not be too easily assumed that delinquency is a symptom of a *general* failure of the educational process.

DIFFERENTIATION AND SELECTION IN THE SECONDARY SCHOOL

It will not be possible to discuss the secondary school phase of education in nearly as much detail as has been done for the elementary school phase, but it is worthwhile to sketch its main outline in order to place the above analysis in a wider context. Very broadly we may say that the elementary school phase is concerned with the internalization in children of motivation to achievement, and the selection of persons on the basis of differential capacity for achievement. The focus is on the *level* of capacity. In the secondary school phase, on the other hand, the focus is on the differentiation of *qualitative types* of achievement. As in the elementary school, this differentiation cross-cuts sex role. I should also maintain that it cross-cuts the levels of achievement which have been differentiated out in the elementary phase.

In approaching the question of the types of capacity differentiated, it should be kept in mind that secondary school is the principal springboard from which lower-status persons will enter the labor force, whereas those achieving higher status will continue their formal education in college, and some of them beyond. Hence for the lower-status pupils the important line of differentiation should be the one which will lead into broadly different categories of jobs; for the higher-status pupils the differentiation will lead to broadly different roles in college.

My suggestion is that this differentiation separates those two components of achievement which we labelled "cognitive" and "moral" in discussing the elementary phase. Those relatively high in "cognitive" achievement will fit better in specific-function, more or less technical roles; those relatively high in "moral" achievement will tend toward diffuser, more "socially" or "humanly" oriented roles. In jobs not requiring college training, the one category may be thought of as comprising the more impersonal and technical occupations, such as "operatives," mechanics, or clerical workers; the other, as occupations where "human relations" are prominent, such as salesmen and agents of various sorts. At the college level, the differentiation certainly relates to concern, on the one hand, with the specifically intellectual curricular work of college and, on the other hand, with various types of diffuser responsibility in human relations, such as leadership roles in student government and extracurricular activities. Again, candidates for post-graduate professional training will probably be drawn mainly from the first of these two groups.

In the structure of the school, there appears to be a gradual transition from the earliest grades through high school, with the changes timed differently in different school systems. The structure emphasized in the first part of this discussion is most clearly marked in the first three "primary" grades. With progression to the higher grades, there is greater frequency of plural teachers, though very generally still a single main teacher. In the sixth grade and sometimes in the fifth, a man as main teacher, though uncommon, is by no means unheard of. With junior high school, however, the shift of pattern becomes more marked, and still more in senior high.

By that time the pupil has several different teachers of both sexes[15] teaching him different subjects, which are more or less formally organized into different courses—college preparatory and others. Furthermore, with the choice of "elective" subjects, the members of the class in one subject no longer need be exactly the same as in another, so the pupil is much more systematically exposed to association with different people, both adults and age-peers, in different contexts. Moreover, the school he attends is likely to be substantially larger than was his elementary school, and to draw from a wider geographical area. Hence the child is exposed to a wider range of statuses than before, being thrown in with more age-peers whom he does

[15] Men make up about half (49 per cent) of the public secondary school instructional staff. *Biennial Survey of Education in the United States, 1954–56, op. cit.,* chap. ii, p. 7.

not encounter in his neighborhood; it is less likely that his parents will know the parents of any given child with whom he associates. It is thus my impression that the transitions to junior high and senior high school are apt to mean a considerable reshuffling of friendships. Another conspicuous difference between the elementary and secondary levels is the great increase in high school of organized extracurricular activities. Now, for the first time, organized athletics become important, as do a variety of clubs and associations which are school-sponsored and supervised to varying degrees.

Two particularly important shifts in the patterning of youth culture occur in this period. One, of course, is the emergence of more positive cross-sex relationships outside the classroom, through dances, dating, and the like. The other is the much sharper prestige-stratification of informal peer groupings, with indeed an element of snobbery which often exceeds that of the adult community in which the school exists.[16] Here it is important that though there is a broad correspondence between the prestige of friendship groups and the family status of their members, this, like the achievement order of the elementary school, is by no means a simple "mirroring" of the community stratification scale, for a considerable number of lower-status children get accepted into groups including members with higher family status than themselves. This stratified youth system operates as a genuine assortative mechanism; it does not simply reinforce ascribed status.

The prominence of this youth culture in the American secondary school is, in comparison with other societies, one of the hallmarks of the American educational system; it is much less prominent in most European systems. It may be said to constitute a kind of structural fusion between the school class and the peer-group structure of the elementary period. It seems clear that what I have called the "human relations" oriented contingent of the secondary school pupils are more active and prominent in extracurricular activities, and that this is one of the main foci of their differentiation from the more impersonally- and technically-oriented contingent. The personal qualities figuring most prominently in the human relations contingent can perhaps be summed up as the qualities that make for "popularity." I suggest that, from the point of view of the secondary school's selective function, the youth culture helps to differentiate between types of personalities which will, by and large, play different kinds of roles as adults.

The stratification of youth groups has, as noted, a selective function; it is a bridge between the achievement order and the adult stratification system of the community. But it also has another function. It is a focus of prestige which exists along side of, and is to a degree independent of, the achievement order focussing on school work as such. The attainment of prestige in the informal youth group is itself a form of valued achievement. Hence,

[16] See, for instance, C. W. Gordon, *The Social System of the High School: A Study in the Sociology of Adolescence* (Glencoe, Ill.: The Free Press, 1957).

among those individuals destined for higher status in society, one can discern two broad types: those whose school work is more or less outstanding and whose informal prestige is relatively satisfactory; and vice versa, those whose informal prestige is outstanding, and school performance satisfactory. Falling below certain minima in either respect would jeopardize the child's claim to belong in the upper group.[17] It is an important point here that those clearly headed for college belong to peer groups which, while often depreciative of intensive concern with studies, also take for granted and reinforce a level of scholastic attainment which is necessary for admission to a good college. Pressure will be put on the individual who tends to fall below such a standard.

In discussing the elementary school level it will be remembered that we emphasized that the peer group served as an object of emotional dependency displaced from the family. In relation to the pressure for school achievement, therefore, it served at least partially as an expression of the lower-order motivational system *out* of which the child was in process of being socialized. On its own level, similar things can be said of the adolescent youth culture; it is in part an expression of regressive motivations. This is true of the emphasis on athletics despite its lack of relevance to adult roles, of the "homosexual" undertones of much intensive same-sex friendship, and of a certain "irresponsibility" in attitudes toward the opposite sex—e.g., the exploitative element in the attitudes of boys toward girls. This, however, is by no means the whole story. The youth culture is also a field for practicing the assumption of higher-order responsibilities, for conducting delicate human relations without immediate supervision and learning to accept the consequences. In this connection it is clearly of particular importance to the contingent we have spoken of as specializing in "human relations."

We can, perhaps, distinguish three different levels of crystallization of these youth-culture patterns. The middle one is that which may be considered age-appropriate without clear status-differentiation. The two keynotes here seem to be "being a good fellow" in the sense of general friendliness and being ready to take responsibility in informal social situations where something needs to be done. Above this, we may speak of the higher level of "outstanding" popularity and qualities of "leadership" of the person who is turned to where unusual responsibilities are required. And below the middle level are the youth patterns bordering on delinquency, withdrawal, and generally unacceptable behavior. Only this last level is clearly "regressive" relative to expectations of appropriate behavior for the age-

17 J. Riley, M. Riley, and M. Moore, "Adolescent Values and the Riesman Typology" in S. M. Lipset and L. Lowenthal (eds.), *The Sociology of Culture and the Analysis of Social Character* (Glencoe, Ill.: The Free Press, to be published in 1960).

grade. In judging these three levels, however, allowance should be made for a good many nuances. Most adolescents do a certain amount of experimenting with the borderline of the unacceptable patterns; that they should do so is to be expected in view of the pressure toward independence from adults, and of the "collusion" which can be expected in the reciprocal stimulation of age-peers. The question is whether this regressive behavior comes to be confirmed into a major pattern for the personality as a whole. Seen in this perspective, it seems legitimate to maintain that the middle and the higher patterns indicated are the major ones, and that only a minority of adolescents comes to be confirmed in a truly unacceptable pattern of living. This minority may well be a relatively constant proportion of the age cohort, but apart from situations of special social disorganization, the available evidence does not suggest that it has been a progressively growing one in recent years.

The patterning of cross-sex relations in the youth culture clearly foreshadows future marriage and family formation. That it figures so prominently in school is related to the fact that in our society the element of ascription, including direct parental influence, in the choice of a marriage partner is strongly minimized. For the girl, it has the very important significance of reminding her that her adult status is going to be very much concerned with marriage and a family. This basic expectation for the girl stands in a certain tension to the school's curricular coeducation with its relative lack of differentiation by sex. But the extent to which the feminine role in American society continues to be anchored in marriage and the family should not be allowed to obscure the importance of coeducation. In the first place, the contribution of women in various extra-familial occupations and in community affairs has been rapidly increasing, and certainly higher levels of education have served as a prerequisite to this contribution. At the same time, it is highly important that the woman's familial role should not be regarded as drastically segregated from the cultural concerns of the society as a whole. The educated woman has important functions *as wife and mother,* particularly as an influence on her children in backing the schools and impressing on them the importance of education. It is, I think, broadly true that the immediate responsibility of women for family management has been increasing, though I am very skeptical of the alleged "abdication" of the American male. But precisely in the context of women's increased family responsibility, the influence of the mother both as agent of socialization and as role model is a crucial one. This influence should be evaluated in the light of the general upgrading process. It is very doubtful whether, apart from any other considerations, the motivational prerequisites of the general process could be sustained without sufficiently high education of the women who, as mothers, influence their children.

CONCLUSION

With the general cultural upgrading process in American society which has been going on for more than a century, the educational system has come to play an increasingly vital role. That this should be the case is, in my opinion, a consequence of the general trend to structural differentiation in the society. Relatively speaking, the school is a specialized agency. That it should increasingly have become the principal channel of selection as well as agency of socialization is in line with what one would expect in an increasingly differentiated and progressively more upgraded society. The legend of the "self-made man" has an element of nostalgic romanticism and is destined to become increasingly mythical, if by it is meant not just mobility from humble origins to high status, which does indeed continue to occur, but that the high status was attained through the "school of hard knocks" without the aid of formal education.

The structure of the public school system and the analysis of the ways in which it contributes both to the socialization of individuals and to their allocation to roles in society is, I feel, of vital concern to all students of American society. Notwithstanding the variegated elements in the situation, I think it has been possible to sketch out a few major structural patterns of the public school system and at least to suggest some ways in which they serve these important functions. What could be presented in this paper is the merest outline of such an analysis. It is, however, hoped that it has been carried far enough to suggest a field of vital mutual interest for social scientists on the one hand and those concerned with the actual operation of the schools on the other.

Work and the Adolescent Transition to Maturity*

DALE B. HARRIS

According to U.S. Department of Labor reports, the number of adolescents seeking work increases proportionately year by year. But what role does work play in the socialization of adolescents? In this selection, Harris scrutinizes the nature of work experience and in his analysis contends that it has a significant function, quite apart from vocational guidance or training objectives. In outlining a theory of work experience, Harris shows how employers facilitate adolescents' adjustment toward authority figures and how such elements as responsibility, status, wages, and attitudes toward work function in this context of the socialization process.

Freedman[1] has insisted that "the successful transition from school to work is central to the process of coming of age in America." Certainly, the 1950's saw a marked shift from social concern with exploitative child labor to social concern with the developmentally constructive aspects of work experience for youth. Increasing proportions of young people—not merely increasing numbers, but increasing proportions—are at gainful work, except during occasional recessions in the nation's business. The hypothesis here is that part-time, casual work experience can be valuable in the socialization of adolescents. In exploring this contention, we shall not be occupied with the social or educational significance of vocational guidance, vocational training, or the need to make career choices. Rather, we shall focus on the young teenager's introduction to the world of work and its psychological significance.

ATTITUDES TOWARD WORK

The work of several decennial White House Conferences on children has been well done. We have been thoroughly imbued with the notion that

[1] Marcia Freedman, "Work and the Adolescent," *Children and Youth in the 1960's* (Washington, D.C.: White House Conference, 1960), pp. 137–153.

* From *Teachers College Record*, LXIII (1961), pp. 146–153. Reprinted by permission of the author and the publisher.

children and youth should not be at work, but should be in school. Even in the past decade, one not infrequently met in welfare and labor circles the notion that work is inherently bad for children and that a signal victory is won when some part-time work opportunity is closed to youth. In discussion after discussion, the emphasis has been on the physical, mental, and social hazards of employment to young people, very seldom (until recently) on the possible socializing, training, or educational features of work experience for them.

This emphasis may only be part of the large assumption that work is dull and debilitating, tolerable only because it is necessary to buy leisure and fun, which are what we really want. As David Riesman,[2] William Whyte, Jr.,[3] and others have observed, we seem to be reversing the older American ethos with respect to work, the concept of work as intrinsically good, virtuous, and satisfying. There are, of course, other factors involved in eliminating the employment of youth. There is, for example, the wish to eliminate a cheap labor group and to maintain high minimum wages, which have grown steadily as our social awareness has grown.

Yet in recent years we have heard another point of view. We have been warned that idleness in the 'teen years plays directly into the hands of juvenile delinquency. We have heard that the school drop-out problem (which persists in the face of determined efforts to keep all youth in school) indicates that the school and its program are not meeting the needs of a large number of adolescents. Nor will this condition grow less as we return to a more academic emphasis in high schools.

The fact is that the proportion of young people enrolled in high school— and in the last few years their absolute numbers as well—has increased for two decades. Yet in spite of this increase, almost half the youth between the ages of 14 and 17 report some paid employment during the year. The *proportion* of this age group who are both enrolled in school and working has been steadily climbing for 15 years. This fact reflects a shift that arose in the necessities of World War II. It has been temporarily checked by short periods of economic recession, but the trend is clear and seems to be here to stay in spite of laws and court decisions increasingly restrictive to the employment of young people under 18. Adolescents *want* work, paid work. But it is well to remember that we are talking about part-time employment. A sizeable proportion of the under-18 youth who are not in school at all are in the ranks of the unemployed. One study[4] showed that those who quit school "to find work" actually took twice as long to start looking for it as those who completed school first!

[2] D. Riesman, N. Glazer and R. Denny, *The Lonely Crowd* (New Haven: Yale University Press, 1953).

[3] W. H. Whyte Jr., *The Organization Man* (New York: Doubleday, 1956).

[4] N. Riches, "Education and Work of Young People in a Labor Surplus Area," *U.S. Month. Labor Rev.* LXXX (1957), pp. 1457–1463.

It should be recognized that this discussion refers to the work experiences of all youth, not just the school-leavers. Indeed, school-leavers, as many studies show,[5] do not have a hopeful future. More are unemployed than their classmates who finished high school. They earn less, hold lower status jobs and have a greater record of irregular employment. The inference in many studies of the early school-leaver is that remaining in school improves prospects for these youth. Those who leave school, however, are a selected group in other ways. They have a lower academic intelligence and earn poorer grades, the latter factor often being directly or indirectly the reason for early school leaving.[6] Matching a group of early school-leavers with high school graduates in both intelligence and general socio-economic status, the author[7] has shown that as early as the sixth grade, those destined to drop out early do significantly more poorly on a number of personality and social background indices. While keeping these youth in school may possibly improve their employment prospects, they evidently do not constitute a significant pool of unrealized abilities of a very high order. Furthermore, with high schools tending toward more academic emphasis, this group is not likely to be better served or to diminish in size.

ADOLESCENT TRAITS

Let us now turn to some characteristics of the adolescent period which seem to be quite characteristic of youth regardless of time and place. In the first place, adolescents are healthy in a physical sense, with a tremendous capacity for marshalling and expending energy. We may be socially concerned about the health of young people, but the fact remains that the years of early adolescence represent just about the healthiest of one's entire life in resistance to infectious disease and onset of various disabilities.

In the second place, normal healthy adolescents are, by adult standards, notably psychopathic, manic, and schizoid in their psychological makeup and behavior.[8] A less dramatic statement is that in assent to statements of attitudes which notably characterize adults with psychopathic, manic, or schizoid disorders, the *average* American adolescent is surpassed only by 15% of the total adult population. Such findings suggest psychologically that adolescents are excitable, show a high level of activity and drive, have

5 L. P. Adams, "When Young People Leave School," *I.L.R. Research,* IV (1958), pp. 9–11; H. J. Dillon, *Early School Leavers* (New York: National Child Labor Committee, 1949); U.S. Department of Labor, *Hunting a Career* (Washington, D.C.: U.S. Government Printing Office, 1949).

6 D. E. Kitch, "Does Retardation Cause Drop-outs? *Calif. J. Elem. Educ.,* XII (1952), pp. 25–28.

7 D. B. Harris, "Psychological and Social Characteristics of a Group of School Drop-outs," *Child Development,* XXXI (1960), pp. 230–233.

8 S. R. Hathaway and E. D. Monachesi, *Analyzing and Predicting Juvenile Delinquency with the MMPI* (Minneapolis: University of Minnesota Press, 1953).

little regard for official social norms, are iconoclastic, and exhibit marked contrasts and inconsistencies in attitudes and behavior. Anyone who has ever lived with a normal teenager needs not be told this! Coupled with the high energy output of the period, this personality structure gives rise to the behavior which distresses adults so much, creates a so-called youth problem, and, indeed, seems to accentuate the delinquency rate, because this rate falls sharply in age groups past 20 years.

In the third place, adolescents seek to establish roles. The word "quest" has always seemed appropriate to characterize their restless, searching behavior. The adolescent needs to find a sense of identity and a sense of personal worth. He needs to clarify his sex role as a developing young man or young woman. He needs to find social skill, a sense of assurance, and a place with his peers. His desire to conform to the peer standard has been so often remarked that we need not mention it. And, finally, he searches for ways to realize his independence socially, emotionally, financially, and intellectually, changing from his childhood dependency on adults.

All these characteristics occur in persons who live in a very rapidly changing social scene. Mature, stable adults are often bewildered by the loss of familiar behavior norms and landmarks. Institutional and ritual supports to the development of roles which existed in the rural village and extended family have disappeared. In mid-century American society, there is a relative lack of restraint on and supervision of youth's behavior. And we must admit in our culture to a considerable exacerbation of two very powerful drives—the drive toward aggression and the drive toward sexual expression.

Given the characteristics of good health and an amazing capacity for energy mobilization; given in the average youth qualities which in adult life are identified as bizarre or deviant; given a driving need to establish mature roles—place these givens in a rapidly changing social context where the clear guide lines of a stable culture seem to be missing, and it is not surprising that we identify youth problems!

It seems probable that serious study and exploration of the significance of work can assist in the solution of some of these problems. This hypothesis cannot be defended directly by data, either observational or experimental. Rather, one must induce from indirect evidence and deduce from the logic of dynamic psychological theory to develop the case. Although the argument rests on no stronger grounds than these, it may serve to provoke thought and investigation.

RESPONSIBILITY AND ROLE

We may now turn to a discussion of the elements of a theory of adolescent work experience. First of these is the significance of responsibility. Responsibility, by which we mean dependability and accountability as well as the production of high-quality work, is much valued in society. Industry, business, and the professions all want a steady person—a dependable, self-starting, stable functioning, productive individual. Yet a common complaint about adolescents is their irresponsibility. Most of the problems adults have with youth arise in trying to inculcate dependable, conforming behavior to adult norms or from the failure of youth to realize such behavior.

Research on responsibility[9] indicates that although its roots seem to be sowed early and crucially in parent attitudes and family relationships, this trait increases with age. The learning process is certainly not completed at adolescence, and it seems clear that the learning of responsibility is rooted in the significant interpersonal relations of a responsible adult with the child and youth. One of the few positive findings of these studies indicated that responsibility in children is associated with certain evidences of social responsibility in their parents. It does not seem to be at all associated with particular training or child-rearing techniques that are often thought to inculcate this quality.

Super's[10] study of vocational maturity in ninth grade boys formulated an index of Independence of Work Experience, based on evidence that a boy has obtained paid work on his own initiative, worked for non-family persons, and worked in situations in which he was "on his own," relatively free of supervision. Indications that the work required responsibility for materials, for the satisfaction of persons, and for handling money also enter the index. Super found his measure internally consistent and reliably evaluated, but it did not relate significantly to other measures of vocational maturity, although it did correlate with a measure of Acceptance of Responsibility. Super did not use his index as a *predictor* variable, however, which is the significance the present writer would put upon it. Nor would the variance in the index possible with ninth grade boys be as great as that possible with fifteen- or sixteen-year-olds eligible for working permits. Hence, the index may be more functional above the ninth grade.

The incomplete development of responsibility in the teen years suggests, then, that if work experience can be shown to evoke stable and efficient work habits and dependable and accountable attitudes toward work, such experience would be very important. Studies indicate that children more willingly perform around the house those tasks in which they are more nearly equal to adults. They assume readily serious and demanding assignments in contrast to trivial chores which make little demand on ability or

9 D. B. Harris, *et al.*, "The Measurement of Responsibility in Children," *Child Development*, XXV (1954), pp. 21–28; D. B. Harris, *et al.*, "The Relation of Children's Home Duties to an Attitude of Responsibility," *Child Development*, XXV (1954), pp. 29–33.

10 D. E. Super and Phoebe L. Overstreet, *The Vocational Maturity of Ninth Grade Boys* (New York: Bureau of Pub., Teachers College, Columbia University, 1960).

interest. Significant work experience should therefore be serious and place performance demands on the person. Super's finding of a correlation between Independence of Work Experience and Acceptance of Responsibility should be followed up in further studies.

A second element of importance is the significance of occupation or work role. Society generally views work role in terms of status or prestige. Jobs are graded along a continuum of "respectability" and give status to the persons holding them. Youth, however, quite generally view occupation in terms of self-development and independence. From the studies of adolescents conducted by both the Boy and Girl Scouts,[11] it appears that young people regard the post-high-school years in terms of further education, work, or marriage, and interpret all these in relation to self-development and self-realization. Youth, then, perceive the work role in terms of the independence it will give them and the chance to realize abilities and to enhance the self. Hence any work *often* appears desirable and is eagerly sought. Industrial psychologists have noted a pronounced drop in job satisfaction indices as characteristic of workers in their early twenties. It is quite possible that this phenomenon signals a shift from an adolescent to a more mature expectation from the job.

There is a third aspect to the work role in the adolescent years. About half of mid-teenagers work for pay during the school year and about three-fourths work for pay during the summer months. The bulk of this work is done for "strangers," persons outside the immediate family. Indeed, it seems that young people *prefer* to work for pay outside the home. This is not difficult to understand. A child recognizes that though he may be valued by his parents, they *must* support him. Both legally and morally, it is their obligation. To be able to do something someone else will pay for is tangible evidence of worth on a different basis. This realization is by no means unimportant to the adolescent struggling to realize his self-image and a sense of identity while at the same time weaning himself from dependency on his parents.

Moreover, in paying a wage, the employer represents society in its more objective relationships to the teenager. This may be useful in developing a sense of accountability in young people. A child may be expected by family tradition to participate in household chores. Whether they are done well or poorly, willingly or grudgingly, becomes as much a matter of the parents' skill or the amount of irritation they can induce in the child as of the youngster's pride or sense of responsibility. Neither the parent nor the immature child can voluntarily give up the other. In the employer-employee

[11] Survey Research Center, *Adolescent Girls* (New York: Girl Scouts of America, 1957); Survey Research Center, *A Study of Adolescent Boys* (New Brunswick, New Jersey: Boy Scouts of America, 1955).

relationship, there is a degree of freedom or option which seems desirable and important for young people to experience and to live with successfully for a time.

MONEY AND ATTITUDES

There is, of course, also the point that money is important to teenagers. It gives direct access to many social experiences. Studies show that both high school and college students today have much more money for entertainment than similar age groups less than a generation ago. In one study,[12] this difference is estimated to be in the neighborhood of around 1,000% more cash available for entertainment to post-World War II college students in contrast to pre-World War II students. This is a far greater increase than can be accounted for in terms of a general inflation or a change in general standards of living. It represents a very real change in circumstances for the contemporary adolescent generation. Yet money continues at the head of lists of problems claimed by youth![13]

The fourth element in a theory of adolescent work experience is the significance of attitudes, both self-attitudes and work attitudes. Erickson[14] has, perhaps more forcefully than any other, emphasized the teen years as the period of achievement of a sense of identity. The sense of self-worth has been held to be the core of all human values. The ego, as a psychological construct, is important in many theories of personality development. If adolescence truly is a time of achievement of this sense of identity, the age is of peculiar importance in the development of personality. We have seen that being able to do work considered payworthy by an unrelated, objective adult can be important in confirming a child's sense of worth, no matter how significant his parental relationships may have been originally in establishing his self-esteem. Simply being aware that one is learning significant "tricks of the trade" can also be an important reinforcer of this attitude. Discovering that he can make suggestions on the job which others accept is a tremendously reinforcing experience.

Much has been made of early work experience as occasioning floundering and failure. Such experiences need not be devastating to the self-image, provided the individual understands them as exploratory and as necessary in developing the best use of his abilities. Too much floundering and too much failure, as clinicians have amply demonstrated, can have a serious, negative effect on the self, despite firmly laid foundations in childhood experiences

---

12 E. G. Williamson, W. L. Layton and M. L. Snoke, *A Study of Participation in College Activities* (Minneapolis: University of Minnesota Press, 1954).
13 D. B. Harris, "Life Problems and Interests of Adolescents," *Sch. Rev.* LXVII (1959), pp. 335–343.
14 E. H. Erickson, *Childhood and Society* (New York: Norton, 1950).

of acceptance. Fortunate is the young person who is able to get work experience which reveals his developing abilities adequately, thus providing positive rather than negative reinforcement for his sense of identity.

Work attitudes are also important. While much of the adolescent's adjustment to authority is in relation to parents and teachers, the primary authority symbols, we have seen that the employer also is a significant representative of authority. Industrial and personnel psychologists frequently remind us that two important aspects of work adjustment are the adjustment to authority and adjustment to co-workers. More individuals fail on the job for these reasons than for a lack of specific skills. It has been said that industry interprets docility in the worker as "responsibility." However that may be, the young worker must somehow learn to be willing to take directions and to progress slowly toward goals—that is, to serve his apprenticeship or to "win his spurs." Studies show that the younger worker is often more dissatisfied on the job than the older worker. Somehow, the young worker must learn willingness to go through the training program, to bring his skills to the level of the reward he hopes for. This is not easy when work operations are simple, dull, and intrinsically uninteresting.

Finally, in the formation of work attitudes, the young worker's relationship to a responsible adult is of considerable importance. As jobs become more fragmented and specialized and require less craft or skill, it is harder to locate appropriate work experience which reinforces responsible work attitudes. The teenager who can work as a part-time helper to the craftsman is in a much better position to learn attitudes than the youth who pushes a broom or the errand boy in the large office. The boy who helps load cars at the super-market gets much more direct personal reinforcement than the one who fills shelves in the stock room. In every case, contact with adult models seems to be helpful to the formation of the desired attitudes, and such contact is increasingly hard to get. Both business and industry and organized labor often seek to avoid bothering with the teenager. He is an uneconomical producer, on the one hand, and too economical on the other!

IMPLICATIONS

To implement the point of view affirmed by this paper is not easy for a number of reasons, not least of which is the great dearth of research on work experiences of youth, work attitudes of youth, evaluations of training experiences, and the like. But at the present time two or three general patterns of prevocational work experience are available to teenage youth. One of these, in some respects the most hopeful in theory and with definite prevocational significance, has proved rather disappointing in practice. This is the work-experience program in the high school, where part-time paid employment is offered under the supervision of the school and related to courses in the regular school curriculum. Only a very small number of young people are reached by this type of program, and there has been a general resistance to developing this program both by industry and labor.

Schoolmen find real problems in the adequate administration and supervision of these programs. They are costly. There is some evidence from one study[15] that such programs are more helpful to individuals lower rather than higher in ability and scholarship. Thus, this program may have some potential value for the school dropout. The effort has not caught on widely, however, and one of the significant challenges to educators is to do something about the development of work attitudes in youth who more and more must stay in school.

Another pattern has been to encourage "job-exchanges" for summer employment. Newspapers, PTA, service clubs, and other agencies sometimes sponsor campaigns to list young people seeking work, or to sponsor job-finding campaigns. The National Committee on the Employment of Youth (NCEY), a division of the National Child Labor Committee, has done pioneer work in this field, stimulating local agencies to undertake projects in specific communities. This is a recent and hopeful development, yet too young to appraise adequately.

Volunteer work programs are becoming increasingly popular with youth-serving groups having character-building or international relations goals. The pattern was set early by the American Friends Service Committee and has been adopted rather widely by church groups. And now we hear of a Peace Corps. These enterprises have been and promise to continue to be very highly selective, taking the youth with the greatest early development of the qualities they seek to foster. On a lesser scale, and perhaps more meaningful to the average youth, are volunteer service jobs in school, civic or citizenship education assignments in the community or projects in settlement houses, summer playgrounds, and the like. Most of these tasks are unpaid, a drawback from the point of view of the objectives urged here as developmentally important.

Outstandingly successful has been a program of paid summer work combined with recreation in the city parks of Berkeley, California, where particular attention is paid to youth needing both money and group experiences.

In summary, we have argued for the significance to youth of part-time job experience, quite apart from vocational guidance or training objectives. We have tried to show that such experiences are actively sought by youth, are often quite difficult to find, and that providing them as a significant part of the transition to adult status constitutes a real challenge to education and the community.

[15] W. C. Brown, "Diversified Occupations of Graduates of 1952," (*University of Missouri Bull.,* Education Series, No. 60, 1959).

Culture Pattern and Adolescent Behaviour*[1]

FRANCIS L. K. HSU,
BLANCHE G. WATROUS, AND
EDITH M. LORD

Virtually every social scientist now accepts the assumption that culture exerts critical, formative influences upon personality. In recent years extensive cross-cultural research has been directed toward exploring this viewpoint. In the cross-cultural study presented below, Chinese American adolescents living in Hawaii are compared with white American adolescents living in Chicago. Several important socialization influences are investigated: childhood experiences, parental attitudes, peer group roles, and societal demands.

The findings show that Chinese youth are initiated into the world of their elders at an early age and conform to traditional social and political institutions easily; the American youth, however, are separated from the adult world until a relatively late age and learn to be self-reliant. In contrast to the Chinese youth, who "are not often stirred by issues," American youngsters grow up "equipped with an idealistic attitude toward life." Eventually American adolescents, as a consequence, experience a degree of trauma when they encounter an imperfect world. But Hsu, Watrous and Lord observe beneficial features in the stresses generated by the American society: "American youth tend to go out to improve things, to fight toward a better living, or at least to do things differently from their parents and to explore unknown possibilities."

[1] The Rorschach tests were administered in 1949 by Francis L. K. Hsu as part of a more inclusive field-work project among the Chinese in Hawaii. The 28 protocols were first scored and analysed by Edith Lord. Later they were reanalysed and in part rescored by Blanche Watrous according to Beck to facilitate comparison with a study of Chicago adolescents. Hsu and Watrous are responsible for the writing and final interpretation of the Rorschach findings.

* From The International Journal of Social Psychiatry VII (1961), pp. 33–53, abridged. Reprinted by permission of the authors and the publisher.

The attention focused on adolescence in this country during the past decade and a half is probably without parallel in human history. The psychiatrist, the educator, the juvenile court officer, the business man, the newspaper reporter and, frequently, bewildered parents have all contributed to this emphasis on teenage problems and behaviour. The increased concern with every facet of adolescent life is apparent from the many conferences, including those in the White House, on juvenile problems and by counting the number of articles related to teenagers in the *Readers Guide to Periodical Literature*. From 1955 to 1957 there were fifty-one articles on the subject, as compared with sixteen in the years 1941–43, and only three in 1919–21.

Although much of the emphasis on this transitional period between childhood and maturity lies in the realm of sensationalism related to pathological behaviour—to the 5 per cent or so of deviant adolescents who are "acting out" their frustrations in an unhealthy manner—the increasing trend in the U.S. towards juvenile violence, with concomitant emotional disturbance, is a matter of realistic concern to social scientists. Psychologists and sociologists generally assume that adolescent stresses stem from major biological and social adjustments, which seem to be an unavoidable part of the transitional period. Cultural anthropologists, on the other hand, are less pessimistic. They have been interested in certain cultural factors which may be linked with relatively low incidence of violence among adolescents, as well as those cultural factors which appear to make the process of growing-up less traumatic than others.

I. THE RORSCHACH FINDINGS

In 1949 one of the co-authors of this article carried out a seven-month period of field work among the Chinese in Hawaii.[2] Part of this field research was to collect Rorschach protocols. Of the 115 Chinese tested, the records of 28 boys and girls, aged 14 to 19 years (mean age 16.03 years), are examined. These individuals, selected on a random basis from two high schools, one public and one private, were estimated by their teachers to be "fairly good" students of average to high average intelligence with no outstanding academic or emotional problems.

. . . When our adolescent records are compared with those in the Thetford, Molish and Beck study,[3] certain significant differences as well as similarities stand out. In the following pages, for the sake of brevity, the subjects in the Thetford, Molish and Beck study will be designated as "Chi-

2 The field work was undertaken by F. L. K. Hsu under the auspices of the S.S.R.C. and Northwestern University's Graduate Committee on Research, between May and December 1949. For some aspects of the Chinese in Hawaii, see F. L. K. Hsu, "The Chinese of Hawaii: Their Role in American Culture." *New York Academy of Sciences,* XII (April, 1951), pp. 244–250.

3 W. N. Thetford, H. B. Molish and S. J. Beck, "Developmental Aspects of Personality Structure in Normal Children," *J. Proj. Tech.,* XV (1951), pp. 58–78.

cago" group or "Chicagoans," and the subjects in the Hsu study as "Hawaii" group or "Hawaiians." The 24 adolescents in the former study are among 155 Chicago public school children selected with the same criteria used by Hsu. . . . even the ages of the two groups of subjects are nearly identical, as shown by Table 1.

Table 1
Age of Adolescents

	Total No.	Boys	Girls	Age Range	Mean C.A.
Hawaii	28	19	9	14–19 yrs.	16.03 yrs.
Chicago	24	14	10	14–17 yrs. 11 mos.	15 yrs. 8 mos.

A detailed comparison of the Hawaiian adolescents with the Thetford, Molish and Beck study of 24 normal Chicago adolescents yields the following similarities and differences:[4]

(1) The intellectual approach of the two groups is roughly similar, with the Chicago youth having a greater amount of intellectual energy at their disposal, but with the Hawaiians exploiting their mental resources in a somewhat more constructive, ambitious manner.

(2) Both quantity and quality of Hawaiian fantasy depart from the white American pattern. The Chicago youth show greater dependence upon inner living, with the Hawaiian adolescent more reluctant to internalize stresses; Hawaiian fantasy, when expressed, is predominantly passive in nature, suggesting submissive acceptance of the environment. The incidence of creative imagination among the Hawaiians is, however, optimally proportionate to their level of drive. Also significantly, the Hawiians show a lower incidence of autistic, pathological fantasy than the American youth.

(3) The Hawaiian Chinese seem to have fewer self-appraisal tendencies and fewer dysphoric reactions than the Chicago group.

(4) The two groups show a surprisingly similar quantity of affective energy. However, the Hawaiians exhibit less emotional immaturity, more empathy and greater sensitivity to the needs of others. The affect expressed is less egocentric than among the Chicago group.

(5) Both groups show healthy intellectual adaptivity. However, the Chicago sample suggests more inhibitory, more wary behaviour with respect to other individuals than the Hawaiians.

II. THE WIDER CULTURAL PERSPECTIVE

Margaret Mead was the anthropological pioneer who first pointed out that adolescent turbulence, regarded as universal by the Westerners, was absent

[4] [*Ed.*] For the analytical details that form the basis of this comparison the reader must consult the original publication (F. L. K. Hsu, Blanche G. Watrous and Edith M. Lord, "Culture Pattern and Adolescent Behaviour," *Int. J. Soc. Psychiat.*, **VII** [1961], pp. 33–53).

in Samoa.[5] The Chinese in Hawaii are also rarely troubled by adolescent difficulties. In racial composition the Chinese make up a little less than 6 per cent of the total population in Hawaii. The majority of the original Chinese migrated to the islands during the latter half of the 19th century. Today most of the Chinese in Hawaii are second, third and fourth generation Americans, spreading over the entire economic and social ladder of the state. Even by 1930, 50 per cent of the males and 70 per cent of the females were engaged in "preferred" occupations. In 1949 there were no Chinese hand laundry establishments in the islands. Instead there were Chinese banks, department stores, and a wide variety of business and industrial establishments. A majority of the Chinese live outside the bounds of "Chinatown" in Honolulu. By 1949, the Chinese had a greater percentage of school attendance than all other racial groups. Most Chinese speak excellent English and live in American style. According to the usual standards, the Chinese of Hawaii, except for physical type, seem very American. Certain cultural differences from the average American are, however, apparent: though most present-day Chinese in Hawaii have become Catholics or Protestants, there are also Chinese Mormons, Chinese Bahaians and Chinese Buddhists. As a rule, rather than the exception, members of the same family have different religious affiliations: for example, there may be a Catholic father, a Methodist son, an Episcopalian daughter, while the mother continues to worship at Chinese temples. Differences in religion do not seem to affect family solidarity, and Christian children frequently go with their elders to Chinese temples—seeing no inconsistency in this behaviour. The relationships between marriage partners and between parents and children appear more casual and less intense than among white Americans. But their adolescents are family oriented to a much greater degree than the average teenager on the mainland of the U.S. It is not that the Chinese boys and girls in Hawaii do not desire independence. They do, but, at the same time, they accept parental injunction and control in general. For example, the adolescents prefer to choose their own mates, set up their independent households, name their children and themselves according to prevailing fashion. However, if parental wishes are opposed, they tend to be less insistent upon these prerogatives than would most young white Americans. They seem to be less sensitive about parental interference. They are more inclined to accept a compromise situation, reconciling the wishes of their parents with their own preferences, even in the matter of mate selection. The most striking difference, in fact, between the Chinese American adolescents in Hawaii and white American adolescents on the mainland is the absence of overt rebellion against authority. The "big fight" with parents is lacking. The Chinese in Hawaii are simply not

[5] Margaret Mead, *Coming of Age in Samoa* (first published in 1928; reprinted in *From the South Seas,* New York: William Morrow and Co., 1939).

troubled by adolescent difficulties. Both police files and interviews with parents and social workers suggest that the "problem adolescent," when found, is an exception. It is a common fact among Chinese parents in Hawaii that, while white Americans anticipate more problems as their children approach adolescence, they expect less and less problems as their children progress in age.[6]

All these observations bear out our Rorschach findings. We must ask, then, what are the factors which make for a relative lack of adolescent turbulence among Chinese Americans and a relative abundance of it among white Americans?

Our hypothesis is that the Chinese way of life is situation-centered and that of the Americans is individual-centered. (The hypothesis and its application which follow were developed by Hsu, with which Watrous and Lord do not necessarily concur.) The situation-centred way of life encourages the individual to find a satisfactory adjustment with the external environment of men and things, while the individual centred pattern enjoins the individual to find means of fulfilling his own desires and ambitions. The individual-centred man tends not only to view the world in absolutist terms, but also to insist on standing or falling alone. As a result he is likely to experience much emotional conflict. His triumphs are moments of effusive and public ecstasy, and his failures are moments of deep and secret misery. In neither can he really share with others, especially the latter. Never being sure of his human relations, he has a perpetual fear of failure, though he jealously guards his privacy, however dear that privacy costs. The situation-centered man tends not only to view the world in relativistic terms, but also consciously to seek mutual dependence with circles of fellow men. As a result he enjoys a great deal of mental ease. His triumphs are never solely a vindication of his own noble qualities, for his parents, relatives and departed ancestors have all generously contributed. Similarly, his failures are never a complete proof of his own inability to make the grade, for his parents, relatives and departed ancestors share the blame. Securely anchored in his primary groups, he is always protected from being a complete failure, though often he suffers

---

[6] During the last ten years there have appeared in the newspapers (last one to come to my notice: The *Washington Post,* April 17, 1960) and some magazines (such as "Youth without a Delinquency Problem," *Look,* XXII, April 29, 1958, pp. 75–78) reports indicating the absence of juvenile delinquency in Chinatowns in the U.S.A. Such reports, though interesting, are not scientific evidence for the conclusion they draw. Rose Hum Lee (see Rose Hum Lee, "Official Cases for Delinquent, Neglected and Dependent Chinese Boys and Girls, San Francisco Bay Region," *J. Soc. Psychol.,* XXXVI [1952], pp. 15–31) pointed out rightly that the picture of Chinese delinquency in the San Francisco Bay region remains unclear because of the small size of the juvenile in proportion to the total adult population, due to U.S. Immigration restrictions up to 1940. Up to about that time the Chinese population in the San Francisco Bay area and elsewhere had a drastically unbalanced sex ratio, in some instances over ten males to one female. But the Chinese population in Hawaii has exhibited relatively normal ratios for many decades.

from too many relatives. (A complete statement of this hypothesis and extensive qualitative documentation of it are given in the work by Francis L. K. Hsu.[7])

In order to show how this hypothesis can help us to explain the psychological contrasts between our Hawaii and Chicago adolescents we propose to examine four factors bearing on the life of the adolescent: (a) childhood experiences; (b) parental attitudes; (c) the rôle of the peer group; and (d) the demands of the wider society.

(a) Childhood Experiences

Before two years of age Chinese children have, as a rule, a secure environment. Among both the wealthy and the poor the customary Chinese practice is to feed the baby, or heed it in some other way, whenever it cries. The wealthy parents do so with the aid of wet nurses and servants. The poor mothers carry their young ones on their backs when they go to the fields. As soon as the child is weaned the picture is, however, somewhat different. In matters of food and clothing, the basic pattern remains one of complete and nearly unregulated satisfaction. The children of the poor may be forced to undergo uncertainty and want by necessity, but that is not the intention of their parents and the little ones can see it for themselves. The children of the rich can get anything they want. They are constantly spoiled by servants. But in social and ceremonial matters the attitudes of the Chinese parents are less tolerant. In the first place, children are praised and rewarded, or rebuked and punished, in direct proportion to their ability to measure up to adult behaviour standards. Chinese parents do not seem to worry about frustration or security in their children. They are much more concerned with the question of social and ritual propriety. While in every society it is the wealthy families who try to conform to the culturally upheld ideal, the weight of this Chinese pattern was often even felt by the children of the comparatively poor. There is a widely circulated and dramatized folk-tale which, though extreme, is nevertheless revealing. Once upon a time there lived a man with his sickly mother, a wife and son. The family being poor, he soon found that he could not support all four. With the consent of his wife he decided to bury his son alive. But as soon as he dug into the ground, quantities of gold came up with his spade. Heaven was moved by his filial feelings, so that a would-be tragedy concluded happily for all. In real life, whenever warranted by economic necessity, it is not unusual for grandparents to be served at the expense of grandchildren.

In the second place, infantile or childish behaviour, though often providing amusement for adults, is not emphasized, nor idealized, nor played up

7 F. L. K. Hsu, *Americans and Chinese: Two Ways of Life* (New York: Abelard-Schuman Ltd., 1953).

through research. Up to the time of World War II there were few toys, and little academic effort at understanding the psychology of children. In fact, Chinese parents do not seem to assume the existence of a children's world qualitatively different from that of the adults. Children are regarded as little adults who will become adults after adult models. The traditional Chinese terms for education, when translated into English, approximate the words "instruction," "restraint," "learning."

In the third place, the maturing Chinese child will experience a good deal of inconsistency in his social relationship. Chinese, especially the mothers, are not too concerned about consistency in discipline. Even if the mother wants such consistency, various relatives will make her discipline inconsistent. The child's grandmother is always there ready to go over his mother's head. Aunts, uncles, older cousins and grandfather will all be unconcerned about giving the child some forbidden articles while his mother is not looking. The customary family ideal is such that even if parents object to such interferences it would appear socially unreasonable for them to make an issue of it. In other words, Chinese parents are seldom the absolute and exclusive masters within the four walls of their homes.

Fourth, and above all, the growing Chinese male is initiated into the adult world imperceptibly. The inconsistency in his early experiences would have already given him a head start in this direction. Then he begins to participate in adult activities as early as he can manage it. By accompanying his father to business meetings, temple fairs and on social calls he becomes almost effortlessly, and at an early stage of his development, acquainted with his place in society. Except in matters pertaining to sex, parents make little effort in keeping their own affairs from the male child. If the family has just suffered a major catastrophe the parents do not discuss among themselves whether they should let Johnny know. Johnny suffers with them right away.

From ten or twelve years of age onwards, Chinese males do not experience any sudden change of status. The same gradual initiation into their adult rôles continues.

Like the Chinese children, American children also suffer from few significant frustrations before weaning. But between the time of weaning and the legal age of 18 or 21, the circumstances surrcunding the average American child tend to be drastically different from those within the experience of the average Chinese child. Like Chinese parents, American parents emphasize adequate satisfaction in food and clothing for their children. But while the lots of the wealthy children and the poor differ widely in China because of necessity, there is less discrepancy of this sort in America. There are few American parents who have to starve their children because of dire want. But in other matters the differences are more intensive and far-reaching.

First, with the possible exception of the very poor, or fresh immigrants from southern and eastern Europe, Americans from middle classes upward tend to apply themselves diligently toward giving their children a qualitatively different world from that of themselves. Nearly ideal conditions prevail in this world of the young. It is further buttressed by Santa Claus, tales about the love and sorrow of animals, a nearly complete correlation between reward and good conduct on the one hand and between punishment and bad conduct on the other. In time of family distress artificial behaviour on the part of the parents keeps the children away from the shock of reality. Many parents send their children to Sunday schools when they have doubts, in order to bring their children up "right." In time of want children are more likely to be served than parents. The many arms of the Society for the Prevention of Cruelty to Children in America, when contrasted with the many societies "for Saving Papers With Written Characters On" or societies "for Giving Away Free Coffins" in China, make the differences of the two cultures very apparent.

Secondly, infantile and childish behaviour is endorsed by American parents, constantly boosted by American business and permanently played up by American research. One of the major duties of the American parents is to enable their children to play and see that they do. The over $800 million a year toy industry, the myriad of commercialized juvenile literature, and the variety of occasions and days during the year on which gifts are expected and given are all strong evidence indicating who are centres of the society.

Thirdly, American parents as a whole emphasize consistency in discipline to an extent unknown among Chinese parents. It is not supposed, of course, that in their actual day-to-day life American parents can be as consistent as they wish to be. But their difference from the Chinese comes first from the ideal they emphasize (and which their family counsellors and child psychologists tell them to emphasize), and secondly from the fact that they live in individual families where few occasions for interference of grandparents or other in-laws exist. Furthermore, even when grandmothers take over during an emergency the older lady is only supposed to administer things according to laws laid down by the younger woman. This consistency tends to suppose a complete or nearly complete correlation between reward and good conduct on the one hand, and punishment and bad conduct on the other.

Lastly, from an early date American parents encourage their children to be self-reliant. When they are a little older, the label of "sissy" or "cry-baby" will shame most youngsters into reacting promptly. Here again we are aware of the fact that many American children do in fact fall back on their parents when the going is tough and the hands of their parents, especially those of their mothers, are very heavy. In fact, Irene M. Josselyn, a practising psychiatrist and psychoanalyst, describes vividly how difficult this struggle for independence is for many youngsters and how one young 14-

year-old girl resents her mother for dictating what she should wear and for letting her choose what she desires to wear. In other words, independence is both desired and feared. Clinical psychologists can usually confirm the impression that they see an inordinate number of cases in which the problems of children are rooted in the heavy hands of their mothers. It is to be expected, in a culture where self-reliance is equivalent to self-respect, most of those individuals who are in need of clinical help to be those who have failed in some way to measure up to the accepted pattern of self-reliance. The reason why some American mothers' hands are heavy will be discussed in the next section. In three years of work, first as a medical social worker and later as a psychiatric social worker in Peking Union Medical College Hospital between 1934 and 1937, Hsu did not find the type of mother-child problem known to American clinicians. From Hsu's experiences in China, both as an individual and as an anthropological field worker, he can state that, among Chinese children, the type of struggle for independence described by Josselyn was rare.

All these are understandable once we appreciate the high American premium on self-reliance as contrasted to its low esteem in the Chinese situation. Furthermore, American parents foster this sense of self-reliance by separating their children from the adult world. In this culture, children have no social rôles in the adult world except for being children. Besides family visits to grandmothers or aunts or during vacations, children are not involved with affairs of the parents. Parents frequently see their friends after having put their children to bed and in the charge of a sitter. Youngsters have their own playmates, whom the parents may not know, and their own jargons, which often take the adults by surprise.

The results of these differing childhood experiences are far-reaching. A majority of Chinese youngsters grow up equipped with a much more realistic view of life and the world around them than their American counterparts. Theirs is a world in which basic satisfactions often intertwine with frustrations, in which principles are frequently affected by compromises, in which hypocrisies and circuitous means of getting out of trouble are not uncommon. Adolescence is a time when the Chinese youngsters have already become acquainted with, and in many cases initiated into, their rôles in society. The shortcomings of the greater world do not give Chinese adolescents any sudden emotional trauma; they have sampled many of them before. The intricacies of the adult society fail to cause them confusion and bewilderment. They have long known differences between what adults do and what they say, and have nearly perfected the art themselves.

The majority of American youngsters grow up, in contrast to the Chinese, equipped with an idealistic attitude towards life and the world around them. Theirs is a world in which light and shadow in human affairs are crystal clear, in which God invariably punishes the bad and rewards the deserving, and in which hypocrisies are banished and frustrations at a minimum. The imperfect world of which American youngsters become aware at adolescence is therefore full of sudden emotional shocks. They are confused because the rules they have been used to often no longer apply. They may refuse to heed their parents at this time simply because they are disillusioned by what they had been told thus far and what they have now found.

(b) Parental Attitudes

The Chinese parents, having never been complete masters of their children in the first place, do not feel especially rejected as the youngsters become more independent. Furthermore, the nature of the Chinese way of life has been such that age, far from being a liability, is a premium. To the Chinese parents, maturity and independence of the children mean only an assurance of a more permanent place in life for themselves.

The American adolescent is a person who has physically grown into the adult world, but with his social and cultural development lagging behind. Having been taught to be self-reliant and aggressive, he is now ready to explore on his own. Facing this, the American parents' attitude towards their children is a seeming paradox.When they say they want Johnny to be independent they mean he can wash his own hands, turn on the light or take the bus by himself, but they decidedly do not mean that Johnny can refuse to eat of his own choice. So when the adolescent is physically ready to explore this confusing world on his own, the parents, accustomed to being complete masters of their children, suddenly find themselves incapable of control. American parents feel the danger of rejection more vividly than the Chinese parents because, in America, once the children become independent parents will have few honoured places in the scheme of things. They therefore want to retain their parental power as long as they can. This is why, as we saw above, the hands of American parents on their children, especially those of American mothers, tend to be heavy. To the American adolescent this is often unbearable. The infant at birth can be satisfied with a bottle. At three or four he gets excited about being dressed like Daddy. He will demand to be thrilled by more and bigger things as his physical power grows. According to psychologists children are most suggestible at the age of eight or nine, after which the suggestibility decreases. Seen from the present analysis, this climax of suggestibility is probably a time when American children find their best adjustment between parental restraint and their own physical capability, after which the latter has outgrown the former.

In this way the Chinese adolescent has less desire to rebel against parental authority not only because his process of initiation into the wider society has begun much earlier in life but also because his parents have little psychological need to hold on to him. The American adolescent experiences more difficulties not only because his life so far has had little reference to the wider society but also because his parents have the strong urge to hold on to him.

(c) The Role of the Peer Group

It is a foregone conclusion that human beings, in order to be human, must lead their existence in a human group, not only for food, sex and language but also for a sense of affiliation and importance. Elsewhere Hsu has classified these latter needs into sociability, security and status and examined how this classification is preferable to that of some others and can help to explain the qualitative and quantitative differences in human behaviour in different societies. But whether scholars agree on these categories, we do not believe that there is any doubt that all human beings, in one manner or another, seek group affiliations. However, while the Chinese situation-centred orientation of life stresses mutual dependence between the generations, the American individual-centred orientation of life emphasizes reliance upon the self. The Chinese, with their ideals of filial piety and reverence to tradition, authority and the past, enjoin their youngsters never to sever their relations with their elders. The Americans, with their ideals of freedom, equality, and drive for creativity and for future, encourage their youngsters to be independent of the adults almost from the beginning of life. In the last section we saw how this independence on the part of the young affects the thinking and behaviour of parents when their children really grow up. The same independence affects the young as soon as they go to school. Independence from parents simply means that they must seek affiliation with peer groups. The greater the sense of independence from parent, the more urgent the need for affiliation with peer groups. In other words, the Chinese youngsters have greater relationship along the vertical line with their elders, but the American youngsters are more deeply involved along the horizontal line with their peers. The resulting psychological difference is significant. The individual who has chiefly to maintain horizontal relationships, must make greater exertions than those who have mainly to deal with vertical relationships. For, from the children's point of view, parents, whether in China or the U.S., can almost be taken for granted but peers cannot. In fact, while parents in all societies tend to express their affection for their children and, in most societies, work hard to make sure their children are affectionate towards them even when harshly treated in return, peers nowhere have any great love for each other. In fact, peers, whether in highly individualistic societies or not, always compete with each other, and therefore one must be continuously on the look-out for trouble with them, trouble which might lead to rejection.

The American adolescent is therefore likely to be far more under the tyranny of his peers than his Chinese counterpart. This gives the former far greater reason for anxiety, for conformity, for violent gestures, including immoral acts and even murder and mayhem, if these are dictated by his needs for retaining or improving his status in his peer group.[8]

Among those who operate within the legal bounds, the extent to which American youngsters are tied to their peers may be gauged from a "Cornell Study of Student Values," which covers a total of 2,760 undergraduate men and women attending Cornell and 4,585 undergraduate men and women attending ten universities (U.C.L.A., Dartmouth, Fisk, Harvard, Michigan, North Carolina, Texas, Wayne, Wesleyan and Yale). Suchman, in a summary report on this study, concludes that "much of the student's development during four years in colleges does *not* take place in classrooms. The conformity, contentment and self-centred confidence of the present-day American students are not academic values inculcated by the faculty, but rather the result of a highly organized and efficiently functioning extra-curricula social system."[9] We do not have a comparative inquiry conducted among the Chinese in China or in Hawaii. However, it is well known that, even as late as 1949, Chinese high schools rarely had any kind of intra-school organizations besides athletic ones, and in Chinese colleges and universities there mostly flourished "native place" organizations, each composed of youngsters from the same province. A recurrent complaint by many observers was that all such voluntary associations did not last, for the students lacked lasting interest in them. In fact it has often been said, by Chinese and Westerners, that the Chinese were like loose sands which do not stick together. In the light of our analysis here, the Chinese youngsters lacked the urge to cohere with their peer groups because they had a far more tenacious relationship with their elders on the vertical plane. Hawaii's high school and college in 1949 had more American type of peer organizations. In the University of Hawaii there are even Chinese fraternities and sororities. But, as reported elsewhere,[10] they entered into the affairs of their elders in a manner and to an extent unknown among Americans to the U.S.

[8] In 1952 an adolescent in Michigan assaulted one nurse and killed another. Subsequent investigations showed no "obvious" motive for the crime. A whole series of articles on this crime was written by John Bartlow Martin in the *Saturday Evening Post* (Grayson Kirk as told to Stanley Frank, "College Shouldn't Take Four Years," *Saturday Evening Post* March 26, 1960). It turned out that the boy in question wanted to prove to his gang that he was "good" enough to belong. A recurrent finding in adolescent crimes has been the absence of "obvious" motives—"obvious," that is, to the investigators and writers.

[9] E. S. Suchman, "The Values of American College Students," *Long-Range Planning for Education* (Washington, D.C.: American Council for Education, 1958), pp. 119–120.

[10] F. L. K. Hsu, "The Chinese of Hawaii: Their Role in American Culture," *op. cit.*

(d) The Demands of the Wider Society

Adolescence, particularly later adolescence, is a time when the individual is well within range of the adult in physical capabilities. We have seen that in the Chinese situation the adolescent's physical growth is accompanied by a corresponding process of his gradual entry into adult society, while in the American situation it is not. However, regardless of whether he is or is not initiated into adult society the adolescent, with his increased mobility, contact and perception, cannot help but be influenced by the dominant patterns of culture governing the society. In America the most desired position of the individual is a combination of (a) economic and social independence and (b) success to this end with speed. Economic independence means to find a job and that one must no longer live on an allowance. That achievement in turn helps him to establish social independence which includes, among other things, full control of one's own hours, movements and activities. As to success with speed, nothing expresses the sentiment better than the recent proposal by Grayson Kirk, President of Columbia University, to shorten our college education from four years to three years, and the enthusiastic and favourable comments this proposal has received so far. The increasingly lowered age of dating is an indication of the same thing. Coupled with these is the fact that individualistic competitiveness has increasingly driven adults to indiscriminate and irresponsible use of any means to pursue their own selfish ends, the high ethical standards preached in the society becoming increasingly a mockery both to the adults but especially to the youngsters.[11]

The American adolescent, confronted with these forces in adult society, often does not know how to cope with them. He may try to take social independence first, or he may seize upon the idea of speed first. When easy outlets are not available he may be driven to unusual ones such as those of the criminal, or to express himself in quarrelsomeness, family explosions,

[11] Studied analyses of these conditions are available (see L. K. Frank, *Society as the Patient* [New Brunswick: Rutgers University Press, 1950]; E. H. Sutherland, *White-Collar Crime* [New York: Dryden Press, 1949]). It will have been evident to the reader, however, that the interpretation of adolescent crime and difficulties we have presented in this paper is very different from that given by Sutherland. The crux of Sutherland's theory of crime is differential association. "Criminal behaviour is learned in association with those who define such behaviour favourably and in isolation from those who define it unfavourably, and that a person in an appropriate situation engages in such criminal behaviour if, and only if, the weight of the favourable definitions exceed the weight of the unfavourable definitions" (*ibid.*, 234). What this theory says is that the social context of the individual determines his tendency to criminality or otherwise. This view agrees with findings in modern social sciences but it does not go far enough. What we have tried to show in this paper is the *forces* which propel the youngsters in the Chinese culture pattern to give greater weight to their vertical associations and which, in turn, lead to lesser adolescent difficulties and criminality, and those which propel the youngsters in the American culture pattern to be more tied to the horizontal associations which in turn lead to greater adolescent difficulties and criminality.

hostility and sulkiness against parents and other adults. These same forces in adult society tend to affect the Chinese adolescent far less than they would the American, even though the two live in the same society and are subject to the same demands of that society. In the first place, at adolescence the Chinese is likely to have become wise in adult ways because of his gradual transition from childhood to adulthood. In the second place, being more oriented towards veridical relationships, he is less involved in and affected by forces prevailing in the wider society than is his horizontal-relationship-bound American counterpart.

In every culture individuals vary, so that not all Chinese adolescents are free from difficulties and not all American adolescents present problems. But forces current in each culture tend to dispose the youths of that culture in one or another direction, so that we are in a better position to appreciate why adolescence presents far less of a problem to the Chinese than to the Americans. In fact, before contact with the West the Chinese had no term meaning adolescence. The individual went from childhood and puberty straight to adulthood. But there are more concrete evidences which we can briefly examine. In inter-societal comparisons we are, of course, limited by the availability of data and by the comparability of the data if found. But a comparison of adolescent crime during the best years of the Nationalist administration in China with that of a corresponding period in the U.S. yields the following interesting points (the Chinese data are taken from police files of fourteen capital cities—*Ministry of the Interior Year Book, 1936*.[12] The American statistics are taken from *Uniform Crime Reports*.[13] Both sets of facts pertain to the years 1931, 1932 and 1933):

(*a*) American males between 16 and 21 committed more felonies than misdemeanours; Chinese males between 13 and 20 committed more misdemeanours than felonies.

(*b*) American males beween 16 and 21 committed more crimes than all other seven-year groups under 51; Chinese males of 13 to 20 committed fewer crimes than all other seven-year groups under 51.

These contrasts are startling when we realize that both Chinese and Americans are subject to the same biological changes, but that during the first half of the century Chinese youth lived in an environment far less socially, politically and economically secure than the Americans. These contrasts become understandable, however, when seen in the light of our hypothesis and analysis so far.

Theoretically, as the Chinese in America become more integrated with

[12] National Government of China, *Ministry of the Interior Year Book* (Shanghai, 1936).

[13] United States Government, *Uniform Crime Reports*, XI, No. 4 (1931, 1932, 1933).

the host society and more acculturated to its way of life, they are likely to experience the same sort of adolescent difficulties which seem to form part of the American way of life. This expectation is a logical sequence of our view that adolescent turbulence is basically a function of culture pattern and not heredity or poverty or lack of playgrounds. But the Chinese in Hawaii have up to date been able to keep some of the essential content of their culture pattern alive among them. This is due probably to two reasons. First, their family system, which as among all peoples is the cradle of their culture from generation to generation, is of prodigious strength which exerts a strong centripetal influence on the individual. Secondly, being on an insular island of small size, they tend to keep close touch with each other through their associational and other activities, though they mix freely with persons of other ethnic stocks. (Over 80 per cent of the total population of Hawaii are found on the island of Oahu, where Honolulu is located.)

III. CULTURE PATTERN AND ADOLESCENT PSYCHOLOGY

We can now see how our Rorschach findings fit in with the wider cultural perspective. We can understand the reason why, psychologically, and compared with the Chicago adolescents, the Hawaii adolescents have a smoother transition from childhood to adulthood, less rebellious strivings on the surface and within, fewer signs of autistic fantasy, less uncontrolled emotionality and bodily anxiety, more empathy, greater sensitivity to the needs of others and more submissive acceptance of their rôles.

However, adolescent difficulties generated by American culture are not altogether a disadvantage, just as their relative absence in Chinese culture is not altogether an advantage. At the end of Section I of this paper we noted that the Hawaiian adolescents have no passionate wish to change, no felt need to alter environment, and that they are unlikely to become "discontents." Put differently, this means they are not often stirred by issues and not easily moved enough so as to strive for reform.

The white American youth, because of discontinuity between their early and later experiences, sometimes come to the position of responsibility with an idealism far less known among their counterparts in China. American youths tend to go out to improve things, to fight towards a better living, or a least to do things differently from their parents and to explore unknown possibilities. This is one of the secrets of strength of American culture. The Chinese youths, because of their early initiation into the world of their elders, cross the threshold of adulthood like old rogues who know all the ropes. They tend to follow well-beaten paths, to talk wisely and to compromise. This is one of the reasons why for the last twenty centuries Chinese social and political institutions and technology, while remarkable in their own right, have shown little change.

The evolution of a culture may come about by way of internal forces or external pressure. External pressure for change is exemplified by contact between different nations. Internal pressure for change is present when there are differences in outlook between successive generations. The greater the latter differences, the greater will be the tendency to change.

However we look at it, adolescent unrest is simply one of the prices of the American type of culture. By wise manipulation we shall be able to reduce the price, but we cannot eradicate it. To eradicate the price means to eradicate much of the potentialities of the culture.

Adolescent Initiation Rites Among Preliterate Peoples*

JUDITH K. BROWN

In many preliterate societies a phenomenon occurs at adolescence that must seem strange to citizens of literate, western societies. Generally labeled the "initiation rite," it provides a formal, institutionalized procedure for inducting youth into adulthood. The initiation may be of short or prolonged duration, and it lays stress upon external and outwardly impressive ceremonials. Nevertheless, a completely acceptable explanation for the necessity of initiation rites is still lacking. In the following paper, Brown discusses several hypotheses based, respectively, upon the Oedipal complex, sex identity conflict, and stabilization of sex role. Interpretations of the rite notwithstanding, Brown and the anthropologists whom she cites affirm that usually it makes men of boys and women of girls.

When is an adolescent ready to accept the rights and duties of adulthood in our own society? Although each state sets certain legal requirements for the right to vote, to drive a car, to have a job, and to get married, no specific event marks the transition from adolescence to adulthood. Gradually, with the passage of successive birthdays and commencements, adulthood is reached. No commonly accepted definition for this stage of life is reached. No commonly accepted definition for this stage of life exists, and it is possible for us to say even of a thirty-year old, "He is too immature for marriage."

Many preliterate societies are as vague as we ourselves are in their criteria for adulthood. Many others, however, celebrate a definite rite to mark the end of adolescence. In these societies, all those who have been initiated have the privileges and responsibilities of adults, and those who have not been initiated do not. Those who have been initiated are adults by definition; those who have not been initiated are not.

---

* Paper prepared especially for this volume from "A Cross-Cultural Study of Female Initiation Rites" (unpublished Ed.D. dissertation, Harvard University, 1961).

Adolescent initiation rites have presented a difficult area for study due to their great variety, and due to the fact that no analogous observances exist in our own society. The ceremonies are generally different for each sex. They are celebrated some time between the eighth and the twentieth year, and are absolutely mandatory.[1] However, some ceremonies are elaborate and take years to complete. Others are relatively simple observances that take only part of a day. In some ceremonies the initiate is treated harshly and subjected to great pain. Others are joyous events that are eagerly anticipated. Some ceremonies are observed under great secrecy. In others, the whole community participates, and guests arrive from afar. Such variety is not surprising considering the wide geographic distribution of initiation rites. They have been reported in every continent except Europe.

Early travellers and missionaries were puzzled and intrigued by the initiations they found in far away lands. They registered strong disapproval of those rites in which the initiate was treated harshly, ritually deflowered, or subjected to a genital operation. Such observances were regarded as needlessly cruel or as immoral. No discernible purpose seemed to be served by the rites, for no analogous celebrations existed in our own society. The tribes themselves, however, ascribe very definite functions to their rites. Among the Bemba of Africa, female initiation is practised to make the girl "a woman as we are" and "to teach her." Richards writes:

. . . The chisungu [initiation rite] teaches, not the technical activities of the wife, mother and housewife, but the socially approved attitudes toward them. The women themselves see this point and, in fact, made it to me. An intelligent *nacimbusa* [mistress of ceremonies] will admit that the girls know how to cook and grind but will say that after her chisungu a girl does her work in a different way.[2]

Although much has been written about both male and female initiation rites, only a limited review of this literature is possible here. One of the older works on the subject, which is still highly regarded is Arnold Van Gennep's *Les Rites de Passage*.[3] In this book, Van Gennep placed initiation rites in context with other events in the life cycle of the individual. Societies arrange their members in certain categories, e.g., infants, children, adolescents, adults. As the individual passes from one category to another various rites serve to mark this transition. There are rites which mark the end of one period of life, rites which mark the fact that the individual is in a stage

---

[1] Observances in our own society, such as confirmation, graduation from high school, initiation into a Greek letter organization and the coming out party do not meet this definition, and can therefore not be considered as true initiation rites.

[2] Audrey Richards, *Chisungu: a Girl's Initiation Ceremony among the Bemba of Northern Rhodesia* (New York: Grove Press, 1956).

[3] Arnold Van Gennep, *Les Rites de Passage* (Paris: Libraire Critique Émile Nourry, 1909).

of transition, and rites which mark his admission into the new category. Rites celebrated at adolescence are but one of a series of such observances. Numerous studies of initiation rites have been written from a psychoanalytic point of view. One such recent book is Bruno Bettelheim's *Symbolic Wounds*.[4] Based on Bettelheim's observations of emotionally disturbed children and on a very limited sampling of the ethnographic literature, this book proposes that an unconscious desire for the genitals of the opposite sex underlies those initiation rites characterized by genital mutilation. Bettelheim suggests that this desire is universal, however, such initiation rites are not. Although Bettelheim's hypothesis is an interesting one, it lacks adequate substantiation.

In recent years, a number of cross-cultural studies have been devoted to initiation rites. These ceremonies have come to be regarded as very sensible solutions to specific problems inherent in certain forms of family structure and in certain types of infant and child rearing. In the following, three recent hypotheses concerning the purpose of male initiation rites will be presented. Next several hypotheses dealing with the initiation of girls will be reviewed. The knowledge gained from a study of these ceremonies has been found to have definite relevance to certain problems in our own society. Therefore a final section will be devoted to the application of these findings.

THE FUNCTION OF MALE INITIATION RITES

Published in 1958, Whiting, Kluckhohn and Anthony's paper, "The Function of Male Initiation Ceremonies at Puberty,"[5] attempts to explain why some societies celebrate male initiation rites, and why others, such as our own, do not. The authors restrict their definition of these ceremonies to those that contain one or more of the following elements: painful hazing, isolation from women, tests of manliness and genital operations. As an example of a particularly severe rite they cite from an account of the ceremony of the Thonga tribe of Africa recorded by Junod:[6]

When a boy is somewhere between ten and sixteen years of age, he is sent by his parents to a "circumcision school" which is held every four or five years. Here in company with his age-mates he undergoes severe hazing by the adult males of the society. The initiation begins when each boy runs the gauntlet between two rows of men who beat him with clubs. At the end of this experience, he is stripped of his clothes and his hair is cut. He is next met by a man covered

4 Bruno Bettelheim, *Symbolic Wounds* (Glencoe: The Free Press, 1954).

5 J. W. M. Whiting, R. C. Kluckhohn and A. Anthony, "The Function of Male Initiation Ceremonies at Puberty," *Readings in Social Psychology,* ed. Eleanor Maccoby, T. M. Newcomb and E. L. Hartley (New York: Henry Holt and Co., 1958), pp. 359–370.

6 Henri A. Junod, *The Life of a South African Tribe* (London: Macmillan, 1927).

with lion manes and is seated upon a stone facing this "lion man." Someone then strikes him from behind and when he turns his head to see who has struck him, his foreskin is seized and in two movements cut off by the "lion man." Afterwards he is secluded for three months in the "yards of mysteries," where he can be seen only by the initiated. It is especially taboo for a woman to approach these boys during their seclusion, and if a woman should glance at the leaves with which the circumcised covers his wound, and which form his only clothing, she must be killed.

During the course of his initiation, the boy undergoes six major trials: beatings, exposure to cold, thirst, eating unsavory foods, punishment and threat of death. On the slightest pretext he may be severely beaten by one of the newly initiated men who is assigned to the task by the older men of the tribe.[7]

Whiting, Kluckhohn and Anthony's hypothesis is based on the psychoanalytic assumption that very early experiences continue to exert an influence in later life, and that the Oedipal situation exists among mother, father and son. Although the original formulation of the Oedipus complex was based on observations in our own Western society, Whiting, Kluckhohn and Anthony believe that child rearing conditions in certain preliterate societies heighten the "family romance." Thus when the mother-son bond is particularly strong, and when the father-son rivalry is accentuated, initiation rites are celebrated at adolescence in order to prevent the son's incestuous approaches to the mother and his open hostility toward the father.

In certain preliterate societies, mother and infant enjoy an exclusive sleeping arrangement during the first two or three years of the child's life. In many of these same societies there is also a taboo on sexual relations between the father and mother during this same period. The mothers devote themselves to their infants in a manner that would be impossible and deemed improper in our own society. It is under circumstances like these that Whiting, Kluckhohn and Anthony believe a particularly strong bond develops between mother and son.

This relationship is then abruptly terminated when the child is weaned, at age two or three. The exclusive sleeping arrangements are ended, and the mother resumes sexual relations with the father. Under these circumstances Whiting, Kluckhohn and Anthony believe that the young boy is subject to particularly strong feelings of rivalry toward the father. At adolescence both the incestuous feelings toward the mother and the rivalrous feelings toward the father could be dangerously disruptive to the society. The initiation rite serves to counteract such a possibility.

Societies like our own, in which the infant does not enjoy such exclusive possession of the mother during the early years, and in which the rivalry with the father never reaches such intensity, do not need an initiation at

---

[7] Whiting, Kluckhohn and Anthony, p. 360.

adolescence to check the potentially disruptive Oedipal strivings of its adolescent boys. Whiting, Kluckhohn and Anthony tested this hypothesis on a sample of fifty-six societies distributed around the world, and found that a statistically significant number of the cases corresponded to their prediction.

In a recent paper, Young[8] rejects the hypothesis suggested by Whiting, Kluckhohn and Anthony, and sets forth his own explanation of the function of male initiation rites. He expands the definition of the latter also to include observances such as tattooing, tooth filing, fasting, special taboos, gifts, dances, participation in raids and change of name. Young does not accept the basic psychoanalytic assumption that events in infancy and early childhood determine behavior later in life, and that problems generated in the early years need resolution in the form of an initiation at adolescence. His explanation of these ceremonies is that they serve to stabilize the sex role of the young boy when he enters adult life, and that this stabilization is of particular importance in those societies characterized by a high degree of male solidarity. The latter, Young describes as follows:

Such solidarity may be defined as the co-operation of men in maintaining a definition of their situation as one which is not only different from that of women, but which involves organized activities requiring the loyalty of all males.[9]

Male solidarity is generally found in conjunction with polygyny, as it seems to take several women to support a man devoting his time to the activities of a cooperating male group. Young suggests that the child rearing factors which necessitate adolescent initiation rites according to Whiting, Kluckhohn and Anthony are actually merely aspects of polygynous family life, and are spurious explanations of the need for male initiation ceremonies. According to Young, it is the presence of a high degree of male solidarity that best explains the initiation of adolescent boys. In societies like our own, where there is a low degree of male solidarity, such rites are not celebrated.

A further criticism of Whiting, Kluckhohn and Anthony's research has been made by Norbeck, Walker and Cohen.[10] They attempted to replicate Whiting, Kluckhohn and Anthony's ratings on seven of the societies in the sample, and found that their own ratings differed. They felt that Whiting, Kluckhohn and Anthony were not specific enough in their definition of the

[8] Frank W. Young, "The Function of Male Initiation Ceremonies: a Cross-Cultural Test of an Alternate Hypothesis," *The American Journal of Sociology,* LXVII, No. 4 (January, 1962), 379–396.

[9] *Ibid.,* p. 381.

[10] Edward Norbeck, Donald E. Walker, and Mimi Cohen, "The Interpretation of Data: Puberty Rites," *American Anthropologist,* LXIV, No. 3, Part 1 (June, 1962), pp. 463–485.

variables they used, that often the ratings were made without regard for their context in the ethnographic accounts, and that Whiting, Kluckhohn and Anthony often reinterpreted ethnographic works that were already interpretative. They also criticized the statistical method Whiting, Kluckhohn and Anthony used. Norbeck, Walker and Cohen concluded that Whiting, Kluckhohn and Anthony's study was overburdened with hypotheses, and that present ethnographic data is inadequate for the kind of research Whiting, Kluckhohn and Anthony attempted.

Norbeck, Walker and Cohen's article is of interest as it points out many of the problems that beset cross-cultural research. The complexity of the ethnographic accounts makes the definition of specific variables difficult. These variables are of necessity treated out of context to some extent. All ethnographic accounts are somewhat interpretative, as the observer is selective in what he reports of a preliterate society. Although replication is an important aspect of research, Norbeck, Walker and Cohen attempted to carry out their work without much of the necessary information. The article by Whiting, Kluckhohn and Anthony was a mere summary and did not contain all the facts that would be needed to make replication possible. Due to the complexity of the material, elaborate instructions would be necessary, embodying all the decisions that the raters have made. The criticism that Whiting, Kluckhohn and Anthony's study was overburdened by hypotheses has some justification. However, the material with which the research dealt was such as to invite numerous conjectures. Ethnographic accounts are never as complete as one would wish for the purposes of cross-cultural research. It is therefore all the more amazing that a hypothesis like that of Whiting, Kluckhohn and Anthony finds the kind of cross-cultural confirmation that it does.

The hypothesis proposed by Whiting, Kluckhohn and Anthony has recently been revised in an article by Burton and Whiting.[11] This revision contains what is probably the most convincing explanation of male initiation rites suggested to date. Burton and Whiting restrict their definition to those ceremonies which contain circumcision as a component. No longer are male initiation rites seen to counteract Oedipal strivings, but rather to counteract a conflict in sex identity. According to Burton and Whiting, "The process of identification consists of the covert practice of the role of an envied status."[12] Envy is in turn based on the distribution of "resources." This is the term by which the authors refer to anything one person wants but over which someone else has control; e.g. food, water, freedom from pain, love, solace, praise, etc. When a parent withholds a resource from a child, the child envies that parent. According to Burton and Whiting, the

[11] Roger V. Burton and J. W. M. Whiting, "The Absent Father and Cross-Sex Identity," *Merrill-Palmer Quarterly of Behavior and Development*, VII, No. 2 (1961), pp. 85–95.
[12] *Ibid.*, p. 85.

envy thus generated will drive the child to wish to be like, and thus to identify with the parent.

The setting in which the young infant spends the greatest part of his time is his bed. It is in this setting that he receives resources or that resources are withheld from him. If he shares his bed with both parents, he will come to envy and to identify with the adult status. If, however, he sleeps with his mother in the exclusive mother-child sleeping arrangements described by Whiting, Kluckhohn and Anthony, the infant will envy and identify with the female status. (Our own society is unique in that the infant usually sleeps in a bed of his own, apart from both parents.)

When the infant grows into a child and enters the world of the family and the household, he is confronted with new possibilities for envy and identification. In those societies in which the married daughters continue to live near or with their mothers (matrilocal societies), women hold a position of power in the household. In those societies in which the married sons continue to live near or with their faithers (patrilocal societies), men hold a position of power in the household. (In our own society, and in several others, the married couple lives away from both the husband's and the wife's family.)

According to Burton and Whiting, sex identity conflict arises in those societies in which the infant experiences the exclusive mother-infant sleeping arrangement, and in which the family structure is patrilocal. In his early years, the infant envies and identifies with the female status, but in childhood, men hold the envied status. Conditions for sex identity are confusing, and the male rite at adolescence serves to force the initiate to relinquish his unacceptable female identification and to identify once and for all with his male initiators. Societies like our own are not characterized by conditions which foster sex identity conflict, and therefore do not practise initiation ceremonies. Burton and Whiting tested this hypothesis on a sample of sixty-four societies distributed around the world, and found that a statistically significant number of the cases conformed to their prediction.

THE FUNCTION OF FEMALE INITIATION RITES

The initiation of girls presents a very different picture. Only very rarely do these rites subject the initiate to harsh treatment or to genital operations. The usual female initiation rites contain one or more of the following elements: bathing, beautification such as a new hair arrangement, isolation in a special place, dietary restrictions, an announcement of the initiate's changed status and instruction in such matters as womanly tasks, etiquette, behavior toward in-laws, menstrual observances, contraceptive devices and observances during pregnancy. The ceremony is often closely related to other events in the young girl's life, such as menarche, betrothal and marriage. Menarche is often prerequisite for initiation, and initiation in turn is often prerequisite for betrothal and marriage.

The following account of the initiation of girls among the Cheyenne Indians of North America contains many of the typical elements:

The passage of a girl from childhood to young womanhood was considered as hardly less important to the tribe than to her own family. She was now to become the mother of children and thus to contribute her part toward adding to the number of the tribe and so to its power and importance.

When a young girl reached the age of puberty and had her first menstrual period, she, of course, told her mother, who in turn informed the father. Such an important family event was not kept secret. It was the custom among well-to-do people for the father of the girl publicly to announce from the lodge door what had happened and as an evidence of his satisfaction to give away a horse.

The girl unbraided her hair and bathed, and afterward older women painted her whole body with red. Then, with a robe about her naked body, she sat near the fire, a coal was drawn from it and put before her, and sweet grass, juniper needles, and white sage were sprinkled on it. The girl bent forward over the coal and held her robe about it, so that the smoke rising from the incense was confined and passed about her and over her whole body. Then she and her grandmother left the home lodge, and went into another small one near by, where she remained for four days.[13]

The few female initiation rites which inflict extreme pain on the young girl are those involving a genital operation or extensive tattooing. Brown[14] found that such rites are practised by societies characterized by those conditions, specified by Burton and Whiting, that foster a conflict of sex identity. The societies that practise painful female initiation rites also practise male rites involving a genital operation and seclusion. It appears that when the conflict in sex identity arises both sexes are subject to dramatic and painful rites in order to compel them to accept their respective roles.

The usual female rite is celebrated in matrilocal societies. Since the young girl lives among the same people throughout her life, the initiation serves to announce her changed status when she reaches adulthood. In non-matrilocal societies the change in residence at marriage seems to serve the same purpose.

Female initiation rites are also characteristic of those societies in which women do a major share of the bread-winning. It seems as if the rite serves to assure the girl and those around her that she will be competent to carry on the vital activities of the society. Thus for example, among the Jivaro Indians of South America, women carry on most of the subsistence

---

[13] G. B. Grinnell, *The Cheyenne Indians, Their History and Ways of Life* (New Haven: Yale University Press, 1923), Vol. I, p. 129.

[14] J. K. Brown, "A Cross-Cultural Study of Female Initiation Rites," *American Anthropologist,* in press.

activities. At initiation, tobacco medicine is administered to the young girl in order that the spirit of tobacco will give her the strength to carry out her womanly tasks, give her skill with the domestic plants and animals, and make her a successful wife and mother. After the rite, she undergoes a prolonged period of training in womanly activities.

In those societies, like our own, in which women merely share in the subsistence activities, or in which men carry on the major part of these activities, female initiation rites are not celebrated. The hypotheses concerning female initiation rites were tested on a sample of seventy-five societies distributed all over the world, and a statistically significant number of cases conformed to each of the predictions.

RELEVANCE OF THE FINDINGS
FOR CONDITIONS IN WESTERN SOCIETY

At first glance, the observance of initiation rites at adolescence may appear as an exotic custom far removed from our own experience. Yet the research dealing with these ceremonies has given a new perspective to certain problems in our own society. For example, Burton and Whiting summarize a number of studies in our own society which clearly show that family structure can produce a sex identity conflict which may find its resolution in initiation into the delinquent gang. Brown's findings concerning the initiation ceremonies of girls have a definite bearing on that controversal subject, the education of women.

The father-absent household is not unknown in our own lower class. Burton and Whiting summarize a number of investigations in which this particular type of family structure had been studied. Although these investigations were concerned with lower class culture and delinquency, rather than sex identity conflict, their data do in effect corroborate the Burton and Whiting hypothesis.

The boy growing up in the "female based" household in our own lower class grows up under conditions very much like those found in certain preliterate societies. As he gets older and moves into the world of the lower class community he finds himself under the domination of the older men and boys who constitute the gang. Often admission into the gang very much resembles the tests of manhood required in male initiation ceremonies. The strongest evidence of sex identity conflict comes from the lower class youth's preoccupation with masculinity and "toughness," and his compulsive rejection of all things feminine. Due to his early experiences femininity is also equated with authority. Delinquent acts appear to serve as part of this reaction against the early feminine identification. Thus although the initiation of boys in preliterate tribes may appear far removed from the problems we encounter in our own society, the study of these ceremonies has shed new light on the delinquent gang in our own lower class culture.

The conditions which Brown found to be present in those preliterate societies which practise the more usual initiation ceremonies for girls (matrilocality and women as the major bread-winners) are not characteristic of our own society. However, the study gives a new perspective to the status of women in our own society and to the type of education they receive.

Female initiation rites are observed in order to make young girls womanly, an attribute for which the society has a clear definition, and one which is highly valued. Among the Bemba tribe of Africa, the womanly role has the following definition:

Women, unlike men, are admired for industry and for resource in finding food in the bush. They are honoured for bearing and rearing many children and for courage in childbirth which is often, under Bemba conditions, a terrible ordeal. They are expected to be loyal to their own sex and to accept the domination of older women.[15]

Not only do these societies have a definition for the womanly role, but the areas of womanly endeavor are also clearly defined. Competence in these activities is sufficiently valued that definite steps are taken to assure the proficiency of the young girl.

In our own society, the domain of women is not clearly designated, and the few truly feminine occupations are not prestigeful. This condition is reflected by our educational system, in which preparation for womanhood is not undertaken with seriousness. Training in grooming, womanly demeanor, household tasks and child care is usually given informally in the home. When specific instruction is offered in these areas, it is not accorded the same prestige as other subjects. Reflecting the attitudes of our society, our system of education trains girls for what is considered important work, that work in which women compete with men.

The young girl of today finds herself confronted by a perplexing array of opportunities. Unlike her grandmother, she may choose her life work from a vast number of occupations as well as the age-old tasks of the homemaker and mother. The greatest recognition will be accorded to that work in which she competes successfully with men. There is no doubt but that our society has benefited by drawing indiscriminately on both its men and its women to do its work. But this is not necessarily the best way of using women's peculiarly feminine gifts. Also, it is perhaps the lack of societal valuation of specifically feminine endeavors that brings on the penis envy which our psychoanalysts find characteristic of their women patients. Would this phenomenon perhaps be absent in a society in which the work of women was a specific and independent domain, and in which

---

[15] Richards, *op. cit.*, p. 48.

this work was highly valued? On this subject, Margaret Mead makes the following statement:

. . . This Western experience, which undoubtedly does occur often enough to be a very frequent characteristic of the woman who finds her way to the analyst's couch, occurs . . . in a society that has so over-rewarded male positions that envy for the rôle which is played by the father can coalesce with an experience of the little brother's or boy companion's more conspicuous anatomical equipment.[16]

No attempt will here be made to suggest what would constitute the best possible education for women, or what constitutes the best possible use of their talents within a society. We should be aware, however, that educating women to be successful men is only one of many possible alternatives. The female initiation rite represents the opposite extreme.

[16] Margaret Mead, *Male and Female* (New York: William Morrow and Co., 1949), p. 85.

PART TWO

SOCIALIZATION: THEORY AND PRACTICE

Prepuberty and Adolescence*

GERALD S. BLUM

Of the personality theories biased toward a genetic interpretation of personality development, the formulations of Freud and his followers long have commanded the most attention. According to orthodox psychoanalytic theory, personality development proceeds sequentially through oral, anal, phallic, latent, and adolescent stages before adulthood is attained. Although inability to control impulses, curb anxieties, or delay gratifications may initiate crises at any stage, maturation of sexuality at adolescence marks this period as particularly susceptible to psychological turbulence. One psychoanalytic writer (J. C. Gustin, "The Revolt of Youth," *Psychoanalysis and the Psychoanalytic Review*, XLVIII [1961], p. 83) offers this vivid description of adolescence: "Picture an adolescent now poised at the brink of adulthood. Racked by sexual desire, frustrated by outer prohibitions and inner inhibitions; desperately longing for independence yet fearful of isolation; eager for responsibilities yet fraught with anxieties about inferiority; flooded by irrational impulses yet committed to rules of propriety, he is hopelessly and helplessly confused and an enigma to everyone and himself."

Certain factors mitigate the rather dismal picture of adolescence favored by psychoanalytic theorists: (a) equally plausible alternative explanations of adolescent behavior frequently are available; (b) the majority of the interpretations are based upon nonreplicable subjective observations; and (c) several key inferences appear contradictory. In the paper presented below, Blum presents a review of orthodox and neo-orthodox psychoanalytic concepts as they relate to adolescence, and in his excellent commentary, he clarifies the implications of these points of view for adolescent development.

If there has been relative peace and quiet in the latency period, it comes to an abrupt end with the onset of puberty. Attainment of sexual maturity

_____

* From G. S. Blum, *Psychoanalytic Theories of Personality* (New York: McGraw-Hill, 1953), pp. 136–155. Copyright, 1953, by the McGraw-Hill Book Company, Inc. Reprinted by permission of the author and the publisher.

brings in its wake a wave of disturbance, not only in the sexual area but also in the broader realm of social behavior. According to psychoanalytic theory, the adolescent, flooded by his own resurgent impulses, must regroup the defensive forces of his ego in an attempt to meet this new onslaught.

ORTHODOX VIEWS

Psychosexual Development

The interval between latency and puberty—known as "prepuberty" or "preadolescence"—is preparatory to physical sexual maturity. There are no qualitative changes, says Anna Freud, but the quantity of instinctual energy has increased (see Note 1). The increase is not confined to the sexual life. There is more libido at the id's disposal and it cathects indiscriminately any impulses which are at hand. In her own words:[1]

Aggressive impulses are intensified to the point of complete unruliness, hunger becomes voracity and the naughtiness of the latency-period turns into the criminal behaviour of adolescence. Oral and anal interests, long submerged, come to the surface again. Habits of cleanliness, laboriously acquired during the latency-period, give place to pleasure in dirt and disorder, and instead of modesty and sympathy we find exhibitionistic tendencies, brutality and cruelty to animals. The reaction-formations, which seemed to be firmly established in the structure of the ego, threaten to fall to pieces. At the same time, old tendencies which had disappeared come into consciousness. The Oedipus wishes are fulfilled in the form of phantasies and day-dreams, in which they have undergone but little distortion; in boys ideas of castration and in girls penis-envy once more become the centre of interest. There are very few new elements in the invading forces. Their onslaught merely brings once more to the surface the familiar content of the early infantile sexuality of little children. [See Note 2.]

Deutsch[2] presents a different account of prepuberty in girls. She characterizes it as a period of greatest freedom from infantile sexuality and from aggression. The increased activity is interpreted, not as a manifestation of aggression, but rather as an intensive process of adaptation to reality and mastery of the environment, which precedes the passivity of puberty. Spiegel,[3] in a review of psychoanalytic contributions to adoles-

[1] Anna Freud, *The Ego and the Mechanisms of Defence*, trans. by C. Baines (New York: International University Press, 1946), p. 159.
[2] Helene Deustch, *The Psychology of Women* (New York: Grune and Stratton, 1944), I.
[3] L. A. Spiegel, "A Review of Contributions to a Psychoanalytic Theory of Adolescence," *Psychoanal. Study of the Child*, VI (1951), pp. 375–393.

cence, questions these conclusions on the basis of Deutsch's own materials. He points out that it is difficult to reconcile the supposed freedom from infantile sexuality with evidences of strong interest in the function of the sexual organs, the preoccupation with prostitution fantasies, and sadomasochistic interpretations of intercourse. Also the prepubertal girl is described as being full of rage and hatred as well as of dependent, clinging feelings toward the mother.

With the arrival of bodily sexual maturity (puberty proper), there is, according to Anna Freud, a further change of a qualitative character (see Note 3). Previously the heightening of instinctual cathexis was general and undifferentiated; now libido, especially in males, is concentrated specifically on genital feelings, aims, and ideas. Pregenital tendencies are relegated to the background, which results in an apparent improvement in behavior. The boorish aggressiveness of preadolescence gives way to the more refined genital masculinity. What seems to be a spontaneous cure of pregenitality is largely deceptive, though. The temporary triumph of genitality over early fixations recedes in adult life, when the pressure of the instinct sinks to its normal level and all the old anxieties and conflicts reappear unchanged.

Heterosexual outlets, however, are limited by the fact that society strongly opposes sexual intercourse during adolescence (see Note 4). According to Fenichel, the conflicts between drives and anxieties are felt consciously by present-day adolescents principally in the form of conflicts around masturbation. The heightened genital strivings sooner or later find expression in masturbatory activity, unless the infantile repressions have been too intense. The fears and guilt feelings originally connected with the accompanying oedipal fantasies are displaced to the masturbation. Adolescents react to these fears and guilt feelings by taking sides with the drive and fighting with anxiety and the parents, or they may more frequently side with the anxiety and the parents and try to fight off instinctual temptations. Often they do both (see Note 5).

For the boy, sexual developments in puberty are said to be a reawakening and continuation of infantile sexuality. He maintains his interest in the penis, whereas for the girl there is a change of direction. During adolescence she becomes aware of her vagina as a source of pleasure, while previously she had been interested solely in her clitoris and the desire to be boyish. At puberty the feminine function and its passive role must be accepted. Where strong penis envy exists, this switch is seriously impeded. The first menstruation, says Spiegel,[4] may play an important role in the process, either by supporting the feminine tendencies with all the fantasies concerning passive-masochistic gratification, pregnancy, and childbirth; or, on the contrary, leading to a rejection of femininity by increasing penis envy and

4 *Ibid.*

the castration complex (see Note 6). Buxbaum[5] reports that, unconsciously, the first menstruation is experienced as an injury to the genitals, as a castration, and as punishment for masturbation. Deutsch[6] also emphasizes the double sexual role of mother and lover which the girl must ultimately integrate.

Sex differences in narcissism at puberty, originally formulated by Harnick, are summarized in Spiegel's review. The male is said to retain the narcissistic estimation of his own penis to a great extent throughout his life, while the woman, on reaching maturity at puberty, tends to prize the beauty of her face and figure. The basis for this female libidinal shift from the genitals to the body as a whole is found in the wave of repression, occurring at puberty, which relates especially to sexuality associated with the clitoris. The male undergoes a similar but less extreme shift in setting up ideals of bodily strength and manliness.

EGO AND SUPEREGO FORMATION

With the advent of preadolescence, as we have seen, the balanced relationship or truce between the ego and the id in latency is disrupted. Physiological forces stimulate the instinctual processes and upset the balance. The ego, already strengthened and consolidated, struggles desperately to regain the equilibrium by using all the defenses in its repertory. The conflict is translated readily into behavior. While the id is winning out, there is an increase in fantasy, lapses into pregenital sexual gratification, and aggressive or even criminal actions. While the ego is ahead, there are various forms of anxiety, neurotic symptoms, and inhibitions.

In adolescence there are two extremes in which the conflict may possibly end. Either the id, now grown strong, may overcome the ego, in which case no trace will be left of the previous character of the individual and the entrance into adult life will be marked by a "riot of uninhibited gratification of instinct," in Anna Freud's words. Or the ego may be victorious, in which case the character of the individual during the latency period will remain permanently. When this happens, the id impulses of the adolescent are confined within the narrow limits prescribed for the instinctual life of the child. No use can be made of the increased libido and there has to be a constant expenditure on countercathexes, defense mechanisms, and symptoms. The ego generally remains rigid and inflexible throughout life. As a result of these conflicting forces, adolescent personality characteristically manifests such contradictory traits as altruism and selfishness, gregariousness and solitariness, indulgence and asceticism.

[5] Edith Buxbaum, "Angstäusserungen von Schulmädchen im Pubertätsalter," *Z. psa. Pädagogik,* VII (1933).

[6] Deutsch, *op. cit.*

The factors which determine whether the outcome will be a one-sided or a happier solution are threefold: (1) the strength of the id impulses, which is conditioned by the physiological process at puberty; (2) the ego's tolerance or intolerance of instinct, which depends on the character formed during the latency period; and (3) the nature and efficacy of the defense mechanisms at the ego's command (see Note 7).

The ego also alienates itself from the superego during adolescence. Since the superego is still intimately related to the parents, it is itself treated as a suspicious incestuous object. The principal effect of this break between ego and superego is to increase the danger which threatens from the instincts. The individual tends to become asocial, since the former alliance of ego and superego is at an end. The defensive measures prompted by superego anxiety become inoperative and the ego is thrown back to the level of pure instinctual anxiety, accompanied by its primitive protective measures (see Note 8). Conditions are then ripe for the development of what Fenichel describes as an "impulsive character." At the other extreme is Spiegel's[7] commentary on the growing stress which society places upon superego formation during adolescence. This tendency to maximize compliance may be responsible for the frequent appearance of the pseudo-mature adolescent who, although he complies with the serious demands of present-day society, is nevertheless emotionally very close to blind revolt against these demands. The revolutionary type of adolescent, he adds, does not seem to be found so frequently nowadays.

Bernfeld,[8] in a series of papers, has attempted to classify reactions of adolescents to the libidinal changes of puberty and also to the shifting ego-superego relations. With respect to the former, he distinguishes two types: the neurotic and the simple or uncomplicated. The neurotic group tries to deny the pubertal changes and to live as if nothing new has occurred. Anxiety and defense against anxiety characterize their behavior. The simple group, on the other hand, maintains the ideal of being grown up and consequently assumes a positive, welcoming attitude to the signs of sexual maturity. On the ego-superego variables Bernfeld differentiates the adolescent who is extremely compliant to the wishes of the environment, the one who is extremely rebellious, and the one who is mixed in his reactions. Wittels[9] suggests a chronological type of breakdown of adolescent phases into a second phallic period, a second latency, and finally a mature ego stage.

---

[7] Spiegel, *op. cit.*

[8] S. Bernfeld, "Uber eine typische Form der männlichen Pubertät," *Imago. Lpz.,* IX (1923); S. Bernfeld, *Vom dichterischen Schaffen der Jugend* (Vienna: Verlag, 1924); S. Bernfeld, "Uber die einfache männliche Pubertät," *Z. psa. Pädagogik,* IX (1935); S. Bernfeld, "Types of Adolescence," *Psychoanal. Quart.,* VII (1938), pp. 243–253.

[9] F. Wittels, "The Ego of the Adolescent," *Searchlights on Delinquency,* ed. K. R. Eissler (New York: International Univer. Press, 1949).

RELATIONSHIPS WITH OTHERS

In the preadolescent phase libido is again directed toward the love objects of childhood. Incestuous oedipal fantasies are prominent. The adolescent ego's first task is to revoke these tendencies at all cost. Typically, the young person isolates himself and behaves like a stranger with members of his own family (see Note 9). He substitutes new attachments to replace the parental ties. Sometimes the individual becomes attracted to young people of his own age, in which case the relationship takes the form of passionate friendship or of actually being in love; sometimes the attachment is to an older person, whom he takes as his leader—clearly a substitute for the abandoned parents. While they last, these love relations are passionate and exclusive, but they are of short duration. Persons are selected as objects and abandoned without any consideration for their feelings, and others are chosen in their place. The abandoned objects are quickly and completely forgotten, but the form of the relation to them is preserved down to the minutest detail and is generally reproduced, with an exactness which almost suggests obsession, in the relation to the new object. Spiegel makes the point that the reanimation of the Oedipus complex often does not appear in clear form, espocially after adolescence has been under way for some time. Parent substitutes who have less and less in common with the original parent images are chosen with increasing frequency as maturation continues.

According to Anna Freud, these fleeting love fixations are not really object relations, but rather identifications of the most primitive kind. The fickleness characteristic of puberty does not indicate any inner change in the love or convictions of the individual, but instead a loss of personality as a consequence of a change in identification. Fenichel says that in many ways objects are used as mere instruments to relieve inner tensions, as good or bad examples, as proofs of one's own abilities, or as reassurances. Objects are easily abandoned if they lose their reassuring significance.

Anna Freud goes on to state that the adolescent regresses in his libidinal life from object love to narcissism. He avoids complete collapse by convulsive efforts to make contact with external objects once more, even though by a series of narcissistic identifications.

Following this wave of narcissism, orthodox theory describes a normal, temporary phase of homosexual object choices (see Note 10). Fenichel elaborates this topic by maintaining that homosexual preferences are due to social factors as well as a narcissistic orientation. Adolescents prefer to meet in homosexual gatherings so as to avoid the exciting presence of the other sex and at the same time avoid being alone. In this way they hope to find the reassurance they are looking for. However, the friendships that were formed in the hope of avoiding sexual object relationships often assume a sexual character themselves.

In her discussion of the girl's development Deutsch[10] says that object choice changes from homosexual in preadolescence to bisexual in early puberty and to heterosexual in later puberty. The homosexual relationship at times shows a sado-masochistic quality. There are typical crushes on some older girl, as well as very close contacts with another girl of the same age. The bisexuality of early adolescence is emphasized in frequently occurring love triangles. Along with the growing sexual desires come numerous fantasies, the most common concerning pregnancy and prostitution and, to a lesser extent, rape.

Psychologically, there is the appearance of narcissism, which is one of the important parts of the feminine core, along with passivity and masochism. The development of passivity is aided by the fact that women cannot be active and aggressive because of the double standard. Also, the trauma associated with the lack of an active organ, the penis, leads the girl to seek passive means of sexual gratification. Since activity and aggression cannot be expressed toward the outside world, they are turned against the self in a masochistic fashion. Narcissism, the intensification of self-love, serves as a defense against the masochistic urges.

MECHANISMS

Prepubertal Defenses

In an effort to regain the equilibrium of the latency period, the prepuberty ego indiscriminately calls upon all the defense mechanisms at its command. Even the breakthroughs of pregenital tendencies, while representing a failure in defense, are considered by Lander[11] to serve as regressive protection against delinquency. Greenacre[12] describes a specific defense of this period—the "prepuberty trauma," in which the young girl provokes or cooperates in a sexual act with an adult. By shifting her feelings of guilt to the adult, she can keep the experience in consciousness and use it as a "real defense" against the demands of puberty. Spiegel[13] cites this illustration as evidence for the fact that external reality may be used primarily for defensive purposes.

Asceticism

A common mechanism in adolescence is the repudiation of all instinctual impulses, so-called "asceticism." The individual mistrusts enjoyment in general, and the safest policy for him is to counter his urgent desires with

---

[10] Deutsch, *op. cit.*

[11] J. Lander, "The Pubertal Struggle against the Instincts," *Amer. J. Orthopsychiat.,* XII (1942), pp. 456–461.

[12] Phyllis Greenacre, "The Prepuberty Trauma in Girls," *Psychoanal. Quart.,* XIX (1950), pp. 298–317.

[13] Spiegel, *op. cit.*

more stringent prohibitions, similar to those of strict parents in early training. The mistrust of instinctual wishes has a tendency to spread, extending
even to the ordinary physical needs. Examples are adolescents who avoid
the society of those of their own age, decline to join in any entertainment,
and refuse to have anything to do with plays, music, or dancing. More
extreme forms of asceticism are exposures to unnecessary health risks,
like wearing inadequate clothing, giving up food pleasures, rising very early
in the morning, and so on.

Anna Freud[14] differentiates asceticism from repression on two grounds:
(1) Repression deals with a specific instinctual relationship and is concerned with the nature and quality of the instinct. Anal-sadistic tendencies
may be repressed and oral ones gratified. Asceticism, on the other hand, is
concerned with the quantity of the instinct, and all instinctual impulses are
regarded as dangerous. (2) In repression there is some form of substitute
expression, such as a hysterical symptom, whereas asceticism can be altered
only by a sudden switch to instinctual excesses. Generally, asceticism is a
more primitive and less complex process.

Intellectualization

A second mechanism in adolescence is intellectualization. The aim of
asceticism is to keep the id within limits simply by imposing prohibitions.
The aim of intellectualization is to link up instinctual processes closely with
ideational contents in order to render them accessible to consciousness and
amenable to control. This mechanism has its origin in the increased effectiveness of intellectual functioning. Interests change from the concrete ones
of latency to abstractions (see Note 11). There are all sorts of abstract discussions on such topics as marriage, political philosophy, religion, professions, and so on. However, the superiority of intellectual performance at
this time makes very little imprint on the adolescent's actual behavior.
Despite his lofty views he remains preoccupied by his own mundane personality problems. The intellectualization is not reality oriented, but rather
serves as a defense against instincts. Instead of an ascetic flight from instinct, there is a turning toward it, but only in thought. Anna Freud
describes the situation as follows:[15]

The abstract intellectual discussions and speculations in which young people
delight are not genuine attempts at solving the tasks set by reality. Their mental
activity is rather an indication of a tense alertness for the instinctual processes
and the translation into abstract thought of that which they perceive. The philosophy of life which they construct—it may be their demand for revolution in
the outside world—is really their response to the perception of the new instinc-

[14] Freud, op. cit.
[15] Ibid., pp. 177–178.

tual demands of their own id, which threaten to revolutionize their whole lives. Their ideals of friendship and undying loyalty are simply a reflection of the disquietude of the ego when it perceived the evanescence of its new and passionate object-relations. The longing for guidance and support in the often hopeless battle against their own powerful instincts may be transformed into ingenious arguments about man's inability to arrive at independent political decisions. We see then that instinctual processes are translated into terms of intellect. But the reason why attention is thus focussed on the instincts is that an attempt is being made to lay hold of and master them on a different psychic level.

Creativity as a Defense

Spiegel[16] summarizes the writings of several psychoanalytic authors who interpret adolescent creativity as a defense against impulses aroused by the reenactment of the oedipal conflict. The most common form of creative endeavor at this time is the diary, which contains in addition to actual events all sorts of reflections, plans, and recollections. Poetry and other literary efforts have also been studied in this connection. Bernfeld states that the incestuous libidinal drives are deflected to other permissible objects, fantasies, values, and ideas, which he calls "also-objects." Creativity in this form is approved by the ego ideal. Rank points out that dramas written in adolescence concern themselves primarily with problems of incest. The frequent sudden cessation of creative activity toward the end of adolescence is accounted for by the inability to master the incest conflict.

The transformation of defensive into true creativity comes about when the adolescent sacrifices his private needs to the demands of communicability, thus finding his way back from fantasy to reality. The motive for renunciation of gratification derived from private daydreams, as recorded in diaries, is to be found in the ambitious strivings of the adolescent for fame and power gained from impressing a wide audience. The hero of these literary products represents the author's ego ideal, for whom he pleads in order to obtain sympathy, recognition, and love.

RANKIAN VIEW: HANKINS

Blanchard[17] describes Rankian theories of adolescence, as expounded in a paper by Hankins. According to the latter, the period of adolescence brings new developments in the child's continuing struggle for independence and sense of self. The sexual drives appear as generic forces within the individual which offer a threat to this recently increased self-assertiveness

---

[16] Spiegel, *op. cit.*
[17] Phyllis Blanchard, "Adolescent Experience in Relation to Personality and Behavior," *Personality and Behavior Disorders*, II, ed. J. McV. Hunt (New York: Ronald, 1944), pp. 691–713.

and self-differentiation. The adolescent fears and resists his sexual impulses because they might dominate him and force him to renounce his capacity to act as a total self. The reconciliation, provided by our culture, between sexual drives and individual self-expression is in a love relationship with another person. However, the adolescent is reluctant to enter such a relationship because he would have to give up total personal control and to accept partial control from the other person.

Hankins states that the normal outcome of adolescence is an acceptance of the fact that new experiences and relationships enrich the personality, despite some element of self-sacrifice. She criticizes Anna Freud's explanation of adolescent asceticism on the grounds that it serves mainly to promote individuality by denying sexuality or keeping it under strict control. Also sexual promiscuity is to be viewed, not as an uninhibited effort for instinctual gratification, but rather as an attempt to preserve the individual self. This kind of transitory relationship can be used to dominate the other person through his sexual needs, while at the same time refusing to yield any part of the self.

NEO-FREUDIAN VIEWS: SULLIVAN

In the preadolescent era, according to Sullivan, the capacity to love matures. Love exists only when the satisfactions and security of the loved one are as important as one's own satisfactions and security. Since boys feel more at ease with each other than with girls at this time, the capacity to love first involves a member of the same sex, the chum. When this happens, there is a great increase in the consensual validation of symbols. The preadolescent learns to see himself through the other's eyes, so that there is a consensual validation of one's own personal worth. In Sullivan's words:[18]

In this period there begins the illumination of a real world community. As soon as one finds that all this vast artistic and somewhat validated structure to which one refers as one's mind, one's thoughts, one's personality, is really open to some comparing of notes, to some checking and counter-checking, one begins to feel human in a sense in which one has not previously felt human. One becomes more fully human in that one begins to appreciate the common humanity of people—there comes a new sympathy for the other fellow, whether he be present to the senses or mediated by rumors in the geography, or the like. In other words, the feeling of humanity is one of the aspects of the expansion of personality which comes in adolescence. Learning at this stage begins to assume its true aspect of implementing the person in securing satisfactions and maintaining his security in interpersonal relations through the rest of life.

[18] H. S. Sullivan, *Conceptions of Modern Psychiatry* (Washington, D.C.: William Alanson White Psychiatric Foundation, 1947), pp. 20–21.

Preadolescence, for most people in our culture, is the period closest to untroubled human life (see Note 12). From that time on life's problems reduce them to "inferior caricatures of what they might have been." Difficulties in adolescence center around the maturation of the "genital lust mechanism." Sex finally comes into its own, but conflicts concerning sex are a function of two cultural factors: (1) premarital sexual experience is frowned upon; and (2) early marriage is discouraged, so that the gap between the adolescent awakening of lust and the proper circumstances for marriage is progressively being widened.

Lust cannot be dissociated easily when the sexual impulses collide with the self-system. In most people it cannot be dissociated at all; in some it can, but only at grave risk to effective living. Generally, sexual feelings operate again and again to threaten security and produce anxiety. One method which may or may not work is sublimation, or as Sullivan phrases it, the sublimatory reformulation of interpersonal relations. He describes sublimation as follows:[19] "A motive which is involved in painful conflict is combined with a social (culturally provided) technique of life which disguises its most conflict-provoking aspect and usually provides some representation for the opposing motive in the conflict." An illustration is the young woman with fantasies of prostitution who devotes her time to philanthropic work with fallen women in the city slums. Mullahy[20] claims that Sullivan's use of the term "sublimation" is much broader than the orthodox, since it can refer to any tendency system or drive (see Note 13).

If adolescence can be successfully negotiated, the person emerges with self-respect adequate to almost any situation. Along with this self-respect goes respect for others and a freedom of personal initiative which allows him to adapt his personal characteristics to the social order.

SUMMARY

Anna Freud describes the prepuberty phase as one in which impulses once again break through, accompanied by aggression, pregenital symptoms, and oedipal fantasies. Deutsch, on the other hand, says that for girls this is the period of greatest freedom from infantile sexuality and aggression. At the onset of puberty, according to orthodox theory, libido becomes concentrated specifically on genital feelings, aims, and ideas, with an apparent improvement in behavior. Heterosexual outlets, however, are limited by society, so that conflicts around masturbation are common. The adolescent girl is said to become aware of the vagina as a source of pleasure while previously she had been interested solely in the clitoris and the desire to be boyish. At this time she faces the problem of accepting the feminine func-

[19] *Ibid.,* p. 62.
[20] P. Mullahy, *Oedipus Myth and Complex* (New York: Hermitage, 1948).

tion and its passive role. Narcissism is high-lighted in both sexes during adolescence.

Conflict between the ego and the id is characteristic. Two possible extremes can result: if the id wins out there is a "riot of uninhibited gratification of instinct," and if the ego is victorious impulses are confined within narrow limits and there has to be constant expenditure of energy on countercathexes, defense mechanisms, and symptoms. The ego also alienates itself from the superego in this period, which further increases the danger from instincts and tends to make the individual asocial.

In the area of relationships to others, the adolescent has to fight off the oedipal fantasies stirred up again during prepuberty. He substitutes new attachments to replace parental ties. These love relations, whether to a person of his own age or a parental substitute, are passionate and exclusive but typically of short duration. Others are selected as objects and then abandoned without any consideration for their feelings. Fleeting love fixations of this sort, says Anna Freud, are highly narcissistic and really represent primitive forms of identification. Following this wave of narcissism is a normal, temporary phase of homosexual relationships. In the case of the girl Deutsch states that there is a change in object choice from homosexual in prepuberty to bisexual in early puberty to heterosexual in later puberty. Significant elements in the feminine core are said to be narcissism, passivity, and masochism.

In prepuberty the ego has to call indiscriminately upon all the defense mechanisms at its command. During adolescence two frequent mechanisms are asceticism, the repudiation of all instinctual wishes, and intellectualization, the linking of instinctual processes to ideational contents. Adolescent creativity, such as the diary, is also interpreted as a form of defense.

The Rankian view of adolescence stresses the continuing struggle for independence and sense of self. The individual fears and resists his sexual impulses because they might dominate him and force him to renounce his capacity to act as a total self. Sullivan describes prepuberty as the most untroubled phase of human life, during which the capacity to love matures. Difficulties in adolescence occur in relation to the "genital lust mechanism." Sex becomes conflict-laden because premarital sexual experience is frowned upon and early marriage is discouraged. If adolescence can be successfully negotiated through the use of sublimation, Sullivan adds, then the person emerges with self-respect adequate to almost any situation.

NOTES

1. **Energy Complications Once More.** Anna Freud's reference to the increased quantity of instinctual energy in prepuberty seems to be at variance with the orthodox notion of a closed system containing a fixed amount of

energy. Perhaps she intends to convey an increase in the amount of energy actively mobilized at this time. In any case, the psychic energy concept, with all its attendant confusions and limitations, stands as something less than a cure-all for what ails personality theory.

2. The Problem of Individual and Class Differences. A difficulty inherent in many psychoanalytic formulations is the unknown extent to which they apply to the population at large. A prime example here is Anna Freud's description of the unruly, boorish behavior of the preadolescent. The issue of how many preadolescents conform to this picture is not treated, so the reader is left with the impression that such characteristics are at least typical. Doubtless there are wide individual differences. The crucial effects, in this connection, of social class membership have been sharply delineated by sociologists. Allison Davis,[21] for example, describes adolescent aggression as an approved, socially rewarded form of behavior in the lower classes. Until adequate normative evidence becomes available, judgments concerning frequency should probably be reserved.

3. Onset of Physical Changes in Adolescence. Kinsey *et al.*[22] state that the onset of adolescent physical changes in boys is more or less abrupt, usually occurring between eleven and fourteen years of age. In girls adolescent development is said to be more gradual, spread over a longer period of time, and does not reach its peak until a good many years after boys are sexually mature. Stolz and Stolz[23] describe three phases of adolescent growth: prepubertal, pubertal, and postpubertal. The first phase takes place sometime before age thirteen in boys and before eleven in girls. Its duration for boys is approximately a year and a quarter and for girls slightly shorter. The pubertal phase, which contains the most noticeable growth spurt, occurs between thirteen and fifteen for males and between eleven and fourteen for females. The third phase in the girl lasts for a year and a half and is somewhat shorter in the case of the boy. The legal definition of puberty, according to Webster's Dictionary, is usually given as fourteen for boys and twelve for girls.

4. Sexual Activities. Surveys of the sexual habits of adolescents confirm the widespread use of masturbatory and homosexual outlets. Kinsey *et al.*[24] report the incidence of masturbation in boys by age fifteen to be 82 per cent. For the period of preadolescence 60 per cent of the boys re-

---

[21] A. Davis, "Socialization and Adolescent Personality," *Readings in Social Psychology,* ed., T. M. Newcomb and E. L. Hartley (New York: Holt, 1947), pp. 139–150.
[22] A. C. Kinsey, W. B. Pomeroy and C. E. Martin, *Sexual Behavior in the Human Male* (Philadelphia: Saunders, 1948).
[23] H. R. Stolz and L. M. Stolz, "Adolescent Problems Related to Somatic Variations," *Yearb. Nat. Soc. Stud. Educ.,* XLIII (1944), pp. 80–99.
[24] Kinsey, Pomeroy and Martin, *op. cit.*

called some homosexual activity, with the average initial contact occurring at 9.2 years, in comparison with 40 per cent who recalled heterosexual activity, beginning typically at 8.8 years. Between the ages of twelve and fifteen the reported frequency of homosexual play ranged from 20 to 29 per cent, of heterosexual play from 16 to 23 per cent. Willoughby's[25] survey of the literature in 1937 revealed adolescent masturbation to be more characteristic for boys than for girls. Concerning homosexuality he inferred that many individuals were so inclined, but for the most part their homosexual activity was a function of restricted heterosexual companionship. In a study of normal and psychotic women Landis and his coworkers[26] noted that masturbation and emotional attachments to other women were frequent in adolescence.

The forms of expression of sexuality are, of course, culturally determined. Malinowski[27] and Mead[28] have described primitive cultures in which adolescents have much more sexual freedom than in our own. In the latter connection Mead stresses the inconsistency of American customs with respect to heterosexual activity. "Dating" now begins as early as the prepubertal period and follows the rules of the game, especially in the middle classes, according to social rather than sexual motives. Later, when sexual urges become dominant, their permitted expression in adolescence is distorted in such a way as to hinder future sexual adjustment in marriage. Cattell[29] points out the differences between Western culture, in which the lack of structure and signposts confuse the adolescent in his new role, and the comfortingly clear expectations and initiation rites among the Arunta, Andamanese, and Kwoma.

5. Adolescent Fantasy. Symonds[30] administered 42 pictures, similar in type to those in the Thematic Apperception Test series, to 20 normal adolescent boys and 20 girls. They were asked to make up stories about each one as a "test of creative imagination." The resulting 1,680 stories revealed, among others, a frequently occurring theme of "Oedipus longing and conflict." In addition, almost everyone in the group gave at least three stories revolving about aggression and love. Other characteristic themes concerned depression, anxiety, ambition, guilt, independence, injury, popularity, appearance, and dominance. While this study cannot itself be considered definitive, on the basis of the limited sample of subjects and the

[25] R. R. Willoughby, "Sexuality in the Second Decade," *Monogr. Soc. Res. Child Develpm.*, II, No. 10 (1937).

[26] C. Landis, *et al.*, *Sex in Development* (New York: Hoeber, 1940).

[27] B. Malinowski, *Sex and Repression in Savage Society* (New York: Harcourt, Brace, 1927).

[28] Margaret Mead, *Male and Female* (New York: Morrow, 1949).

[29] R. B. Cattell, *Personality* (New York: McGraw-Hill, 1950).

[30] P. M. Symonds, *Adolescent Fantasy* (New York: Columbia University Press, 1949).

absence of comparative data for other age groups, it offers a fruitful method for further explorations of fantasy.

6. The First Menstruation. Mead[31] emphasizes the significance in primitive cultures of the first menstruation (menarche) as a sharp dividing line between childhood and womanhood. She goes on to describe in detail the variety of customs which have arisen. The puritanical Manus women have an important, festive ceremony for the adolescent girl at menarche, but all later menstruations are concealed with great secrecy. Among the Arapesh, the girl's first menstruation, which takes place several years after she has been betrothed, is also an occasion for ceremony. Her brothers come and build her a menstrual hut, placing it beyond the edge of the village to keep the village safe from the dangerous supernatural strength attached to menstruating women. In contrast the peoples of Iatmul, Tchambuli, Mundugumor, and Samo place little or no social stress on menarche.

Apart from anthropological sources, there are two well-controlled studies by Stone and Barker,[32] who compared the interests and attitudes of pre- and post-menarcheal girls. The latter group showed greater heterosexual interests and activities, regardless of chronological age; indulged in daydreaming more frequently; avoided vigorous physical exercise; and showed more concern over their physical appearance. A similar investigation in boys was conducted by Sollenberger,[33] who separated more and less mature boys on the basis of amount of male sex hormone content in their urine. The sexually mature group proved to be more interested in heterosexual activities, strenuous competitive sports, and personal appearance.

7. Factors Determining Outcome of the Adolescent Struggle. A fourth factor affecting adolescent development, in addition to impulse strength, ego tolerance, and efficacy of defenses, is omitted by Anna Freud. This relates to the degree and type of stress provided by the environment. Presumably two equally equipped adolescents, from the point of view of the three listed attributes, will react differently if one becomes subjected to a malevolent social climate and the other does not.

8. Explanations of Asocial Behavior. An alternative way of looking at asocial behavior, other than the ego-superego split, is in terms of the adolescent's marginal position. Being no longer a child and yet a man, he is

[31] Mead, *op. cit.*

[32] C. P. Stone and R. G. Barker, "Aspects of Personality and Intelligence in Post-menarcheal and Pre-menarcheal Girls of the Same Chronological Ages," *J. Comp. Psychol.*, XXIII (1937), pp. 439–455; C. P. Stone and R. G. Barker, "The Attitudes and Interests of Pre-menarcheal Girls and Post-menarcheal Girls," *J. Genet Psychol.*, LIV (1939), pp. 27–71.

[33] R. T. Sollenberger, "Some Relationships Between the Urinary Excretion of Male Hormone by Maturing Boys and Their Expressed Interests and Attitudes," *J. Psychol.*, IX (1940), pp. 179–190.

placed in a very tenuous situation by society. One conceivable reaction to this anomalous role is social withdrawal.

9. Adolescent Revolt against Parents. Dollard *et al.*[34] interpret the adolescent's commonly observed rebelliousness, directed against his parents and authority figures in general, as a response to frustration. The source of the frustration lies in the situation described in Note 8. However, according to this group of authors, aggressive reactions are most typical of early adolescence, since substitute satisfactions tend to be worked out gradually by trial and error. Placing the focus of aggression in early adolescence is in disagreement with Tryon's[35] observation that the period of greatest resistance to adults is middle adolescence, when growth is most accelerated. Thus our knowledge of adolescent relationships, if we can generalize from this particular form, seems to be deficient in the facts of actual behavior, to say nothing of underlying reasons.

A few isolated studies have been done in this area, but even the surface has hardly been scratched. Kitay[36] found that the majority of children between eleven and fourteen, responding to a questionnaire, felt that their parents understood them, whereas from age fifteen on there was a much greater feeling of being misunderstood. Stott,[37] averaging ratings on several personality tests, noted poorer adjustment in those adolescents who criticized their parents most. Another suggestion of the connection between disturbance and rebelliousness comes from Watson's study, reported by Cattell,[38] in which those individuals with radical antiauthority views turned out to have been punished more frequently and more severely by their parents.

10. Homosexual Behavior. See Note 4 for a summary of existing data on homosexuality during adolescence.

11. Interests and Attitudes. This general area is one which has received considerable attention from investigators, though not specifically on the concrete-abstract dimension stressed by Anna Freud. Beginning with the preadolescent period, we have available a foreign study by Zillig[39] (summarized by Cattell[40]), who used recorded spontaneous conversations of a

[34] J. Dollard, L. W. Dobb, N. E. Miller and R. R. Sears, *Frustration and Aggression* (New Haven, Yale University Press, 1939).
[35] Caroline M. Tryon, "The Adolescent Peer Culture," *Yearb. Nat. Soc. Stud. Educ.*, XLIII (1944), pp. 217–239.
[36] P. M. Kitay, "A Comparison of the Sexes in Their Attitude and Beliefs about Women: A Study of Prestige Groups," *Sociometry*, III (1940), pp. 399–407.
[37] L. H. Stott, "Adolescents' Dislikes Regarding Parental Behavior and Their Significance," *J. Genet. Psychol.*, LVII (1940), pp. 393–414.
[38] Cattell, *op. cit.*
[39] M. Zillig, "Prollereien unter Schulkindern," *Z. pädag. Psychol.*, XXXIX (1938), pp. 241–250, 263–270.
[40] Cattell, *op. cit.*

large number of boys and girls ranging from nine to twelve years of age. The group manifested a boastful and fantastic tone, wishful thinking, and a lack of modesty and ethics. Boys talked mainly about physical strength and daring exploits, whereas girls were concerned with appearance, possessions, and social prominence. In connection with this research, it is interesting to note the congruence with Anna Freud's description of preadolescent behavior, which was based largely on observations of children in Austria. The need for more extensive cross-cultural checks again makes itself felt at this point.

The early adolescent, as portrayed by Tryon,[41] Zeligs,[42] Jones,[43] James and Moore,[44] and others, indulges in like-sex clubs or gang activities. These cliques, formed slightly earlier in the case of girls, emphasize in-group secrets, slang, loyalties, and by and large, tend to suppress individuality. Twelve-year-old boys behave in an active, aggressive, competitive, boisterous manner, whereas girls of the same age are generally neat, docile and prim, though some tomboyishness is acceptable. Interests in boys emphasize political and social questions, personal development, and possessions and pleasures; in girls family welfare. With respect to superego functioning, Buck[45] notes that twelve- and thirteen-year-olds consider about 50 per cent more activities to be morally wrong than do twenty-year-olds.

The period of middle adolescence, according to Tryon,[46] features the striving for social conformity. Boys of fifteen become less boisterous and more interested in social poise. Early maturing girls at this age stress sophistication; others attach importance to being "good fellows." Parties are especially attractive. Using the Strong Vocational Interest Blank, Taylor[47] found relatively greater stability of interests during the later rather than the earlier years of mid-adolescence. Subsequently, around the ages of seventeen and eighteen. Tryon reports boys to be concerned with social maturity, athletics, and leadership, whereas girls are absorbed with feminine ideals and security. James and Moore,[48] analyzing leisure activities by keeping diaries, noted increasingly heterosexual and social interests at these ages.

[41] Tryon, *op. cit.*
[42] R. Zeligs, "Social Factors Annoying to Children," *J. Appl. Psychol.*, XXIX (1945), pp. 75–82.
[43] H. E. Jones, *Development in Adolescence* (New York: Appleton-Century-Crofts, 1943).
[44] H. E. O. James and F. F. Moore, "Adolescent Leisure in a Working-Class District," *Occup. Psychol.*, XIV (1940), pp. 132–145.
[45] W. Buck, "A Measurement of Changes of Attitudes and Interests of University Students over a Ten-Year Period," *J. Abnorm. Soc. Psychol.*, XXXI (1936), pp. 12–19.
[46] Tryon, *op. cit.*
[47] K. Van F. Taylor, "The Reliability and Permanence of Vocational Interests of Adolescents," *J. Exp. Educ.*, XI (1942), pp. 81–87.
[48] James and Moore, *op. cit.*

Symonds[49] characterizes the older adolescent boy as intrigued primarily by an urge toward success, and the girl as being more passive, receptive, and interested in people.

12. Conflicting Views on Preadolescence. Sullivan's description of preadolescence as the period closest to untroubled human life is in sharp contrast to Anna Freud's. The latter, as we have seen, stresses unruliness, brutality, exhibitionism, and pregenital breakthroughs. Deutsch's portrayal of the preadolescent girl as showing the greatest freedom from infantile sexuality and aggression corresponds to Sullivan's, whereas Spiegel's reinterpretation of Deutsch's data follows Anna Freud. These discrepancies point to the necessity for systematic, reliable observations of behavior.

13. The "Sublimatory Reformulation of Interpersonal Relations." The merit, if any, in Sullivan's attempt to redefine sublimation obviously requires greater substantiation than Mullahy provides. Broader coverage alone is frequently not a virtue.

[49] P. M. Symonds, "Changes in Sex Differences in Problems and Interests of Adolescence with Increasing Age," *J. Genet. Psychol.*, L (1937), pp. 83–89.

The Absent Father and Cross-Sex Identity*[1]

ROGER V. BURTON AND
JOHN W. M. WHITING

Simple analyses of socialization processes are complicated by the fact that in some instances several hypotheses may be advanced to account for the same behavior. For example, everybody agrees that children and adolescents acquire the characteristic behavior patterns of adult models, but why does this identification occur? Some theorists assert that it stems largely from genetic factors; others argue that it results primarily from cultural and environmental influences. Based upon the latter view, Burton and Whiting offer an intriguing, new theory to account for this identification process. Named the *"status envy* hypothesis," it predicts that persons will identify with models who control resources they covet. Boys from father-absent households, where the mother's status is particularly likely to be envied, are shown to experience considerable cross-sex identity conflict. The theory suggests that some delinquent acts of boys in gangs may be exaggerated expressions of masculine behavior resulting from conflict in sex identity.

The *status envy* hypothesis is a valuable contribution to socialization theory, and students interested in the identification process will find it helpful in explaining the function of role models and the nature of motivation during adolescence.

[1] This paper is a shortened revision of the paper read at the symposium. The first portion of this paper constituting the theoretical formulation and supporting cross-cultural material is based on a presentation of the status envy hypothesis given by John W. M. Whiting at Tulane University as part of the Mona Bronsman Sheckman Lectures in Social Psychiatry, March 17–19, 1960. These lectures, called "Social Structure and Child Rearing: A Theory of Identification," provide a more extended presentation of this material and will be published as a monograph at a later date.

* From *Merrill-Palmer Quarterly of Behavior and Development*, VII (1961), pp. 85–95. Reprinted by permission of the authors and the publisher.

THE STATUS ENVY HYPOTHESIS

Before presenting the evidence, however, we would like to state our view on the process of identification and the development of identity. This view we would like to call the *status envy hypothesis*. This hypothesis may be summarily stated as follows: The process of identification consists of the covert practice of the role of an envied status. Identification consists of learning a role by rehearsal in fantasy or in play rather than by actual performance, and this rehearsal is motivated by envy of the incumbent of a privileged status.

Let us consider the mother-infant relationship in which the mother attempts to satisfy all of the infant's needs. According to our theory, if it were possible for the mother to supply everything the infant wanted, he would not identify with her as he already occupies the privileged status. Some learning does, of course, take place in such a complementary relationship. The child learns to give the proper signals when he wants something and to accept and consume it when it is offered. Furthermore, he learns to predict certain sequences of events determined by his mother's behavior. In other words, he has cognizance of his mother's role. Although this cognizance may provide some savings in later training, if and when he is motivated to perform her role, we would like to distinguish cognizance of a complementary role from identification with its incumbent.

To clarify our view of the motivation leading to identification, we would like to introduce the concept of a resource. A resource is anything, material or nonmaterial, which somebody wants and over which someone else may have control. Resources include food, water, optimum temperature, freedom from pain, and the derived symbolic resources such as love, solace, power, information, and success. Were these resources inexhaustible, and equally and completely available to all, there would be no such thing as status envy and, by our hypothesis, no learning by identification. Such, however, is not the case. As part of the cultural rules of every society, there is a status system which gives privileged access to resources for some positions in the system and, at the same time, disbars other positions from controlling and consuming them.

Returning to our mother-child example: As soon as the mother withholds a resource from her child and, by virtue of her position in the family, either herself consumes it or gives it to someone else, the conditions for status envy obtain. Even during infancy in societies where an infant occupies the most privileged status, complete nurturance is practically impossible. No matter how much a mother might wish to be ever-loving the exigencies of life are such that there are times when she must withhold some resource that the child wants.

This is particularly true during the process of socialization. By definition this process involves teaching the child to delay gratification and to defer to the rights of others. More specifically, socialization involves teaching the child the privileges and disabilities which characterize the social structure of his society.

We may now restate our major hypothesis: If there is a status that has privileged access to a desired resource, the incumbent or occupant of such a status will be envied by anyone whose status does not permit him the control of, and the right to use, the resource. Status envy is then a motivational component of status disability, and such motivation leads to learning by identification.

This view differs from some other theories of identification in that we hold that a completely satisfying complementary relation between two people will not lead to identification. By this hypothesis, a child maximally identifies with people who consume resources in his presence but do not give him any. He does not identify with the people he loves unless they withhold from him something he wants. Love alone will not produce identification. Thus, the status envy hypothesis advanced here makes identification with the aggressor just a special case, and the Oedipal situation is also simply a special case.

The actual process of learning by identification consists of the covert practice in fantasy or in play of the role of the envied status. So when the child wants to stay up late, for example, and his parents make him go to bed while they themselves stay up, the child says to himself, "I wish I were grown up. Perhaps if I acted as they do I would be grown up," and he goes to sleep rehearsing, in fantasy, grown-up behavior.

ATTRIBUTED, SUBJECTIVE, AND OPTATIVE IDENTITY

We would now like to present our views on another concept which we believe will be useful in distinguishing households with fathers absent from those with fathers present. This is the concept of identity.

In every society, statuses have names or labels. In our society, for example, there are the familiar kinship statuses of mother, father, uncle, aunt, brother, sister; the age-determined statuses of infant, child, adolescent, adult, and aged; the occupational statuses of doctor, lawyer, clerk, workman, etc.; and, especially important to our thesis, the sex-determined statuses of male and female.

We would like to define a person's position or positions in the status system of this society as his identity. Furthermore, we would like to distinguish three kinds of identity: attributed, subjective, and optative. *Attributed identity* consists of the statuses assigned to a person by other members of his society. *Subjective identity* consists of the statuses a person sees himself as occupying. And finally, *optative identity* consists of those statuses a person wishes he could occupy but from which he is disbarred. It is this last kind of identity that is most important for this paper.

Obviously, one's optative identity derives from status envy, and nothing much would be added to our theory by introducing this concept if one's optative identity were always objective and realistic. The wish being father to the thought, however, this is frequently not the case, and people often feel "I am what I would like to be." In such a case, the subjective and optative identities merge and become discrepant with the attributed identity.

It is our thesis that the aim of socialization in any society is to produce an adult whose attributed, subjective, and optative identities are isomorphic: "I see myself as others see me, and I am what I want to be." It is further presumed, however, that such isomorphism can only be achieved by passing through a stage in which there is status disbarment, status envy, and thus a discrepancy between one's optative and attributed identities. That is, to become such an adult, a person must have been deprived of the privileged consumption of resources accorded only to adults. This disbarment results in his wanting to be a member of that class. When society then permits him to occupy this privileged status, there is agreement in what he wants to be, in what society says he is, and in what he sees himself to be.

CROSS-CULTURAL EVIDENCE

Having briefly presented our views on learning by identification and on identity, let us now turn to the consideration of some empirical data which may provide a test of these notions. The first such test will be cross-cultural. The independent variables are judgments as to the distribution of resources during infancy and during childhood. Specifically, social structure of a sample of societies was judged for the degree to which the father and adult males in general, or the mother and adult females in general, occupied privileged or equivalent statuses as perceived by the infant and later by the child. Arrangements in infancy lead to *primary identification;* whereas those in childhood lead to *secondary identification.*

It is our assumption, and this has been supported by a previous study,[2] that sleeping arrangements provide the best index of status envy during infancy. The bed seems to be the center of a child's world during the first year or two of his life. This is where the resources of greatest value to him are given or withheld, and those who share this setting with him become the models for his first or primary identification.

In most societies the world over, an infant sleeps during the nursing period either in his mother's bed, or in a crib or cradle right next to it, and

[2] J. W. M. Whiting, R. Kluckhohn, and A. Anthony, "The Function of Male Initiation Ceremonies at Puberty," *Readings in Social Psychology,* ed., Eleanor E. Maccoby, T. M. Newcomb and E. L. Hartley (New York: Holt, 1958), pp. 359–370.

within easy reach. Of over 100 societies on which we have data on sleeping arrangements, the American middle class is unique in putting the baby to sleep in a room of his own.

For our purposes, the big difference lies in whether or not the father also sleeps with the mother. In a sample of 64 societies which we would like to report now, 36 of them have the pattern of the father and mother sleeping apart, and the infant thus has the exclusive attention of the mother at night. In the remaining 28 societies, the infant either shares his mother's bed with his father or in a few instances sleeps alone. According to our theory, these two arrangements should be profoundly different in their effect on the infant's first or primary identification.

In the exclusive mother-infant case, the mother should be seen as all-powerful, all-important, and, insofar as she sometimes withholds resources, the person to be envied; and we predict the infant will covertly practice her role, and his optative identity will be female. In societies where the father sleeps with the mother, quite a different picture obtains with respect to valued resources. In this instance, both parents give and withhold important resources. Under these conditions, therefore, we assume the envied status to be that of a parent of either sex. For the infant, the juxtaposition of privilege is seen as between self and adult, rather than between self and female.

Thus the male infant in societies with exclusive mother-child sleeping arrangements should have a primary cross-sex optative identity, whereas the boy reared in societies in which the father sleeps with the mother should have a primary adult optative identity.

After a child is weaned and becomes what Margaret Mead calls a yard child, conditions may change drastically from those of infancy. Privilege may now be defined by marital residence. Three major patterns emerge in our samples of societies: patrilocal, matrilocal, and equilocal.

In societies with patrilocal residence, a man will remain throughout his life in or near the house in which he was born, his wife or wives moving in from another village. In such societies, the domestic unit consists of a group of males closely related by blood, and a group of inmarrying and interloping females. Prestige and power are clearly vested in this group of men, and adult males are the ones to be envied.

Societies with matrilocal residence are a mirror image of the patrilocal case. Here the daughters stay at home and their husbands are the interlopers. In such societies, by contrast with the patrilocal, women occupy the privileged and envied statuses.

Equilocal societies are more familiar to us. Here a young husband and wife set up a household of their own apart from the parents of either, as is generally the case in our own society; or they may choose between, or alternate between, living with the wife's parents and the husband's parents.

In this instance, residence does not automatically give advantage to either men or women, and sex identity is thus not an important issue.

Thus residence patterns may provide the conditions for the envy of males or the envy of females; or sex-determined statuses may be relatively un-privileged. This distribution of resources in the domestic unit provides the conditions for what we would like to call secondary identification.

SOME PRIMARY AND SECONDARY OPTATIVE IDENTIFICATION COMBINATIONS

Although the two types of sleeping arrangements and three residence patterns yield six combinations of conditions for primary and secondary identification, we would like here to concentrate on only two of them in contrast to all others. These are, first, the societies which should produce the maximum conflict between primary and secondary optative sex identity: e.g., societies with both exclusive mother-infant sleeping arrangements, which should lead a boy initially to wish he were feminine, and patrilocal residence patterns, which should lead him subsequently and secondarily to want to be masculine. The other societies of interest to us are those which promote feminine identification, both initially and secondarily; that is, societies with both exclusive mother-child sleeping arrangements and matri-local residence.

Having described our independent variables, let us now turn to the de-pendent variables which should be predicted by our theory from (a) maxi-mum conflict in optative sex identity and (b) maximum feminine optative sex identity.

Initiation Hypothesis

In a previous study,[3] male initiation rites at puberty were shown to be strongly associated with exclusive mother-child sleeping arrangements and a long post-partum sex taboo. Although cross-sex identification was mentioned in a footnote as a possible interpretation of these findings, the authors' major explanation was based on the assumption that these condi-tions exacerbated the Oedipal conflict, and that initiation rites were the symbolic expression of resolution of this conflict.

We now believe, and would like to present evidence, that the sex identity interpretation is the more valid and fruitful. We would like to present the cross-sex identity and initiation hypothesis explicitly as follows: In societies with maximum conflict in sex identity, e.g., where a boy initially sleeps exclusively with his mother and where the domestic unit is patrilocal

[3] *Ibid.*

and hence controlled by men, there will be initiation rites at puberty which function to resolve this conflict in identity.

This hypothesis suggests that the initiation rites serve psychologically to brainwash the primary feminine identity and to establish firmly the secondary male identity. The hazing, sleeplessness, tests of manhood, and painful genital operation, together with promise of high status—that of being a man if the tests are successfully passed—are indeed similar to the brainwashing techniques employed by the Communists. Indicating how traumatic these rites may be, one ethnographer[4] reports that boys returning home after initiation did not know their village or recognize their parents.

Native theory also supports our interpretation. In most societies with elaborate initiation rites at puberty, there are two terms labeling one's sex identity which are different from the ones with which we are familiar. One term refers to all women and uninitiated boys, whereas the other refers to initiated males only. In these societies, according to native theory, a male is born twice; once into the woman-child status, and then at puberty he symbolically dies and is reborn into the status of manhood.

Let us now turn to our data. In our sample of 64 societies, there were 13 in which there were elaborate initiation ceremonies with genital operations. All 13 of these had the exclusive mother-infant sleeping arrangements which we predicted would cause a primary feminine identification. Furthermore, 12 of these 13 had patrilocal residence which we predicted would produce the maximum conflict in identity and hence the need for an institution to help resolve this conflict. A chi-square test of the association is fantastically beyond chance. Expressed simply, 87½ per cent of the 64 societies fall in the cells predicted by our hypothesis.

But what of societies where the female status is seen as privileged both in infancy and in childhood, where the infant sleeps exclusively with his mother and in childhood moves into a world controlled by his mother, his aunts, and his tyrannical maternal grandmother? Here our theory would predict that a man would have a strong optative feminine identity, and the society should provide him some means to act out, symbolically at least, the female role.

From the beginnings of ethnographic reporting, a strange custom has been described for various societies over the world. This custom consists of the husband going to bed and undergoing all the same taboos as his wife during the time she is in labor. This custom is known as the *couvade* and has long been a favorite example for undergraduate texts in anthropology to exemplify the curious customs of primitive peoples. As a test of our

[4] J. Staub, "Beitrage zur Kenntais der Materiellen Kultur der Mendi in der Sierra Leone (Contributions to a Knowledge of the Material Culture of the Mende in Sierra Leone) Solothurni Buchdruckerei Vogt-Schild," translated for the Human Relations Area Files by C. Wood (1936), p. 61.

hypothesis, however, the couvade is most apt. What event more than child-birth defines that part of a woman's role that is uniquely feminine? It seems to us, at least, that when a man attempts to participate in the birth of his child by closely imitating the behavior of his wife, this should be a good index of his wish to act out the feminine role and thus symbolically to be in part a woman.

Our hypothesis is again strongly confirmed by the data. Of the 12 societies with couvade in our sample, 10 had exclusive mother-child sleeping arrangements and 9 had matrilocal residence. Again, the results are highly significant statistically. In this instance, 90 per cent of the cases fall in the predicted cells.

AMERICAN CULTURE EVIDENCE

Cross-cultural evidence thus seems to confirm the status envy hypothesis with respect to sex identity. Now let us turn to other studies done within our own cultural context which seem relevant and yet were not specifically designed with this theory in mind. A recent book by Rohrer and Edmonson, *The Eighth Generation,*[5] seems especially significant. This study is a follow-up twenty years later of the people described in *Children of Bondage* by Davis and Dollard.[6] The problems of identification and identity are stressed throughout, and the importance of what we have called primary feminine identification clearly presented.

The girls raised in the matriarchy, which coincides with our exclusive mother-infant case, are very likely to establish a matriarchal home of their own and to live with their mothers or very close to them. The boys from this kind of household also seem to conform to our theoretical expectations. If the boy finds that he falls under the dominance of older men when he leaves his house, in these cases a gang of older boys, he shows evidence of a sex role conflict in compulsive denial of anything feminine. Rohrer and Edmonson conclude that "the gang member rejects this femininity in every form, and he sees it in women and in effeminate men, in laws and morals and religion, in schools and occupational striving."[7]

This compulsive masculine behavior is also described by Walter Miller[8] in his discussion of the "focal concerns" of the lower-class culture. He emphasizes that the "female-based" household and "serial monogamy"

---

[5] J. H. Rohrer and M. S. Edmonson, *The Eighth Generation* (New York: Harper and Bros., 1960).

[6] A. Davis and J. Dollard, *Children of Bondage* (Washington: American Council on Education, 1941).

[7] Rohrer and Edmonson, *op. cit.,* 163.

[8] W. B. Miller, "Lower Class Culture as a Generating Milieu of Gang Delinquency," *Journal of Social Issues,* XIV (1958), pp. 5–19.

are characteristic of the "hard core" of this lower class and closely associated with delinquent gang behavior. He argues that delinquent acts function as means of resolving dominant motivational themes in the lower-class community, which he views as "a long-established, distinctively patterned tradition with an integrity of its own—rather than a so-called 'delinquent subculture' which has arisen through conflict with middle class culture."[9]

In Miller's writings and in *The Eighth Generation* are descriptions of the requirements for gang membership, requirements which closely resemble the attributes of the initiation ceremonies of primitive societies, especially the "tests of manhood." Miller specifically relates the focal concern of "toughness" to conflict over sexual identity:

. . . Among its [toughness] most important components are physical prowess, evidenced both by demonstrated possession of strength and endurance and athletic skill; "masculinity," symbolized by a distinctive complex of acts and avoidances (bodily tattooing; absence of sentimentality; non-concern with "art," "literature," conceptualization of women as conquest objects, etc.); and bravery in the face of physical threat.[10]

The attributes of this male model are seen in the prototypical "private eye" of television: "hard, fearless, undemonstrative, skilled in physical combat," and irresistible as Don Juan.[11] Behavior deviating from this stereotype is evidence of one's being a homosexual. Miller also attributes the genesis of this obsessive concern with masculinity to a cross-sex primary identification and considers the behavior a type of compulsive reaction formation. This interpretation is, of course, closely attuned to the status envy hypothesis we have described.

In their study of delinquency, the Gluecks report that more of the delinquent boys, as compared with the nondelinquents, came from homes "broken by desertion, separation, divorce, or death of one or both parents, many of the breaches occurring during the early childhood of the boys."[12] They further indicate that the fathers of the delinquents tend to be irresponsible in family matters and to have far poorer work habits than the fathers of the nondelinquents. If many of these broken homes were actually exclusive mother-infant or female-based households, and it seems from most reports on the lower class that this is a fairly safe assumption, these results are consonant with Miller's interpretation that delinquent acts conform to the focal concerns of boys raised in the mother-child household.

Concentrating on the "good" boy in a high delinquency area, Reckless,

9 *Ibid.,* pp. 5–6.
10 *Ibid.,* 9.
11 *Ibid.*
12 S. Glueck and Eleanor T. Glueck, *Unraveling Juvenile Delinquency* (New York: Commonwealth Fund, 1950), p. 280.

Dinitz, and Murray,[13] and more recently with Scarpitti,[14] found that the nondelinquent boy comes from an intact family which is quite stable. These boys also felt accepted by their parents and expressed acceptance of them. These relationships with their parents were markedly different from those of a group of boys being held in a detention home.

The studies we have just considered found family structure an important factor in the early lives of the subjects. This relationship was found as a result of the analyses of the data which the investigators had gathered in order to study the culture as a whole or with special focus on delinquency. Let us now turn to some investigations which have the presence or absence of the father as the selected variable for study.

FATHER ABSENCE AND PRESENCE

The draft at the beginning of World War II made possible several studies comparing middle-class children from father-absent homes with those from father-present households.[15] These studies indicated that boys from father-absent households behaved like girls both in fantasy behavior and in overt behavior, especially with respect to producing very little aggression. Investigating the effect on the child of the father's return, Stolz[16] found that boys whose fathers had been absent but were then returned, continued to be effeminate in overt behavior, but there was a marked change in their fantasy behavior. This group now produced the maximum amount of aggression in fantasy. These conditions of father absence for the initial years and then control by an adult man are the conditions we have indicated should produce conflict over sexual identification.

The influence of father absence on the child has also been studied in Norway.[17] The families of sailors were compared with other families of

[13] W. C. Reckless, S. Dinitz and E. Murray, "Self Concept as an Insulator Against Delinquency," *Amer. Socio. Rev.,* XXI (1956), pp. 744–746.

[14] F. R. Scarpatti, E. Murray, S. Dinitz and W. C. Reckless, "The 'Good' Boy in a High Delinquency Area: Four Years Later," *Amer. Socio. Rev.,* XXV (1960), pp. 555–558.

[15] G. R. Bach, "Father-Fantasies and Father-typing in Father-separated Children," *Child Development,* XVII (1946), pp. 63–79; P. S. Sears, "Doll Play Aggression in Normal Young Children: Influence of Sex Age, Sibling Status, Father's Absence," *Psychol. Monogr.,* LXV, Whole No. 323 (1951); Lois M. Stoltz, *Father Relations of Warborn Children* (Palo Alto: Stanford University Press, 1954).

[16] Stoltz, *op. cit.*

[17] E. Gronseth, "The Impact of Father Absence in Sailor Families upon the Personality of Structure and Social Adjustment of Adult Sailor Sons," *Studies of the Family,* II, Part I, ed., A. Anderson (Gottingen: Vandenhoeck and Ruprecht, 1957), pp. 97–114; D. B. Lynn and W. L. Sawrey, "The Effects of Father-absence on Norwegian Boys and Girls," *J. Abnorm. Soc. Psychol.,* LIX (1959), pp. 258–262; P. O. Tiller, "Father Absence and Personality Development of Children in Sailor Families: A Preliminary Research Report," *Studies of the Family,* II, Part II, ed., N. Anderson, *op. cit.,* 115–137.

the same social class in which the fathers were present. The absence of these fathers often extended for two or more years. The results showed the wives of the sailors were more isolated from social contacts, more over-protective, and more concerned with obedience rather than happiness and self-realization for their children than were the nuclear household mothers, i.e., mothers whose husbands were not away from the household. The boys of the sailor families tended to be infantile and dependent and to manifest conflict over identification through compensatory or overly masculine behavior as compared with the father-present boys.

These data are suggestive for our theory, but we would also be interested in what happens to those boys later on. It would be interesting to know whether or not these boys themselves tend to become sailors, an occupation which would be suitable for a man who places a high value on obedience and also permits a man to perform acts of the female role in cleaning his quarters, sewing, etc., that are necessary on an extended sea voyage. The age of their first voyage and a description of the treatment accorded them as novitiate seamen would be pertinent. We would not be surprised, according to our theory, if these boys from sailor households themselves became sailors, made their first voyage during adolescence, and underwent a rather severe initiation ceremony on their first trip.

These studies, then, seem generally consistent with our cross-cultural findings in that the absence of the father produces in the boy cross-sex iden-tification which is either acted out or, more usually, defended against by exaggerated masculine behavior. Although the conditions differentiating primary and secondary identification are not as clearly specified in these studies as in the cross-cultural study, it does seem clear that the gang is an institution with a function similar to that of initiation, and that at least certain types of delinquent behavior are equivalent to the tests of manhood in those societies with conflict in sex identity.

Further Research

Although the general effect of father absence seems evident, the details of the process are not. For example, are there critical periods when the absence of a father is more crucial than other times? How long does it take for a child to establish identity? What are the relative effects of a weak father and an absent father? What is the effect of the absent father on the development of a girl?

Some of these details are being investigated at the Laboratory of Human Development at Harvard University, and others at the National Institutes of Health at Bethesda, Maryland, but these studies are not far enough along to warrant reporting here. It seems to us, however, that the effect of the household structure on the process of identification provides a very fruitful area for research.

Some Effects of Paternal Absence on Male Children* [1]

JOAN MCCORD,
WILLIAM MCCORD, AND
EMILY THURBER

The effects of paternal absence upon boys' sex role identification, sex anxiety, and antisocial behavior are investigated in the following study of adolescent boys from lower-class homes. The findings reveal, as Burton and Whiting predicted in the preceding paper, that "feminine-aggressive behavior" results from "paternal absence." The data also suggest that the years of middle childhood and the nature of the boys' relations with their mothers may be particularly critical factors in boys' sex role conflicts. Contrary to expectation, however, the researchers do not find heightened anxiety or increased delinquent gang activity among the boys whose fathers are absent. Rather than resulting from paternal absence per se, these attributes are interpreted as stemming from homes characterized by "intense parental conflict" or from homes where the mother is "deviant or rejecting."

"That children are best reared in a home with two loving and understanding parents is so obvious as to need no statement" Dorothy Barclay[2] has commented, typifying current opinion. This viewpoint is so prevalent that it

[1] This research has been generously supported by the Ella Lyman Cabot Foundation, the Harvard Laboratory of Social Relations, and the National Institute of Mental Health (Grant M-2647).
Additional tables from this study have been deposited with the American Documentation Institute. Order Document No. 7059 from ADI Auxiliary Publications Project, Photoduplication Service, Library of Congress; Washington 25, D.C., remitting in advance $1.25 for microfilm or $1.25 for photocopies. Make checks payable to: Chief, Photoduplication Service, Library of Congress.
[2] D. Barclay, "When One Parent Plays the Double Role," *The New York Times Magazine*, LXIX (April 5, 1959).

* From the *Journal of Abnormal and Social Psychology*, LXIV (1962), pp. 361–369. Reprinted by permission of the authors and the American Psychological Association.

comes close to heresy to question it. Although William Goode,[3] in his comprehensive study of divorce, points to the almost total lack of research on the effects of divorce on children, he concludes:

> At every developmental phase of childhood, the child needs the father (who is usually the absent parent) as an object of love, security, or identification, or even as a figure against whom to rebel safely. . . . It would be surprising if the absence of the father had no effect on the child.

The same view prevails throughout social science. Few empirical studies of child development fail to include the words "intact homes" as a criterion of sample selection. It has long been the tradition to view anxiety as a primary outcome of father absence.[4] Such disorders as alcoholism, homosexuality, and totalitarian tendencies have been attributed to paternal absence.[5] The high incidence of broken homes among the delinquent population has led to theories which might account for the apparent causative relationship.[6]

In research comparing united homes with those in which the father is permanently or temporarily absent, and in psychological and psychoanalytic theory concerning paternal absence, attention has been particularly centered on three areas of personality development: the extent to which the child develops a feminine as opposed to a masculine self-image, the intensity and type of anxiety which he experiences, and the probability of his engaging in antisocial behavior. In the following pages, we will examine various hypotheses in these areas as they relate to a (primarily) lower-class sample of boys. In the analyses, comparisons are made between boys raised in permanently broken homes and those in united homes. By varying the subgroups compared, the dynamic relationship between family disorder and abnormal behavior is assessed.

METHOD

Design of the Research

During the 1930s, Richard Clark Cabot initiated the project, from which the subjects for this study of broken homes were taken, as an adjunct of an experi-

[3] W. J. Goode, *After Divorce* (Glencoe, Ill.: Free Press, 1956).

[4] O. Fenichel, *The Psychoanalytic Theory of Neurosis* (New York: Norton, 1945); S. Freud, "Three Essays on Sexuality," *Standard Edition,* VII (originally published 1905; London: Hogarth, 1953); G. E. Gardner, "Separation of the Parents and the Emotional Life of the Child," *The Problems of Delinquency,* ed., S. Glueck (Boston: Houghton Mifflin, 1959), pp. 138–143.

[5] J. A. M. Meerloo, "The Father Cuts the Cord: The Role of the Father as Initial Transference Figure," *Amer. J. Psychother.,* X (1956), pp. 471–480.

[6] R. V. Burton and J. W. M. Whiting, "The Absent Father: Effects on the Developing Child" (rev.); paper read at American Psychological Association Convention, Chicago, 1960; J. W. M. Whiting, R. Kluckholn and A. Anthony, "The Function of Male Initiation Ceremonies," *Readings in Social Psychology,* ed., Eleanor E. Maccoby, T. M. Newcomb and E. L. Hartley (New York: Holt, 1958), pp. 359–370.

mental program aimed at the prevention of delinquency in Cambridge and Somerville, Massachusetts.[7]

For an average period of 5 years, between the ages of 10 and 15, 255 boys[8] were observed at home, at school, and at play. Trained social workers, who visited the families approximately every other week, noted the behavior of the parents as well as the child. The counselors would appear unannounced, with a frequency which made it possible to observe the families at meals, during their leisure, in the midst of crises, and during their ordinary daily routines. They recorded their observations after each visit. Thus, running records were kept for 255 subjects between 1939 and 1945.[9]

In 1956 and 1957, trained researchers read each case record and rated the boy and his parents on a number of variables ranging from occupation and religion to affectional interaction. Interrater agreement, tested on a random sample, was high[10] and several factors point to the validity of the information obtained in this manner. Expected relationships which might have indicated a middle-class bias or operation of a halo effect were not found (e.g., the lower-class boys were not pictured as more aggressive and the brighter boys were not pictured as leaders). Most importantly, the categorized ratings of the case records yielded strong relationships to completely independent measures of social deviance among the subjects when they had become adults.[11]

Sample Characteristics

Among the 255 boys[12] in the study, 105 had lost one or both parents. Because we wished to focus on the effects of paternal absence, we dropped boys

[7] E. Powers and Helen Witmer, *An Experiment in the Prevention of Delinquency* (New York: Columbia University Press, 1951).

[8] Originally 325 boys had been included. Because of heavy case load, 65 boys were retired from the project in 1941, 5 additional boys were dropped because of their death or moving out of Massachusetts. The original sample was selected as follows: Teachers, police, and other officials recommended boys whom they believed showed signs of incipient delinquency. The Cambridge-Somerville Youth Study staff gathered information about them for the matching procedure (one boy to receive treatment and the other to be placed in a control group) so that the criteria of selection consisted in a willingness to participate and ability to find two boys with similar backgrounds in family structure, age, and "general personality." To avoid stigmatizing the boys in the project, an approximately equal number were added who were considered "normal" by the same authorities (again, equally divided between the treatment and the control groups).

[9] Between 1955 and 1957, these subjects and a matched control group who had received no direct attention from the project were traced through Massachusetts Board of Probation, mental hospitals, and various agencies dealing with alcoholism. It was found that the treatment program had no discernible effect upon criminality or alcoholism (see W. McCord and Joan McCord, *Origins of Crime* [New York: Columbia University Press, 1959]; and W. McCord and Joan McCord, *Origins of Alcoholism* [Stanford, Cal.: Stanford University Press, 1960]).

[10] The reliability of each of the ratings is fully discussed in McCord and McCord, *Origins of Alcoholism,* 1960.

[11] McCord and McCord, *Origins of Alcoholism,* 1960.

[12] From 237 families.

who were not living with their natural mothers (12 had lost both parents and 20 had lost their mothers) and the 18 who had step- or foster fathers. The remaining 55 boys from broken homes were living with their natural mothers; these were children whose fathers had died (24), deserted (8), been placed in mental hospitals (4), were serving long prison terms (3), or whose parents had been divorced or legally separated (16). The 150 boys whose natural parents were living together were used for the control group.

A number of studies have indicated that broken homes are associated with low socioeconomic status.[13] To the extent that social class affects personality development, this relationship between social class and family stability may lead to false conclusions regarding the effects of broken homes. Since the Cambridge-Somerville Youth Study centered upon the congested areas of these two cities, the entire sample had a strong lower-class representation. A comparison of fathers' occupations between broken and united homes within the sample showed slight (not statistically significant)[14] differences between the groups.

Various studies have indicated that Catholic families may be slightly more stable, although they seem to contribute more than their share of desertion cases.[15] In our sample, records of the mother's religion showed that 65% of the boys raised in united homes and 64% of the boys in broken homes had been raised by Catholic mothers.

Theorists have also suggested that the wife may alter her behavior to compensate for her husband's absence. P. O. Tiller[16] reports that Norwegian sailors' wives whose husbands were absent for extended periods of time exceeded matched mothers whose husbands were not absent in being overprotective and stressing obedience and politeness (in contrast to happiness and self-realization). In our sample, we did not find a significantly greater incidence of either maternal overprotection (31%/29%) or punitiveness (49%/44%) in the broken homes than in the united homes. Nor did we find significant differences between the mothers' attitudes toward their sons[17] in united homes and broken homes.

Two potentially important variables, however, strongly differentiated broken

[13] E. W. Burgess, "Predictive Methods and Family Stability," *Ann. Amer. Acad. Pol. Soc. Sci.,* CCLXXII (1950), pp. 47–52; A. B. Hollingshead, "Class Differences in Family Stability," *Ann. Amer. Acad. Pol. Soc. Sci.,* CCLXXII (1950), pp. 39–46; A. H. Weeks, "Differential Divorce Rates by Occupations," *Social Forces,* XXII (1943), pp. 334–337.

[14] Throughout the research, the chi-square test, two-tailed, was used when $N > 30$ and the Fisher test, two-tailed, was used when $N < 30$. Differences were considered significant if $p < .05$.

[15] H. Bell, *Youth Tell Their Story* (Washington, D.C.: American Council on Education, 1938); T. P. Monahan and W. M. Kephart, "Divorce and Desertion by Religious and Mixed-religious Groups," *Amer. J. Sociol.,* LIX (1954), pp. 454–465.

[16] P. O. Tiller, "Father-Absence and Personality Development of Children in Sailor Families: A Preliminary Research Report," *Nord. Psykol.,* Monograph No. 9 (1958).

[17] "Warm" mothers openly expressed their affection; "cold" mothers showed passive concern, but seldom demonstrated affection; "ambivalent" mothers displayed extreme variation between overt affection and overt rejection; and "rejecting" mothers cared little for their children or their welfare.

home boys from boys in united homes. William Goode[18] reported that about a third of his sample of divorced women cited sexual or alcoholic deviance of their husbands as the primary cause of divorce. We found a significantly higher proportion of deviant (i.e., alcoholic, criminal, or promiscuous) fathers ($p <$ .001) and deviant mothers ($p < .025$) among the boys from broken homes than among the boys whose parents were living together (see Table 1).

Table 1
Parental Deviance

Condition	Broken homes ($N = 55$)	United homes ($N = 150$)
Father deviant	30%	31%
Mother deviant	1	4
Both deviant	24	5
Neither deviant	45	60

In addition, a significantly lower proportion of the boys in broken homes had immigrant fathers ($p < .001$). Fifty-eight percent of the fathers in united homes, compared to 29% in broken homes, were immigrants.

To insure that the effects of these differences were not attributed to paternal absence, we matched each boy from a broken home to a boy similar in background whose parents were living together. Besides parental deviance and father's birthplace, the mother's attitude toward the boy, her disciplinary technique, her degree of control over her son, and the consistency of her discipline were used as criteria for matching.

We anticipated that paternal absence might have different effects under various conditions. Therefore, we divided the broken home boys on three dimensions:

1. The reason for the father's absence. The father's death might be presumed to have a different effect on the child than would his disappearance from the home after preliminary quarrels.

2. The age of the boy at the time when his father left. The child's age at the time of the break was divided roughly into preschool, preadolescent (or middle childhood), and adolescent.

3. The affectional relationship and stability (non-deviance) of the mother. Warm, nondeviant mothers were considered "normal." The distribution of the boys in broken homes on these three dimensions is shown in Table 2.

Since overt conflict probably precedes divorce and separation, and may have preceded desertion or death, the putative effects of broken homes may actually be the result of parental conflict. Ratings from direct observation of parental interaction were used to divide the boys whose parents were living together into two groups: the 30 whose parents quarreled constantly and were in overt conflict, and the 120 whose homes were relatively tranquil.

18 Goode, op. cit.

Table 2
Distribution of Broken Homes

		Age of boy at time of break		
Father	Mother	0–5	6–12	Over 12
Dead	Normal*	4	6	4
Living	Normal*	4	6	1
Dead	Abnormal†	3	3	4
Living	Abnormal†	7	11	2

* Warm, nondeviant.
† Deviant, cold, ambivalent, or rejecting.

RESULTS

Feminine Identification

One of the most widely held beliefs about the effects of paternal absence is that male children will develop unusually strong feminine components in their personalities. Three sets of ratings on the 205 boys in our study were used to test feminization in the father-absent group: homosexual tendencies, dependency, and lack of aggressiveness.[19] Although the trend of past evidence would suggest that father-absent boys would be relatively more feminine,[20] more dependent,[21] and less aggressive,[22] we found that neither homosexuality nor dependency differentiated significantly between the boys whose fathers were absent and those whose fathers were present and that the aggression scale was significantly related—but in the opposite direction from that predicted. (Eighty-seven percent of the broken home boys as opposed to 67% of those from tranquil homes, were moderately or strongly aggressive.)

[19] Boys were considered to have strong homosexual tendencies if they played with dolls, sometimes wore dresses, frequently expressed the wish to be a girl, or were overtly homosexual. They were considered to be dependent if they showed an unusually strong desire for adult approval. Femininity and dependency were not significantly related to each other. A three-point scale of behavioral aggression, ranging from little to unrestrained, was used.

[20] Burton and Whiting, *op. cit.;* M. Leichty, "The Absence of the Father during Early Childhood and Its Effect upon the Oedipal Situation as Reflected in Young Adults," *Merrill-Palmer Quart.,* VI (1960), pp. 212–217; D. B. Lynn and W. L. Sawrey, "The Effects of Father-Absence on Norwegian Boys and Girls," *J. Abnorm. Soc. Psychol.,* LIX (1959), pp. 258–262; R. F. Winch, "The Relation Between the Loss of a Parent and Progress in Courtship," *J. Soc. Psychol.,* XXIX (1949), pp. 51–56.

[21] L. M. Stoltz *et al., Father Relations of War-Born Children* (Stanford, Cal.: Stanford University Press, 1954).

[22] G. R. Bach, "Father-Fantasies and Father-typing in Father-Separated Children," *Child Development,* XVII (1946), pp. 63–79; R. R. Sears, M. H. Pintler and P. S. Sears, "Effects of Father-Separation on Preschool Children's Doll Play Aggression," *Child Develpm.,* XVII (1946), pp. 219–243.

Since aggressive behavior may be considered as an exhibition of "masculinity," it seemed probable that those who were both aggressive and showed signs of feminine identification[23] were expressing an instability in sex role identification or defending against feminine identification. This combination of feminine-aggressive behavior (as compared to feminine-nonaggressive behavior) was found significantly more frequently among boys in broken homes than among boys in tranquil homes ($p < .001$).

Since both parental conflict and paternal absence were related to feminine-aggressive behavior, it seemed likely that either parental conflict or parental deviance (found in almost equal proportions among broken and conflictful homes)[24] might fully account for the difference. Neither of these explanations, however, fit the data. We reasoned that parental conflict would have been less among homes severed by death of the father; yet a higher proportion (58%) of the sons in these homes showed feminine-aggressive behavior (see Table 3).

Table 3
Sex Role Behavior

Sex role	Broken home ($N = 55$)	Conflictful home ($N = 30$)	Tranquil home ($N = 120$)
Masculine*	49%	43%	58%
Feminine-nonaggressive	4	14	20
Feminine-aggressive	47	43	22

* Nine percent of the broken home boys, none of those in conflictful homes, and 13% of those in tranquil homes showed masculine role behavior but were not aggressive.

To check whether the home milieu rather than paternal absence itself was responsible for the high rate of feminine-aggressive behavior, we used the group of boys with similar backgrounds in united homes.

Because the comparison with matched controls (see Table 4) showed higher feminine-aggressive behavior among broken home boys ($p < .005$), the difference in sex role behavior could not be attributed simply to conditions which might have precipitated the family break.

Analysis of the father-absent boys provided a clue to their reasons for

[23] Boys who evidenced high dependency or strong homosexual tendencies were classified as showing feminine identification. We hypothesized that feminine identification (with or without aggression) would arise from the "teasing" effect of an ambivalent nondeviant mother or from the combination of rejection from a stable father and affection from a stable mother; among the 22 boys whose parents were of these types, 77% evidenced feminine identification.

[24] Immigrant families, too, were found in almost equal proportions among broken and conflictful homes, i.e., they were less likely to be either conflictful or severed.

Table 4
Sex Role Behavior

Sex role	Father absent	Matched controls
Masculine	49%	45%
Feminine-nonaggressive	4	24
Feminine-aggressive	47	31

sex role conflict. We contrasted sons whose mothers were normal (affectionate and nondeviant) with those having mothers rated abnormal. In these two groups of boys, the age at which paternal absence began and the reason for such absence had different relationships to sex role behavior. These differences suggest that feminine-aggressive behavior has different origins in broken homes in which a normal, as opposed to an abornal, mother had remained.

Whereas the child's age when his father left was of great importance among boys whose mothers were warm and nondeviant, it had slight relationship to feminine-aggressive behavior for boys raised by abnormal mothers (see Table 5).

Table 5
Percentage Who Exhibited Feminine-Aggressive Behavior

	Boy's age when father left		
	0–5	*6–12*	*Over 12*
Normal mother	$(N = 8)$ 0	$(N = 12)$75*	$(N = 5)$ 0†
Abnormal mother	$(N = 10)$70	$(N = 14)$50	$(N = 6)$50

* Twenty-five percent of matched group exhibited feminine-aggressive behavior ($p < .05$).
† $p < .01$.

Boys reared by normal mothers showed feminine-aggressive behavior only if their fathers left when the boys were between the ages of 6 and 12 ($p < .01$). Since only 25% of their matched controls indicated sex role conflict of this type, the home milieu of these boys were apparently not responsible for their high rate. Studies of children's sex differentiated behavior give reason to believe that the years of middle childhood may be critical ones in the development of sex identification. In an early study, P. H. Furfey[25] noted little sex differentiation in the play of 6–8 year olds, with increasing separation and differentiation after that age. Observations of recreational clubs at the Merrill-Palmer School in Detroit indicated that

[25] P. H. Furfey, "Some Factors Influencing the Selection of Boys' Chums," *J. Appl. Psychol.*, XI (1927), pp. 47–51.

5- and 6-year-olds seem to ignore sex as a basis for choosing play groups, but that sex segregation is almost complete for 10- and 11-year-olds.[26] Studies of friendship choices point to the same phenomenon.[27]

Previous research with father-separated samples whose mothers were probably "normal" by our criteria tend to point also to the importance of age at the time of separation. A study by Sears *et al.*[28] found that early differences in sex role behavior between father-absent and father-present boys had begun to disappear by age 5. Bach,[29] however, reported evidence of femininization among 6–10 year olds whose fathers had been absent 1–3 years.

Early separation, as Sears *et al.*[30] suggested, may result in sex typing delay—but both theirs and our evidence indicates that this effect is of relatively short duration: probably because the boy is able to find substitute role models during the period of sex identification. During the critical years of sex identification, perhaps because memory of the father interferes with adoption of a substitute model, loss of the father seems to have a more permanent affect on sex role identification. By age 12, the process of sex role identification is probably fairly complete, thus, explaining the absence of feminine-aggressive behavior among the older boys raised by normal mothers.

Among boys raised by abnormal mothers, age at the time of separation was of relatively minor importance in relation to feminine-aggressive behavior; death of the father (see Table 6), however, seemed to be highly productive of this type of confused sex role behavior ($p < .05$).

One can argue that death of the father raises a conflict in the male child between his desire to replace the father and his denial of this desire; yet

Table 6
Percentage Who Exhibited Feminine-Aggressive Behavior

Reason for father's absence

	Death	Other
Normal mother	($N = 14$) 36	($N = 11$) 36
Abnormal mother	($N = 10$) 90*	($N = 20$) 40†

* Ten percent of matched group exhibited feminine-aggressive behavior ($p < .01$).
† $p < .05$.

[26] E. H. Campbell, "The Social-Sex Development of Children," *Genet. Psychol. Monogr.*, XXI (1939), pp. 461–552.

[27] J. L. Moreno, *Who Shall Survive?* (Washington, D.C.: Nervous and Mental Disease Publishing Co., 1934).

[28] Sears, Pintler and Sears, *op. cit.*

[29] Bach, *op. cit.*

[30] Sears, Pintler and Sears, *op. cit.*

this theory does not explain the *lower* proportion among those whose mothers were affectionate ($p < .05$) who showed feminine-aggressive behavior.

It seems reasonable to explain this type of sex role instability among boys exposed to cold or rejecting mothers in terms of dependency needs and their satisfactions: When resources for satisfaction of dependency needs are limited (as they would be in broken homes of this type), the child becomes both more dependent on this limited source and also more resentful of his dependency because it fails to bring satisfaction.[31] Thus, such children responded to the conflict by being relatively dependent and feminine, and simultaneously behaving aggressively, in a compensatory masculine fashion.

Anxiety

Although it has received less research attention, the belief that paternal absence results in anxiety is widespread. Specific research relating anxiety to paternal absence has yielded conflicting results. A number of studies have linked such various manifestations of anxiety as feelings of inferiority, poor school performance, immaturity, and tensions to paternal absence.[32] Other studies have found no evidence of increased anxiety.[33] In an attempt to clarify this confusion in the literature, we tested three hypotheses derived from clinical theories.

Hypothesis 1. Father-separated boys should manifest many or intense fears because their heightened Oedipal desires cannot be brought to gratification,[34] or because the child fears that his mother will desert him.[35] We found no confirmation of this hypothesis that loss of the father results in

[31] It seems likely that a relationship between maternal rejection and parental separation or divorce (see H. W. Newell, "The Psycho-Dynamics of Maternal Rejection," *Amer. J. Orthopsychiat.*, VI [1936], pp. 575–588) leads to disproportionate representation of this type of home in some studies of the effects of broken homes on sex role identification. Whiting (J. W. M. Whiting, Paper read to Graduate Colloquium in Psychology [Stanford Univer., Jan. 19, 1961]) suggested that cultures in which there are exclusive mother-child sleeping arrangements also tend to define the maternal role in terms which would be considered abnormal in our society (i.e., maternal rejection and promiscuity are common among them). It seems possible that the cross-cultural relationship found between father separation in infancy and evidence of sex role conflict is dependent upon the limited resources for satisfaction of dependency needs in these cultures.

[32] M. C. Hardy, "Aspects of Home Environment in Relation to Behavior at the Elementary School Age," *J. Juv. Res.*, XXI (1937), pp. 206–225; Lynn and Sawrey, *op. cit.*; J. Rouman, "School Children's Problems as Related to Parental Factors," *J. Educ. Res.*, L (1956), pp. 105–112; Stolz, *et al.*, *op. cit.*

[33] Leichty, *op. cit.*; G. Rowntree, "Early Childhood in Broken Families," *Popul. Stud.*, VIII (1955), pp. 247–263; I. L. Russell, "Behavior Problems of Children from Broken and Intact Homes," *J. Educ. Sociol.*, XXXI (1957), pp. 124–129.

[34] Freud, *op. cit.*

[35] Gardner, *op. cit.*

abnormal fears. Forty percent of the broken home boys and 40% of those raised in tranquil homes gave evidence of abnormal fears (e.g., fear of the dark or excessive fear of bodily injury). Among boys reared in conflictful homes, 50% had abnormal fears. These negative results relating paternal absence to abnormal fears tend to confirm the findings of Rowntree[36] for matched pairs of preschool children in Britain and Russell[37] for matched pairs of school age children in America.

Hypothesis 2. Father-separated boys should have anxiety about sex; this should be particularly strong for those whose fathers have died.[38] A number of boys expressed to their counselors their concern over achieving normal sexual relations or about their sexual adequacy; others publicly masturbated during periods of tension.[39] These boys were considered to be sexually anxious. Although a significantly higher proportion of those whose fathers were absent than of those whose homes were tranquil evidenced sex anxiety ($p < .02$), roughly the same proportion of those whose parents were in open conflict were sexually anxious (see Table 7).

Table 7
Percentage Who Exhibited Sex Anxiety

Condition	Percentage
Broken home ($N = 55$)	47*
Conflictful home ($N = 30$)	57
Tranquil home ($N = 120$)	27

* Forty-nine percent of the matched group exhibited sex anxiety.

There was little variation within the father-absent group in the proportions who showed sex anxiety: 45% of those whose fathers were living, compared to 50% of those whose fathers had died; 54% of those whose mothers were rejecting and 41% of those whose mothers were affectionate evidenced sex anxiety. None of the four boys with affectionate deviant mothers evidenced sex anxiety. Although sex anxiety was prominent among boys raised without their fathers, the fact that 49% of the matched controls (compared to 47%) exhibited sex anxiety suggests that high sex anxiety may not be specifically related to paternal absence.

Hypothesis 3. Father-separated boys should show signs of regression.[40] Thumb sucking, nail biting, excessive smoking, and constant playing with the mouth used as behavioral signs of oral tendencies. Since these

36 Rowntree, *op. cit.*
37 Russell, *op. cit.*
38 Fenichel, *op. cit.*
39 The two measures were significantly related in the sample ($p < .01$).
40 Fenichel, *op. cit.*

forms of behavior may also indicate general anxiety, only those who did not exhibit abnormal fears were classified as showing oral regression. Oral regression, though not oral anxiety, was found most frequently among the father-absent group. The relationship was not, however, strong enough to reject the possibility that it had occurred by chance (see Table 8).

Table 8
Oral Tendencies

	Broken home (N = 55)	Conflictful home (N = 30)	Tranquil home (N = 120)
Oral regression	22%*	13%	10%
Oral and anxious	15	23	16
Neither	63	64	74

* Thirteen percent of the matched group exhibited oral regression.

As a further check, we examined oral regression in relation to normal and abnormal mothers among the father-absent boys. Although the proportion showing oral regression was not higher among the normal mother group than among those raised in tranquil homes (8%/10%), the comparison revealed a significantly higher proportion (see Table 9) showing

Table 9
Percentage Who Showed Signs of Oral Regression

	Father absent	Matched controls
Normal mother	(N = 25) 8%	(N = 25) 20%
Abnormal mother	(N = 30) 33	(N = 30) 7*

* $p < .025$.

signs of oral regression (33%) among those whose mothers were rejecting or deviant ($p < .005$).

Rejection or deviance, with or without paternal absence, might have explained oral regression. Comparison with the matched group led to rejection of this hypothesis.

Reasoning that death of the father would most fully realize the Oedipal wish, we hypothesized greater regression among boys whose fathers had died. This hypothesis, too, was not supported. These comparisons indicate that paternal absence, probably following conflict, *in combination with* maternal deviance or rejection result in oral regression.

Antisocial Behavior

The lay public as well as professional criminologists have linked broken homes to antisocial behavior. There seems to be general agreement that the proportion of broken homes among criminals is greater than that of the general population.[41] It was possible to use two measures of antisocial behavior for our sample. The counselors' reports of direct observations permitted ratings of primary reference groups during adolescence. Boys whose primary reference groups were delinquent gangs participated in behavior disapproved by the majority in their community. In 1955, court records for each of the subjects were obtained as an additional independent record of criminality; these traced the boys into adulthood. Those who had been convicted for a felony (or for a crime which would be a felony if the boy were an adult) were considered criminals.

There was little support for the theory that paternal absence led to delinquent gang activities. A significantly higher proportion of those boys whose parents continued to live together despite considerable overt conflict than *either* those whose parents were in little conflict ($p < .01$) or those whose fathers were absent ($p < .05$) were gang delinquents (see Table 10).

Table 10
Percentage Who Had Delinquent Reference Groups

Condition	Percentage
Broken home ($N = 55$)	20
Conflictful home ($N = 30$)	43
Tranquil home ($N = 120$)	18

That parental conflict rather than paternal absence tends to result in gang delinquency is given further support by the fact that the older the boy at the time of the break, the more likely he was to become a gang delinquent. It should further be noted that a significantly higher proportion of those who had parent substitutes (34%) than of those who lived in tranquil homes had become gang delinquents. This latter group, it appears, is responsible for the apparently high rate of juvenile delinquency among the broken home population of the lower class—a correlation which has been erroneously attributed to the absence of a paternal model.[42]

Using convictions for felonies as a measure of antisocial behavior, the expected relatively high rate of criminality was found among the father-absent group (see Table 11). Tranquil homes produced a significantly lower

[41] H. M. Shulman, "The Family and Juvenile Delinquency," *The Problems of Delinquency,* ed. S. Glueck, *op. cit.,* pp. 128–136.

[42] With this theory in mind, we recomputed the Glueck (S. Glueck and Eleanor T. Glueck, *Unraveling Juvenile Delinquency* [Cambridge, Mass.: Harvard University Press, 1950]) figures reported in *Unraveling Juvenile Delinquency,* breaking down the broken home boys into those who did and those who did not have parent substitutes. Recomputed, the Glueck figures no longer support the theory that broken homes as such are causally related to delinquency: Among their 500 nondelinquents, 111 were from broken homes without parent substitutes. In contrast, 230 of the delinquents, compared to 60 of the nondelinquents, had substitute parents.

Table 11
Percentage Who Became Criminals

Condition	Percentage
Broken home ($N = 55$)	36
Conflictful home ($N = 30$)	40
Tranquil home ($N = 120$)	22

proportion of criminals than did the father-absent homes and the conflictful homes ($p < .025$).

Several findings point to the fact that the absence of a generally stable home environment, rather than the specific absence of the father, is related to criminality: (*a*) boys reared by parents who were in overt conflict were as likely to become criminals as boys from father-absent families; (*b*) the criminal rate among boys who had parent substitutes was identical (i.e., 36% became criminals) to that of the father-absent boys; (*c*) the criminal rate increased with an increase in the age of the boy at the time of the family break; and (*d*) none of the 13 father-absent boys cared for by warm nondeviant mothers whose fathers had not been deviant became criminals.[43]

SUMMARY

Repeated direct observations of 205 boys and their families during a period of approximately 5 years of their early adolescence and court records for convictions for felonies were used to assess the effects of paternal absence upon boys. The sample, drawn from former members of the Cambridge-Somerville experiment, came from a lower-class, relatively deprived environment. The results of this study suggest the following conclusions:

1. Although feminine-nonaggressive behavior was negatively related to paternal absence, feminine-aggressive behavior appeared to be produced by paternal absence if the boy was between 6 and 12 when his father left, or the mother was deviant or rejecting (especially if the father had died).

2. No support was found for the theory that paternal absence leads to abnormal fears.

3. Intense sexual anxiety was found among almost half of the boys who had lost their fathers. Yet this anxiety seemed to be a response to a generally unstable environment rather than to paternal absence per se.

4. Oral regression was related to father-absence only among those whose mothers were deviant or rejecting.

5. Gang delinquency was found to be unrelated to paternal absence, al-

---

[43] Nine of the 10 father-absent boys whose mothers were both rejecting and deviant had been convicted for felonies.

though it did occur more frequently in broken homes in which the father or mother had been replaced by substitutes. In fact, the proportion of gang delinquents among boys whose parents quarreled but remained together was significantly higher than among those whose fathers were absent.

6. The relationship between criminality and paternal absence appears to be largely a result of the general instability of broken homes rather than of paternal absence in itself.

The evidence drawn from this sample indicates that many of the effects often presumed to result from paternal absence can, largely, be attributed to certain parental characteristics—intense conflict, rejection, and deviance —which occur more commonly in broken families.

Family Patterns Correlated with Adolescent Personality Structure*

ROBERT F. PECK

In the following study, Peck factor analyzes ten family variables and twenty-nine personality variables in an attempt to discover patterns of relationships between dimensions of family interaction and personality ratings of adolescents. From the analyses, four family and six personality trait clusters emerge. The intercorrelations of the traits provide an empirically grounded description of some of the relationships between family experience and adolescent personality characteristics.

In present day theories of personality development it is almost axiomatic that the emotional dynamics of the child's family play a dominant part in shaping his personality. Even today, however, the most detailed and persuasive evidence for this proposition comes largely from individual case studies and, chiefly, from clinical studies of maladjusted individuals, who most often seem to present a compelling reason for investigating their histories. There have been, of course, a sizable number of studies that relate certain overt traits of child behavior to similar traits in parents.[1] Perhaps the most comprehensive effort to relate child behavior patterns to parental practices has been the Yale cross-cultural survey.[2]

For the most part, these studies have adhered to overt behavioral characteristics that are readily observable in a common-sense way, both in children and in parents. Conceptual constructs about "inner" personality dimensions, on the other hand, have rarely been tested in any quantified way,

---

[1] R. R. Sears, J. W. M. Whiting, E. Nowlis and P. S. Sears, "Some Child Rearing Antecedents of Aggressions and Dependence in Young Children," *Genet. Psychol. Monogr.*, XLVII (1953), pp. 135–234.

[2] J. W. M. Whiting and I. L. Child, *Child Training and Personality* (New Haven: Yale University Press, 1953).

---

* From the *Journal of Abnormal and Social Psychology*, LVII (1958), pp. 347–350. Reprinted by permission of the author and the American Psychological Association.

or on more than a few individual cases. In short, most studies susceptible of rigorous hypothesis-testing have dealt with surface traits which psychodynamically oriented people sometimes regard with misgivings as an oversimplified correlating of symptoms, rather than a study of the persistent inner roots of behavior. Conversely, not many "depth" studies of personality structure have provided systematic measurements of child and family characteristics in samples large enough to allow mathematical tests of significance; and where such work has been done, it has generally been on "problem" samples, such as delinquents.[3]

METHOD

Sample

In the course of an eight-year longitudinal study of adolescent character development, data became available that offered an opportunity to measure certain key dimensions of personality structure, and to relate them to fairly universal dimensions of family experience in a quantitative way. The sample population represented a relatively even cross section of all the children born in the year 1933 in a sociologically typical midwestern town, known here as "Prairie City." The intensity of the study limited the sample to 34 children (half girls and half boys) and their 34 families, but at least some tests could be made of some of the salient propositions now current about the influence of family constellations on dimensions of personality structure. Indirectly, the data permit a test of the validity of such constructs as "ego strength," "superego strength," and the like.

The population consisted of 34 children, selected from the 120 children living in Prairie City in 1943 who had been born there ten years before. The original selection was based on a composite assessment of personal adjustment, comprised of teacher-ratings, test scores and clinician ratings. A pilot study indicated that the 34 children were quite evenly distributed along a scale from the best adjusted to the most poorly adjusted in the total group of 120. (As a bit of parallel evidence, they were evenly distributed, also, from top to bottom of the total group on a composite rating or moral character reputation, based on peer and teacher ratings.)

The Research Data

Each child was intensively observed, tested, and otherwise studied from age 10 to age 18. There were annual interviews by resident field workers with the child, his or her parents, and with friends and other informants. Sociometric tests of varied kinds were obtained annually, as were projectively analyzable essays. The Rorschach was administered at 13 and 14; the TAT at 13, 15, and 17; and a Sentence Completion test at 16. Numerous intelligence tests were

---

[3] S. Glueck and Eleanor Glueck, *Unraveling Delinquency* (Cambridge: Harvard University Press, 1950).

repeated each year or two. A variety of self-rating questionnaires on values, attitudes, personal adjustment, family adjustment, etc. were obtained annually. Teacher ratings of several kinds, anthropometric measures and certain other data were also gathered.

Procedure

In 1946 a research staff of 12, under the direction of William E. Henry and the late Caroline Tryon, was engaged in a study of the adolescent role behavior of the children in the sample. Interested in the developmental backgrounds of the subjects, the staff, among other things, rated the children's families on eight aspects of their emotional relationships and child-rearing practices. These data were subsequently filed away and remained unexamined until the work of the 1950 conference had been completed.

In 1949–50, a new staff of ten, under the direction of Robert J. Havighurst and the writer, conducted a study of the character development of the same 34 adolescents. An intensive case study was made of each child. Among other things, the staff made ratings (as of the subjects' sixteenth year) on some 30-odd personality variables and, also, on two aspects of parental discipline.[4] The estimated—Spearman-Brown—reliability of the judges' pooled-average ratings for any subject on any trait was .96.

Thus, two independent sets of data were available: one on the characteristics of the children's families, and the other on the personalities of the children. (The two additional family ratings by the 1950 staff were retained for analysis, although these were not strictly independent of the personality ratings, being made by the same judges.) A quantitative comparison of the measures of family dynamics with the personality dynamics of the children supplies the basis for the present report.

RESULTS AND DISCUSSION

Dimensions of Family Interaction

The ten family variables were intercorrelated and factor analyzed. Four trait-clusters were defined, with the following composition:[5]

F1 Consistency in Family Life
   Regularity of home life
   Consistency of parental control
   Common family participation in activities

[4] R. F. Peck, "The Psychology of Moral Character" (unpublished Doctoral dissertation, University of Chicago, 1951).
[5] See Table 1 for intercorrelations of these four trait clusters. These were factorially distinct clusters, not "pure," uncorrelated factors. See Peck, *op. cit.*, Appendix, for the rationale for this use of what Stephenson calls "mixed" factor types or clusters.

F2 Democracy–Autocracy
   Child's degree of sharing in family decisions
F3 Mutual Trust and Approval
   Good father-mother relations
   Parental trust and faith in the child
   Child's willingness to share confidences with parents
   Parental approval of the child
   Parental approval of child's peer activities
F4 Severity–Leniency
   Severity of parental control

Dimensions of Adolescent Personality Structure

Twenty-nine of the personality variables rated by the 1950 conference were intercorrelated and factor analyzed.[6] Six distinct trait clusters emerged as follows (the traits in each cluster are listed in descending order of their factor-loadings):

P1 Ego Strength[7]
   Emotional maturity
   Locus of concern (egocentric to altruistic)
   Internal consistency (roughly, personality integration)
   Rationality of behavior
   Accuracy of self-perception
   Accuracy in assigning responsibility (to self or others)
   Accuracy of social observation
   Functioning intelligence (largely, test-IQ)
   Insight into others' motives
   Autonomy (inner-directed)
   (Positive) Relations with the same-sex peers
   Positive feeling toward mother
P2 Superego Strength
   Superego strength (presence of an effectively behavior-guiding conscience)
P3 Willing Social Conformity
   Overt conformity to the (conference defined) moral code
   Emotional stability (largely, overt conformity to expected, "controlled" behavior)
   Range of moral horizon (the range of people and groups toward whom S is overtly moral)
   Overt acceptance of mother's expectations

[6] Peck, op. cit.
[7] See Table 1 for intercorrelations of these six trait clusters. The factoring was done in order to reduce the original, overlarge set of variables to a small number of more stable variables, with the result that six distinctly separate traits or trait clusters were found, defined by a three-factor system.

Absence of overt hostility
(Positive) Relations with opposite-sex peers
P4 Spontaneity
  Identity of behavior with impulse
  Positive feeling toward father
  Empathy (with others' feelings)
  Positive feeling toward same-sex peers
  (Lack of) Guilt about overt behavior
P5 Friendliness
  Absence of covert hostility
P6 Hostility-Guilt Complex
  Guilt about inner impulses
  Inner feelings of hostility toward mother
  (Lack of) Overt acceptance of father's expectations
  (Lack of) Inner liking for opposite-sex peers

Relationships of Personality Dimensions to Family Characteristics

In order to compare the two sets of data, each child's standard score on each of the six personality dimensions was computed. Similarly, a standard score was derived for each family on each of of the four family dimensions. It was thus possible to correlate the children's scores on the personality dimensions with the characteristics of their families.

From Table 1, the significant correlations suggest the following relationships, presumably causal in nature, between family experience and personality:

Ego Strength seems largely produced by Trust (.73) and Consistency (.56).
Social Conformity also seems importantly influenced by Trust (.60) and Consistency (.53).
Superego Strength seems influenced by Consistency (.50) and perhaps Trust (.33).
Spontaneity seems influenced by Democracy (.36) and perhaps Trust (.27), plus lack of Severity (−.38).
Friendliness seems most influenced by Trust (.44) and Democracy (.33).
The Hostility-Guilt Complex seems influenced by Severity (.40) combined with a lack of Trust (−.40) and of Democracy (−.40).

The over-all pattern shown in Table 1, suggests that mutual trust among family members (F3) is rather closely related (.66) to consistency in family life (F1). It might be inferred from the correlation pattern that these two family characteristics, working together, are responsible for the development of healthy *ego strength* (P1) and willing *social conformity* (P3). That is, a child's emotional maturity, personal integration, autonomy, rationality of behavior, and his willingness to adapt to society's expectations, appear

Table 1
Correlations of Family and Personality Vectors

Variable	F1	F2	F3	F4	P1	P2	P3	P4	P5	P6
F1 Consistency in Family Life		-.01	.66†	.37*	.56†	.50†	.53†	.05	.19	-.10
F2 Democracy–Autocracy			.53†	-.65†	.43*	-.07	.16	.36*	.33	-.40*
F3 Mutual Trust & Approval				-.22	.74†	.33	.60†	.27	.44†	-.40*
F4 Parental Severity					-.16	.26	-.08	-.38*	-.38*	.40*
P1 Ego Strength						.48†	.73†	.56†	.43*	-.33
P2 Superego Strength							.66†	-.24	.02	-.23
P3 Social Conformity								.11	.48†	-.37*
P4 Spontaneity									.39*	-.28
P5 Friendliness										-.75†
P6 Hostility-Guilt Complex										

* Significant at .05 level.
† Significant at .01 level.

138

to be directly related to the degree of consistency, mutual trust, and mutual approval he experiences within his family.

Superego strength (P2) is not unrelated (.48) to ego strength (P1), but insofar as it is a separate entity, it appears to be the product of a somewhat different pattern of these family forces. It seems mainly to come from a regular, consistent family life. Superego strength is not at all the same thing as the hostility-guilt complex (P6); indeed, they correlate slightly negatively, −.23. Moreover, superego strength is unrelated to the generalized attitude of friendliness (−.02). One might therefore think that superego strength would be associated with severe parental autocracy (F2, F4); but it is not. Judging from the case studies, the reason appears to be that while some children with strong, *rigid* superegos do tend to come from severe, autocratic families, there are other children who have equally strong internal principles but who test and apply them rationally. These latter children came from families that have been quite democratic and unsevere. Other data from the study suggest the existence of these two different *kinds* of strong superego, each of which has a different relationship with the democratic-autocratic family dimension. Spontaneity (P4) and ego strength (P1) are moderately related. Both characteristics appear to be favored by a lenient, democratic family atmosphere which actively promotes a self-accepting, good-natured spontaneity in the child.

Friendliness is significantly related to the degree of mutual trust and affection within the family, whether or not there is stable consistency in it. There are some friendly children who have weak egos and weak superegos. These come (in the present study, at least) from inconsistent, irregular families who follow a policy that might better be called laissez-faire than "democratic," though the parents show an uncritically acceptant attitude toward the children in a desultory, rather inattentive way.

The hostility-guilt complex (P6) might readily be called a hostile but dependent, unresolved Oedipal complex, upon examination of the variables that comprise it (see above). Not surprisingly, it tends to occur in children whose families are severe, autocratic, but unloving and inconsistent.

SUMMARY AND CONCLUSIONS

The purpose of the study was to test and measure the relationships between key elements in personality structure and certain characteristics of family emotional and regulatory patterns. Thirty-four adolescents were selected as a representative cross section of all children born in Prairie City in 1933. They were interviewed and diversely tested each year from age 10 to age 18.

Independent ratings were made on the families, and on the children, by two separate research staffs, following intensive individual case studies. The family ratings were intercorrelated and factor analyzed, yielding four dimensions of family interaction: Consistency, Democracy, Mutual Trust and Approval, and Parental Severity. The personality ratings, similarly analyzed, yielded six dimensions of personality: Ego Strength, Superego Strength, Willing Social Conformity, Spontaneity, Friendliness, and a Hostility-Guilt Complex.

Scores for each child were then computed on each personality dimension and these were correlated with the corresponding families' scores on each family dimension. The intercorrelations were analyzed, to discover general patterns of relationship between family experience and personality.

In this sample of adolescents, covering the full range of personal adjustment and moral responsibility, there proved to be a significant pattern of relationships between family experience and personality. Specifically:

1. Ego strength occurred in association with a family life which was characterized by stable consistency and warm, mutual trust and approval between the parents and between parents and child.

2. Superego strength was partially related to ego strength, but was chiefly related to the regularity and consistency of family life. It was *not* systematically related to severely autocratic rearing; or, at least, there appeared to be two different kinds of superego, produced in two different ways: (*a*) a strong, rigid, compartmentalized superego created by sternly autocratic rearing; and (*b*) a strong superego which was closely knit with ego functions, open to rational appraisal, and created by consistent, democratic, nonsevere rearing in a trustful, approving family. This interpretation rests, of course, on the qualitative case studies.

3. Generalized friendliness and spontaneity appear to be allied and to be associated with a lenient, democratic family atmosphere. Probably because the family background may or may not be consistent, these personality characteristics therefore may or may not be allied with ego strength and superego strength.

4. The hostility-guilt complex might reasonably be considered a hostile but dependent, unresolved Oedipal complex. It tends to occur in association with a severely autocratic, untrusting, and disapproving family.

In general, insofar as the findings of this study bear on the concepts of present day theory about personality development, they tend to corroborate that theory. These adolescents' personality characteristics proved to be significantly related to the emotional relationships and the disciplinary patterns which they experienced in living with their parents.

Maternal Behavior and Personality Development Data from the Berkeley Growth Study*

NANCY BAYLEY AND
EARL S. SCHAEFER

The aphorism that "the child is father of the man" is equally applicable to adolescence; in brief, the child is also father of the adolescent. To assay the extent to which this is true, studies of a longitudinal design are frequently employed. In 1928 and 1929 the Institute of Child Welfare at the University of California initiated "The Berkeley Growth Study," and during the ensuing years the imaginative researchers involved in the project have increased immeasurably our knowledge of the effects of one period of life upon another. The paper included here is one of four papers in this book of readings that is based upon the Study. Bayley and Shafer are concerned primarily with the long-range influence of certain maternal behaviors. Their findings suggest that boys tend to do well "if the mothers were loving at an early age and at adolescence also granted autonomy." For girls, the data suggest "little carry-over from the influences of early maternal behavior;" however, adolescent girls "seem to be well attuned to their mothers' present attitudes."

This report is concerned with one segment of an investigation of social interaction patterns as they were observed in a longitudinal study, and as they bear on several aspects of the development of a group of normal children. The data with which we are working are very complex, and we are still struggling with the process of organizing them into meaningful patterns, and with presenting them in useful form. This report should, therefore, be viewed as an example of an ongoing effort, and not as a finished research. But hopefully, it may serve as a stimulant to more research in this area,

* From *Psychiatric Research Reports 13* (1960), pp. 155–173, abridged and slightly revised. Reprinted by permission of the authors and the American Psychiatric Association.

both to utilize some of the methods we have developed, and to test by specifically designed studies, the validity of our findings and interpretations that, because of the nature of our materials, are necessarily tentative.

This part of the research is an exploration into interactions between the child and his mother, as they bear on the formation and establishment of emotional and attitudinal patterns of behavior in the child. This study involves both the development of *conceptual schemes* of relevant maternal and social-emotional child behaviors and a preliminary empirical testing of them. Our empirical data are from the Berkeley Growth Study, and our conceptual schemes have, to a considerable extent, grown out of these same empirical data. This bootstrap type of operation can thus only be utilized to formulate hypotheses and to point out possibly fruitful areas for further research. It is also true that the data were not collected for the purposes to which we are putting them here, and accordingly they have many inadequacies. But we have done some testing and partial verifying of hypotheses by applying them to other published studies. To this extent, then, we hope we are on at least moderately firm ground.

SAMPLE AND OUTLINE OF STUDY

The main emphasis in the Berkeley Growth Study has, until recently, been directed toward the mental, motor, and physical growth of this group of children who were seen first as healthy neonates. But in the thirty-year records of their growth we have accumulated much information about their emotions, attitudes, and ways of coping with their environments. The evident relevance of these social-emotional behaviors to the other aspects of growth, as well as the importance for study of these processes of growth themselves, have led us in the last several years to try a new approach to the Berkeley data. Some of the resulting studies have already been reported by Schaefer, Bell and Bayley, and are published or in the process of being published.[1] A brief review here of these preliminary studies seems in order, to set the background for the material we wish to present today.

The children of the Berkeley Growth Study have been observed at the Institute of Child Welfare at frequent intervals from the time they were born in Berkeley, California in 1928 and 1929.[2] The criteria for their in-

[1] Nancy Bayley and E. S. Schaefer, "Relationships Between Socioeconomic Variables and the Behavior of Mothers Toward Young Children," *J. Genet. Psychol.*, XCVI (1960), pp. 61–77; E. S. Schaefer, "A Circumplex Model for Maternal Behavior," *J. Abnorm. Soc. Psychol.*, LIX (1959), pp. 226–235; E. S. Schaefer and Nancy Bayley, "Consistency of Maternal Behavior from Infancy to Preadolescence," *J. Abnorm. Soc. Psychol.*, LXI (1960), pp. 1–6; E. S. Schaefer, R. Q. Bell and Nancy Bayley, "Development of a Maternal Behavior Research Instrument," *J. Genet. Psychol.*, XCV (1955), pp. 83–104.

[2] H. E. Jones and Nancy Bayley, "The Berkeley Growth Study," *Child Development*, XII (1941), pp. 167–173.

clusion in the study were that they be full-term, healthy infants of white, English-speaking parents who were willing and able to cooperate in the planned series of tests and measurements. The babies were born in two Berkeley hospitals and were first seen by the pediatrician in the study at about four days of age. In a six-month period 61 babies (31 boys and 30 girls) were registered in the study. A few of these dropped out and a few replacements were made. Of the total, there are fairly complete records on 54 of the children through at least their first six years, and on 48 of them to adult or almost adult status.

In addition to the measurements of mental, motor, and physical growth, a variety of ratings and notes were made on the children's emotional and attitudinal behaviors. Also, among the records are some fairly extensive descriptions of the mothers' behaviors as observed during the children's first three years, when the mothers were present while their babies were being tested and measured (usually about 20 visits during this period). For 34 of the mothers there is an additional set of descriptive characterizations that are based on interviews made when the children were between the ages of nine and 14 years.

We have converted descriptive notes on both the mothers and the children into scores that can be treated statistically. These, together with various ratings made at the times of observation and with other measures and scores, have been intercorrelated and further analyzed statistically. From these data we have derived patterns of maternal and child behaviors and have been able to study some of their interrelations and their consistencies over time.

Maternal Behaviors

The maternal records were converted into objective scores by Schaefer and Bell, who devised what they have called a Maternal Behavior Research Instrument.[3] This is a series of rating scales for 32 variables representing those maternal behaviors that were considered to be theoretically relevant, and that also could be judged from the available material in the notes. They then adapted 28 of the scales and applied them to the descriptions that had been made of the mothers at the preadolescent (9-14 year) interviews. Schaefer has found that most of these maternal behavior rating scales can be arranged in a circular order with two reference dimensions of Autonomy-Control and Love-Hostility. This circumplex reveals a sequential ordering of scales according to a law of neighboring.[4]

Utilizing the two circumplex orderings and other published data on

---

[3] Schaefer, Bell, and Bayley, *op. cit.*

[4] L. Guttman, "A New Approach to Factor Analysis: The Radex," *Mathematical Thinking in the Social Sciences,* ed., P. F. Lazarsfeld (Glencoe, Ill.: Free Press, 1954).

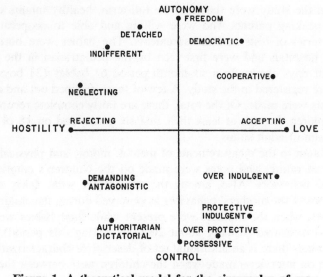

Figure 1. A theoretical model for the circumplex of maternal behavior. (From Schaefer, *op. cit.*, p. 232.)

maternal attitudes and behaviors, Schaefer[5] has developed a theoretical circumplex model of maternal behavior, shown in Figure 1. Most of the relevant mother-child personal-social interactions seem to fall into this two-dimensional space. We have based our further ordering of maternal and child behavior on hypotheses derived from this model. Intercorrelations between behaviors can be arranged into sequential orders of neighboring, and often into fairly complete circumplexes. With this procedure, we may explore patterns of interaction by relating one ordered set of variables (*e.g.,* maternal behavior) with another ordered set (*e.g.,* child behavior).

One of our first explorations has been a study of the consistency over time of maternal behavior. Presumably those characteristics that are more stable will have a greater, cumulative effect on the children and their behaviors. It was possible to correlate the maternal traits that appeared to be very similar as they had been rated from the protocols obtained at the two periods, roughly 10 years apart.[6] These correlations show rather high consistency for items in the Love-Hostility dimension, but low intercorrelations for those in the Autonomy-Control dimension. That is, the mothers of children under three years who were seen to be affectionate and warm in the testing situation were usually also seen by an independent interviewer as affectionate in their attitudes toward their young adolescents. However, the other dimension, Autonomy-Control, was not stable, as here measured.

[5] Schaefer, *op. cit.*
[6] Schaefer and Bayley, *op. cit.*

These differences in consistency may be summarized in the cluster correlations: That is, when the ratings representing love *vs.* hostility and those representing autonomy *vs.* control are combined into two sets of scores for the two sets of data, behavior toward infants is correlated with expressed attitudes toward preadolescents .68 for love-hostility, and .26 for autonomy-control. If these two correlations are true descriptions of degrees of maternal consistency over time, then we may say that affectional attitudes tend to be stable, but that factors in the age of the child, such as his needs for freedom, and his abilities to exercise autonomy, together with the mothers' awareness of these factors, appear to operate to change the mother in the degree of control she exercises.

Before we leave this description of the organization of maternal behaviors, we should note several conditions that affect the ways in which these behaviors were found to vary. First, . . . the more educated, higher socioeconomic-status mothers tend more to grant autonomy and to be cooperative and equalitarian toward their children. The low-status mothers are more often controlling and punitive.

Another aspect of variation in maternal behavior is the sex of her child. The relation between socioeconomic status and maternal behavior is consistently greater for mothers of boys than for mothers of girls. There is even a suggestion of a reversal in the Autonomy-Control dimension: For this sample at least, the higher-status mothers grant their infant sons more autonomy and their daughters less than do the lower-status mothers.

Children's Behaviors

Given these characterizations of the mothers, what information have we on the children which we can relate to maternal behavior? The most readily available scores on child behavior are a series of ratings that had been made by the examiner (most often Bayley), immediately after the child's visit. These ratings were all made on seven-point scales; they are concerned with emotional and attitudinal aspects of the children's behavior in the testing-measuring situation. Three different rating forms were used (each appropriate for the child's age), and the ratings included all ages between nine months and 12 years. In order to have a measure of the children's adolescent behavior, we utilized descriptive notes that were written after each examination, but it was necessary first to convert them into a meaningful array of scores. Ratings (seven-point) were made from these notes on 96 adjectives that covered a wide range of personality variables.

We have thus, in the form of ratings, some evaluations (more or less restricted in nature) of the children throughout almost their entire period of growth. We should emphasize that we are dealing with observed overt behaviors, and can thus make no direct tests of underlying conflicts or motivations.

In working with these ratings we have found sufficient evidence of sex differences, both in the mothers' treatments of their children and in the children's behaviors, that it has been necessary to make our analyses for the sexes separately.

*   *   *

For the purposes of mother-child comparisons it would be advantageous to use a circumplex arrangement of the child's emotional-behavioral traits that might theoretically relate systematically to the circumplex of maternal behaviors. Schaefer used Guttman's circumplex model to organize several published sets of correlational data on ratings of social and emotional behavior that had been made of children's behaviors. He found that he could arrange these tables of correlations into meaningful circumplex orders with reference dimensions of Love-Hostility and Extraversion-Introversion.

On the basis of these empirical orderings, Schaefer constructed a hypothetical circumplex model for social and emotional behavior, shown in Figure 2.

*   *   *

Early Maternal Behavior and Adolescent Traits

We should expect some changes in mother-child relationships during the period of adolescence. This is notorious as a time when children rebel against parental controls and often experience strong emotions in the process of adjusting to adult status.

How do these adolescent traits relate to early maternal behavior? Among the girls, the correlation charts show only hints of resemblance between their behavior-tendencies and the way their mothers treated them as infants. The *r*'s are so low that we are not justified even in speculating. The boys, however, as usual show some clear patterns.

In the mother-son relationships, it appears that the Love-Hostility dimension is less important than at earlier ages, although positively evaluating equalitarian mothers more often had well-adjusted adolescent sons. It is the early maternal pattern of Autonomy-Control that is most clearly correlated with adolescent extraversion-introversion. That is, the pattern of correlation coefficients shows that autonomy-granting, ignoring (and to some extent punitive) mothers more often had sons who at adolescence were reserved, timid, and tactful. The mothers who were close, involved, and controlling toward infant sons (emotionally involved, fostered dependency, made excessive contact, demanded achievement, and were concerned about their sons' health) had adolescent boys who were more often characterized as rude, irritable, impulsive, and independent. In other words, the adolescent revolt appears to be strongest in those boys whose mothers were closely interacting and involved with them as infants.

A HYPOTHETICAL CIRCUMPLEX MODEL FOR SOCIAL AND EMOTIONAL BEHAVIOR

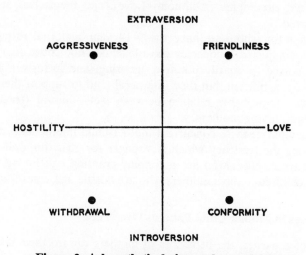

Figure 2. A hypothetical circumplex model for social and emotional behavior. (From E. S. Schaefer,
"Converging Conceptual Models for Maternal Behavior and for Child Behavior," *Parental Attitudes
and Child Behavior*, ed. J. C. Glidewell [New York:
Charles C. Thomas, 1961]).

Concurrent Mother-Child Interactions at Adolescence

So far, we have talked about children's behavior as related to the maternal behavior when they were infants. When we turn to the mother's attitudes toward their children at a later age we again find sex differences in
correlation. The ratings of mothers made from interviews when the children
approximated 12 to 13 years show similar concurrent correlational patterns
toward both daughters and sons, but they are much clearer for the daughters. The adolescent girls, who evidence little carry-over from the influences
of early maternal behavior, seem to be well attuned to their mothers' present
attitudes. Although there are only 13 girls on whom we have the later
maternal ratings, many of the correlation coefficients are high enough to
reach statistical significance. Girls who are maladjusted (*i.e.,* rated as
gloomy, unhappy, sulky, and hostile), more often have mothers who are
hostilely controlling (*i.e.,* punitive, irritable, controlling, isolating, and make
excessive contact with their daughters).

Girls who are rated as popular and not nervous, and who on the adolescent behavior circumplex are well-adjusted, show high correlations with

mothers who are social, and outgoing, and on the maternal circumplex grant their daughters autonomy, are equalitarian, and evaluate them positively: That is, these mothers' scores tend to fall in the upper right quadrant of the maternal circumplex (Autonomy-Love), and themselves are somewhat extraverted.

The 13 boys for whom we have the 9-14 year maternal ratings more often show maladjusted tendencies (hostile, cold, not courteous) if their mothers are hostile (primarily punitive, ignoring, and intrusive). None of the other r's are significant, but they in general tend to support this relation and to indicate a probable relation between well-adjusted (friendly, sociable) boys and loving mothers.

We may summarize these concurrent mother-child interactions at adolescence by noting the tendency which is stronger for girls, for well-adjusted children to have mothers who are autonomy-granting and loving, and for maladjusted children to have mothers who are hostile and controlling.

Sex Differences in Mother-Child Patterns Over Time

As was noted earlier, the behaviors of mothers toward their infant sons continued to show significant relations to these boys' characteristics even through adolescence. The only exception is a brief period around three and one-half to four and one-half years when the correlations dropped very low. However, the mother-daughter correlations that were strongly clear in infancy, faded out as the girls grew older.

When we reverse the picture and compare the ratings on the mothers made when the children were around 12 to 13 years old with the children at all ages, we again find the sex differences in constancy over time. The boys' scores at adolescence show a moderate pattern of correlations in the predicted directions with these concurrent maternal scores. And also the patterns of correlation are present retrospectively and often rather strongly clear back to the 10-36 month ratings. Again the relations drop out briefly around three and one-half to four and one-half years. With this exception, the boys appear to establish early certain characteristic behaviors or attitudes and interactions with their mothers that persist over time.

The mothers' later scores, as we have noted, show a marked pattern of correlation with the girls' scores at adolescence. But there is no correlation with the girls at younger ages. The mother-daughter interactions appear to be strong, but continuously changing over time, so that for them it is the present that determines the nature of their interpersonal behavior. It is as though the girl is attuned to adapt to the important aspects of her present interpersonal milieu rather than to persist in an established set of habit patterns.

In reviewing these patterns of correlation there appears to be at least one area of incompatibility of findings. Comparisons of the children's own scores over time indicate somewhat greater consistency in girls than in boys. But when we turn to mother-child relations the boys' behaviors are the ones that maintain the clearer relations to maternal behaviors whether the mothers are rated before or after the boys' ages at comparison. Perhaps these two conditions are not mutually exclusive. There is still room for freedom in correlations of the magnitude under consideration here. It is also possible that, in the close mother-daughter ties the daughters' behaviors have considerable effect on their mothers' concurrent behavior. The boys, on the other hand, might show in later childhood and adolescence close relations to their fathers, if such data were available to us.

Individual Patterns of Interaction

In this presentation, so far, we have treated these mother-child interactions entirely by manipulating correlations between groups. The question arises whether, and to what extent, we can apply these findings to individual cases.

To explore this question, we have plotted individual scores for mothers and adolescent children on circumplex charts. The analyses of these cases has not yet been completed. But in looking them over it is evident that although many of the cases fit the expected pattern of relations, a fair number do not. For example, Jim's mother is hostile and controlling toward him, both as an infant and as a preadolescent. Jim was an unhappy, and unfriendly, little boy, and a hostile and maladjusted adolescent. For comparison, the mother of another boy, Tom, is also somewhat controlling but is definitely loving and not hostile. Her son Tom has at adolescence a very similar profile to Jim's, though he is even more hostile. It is difficult to explain these discrepant relationships, but some information about the boys may be relevant. For one thing, these boys are brothers. The same woman has obviously different attitudes and behaviors toward her two sons, so much so that she was never recognized by the raters as the same person. We might have expected Tom to be less hostile and in general better adjusted than Jim. In the senior author's personal experience with Tom, it is her belief that he is better adjusted, but less inhibited and freer to express his hostility. Also there was evidence in his behavior that Tom tried hard to emulate his older brother. But there are, of course, also many other relevant factors that must be called into the picture for an adequate understanding of these boys' similarities and differences.

Another mother was loving and autonomy-granting toward Dan, her firstborn. Dan was a calm, happy baby and a friendly, social, attentive little boy. As an adolescent, he is extraverted, with no clear-cut evidence for either poor or good adjustment.

The mother of Anna is loving and controlling toward her infant daughter. As her daughter approached adolescence, she has shifted from control to autonomy-granting, remaining loving. Anna is a well-adjusted, friendly adolescent.

Let us now select on the basis of some characteristic of the child. Morgan has had serious problems as an adult, having been hospitalized briefly after 21 years with a diagnosis of catatonic schizophrenia. The ratings on his mother show some congruence between her controlling behavior and theories of schizophrenogenic mothers. Morgan himself, as an adolescent, was maladjusted, though his scores are not extreme.

Another boy who was in a mental hospital briefly is Elbert. His mother is rated consistently as loving and autonomy-granting. One would never suspect maladjustment in her son. We do not have ratings on Elbert at adolescence because he was so upset by having to go through the physical examinations that he refused to come in for any tests. In retrospect, he is remembered as a quiet, rather withdrawn, sensitive, painfully self-conscious adolescent who was also very small and slow in maturing physically. It may be relevant to note that both Morgan and Elbert became ill while in the armed services, and both boys though very different from each other, would (in the examiner's opinion) have problems in adapting to the gregarious and conforming army life. With two such different mothers, we must look to some of these other factors as precipitating causes of their difficulties.

Nora and her mother make an interesting pair. The mother was very involved and controlling, more affectionate at first, then later a little more punitive. As an adolescent Nora was very hostile and extraverted. Her behavior appears to be a strong rebellion against maternal control. The impression Nora gave the examiners at this period was that she now controlled her parents. For example, she obtained from them written consent to marry at 16. When she came in for tests at this age, she gave the name and a description of her fiancé. Three days later there was a newspaper account, with picture, of Nora's marriage to an obviously different man. This is only a small episode in Nora's history. But her behavior has always been extraverted, tending after her first eight or 10 years toward hostile extraversion.

These are only meager samples of data from a few cases. When all the case studies have been worked out in more detail, we shall be able more adequately to evaluate the meaningfulness for individuals of the correlational patterns of mother-child relations. At present, our case studies point up the need for caution. We must not make hasty generalizations from the trends in mother-child correlations. After all, these correlations are only moderate: There is ample room for the effects of other variables (genetic and environmental) in determining behavioral tendencies in individual children.

What we do have is some evidence for trends in mother-child relations for a group of normal children. These trends show both sex differences and changes over time as the children grow older. The boys in this study tended to do well if their mothers were loving at an early age and at adolescence also granted autonomy. The girls appear to be a little more consistent in their own behavior patterns, and also to show more correlation with their mothers' concurrent maternal behavior. From our data we can not say whether the mother-child interactions are determined primarily by the behavior tendencies of the mother or the child.

Stability of Achievement and Recognition Seeking Behaviors from Early Childhood Through Adulthood*[1]

HOWARD A. MOSS AND
JEROME KAGAN

When a citizen of contemporary America expresses an ambition "to do well" or "to get ahead," cultural approval is nearly unanimous. A certain amount of achievement motivation appears to be one of the prime requisites for successful citizenship in the twentieth century. In the following study, drawn from longitudinal data collected at the Fels Research Institute at Yellow Springs, Ohio, Moss and Kagan describe several achievement and recognition seeking behaviors that are characteristic of individuals at different ages. Concerned principally with the stability of achievement and recognition behaviors from early school years through young adulthood, the researchers show, in essence, that "achievement strivings during the first four years of school are a moderately good index of future achievement behavior during adolescence and adulthood." Their data also suggest that intellectual activities rather than athletic activities for the ten to fourteen age range are positively related to achievement behavior in adulthood.

The supposition that selected adult response patterns are established at an early age is a primary assumption of developmental theory. Although literary documents and psychotherapy protocols have provided anecdotal support for this hypothesis, more objective validation has been difficult to obtain. The present paper is a second report that has emerged from a larger project on the stability of childhood behavior. The first paper indicated

[1] This research was supported, in part, by Research Grant M-1260 from the National Institute of Mental Health, United States Public Health Service.

* From the *Journal of Abnormal and Social Psychology*, LXII (1961), pp. 504–513. Reprinted by permission of the authors and the American Psychological Association.

that dependent behavior in girls showed moderately high stability from the early school years through young adulthood.[2] The present report is concerned with the developmental consistency of two related behaviors: the tendency to strive for (*a*) mastery of selected skills (achievement behavior), and (*b*) social recognition through acquisition of specific goals or behaviors (recognition behavior).

The achievement variable emphasizes mastery of intellectual, athletic, mechanical, and artistic skills as well as competence in specialized crafts. Social recognition is obtained through acquisition of most of the above behaviors. For intellectual competence, athletic ability, acquisition of money, and positions of power in social groups are the primary methods of obtaining social recognition in the cultural milieu of our middle class population. Thus, the overt behaviors involved in achievement and recognition strivings overlap to some degree.

In an attempt to differentiate between these two variables, the investigators evaluated the degree to which the individual's mastery behavior was directed at satisfaction of an internal standard of excellence in order to gain self-approval (achievement motivation), in contrast to seeking approval from the social environment (recognition motivation). This is a difficult differentiation to make. The data to be presented reveal a high, positive correlation between ratings of these two behavioral variables. This interdependence suggests that it may be impossible to measure the "desire to improve at a skill" independent of the individual's "desire for social recognition" for this improvement.

METHOD

Subjects and General Procedure

The subjects were 36 males and 35 females from the Fels Research Institute's longitudinal population. They were enrolled in the project at birth, during the years 1929–1939. At the time of a recent adult assessment (1957–1959) they were between 20 and 29 years of age. The subjects came from predominantly middle class backgrounds, over half of the group were married; 70% had college degrees or were enrolled in a college, and the majority were living within a 30-mile radius of the institute. The adult group included 5 Protestants, 15 Catholics, and 1 Jew.

The heart of this study consists of correlations between the childhood information on these subjects and their adult behavior. The childhood data included (*a*) longitudinal observations of the child's behavior during the first 14 years of life in a variety of settings, (*b*) observations of the mother-child interaction during these years, (*c*) TAT protocols obtained in adolescence, and

2 J. Kagan and H. A. Moss, "The Stability of Passive and Dependent Behavior from Childhood Through Adulthood," *Child Development*, XXXI (1960), pp. 577–591.

(*d*) annual Stanford-Binet intelligence test scores during the ages 5–11. Although the data collected during adulthood (age range 20–29) sampled a variety of techniques, this report utilizes only two sources of adult information, 5 hours of interview, and a TAT protocol.

Longitudinal Observations: Birth to Age 14

As a standard procedure of the Fels longitudinal program, psychologists or psychologically trained personnel summarized their observations of the child in the home, in the Fels nursery school and day camp, and in the subject's public school. The home reports were based on a visit to the home where mother and child were observed for half-day sessions. These home visits were generally made semiannually for the first 6 years of life and annually from 6 to 12. Most of the mothers were interviewed each year for the first 14 years of the child's life. The nursery school summaries were based on semiannual, free-play sessions from age 2.5 to 5. The sessions usually consisted of 15 consecutive half-day periods in groups of 10–12 children. Day camp typically consisted of an annual 2 week session of half-day periods during age 6–10 in which free and structured group activities were observed. Public school visits, made semiannually, consisted of a half-day observation of the child in his routine classroom activities. Finally, the subjects of age 6–14 were interviewed each year at the institute and a summary of the interview was prepared. All of the longitudinal reports for each subject were collated in chronological order and placed in the subject's individual file.[3]

Scoring of longitudinal variables. A comprehensive list of rating scale variables (seven-point scale) was defined for the purpose of evaluating the narrative material just outlined. The material for each subject was divided into four age periods: 0–3, 3–6, 6–10, and 10–14. The senior author, who had no knowledge of the adult psychological status of the subjects, first read all the information for each subject for age 0–3 and made those ratings for which he had adequate information. Following a period of interpolated work, he studied each subject's material for age 3–6 and again made his ratings. This procedure was repeated for ages 6–10 and 10–14. A period of approximately 6 months intervened between the evaluation of the data for any one subject for each age period. This paper deals only with the stability of achievement and recognition behaviors and abridged definitions of these variables follow.

Childhood Variables

Achievement behavior: (*Rated for ages 0–3, 3–6, and 6–10*). This variable assessed the degree to which the subject tended to persist with challenging

---

[3] The staff of the institute during the 24 years of data collection included Alfred L. Baldwin, Thomas W. Richards, Horace Champney, Virginia L. Nelson, assisted by Leah Levinger, Helen Marshall, Mary Frances Hartson, Joan Kalhorn Lasko, Faye Breese, Margaret Slutz, Marjorie Powell, Frances Best, and a group of assistants to whom the authors are indebted. Their efforts made this project possible.

tasks, games, and problems, and his involvement in activities in which a standard of excellence was applicable. For 0–3, emphasis was given to persistence with perceptual-motor activities (e.g., making block towers, stringing beads, drawing, and coloring). For ages 3–6 and 6–10 the greatest weight was given to interest in and persistence with intellectual, mechanical, athletic, and fine motor activities.

For age 10–14 the general achievement variable defined above was differentiated into three variables dealing with different achievement areas (intellectual, mechanical, and athletic).

Intellectual achievement: (Rated for age 10–14). This variable assessed the degree to which the subject attempted to master language and numerical skills and showed involvement in the acquisition of knowledge.

Mechanical achievement: (Rated for age 10–14). This variable assessed the degree to which the subject attempted to master mechanical skills and manifested involvement in activities such as carpentry, construction of model vehicles, engines and motors, and craft work.

Athletic achievement: (Rated for age 10–14). This variable assessed the degree to which the subject attempted to master and showed involvement in athletic activities. These behaviors included swimming, hiking, baseball, football, basketball, tennis, acrobatics, and track events.

Recognition seeking behavior: (Rated for ages 6–10 and 10–14). This variable assessed the subject's striving to obtain goals that led to recognition from parents, teachers, and peers. The behaviors emphasized in the rating were (*a*) grades in school and school honors, (*b*) stated desire for status-laden vocations or ostentatious material goods, (*c*) striving for leadership in teams or clubs, (*d*) attempts to get recognition from farm activities (e.g., raise the best calf, the highest corn, etc.).

Maternal Variables

Maternal acceleration of developmental skills in child: (Rated for ages 0–3, 3–6, and 6–10). The home visits and maternal interviews yielded information on the mother's behavior and attitudes toward her child. The maternal variable that is directly relevant to the subject's achievement behavior was called *maternal acceleration.* It was defined in terms of the degree to which the mother showed concern over the subject's cognitive and motor development, and the degree to which she exhibited desires for precocious achievement in her child. The rating reflected the degree to which the mother "pushed" the subject's development beyond his abilities and her concern with his general achievement level.

Adult Interview

The junior author, who had no knowledge of the subject's childhood information, interviewed each subject and rated him (seven-point scale) on a variety of variables. The definitions of the variables related to achievement and recognition seeking behaviors follow.

Achievement behavior. This variable evaluated the subject's behavioral attempts to master tasks for which "self-satisfaction" rather than social recognition was the *salient* goal. In achievement behavior, the subject was striving to attain a *self-imposed* standard of excellence. The rating was based on the subject's emphasis and concern with task mastery in his job and avocational pursuits.

Recognition seeking behavior. This variable evaluated the subject's behavioral attempt to obtain symbols of status and social recognition. The rating was based on evidences of strivings for (a) vocational recognition, (b) academic awards and honors, (c) positions of leadership or recognition in community or vocational groups, (d) concern with conspicuous material display, (e) striving for upward mobility in social class position.

Concern with intellectual competence. This variable assessed the value the subject placed upon intelligence, knowledge, academic achievement, and intellectual superiority regardless of whether the goal was to satisfy inner standards or to obtain social recognition.

Reliability of Longitudinal and Adult Interview Ratings

A random sample of 32 tape recorded adult interviews were independently studied and rated by a second judge to assess the reliability of the junior author's adult ratings. The reliabilities of the longitudinal variables were also assessed through independent ratings, by a second judge, of samples of 50–60 cases at each of the four age periods. The reliabilities of the adult and child ratings were determined by product-moment correlation coefficients.[4] For the adult ratings of achievement behavior, recognition behavior, and intellectual concern the reliability coefficients were .84, .99, and .98, respectively. With the exception of one child behavior variable, the reliabilities of the longitudinal ratings ranged from .74 to .90 with a median coefficient of .81. The one low longitudinal reliability was for child's achievement for age 0–3 ($r = +.35$; $p < .01$; two-tailed).

TAT Achievement Fantasy: Adolescent and Adult Protocols

Early adolescent (median age of 14–6) protocols were available for 67 of the 71 subjects, and all 71 subjects were administered TAT stimuli following the adult interview. The adolescent protocol was based on seven cards from the Murray[5] series (Cards 1, 5, 14, 17BM, 3BM, 6BM, and 3GF). The male adult protocol was based on 13 cards (4, 8BM, 7BM, 6BM, 12M, 17BM, 13MF, 14, 3BM, 5, 1, 3GF, and 18GF). The adult females were also administered 13 cards (4, 6GF, 12F, 2, 8GF, 17BM, 13MF, 14, 3BM, 5, 1, 3GF, and 18GF).

[4] All correlations were corrected for restricted range of scores using a procedure described by C. C. Peters and W. R. Van Voorhis, *Statistical Procedures and Their Mathematical Bases* (New York: McGraw-Hill, 1940), pp. 395–398.

[5] H. A. Murray, *Thematic Apperception Test Manual* (Cambridge: Harvard University Press, 1943).

For both the adolescent and adult protocols achievement themes were scored according to the scheme described by McClelland, Atkinson, Clark, and Lowell.[6] Since incidence of the subcategories of the McClelland scoring system were infrequent, only stories in which achievement behavior was the major aspect of the plot were considered. These are scored Ach Th in the McClelland scheme. For the adolescent protocol, there was a lack of comparability among the examiners with respect to the inquiry questions and only the spontaneous verbalization of the subject was scored. Agreement between two independent coders was 95%. The longitudinal and interview ratings of achievement and recognition behavior were made *without knowledge* of the subject's adolescent or adult TAT stories. Thus, the behavior and interview ratings were independent of each other and of the TAT thematic scores.

IQ Change

Each child was given the Stanford-Binet, Forms L and M alternately, annually from ages 5 through 11 by the same psychologist.[7] The mean IQ for the entire Fels population is about 120 (*SD* of 15). For each subject, a smoothed plot of his IQ scores was obtained by averaging his three IQ scores around each age. For example, a child's smoothed or average IQ at age 6 was the result of averaging his IQ scores at ages 5, 6, and 7; his smoothed IQ at age 10 was the average of his IQs at ages 9, 10, and 11. This procedure tends to remove the chance variation associated with any one IQ score and has been used in other studies.[8] Each subject's smoothed IQ at age 6 was then subtracted from his smoothed IQ at age 10 and the resulting difference was used as a measure of IQ change. As with achievement themes, the child and adult achievement ratings were made without knowledge of the subject's IQ or his IQ change score.

In summary, four independent sources of data were analyzed: child and maternal behaviors for the first 14 years of life, adult behavior, adolescent and adult achievement themes, and childhood IQ change scores.

Statistical Analysis

Relationships among the following variables were evaluated: (*a*) childhood achievement and maternal acceleration ratings with the adult interview ratings, (*b*) adolescent achievement themes with adult achievement themes, (*c*) adolescent and adult achievement themes with the longitudinal and adult ratings, and (*d*) IQ change scores with the childhood and adult ratings. Product-moment correlations were used except when the TAT achievement score was involved. Since achievement themes were not normally distributed, contingency

---

[6] D. C. McClelland, J. W. Atkinson, R. A. Clark and E. L. Lowell, *The Achievement Motive* (New York: Appleton-Century-Crofts, 1953).

[7] Virginia L. Nelson administered all of the IQ tests.

[8] J. Kagan, L. W. Sontag, C. T. Baker and V. L. Nelson, "Personality and IQ Change," *J. Abnorm. Soc. Psychol.*, LVIII (1958), pp. 261–266; L. W. Sontag, C. T. Baker and V. L. Nelson, "Mental Growth and Personality Development," *Monogr. Soc. Res. Child Development*, XXIII (1958), No. 68.

coefficients[9] were used for all tests of association using this variable. Mechanical achievement for age 10–14 was the only variable for which there was a significant sex difference; the boys having a higher mean rating than the girls ($p < .05$; two-tailed).

RESULTS

Stability of Achievement and Recognition Behaviors

Table 1 presents the relationships between the child and adult ratings of achievement and recognition behavior, as well as the relation between maternal acceleration and the adult achievement variables. There are several important results in this table. The rating of achievement behavior for age 6–10 showed a significant, positive association with all three adult variables for both sexes. The rating of achievement for age 3–6 was predictive of adult behavior for the females but not for the males, a finding that suggests

Table 1
Relation between Longitudinal Ratings of Childhood Achievement and Early Maternal Acceleration with Adult Achievement Behavior
(product-moment correlations)

| | | ADULT VARIABLES | | | | | |
| | | Achievement | | Recognition | | Intellectual Concerns | |
CHILDHOOD VARIABLES	AGE	Males	Females	Males	Females	Males	Females
Recognition	6–10	.47‡	.40†	.42†	.48‡	.37†	.55**
	10–14	.25	.20	.36*	.39†	.24	.40†
Achievement	0–3	−.12	−.02	.01	−.22	−.08	−.02
	3–6	−.03	.45†	−.11	.49‡	.13	.44†
	6–10	.46‡	.38†	.57**	.51‡	.69**	.49‡
Achievement							
Intellectual	10–14	.40†	.42†	.60**	.56‡	.66**	.49‡
Mechanical	10–14	.20	.20	.46†	.02	.47†	.27
Athletic	10–14	−.18	.01	−.17	−.09	−.47†	.02
Maternal acceleration	0–3	.22	.36*	.44*	.41*	.09	.36*
	3–6	.31	.09	.24	.12	.42†	.12
	6–10	.14	.33*	.16	.23	.32*	.43†

* $p < .05$; one-tailed.
† $p < .02$; one-tailed.
‡ $p < .01$; one-tailed.
** $p < .001$; one-tailed.

[9] The contingency coefficients were based on chi squares computed from Mood's likelihood ratio test for a 3×2 distribution (A. M. Mood, *Introduction to the Theory of Statistics* [New York: McGraw-Hill, 1950], p. 257).

the earlier emergence of a stable achievement strivings in girls' development than in boys. Of the three achievement behaviors rated for age 10–14, only intellectual mastery was predictive of adult achievement for both sexes. Involvement in mechanical activities was predictive of adult achievement for boys but not for girls. Athletic achievement showed no relationship to the rating of general adult achievement, and was negatively associated with intellectual concern for adult males ($p < .02$).

Recognition seeking behavior for age 6–10 was also predictive of adult achievement behavior. A few of the child variables were moderately intercorrelated and the three adult variables were highly intercorrelated (Tables 4, 5, and 6). This lack of independence makes some of the stability correlations between childhood and adulthood somewhat redundant.

Maternal Acceleration and Adult Behavior

Maternal concern with the child's developmental progress during the first 10 years of life showed low to moderate correlations with adult achievement behavior. The maternal rating for age 6–10 was not a better predictor of adult behavior than the maternal rating for the first 3 years of life. Moreover, the age 0–3 rating was associated with all three adult, achievement variables for girls, while it predicted only recognition behavior for adult males.

Stability of TAT Achievement Fantasy

Although different sets of TAT pictures were used in obtaining the adolescent and adult protocols, the three pictures that usually elicited achievement stories were presented at both administrations. Cards 1, 14, and 17BM, which elicited 77% of all the achievement themes, were common to both protocols. The strong tendency for these particular cards to elicit achievement themes has been noted in another study.[10] A typical achievement theme to Card 1 concerned a boy who wanted to master the violin and/or become a famous violinist. A typical achievement story to Card 17BM involved a person who was in a rope climbing contest and wanted to do his best to win. A common achievement story to Card 14 concerned an artist or student who had been working hard and was looking forward to fame and success as a result of his accomplishments.

The stability of the TAT achievement score between the adolescent and adult protocols was determined through the use of contingency coefficients. The stability coefficients were .34, .36, and .31 for boys, girls, and total group ($p < .10$, $< .05$, $< .02$; one-tailed). Thus, achievement themes also

[10] J. Kagan and H. A. Moss, "The Stability and Validity of Achievement Fantasy," *J. Abnorm. Soc. Psychol.*, LVIII (1959), pp. 357–364.

showed some degree of stability over this 10-year period. These data extend
the findings of an earlier investigation,[11] in which the authors reported a
3 year stability coefficient of .32 ($p < .01$) for achievement themes obtained
at median ages of 8–9 and 11–6. The stability coefficients between the
adolescent and adult protocols are of the same magnitude as those found
for the earlier age period.

Validity of Achievement Themes: Relations with Child and Adult Behavior

Contingency coefficients were computed relating the occurrence of
adolescent and adult achievement themes with the longitudinal and adult
achievement ratings. These results are presented in Table 2. The highest
and most consistent relations were between the adult achievement themes
and adult interview ratings. The only significant relation between adult

Table 2

**Relation between TAT Achievement Themes and Child
and Adult Achievement Behavior
(contingency coefficients)**

		ADOLESCENT TAT (Median age 14–6)		ADULT TAT (Median age 25)	
LONGITUDINAL VARIABLE	AGE	Males	Females	Males	Females
Recognition	6–10	.21	.17	.26	.22
	10–14	−.20	−.18	−.31	.39
Achievement	0–3	−.15	−.25	−.20	.16
	3–6	.42*	.19	.19	.36
	6–10	.24	.15	.13	.30
Achievement					
Intellectual	10–14	.30	−.25	.26	.16
Mechanical	10–14	.31	−.62‡	.63**	−.50†
Athletic	10–14	−.20	.12	.12	.17
Maternal ac-					
celeration	0–3	.11	.51†	.25	−.08
	3–6	.37	.23	.27	.28
	6–10	.51‡	.26	.24	.41*
Adult interview variables					
(median age 25)					
Recognition		.17	.25	.40†	.52**
Achievement		.19	.44‡	.37	.52**
Intellectual Concerns		.44‡	.25	.31	.59**

* $p < .05$; one-tailed.
† $p < .02$; one-tailed.
‡ $p < .01$; one-tailed.
** $p < .001$; one-tailed.

[11] *Ibid.*

themes and the childhood ratings held for mechanical achievement (C = +.63; $p < .001$ for boys, and $-.50$; $p < .02$ for girls).

The adolescent TAT was also more predictive of adult behavior than it was of the childhood ratings. Adolescent achievement themes predicted adult achievement behavior for women (C = +.44; $p < .01$) and intellectual concerns for men (C = +.44; $p < .01$). Adolescent achievement themes showed minimal association with the child's achievement behavior. The only significant positive association was with age 3–6 achievement for boys. Once again the rating of mechanical achievement for girls was negatively associated with achievement themes. This negative correlation may be due to the fact that this is the only variable for which markedly different behavioral referents were used in rating the two sexes. For boys, involvement in carpentry, engines, motors, and model airplanes was emphasized in the rating. These activities are sex-typed and girls showed no interest in them. Participation in craft work (making jewelry, leather articles) and sewing was also used as evidence of involvement in mechanical activities and girls tended to choose these behaviors.

Maternal acceleration during the first 10 years of life showed suggestive relationships with the adolescent achievement themes. For example, maternal acceleration for age 0–3 predicted achievement themes at adolescence for girls (C = +.51; $p < .02$), but not for boys. Maternal acceleration for age 6–10 predicted adolescent achievement themes for boys (C = +.51; $p < .01$) and adult achievement themes for girls (C = +.41; $p < .05$).

In summary, the adult and adolescent TAT stories showed moderate correlations with adult achievement but minimal association with the childhood achievement ratings. Maternal acceleration was associated, to some degree, with adolescent achievement themes.

IQ Increase and Achievement Behavior

The difference between the child's smoothed IQ at age 6 and 10 was used as a measure of IQ change. Earlier studies[12] have demonstrated that the amount of increase in IQ correlated both with independent behavioral indices of achievement strivings for age 6–10, and with early adolescent (age 10–14) achievement stories. These latter relations remain significant when the influence of the child's IQ at age 6 is statistically controlled. The present data allowed for a partial validation of these results and an extension of the Sontag *et al.* findings for adolescence and adulthood.[13]

[12] Kagan, *et al., op. cit.;* Sontag, *et al., op. cit.*

[13] In the present sample of 71 subjects, 50% of the males and 20% of the females overlapped with the group of 70 subjects studied by Sontag, Baker, and Nelson (see Sontag, *et al., op. cit.*). However, their data only dealt with the period from 3 to 10 years of age. The present behavioral material covered adolescence and early adulthood.

Table 3
Relation Between IQ Change and Childhood and
Adult Achievement Variables
(product-moment correlations)

Longitudinal Variables	Age	Males	Females
Recognition	6–10	.24	.21
Recognition	10–14	.41†	.09
Achievement	0–3	.13	.04
Achievement	3–6	−.02	.24
Achievement	6–10	.39‡	.47‡
Achievement-intellectual	10–14	.37*	.41†
Achievement-mechanical	10–14	.15	.14
Achievement-athletic	10–14	−.16	−.46†
Maternal acceleration	0–3	−.06	.20
Maternal acceleration	3–6	−.03	−.12
Maternal acceleration	6–10	.10	.54‡
Adult interview variables			
Recognition		.48‡	.25
Achievement		.38‡	.38†
Intellectual concern		.49‡	.42‡

* $p < .05$; one-tailed.
† $p < .02$; one-tailed.
‡ $p < .01$; one-tailed.

Table 3 presents the correlations between changes in IQ during age 6–10 and the longitudinal and adult behaviors. The amount of IQ increase was a fairly sensitive predictor of both intellectual achievement for age 10–14 ($r = .37$ and .41 for boys and girls; $p < .01$), and concern with intellectual competence in adulthood ($r = .49$ and .42; $p < .01$). These results support and extend the earlier studies and indicate that amount of IQ increase during the first 4 years of school is a moderately accurate index of the subject's motivation to master intellectual tasks during adolescence and early adulthood. It is important to note that IQ change showed no relation to mechanical or athletic strivings for boys, and was negatively associated with athletic achievement for girls ($r = −.46$; $p < .02$). Thus, IQ increase is not a general measure of achievement strivings for all areas of task mastery. The IQ change measure predicts all three adult achievement ratings because the three adult variables are heavily weighted with concern over intellectual competence. Finally, the maternal acceleration rating for age 6–10 showed a positive relation with IQ change for girls ($r = +.54$; $p < .01$) but not for boys.

Intercorrelations Among the Measures

There were, as might be anticipated, positive correlations among the achievement and recognition ratings. Tables 4, 5, and 6 present the inter-

Table 4
Intercorrelations Among Variables Rated for Age 6–10

	Recognition	Achieve- ment	Maternal Acceleration
Recognition	—	.77‡	.57‡
Achievement	.60‡	—	.59‡
Maternal acceleration	.39*	.44‡	—

Note.—Data for males are in upper right; for females, in lower left.
* $p < .05$; two-tailed.
‡ $p < .01$; two-tailed.

Table 5
Intercorrelations Among Variables Rated for Age 10–14

	Recog- nition	Intellec- tual Achieve- ment	Mechan- ical Achieve- ment	Athletic Achieve- ment
Recognition	—	.74‡	.23	.04
Intellectual achievement	.60‡	—	.53‡	−.11
Mechanical achievement	.17	.32	—	−.23
Athletic achievement	.24	.12	.07	—

Note.—Data for males are in upper right; for females, in lower left.
‡ $p < .01$; two-tailed.

Table 6
Intercorrelations Among Adult Interview Variables

	Achieve- ment	Recog- nition	Intellec- tual
Achievement	—	.72‡	.73‡
Recognition	.79‡	—	.72‡
Intellectual	.77‡	.84‡	—

Note.—Data for males are in upper right; for females, in lower left.
‡ $p < .01$; two-tailed.

correlations among the variables that were rated for ages 6–10, 10–14, and adulthood. The correlations for the males are above and to the right of the diagonal; the female data are to the left and below the diagonal.

For all three age periods there were high, positive correlations among the achievement and recognition variables. For age 10–14, recognition behavior was highly correlated with achievement strivings in the intellectual area, but only minimally related to mechanical or athletic achievement. This finding suggests that, for this middle class sample, mastery of intellectual skills is the primary method chosen to obtain social recognition. Perhaps for lower class samples this generalization might be less valid. The high correlations between recognition behavior and intellectual concern in adulthood, together with the fact that maternal acceleration predicted both variables, suggests that it is difficult to separate "recognition seeking behavior" from "attempts to improve intellectual competence."

DISCUSSION

Stability of Achievement Strivings

The results indicate that strivings for intellectual mastery are moderately stable from the school years through early adulthood. This behavioral disposition emerges as a stable phenomenon at ages 3–6 for girls and 6–10 for boys. The stability of the behavior ratings is paralleled by the moderate stability of TAT achievement stories over a shorter age span. Moreover, achievement stories in adolescence and adulthood also predicted the adult behavior ratings. This consistent cluster of correlations adds construct validity to the TAT achievement variable and support to the conclusion that this class of behaviors is stable over time.

Involvement in athletics for age 10–14 showed no strong, positive relation to either IQ increase or adult achievement behavior and, in a few instances, negative relationships occurred. This was not because the interviewer failed to assess adult involvement in this particular activity. Rather, many of the adults who had been involved in athletics as early adolescents were not overly concerned with task mastery as adults and they tended to avoid intellectual activities.

The majority of the sample regarded positions of responsibility, intellectual challenge, and knowledge of the environment as highly desirable goals. If a subject had strong achievement motives he tended to gratify them through intellectually oriented endeavors. It is suggested that the mass media and social environment differentially emphasize the importance of different skills in accordance with the sex and age role characteristics of the individual. For adults, there tends to be an emphasis on intellectual competence and a de-emphasis on active mastery of athletic skills. Moreover, intellectual mastery is less involved in potential sex role conflict than mechanical or athletic behaviors. To excel at sports is one of the defining characteristics of masculinity. Some boys become involved in athletics in order to maintain their sex role identity and avoid peer rejection. An athletic girl will be subject to peer rejection for excessive participation in athletics. Thus, athletic mastery is under the control of motives and conflicts related to sex role identification in addition to needs for task mastery.

This latter point raises the question of the appropriate definition of achievement behavior and motivation. It is suggested that the concept of a general achievement motive is too broad a term, and it may be useful to replace this construct with a series of variables that relate to more specific behaviors. It seems more reasonable to talk about "desire to improve intellectual skills," or "desire to improve athletic skills" than to use the more global concept of need achievement. Individuals strive to perfect skills in different areas, and the motivations for these strivings are multiple. Prediction and comprehension of these phenomena might be facilitated if there was some differentiation among the behaviors and motives that are involved in task mastery.

The lack of predictive power of age 0–3 mastery behavior might have been due to the greater difficulty in rating this variable (the interrater reliability was .35). On the other hand, the behavioral referents for this rating differed from those used to assess mastery for the older age periods. Since 2-year-olds do not initiate intellectual or athletic mastery behavior, persistence with simple, perceptual-motor tasks (stringing beads, building towers) was the basis for this early rating. A high rating for 0–3 reflected a high threshold for satiation with simple, sensori-motor activities. At the older ages, the achievement rating was based on involvement with problem solving behaviors that were more similar in form to adult achievement behavior. The age 0–3 rating is dynamically different from the symbolic behaviors that characterize achievement during the preschool and school years.[14] This statement is supported by the fact that achievement for age 0–3 was negatively correlated with achievement for age 3–6 ($r = -.20$) and age 6–10 ($r = -.03$), and showed no relationship to achievement themes or IQ change. Persistence with simple sensori-motor tasks during the first 2 or 3 years of life is not an index of future intellectual, achievement strivings. The 2-year-old who will sit for 20 minutes trying to put a peg in a hole is not necessarily the ambitious scholar of the fifth grade.

Maternal Acceleration and Achievement

The ratings of maternal concern with the child's developmental skills were heavily weighted with encouragement of intellectual progress. The most consistent correlates of maternal acceleration were found with the ratings of adult concern with intellectual competence. Maternal acceleration for age 0–3 was slightly more predictive of adult behavior for girls than for boys. Similarly, maternal acceleration for age 6–10 was more predictive of IQ increase for daughters than for sons. The sex difference between these latter two correlations was significant at the .05 level. It is suggested that since the girl was more likely than the boy to identify with

[14] The differences in the content of mastery behaviors for ages 0–3 and 3–6 are analogous to Piaget's (J. Piaget, *The Origins of Intelligence in Children.* [New York: International University Press, 1952]) description of intellectual development. Piaget suggests that during the first 2 years the child is in the sensori-motor stage of intelligence in which simple perceptual-motor activity is salient. During the subsequent preschool years the child's intellectual activity becomes more symbolic and more comparable to adult problem solving behavior.

the mother, maternal encouragement of intellectual mastery should have had a greater effect on the development of the girl than on the boy.[15]

TAT Achievement Stories

Achievement themes on the TAT were moderately stable and were correlated with adult achievement behavior. The fact that the correlations were as high for females as for males, although the three critical cards illustrated male heroes, raises some question concerning the validity of the hero hypothesis. Since Cards 1, 14, and 17BM all picture a male in a potential achievement situation, one might expect that achievement themes for women would not be highly correlated with their achievement behavior. The present results indicate that the production of achievement themes may be more influenced by the subject's conception of what behaviors are appropriate for the hero, than by the degree of identification of storyteller with hero. Perhaps high achievement girls conceptualize the male role as being more associated with task mastery than do low achievement girls.

Atkinson[16] has suggested that achievement themes have differential validity depending on whether or not the criterion task engages the subject's motivation. The achievement variables used in this study (ratings of overt behavior, IQ increase scores) measured "real life" behaviors that would be expected to engage the subject's motivation. The positive correlations obtained indicate that achievement themes are valid indices of intellective mastery when the conditions under which the behavioral samples are obtained are motive arousing.

Limitations on Generalizability

Although the stability correlations for achievement behavior are fairly high, the nature of this particular sample favored stability. The social milieu of these subjects remain constant throughout the first 17 years of their lives, and the parents and peers of these subjects retained their same values. The degree of stability obtained with this sample might not hold for populations that were more mobile, for different ethnic or social class groups, or for children subjected to major developmental traumata.

Social Reinforcement and Stability

The stability of achievement behavior is congruent with general reinforcement theory. Each time achievement strivings are rewarded through

---

[15] Research in progress at the institute, under the direction of Vaughn J. Crandall and Walter Katkovsky is assessing the role of both mother and father in the adoption of achievement motives and behaviors.

[16] J. W. Atkinson, "Motivational Determinants of Risk Taking Behavior," *Psychol. Rev.*, LXIV (1957), pp. 359–372.

social approval or internal feelings of satisfaction, the strength of this behavioral tendency should be increased. If achievement strivings lead to failure, these behaviors should extinguish. The child who attains scholastic honors through effort is rewarded by the social environment, and this experience frequently leads to an expectancy of future success for similar behavior. This rewarding experience, coupled with the strong cultural approval for intellectual competence, increases the probability that the child will continue to engage in intellectual tasks. On the other hand, persistent failures in intellectually challenging situations are likely to lead to an expectancy of failure, and these expectancies can result in avoidance and/or withdrawal from involvement in intellectual behavior.

SUMMARY

This paper summarized results from a larger investigation on the stability of behavior from childhood through adulthood. This investigation dealt specifically with the long term stability of achievement and recognition seeking behaviors in subjects who were part of the Fels Research Institute's longitudinal population.

The subjects were 36 males and 35 females for whom extensive longitudinal information was available from birth through 14 years of age. One psychologist, who had no knowledge of the adult behavior of these subjects, studied narrative reports based on observations of the child in a variety of settings, and rated each child on achievement and recognition seeking behaviors for four age periods: 0–3, 3–6, 6–10, and 10–14. In addition, ratings were made for maternal acceleration of developmental skills for the first three age periods. A second psychologist, who had no knowledge of the childhood information, interviewed each subject in adulthood (age range 20–29) and rated him on three variables related to achievement and recognition seeking behavior in adulthood.

In addition, the following information was available for most subjects: (*a*) a 7 card TAT protocol administered during early adolescence (median age 14–6) and a 13 card TAT protocol following the adult interview, and (*b*) annual Stanford-Binet IQ tests from ages 5 through 11 which furnished an IQ change score over the years 6–10.

The major results were as follows:

1. Both achievement and recognition striving behaviors for age 6–10 showed significant positive correlations with similar behaviors during adulthood, the correlations ranged from .38 to .68 and all were significant at the .05 level or better.

2. Involvement in intellectual activities for age 10–14 showed high positive correlations with achievement behavior in adulthood while involvement in athletics during these years showed no positive relationship with

adult achievement behavior. Involvement in mechanical tasks for age 10–14 showed positive correlations with adult achievement behavior for boys but not for girls.

3. Maternal acceleration of the child's developmental skills during the first 3 years of life predicted adult achievement behavior for women but not for men. Maternal acceleration of developmental skills during age 6–10 showed moderate correlations with adult concern with intellectual competence in both sexes.

4. Achievement stories told during adolescence and adulthood showed high positive correlations with adult achievement behavior. Maternal acceleration of developmental skills showed suggestive correlations with the occurrence of achievement stories in both adolescence and adulthood.

5. The amount of increase in IQ score during the years 6–10 showed high positive correlations with the ratings of achievement behavior during adulthood. In addition, increase in IQ showed positive correlations with age 6–10 achievement behavior, and with strivings for intellectual competence during age 10–14. Amount of IQ increase showed negative correlations with athletic achievement for age 10–14.

The results suggested that achievement strivings during the first 4 years of school are a moderately good index of future achievement behavior during adolescence and adulthood. There were high correlations between strivings for social recognition and intellectual achievement and it was suggested that these variables are intimately related in a middle class population.

Family Structure and Achievement Motivation*

BERNARD C. ROSEN

Among the influences upon achievement motivation, those associated with demographic factors are especially difficult to pin down for analysis. Generally speaking, children develop strong achievement motivation when parents compel them to excel and to rely upon their own resources. However, child training for acquisition of achievement motivation, as well as for other attributes, varies from family to family on the basis of several family differences other than those specific to child rearing. In the paper presented below, Rosen investigates the ways in which such variables as family size, ordinal position, mother's age, and social class relate to the socialization process and to the development of achievement motivation in boys. An analysis of the data indicates that "it is exceedingly unwise to single out any one demographic factor as an explanation of achievement motivation."

This paper is a study of the relationship of certain demographic factors to family structure and personality development. Specifically, it examines the ways in which family size, ordinal position, mother's age, and social class

* From *American Sociological Review*, XXVI (1961), pp. 574–585. Reprinted by permission of the author and the American Sociological Association. This paper is part of an address before the annual meeting of the Brazilian Society for the Advancement of Science (Sociedade Brasileira Para O Progresso Da Ciencia), Piracicaba, Brazil, July 6, 1960. This research was supported by a research grant (M2283) from the National Institute of Mental Health, United States Public Health Service. The paper was written while the author held a Special Research Fellowship (MF-10,795) awarded by the Research Fellowships Branch of the National Institute of Mental Health and sponsored by the Universidade de Sao Paulo, Brazil. The contributions of Marian Winterbottom for her work in scoring the TAT protocols, and June Schmelzer, Miriam Witkin, and William Erlbaum for their assistance in reviewing the literature are greatly appreciated. Thanks also to Dr. Carolina Martuscelli Bori of the Faculdade Filosofia, Ciencias e Letras, Universidade de Sao Paulo for her helpful comments.

169

influence the quality and quantity of patterned parent-child interaction and their impact upon the development of achievement motivation.

Achievement motivation has been defined as the redintegration of affect aroused by cues in situations involving standards of excellence.[1] Such standards are typically learned from parents who urge the child to compete against these standards, rewarding him when he performs well and punishing him when he fails. In time parental expectations become internalized, so that when later exposed to situations involving standards of excellence the individual re-experiences the affect associated with his earlier efforts to meet them. In our culture, the behavior of people with strong achievement motivation is characterized by persistent striving and general competitiveness.

Recent empirical data show that strong achievement motivation tends to develop when parents set high goals for their child to attain, when they indicate a high evaluation of his competence to do a task well, and impose standards of excellence upon problem-solving tasks, even in situations where such standards are not explicit. This complex of socialization practices has been called *achievement training*. Also related to achievement motivation is another set of socialization practices called *independence training*. This type of training involves expectations that the child be *self-reliant* in situations where he competes with standards of excellence. At the same time the parent grants him relative *autonomy* in problem-solving and decision-making situations where he is given both freedom of action and responsibility for success or failure. The role of independence training in generating achievement motivation is exceedingly complex and can only be understood in the context of what appears to be a division of labor between the fathers and mothers of boys with high achievement motivation. Observation of parent-child interaction in an experimental problem-solving situation has shown that both of the parents of boys with high achievement motivation stress achievement training. When compared with parents of boys with low achievement motivation, it was found that the fathers and mothers of boys with high achievement motivation tend to be more competitive and interested in their sons' performance; they set higher goals for him to attain and have a greater regard for his competence at problem solving. They also react to good performance with more warmth and approval, or with disapproval if he performs poorly. The pattern changes with respect to independence training. Much of this type of training comes from the father, who (in an experimental situation at least) expected his son to be self-reliant in problem solving, and gave him a relatively high degree of autonomy in making his own decisions. The mothers of boys with high achievement motivation, on the other hand, were likely to be

[1] D. C. McClelland, J. Atkinson, R. Clark, and E. Lowell, *The Achievement Motive,* New York: Appleton-Century-Crofts, 1953.

more dominant and to expect less self-reliance than the mothers of boys with low motivation.

It appears that the boy can take, and perhaps needs, achievement training from both parents, but the effects of independence training and sanctions (a crucial factor determining the child's affective reaction to standards of excellence) are different depending on whether they come from the father or mother. In order for strong achievement motivation to develop, the boy seems to need more autonomy from his father than from his mother. The authoritarian father may crush his son—and in so doing destroy the boy's achievement motive—perhaps because he views the boy as a competitor and is viewed as such by his son. On the other hand, the mother who dominates the decision-making process does not seem to have the same effect, possibly because she is perceived as imposing her standards on the boy, while a dominating father is perceived as imposing himself on his son. It may be that mother-son relations are typically more secure than those between father and son, so that the boy is able to accept higher levels of dominance and hostility from mother than father without adverse effect upon his achievement motivation. It should be remembered, however, that while the mother of a boy with high achievement motivation is willing to express hostility at poor performance she is also more likely to show approval and warmth when he does well then is the mother of a boy with low motivation.[2]

A number of investigators have remarked upon the differences in parent-child relationships associated with certain demographic characteristics of the family. It has been said that life in a small family is more competitive than in a large family, and that the parents of the former are more likely to have higher aspirations for their children and to place a greater stress upon personal achievement. Furthermore, fathers of small families, particularly in the middle class, are described as less authoritarian than those of large, lower class families. With respect to the variable of ordinal position, early born children are said to be reared more anxiously, to be more "adult-oriented," and to command more of their parents' attention than later born. And as regards parental age, it has been noted that parents as they grow older have less energy to enforce their socialization demands. They are also said to be more indulgent and solicitous, placing less emphasis upon self-reliance and achievement in child rearing. For these and other reasons which will be spelled out in more detail, this study hypothesized that (a) children from small families will tend to have stronger achievement motivation than children from larger families, (b) early born (first or only) would tend to have higher achievement motivation scores

[2] The above two paragraphs are paraphrased from B. C. Rosen and R. D'Andrade, "The Psychosocial Origins of Achievement Motivation," *Sociometry*, 22 (September, 1959), pp. 185–218.

than later born, and (c) children of young mothers would tend to have higher motivation than the children of old mothers.

RESEARCH PROCEDURE

The data for this study were collected from two independent samples. The first was a purposive sample of 427 pairs of mothers and their sons who resided in four Northeastern states. This sample (which we will call sample "A") was deliberately designed to include subjects from a very heterogeneous population.[3] The interviewers, all of whom were upperclassmen enrolled in two sociology courses, were instructed to draw respondents from six racial and ethnic groups: French-Canadians, Greeks, Italians, Jews, Negroes, and white Protestants, as well as from various social classes. Most of the mothers and all of the sons were native-born. The boys ranged in age from 8 to 14, with a mean age about eleven. At a later date, a second group of respondents (Sample "B") was obtained in connection with another and larger research program by interviewing systematically virtually the entire universe of boys, nine to eleven years of age, in the elementary schools of three small Northeastern Connecticut towns. This sample of 367 subjects had a mean age of about ten years, and was much more homogeneous with respect to race and ethnicity. All the respondents were white, and predominantly Protestant or Roman Catholic. Also, the interviewers were two carefully trained graduate assistants employed specifically for this purpose. For both samples, the respondent's social position was determined by a modified version of Hollingshead's Index of Social Position, which uses the occupation and education of the main wage-earner, usually the father, as the principal criteria of status. Respondents were classified according to this index into one of five social classes, from the highest status group (Class I) to the lowest (Class V).

A measure of the boy's achievement motivation was obtained by using a Thematic Apperception-type test.[4] This projective test involves showing the subject four ambiguous pictures and asking him to tell a story, under time pressure, about each one. The stories are then scored by counting the frequency of imagery about evaluated performance in competition with a standard of excellence. This test assumes that the more the individual shows indications of connections between affect and evaluated performance in his fantasy, the greater will be the degree to which achievement motivation is a part of his personality. The boys in both samples were given

[3] Cf. B. C. Rosen, "Race, Ethnicity, and The Achievement Syndrome," *American Sociological Review*, 24 (February, 1959), pp. 47–60.
[4] The test was administered under neutral conditions, using pictures 33, 26, 9, 24 in that order. For more information about this test see, D. C. McClelland, *et al.*, *op. cit.*

this test privately and individually. In the case of the first sample the testing was done in the home; in the second at school in a private office. The subject's imaginative responses were scored by two judges, and a product-moment correlation between the two scorings of .86 for the first sample and .92 for the second was obtained.

For Sample "A," information about the size of the family, ordinal position of the boy, mother's age, and occupation-education characteristics of the father was obtained from the mother in personal interviews in the home. In the case of Sample "B," these data were secured from the boy through questionnaires administered in the classroom. Data on the age of mother are lacking for subjects in Sample "B," as the boys were frequently uncertain of their mother's age.

RESEARCH FINDINGS

Family Size and Achievement Motivation

Considering the sociologist's traditional and continuing concern with group size as an independent variable (from Simmel and Durkheim to the recent experimental studies of small groups), there have been surprisingly few studies of the influence of size upon the nature of interaction in the family. However, such studies as do exist (Bossard's work especially) strongly point to the importance of family size as a variable affecting the socialization process in ways that are relevant to the development of achievement motivation. In fact, when comparing small and large families, investigators tend to regard what we have called achievement and independence training as among the more important criteria differentiating one type of family from the other.[5]

The small family has been described as a planned unit driven by ambition. Middle class small families are regarded as particularly oriented towards status striving and upward mobility. To achieve this end, the parents stress planning and achievement not only for themselves but for their children as well. Considerable attention can be given to the child's progress in the small family since its limited size affords the parents a relatively greater opportunity to devote more of their time and effort to each child than would be possible in the large family. In fact, life in many small families seems to be organized around plans for the child's development

[5] See, for example, J. H. Bossard, *Parent and Child,* Philadelphia: University of Pennsylvania Press, 1953; J. H. Bossard and E. S. Boll, "Personality Roles in the Large Family," *Child Development,* 26 (March, 1955); D. E. Damrin, "Family Size and Sibling Age, Sex, and Position as Related to Certain Aspects of Adjustment," *The Journal of Social Psychology,* 29 (February, 1949) pp. 93–102; R. Stagner and E. T. Katyoff, "Personality as Related to Birth Order and Family Size," *Journal of Applied Psychology,* 20 (May-June, 1936) pp. 340–346.

and future achievement. There may be, for example, an intense concern with his performance in school. In such families, parental reaction to the child's success or failure in competition with his peers is frequently immediate and strong. Evidences of achievement are likely to be lavishly applauded and rewarded, while failure will elicit numerous signs of parental disappointment or displeasure. Of course, the parent's motives are not always altruistic. In some cases the child's achievements serve to improve the family's status or may represent the working out through the child of the parent's unfulfilled personal aspirations. McArthur suggests that children in small families are sometimes "exploited to fulfill the expectations, even the frustrated desires of the parents."[6] Whatever the motives may be, and surely they are many and complex, it seems safe to say that in cases where parents are ambitious for themselves and their children, we may expect to find much emphasis upon standards of excellence, coupled with expectations for high achievement and intense parental involvement in the child's performance. Competition with standards of excellence, and rivalry with peers and siblings are, in fact, oft noted characteristics of the behavior of children from small, particularly middle class, homes.[7]

The pattern of independence training known to be related to the development of achievement motivation is also believed to be more characteristic of life in the small family. The achievement-oriented values of parents of small families and their recognition of the importance of self-reliant mastery for advancement in our competitive society will cause them to urge the child to be self-reliant *in situations where he competes with standards of excellence*. Also, the small family is said to be more democratic and relatively free from the authoritarian, patriarchal leadership that is more common to the large family. In the small family, particularly in the middle class, the parent typically seeks to obtain the cooperation of the child through the employment of conditional love and the manipulation of guilt feelings rather than by the use of coercion. Of course, the very intensity of parent-child relations in this type of family, especially between mother and son, sets definite limits to the child's freedom of action. But an intensely

[6] C. McArthur, "Personalities of First and Second Children," *Psychiatry*, 19 (February, 1956), pp. 47–54.

[7] Cf. M. Mead, *And Keep Your Powder Dry*, New York: William Morrow and Co., 1943, especially Chapter VI–VII. The variables examined in this paper do not, of course, exhaust the list of possible causal factors. It is quite possible that other demographic factors, such as the number and ordinal position of male and female siblings and the number of years separating each child, may also be important. Furthermore, non-demographic factors, such as parental values, could also play a significant role in the development of achievement motivation. Thus family size and achievement motivation may *both* reflect the achievement oriented values of the parents. We know, also, that other persons besides parents, for example, peers, play an important part in the socialization process. Cf. B. C. Rosen, "Multiple Group Membership: A Study of Parent-Peer Group Cross-Pressures," *American Sociological Review*, 20 (April, 1955), pp. 155–161.

involved, "pushing" mother appears to promote the development of achievement motivation in boys. It is the authoritarian father, not the mother, who represents a greater threat to the boy and inhibits the development of achievement motivation.

The large family is a different social system, both qualitatively as well as quantitatively. The large number of persons in the group creates a greater degree of interdependence between members and an increased need for cooperative effort and consensus. The precarious equilibrium of the large family would be threatened by excessive emphasis upon competition and achievement. Rivalry exists, of course, but it must be muted. Hence, in contrast to the small family, the large family is more likely to value responsibility above individual achievement, conformity above self-expression, cooperation and obedience above individualism. Children are more likely to be disciplined for the sake of family harmony than to assure their meeting achievement goals. Bossard maintains that there is a greater degree of specialization of roles in the large family. Each child tends to become functionally specialized, his behavior being more influenced by the family division of labor than by parental aspirations for achievement. He notes that his material on the large family contains "little mention of a child who excels at large, as is so common with small family children; there is little comparison with neighbor's children; there is emphasis on duty, not spectacular achievement."[8]

As the size of the family increases, better internal organization and a higher degree of discipline are required. It is perhaps for this reason that the authoritarian father is often associated with the large family system. But in families where the father is overly-dominant the amount of autonomy permitted the son will be severely curtailed. The child will have little opportunity to experience the pleasures of autonomous mastery that appear important to the development of strong achievement motivation. On the other hand, although the child may not be granted very much autonomy in the large family, he typically receives considerable training in self-reliance. In the large family the child normally receives a smaller amount of attention and surveillance from his parents than would be the case in the small family. Hence, he is expected to be self-reliant, but usually in areas involving self-care-taking (e.g., feeding, dressing, amusing and defending oneself) rather than in situations where he competes with standards of excellence. Research has shown that self-reliance training in care-taking areas is not related to high achievement motivation.

In view of these differences between the socialization practices of parents with families of different sizes, we predicted that the children from small families would tend to have higher achievement motivation than those from

---

[8] J. H. Bossard, *The Large Family System*, Philadelphia: University of Pennsylvania Press, 1956.

large families. To test this hypothesis, we divided the families into three groups. Families with one or two children were called "small," those with three or four children, "medium," and those with five or more children "large." This procedure was performed for both samples. In Table 1 are shown the boys' mean achievement motivation scores, cross-tabulated by family size and social class[9] for samples "A" and "B." The data tend to support our hypothesis, especially for subjects in sample "A." Considering for the moment only the means for family groups without regard to social class, we find a clear inverse relationship between family size and achievement motivation: the mean score for boys from small families in sample "A" is 5.43, medium families 4.64, and large families 2.48. Thus, the mean score of boys from small families is more than twice as great as that of boys from large families, and the mean score of boys from medium size families

Table 1
Mean Achievement Scores by Family Size and Social Class

SOCIAL CLASS	SAMPLE A* Family Size Small	Medium	Large	$\bar{x}$	SAMPLE B† Family Size Small	Medium	Large	$\bar{x}$
I–II	5.20	6.41	2.33	5.46	7.28	7.93	2.25	7.11
III	6.49	6.14	5.83	6.28	7.67	7.36	6.13	7.32
IV	5.06	3.40	2.82	4.00	6.33	6.15	7.29	6.29
V	4.57	3.67	1.48	3.31	4.15	5.00	2.00	4.69
$\bar{x}$	5.43	4.64	2.48		6.61	6.57	6.22	
N	178	193	54		155	166	45	

* Information lacking for two cases.
† Information lacking for one case.

almost twice as great. The difference between the scores of boys from large families and those from medium and small families is statistically significant at the .001 level. However, the difference between small and medium families is not statistically significant. Social class is also related to achievement motivation, as has been reported elsewhere,[10] and, in fact, accounts

[9] An analysis was made to determine the relationship of religion and race to family size, since achievement motivation is known to be related to these factors. (See footnote 3.) It was found that Roman Catholics and Negroes have larger families than white Protestants, Greeks, and Jews. But these differences virtually disappear when social class is controlled. For example, in the middle class the average number of children in Negro families is 3.0, Catholic families 2.7 as compared with 2.5 for Greek, 2.6 for Jews, and 2.8 for white Protestants. In the lower class the differences are somewhat larger but not statistically significant: Jews 2.1, Greek 2.4, white Protestants 3.0, Catholics 3.3, and Negroes 3.6. This finding is one reason why social class was introduced as a controlling variable throughout this study.

[10] See B. C. Rosen, "The Achievement Syndrome: A Psychocultural Dimension of Social Stratification," *American Sociological Review,* 21 (April, 1956), pp. 203–211.

for more of the variance (F = 5.67, P < .01) than family size
P < .05). However, for sample "A," the relationship between
and achievement motivation tends to persist even when social cl
trolled. An internal examination of the table reveals that for each social
class, in eleven out of twelve cells, the boys from small families have the
highest mean scores, with somewhat lower motivation scores for boys from
medium size families, while the scores of boys from large families are the
lowest in every social class.

For sample "B," the relationship of family size to achievement motivation is also an inverse one (small family 6.61, medium 6.57, large 6.22),
but the differences between groups are small and statistically insignificant.
Social class continues to be related significantly to achievement motivation
—this time at the .05 level—and displays a pattern identical to that found
in Sample "A": the highest score is in class III, a somewhat lower score in
class I–II, with progressively declining scores in classes IV and V.

There are other similarities between samples "A" and "B." For example,
the *rank* of mean scores for class I–II and III are similar for both samples.
That is, in class I–II the relationship between family size and motivation is
curvilinear: highest score in medium size families, a somewhat lower score
in the small family and a considerably lower score in large families. In class
III there is an inverse relationship between motivation and family size: the
smaller the family the larger the motivation score. Furthermore, in both
samples the large size families in classes I–II and V have the lowest scores
of all groups. Why should this be so? Perhaps because at both extremes of
the status continuum the pressure to excel is not so intense; there may be
less stress on striving, less emphasis on standards of excellence and fewer
pressures on the child to compete with them, possibly because in one class
the need to succeed is not as great, and in the other because the objective
possibility is so limited.

Generally, then, boys from large families tend to have lower achievement
motivation than those from small and medium families (with one exception:
class IV in sample "B"), but it must be added that any statement about the
relationship of family size to achievement motivation would be on firmer
ground if the F ratio for sample "B" had been statistically significant.

Birth Order and Achievement Motivation

Influenced, perhaps, by Freud's observation that "a child's position in the
sequence of brothers and sisters is of very great significance for the course
of his later life,"[11] a considerable number of researchers have studied the
relationship between ordinal position, socialization and a variety of person-

[11] S. Freud, *A General Introduction to Psycho-Analysis,* Garden City, N.Y.:
Doubleday & Co., 1938, p. 182.

ality characteristics. Though sometimes conflicting, many of their findings have relevance for a study of the development of achievement motivation.[12]

A disproportionate degree of attention has been concentrated on the first born, so that an impressive amount of data has been collected on this position. While the term "achievement training" is not used explicitly, several studies indicate that the first born child (i.e., eldest child in a family containing two or more children) typically receives more achievement training than the later born. To begin with, the amount and degree of interaction between parent and first born is likely to be large and intense. Also, as the only child (at least for a time), he is the sole object of parental expectations. These tend to be high, and sometimes involve an overestimate of the child's abilities, in part because there are no other children to provide a realistic standard against which his performance may be evaluated. This may lead the parent to accelerate his training, a process which receives further impetus with the arrival of younger siblings. Thus, it has been noted that the first born child tends to talk earlier than the later born. Koch has found that first born children are more competitive than the later born.[13] Furthermore, in part because of his greater access to his parents, the first born tends to become intensely involved with them and very sensitive to their expectation and sanctions. The first born child has been described as "adult-oriented," serious, conscientious and fond of doing things for his parents, while the second born is said to be more "peer oriented."[14] Of course, this close association may make him more dependent upon his parents, although with the advent of younger siblings he is likely to receive considerable and even abrupt independence training. Frequently, where the family is large, the oldest child will act as a parent-surrogate, and is given very early self-reliance training, so that at times he may behave more like a responsible little man than a child. However, in the absence of achievement training this type of self-reliance training is likely to generate a personality oriented more towards accepting responsibility than striving for achievement.

In the beginning, the positions of the oldest and the only child are identical—neither have siblings, and one would expect that their socialization ex-

[12] A. Adler, "Characteristics of First, Second, and Third Child," *Children, the Magazine For Parents,* 3 (May, 1928), pp. 14–52; H. E. Jones, "Order of Birth," in *Handbook of Child Psychology,* C. Murchison, editor, Worcester: Clark University Press, 1933; M. H. Krout, "Typical Behavior Patterns in Twenty-six Ordinal Positions," *Journal of Genetic Psychology,* 55 (September, 1939), pp. 3–30; J. P. Lees, "The Social Mobility of a Group of Eldest-born and Intermediate Adult Males," *British Journal of Psychology,* 43 (August, 1952), pp. 210–221; R. R. Sears, "Ordinal Position in the Family as a Psychological Variable," *American Sociological Review,* 15 (June, 1950), pp. 397–401.

[13] H. L. Koch, "Some Personality Correlates of Sex, Sibling Position and Sex of Siblings Among Five and Six Year Old Children," *Genetic Psychology Monographs,* 52 (August, 1955), pp. 3–50.

[14] C. McArthur, *op. cit.,* p. 54.

periences would be similar. This is likely to be the case with respect to achievement training, although the only child will miss the extra push that the oldest child receives with the advent of the next-born. The major difference seems to be with respect to independence training. Only children are said to be anxiously trained: some are reared over-strictly, others are excessively indulged. They run the risk of being "smothered" by their parents and of becoming excessively dependent. An over-dominated child may be only externally driven and "run out of gas" as soon as parental pressures are removed. The excessively indulged child may simply not internalize the expectations of his parents. Thus, Sears reports that "high conscience" is found more frequently in children whose parents employed both rewards and punishments than among children who experienced only rewards.[15] In either event, the only child is not likely to receive the training in self-reliance and autonomy that is more frequently the experience of the oldest child with several siblings.

The socialization experiences of the youngest child may involve considerable achievement training, for with approaching freedom from child care the mother tends to accelerate the youngest child to the level of mastery attained by his elder siblings. Thus, Lasko found, in comparing second children who are youngest with second children who have younger siblings, that parents tend to accelerate the younger in a two child family to the level imposed upon the oldest child.[16] Where there were younger sibs no such attempt was made, since the parents were able to estimate more realistically the child's capabilities. The youngest child, however, does run considerable risk with regard to independence training. Research in this connection indicates that parents are more warm and solicitous towards the youngest child than towards other children in the birth order. The youngest child is likely to be pampered, over-protected, and over-indulged, not only by his parents but also by elder siblings. Such indulgence and over-protectiveness is antithetical to the development of achievement motivation, which requires that parents set and enforce high expectations for achievement, self-reliance, and autonomy.

Very little has been written about the socialization of the intermediate child in the birth sequence. Perhaps this is because the intermediate child is not so much a fixed position in the birth order as a residual category. The intermediate child could be anyone of several children in the ordinal sequence; e.g., the second child in a three-child family, the third or fourth child in a five-child family, and so on. Despite this ambiguity, there has been

[15] R. R. Sears, E. E. Macoby and H. Levin, in collaboration with E. L. Lowell, P. S. Sears and J. W. M. Whiting, *Patterns of Child Rearing*, Evanston: Row, Peterson, 1957.

[16] J. K. Lasko, "Parent Behavior Towards First and Second Children," *Genetic Psychology Monographs*, 49 (February, 1954), pp. 97–137.

some speculation that the position of the intermediate child is the most comfortable in the birth order.[17] There is less pressure on the intermediate child to conform to the levels of mastery attained by his siblings and less anxiety about his development. Furthermore, the intermediate child is more likely to come from a large family than a small family; he must, of course, come from a family with at least three children. It is probable, then, if our observations about socialization in the large family are correct, that his training will involve a greater emphasize upon cooperation and responsibility than on achievement.

Given these descriptions of the socialization experiences associated with different positions in the birth order, we predicted that achievement motivation would be highest among boys who are oldest in the birth sequence, somewhat lower among only and youngest children, and lowest among the intermediate boys. As can be seen in Table 2, the data do not confirm our

Table 2
Mean Achievement Scores by Birth Order and Social Class

| | SAMPLE A* Birth Order | | | | | SAMPLE B† Birth Order | | | | |
SOCIAL CLASS	Only	Oldest	Inter- medi- ate	Young- est	x̄	Only	Oldest	Inter- medi- ate	Young- est	x̄
I–II	3.50	6.03	4.28	5.34	5.46	5.33	7.76	5.76	8.29	7.11
III	8.50	6.38	5.61	5.62	6.28	9.83	6.63	7.16	7.88	7.32
IV	2.92	3.73	4.02	4.70	4.00	3.91	7.36	7.27	4.29	6.29
V	4.14	3.36	2.89	4.95	3.31	4.28	5.84	4.21	2.66	4.69
x̄	5.08	4.97	3.45	5.12		5.41	7.02	6.59	5.97	
N	36	162	103	124		31	139	106	90	

* Information missing for two cases.
† Information missing for one case.

hypothesis. It is true that the mean score for oldest boys in sample "B" is higher than those for other ordinal positions, as predicted. But, unfortunately for our hypothesis, the oldest boys in sample "A" have a lower mean score than only or youngest although the differences between the positions are very small and statistically insignificant. The intermediate boys in sample "A" have the lowest mean score, again as predicted, but in sample "B" their mean score is higher than that for only or youngest boys. Most significant is the fact that an analysis of the variance for each sample revealed that the effects of ordinal position are not statistically significant. The effects

[17] W. Toman, "Family Constellation as a Basic Personality Determinant," *Journal of Individual Psychology,* 15 (November, 1959), pp. 199–211.

of social class, however, are statistically significant; at the .01 level for sample "A," and the .05 level for sample "B."

Since family size has been shown to be related to achievement motivation, it occurred to us that the difference between these two samples might be a function of the effects of this variable. That is, perhaps the oldest boys in sample "A" come from large families, while those from sample "B" tend to be from small families. Similarly, youngest and intermediate boys in the two samples might also come from families of markedly different size. We decided to introduce family size as a test variable. Table 3 shows the rela-

Table 3
Mean Achievement Motivation Scores by Birth Order,
Family Size and Social Class

	SOCIAL CLASS I–II–III Family Size			SOCIAL CLASS IV–V Family Size		
BIRTH ORDER	Small	Medium	Large	Small	Medium	Large
Oldest	5.82	7.52	5.75	4.31	2.86	1.00
Intermediate	*	5.44	10.00	*	3.43	1.96
Youngest	5.94	5.21	2.00	5.93	3.90	2.84

* There are, of course, no intermediate children in a two-child family.

tionship between birth order and achievement motivation with family size and social class controlled. Class III has been grouped with classes I–II, and class IV with class V in order to reduce the number of cells without cases. We will call the former group middle class, the latter group lower class. Only the data derived from sample "A" are presented. Unfortunately, the smaller number of cases in sample "B" made a multivariate analysis of this complexity impossible—there proved to be too many empty cells or cells with very few cases—so we were not able to test our hypothesis about the different composition of the two samples. Only children, for whom of course family size is not a variable, are also not included.

Table 3 shows how perilous it is to speak about the relationship of birth order to achievement motivation without taking into account the influence of family size and social class. For each ordinal position, with the exception of only two out of seventeen cells, achievement motivation declines as the size of the family increases. The decline is greatest and most consistent in the lower class. For example, the mean score for oldest children from small families is 4.31, medium families 2.86 and large families 1.00. Similar consistent declines also apply to lower class intermediate and youngest children. The motivation score of the youngest child is most consistently affected by family size: the mean scores for both middle and lower class boys who are youngest in the birth sequence decline as the size of the family increases.

In the middle class, the mean score for youngest boys from small families is 5.94, from large families 2.00. In the lower class the score for youngest boys from small families is 5.93, from large families 2.84. On the other hand, only in the lower class does family size affect the scores of the oldest child. In the middle class, the mean motivation scores for oldest boys increase from 5.82 in small families to 7.52 in medium families and drop negligibly to 5.75 in large families. But in the lower class the scores for oldest boys drop rapidly as family size increases: small family 4.31, medium 2.86, large 1.00.

Why should family size have this differential effect? Probably because the socialization practices associated with ordinal position vary with the size of the family and its social class. We have noted that oldest children in large, lower class families are often expected to be parent-surrogates, performing some of the child-rearing duties for which the overburdened parents have neither the time nor energy. This condition is especially likely to occur when both parents are working (as is increasingly the case for both middle and lower class families), and are unable or unwilling to hire help. In situations where the mother is absent from the home, or where one parent is missing for some reason, the oldest child must frequently assume her functions. Often he must defer his own ambitions and gratifications in order to help raise the family and to insure the education of younger siblings. Under these conditions a concern with training him for achievement may go by the board. In the middle class, however, financial pressures are not as likely to force parents to place so much of the burden of child rearing on the oldest child. If the mother is working, it is usually possible for the family to hire someone to perform some of her functions.

The situation is quite different for the youngest child. In large families the youngest child is frequently indulged, over-protected, and may in general be exposed to few of the socialization experiences associated with the development of high achievement motivation. *In this connection it is particularly interesting that the impact of family size on achievement motivation scores of boys who are youngest in the birth order appears to be more important than social class.* The pervasive achievement orientation of the middle class, which may have been responsible for the maintenance of relatively high scores among oldest boys of large middle class families, seems *not* to have had the same effect on the youngest child; i.e., the youngest child from a large family has a lower mean achievement motivation score than any other middle class group.

Social class seems clearly to influence the impact of family size on ordinal position and achievement motivation. As we have noted, *in the lower class* the scores for oldest, intermediate, and youngest children all decline as family size increases. This decline is more precipitate among oldest than intermediate or youngest children. Also the mean motivation scores of the youngest and intermediate boys are higher than those for oldest children. Thus in the lower class the mean scores for youngest boys is as follows: small family 5.93, medium 3.90, large 2.84. The scores for oldest boys are consistently lower: small family 4.31, medium 2.86, large 1.00. But *in the middle class* the scores for oldest children are higher than those for intermediate and youngest, except in small families where the score for youngest children is slightly and negligibly higher.

It is difficult to assess the relative effects of these three variables—ordinal position, family size, and social class—since unfortunately the empty cells in this table make an analysis of variance impracticable. But it appears probable that social class is the greatest and most consistent factor, followed by family size and ordinal position.

Mother's Age and Achievement Motivation

When considering the relationship of mother's age to the achievement motivation of the child, the question arises as to the nature of the changes that occur in the socialization process with increments in the parent's age. Systematic data on this factor are exceedingly skimpy, although the frequent use of such terms as "young mother" or "old mother" suggest that the parent's age is commonly considered important.[18]

Perhaps the most obvious difference between young and older women is that of sheer physical stamina. Older mothers on the average have less energy to cope with very young children, who normally seethe with activity, and may have difficulty enforcing their socialization demands. It is said, also, that older mothers tend to be more solicitous and indulgent towards children than their younger counterparts. The older mother, particularly where the child represents a long delayed fulfillment, may be unwilling to make strong demands upon her child for self-reliance and achievement. Or, if the demands are made, she may not enforce them with the negative sanctions that appear important to the development of achievement motivation. The tendency for the young mother, on the other hand, especially in the middle class, to be intensely competitive about the speed with which her child learns to master his environment—as compared with his peers—has excited frequent and disapproving comment. She may, for example, constantly compare her child's skill in walking or talking with that of his playmates. Later in school, his performance relative to that of his peers is closely watched and strong pressure may be exerted if he falls behind. Where the competitive spirit is not a factor, the young mother may accelerate her child's training simply through inexperience and an inability to correctly gauge his abilities. It was for these reasons that we hypothesized

[18] See J. H. Bossard, *Parent and Child,* Philadelphia: University of Pennsylvania Press, 1953.

that children of younger mothers would tend to have higher achievement motivation than those of older mothers.

In order to test this hypothesis the mothers were divided into three age groups: mothers 34 years of age or less are called "young," those between 35 and 44 "middle age," and those 45 years or more "old." These data were obtained only from subjects in sample "A," where it was possible to interview the mother personally.

Table 4 shows the relationship between mother's age and the boy's

Table 4
Mean Achievement Motivation Scores by Mother's Age and Social Class

SOCIAL CLASS	Mother's Age			
	Young	Middle	Old	$\bar{x}$
I–II	5.00	5.57	6.50	5.65
III	9.14	5.78	6.18	6.32
IV	2.37	4.78	3.58	4.01
V	0.57	4.33	2.87	3.43
$\bar{x}$	3.61	5.09	4.75	
N	75	266	69	

Information missing on seven cases.

achievement motivation with social class controlled. An analysis of variance of the data revealed that mother's age is significantly related to achievement motivation ($F = 5.56$, $P < .01$). The effects of social class are also significant ($F = 5.79$, $P < .01$): *within all mother's age groups* the boy's mean achievement motivation scores decline as the mother's status decreases, except for a slight increase from class I–II to class III. However, our hypothesis that the children of young mothers would have higher achievement motivation scores than those of older mothers was not confirmed. Disregarding social class, the relationship between mother's age and the boy's motivation is curvilinear: children of young mothers have the lowest mean scores (3.61), those of middle age mothers the highest (5.09), and the sons of old mothers the intermediate score (4.75). However, when social class is controlled the picture becomes quite confused. In class I–II, the achievement motivation scores of the boys increase as mother's age increases—just the opposite of what we had predicted. However, in class III, the reverse is true: the boys of younger mothers have higher scores than those of old mothers.

Some of this confusion is reduced when family size is introduced as a specifying variable. The data in Table 5 show the relationship of mother's

Table 5
Mean Achievement Motivation Scores by Mother's Age, Family Size and Social Class

MOTHER'S AGE	SOCIAL CLASS I–II–III Family Size			SOCIAL CLASS IV–V Family Size		
	Small	Medium	Large	Small	Medium	Large
Young	7.64	7.33	*	4.32	0.02	0.33
Middle	5.79	5.70	4.50	5.58	4.29	2.70
Old	5.86	7.60	5.33	3.81	3.53	2.36

* No cases.

age to son's achievement motivation when the variables of social class and family size are controlled. In small size families the sons of young mothers have higher mean scores than the sons of old mothers, but this relationship is reversed as the size of the family increases. In medium and large size families of both the middle and lower classes, the sons of old mothers have higher scores than the sons of young mothers. The effect of increased family size, however, is much greater in the lower than in the middle class and greatest of all upon the sons of young, lower class mothers. Thus, the mean scores of the sons of young, lower class mothers drop precipitately as the size of the family increases: from 4.23 in small families to 0.02 in medium size, and 0.33 in large families. The mean scores of the sons of older mothers also decline as family size increases, but the drop is more modest; i.e., small family 3.81, medium family 3.53, large family 2.36. Why should the motivation scores of sons of young mothers be so much more adversely affected by increased family size than are the scores of sons of older mothers? Perhaps because the children of a young mother with a large family are all young, so that the older children are not able to provide much help in taking care of younger siblings. In this case the young mother, particularly if she is lower class and unable to obtain help, may simply be overwhelmed. She will have little time or energy for the supervision and complex training in achievement that the development of achievement motivation requires.

The introduction of family size as a specifying variable requires a rephrasing of our original hypothesis about the relationship of mother's age to achievement motivation. Our prediction that the sons of young mothers would have higher motivation than the sons of old mothers is correct *but only when the family is small and primarily when the parents are middle class.* As the family increases in size, the motivation scores of children of older mothers are higher than the scores of children of younger mothers, and indeed in the lower class the sons of middle age mothers have the highest scores of all.

CONCLUSION

Perhaps the most important generalization to be drawn from this study is that it is exceedingly unwise to single out any one demographic factor as an explanation of achievement motivation. It is true that social class is consistently related to achievement motivation: the data show that the motivation scores of classes I–II–III boys are significantly higher than are the scores of boys from classes IV–V. Also, we have noted time and again that boys from small families tend to have higher achievement motivation than their peers from large families. But the effects of social class and family size, as well as the impact of birth order and mother's age, can only be properly understood in a large context in which all of these variables (and others, undoubtedly) interact.

For example, the impact of family size on the boy's achievement motivation varies with his social class. It was shown that while, in general, motivation scores decline as family size increases, the effect of family size on motivation scores is much greater at the upper-middle (class I–II) and lower class (class V) levels than at the lower-middle (class III) and upper-lower class (class IV) levels. Furthermore the effect of birth order is intimately related to family size and social class. Hence it is not very helpful in predicting an individual's achievement motivation to know his position in the birth order—indeed this information may be misleading rather than useful—unless the social class and size of his family of orientation are also known. In small middle class families, for example, the effect of ordinal position seems to be relatively unimportant: the oldest and youngest child in a two-child, middle class family have almost identical motivation scores, but *as the size of the family increases* the scores for the oldest child *in the middle class* become higher than those for the youngest child. However, *in the lower class* the reverse is true: the youngest child has a higher achievement motivation score on the average than the oldest child—a position that is maintained even when the size of the family increases. Similarly, the effect of mother's age upon the child's achievement motivation varies with the size of her family and social class. Thus the hypothesis that the sons of young mothers would have higher achievement motivation than the sons of old mothers proved to be correct, *but only when the family is small.* As the size of the family increases, *particularly in the lower class,* the scores of sons of young mothers drop rapidly and are surpassed by the scores of sons of middle age and old mothers.

These data, then, indicate that the demographic factors examined in this study have relevance for the development of achievement motivation, but their effects are complicated, interconnected, and interdependent upon one another, and difficult to assess individually.

Social Class and Parental Values[*][1]

MELVIN L. KOHN

In the paper below, the author's data show "that parents, whatever their social class, deem it very important indeed that their children be honest, happy, considerate, obedient, and dependable." But aside from the residue reflected by these virtues, middle- and working-class parents differ in that the former stress "internalized standards for governing one's relationships with other people" and the latter, "qualities of honesty and neatness." The evidence of Kohn's study clearly demonstrates the importance of social class stratification as a factor in the socialization process.

We undertake this inquiry into the relationship between social class and parental values in the hope that a fuller understanding of the ways in which parents of different social classes differ in their values may help us to understand why they differ in their practices.[2] This hope, of course, rests on two assumptions: that it is reasonable to conceive of social classes as subcultures

[1] Revision of paper presented at the annual meeting of the American Sociological Society, August, 1957. This is the first portion of a more general inquiry into the relationship of class and family directed by the author and John A. Clausen, with the collaboration and aid of Eleanor Carroll, Mary Freeman, Paul Hanlon, Alexander Shakow, and Eleanor Wolff.

[2] There now exists a rather substantial, if somewhat inconsistent, body of literature on the relationship of social class to the ways that parents raise their children. For a fine analytic summary see Urie Bronfenbrenner, "Socialization and Social Class through Time and Space," in Eleanor E. Maccoby *et al., Readings in Social Psychology* (New York: Henry Holt & Co.; new edition in press). Bronfenbrenner gives references to the major studies of class and child-rearing practices that have been done.

For the most relevant studies on class and *values* see Evelyn M. Duvall, "Conceptions of Parenthood," *American Journal of Sociology*, LII (November, 1946), 193–203; David F. Aberle and Kaspar D. Naegele, "Middle Class Fathers' Occupational Role and Attitudes toward Children," *American Journal of Orthopsychiatry*, XXII (April, 1952), 366–78; Herbert H. Hyman, "The Value Systems of Different Classes," in Reinhard Bendix and Seymour M. Lipset (eds.), *Class, Status, and Power* (Glencoe, Ill.: Free Press, 1953), pp. 426–42.

[*] From the *American Journal of Sociology*, LXIV (1959), pp. 337–351. Reprinted by permission of the author and the University of Chicago Press.

of the larger society, each with a relatively distinct value-orientation, and that values really affect behavior.

SAMPLE AND METHOD OF DATA COLLECTION

Washington, D.C.—the locus of this study—has a large proportion of people employed by government, relatively little heavy industry, few recent immigrants, a white working class drawn heavily from rural areas, and a large proportion of Negroes, particularly at lower economic levels. Generalizations based on this or any other sample of one city during one limited period of time are, of course, tentative.

Our intent in selecting the families to be studied was to secure approximately two hundred representative white working-class families and another two hundred representative white middle-class families, each family having a child within a narrowly delimited age range. We decided on fifth-grade children because we wanted to direct the interviews to relationships involving a child old enough to have a developed capacity for verbal communication.

The sampling procedure[3] involved two steps: the first, selection of census tracts. Tracts with 20 per cent or more Negro population were excluded, as were those in the highest quartile with respect to median income. From among the remaining tracts we then selected a small number representative of each of the three distinct types of residential area in which the population to be studied live: four tracts with a predominantly working-class population, four predominantly middle-class, and three having large proportions of each. The final selection of tracts was based on their occupational distribution and their median income, education, rent (of rented homes), and value (of owner-occupied homes). The second step in the sampling procedure involved selection of families. From records made available by the public and parochial school systems we compiled lists of all families with fifth-grade children who lived in the selected tracts. Two hundred families were then randomly selected from among those in which the father had a "white-collar" occupation and another two hundred from among those in which the father had a manual occupation.

In all four hundred families the mothers were to be interviewed. In every fourth family we scheduled interviews with the father and the fifth-grade child as well.[4] (When a broken family fell into this subsample, a substitute

[3] I owe a considerable debt of gratitude to Samuel W. Greenhouse, chief of the Section on Statistics and Mathematics, Biometrics Branch, NIMH, for his expert help in sample design, as well as for his advice on general statistical problems of the research.

[4] The interviewing staff was composed of Eleanor Carroll, Mary Freeman, Paul Hanlon, and Melvin Kohn. We were aided from time to time by three volunteers from the NIMH staff: Leila Deasy, Erwin Linn, and Harriet Murphy. Field work was conducted between March, 1956, and March, 1957.

We secured the co-operation of 86 per cent of the families where the mother alone

was chosen from our over-all sample, and the broken family was retained in the over-all sample of four hundred families.)

When interviews with both parents were scheduled, two members of the staff visited the home together—a male to interview the father, a female to interview the mother. The interviews were conducted independently, in separate rooms, but with essentially identical schedules. The first person to complete his interview with the parent interviewed the child.

INDEXES OF SOCIAL CLASS AND VALUES

Social Class. Each family's social-class position has been determined by the Hollingshead Index of Social Position, assigning the father's occupational status a relative weight of 7 and his educational status a weight of 4. We are considering Hollingshead's Classes I, II, and III to be "middle class," and Classes IV and V to be "working class." The middle-class sample is composed of two relatively distinct groups: Classes I and II are almost entirely professionals, proprietors, and managers with at least some college training. Class III is made up of small shopkeepers, clerks, and salespersons but includes a small number of foremen and skilled workers of unusually high educational status. The working-class sample is composed entirely of manual workers but preponderantly those of higher skill levels. These families are of the "stable working class" rather than "lower class" in the sense that the men have steady jobs, and their education, income, and skill levels are above those of the lowest socioeconomic strata.

Values. We shall use Kluckhohn's definition: "A value is a conception, explicit or implicit, distinctive of an individual or characteristic of a group, of the desirable which influences the selection from available modes, means, and ends of action."[5]

Our inquiry was limited to the values that parents would most like to see embodied in their children's behavior. We asked the parents to choose, from among several alternative characteristics that might be seen as desirable, those few which they considered *most* important for a child of the appropriate age. Specifically, we offered each parent a card listing 17 characteristics that had been suggested by other parents, in the pre-test interviews, as being highly desirable. (These appear down the left margin of Table 1. The order in which they were listed was varied from interview to interview.) Then we asked: "Which three of the things listed on this card would you say are the *most* important in a boy (or girl) of (fifth-grade

---

was to be interviewed and 82 per cent of the families where mother, father, and child were to be interviewed. Rates of non-response do not vary by social class, type of neighborhood, or type of school. This, of course, does not rule out other possible selective biases introduced by the non-respondents.

[5] Clyde Kluckhohn, "Values and Value Orientations," in Talcott Parsons and Edward A. Shils (eds.), *Toward a General Theory of Action* (Cambridge, Mass.: Harvard University Press, 1951), p. 395.

Table 1

Proportion of Mothers Who Select Each Characteristic as One of Three "Most Desirable" in a Ten- or Eleven-Year-old Child

CHARACTERISTICS	FOR BOYS		FOR GIRLS		COMBINED	
	Middle Class	Working Class	Middle Class	Working Class	Middle Class	Working Class
1. That he is honest	0.44	0.57	0.44	0.48	0.44	0.53
2. That he is happy	.44*	.27	.48	.45	.46*	.36
3. That he is considerate of others	.40	.30	.38*	.24	.39*	.27
4. That he obeys his parents well	.18*	.37	.23	.30	.20*	.33
5. That he is dependable	.27	.27	.20	.14	.24	.21
6. That he has good manners	.16	.17	.23	.32	.19	.24
7. That he has self-control	.24	.14	.20	.13	.22*	.13
8. That he is popular with other children	.13	.15	.17	.20	.15	.18
9. That he is a good student	.17	.23	.13	.11	.15	.17
10. That he is neat and clean	.07	.13	.15*	.28	.11*	.20
11. That he is curious about things	.20*	.06	.15	.07	.18*	.06
12. That he is ambitious	.09	.18	.06	.08	.07	.13
13. That he is able to defend himself	.13	.05	.06	.08	.10	.06
14. That he is affectionate	.03	.05	.07	.04	.05	.04
15. That he is liked by adults	.03	.05	.07	.04	.05	.04
16. That he is able to play by himself	.01	.02	.00	.03	.01	.02
17. That he acts in a serious way	0.00	0.01	0.00	0.00	0.00	0.01
N	90	85	84	80	174	165

* Social-class differences statistically significant, 0.05 level or better, using chi-squared test.

child's) age?" The selection of a particular characteristic was taken as our index of value.

Later in this report we shall subject this index to intensive scrutiny.

CLASS AND VALUES

Middle- and working-class mothers share a broadly common set of values—but not an identical set of values by any means (see Table 1). There is considerable agreement among mothers of both social classes that happiness and such standards of conduct as honesty, consideration, obedience, dependability, manners, and self-control are highly desirable for both boys and girls of this age.

Popularity, being a good student (especially for boys), neatness and cleanliness (especially for girls), and curiosity are next most likely to be regarded as desirable. Relatively few mothers choose ambition, ability to defend one's self, affectionate responsiveness, being liked by adults, ability to play by one's self, or seriousness as highly desirable for either boys or girls of this age. All of these, of course, might be more highly valued for children of other ages.

Although agreement obtains on this broad level, working-class mothers differ significantly[6] from middle-class mothers in the relative emphasis they place on particular characteristics. Significantly fewer working-class mothers regard happiness as highly desirable for *boys*. Although characteristics that define standards of conduct are valued by many mothers of both social classes, there are revealing differences of emphasis here too. Working-class mothers are more likely to value obedience; they would have their children be responsive to parental authority. Middle-class mothers are more likely to value both consideration and self-control; they would have their children develop inner control and sympathetic concern for other people. Furthermore, middle-class mothers are more likely to regard curiosity as a prime virtue. By contrast, working-class mothers put the emphasis on neatness and cleanliness, valuing the imaginative and exploring child relatively less than the presentable child.[7]

Middle-class mothers' conceptions of what is desirable for boys are much

[6] The criterion of statistical significance used throughout this paper is the 5 per cent level of probability, based, except where noted, on the chi-squared test.

[7] Compare these results with Bronfenbrenner's conclusion, based on an analysis of reports of studies of social class and child-rearing methods over the last twenty-five years: "In this modern working class world there may be greater freedom of emotional expression, but there is no laxity or vagueness with respect to goals of child training. Consistently over the past twenty-five years, the parent in this group has emphasized what are usually regarded as the traditional middle class virtues of cleanliness, conformity, and (parental) control, and although his methods are not so effective as those of his middle class neighbors, they are perhaps more desperate" (*op. cit.*).

Table 2
Proportion of Fathers Who Select Each Characteristic as One of Three "Most Desirable" in a Ten- or Eleven-Year-Old Child

CHARACTERISTICS	FOR BOYS		FOR GIRLS		COMBINED	
	Middle Class	Working Class	Middle Class	Working Class	Middle Class	Working Class
1. That he is honest	0.60	0.60	0.43	0.55	0.52	0.58
2. That he is happy	.48	.24	.24	.18	.37	.22
3. That he is considerate of others	.32	.16	.38	.09	.35*	.14
4. That he obeys his parents well	.12*	.40	.14	.36	.13*	.39
5. That he is dependable	.36*	.12	.29*	.00	.33*	.08
6. That he has good manners	.24	.28	.24	.18	.24	.25
7. That he has self-control	.20	.08	.19	.00	.20*	.06
8. That he is popular with other children	.08	.16	.24	.45	.15	.25
9. That he is a good student	.04	.12	.10	.36	.07	.19
10. That he is neat and clean	.16	.20	.14	.09	.15	.17
11. That he is curious about things	.16	.12	.10	.00	.13	.08
12. That he is ambitious	.20	.12	.14	.00	.17	.08
13. That he is able to defend himself	.04	.16	.00*	.18	.02*	.17
14. That he is affectionate	.00	.04	.05	.18	.02	.08
15. That he is liked by adults	.00	.08	.00	.09	.00	.08
16. That he is able to play by himself	.00	.08	.05	.00	.02	.06
17. That he acts in a serious way	0.00	0.04	0.00	0.00	0.00	0.03
N	25	25	21	11	46	36

* Social-class differences statistically significant, 0.05 level or better, using chi-squared test.

192

the same as their conceptions of what is desirable for girls. But working-class mothers make a clear distinction between the sexes: they are more likely to regard dependability, being a good student, and ambition as desirable for boys and to regard happiness, good manners, neatness, and cleanliness as desirable for girls.

What of the *fathers'* values? Judging from our subsample of 82 fathers, their values are similar to those of the mothers (see Table 2). Essentially the same rank-order of choices holds for fathers as for mothers, with one major exception: fathers are not so likely to value happiness for their daughters. Among fathers as well as mothers, consideration and self-control are more likely to be regarded as desirable by the middle class; middle-class fathers are also more likely to value another standard of conduct—dependability. Working-class fathers, like their wives, are more likely to value obedience; they are also more likely to regard it as desirable that their children be able to defend themselves.[8]

We take this to indicate that middle-class parents (fathers as well as mothers) are more likely to ascribe predominant importance to the child's acting on the basis of internal standards of conduct, working-class parents to the child's compliance with parental authority.

There are important differences between middle- and working-class parents, too, in the way in which their choice of any one characteristic is related to their choice of each of the others.[9]

[8] A comparison of the values of the fathers in this subsample with those of the mothers in this same subsample yields essentially the same conclusions.

We do not find that fathers of either social class are significantly more likely to choose any characteristic for boys than they are to choose it for girls, or the reverse. But this may well be an artifact of the small number of fathers in our sample; Aberle and Naegele (*op. cit.*) have found that middle-class fathers are more likely to value such characteristics as responsibility, initiative, good school performance, ability to stand up for one's self, and athletic ability for boys and being "nice," "sweet," pretty, affectionate, and well-liked for girls.

[9] A logical procedure for examining these patterns of choice is to compare the proportions of parents who choose any given characteristic, B, among those who do and who do not choose another characteristic, A. But since a parent who selects characteristic A has exhausted one of his three choices, the a priori probability of his selecting any other characteristic is only two-thirds as great as the probability that a parent who has not chosen A will do so. (A straightforward application of probability considerations to the problem of selecting three things from seventeen when one is interested only in the joint occurrence of two, say, A and B, shows that we can expect B to occur 2/16 of the time among those selections containing A and 3/16 of the time among those not containing A.) This, however, can be taken into account by computing the ratio of the two proportions: p_1, the proportion of parents who choose B among those who choose A, and p_2, the proportion who choose B among those who do *not* choose A. If the ratio of these proportions (p_1/p_2) is significantly larger than two-thirds, the two are positively related; if significantly smaller, they are negatively related.

[Ed.] For a discussion of the test of significance and the logic of the testing procedure, the reader must consult the original publication (M. L. Kohn, "Social Class and Parental Values," *Amer. J. Sociol.*, LXIV [1959], pp. 337–351).

We have already seen that parents of both social classes are very likely to accord *honesty* first-rank importance. But the choice of honesty is quite differently related to the choice of other characteristics in the two classes (see Table 3). Middle-class mothers[10] who choose honesty are more likely than are other middle-class mothers to regard consideration, manners, and (for boys) dependability as highly desirable; and those mothers who regard any of these as desirable are more likely to value honesty highly. Consideration, in turn, is positively related to self-control, and manners to neatness. Honesty, then, is the core of a set of standards of conduct, a set consisting primarily of honesty, consideration, manners, and dependability, together with self-control and neatness. As such, it is to be seen as one among several, albeit the central, standards of conduct that middle-class mothers want their children to adopt.

This is not the case for working-class mothers. Those who regard honesty as predominantly important are not especially likely to think of consideration, manners, or dependability as comparable in importance; nor are those who value any of these especially likely to value honesty. Instead the mothers who are most likely to attribute importance to honesty are those who are concerned that the child be happy, popular, and able to defend himself. It is not that the child should conduct himself in a considerate, mannerly, or dependable fashion but that he should *be* happy, *be* esteemed by his peers, and, if the necessity arise, *be* able to protect himself. It suggests that honesty is treated less as a standard of conduct and more as a quality of the person; the emphasis is on being a person of inherent honesty rather than on acting in an honest way.

Note especially the relationship of popularity to honesty. For middle-class mothers these are *negatively* related. To value honesty is to forego valuing popularity; to value popularity is to forego valuing honesty. One must choose between honesty "at the risk of offending" and popularity at the sacrifice of absolute honesty. The exact opposite obtains for working-class mothers: those who accord high valuation to either are *more* likely to value the other. The very mothers who deem it most important that their children enjoy popularity are those who attribute great importance to honesty. Honesty does not interfere with popularity; on the contrary, it enhances the probability that one will enjoy the respect of one's peers.

However, working-class mothers who value obedience, manners, or consideration are distinctly unlikely to value popularity, and vice versa. They

[10] This analysis and those to follow will be limited to the mothers, since the sample of fathers is small. For simplicity, we shall present data separately for boys and for girls only where the relationship under discussion appears to differ for the two sexes considered separately.

do see each of these standards of conduct as inconsistent with popularity.[11] This further substantiates the view that working-class mothers are more likely to view honesty as a quality of the person, a desideratum of moral worth, rather than as one among several highly valued standards of conduct.

Happiness, in distinction to honesty, implies neither constraints upon action nor a moral quality; rather, it indicates a desired goal, achievable in several different ways. One way of specifying what is implied when happiness is regarded as a major value is to ascertain the other values most likely to be related to the choice of happiness.

The two choices positively related to the choice of happiness by middle-class mothers are curiosity and (for boys) ambition. Those middle-class mothers who deem it exceedingly important that their children aspire for knowledge or success are even more likely than are middle-class mothers in general to value their children's happiness highly.

Working-class mothers who value these, however, are no more likely to value happiness. Instead, curiosity is related to consideration, to the child's concern for others' well-being, and ambition to dependability, to his being the type of person who can be counted on. The values that are positively related to happiness by working-class mothers are honesty, consideration (for boys), and popularity (for girls). Not aspirations for knowledge or for success, but being an honest—a worthy—person; not the desire to outdistance others, but, for boys, concern for others' well-being and, for girls, enjoyment of the respect and confidence of peers: these are the conceptions of the desirable that accompany working-class mothers' wishes that their children be happy.

Still the perhaps equally important fact is that no choice, by mothers of either social class, is negatively related to the choice of happiness.

The final bit of information that these data provide concerns the conception of *obedience* entertained in the two classes. Middle-class mothers who value curiosity are unlikely to value obedience; those who value obedience are unlikely to value consideration. For middle-class mothers, but not for working-class mothers, obedience would appear to have a rather narrow connotation; it seems to approximate blind obedience.

---

[11] It may be that these three characteristics have more in common than that they are all standards of conduct. The fact that working-class mothers who value consideration for their *daughters* are especially likely to value manners, and the converse, suggests the possibility that consideration may be seen as a near-equivalent to manners by at least a sizable portion of working-class mothers. If so, all three values negatively related to popularity can be viewed as reflecting close conformance to directives from parents—as contrasted to directives from within. (Note, in this connection, that working-class mothers who would have their daughters be mannerly are distinctly unlikely to deem it important that they be dependable.)

Table 3
All Cases* Where Mothers' Choice of One Characteristic as "Desirable" Is Significantly Related to Their Choice of Any Other Characteristic as "Desirable"

MIDDLE-CLASS MOTHERS

		PROPORTION WHO CHOOSE B AMONG THOSE WHO:		
		Do Not		
CHARACTERISTIC		Choose A	Choose A	
A	B	(p_1)	(p_2)	p_1/p_2
Positive relationships:				
1. Honesty	Consideration	0.42	0.37	1.14
2. Honesty	Manners	.22	.16	1.38
3. Honesty	Dependability (boys)	.33	.22	1.50
4. Consideration	Honesty	.47	.42	1.12
5. Manners	Honesty	.52	.43	1.21
6. Dependability	Honesty (boys)	.54	.41	1.32
7. Consideration	Self-control	.24	.22	1.09
8. Self-control	Consideration	.41	.39	1.05
9. Manners	Neatness	.24	.08	3.00
10. Neatness	Manners	.42	.16	2.63
11. Curiosity	Happiness	.58	.43	1.35
12. Happiness	Curiosity	.23	.14	1.64
13. Happiness	Ambition (boys)	.13	.06	2.17
Negative relationships:				
1. Honesty	Popularity	.04	.24	0.17
2. Popularity	Honesty	.12	.50	0.24
3. Curiosity	Obedience	.03	.24	0.13
4. Obedience	Consideration	0.17	0.45	0.38

WORKING-CLASS MOTHERS

A	B	(p_1)	(p_2)	p_1/p_2
Positive relationships:				
1. Happiness	Honesty	0.51	0.55	0.93
2. Popularity	Honesty	.62	.51	1.22
3. Honesty	Popularity	.20	.14	1.43
4. Honesty	Defend self	.07	.05	1.40
5. Consideration	Manners (girls)	.42	.30	1.40
6. Manners	Consideration (girls)	.31	.20	1.55
7. Consideration	Curiosity	.11	.04	2.75
8. Ambition	Dependability	.29	.19	1.53
9. Happiness	Consideration (boys)	.35	.27	1.30
10. Consideration	Happiness (boys)	.32	.25	1.28
11. Happiness	Popularity (girls)	.25	.16	1.56

Table 3 (Cont.)

WORKING-CLASS MOTHERS

CHARACTERISTIC		PROPORTION WHO CHOOSE B AMONG THOSE WHO:		
			Do Not	
		Choose A	Choose A	
A	B	(p_1)	(p_2)	p_1/p_2
Negative relationships:				
1. Obedience	Popularity	.05	.24	0.21
2. Manners	Popularity	.00	.23	0.00
3. Consideration	Popularity	.02	.23	0.09
4. Popularity	Obedience	.10	.38	0.26
5. Popularity	Manners	.00	.29	0.00
6. Popularity	Consideration	.03	.32	0.09
7. Manners	Dependability (girls)	0.00	0.20	0.00

* Where it is not specified whether relationship holds for boys or girls, it holds for both sexes. In all the relationships shown, p_1 and p_2 are each based on a minimum of 20 cases.

Table 4

Mothers' Socioeconomic Status and Their Choice of Characteristics as "Most Desirable" in a Ten- or Eleven-Year-Old Child

CHARACTERISTIC	PROPORTION WHO SELECT EACH CHARACTERISTIC SOCIOECONOMIC STRATUM (ON HOLLINGSHEAD INDEX)				
	I	II	III	IV	V
Obedience	0.14	0.19	0.25	0.35	0.27
Neatness, cleanliness	.06	.07	.16	.18	.27
Consideration	.41	.37	.39	.25	.32
Curiosity	.37	.12	.09	.07	.03
Self-control	.24	.30	.18	.13	.14
Happiness	.61	.40	.40	.38	.30
Boys	.48		.40	.27	
Girls	.54		.40	.45	
Honesty	0.37	0.49	0.46	0.50	0.65
N	51	43	80	128	37

CLASS, SUBCULTURE, AND VALUES

In discussing the relationship of social class to values we have talked as if American society were composed of two relatively homogeneous groups, manual and white-collar workers, together with their families. Yet it is likely that there is considerable variation in values, associated with other bases of social differentiation, *within* each class. If so, it should be possible to divide the classes into subgroups in such a way as to specify more precisely the relationship of social class to values.

Consider, first, the use we have made of the concept "social class." Are the differences we have found between the values of middle- and working-class mothers a product of this dichotomy alone, or do values parallel status gradations more generally? It is possible to arrive at an approximate answer by dividing the mothers into the five socioeconomic strata delineated by the Hollingshead Index (see Table 4). An examination of the choices made by mothers in each stratum indicates that variation in values parallels socioeconomic status rather closely:

a) The higher a mother's status, the higher the probability that she will choose consideration, curiosity, self-control, and (for boys)[12] happiness as highly desirable; curiosity is particularly likely to be chosen by mothers in the highest stratum.

b) The lower her status, the higher the probability that she will select obedience, neatness, and cleanliness; it appears, too, that mothers in the lowest stratum are more likely than are those in the highest to value *honesty*.

Mothers' values also are directly related to their own occupational positions and educational attainments, independently of their families' class status. (The family's class status has been indexed on the basis of the husband's occupation and education.) It happens that a considerable proportion of the mothers we have classified as working class hold white-collar

Table 5
Working-Class Mothers' Own Occupations and Their Choice of Characteristics as "Most Desirable" in a Ten- or Eleven-Year-Old Child

	PROPORTION WHO SELECT EACH CHARACTERISTIC		
	White Collar Job	*No Job*	*Manual Job*
CHARACTERISTIC			
Obedience	.26	.35	.53
Neatness, cleanliness	.16	.18	.42
Consideration	.39	.21	.05
Curiosity	.10	.04	.00
Self-control	.13	.14	.11
Happiness	.33	.40	.26
Boys	.32	.21	..
Girls	.36	.59	..
N	69	77	19

[12] The choice of happiness is, as we have seen, related to social class for boys only. Consequently, in each comparison we shall make in this section the choice of happiness for *girls* will prove to be an exception to the general order.

jobs.[13] Those who do are, by and large, closer to middle-class mothers in their values than are other working-class mothers (see Table 5). But those who hold manual jobs are even further from middle-class mothers in their values than are working-class mothers who do not have jobs outside the home.

So, too, for mothers' educational attainments: a middle-class mother of *relatively* low educational attainment (one who has gone no further than graduation from high school) is less likely to value curiosity and more likely to value (for girls) neatness and cleanliness (see Table 6). A working-class

Table 6
Mothers' Education and Their Choice of Characteristics as "Most Desirable" in a Ten- or Eleven-Year-Old Child

MIDDLE-CLASS MOTHERS

PROPORTION WHO SELECT EACH CHARACTERISTIC

	Male Child		Female Child	
	At Least Some College	High-School Graduate or Less	At Least Some College	High-School Graduate or Less
CHARACTERISTIC				
Obedience	0.11	0.22	0.13	0.29
Neatness, cleanliness	.03	.09	.03*	.23
Consideration	.47	.35	.41	.37
Curiosity	.31*	.13	.31*	.06
Self-control	.33	.19	.19	.21
Happiness	0.50	0.41	0.59	0.40
N	36	54	32	52

WORKING-CLASS MOTHERS

PROPORTION WHO SELECT EACH CHARACTERISTIC

	Male Child		Female Child	
	At Least High-School Graduate	Less than High-School Graduate	At Least High-School Graduate	Less than High-School Graduate
CHARACTERISTIC				
Obedience	0.29	0.43	0.28	0.32
Neatness, cleanliness	.12	.14	.21	.35
Consideration	.32	.27	.33*	.14
Curiosity	.07	.05	.12*	.00
Self-control	.22*	.07	.16	.08
Happiness	0.27	0.27	0.47	0.43
N	41	44	43	37

* Difference between mothers of differing educational status statistically significant, 0.05 level or better, using chi-squared test.

[13] No middle-class mothers have manual jobs, so the comparable situation does not exist. Those middle-class women who do work (at white-collar jobs) are less likely to value neatness and cleanliness and more likely to value obedience and curiosity.

mother of *relatively* high educational attainment (one who has at least graduated from high school) is more likely to value self-control for boys and both consideration and curiosity for girls. The largest differences obtain between those middle-class mothers of highest educational attainments and those working-class mothers of lowest educational attainments.

Even when we restrict ourselves to considerations of social status and its various ramifications, we find that values vary appreciably within each of the two broad classes. And, as sociologists would expect, variation in values proceeds along other major lines of social demarcation as well. Religious background is particularly useful as a criterion for distinguishing sub-cultures within the social classes. It does *not* exert so powerful an effect that Protestant mothers differ significantly from Catholic mothers of the same social class in their values.[14] But the combination of class and religious background does enable us to isolate groups that are more homogeneous in their values than are the social classes *in toto*. We find that there is an ordering, consistent for all class-related values, proceeding from middle-class Protestant mothers, to middle-class Catholic, to working-class Protestant, to working-class Catholic (see Table 7). Middle-class Protestants and work-

Table 7
Mothers' Religious Background and Their Choice of Characteristics as "Most Desirable" in a Ten- or Eleven-Year-Old Child

PROPORTION WHO SELECT EACH CHARACTERISTIC

CHARACTERISTIC	Middle-Class Protestant	Middle-Class Catholic	Working-Class Protestant	Working-Class Catholic
Obedience	0.17	0.25	0.33	0.36
Neatness, cleanliness	.08	.15	.17	.27
Consideration	.36	.38	.26	.29
Curiosity	.24	.12	.07	.05
Self-control	.28	.15	.15	.09
Happiness	.47	.42	.38	.30
Boys	.48	.32	.35	.13
Girls	0.45	0.52	0.42	0.54
N	88	52	107	56

[14] The index here is based on the question "May I ask what is your religious background?"

Even when the comparison is restricted to Catholic mothers who send their children to Catholic school versus Protestant mothers of the same social class, there are no significant differences in values.

Jewish mothers (almost all of them in this sample are middle class) are very similar to middle-class Protestant mothers in their values, with two notable exceptions. More Jewish than Protestant mothers select popularity and ability to defend one's self—two values that are not related to social class.

ing-class Catholics constitute the two extremes whose values are most dissimilar.

Another relevant line of social demarcation is the distinction between urban and rural background.[15] As we did for religious background, we can arrange the mothers into four groups delineated on the basis of class and rural-urban background in an order that is reasonably consistent for all class-related values. The order is: middle-class urban, middle-class rural, working-class urban, working-class rural (see Table 8). The extremes are middle-class mothers raised in the city and working-class mothers raised on farms.

Table 8
Rural versus Urban Background of Mothers and Their Choice of Characteristics as "Most Desirable" in a Ten- or Eleven-Year-Old Child

PROPORTION WHO SELECT EACH CHARACTERISTIC

CHARACTERISTIC	Middle-Class Urban	Middle-Class Rural	Working-Class Urban	Working-Class Rural
Obedience	0.19	0.24	0.29	0.42
Neatness, cleanliness	.11	.12	.17	.25
Consideration	.42	.27	.31	.18
Curiosity	.19	.12	.07	.04
Self-control	.20	.33	.15	.11
Happiness	.47	.42	.41	.25
Boys	.44	.47	.28	.25
Girls	0.50	0.37	0.57	0.26
N	141	33	110	55

Several other variables fail to differentiate mothers of the same social class into groups having appreciably different values. These include the mother's age, the size of the family, the ordinal position of the child in the family, the length of time the family has lived in the neighborhood, whether or not the mother has been socially mobile (from the status of her childhood family), and her class identification. Nor are these results a function of the large proportion of families of government workers included in the sample: wives of government employees do not differ from other mothers of the same social class in their values.

[15] We asked: "Have you ever lived on a farm?" and then classified all mothers who had lived on a farm for some time other than simply summer vacations, prior to age fifteen, as having had a rural background.

Ordinarily, one further line of cultural demarcation would be considered at this point—nationality background. The present sample, however, is composed predominantly of parents who are at least second-generation, United States-born, so this is not possible.

In sum, we find that it is possible to specify the relationship between so-cial class and values more precisely by dividing the social classes into sub-groups on the basis of other lines of social demarcation—but that social class seems to provide the single most relevant line of demarcation.

ADEQUACY OF INDEX OF VALUES

The form in which our major question was asked enabled us to set the same ground rules for all parents. No premium was put on imaginativeness or articulateness. But the fact that we limited their choice to these particular characteristics means that we denied them the opportunity to select others that they might have regarded as even more desirable. However, we had *previously* asked each parent: "When you think of a boy (or girl) of (child's) age, are there *any* things you look for as most important or most desirable?" Only three additional characteristics were suggested by any ap-preciable number of parents. The first, suggested by a significantly larger proportion of middle- than of working-class parents, was "self-reliance" or "independence"—a result entirely consistent with the rest of this study. The second, variously labeled "friendliness," "co-operativeness," or "ability to get along well with others" was also predominantly a middle-class concern. It indicates that we may have underrepresented the proportion of middle-class parents who value their children's ability to relate to others. Finally, several parents (of both social classes) said that they considered it desirable that the child not "act too old," "too young," or be effeminate (in a boy) or masculine (in a girl). There seems to be a certain concern, not ade-quately indexed by our major question, that the child conform to his parents' conception of what constitutes the proper age and sex role.

Of course, parents might have selected other characteristics as well, had we suggested them. These possible limitations notwithstanding, it appears that the index is reasonably comprehensive.

More important than the question of comprehensiveness is whether or not it is really possible for parents to select characteristics as desirable in-dependently of the way that they rate their own children's behavior. Since each parent was later asked to rate his child's performance with respect to each characteristic, we can compare the ratings given by parents who chose a characteristic with those given by parents of the same social class who did not. Parents who chose each characteristic were no more and no less likely to describe their children as excelling in that characteristic; nor were they any more or less likely than other parents to feel that their children were deficient. The parents have not imputed desirability to the characteris-tics that they feel represent their children's virtues or their children's de-ficiencies.

The final and most important question: Is it wise to accept someone's assertion that something is a value to him? After all, assertions are subject to distortion.[16] To the degree that we can ascertain that parents act in reasonable conformity to the values they assert, however, we gain confidence in an index based on assertions.

This study does not provide disinterested observations of the parents' behavior. Our closest approximation derives from interviews with the parents themselves—interviews in which we questioned them in considerable detail about their relevant actions. Perhaps the most crucial of these data are those bearing on their actions in situations where their children behave in *disvalued* ways. We have, for example, questioned parents in some detail about what they do when their children lose their tempers. We began by asking whether or not the child in question "ever really loses his temper." From those parents who said that the child does lose his temper, we then proceeded to find out precisely what behavior they consider to be "loss of temper"; what they "generally do when he acts this way"; whether they "ever find it necessary to do anything else"; if so, what else they do, and "under what circumstances." Our concern here is with what the parent reports he does as a matter of last resort.[17]

Mothers who regard *self-control* as an important value are more likely to report that they punish the child—be it physically, by isolation, or by restriction of activities; they are unlikely merely to scold or to ignore his loss of temper altogether (see Table 9).

To punish a child who has lost his temper may not be a particularly effective way of inducing self-control. One might even have predicted that mothers who value self-control would be less likely to punish breaches of control, more likely to explain, even ignore. They do not, however, and we must put the issue more simply: mothers who assert the value are more likely to report that they apply negative sanctions in situations where the child violates that value. This response would certainly seem to conform to their value-assertion.

A parallel series of questions deals with the mother's reactions when her child "refuses to do what she tells him to do." Mothers who assert that they regard *obedience* as important are more likely to report that they punish

---

[16] But inferring values from observed behavior may not be satisfactory either, for we cannot be certain that we are correctly distinguishing the normative from other components of action. As Robin Williams states: "No student of human conduct can accept uncritically, as final evidence, people's testimony as to their own values. Yet actions may deceive as well as words, and there seems no reason for always giving one precedence over the other" (*American Society: A Sociological Interpretation* [New York: Alfred A. Knopf, 1951], p. 378).

[17] This comparison and those to follow are limited to parents who say that the child does in fact behave in the disvalued way, at least on occasion. (Approximately equal proportions of middle- and working-class mothers report that their children do behave in each of these ways.)

Table 9
Choice of "Self-control" as "Most Desirable" Characteristic and Most Extreme Actions That Mothers Report They Take When Their Children Lose Their Tempers

PROPORTION

	Middle Class		Working Class		Both	
	Choose Self-control	Don't Choose Self-control	Choose Self-control	Don't Choose Self-control	Choose Self-control	Don't Choose Self-control
Punish physically	0.26	0.20	0.44	0.26	0.32	0.23
Isolate	.20	.11	.11	.12	.17	.11
Restrict activities, other punishments	.06	.05	.17	.14	.10	.10
Threaten punishment	.06	.03	.00	.02	.04	.02
Scold, admonish, etc.	.31	.40	.17	.31	.26	.36
Ignore	0.11	0.21	0.11	0.15	0.11	0.18
	1.00	1.00	1.00	1.00	1.00	1.00
N	35	113	18	113	53	226

in one way or another when their children refuse.[18] There is also evidence that mothers who value *consideration* are more likely to respond to their children's "fighting with other children," an action that need not necessarily be seen as inconsistent with consideration, by punishing them, or at least by separating them from the others.[19]

In all three instances, then, the reports on parental reactions to behavior that seem to violate the value in question indicate that mothers who profess high regard for the value are more likely to apply negative sanctions.

[18] The figures are 47 versus 29 per cent for middle-class mothers; 36 versus 18 per cent for working-class mothers.

[19] The figures are 42 versus 29 per cent for middle-class mothers; 61 versus 37 per cent for working-class mothers.

There is also some indication that *working-class* mothers who value *honesty* have been more prone to insist that their children make restitution when they have "swiped" something, but the number of mothers who say that their children have never swiped something is too small for this evidence to be conclusive. (The figures for working-class mothers are 63 versus 35 per cent; for middle-class mothers, 38 versus 33 per cent.)

The interviews with the children provide further evidence that parents have acted consistently with their values—for example, children whose mothers assert high valuation of dependability are more likely to tell us that the reason their parents want them to do their chores is to train them in responsibility (not to relieve the parents of work).

INTERPRETATION

Our first conclusion is that parents, whatever their social class, deem it very important indeed that their children be honest, happy, considerate, obedient, and dependable.

The second conclusion is that, whatever the reasons may be, parents' values are related to their social position, particularly their class position.

There still remains, however, the task of interpreting the relationship between parents' social position and their values. In particular: What underlies the differences between the values of middle- and of working-class parents?

One relevant consideration is that some parents may "take for granted" values that others hold dear. For example, middle-class parents may take "neatness and cleanliness" for granted, while working-class parents regard it as highly desirable. But what does it mean to say that middle-class parents take neatness and cleanliness for granted? In essence, the argument is that middle-class parents value neatness and cleanliness as greatly as do working-class parents but not so greatly as they value such things as happiness and self-control. If this be the case, it can only mean that in the circumstances of middle-class life neatness and cleanliness are easily enough attained to be of less immediate concern than are these other values.

A second consideration lies in the probability that these value-concepts have differing meanings for parents of different cultural backgrounds. For example, one might argue that honesty is a central standard of conduct for middle-class parents because they see honesty as meaning truthfulness; and that it is more a quality of the person for working-class parents because they see it as meaning trustworthiness. Perhaps so; but to suggest that a difference in meaning underlies a difference in values raises the further problem of explaining this difference in meaning.

It would be reasonable for working-class parents to be more likely to see honesty as trustworthiness. The working-class situation is one of less material security and less assured protection from the dishonesty of others. For these reasons, trustworthiness is more at issue for working-class than for middle-class parents.

Both considerations lead us to view differences in the values of middle- and working-class parents in terms of their differing circumstances of life and, by implication, their conceptions of the effects that these circumstances may have on their children's future lives. We believe that parents are most likely to accord high priority to those values that seem both *problematic,* in the sense that they are difficult of achievement, and *important,* in the sense that failure to achieve them would affect the child's future adversely. From this perspective it is reasonable that working-class parents cannot afford to take neatness and cleanliness as much for granted as can middle-class parents. It is reasonable, too, that working-class parents are more likely to see honesty as implying trustworthiness and that this connotation of honesty is seen as problematic.

These characteristics—honesty and neatness—are important to the child's future precisely because they assure him a respectable social position. Just as "poor but honest" has traditionally been an important line of social demarcation, their high valuation of these qualities may express working-class parents' concern that their children occupy a position unequivocally above that of persons who are not neat or who are not scrupulously honest. These are the qualities of respectable, worthwhile people.

So, too, is obedience. The obedient child follows his parents' dictates rather than his own standards. He acts, in his subordinate role as a child, in conformity with the prescriptions of established authority.

Even in the way they differentiate what is desirable for boys from what is desirable for girls, working-class mothers show a keen appreciation of the qualities making for respectable social position.

The characteristics that middle-class parents are more likely to value for their children are internal standards for governing one's relationships with other people and, in the final analysis, with one's self. It is not that middle-class parents are less concerned than are working-class parents about social position. The qualities of person that assure respectability may be taken for granted, but in a world where social relationships are determinative of position, these standards of conduct are both more problematic and more important.

The middle-class emphasis on internal standards is evident in their choice of the cluster of characteristics centering around honesty; in their being less likely than are working-class parents to value obedience and more likely to value self-control and consideration; and in their seeing obedience as inconsistent with both consideration and curiosity. The child is to act appropriately, not because his parents tell him to, but because he wants to. Not conformity to authority, but inner control; not because you're told to but because you take the other person into consideration—these are the middle-class ideals.

These values place responsibility directly upon the individual. He cannot rely upon authority, nor can he simply conform to what is presented to him as proper. He should be impelled to come to his own understanding of the situation.[20] He is to govern himself in such a way as to be able to act

[20] Curiosity provides a particularly interesting example of how closely parents' values are related to their circumstances of life and expectations: the proportion of mothers who value curiosity rises very slowly from status level to status level until we reach the wives of professionals and the more highly educated businessmen; then it jumps suddenly (see Table 4). The value is given priority in precisely that portion of the middle class where it is most appropriate and where its importance for the child's future is most apparent.

consistently with his principles. The basic importance of relationship to self is explicit in the concept of self control. It is implicit, too, in consideration—a standard that demands of the individual that he respond sympathetically to others' needs even if they be in conflict with his own; and in the high valuation of honesty as central to other standards of conduct: "to thine own self be true."

Perhaps, considering this, it should not be surprising that so many middle-class mothers attribute first-rank importance to happiness, even for boys. We cannot assume that their children's happiness is any less important to working-class mothers than it is to middle-class mothers; in fact, working-class mothers are equally likely to value happiness for *girls*. For their sons, however, happiness is second choice to honesty and obedience. Apparently, middle-class mothers can afford instead to be concerned about their sons' happiness. And perhaps they are right in being concerned. We have noted that those middle-class mothers who deem it most important that their sons outdistance others are especially likely to be concerned about their sons' happiness; and even those mothers who do not are asking their children to accept considerable responsibility.

Some Characteristics of High School Pupils from Three Income Groups*

JOHN K. COSTER

The attainment of free secondary education for all citizens during the past century is one of the great cultural triumphs of this country. Even so, equality in educational experiences appears to lag behind equality in educational opportunities. As Coster indicates below, high school pupils from families representing higher socioeconomic status are more likely than those from middle- and lower-status homes to participate in extracurricular activities, hold an office in an organization, get high marks in school, be named to the school honor roll, complete their courses, and continue their education. There are signs, moreover, that low income pupils accept their lot in "a state of resignation."

In a recent study, a sample of 878 high school pupils was divided into three income groups, and responses to 27 items reflecting attitudes toward high school were analyzed to ascertain variations among income groups. The attitudinal items pertained to such objects as school, teachers, school program, other pupils, and the value of education. The groups varied significantly on only eight of the 27 items. Greatest variations generally were noted on items dealing with interpersonal relationships (e.g., Do you feel that the other students like you?). There was little or no variation in responses to items which suggested an appraisal of the school or school program, such as the number of school subjects and activities offered in the school, the grading system, the administration of the school, the method of teaching, and school equipment and facilities.

After the forementioned study was completed, an analysis was made of other available data from the same sample to compare the three income groups on several items of personal information—such as sex, schooling of

---

* From the *Journal of Educational Psychology*, L (1959), pp. 55–62. Reprinted by permission of the author and the American Psychological Association.

parents, and participation in school and community activities. The purposes of the second analysis were to identify the characteristics on which pupils in the three groups differed significantly, and to compare affective behavior (denoted by responses to attitudinal items) with factual descriptions of the Ss.

Several studies of the characteristics of pupils of diverse socioeconomic groups have been reported in the literature. Hollingshead,[1] for example, found that adolescents in the middle- and lower-upper social classes were more likely to attend athletic events, school dances, evening plays and parties, and participate in extracurricular activities than adolescents in lower classes. Smith[2] reported a high degree of relationship between participation in extracurricular activities and Sims Socio-Economic scale scores. In a study of junior high school pupils, Abrahamson[3] found that middle-class pupils participated in more extracurricular activities, received more scholarship awards, scored higher on social acceptance scales, held more student offices, and participated more frequently in student government, proportionately, than pupils in lower social classes.

An investigation of factors related to social acceptance of pupils living in a small community, the population of which was expanded and changed radically when a war industry was located in the area, was conducted by Morgan.[4] His findings disclosed that the social position of pupils was stabilized rapidly, and that father's income and parents' education were the two most pertinent factors bearing on social acceptance and reputation. Keisler[5] examined the relationship between parental occupation and membership in YMCA and YWCA sponsored clubs, and reported that occupation of parents, grade point average, and scholastic aptitude were related significantly to membership in these clubs.

PROCEDURE

A questionnaire, containing 27 attitudinal items and a number of personal information items, was administered to approximately 3000 pupils in nine Indiana high schools.[6] A sample of 878 cases was selected from the

[1] A. B. Hollingshead, *Elmtown's Youth* (New York: John Wiley, 1949).

[2] P. Smith, "A Study of the Selective Character of American Education: Participation in School Activities as Conditioned by Socio-economic Status and Other Factors," *J. Educ. Psychol.*, XXXVI (1945), pp. 229–246.

[3] A. Abrahamson, "Our Status System and Scholastic Rewards," *J. Educ. Sociol.*, XXV (1952), pp. 441–450.

[4] H. G. Morgan, "Social Relationships of Children in a War-boom Community," *J. Educ. Res.*, XL (1946), pp. 271–286.

[5] E. R. Keisler, "Differences among Adolescent Social Clubs in Terms of Members' Characteristics," *J. Educ. Res.*, XLVIII (1954), pp. 297–303.

[6] J. K. Coster, "Factors Related to Morale in Secondary Schools," (unpublished Doctoral dissertation, Yale Univer., 1955).

returns. The sample included 100 questionnaires, selected randomly, from each of six larger schools, and all usable questionnaires from three smaller schools.

The personal information items included a "House and Home" scale, designed to yield an indication of income level. This scale has been used extensively by Remmers and others in the Purdue Opinion Panel studies to divide pupils into income groups.[7] Remmers and Kirk[8] and Elias[9] have reported on the validity of the scale. The scale consisted of seven items found in the home or provided for the pupil.[10] Based on the number of items checked by each respondent, Ss were divided into high (five to seven items checked), middle (three or four items), and low (zero to two items) income groups. The number and percentage of pupils in each income group are shown in Table 1.

Table 1
Number and Percentage of Pupils in Each Income Group

Number of items checked on house and home scale	Number and percentage of pupils		Income group
0–2	219	24.9	Low
3–4	558	63.6	Middle
5–7	101	11.9	High
Totals	878	100.0	
	N	%	

The personal information items included such categories as sex, size of family, schooling of parents, hours spent working or studying at home, grade received in school, participation in high school and out-of-school activities, and offices held in organizations. Each item in the questionnaire was followed with a list of appropriate responses, one of which was to be checked.

[7] The *Purdue Opinion Panel* is published periodically by the Division of Educational Reference, Purdue University. Permission to use the "House and Home" scale was granted kindly by the publishers of the *Purdue Opinion Panel*. Special acknowledgment is due R. L. Horton, who suggested the items used in this scale.

[8] H. H. Remmers and R. B. Kirk, "Scalability and Validity of the Socio-Economic Status Items of the *Purdue Opinion Panel*," *J. Appl. Psychol.*, XXXVII (1953), pp. 384–386.

[9] G. Elias, "A Study of Certain Methods of Attitude Measurement and Related Variables" (unpublished Master's thesis, Purdue University, 1944).

[10] The items were a vacuum cleaner; an electric or gas refrigerator; a bath tub or shower with running water; two automobiles (excluding trucks); lessons in drama, art, expression, dancing, or music provided outside the school; an automatic dishwasher; and a cabin or cottage for vacations.

For each item a null hypothesis was postulated: There is no difference in the proportion of pupils checking each response category when they are divided into three income levels. Hypotheses were tested by the chi-square technique with tests based on a series of $3 \times n$ contingency tables. Adjacent response categories were combined, whenever necessary, to provide a minimum expected frequency of five in each cell. Additional combinations were made to conserve space in the tables, where reductions in the number of cells did not alter the character of the results.

RESULTS

Analyses were made of 23 personal information items. In marked contrast to the relative homogeneity of responses to the items in the attitudinal study,[11] the pupils in the three groups varied sharply on two thirds of the personal information items. A total of 16 hypotheses were rejected, 13 at the .001 level of confidence, and one each at the .01, .02 and .05 levels.

For the report of the results, the items are grouped into four divisions: Personal Information, Success in School, Participation in School and Community Activities, and Work or Study.

Personal Information

The personal information items include sex, broken homes, size of family, schooling of father and mother, and employment of mother outside the home. Most of the items in this division are associated with income level or socioeconomic status. Results of tests of significance are shown in Table 2. Three of the six hypotheses were rejected at the .001 level of confidence, one was rejected at the .02 level, and two hypotheses failed to be rejected.

Size of family and schooling of parents varied significantly with income level, with $P < .001$. Computed chi-square values greatly exceeded the value required for significance at this level. With regard to family size, high income families were more than twice as likely to have one to three children as low income families, and low income families were more than twice as likely to have four or more children as high income families. Concerning schooling of parents, variations were noted at each level of education, with greatest variations observed in the incidence of college attendance. Approximately one of four high income fathers attended college, as compared with one middle income father in eight, and one low income father in 30. Mothers varied similarly. One high income mother in four attended

[11] J. K. Coster, "Attitudes Toward School of High School Pupils from Three Income Levels," *J. Educ. Psychol.*, XLIX (1958), pp. 61–66.

college, as compared with one middle income mother in seven, and one low income mother in 30.

There were variations in the percentage of boys and girls in each income group, and the attending hypothesis was rejected at the 2% level. The sample included 450 boys and 428 girls, but the difference in proportion of boys and girls was not significant. The percentage of boys exceeded the percentage of girls in the middle income group, whereas the percentage of girls exceeded the percentage of boys in the high and low groups. Additional chi-square tests were made, comparing the high group with the others, the high and middle groups, the low group with the other two groups, and the low and middle groups. A significant chi-square value was obtained when the low group was compared with either the middle group, or with the other two groups. These data probably suggest a higher dropout rate among low income boys than low income girls.

A higher percentage of pupils from the low income group than from the high and middle groups lived with only one parent, a step-parent, or other relatives or persons. The differences in proportions, however, were not sufficiently large to be statistically significant. And the data in Table 2 indicate

Table 2
Results of Tests of Significance of Personal Information Items, Showing Percentage of Pupils Checking Response Categories by Income Groups

	INCOME GROUP				
ITEM	High	Middle	Low	Total	P
1. Sex.					
a. Boy	48.5	54.8	43.4	51.3	
b. Girl	51.5	45.2	56.6	48.7	.02
2. With whom do pupils live?					
a. With father and mother	85.0	84.2	77.6	82.7	
b. Others	15.0	15.8	22.4	17.3	.10
3. Number of children in family.					
a. One to three children	68.3	52.7	29.6	49.5	
b. Four or more children	31.7	46.2	70.3	50.5	.001
4. Schooling of father.					
a. Grade school	18.8	36.2	56.0	39.0	
b. High school	52.5	50.8	40.8	48.5	
c. College	28.7	12.9	3.2	12.4	.001
5. Schooling of mother.					
a. Grade school	9.9	21.8	44.4	26.0	
b. High school	64.3	64.5	52.2	61.5	
c. College	25.7	13.3	3.3	12.5	.001
6. Mother employed outside of home.					
a. Yes	31.7	32.4	23.9	30.2	
b. No	68.3	67.6	76.1	69.8	.10

that a higher percentage of high and middle income mothers are employed outside the home, but, again, the differences were not significant.

Success in School

The "Success in School" items, listed in Table 3, included queries on plans to continue education, failure in school, and average marks. Six hypotheses were tested, and five were rejected at the .001 level. The pro-

Table 3
Results of Tests of Significance of Success in School Items, Showing Percentage of Pupils Checking Response Categories, by Income Group

		INCOME GROUP				
ITEM		*High*	*Middle*	*Low*	*Total*	*P*
7. Plan to graduate from high school?						
	a. Yes	99.0	96.4	89.0	94.9	
	b. Undecided or no	1.0	3.6	11.0	5.1	.001
8. Plan to go to college?						
	a. Yes	49.5	32.1	15.5	30.0	
	b. Undecided or no	50.5	67.9	84.5	70.0	.001
9. Years failed in grade school?						
	a. None	94.1	86.1	77.6	84.9	
	b. One or more	5.9	13.9	22.4	15.1	.001
10. Subjects failed in high school?						
	a. None	93.1	87.9	82.8	87.3	
	b. One or more	6.9	12.1	17.2	12.7	.05
11. Average marks received in high school.						
	a. A or B average	71.3	49.4	31.2	47.4	
	b. C, D or F average	28.7	50.5	68.8	52.6	.001
12. Cited on honor roll during past year.						
	a. Yes	42.4	35.3	20.3	32.3	
	b. No	57.6	64.7	79.7	67.3	.001
13. Field of specialization.						
	a. College preparatory or academic	34.0	19.1	9.0	18.5	
	b. General	13.4	17.7	13.2	16.2	
	c. Vocational	52.6	63.2	77.8	65.3	.001
14. Selected life's work.						
	a. Yes	42.6	34.9	32.7	35.2	
	b. Not definitely or no	57.4	65.1	67.3	64.8	.30

portion of pupils who indicated that they plan to graduate from high school and go to college was significantly higher for the high group than for the other two groups, with $P < .001$ in both instances. There were more failures in grade school and high school subjects for the low income group than the other two groups. Differences in grade school failures were significant at the .001 level. The three groups, however, were more homogeneous with regard to failure in high school subjects, with $P < .05$.

Scholastic success, as measured by average marks in school, varied markedly among the three groups. High income pupils were more than twice as likely to report A or B grade averages than low income pupils. Similar variations were noted when pupils were asked whether their names have appeared on their school honor rolls.

Closely related to the success in school items were the questions on field of specialization and selection of life's work. Results of tests of significance for these two items are included in Table 3. Field of specialization varied significantly with income group, with $P < .001$. A larger percentage of high income pupils than middle or low income pupils were enrolled in the college preparatory or academic curriculums, whereas low income pupils were attracted in greater proportions to one of the vocational programs. Among the three groups, there was very little difference in the percentages of pupils who elected a general program. The relatively high percentage of pupils who were enrolled in a vocational program (including industrial arts in addition to vocational agriculture, homemaking, and industrial education) probably is an indication of limited curricular offerings in small schools. Practically all boys in the smaller schools were enrolled in vocational agriculture, and a large proportion of girls in the smaller schools studied homemaking for at least two or three years.

Approximately one third of the Ss indicated that they definitely had selected their life's work. A higher percentage of the "Yes" responses was from the high income group than from the other two groups, but the differences were not significant.

Participation in School and Community Activities

All five hypotheses pertaining to school and community activities were rejected, four at the .001 level and one at the .01 level, according to data in Table 4. One indication of participation in school activities—and social acceptance—is the extent to which youths associate with fellow pupils. A significantly higher proportion of low income pupils, than high and middle income pupils, reported that they had most of their social activities outside of school with youths who go to other schools or who are not in school.

Extremely wide variations occurred in the number of high school and out-of-school activities in which pupils of the three groups participated.

Table 4
Results of Tests of Significance of Participation in School and Community Activities Items, Showing Percentage of Pupils Checking Response Categories, by Income Groups

	INCOME GROUP				
ITEM	*High*	*Middle*	*Low*	*Total*	*P*
15. With whom do pupils associate					
a. With pupils in the same high school	82.2	84.1	74.0	81.4	
b. With youth in other high schools or not in school	17.8	15.9	26.0	18.6	.01
16. Participation in high school activities.					
a. None	2.0	9.5	19.2	11.1	
b. One or two activities	25.8	44.2	55.7	45.0	
c. Three or four activities	35.6	29.5	21.0	28.1	
d. Five or more activities	36.6	16.7	4.1	15.8	.001
17. Participation in out-of-school activities.					
a. None	3.0	11.3	27.9	14.5	
b. One or two activities	32.0	49.1	52.5	48.1	
c. Three or four activities	39.6	30.9	17.3	28.5	
d. Five or more activities	24.7	8.6	2.3	8.9	.001
18. Held office in an organization.					
a. Yes	78.0	69.7	40.2	63.6	
b. No	22.0	30.3	59.8	36.4	.001
19. Frequency of Church or Sunday School attendance.					
a. Three or more times per month	78.0	66.8	52.1	64.5	
b. Less than three times a month	21.0	28.7	32.8	28.8	
c. Never	1.0	4.5	15.0	6.7	.001

Nearly ten times as many low income as high income pupils did not participate. Whereas nearly three fourths of the high income pupils reported that they participated in three or more high school activities, only one fourth of the low income group reported such extensive participation. And whereas nearly two thirds of the high income pupils indicated that they had participated in three or more out-of-school activities, less than one fifth of the low income group indicated similar participation. A divergence was also noted in the percentages of pupils who have been elected to an office. More than three fourths of the high income pupils and more than two thirds of the middle income pupils have been elected to an office in a high school or out-of-school activity, as compared with only 40% of the low income group.

Differences in the behavior of youths were noted in extent of Sunday School and Church attendance. Slightly more than three fourths of the high income pupils and over two thirds of the middle income pupils reported regular Sunday School and Church attendance, as contrasted with slightly more than one half of the low group. Fifteen per cent of the low income pupils indicated that they never attended Sunday School or Church, as compared with less than five per cent of the middle group and only one per cent of the high group.

Work and Study

The fourth division pertains to an analysis of income group variation with regard to the number of hours spent working or studying outside of school. This aspect of the study has received limited attention in other investigations of income level and social status. To get the necessary information, pupils in the sample were asked these questions:

1. About how many hours do you study at home each week?
2. About how many hours each week (during the school year) do you work at home?
3. Do you receive pay or allowance for the work you do at home?
4. About how many hours each week do you work at a job away from home during the school year from which you earn some money?

The results of tests of significance are shown in Table 5. High income pupils tended to spend more time studying at home than low and middle income pupils, and middle income pupils were more likely to receive pay and allowance for the work they did at home than youths in the other two groups, but the differences were not significant. There was practically no difference among the three groups in the number of hours per week that pupils worked outside of school, either at home or away from home.

DISCUSSION

Some general comments based on a synthesis of the findings of the two studies presented in this paper and in the previous article[12] are here appropriate. High income pupils responded more favorably than middle or low income pupils with regard to the majority of items in both studies; however, there were marked variations in the number of items for which

12 *Ibid.*

Table 5
Results of Tests of Significance of Work or Study Items, Showing Percentage of Pupils Checking Each Response, by Income Group

| | INCOME GROUP | | | | |
ITEM	*High*	*Middle*	*Low*	*Total*	*P*
20. Hours pupils study at home each week.					
a. Less than five hours per week	62.4	73.4	70.4	71.5	
b. Five hours or more per week	37.6	26.6	29.6	28.5	.10
21. Hours pupils work at home each week.					
a. Less than ten hours per week	61.4	61.6	59.8	61.1	
b. Ten hours or more per week	38.6	38.3	40.3	38.9	.90
22. Receive pay or allowance for work at home.					
a. Yes	42.6	50.9	42.7	47.9	
b. No	57.4	49.1	57.3	52.1	.10
23. Hours pupils work outside of home each week.					
a. Less than ten hours per week	73.3	79.0	75.9	77.6	
b. Ten hours or more per week	26.7	20.9	24.1	22.4	.50

null hypotheses were rejected. In the present study, significant differences were obtained for the majority of the items. Responses to attitudinal items which involved an appraisal of the school and school program generally did not manifest these marked differences in school and community experiences.

There are indications that the low income pupil has tended to accept his lot in school in a state of resignation. Perhaps he is conscious of the efforts of his school to provide an appropriate educational program for him. The findings show, nevertheless, that he participates in few school activities, yet complained no more about the number of activities than high or middle income pupils. He tended to receive low grades in school, yet he was as satisfied with the grading system as high and middle income pupils whose average grades were much higher. And his opinions of the subjects offered in the school did not differ from the opinions of pupils from higher income homes, yet the low income pupil is more likely to deprecate his chances of getting the kind of job he wants after high school even though there is a greater possibility that he is enrolled in a vocational program designed to fit him for useful employment.

Responses to attitudinal items dealing with social acceptance, in contrast, varied similarly with the school and community experience items reported in this study. It would seem, perhaps, that low income pupils recognize that there are activities in which they may participate, but that either they do not wish to participate, possibly because of variations in social values attached to these activities, or they feel that they are not welcome to join.

The findings of these two studies tend to suggest that although schools may subscribe to a position of equality of educational opportunity, equality of educational experiences falls somewhat short of the ideal. Even though a predominant theme of the contemporary philosophy of American education is to provide appropriate educational opportunities for all American youth, sociological and psychological factors tend to operate against the attainment of this goal. Then, too, criticisms to the effect that American education has been more concerned with the education of the "masses" at the expense of the "elite" are more apropos when leveled at theory than at practice. The findings from these and other studies of social status and income level suggest that American schools, consciously or unconsciously, have been prone to favor pupils from middle and upper socioeconomic strata which, generally, include a high proportion of academically competent youth.

SUMMARY

In this study, 878 pupils were divided into three income groups, and the pupils in the groups were compared on a number of items of personal information—such as sex, schooling of parents, and participation in school and community activities. High income pupils were more likely than middle and low income pupils to participate in high school and out of school activities, hold an office in an organization, get high marks in school, be named to the school honor roll, attend Sunday School and Church regularly, successfully complete courses in school, and continue education. The number of hours spent studying or working outside of school, during the school year, however, did not differ among the groups. The number of items related to school and community experience·which varied significantly with income level contrasted markedly with the relative homogeneity of responses of the three groups to attitudinal items pertaining to the school and school program, as reported in a previous study of the same Ss.[13] But there seemed to be an essential agreement between differences in responses to attitudinal items dealing with social acceptance and the extent of participation in school and community activities.

[13] *Ibid.*

Sex Differences in the Life Problems and Interests of Adolescents, 1935 and 1957*[1]

DALE B. HARRIS

An adolescent's social interests and problems affect his acquisition of age- and sex-appropriate role behaviors and his identification with models who are exemplars of his ambitions. Issues such as these play a significant part in the socialization process. The socializing agent who attempts to understand the social concerns of adolescents may acquire valuable information about the sources of their motivation and the goals toward which they strive. Unfortunately, for those who would seek closure, adolescent sentiments change over time. In the paper presented below, Harris assays differences in the social concerns of two groups of adolescents, separated by over a generation. His evaluation of the changes that occur provides a useful historical perspective for students who wish to make an analysis of some of the contemporary issues confronting adolescents.

This is a study of interests and problems which uses the method of rank order rather than a check list as its research technique. The items ranked are 15 topics selected from the concerns of adolescents. High school students were asked first to consider the items as personal problems and to construct an order reflecting their own experience with the issues as personal problems. The students then reranked the same items in order of interest, considering the topics as things they would like to read about and discuss or hear discussed.

The problems and instructions for ranking were taken verbatim from a

[1] This study was supported by the Institute of Child Development, University of Minnesota.

* From *Child Development*, XXX (1959), pp. 453–459. Reprinted by permission of the author and the Society for Research in Child Development.

study published by Symonds.[2] He had selected the issues from young people's own discussions and phrased the issues in terms used by young people themselves. His 1641 students attended junior and senior high schools in Tulsa, Oklahoma, and New York City. The 1165 youth in the present study came from the junior-senior high school in a Minnesota community. Twenty-two years and considerable social, cultural, and economic change separate the circumstances of the two studies. Whether geographic or regional differences also influence the data cannot be known. In both studies, the samples represented in general the socioeconomic distribution of the communities from which they were drawn. The comparability of samples drawn from different geographic areas without close control through a stratification procedure is questionable. But the comparability of samples is also problematical across long time intervals, in which social and cultural changes have occurred, even when stratification by some socioeconomic index has been attempted. Changing conditions may themselves affect the index.

The hypothesis of the present study is taken from Symonds' discussion:[3] "Change the social and economic structure of society and you immediately change the relative emphasis of these problems and interests."

In a ranking process as in any *system,* change in one feature or aspect may have widespread effects throughout the system. Thus, there are some limitations to the method. The elements are *relative* to one another. The resulting rank order is not a true *scale* of values. Each' choice made removes a degree of freedom and relates to the choices already made and those yet to be made. The ranks accorded a series of stimuli are systematically affected by the order in which the stimuli are first presented. Symonds removed this effect in his study by presenting the items in reverse order to approximately half his subjects. This study used the same procedure. The sample of children was drawn randomly from the available supply to constitute groups of 100 boys and 100 girls at each grade; half of each sex responded to the items in the order Symonds presented them in his report, and the other half responded to a reversed order.

For 15 items ranked in one experience, a rho value of .535 is required to establish a relationship greater than chance at the 5 per cent level of significance. To interpret differences in rankings accorded items by boys and girls, or changes between two sets of rankings made at different times, one can place more confidence in *mean* ranks of samples than in ranks made by individuals. But the meaning of the magnitude of the differences

[2] P. M. Symonds, "Life Interests and Problems of Adolescents," *Sch. Rev.,* XLIV (1936), pp. 506–518; P. M. Symonds, "Sex Differences in the Life Problems and Interests of Adolescents," *Sch. and Soc.,* XLIII (1936), pp. 751–752.

[3] Symonds, "Sex Differences in the Life Problems and Interests of Adolescents," *op. cit.,* 752.

thus described is still elusive. By building a body of experience with different arrangements of the data, one can possibly increase the insight he brings to bear on any one arrangement.

For example, when means of rankings of items considered as problems, established by 100 boys in each grade, 7 through 12, are compared, the average or typical between grade-group rank order correlation is +.74 (estimated from Kendall's W). For the same items considered as interests, the typical between grade-group rank order correlation is +.78. For girls, the corresponding values are +.70 and +.72. Thus, children's rankings from grade to grade change no more on the average than is suggested by correlation values in the .70's. Putting the data of boys and girls together in each grade, thus increasing reliability through the size of N but also introducing any existing systematic sex differences, the values become +.65 (problems) and +.63 (interests), (both estimated from Kendall's W).

Because there are likely to be intrinsic relationships in any set of values ranked by a group of judges, simply because judges from similar backgrounds are not reacting blindly or randomly to meaningful material, it is instructive to examine some typical interarray correlations estimated from Kendall's W. If we consider the four ranks of mean values accorded by boys and girls in 1935 and 1957 to *problems,* this typical interarray correlation is +.58. For four arrays of *interests* this value is also +.58. Throwing together the eight arrays of problems and interests, the value becomes +.36. These values provide a pragmatic bench-mark to judge the meaning of the correlation values presented below, which have a theoretical top value of +1.00 and describe a chance relationship as .00.

Taking all boys regardless of grade and similarly combining all girls for purposes of comparison with data obtained on the same items by Symonds in 1935, some interesting observations can be made. Youth showed greater consistency in the ordering of these items, considered first as problems and then as interests, in 1935 than they do at present. This change is true both for boys (+.63 compared with −.23) and for girls (+.66 compared with +.25). Thus, in 1957 there is little correspondence between a set of issues considered as problems and the order of interest in the same issues. This was not true in 1935, when there was a noticeable correspondence between the sets of ranks.

But how do young people separated by almost a generation compare in the ordering of their problems and their interests? Boys' rankings of interests across the years are somewhat more consistent (+.76) than their rankings of problems then and now (+.47). For girls, there is little difference between relative positions accorded problems and interests over the years (problems, +.50; interests, +.55).

Do boys and girls accord the same order of importance to a set of adolescent problems? In both periods boys and girls rank their problems similarly. In 1935 the similarity of the rank order of the sexes is expressed by a correlation value of +.80. In the 1957 study the value is +.77. The similarity of boys and girls is as great, on the average, as the similarity of successive grade groups of boys, or of girls. When the items were ranked according to interest in 1935, a value of +.80 expresses the similarity of boys' and girls' judgments. The comparable figure in 1957 is +.58.

The changes described above become more interesting when we look at specific ranks in Tables 1 and 2. As problems (Table 1), three items change five ranks or more across time for both boys and girls (health, mental health, manners), three more for boys only (safety, recreation, schedule), and two more for girls only (love and marriage, and study habits). As interests (Table 2), three items change for both sexes across time (love and marriage, family relations, manners), and one more for each sex singly (recreation for girls, getting along with others for boys). There are as many sex differences now as in 1935. At that time seven topics significantly

Table 1
Ranks Accorded Issues Considered As Problems by High School
Boys and Girls in 1935 and in 1957

| | BOYS | | | | GIRLS | | | |
| | 1935 | | 1957 | | 1935 | | 1957 | |
Issue	Mean Rank	Rank	Mean Rank	Rank	Mean Rank	Rank	Mean Rank	Rank
Health	6.7	(2)	9.1*	(12)	6.6	(2)	8.7*	(12.5)
Love, marriage	10.8	(15)	9.2*	(13.5)	11.0	(15)	8.5*	(10)
Safety	8.3	(8.5)	9.2*	(13.5)	8.8	(12)	10.0*	(14.5)
Money	6.2	(1)	6.3	(2)	6.8	(3)	6.5	(2)
Mental hygiene	8.7	(13)	8.2	(8)	8.2	(9.5)	6.9*	(3.5)
Study habits	6.8	(3)	5.0	(1)	7.4	(6)	6.3*	(1)
Recreation	8.3	(8.5)	10.1	(15)	8.4	(11)	10.0*	(14.5)
Personal, moral qualities	7.1	(4)	6.6*	(3)	7.3	(4)	7.1	(5)
Home, family relationships	8.2	(7)	8.4	(10)	8.2	(9.5)	7.6	(6)
Manners	8.5	(11.5)	7.6*	(5)	7.4	(6)	8.6*	(11)
Personal attractiveness	7.9	(6)	7.7	(6)	6.2	(1)	6.9*	(3.5)
Daily schedule	9.0	(14)	8.3*	(9)	9.4	(14)	8.7*	(12.5)
Civic interest	8.5	(11.5)	7.9*	(7)	9.0	(13)	8.4	(9)
Getting along with other people	8.4	(10)	8.6	(11)	7.9	(8)	8.0	(8)
Philosophy of life	7.5	(5)	7.5	(4)	7.4	(6)	7.7	(7)

* Change from 1935 significant at the 1 per cent level.

Table 2
Ranks Accorded Issues Considered As Interests by High School
Boys and Girls in 1935 and in 1957

| | BOYS | | | | GIRLS | | | |
| | 1935 | | 1957 | | 1935 | | 1957 | |
Issue	*Mean Rank*	*Rank*	*Mean Rank*	*Rank*	*Mean Rank*	*Rank*	*Mean Rank*	*Rank*
Health	5.6	(2)	6.4*	(2)	6.6	(4)	7.0	(6)
Love, marriage	9.3	(13)	7.7*	(8)	9.4	(12)	6.5*	(4.5)
Safety	7.8	(7)	8.7*	(11)	9.2	(10)	10.2*	(14)
Money	7.1	(3)	6.5*	(3)	8.1	(8)	8.2	(10)
Mental hygiene	9.6	(14)	9.5	(13)	9.8	(13.5)	8.0*	(9)
Study habits	8.7	(11)	9.4*	(12)	9.3	(11)	9.9*	(12.5)
Recreation	4.9	(1)	5.6*	(1)	5.6	(2)	7.8*	(8)
Personal, moral qualities	7.7	(5.5)	7.3*	(6)	7.6	(7)	7.1	(7)
Home, family relationships	8.4	(10)	7.2*	(5)	8.3	(9)	6.4*	(2.5)
Manners	7.5	(4)	8.6*	(10)	6.3	(3)	8.5*	(11)
Personal attractiveness	8.1	(8)	8.0	(9)	5.4	(1)	6.0*	(1)
Daily schedule	10.5	(15)	10.9	(15)	10.4	(15)	11.4*	(15)
Civic interest	9.0	(12)	9.6*	(14)	9.8	(13.5)	9.9	(12.5)
Getting along with other people	8.2	(9)	7.1*	(4)	7.0	(5)	6.4*	(2.5)
Philosophy of life	7.7	(5.5)	7.4	(7)	7.3	(6)	6.5*	(4.5)

* Change from 1935 significant at the 1 per cent level.

differentiated the sexes as problems at the .01 level of certainty.[4] Now eight topics satisfy the .01 level.

Sex differences in interests also are about the same. In 1935 boys and girls rated nine topics quite different. In 1957, 10 topics satisfied the .01 level.

Attention to item placements show that a number of topics are relatively high as sources of problems: *Money* is still high as a problem to both boys and girls (ranks 2 and 2, respectively). It is of considerably greater interest to boys than to girls (rank 3 as compared with rank 10).[5] *Health* at rank 2

[4] This index of statistical significance refers to the difference between mean ranks, interpreted in terms of the standard errors of these means. It does not refer to shift in rank order.

[5] In 1935 Symonds attributed the high ranks accorded money to the current economic stress. Studies of allowances show that modern youth "never had it so good" from an economic point of view, but inflation and rising standards of living expectancy keep the 'teen age group keenly aware of the medium of exchange.

as a problem in 1935 is no longer seen as such (rank 12), though interest in it is still relatively high, especially among boys. *Study habits* are somewhat more of a problem now than in 1935, especially for boys, but the topic ranked quite low in interest value in both periods. *Moral qualities* and *philosophy of life* come next in position both as problems and as topics of interest and are of similar relative magnitude in both periods.

Of intermediate concern as problems are the following: Both sexes see *mental health* as somewhat more of a problem to them now than they did in 1935, and for girls it now appears in the top five ranks. It has, likewise, moved up significantly ($p = .01$) in rank of interest to girls, though it remains low on the boys' list. *Home and family relations* is likewise ranked higher as a problem by girls than by boys now ($p = .01$). Relative to 1935, boys rank it slightly lower and girls slightly higher as a problem, though in these intermediate positions such shifting is statistically meaningless. Both boys and girls rank this topic higher on the list of interests than they did in 1935, girls very considerably so (rank of 2.5 compared with 9, $p = .01$). *Manners and courtesy,* up somewhat ($p = .01$) as a problem for boys as compared with the earlier period, is significantly less a problem for girls now (rank 11 compared with rank 6, $p = .01$). As a topic of interest it is down sharply for both sexes. *Attractiveness,* of intermediate value both as a problem and as an interest for boys in both periods, ranks high in both interest value and as a problem for girls in both periods. Likewise, *getting along with others* was and is of considerable interest to girls and has risen (rank 4 compared to rank 9, $p = .01$) as a topic of interest to boys. It is of intermediate significance as a problem. *Civic affairs* was and is of about median significance as a problem to both boys and girls and is of even less relative importance as a topic of interest.

Of least concern as problems now are the following: *Recreation,* of intermediate significance as a problem to both boys and girls in 1935, is negligible now. It was and is number 1 in interest value to boys but has dropped from second to eighth place for girls ($p = .01$). *Health,* of high significance both as a problem and as a topic of interest to boys and girls in 1935, is now negligible as a problem to either sex. It is now only of intermediate interest to girls, though it remains high on the boys' list. *Safety* is of little interest and even less a problem to both boys and girls now than in 1935 ($p = .01$). *Love and marriage,* ranked low as a problem by boys in both periods, has risen to an intermediate rank as a problem for girls. Both sexes now give it an intermediate interest rating, some several ranks higher than 22 years ago. The change in both problem and interest values of this topic is statistically significant, highly so for girls. *Daily schedule* is of little significance then or now, both to boys and girls, as problem or as interest.

This observation concerning the specific rankings accorded the issues should be made. Both psychologically and statistically, the highest and lowest ranks are most differentiated in any ranking or scaling procedure. The method in this study called for the identification of the first three positions, and then positions 13, 14, and 15. The intermediate positions were assigned last and may, particularly in the ranking of interests, represent a state of psychological indifference or lack of discrimination more than a state of intermediate significance. Should this be the case, the significance attributed by Symonds to the "relatively high" rank of philosophy of life (6th in 15 issues) may be modified somewhat. He affirmed[6] that "values and goals are craved" by youth and challenged teacher and counselors by the rank accorded this topic. Symonds attributed the high rank of money as a problem to the depression years and observed "it is a pity" that money drops to a much lower rank in interest value. The problem significance of money was not just a function of depression years, it is now clear.

The lack of concern with love and marriage, identified by Symonds as "sex adjustments," puzzled him, and he explained the low ranks by reference to "repression." His own hypothesis concerning social change appears from the present data to be equally plausible. A similar point can be made about mental health as an issue in adolescence. Symonds dismissed the low ranks attributed to this issue in these words: "Mental health likewise is no concern of healthy, growing adolescents. The crest of life is before them. Their failures and thwartings have not yet turned them back upon themselves."[7] The changed cultural ethos apparently has made a difference in the significance accorded this issue in the adolescent years.

The shifts noted in the tables and in the brief discussion for the most part confirm what observers of recent social trends have noted. Today, youth marry younger and show an earlier interest in social relations, love, and marriage. Our culture appears to recognize more openly now than two decades ago the sex, love, and marriage problems of young people. Physical health is actually less a problem today, and possibly receives less attention in school and in the popular press, whereas mental health discussions, literature, and posters appear in every newspaper, magazine, and waiting room. An increase in informality and casualness in dress and behavior may reflect itself in the decline in concern with manners.

The student of adolescent behavior will not be surprised at the significance of money as a problem, high interest in recreation, lack of concern with and interest in safety, unconcern over daily schedule and civic affairs, considerable concern over study habits as a problem but lack of interest in the topic, nor will he be surprised by the greater interest of girls than boys in attractiveness, love and marriage, mental health, and philosophy and beliefs; of boys than girls in money, health, and recreation.

[6] Symonds, "Life Interests and Problems of Adolescents," *op. cit.*
[7] *Ibid.,* 517.

If adults wish to "view with alarm," they may attend to the adolescent's relative unconcern with safety and hazard, set over against the 'teen-age driving problem, and the young person's continuing unconcern with civic affairs, set over against the continued increased emphasis on "modern problems," and citizenship in the secondary school's curriculum theory and effort.

Personality Factors Related to Juvenile Delinquency[*][1][2]

Donald R. Peterson,
Herbert C. Quay, and
Theodore L. Tiffany

The behavioral scientist who seeks to appraise delinquency proneness from personality characteristics faces difficult problems. First, he must define operationally the delinquent or antisocial act, which may be evaluated along different dimensions, e.g., magnitude of transgression and degree of premeditation. Then, if the nature of delinquency is to be better understood and if asocial behavior is to be constrained and redirected into socially acceptable outlets, he must determine which individuals are delinquency prone. In the paper presented below, questionnaires tapping a wide variety of personality dimensions were administered to over 400 delinquents and nondelinquents in an attempt "to generate a set of unitary, independent, possibly meaningful personality constructs related to delinquent behavior." Factor analyses of the data reveal the existence of several meaningful factors, and the results contribute substantially to our knowledge regarding the relationships between personality and juvenile delinquency.

Research on juvenile delinquency has often been handicapped by the behavioral heterogeneity of the delinquent population. Subjects have ordi-

[1] This study was supported by a grant from the University Research Board, University of Illinois.

[2] So many people have helped in the conduct of this research that we cannot possibly thank them all. We are especially grateful, however, to Earl K. Dryden, Chief Psychologist at the Illinois State Training School for Boys, St. Charles; E. B. Daly, Principal of Thomas Kelly High School in Chicago; C. S. Prigmore, Superintendent, and R. W. Edwards, Psychologist at the Tennessee State Vocational Training School for Boys; and to A. D. Hancock, Principal of Cumberland High School in Nashville, Tennessee, for their help in gathering data for the investigation.

[*] From *Child Development*, XXXII (1961), pp. 355–372. Reprinted by permission of the authors and the Society for Research in Child Development.

narily had one common property, the commission of some legally defined delinquent act, and nothing more. It is little wonder that knowledge about cause and consequence has accumulated so slowly; the behavioral unity required for adequate scientific investigation is lacking.

One major approach to conceptual and methodological refinement has involved the delineation of typological and dimensional constructs of various kinds. Before examining social correlates of delinquency, Reiss[3] classified subjects into three groups, those with relatively weak ego controls, those with defective superego controls, and those with relatively integrated personal controls. Similarly, Jenkins and Glickman[4] have offered a basis for classifying delinquents into an unsocialized aggressive group, a socialized delinquent group, and an emotionally disturbed group. Both these efforts, and others like them, represent a considerable advance over earlier attempts to study juvenile delinquency without further specification, but their value is limited in various ways. Most of them are stated in typological, rather than dimensional, terms, and there is some reason to doubt the very existence of nonarbitrary personality types among juvenile delinquents.[5] Even more fundamentally, the earlier formulations are typically based on case history information, which is necessarily indirect, notoriously vulnerable to subjective bias, and inclined to be unreliable.

A second approach to methodological refinement has led to the construction of a number of tests which distinguish delinquents from nondelinquents on a behavioral rather than a legal basis.[6] Some of these instruments have proved remarkably effective in accomplishing the tasks for which they were designed,[7] but they fail to provide any improvement in conceptual unity. The items comprising the scales are nearly as heterogeneous in meaning as delinquents are in behavior.

Various difficulties with the above approaches can be overcome if data are restricted to behavior observations or products of some known relevance to delinquent activity and if appropriate analytic techniques are employed to define any structural concepts inherent in the data. Many

[3] A. J. Reiss, "Social Correlates of Psychological Types of Delinquency," *Amer. Sociol. Rev.*, XVII (1952), pp. 710–718.

[4] R. L. Jenkins and S. Glickman, "Patterns of Personality Organization Among Delinquents," *Nerv. Child*, VI (1947), pp. 329–339.

[5] T. L. Tiffany, D. R. Peterson, and H. C. Quay, "Types and Traits in the Study of Juvenile Delinquency," *J. Clin. Psychol.*, XVII (1961), pp. 19–24.

[6] H. G. Gough and D. R. Peterson, "The Identification and Measurement of Predispositional Factors in Crime and Delinquency," *J. Consult. Psychol.*, XVI (1952), pp. 207–212; W. C. Kvaraceus, *K D Proneness Scale and Checklist* (World Book, 1950); G. C. Loofbourow and N. Keys, *The Personal Index* (Minneapolis: Educational Testing Bureau, 1933); H. C. Quay and D. R. Peterson, "A Brief Scale for Juvenile Delinquency," *J. Clin. Psychol.*, XIV (1958), pp. 139–142.

[7] W. C. Kvaraceus, *Forecasting Juvenile Delinquency* (World Book, 1956); D. R. Peterson, H. C. Quay, and A. C. Anderson, "Extending the Construct Validity of a Socialization Scale," *J. Consult. Psychol.*, XXIII (1959), p. 182.

kinds of behavior meet the first qualification. For this study, we have chosen questionnaire responses of demonstrated effectiveness in differentiating delinquents from nondelinquents. A number of statistical procedures have been proposed for the elaboration of structural concepts. We have elected to use centroid factor analysis.

In a previous study,[8] two questionnaires which distinguished reliably between delinquents and nondelinquents were administered to 116 inmates of a boys' training school and to 115 male high school students. Responses were factorized, and five reasonably unitary, comprehensible dimensions emerged. The first implied a tendency toward impulsiveness, a lack of emotional involvement with others, and a tough, rebellious, distrustful attitude toward authority. It was called "Psychopathy." The second factor also contained an element of impulsivity, but this was associated with tension, discouragement, guilt, and depression. The factor was labelled "Neuroticism." The remaining three factors accounted for relatively small proportions of variance. One of them implied a sense of failure and incompetence and was called "Inadequacy." The other two were interpreted as background factors relating to family dissension and a history of scholastic maladjustment.

Extension of the meaning and validity of the three personality factors was sought by investigating associations with other logically related variables.[9] For a sample of delinquents, Psychopathy was significantly related to recidivism, length of institutionalization, the occurrence of problem behavior and disciplinary measures during incarceration, and a history of crimes against person rather than against property. Among the variables examined, Neuroticism was correlated reliably only with a measure of manifest anxiety.[10] The Inadequacy factor was related negatively to Army Beta IQ and positively to length of institutionalization. While the correlations were generally of low magnitude, they were in nearly perfect accord with factor interpretations originally developed solely on the basis of item content.

The results of this previous research appeared sufficiently promising to encourage initiation of the present study. Our purpose is the same as before: to generate a set of unitary, independent, possibly meaningful personality constructs related to delinquent behavior in the belief that these will offer a more rigorously defined frame of reference and more powerful

[8] D. R. Peterson, H. C. Quay, and G. R. Cameron, "Personality and Background Factors in Juvenile Delinquency as Inferred from Questionnaire Responses," *J. Consult. Psychol.*, XXIII (1959), pp. 395–399.

[9] H. C. Quay, D. R. Peterson, and C. Consalvi, "The Interpretation of Three Personality Factors in Juvenile Delinquency," *J. Consult. Psychol.*, XXIV (1960), p. 555.

[10] A. Castaneda, B. R. McCandless, and D. S. Palermo, "The Children's Form of the Manifest Anxiety Scale," *Child Develpm.*, XXVII (1956), pp. 317–326.

hypotheses for further research than are now available to investigators of juvenile delinquency. This study differs from the previous one in that the range of behavior has been greatly expanded, and the sample of subjects approximately doubled.

SUBJECTS

Four hundred six subjects (Ss) participated in the investigation. Of these, 93 were in a state training school in Illinois, 93 were attending a Chicago high school, 110 were located in a state training school in Tennessee, and 110 were students at a high school in Nashville, Tennessee.

In selecting Ss, an effort was made to maximize variance along the gross dimension of major concern, i.e., delinquency proneness, and to reduce variance to a minimum along various other dimensions which might be related to delinquent behavior. Thus, both delinquents and nondelinquents were examined, but an attempt was made to equate the groups in respect to several other characteristics. All Ss were white, male, and in the same age range (10 to 18 years). Boys at the Illinois State Training School had all been residents of Chicago, and the residential area for Chicago high school students resembled that of the "average" delinquent in regard to social and cultural factors tending to foster delinquency. Comparability of the latter kind was achieved by locating the home address of each Chicago delinquent, tabulating delinquency rate[11] for the part of town in which he lived, and obtaining the mean of those rates. Choice of a high school was then determined by its location; it was situated in an area with the same delinquency rate as the mean for adjudged delinquents in the sample. The relatively small size of the population in the Tennessee training school, the diversity of background of the inmates, and the lack of information on delinquency rate for home communities prohibited similar rigor in selecting Ss from Tennessee. An attempt to achieve at least urban-rural comparability was maintained, however, by selecting nondelinquent Ss from a high school on the outskirts of Nashville which drew most of its students from the city, but some of them from outlying districts. A majority of the Tennessee delinquents (65) were from the four largest cities in the state, and the remainder (45) were from smaller communities.

PROCEDURES

Questionnaires

A battery of four questionnaires, providing nearly exhaustive coverage of available items which differentiate between delinquent and nondelinquent boys, was administered to all Ss.

[11] Chicago Area Project, *Delinquency Rates in the City of Chicago for Males Age 10–16, During the Years 1945–1951.*

PNI Attitude Schedule (PNI). The first questionnaire, containing 100 items, was called the PNI Attitude Schedule in reference to factors derived in previous research. Fifty-nine of the items had shown the requisite discriminatory power in earlier comparisons[12] and appeared as salient variables marking Psychopathy, Neuroticism, and Inadequacy as defined in the factor analysis mentioned above.[13] To secure better representation of the putative Inadequacy factor, 41 new items were written to express various facets of the dimension as the investigators conceived it. The Psychopathy (P), Neuroticism (N), and Inadequacy (I) items were systematically arranged in the order PINIPINI, etc., and the entire 100 items administered to the Ss.

Only 68 statements, however, were included in the analysis. Since one criterion for selection of items was their ability to distinguish delinquents from nondelinquents, it was necessary to test the discriminatory power of the 41 new items and to cross-validate the results. One hundred fourteen delinquents from the Tennessee training school were compared with an equal number of nondelinquents from Tennessee as to performance on these items. Frequencies of endorsement were tabulated, chi square tests performed, and nine items selected as discriminating "significantly" between the two groups of Ss. At this point, it became necessary to begin further analyses, and the nine items were retained in all subsequent work. On cross-validational comparison of 93 delinquents and 93 nondelinquents from Illinois, unfortunately, the nine-item subtest did not function effectively, and the 68 PNI items which were later factorized can only be described as follows: 25 of them discriminated between delinquents and nondelinquents and loaded on Psychopathy in the previous factorization; 25 differentiated between delinquents and nondelinquents and loaded on the Neuroticism factor; nine showed similar discriminatory power and loaded on Inadequacy; nine items, introduced to fortify measurement of Inadequacy, appeared at first to differentiate between delinquents and nondelinquents, but failed to do so on cross-validation.

The Personal Index (PI). The Personal Index by Loofbourow and Keys[14] was chosen as a second instrument for investigation. The test is fairly old, but we have assumed that the attitudes and other tendencies associated with delinquency have not changed radically since the discriminatory ability of the test was demonstrated, and it has been included, without modification, in the study.

The Personal Opinion Inventory (POI). A third questionnaire was assembled from certain items in the Minnesota Multiphasic Personality Inventory (MMPI), and a set of items developed in rehabilitation research

12 Gough and Peterson, *op. cit.;* Quay and Peterson, *op. cit.*
13 Peterson, Quay, and Cameron, *op. cit.*
14 Loofbourow and Keys, *op. cit.*

in the U. S. Navy.[15] The MMPI items, 33 in number, not only discriminated between previously classified delinquents and nondelinquents, but were, in addition, valid predictors of delinquent activity.[16]

Items written for the Navy research were "designed to uncover individual susceptibility toward delinquent behavior in the military service."[17] From a larger pool, 121 items were selected for their effectiveness in distinguishing Navy and Marine Corps enlisted men serving sentences in Naval retraining commands from enlisted men in various duty stations. The populations involved in this research are thus somewhat different from the delinquents and nondelinquents employed in the present study, but a considerable amount of research indicates that questionnaire items which differentiate between legally and socially defined groups of offenders and nonoffenders have a good deal of discriminatory generality, however the offenses are defined and regardless of subject age range. The Socialization Scale of the California Psychological Inventory, for example, has differentiated not only between delinquent and nondelinquent adolescents, but between guard house prisoners and duty soldiers in the Army, adult reformatory inmates and high school students, judged behavior problems and "good citizens" in school, and it relates rather impressively to assumed socialization over some 20 groups to which the scale has been applied.[18] We cannot claim that the items defined by research on Navy and Marine Corps personnel actually differentiate between delinquent and nondelinquent adolescents, but there is good empirical reason to assume that the items would perform the desired discrimination, and this was our reason for including them in the battery.

The tendency among questionnaire authors to use items from previously developed instruments led to some overlap among tests. Seven of the 33 MMPI items also appeared in the PNI Attitude Schedule and were eliminated from the set now under discussion. Thirty-eight of the 119 items in the Navy questionnaire appeared either in the PNI or the MMPI, and these were also eliminated. Two more statements were omitted because they made reference to affairs of a specifically military kind. The remaining 105 items, 26 from the MMPI and 79 from the Navy scale, were entitled the Personal Opinion Inventory (POI) and were used as one test in this study.

[15] C. H. Hanley, *An Inventory of Personal Opinions, First Technical Report, Rehab. Research* (San Diego, Calif.: U. S. Naval Retraining Command, Camp Elliot, 1954).

[16] S. R. Hathaway and E. D. Monachesi, "The Personalities of Delinquent Boys," *J. Crim. Law Criminol. Police Sci.* XLVIII (1957), pp. 149–163.

[17] Hanley, *op. cit.*, 2.

[18] H. G. Gough, *Manual for the California Psychological Inventory* (Palo Alto: Consulting Psychologists Press, 1957); Gough and Peterson, *op. cit.;* Peterson, Quay, and Anderson, *op. cit.*

The K D Proneness Scale (KD). The K D Proneness Scale by Kvaraceus[19] was employed as a fourth questionnaire. It consists of 75 multiple-choice items which permit differentiation of delinquent and nondelinquent groups. The following item illustrates the format in which statements are presented: "Failure in school is usually due to (a) bad companions, (b) lack of ability, (c) lack of hard work, (d) unfriendly teachers." Since the response alternatives represent discrete choices, rather than points on continua, the separate alternatives were employed as elemental variables in conducting the factorization. Of the 300 variables which thus appear in the scale (75 items × four alternatives) Kvaraceus has claimed discriminatory power for only 135, but the latter number was still too large to permit analysis, and the number of variables had to be reduced even further.

Elimination was accomplished by executing a preliminary factorization of some of the items, retaining those with the highest communalities, and pooling the latter with the remaining variables for a second analysis. The first 106 alternatives which perform the necessary differentiation were intercorrelated, and 10 centroid factors extracted. Eighty variables with communalities over .25 were then combined with the 29 remaining alternatives in the scale for the final factor analysis.

Data Analysis

The following analytic steps were performed with the aid of an electronic computer. First, phi coefficients of intercorrelation were computed for each of the four questionnaires, and 10 centroid factors were extracted from each correlation matrix. Decisions as to how many factors to rotate were largely arbitrary, although plots of variance removed by successive factors generally reinforced our decisions. Three factors were retained in the PNI Attitude Schedule, as directed by the hypothesis that Psychopathy, Neuroticism, and Inadequacy would emerge as factors in the instrument. Four factors were retained in each of the remaining three questionnaires. The four sets of factors were then rotated in accordance with Kaiser's varimax criterion.[20]

The first order factors were given independent interpretation, as discussed below, and further analyses focused on relations among them. To reduce spurious intercorrelations between factors in the same test, factor scores were based on relatively pure items, viz., those with loadings $\geq .30$ on the factor in question and $< .20$ on all other factors. No differential

[19] Kvaraceus, *K D Proneness Scale and Checklist, op. cit.*; Kvaraceus, *Forecasting Juvenile Delinquency, op. cit.*

[20] H. F. Kaiser, "The Varimax Criterion for Analytic Rotation in Factor Analysis," *Psychometrika*, XXIII (1958), pp. 187–200.

weights were employed; scores were derived by algebraic addition, and the correlations among them determined.

As a final integrative analysis, second order questionnaire factors were defined. To permit first order factors statistical freedom to emerge at the second order, two scores had to be computed for each of the first order factors examined in the analysis. One vector in the Personal Index was eliminated because only three variables met our criteria for inclusion as salients, but two scores were obtained for each of the remaining 14 dimensions. The salient variables in each factor were rearranged in the order in which they had originally been presented to Ss. One score was then derived from the first half of the items, and another from the second half of the items. Product-moment intercorrelations were calculated for the resulting 28 variables, 10 centroid factors were extracted, and three of the latter were rotated to orthogonal simple structure as defined by the varimax procedure.

RESULTS

All questionnaires used in the investigation, all centroid and rotated factor matrices, lists of salient variables complete with loadings and item numbers, and various tables pertinent to the second order analysis have been reported elsewhere.[21] Only the salient variables representing each factor will be discussed below, beginning with the first order dimensions derived from the questionnaires. In accordance with the usual convention, omission of sign before any item means that the response "true" is associated with the positive pole of the factor; a negative sign in parentheses at the beginning of an item indicates that the response "false" is associated with the positive pole of the factor.

First Order Factors

PNI Attitude Schedule. Salient variables for the first factor drawn from the PNI emerged as follows:

PNI Factor 1—*Psychopathy.* The only way to make big money is to steal it. It's dumb to trust older people. A lot of times it's fun to be in jail. The only way to settle anything is to lick the guy. If you don't have enough to live on, it's

---

[21] The four questionnaires, centroid factor matrices and rotated factor matrices pertaining to the analyses, complete lists of salient variables, and intercorrelations among first order factors have all been deposited as Document number 6606 with the ADI Auxiliary Publications Project, Photoduplication Service, Library of Congress, Washington 25, D. C. A copy may be secured by citing the Document number and by remitting $5.00 for photoprints, or $2.25 for 35 mm. microfilm. Advance payment is required. Make checks or money orders payable to: Chief, Photoduplication Service, Library of Congress.

OK to steal. I go out of my way to meet trouble rather than try to escape it. I do what I want to, whether anybody likes it or not. I would have been more successful if people had given me a fair chance. A person is better off if he doesn't trust anyone. I'm really too tough a guy to get along with most kids. (—) I would rather be at home when things go wrong. Most brothers and sisters are more trouble than they are worth. I hardly ever get excited or thrilled.

The same amoral, rebellious qualities which characterized the Psychopathy dimension of the earlier factor study[22] are evident here and leave little doubt as to factor identity. Eleven of the 13 variables which appear in the present factor loaded over .30 in the previous one, and the two remaining items (I would have been more successful if people had given me a fair chance; I hardly ever get excited or thrilled) are perfectly consistent with interpretation as psychopathy.

Composition of the second PNI factor is remarkably like that of the Neuroticism dimension isolated before.[23]

PNI Factor 2—*Neuroticism.* I don't think I'm quite as happy as others seem to be. I just don't seem to get the breaks other people do. It seems as if people are always telling me what to do, or how to do things. I often feel as though I have done something wrong or wicked. It is hard for me to act natural when I am with new people. I seem to do things that I regret more often than other people do. People often talk about me behind my back. I sometimes feel that I made the wrong choice in my occupation.(—) Most of the time I feel happy. I get nervous when I have to ask someone for a job. It seems as if I've been caught in every lie I ever told. My folks move (or used to move) from place to place a lot. (—) Most people seem to like me as soon as they meet me.

Of the 13 salient items, nine had been employed in the earlier study, and eight of these occur as markers for Neuroticism. One item previously identified with Inadequacy and four new items complete the present set of defining variables. All are sufficiently indicative of low self-esteem, dysphoric mood, tension, and guilt to justify use of the term "Neuroticism" as a label for the dimension.

The first two PNI factors strongly confirmed hypotheses regarding the structural occurrence of Psychopathy and Neuroticism, but the third PNI factor bears no relation whatsoever to the remaining hypothetical dimension, Inadequacy.

PNI Factor 3—*Delinquent Background.* When I was going to school I played hooky quite often. In school I was sometimes sent to the principal for cutting up. My folks usually blame bad company for the trouble I get into. (—) I have never been in trouble with the law. When I was a little kid, I was

---

[22] Peterson, Quay, and Cameron, *op. cit.*
[23] *Ibid.*

always doing things my folks told me not to. I am behind at least a year in school. I have very strong likes and dislikes.

In fact, the items have no obvious pertinence to any aspect of personality. Most of them have some kind of historical-environmental significance, and the label, "Delinquent Background" implies little more than a history of delinquent behavior, possibly committed in company with other members of a delinquent group. From this point of view, the factor resembles Jenkins and Glickman's[24] "Socialized Delinquency," and from its apparent reference to early history it might be construed as a unification of the "Family Dissension" and "Scholastic Maladjustment" factors distinguished in earlier research with many of these same questionnaire items. An alternative interpretation is suggested by reflecting the factor. When loading signs are reversed, it is clear that covariation among the items could stem from a tendency to deny ever having done anything delinquent, or even naughty. A response set of this kind would be analogous to defensiveness as defined by the K-scale of the MMPI, and appropriately developed measures might be useful in improving the discriminatory effectiveness of other scales. Whether PNI factor 3 should be interpreted as historical background, momentary or dispositional response set, or as something else remains to be seen. At any rate, it does not represent Inadequacy, as we had expected, and only Psychopathy and Neuroticism have been solidly replicated as personality factors defined by this particular group of questionnaire items.

Personal Index. Loofbourow and Keys developed their instrument in an era of psychometric preoccupation with such dimensions as neuroticism and general adjustment. A great many of the items refer to neurotic symptoms, and this concentration of content, quite different from that of the PNI, probably accounts for the emergence of two factors with some kind of neurotic quality.

PI Factor 1—*Conversion Reaction.* Do your eyes often pain you? Do you ever have the same dream over and over? Are you troubled with dreams about your play? Do you ever dream of robbers? Do you get angry so that you "see red"? Did you ever have the habit of jerking your head, neck, or shoulders? Have you often fainted away? Do you feel like jumping off when you are on a high place? Do you giggle a good deal and find you cannot help it? Do you know anybody who is trying to do you harm or hurt you? Have you the habit of biting your finger nails? Have you ever had a vision?

The first factor from the Personal Index implies a variety of conversion symptoms, along with some other hysterical tendencies, and had been correspondingly named "Conversion Reaction."

[24] Jenkins and Glickman, *op. cit.*

PI Factor 2—*Hypersensitivity*. Do you ever wish that you were dead? Do you feel tired a good deal of the time? (—) Do you think people like you as much as they do other people? (—) Do you usually feel well and strong? Do you ever feel that no one loves you? Are your feelings often hurt so badly that you cry? (—) Can you do good work while people are looking at you? Do you often have a hard time making up your mind about things? (—) Can you stand the sight of blood? Do people find fault with you much? (—) Do you hear easily when spoken to?

The second dimension has a noticeable depressive component, but suggests, even more strongly, an extreme vulnerability to stress and especially to social criticism. Such frailty might easily predispose depressive feelings of a reactive kind, and sensitivity itself is conceived as the core of the factor.

PI Factor 3—*Scholastic Maladjustment*. Are you required to take subjects that you dislike? Would you select another teacher in any of your subjects if you were permitted to? Have you often been punished unjustly? Were you ever expelled from school or nearly expelled? Are you ever punished for things you do not do? Do you often fail in subjects that you dislike? Did you ever want to run away from home? Do any of your teachers tell you that you are too noisy or talk too much? Do any of your teachers mark examinations too severely? Did you ever have a nickname you didn't like very well? Did you ever have a real fight? (—) Are you doing as much or as well in school as your parents expect you to? Do you think there should be more tryout or optional classes?

One of the factors drawn from the Personal Index contained only three pure items and will not be discussed. The items in the remaining factor, like those in the third factor of the PNI, have little to do with personality, but refer instead to external matters, principally to school and the unpleasantness of academic life. "Dislike for School" would not be an inappropriate name for the factor, but it is a trifle too specific, and the label we have chosen, "Scholastic Maladjustment," has a more fittingly general meaning.

Personal Opinion Inventory. The PNI Attitude Schedule yielded one "Neuroticism" factor. The Personal Index of Loofbourow and Keys yielded two factors related to more narrowly limited aspects of neuroticism, viz., conversion tendencies and hypersensitivity. Now the Personal Opinion Inventory, made up of items from the MMPI and from research on Naval offenders, has produced still another factor whose content can be subsumed under the general concept of neuroticism, but whose focus is more specifically upon neurotic tension and the social isolation frequently related to such dynamics.

POI Factor 1—*Neurotic Estrangement*. At times I have a strong urge to do something harmful or shocking. No one seems to understand me. It is hard for me to just sit still and relax. Sometimes my conscience makes me do things that get me in trouble. My parents never really understood me. I feel that I have often been punished without cause. One or more members of my family is very nervous. I am so touchy on some subjects that I can't talk about them. My way of doing things is apt to be misunderstood by others. I must admit I find it very hard to work under strict rules and regulations. I have the wanderlust and am never happy unless I am roaming or traveling about. If I am not feeling well I am somewhat cross and grouchy. It makes me uneasy when someone does me a favor I didn't expect. I would rather go without something than ask for a favor. I feel like jumping off when I am on a high place.

Many of the items have something to do with tension or its derivatives. Most of the remaining variables refer in one way or another to misunderstanding and difficulty in open communication with other people. "Neurotic Estrangement" fails to place any particular emphasis on tension, but it summarizes the social distance implied by the variables, and suggests a neurotic basis for this state of affairs.

POI Factor 2—*Egocentricity.* A guy who doesn't look out for himself first is a sucker. We ought to worry about our own country and let the rest of the world take care of itself. It's no use worrying my head about public affairs; I can't do anything about them anyhow. I don't blame anyone for trying to grab all he can get in this world. A person does not need to worry about other people if only he looks out for himself. Any job is all right with me, so long as it pays well. Only a fool would ever vote to increase his own taxes. There are only two kinds of women—the good and the bad. Sometimes I think I'm too nice to some people. When I am cornered I tell that portion of the truth which is not likely to hurt me. I would like to hunt lions in Africa.

The only "psychopathic" factor discussed so far, factor 1 of the PNI Attitude Schedule, contained a variety of elements which permitted unification under the general concept of psychopathy. Disregard for and distrust of authority, positive enjoyment of antisocial activity, rejection of conventional norms, isolation from close family ties, and blunting of strong positive affect were all represented. The second factor from the POI, on the other hand, most strongly emphasizes a single quality, egocentricity, but the self-centeredness is so blunt in its expression that it could hardly occur except in company with other psychopathic tendencies.

POI Factor 3—*Social Desirability.* I would never play cards (poker) with a stranger. If I get too much change in a store, I always give it back. I am embarrassed by dirty stories. It would embarrass me to have a girl tell me a dirty story. Women should not be allowed to drink in cocktail bars. (—) During one period when I was a youngster I engaged in petty thievery. I have lived the right kind of life. (—) I would like to wear expensive clothes. The average policeman is not strict enough about the law. We ought to pay our elected officials better than we do.

The items in the third factor extracted from the POI suggest a prim morality that is too "good" to be genuine. In interpreting the third factor from the PNI Attitude Schedule, tentatively labelled "Delinquent Background," an alternative interpretation was proposed, namely that a reflection of the factor might represent defensive refusal to admit the commission of any socially unacceptable acts. A similar interpretation seems tenable for the present factor, and it has been named "Social Desirability" in the belief that a response set, and nothing deeper, has occasioned coalescence of the variables.

POI Factor 4—*Concern over Others' Opinions.* I really care whether people like me or dislike me. When people dislike me, I figure it's worth while to try to change their opinion. I often think about how I look and what impression I am making on others. I never refuse to play a game because I am not good at it. I find it hard to "drop" or "break with" a friend. It is very important to me to have enough friends and social life. It makes me angry when I hear of someone who has been wrongly prevented from voting. Before I do something, I try to consider how my friends will react to it. There is something wrong with a person who can't take orders without getting angry or resentful. It is easy for me to sympathize with someone who is always doubting and unsure about things. I regard the right to speak my mind as very important.

Some time ago, Gough[25] proposed a role-taking theory of psychopathy whose central postulate was that psychopaths are unable to see themselves from the point of view of other people. The idea led to development of a questionnaire scale for measuring role-taking capacity, and performance on the scale was related rather convincingly to role-taking ability in an experiment by Reed and Cuadra.[26] The fourth factor derived from the POI appears at first to be a fairly pure representation of role-taking concern, if not ability, and it is interesting to note that the factor correlates to a modest but reliable degree $(-.23)$ with the Psychopathy factor of the PNI Attitude Schedule. The cogency of this interpretation is weakened, however, by the fact that the average factor score for delinquents is higher than for nondelinquents and by the collective impression one gets from reading the variables that they constitute an exaggerated overstatement of concern for social approval. Again, some kind of defensive response set may be involved, but this, like the role-taking hypothesis, is difficult to assess from

[25] H. G. Gough, "A Sociological Theory of Psychopathy," *Amer. J. Sociol.,* LIII (1948), pp. 359–366.
[26] C. F. Reed and C. A. Cuadra, "The Role-taking Hypothesis in Delinquency," *J. Consult. Psychol.,* XXI (1957), pp. 386–390.

mere inspection of the items. At least, the statements have clear pertinence to concern over the evaluation of others, and we have chosen a properly conservative label to express this fact.

KD Proneness Scale. The relative complexity of item format in the KD Proneness Scale makes factor interpretation more difficult than for the simpler, forced-choice questionnaires discussed so far. In attempting to discern the meaning of each response tendency, one must not only consider the alternative which has been chosen or denied, but must also note relations with the other available alternatives. Thus, the first item in KD factor 1, presented below, suggests endorsement of the following kind of idea: "Whatever else policemen may do—scare you, boss you, or get something on you—they do *not* try to help you." This item, like all the KD items, is presented with the crucial alternative italicized, and the three remaining alternatives in parentheses. Signs before each item indicate whether a given italicized alternative was chosen (sign omitted) or rejected (—).

KD Factor 1—*Situational Delinquency.* (—) Most policemen try to *help you* (scare you, boss you, get something on you). (—) A boy or girl should be allowed to be his own boss when he is *21 years old* (14 years old, 16 years old, 18 years old). (—) The police *are usually very fair* (make some mistakes, favor the rich, are usually unfair). Most boys stay in school because they *are required by law to do so* (have to learn to make a living, want to go to college, like school). When not in school, I can have the most fun *around midnight* (in the mornings, in the afternoons, around noon). On my report card I usually get *some failure marks* (all honor marks, mostly good marks, fair marks). I have the most fun when I play *on my street* (in my own house, in my own yard, on the playground near my house). If a person called me a dirty name, I would *fight the person* (tell him where to get off, say and do nothing, laugh it off). When I leave school or graduate, I shall *take it easy for a while* (take any job that comes along, find a good job, go to another school or college). Going to high school is *all right for some people but not for me* (a waste of time, all right if you can take the course you want to, necessary for success). (—) If a person called me a dirty name, I would *say and do nothing* (fight the person, tell him where to get off, laugh it off). Going to school right now is doing me *more harm than good* (a great deal of good, some good, a great deal of harm). I have been *unlucky* (extremely lucky, lucky, extremely unlucky). (—) Most boys stay in school because they *want to go to college* (are required by law to do so, have to learn to make a living, like school). When I am with someone else and we want something to drink, I like to *match to see who will pay* (buy my own drink, fix it so the other person usually pays, pay for all the drinks). (—) On my report card I usually get *mostly good marks* (all honor marks, fair marks, some failure marks). Of the following sports, the one I like best to watch is a *prize fight* (baseball game, horserace, basketball game).

Few of the items in the first KD factor have clear relevance to personality as a set of internal dispositions. Most of the referents are outside the individual (policemen, school situations, social regulations, and the like). Insofar as personal characteristics are represented, they apparently constitute desires for early independence, rejection of middle-class beliefs in the value of education and hard work, and wishes just to have a good time without the annoyance of rules or constraints. Factor meaning is anything but obvious, and another psychopathic expression may be involved. The attitudes implied, however, are those commonly said to arise merely from long exposure to a delinquent subculture, with no truly psychopathic basis, and we tentatively propose the name "Situational Delinquency" as a label for the dimension.

KD Factor 2—*Irresponsibility.* In school, my friends *always get me into trouble* (almost always get me into trouble, sometimes get me into trouble, never get me into trouble). I think about what I'll do when I get out of school *not at all* (all the time, most of the time, some of the time). Going to school right now is doing me *a great deal of harm* (a great deal of good, some good, more harm than good). Whenever I get into serious trouble, other people are to blame *always* (almost always, sometimes, seldom or never). Taking part in school clubs is *very unimportant* (very important, quite important, not very important). The best teachers are the ones who are *very easy* (fairly easy, fairly hard, very hard). When I leave school or graduate, I shall *take any job that comes along* (find a good job, take it easy for awhile, go to another school or college). (—) When I leave school or graduate, I shall *find a good job* (take any job that comes along, take it easy for awhile, go to another school or college). Being successful usually means having *your name in the paper* (a big fortune, many friends, the respect of many people). (—) In school, my friends *sometimes get me into trouble* (always get me into trouble, almost always get me into trouble, never get me into trouble). Those who get the best jobs are usually the ones who *are the luckiest* (know the right person, are the best trained, work the hardest).

The tendencies expressed in the second KD factor include denial of personal responsibility for getting into difficulty, a lack of concern over academic and vocational success, a belief that success is tantamount to notoriety, and that it is obtained through luck, rather than effort, training, or even "pull." "Irresponsibility" summarizes these attitudes rather well, and a more central psychopathic tendency may again be represented.

KD Factor 3—*Response Set—Central Tendency.* (—) During the past month I have worried about my family *all the time* (most of the time, some of the time, not at all). During the past month I have worried about my family *some of the time* (all of the time, most of the time, not at all). (—) I think about what I'll do when I get out of school *all the time* (most of the time, some of the time, not at all). I think about what I'll do when I get out of school *some of the time* (all the time, most of the time, not at all). The pupils who have the best attendance records are almost always *good students* (honor students, poor students, sissies). Failure is usually due to *lack of hard work* (bad habits, bad companions, lack of ability). (—) Going to school causes me to be worried and upset *most of the time* (all the time, some of the time, not at all). I usually have the best time when I do things *with two or three friends* (all by myself, with one friend, with a big gang). (—) The secret of success is *ability* (just luck, hard work, money).

It seems unlikely that the variables in KD factor 3 were drawn together by any enduring personal trait. What seems to be involved is consistency in avoiding extreme statements and in selecting moderate, "middle-of-the-scale" alternatives. This is nothing more than a response set, and the title of the factor has been phrased accordingly.

KD Factor 4—*Attitude toward School.* Most teachers are *fair most of the time* (very fair, seldom fair, never fair). (—) The most popular boys are the ones who *almost never get into mischief* (almost always get into mischief, sometimes get into mischief, seldom get into mischief). Going to college is *all right if you can afford it* (necessary for success, all right if you have the ability, just a waste of time and money). Going to high school is *all right if you can take the course you want* (a waste of time, all right for some people but not for me, necessary for success). (—) The best teachers are the ones who are *very hard* (very easy, fairly easy, fairly hard). Cheating in school is usually done by *most of the pupils* (only a few bad pupils, none of the pupils, all of the pupils). Cheating in school is usually done by *none of the pupils* (only a few bad pupils, most of the pupils, all of the pupils).

Six of the seven items in KD factor 4 have something to do with school, but the nature of the attitude represented is difficult to stipulate. Some of the variables seem related to a vague lack of enthusiasm for educational matters, but attitudinal implications are not sufficiently specific to warrant interpretation beyond the obvious reference to academic affairs.

Intercorrelations among Factors

The complete table of correlations among first order factors can be obtained, along with other tabular materials, from the American Documentation Institute.[27] This discussion will principally concern relations between first order factors which were similarly interpreted.

Some concept implying neuroticism was invoked more often than any other in labelling dimensions. Four factors, Neuroticism from the PNI,

---

[27] *See* footnote 21.

Conversion Reaction and Hypersensitivity from the PI, and Neurotic Estrangement from the POI, were alleged to represent neurotic tendencies of one sort or another, and if these propositions are sound the factors ought to be related among themselves. In fact, the mean r for pertinent intercorrelations is .49, which is about as high as one could expect, considering the limited number of items on which factor scores were based.

Except in the case of PNI factor 1, specification of "psychopathic" factors was less clear than for "neurotic" ones. However, intercorrelations for some of the traits generally associated with the concept of psychopathy, e.g., Psychopathy itself from the PNI, Egocentricity from the POI, and Irresponsibility from the KD, are worth considering. The mean intercorrelation for those dimensions is .29. This value is lower than for "neurotic" factors, principally because our measures of Egocentricity (POI-2) and Irresponsibility (KD-2) were not closely related ($r = .17$). The correlation between Psychopathy (PNI-1) and Egocentricity (POI-2) was .34, and the r for Psychopathy and Irresponsibility (KD-2) was .35. With an N of 406, all three rs are significant beyond the .01 level, but none of them is particularly impressive.

Evaluation of the complete matrix of factor intercorrelations also requires consideration of relations among various factors within each test. These should of course be lower than for allegedly similar factors in different tests. The mean r for intratest correlations was .21, which is satisfactorily less than the mean for factors implying neuroticism, but not compellingly different from the mean r of putative "Psychopathy" factors.

The remaining dimensions were sufficiently diverse in meaning to prohibit supraordinate evaluation without additional analysis. To assess relations among them, as well as to test hypotheses regarding the coalescence of "Neuroticism" and "Psychopathy" factors, a second order factorization was conducted.

Second Order Factors

Results are given in Table 1. The salient variables are halves of the first order dimension, presented by indicating second order loadings and first order factor designations, with the letters "a" or "b" to show which half of each primary factor is involved.

Factor I is dominated by elements suggesting neuroticism. Every one of the first order constituents thought to refer to a neurotic tendency has a loading of .60 or more. Below that point, discontinuity appears in the distribution of loadings, and then a second cluster of first order elements can be seen. The latter refer to a history of delinquent activity and difficulty in school and characterize the present neuroticism factor as an alloplastic one. The neurotic tendencies, which would otherwise be indis-

Table 1
Second Order Factors

FACTOR I—NEUROTIC DELINQUENCY		FACTOR II—DELINQUENT BACKGROUND (OR DEFENSIVENESS)		FACTOR III—PSYCHOPATHIC DELINQUENCY	
Loading	First Order Designation	Loading	First Order Designation	Loading	First Order Designation
67	PNI-2a Neuroticism	66	KD-1a Situational Delinquency	56	KD-2a Irresponsibility
67	POI-1b Neurotic Estrangement	−66	POI-3a Social Desirability	56	PNI-1b Psychopathy
65	POI-1a Neurotic Estrangement	63	KD-1b Situational Delinquency	54	PNI-1a Psychopathy
65	PI-2a Hypersensitivity	50	PI-3a Scholastic Maladjustment	52	KD-4b Attitude toward School
65	PI-1a Conversion Reaction	46	PNI-3b Delinquent Background	51	POI-2b Egocentricity
64	PNI-2b Neuroticism	−45	POI-4a Concern, Others' Opinions	49	KD-2b Irresponsibility
62	PI-2b Hypersensitivity	44	PNI-3a Delinquent Background	47	POI-2a Egocentricity
60	PI-1b Conversion Reaction	43	PI-3b Scholastic Maladjustment		
50	PI-3a Scholastic Maladjustment	−40	POI-4b Concern, Others' Opinions		
48	PI-3b Scholastic Maladjustment				
47	PNI-3b Delinquent Background				
44	PNI-3a Delinquent Background				

244

tinguishable from those among the clientele of a typical guidance clinic, are evidently expressed outwardly in this behavioral pattern; they are "acted out" against society.

Factor II is more difficult to interpret than the first one. The pattern of positive and negative loadings suggests that covariation could be determined by a consistent tendency to endorse statements implying a history of misbehavior and to deny items implying concern over society's evaluation of the behavior. The underlying attitudes are those commonly thought to occur among members of delinquent gangs, and this, in the absence of any clear expression of personality disturbance, suggested "Delinquent Background" as a label. Another interpretative possibility, however, becomes apparent when the factor is reflected, namely, that the factor could express a tendency to place oneself in a socially favorable light and deny past commission of delinquent acts. It is difficult to say which interpretation is more likely just by looking at the items, and further study is obviously needed.

Factor III unifies those first order dimensions assumed to reflect psychopathic tendencies and has been labelled accordingly. In general, the primary factors thought to refer to various facets of psychopathy appear as salient variables at the second order. In addition, half of KD factor 4, vaguely defined as "Attitude toward School," appears with a fairly high loading, suggesting that the attitude involved may represent another facet of the psychopathic viewpoint.

Together, the three second order factors define a structure remarkably similar to that developed by Jenkins and Glickman[28] from case history data. The conceptual parallels between "Neurotic Delinquency" and "Disturbed Delinquency," "Delinquent Background" and "Socialized Delinquency" and "Psychopathic Delinquency" and "Unsocialized Aggression" are obvious, but operationally defined associations remain to be established.

In time, further research on these dimensions should proceed to extensive elaboration of antecedent and consequent relationships, but it should probably begin with the establishment of concurrent validity and more thorough examination of such purely psychometric properties of the measures as reliability and independence. Some preliminary checks with military personnel suggest that scales based on the second order factorization are not nearly as independent as one might expect from the nature of their derivation. This is true even when the cooperative elements of factors I and II are excluded, and further purification will probably be necessary.

In the present study, a premature effort was made to relate the first order questionnaire factors to three factors derived from teacher ratings and to a limited number of indicants taken from institutional files. The results were almost wholly incomprehensible, and, while this may mean

[28] Jenkins and Glickman, *op. cit.*

that the questionnaire factors are unrelated to anything outside themselves, we are more inclined to question the adequacy of the ratings and of our own first order factor measures. In some cases, the latter were based on as few as seven items and were never derived from more than 17. Results with previous measures of Psychopathy, Neuroticism, and Inadequacy appeared rather promising.[29] It seems reasonable to suppose that the present more comprehensively defined measures may also be related to crucial extratest variables and that their application may eventually lead to a substantial increase in knowledge about personality factors and the part they play in juvenile delinquency.

SUMMARY

Four questionnaires which differentiate delinquents from nondelinquents were administered to 203 training school inmates and to 203 high school boys. The items in each questionnaire were intercorrelated over the entire sample, and four separate factor analyses conducted. The resulting first order factors were individually interpreted, relations between them were examined, and a second order factorization was performed. The following results emerged.

1. Psychopathy and Neuroticism factors isolated in previous research were almost identically reproduced in the present first order analysis.

2. A factor called "Inadequacy" in the previous study did not appear in this investigation.

3. Differences in item content from questionnaire to questionnaire occasioned differences in meaning of first order factors, but many of the latter could be subsumed under second order concepts of Psychopathic and Neurotic Delinquency.

4. Most of the remaining first and second order dimensions seemed to refer to a history of delinquent behavior, and possibly to previous membership in a delinquent group, but interpretation as test-taking defensiveness was also frequently considered.

[29] Quay, Peterson, and Consalvi, op. cit.

Varieties of Religious Experience in Young Adolescents*

DAVID ELKIND AND
SALLY ELKIND

The Elkinds outline descriptively almost a dozen different religious experiences in the following investigation of the activities in which adolescents either maintain their belief in a Deity or test their faith in Him. The researchers view religiosity as a culturally determined personality trait and couch their explanations in conventional psychological terms. Evidence bearing upon religious behavior of adolescents other than that provided by anecdotal or case material is not plentiful, and this study by the Elkinds contributes valuable information about a very important aspect of development during adolescence that is rarely examined.

In his book, *The Varieties of Religious Experience*,[1] (1902), William James distinguished between institutional and personal religion. Institutional religion involves all the formal aspects of the Church and has as its central aim "winning the favor of Gods."[2] Personal religion, on the other hand, involves the "inner dispositions of man," whose "individual conscience, helplessness, incompleteness form the center of interest."[3] In his writing, James further limited personal religion to "The feelings, acts and experiences of individuals *in their solitude* (our italics) so far as they apprehend themselves to stand in relation to whatever they may consider to be divine."[4]

By limiting personal religion to those experiences which occurred in solitude, James was necessarily led to striking and perhaps extreme forms

[1] W. James, The Varieties of Religious Experience (*Modern Library* Edit.; New York: Longmans Green & Co., 1902).
[2] *Ibid.*, 40.
[3] *Ibid.*
[4] *Ibid.*, 42.

* From the *Journal for the Scientific Study of Religion*, II (1962), pp. 102–112. Reprinted by permission of the authors and the publisher.

of the religious consciousness such as the "sick soul" and the "divided self." There would seem to be, however, a variety of religious experiences which—while remaining personal in the sense of individual apprehension of the divine—do not necessarily occur in solitude nor to persons of a peculiar religious temperament. If we start from the notion that religious experience is a relationship between the individual and God, we can also suppose that this relationship, at least in form, is comparable to a relationship between two individuals. Such a relationship, say friendship, is conditioned by two types of experience. *Recurrent* experiences such as lunching, golfing, or going to the theatre together are consciously chosen and serve to maintain and strengthen the relationship. On the other hand there are also *acute* experiences, such as misunderstandings, breaches of trust, and emotional conflicts which are largely fortuitous and serve to test the strength of the relationship. The same distinction would appear to hold true for the relationship between man and God. Here too we find consciously chosen recurrent experiences, such as going to Church, saying prayers, and performing rituals which can serve to strengthen and maintain the relationship. But there are also acute fortuitous experiences such as death or unanswered prayers which serve to test the strength of the relationship. According to this distinction, the experiences described by James would be extreme types of acute experience and would not exhaust the varieties of religious experience peculiar to personal religion.

In the present study we made an exploratory attempt at discovering the variety of recurrent and acute religious experiences in which adolescents "apprehend themselves in the presence of the divine" regardless of whether such experiences occurred in solitude. We also explored the possibility that there were sex, ability and denominational differences in the frequency with which particular types of religious experience occurred.

It should be said that we are presenting our material at this time not because we regard it as definitive but rather in the hope that the problems raised by our preliminary findings will encourage others to undertake investigations into this aspect of religion.

METHOD

Subjects

One hundred and forty-four ninth-grade students attending the Wilson Jr. High School in Natick, Mass., were tested.[5] All of the students were enrolled in English classes taught by one of the authors (SE). The following characteristics of the students were of importance for the group comparisons made in the study.

[5] We are indebted to Mr. George M. Rogers, principal of the Wilson J. High School, for permission to carry out the study.

Sex. Of the 144 subjects, 67 were boys and 77 were girls.

Ability Grouping. Ability grouping was practiced at the Wilson school and these subdivisions rather than IQ scores were used for group comparisons.[6] Of the 144 students taught by SE, 36 were either in the Honor Group or considered Honor Group material. The Honor Group consisted of those students with IQ's of 155 or better (usually) and with outstanding records of school achievement. The remaining 108 students were in Average Groups. Accordingly in the comparisons to be made the Honor Group will be compared with the remaining children hereafter called the Average Group.

Religion. Questions regarding religious affiliation were not permitted in the Massachusetts schools, so it was not possible to ascertain the exact number of Catholic, Jewish, and Protestant children participating in the study. Information offered spontaneously, however, revealed that there were at least 25 Jewish and 27 Catholic children in the sample. The remaining students were Protestant and largely Congregational. While the indefiniteness regarding the exact number of children in each denominational group precluded statistical texts of religious group differences, general comments about such differences will be made in presenting the results.

Procedure

During the regular class period the students were asked by their teacher (SE) to compose two paragraphs in answer to the following questions:

1. "When do you feel closest to God?"

2. "Have you ever had a particular experience when you felt especially close to God?"

The students were also told that if they could not answer either or both of the above questions they should compose a paragraph in answer to the question:

3. "Why does God permit war, murder, and disease?"

None of the classes was told beforehand that the compositions were to be used for other than English purposes. They were told, however, that the compositions would be corrected for grammar but not graded.

RESULTS

The per cent of boys and girls and of Honor and Average Group students answering each of the three questions is shown in Table 1. As this table indicates, there were significant differences between the Honor and the Average Groups with respect to the frequency with which they answered the

[6] It was decided not to use the IQ's because they were not available for all youngsters and those which were had been obtained with different tests and at different ages.

questions. More Honor than Average Group students answered questions 1 and 2, while the reverse held true for question 3. On the other hand, there were no such differences for boys and girls. The findings shown in Table 1 raise two questions: (1) Why do more Honor than Average students report occurrences of religious feeling and (2) Why do Average, but not Honor, students answer question 3?

With respect to the first question, one possible interpretation is that the Honor Group have a broader conception of God than the Average Group and this broader conception enables them to interpret many more experiences than the Average Group as religious in nature. We will invoke a similar hypothesis to explain other Honor-Average Group differences. Why the Honor Group fails to answer question 3 is a puzzle, since one would expect that the question, "Why does God permit war, murder, and disease?" would challenge their intelligence. Perhaps, and this is just a speculation, the bright students avoid the intellectual issue because of a fear (not necessarily conscious) that if they bring their critical faculties to bear on such questions they will lose their faith. From this point of view the average student, who is probably more apt to accept the explanation of authority or some practical or utilitarian rationale, may not sense the threat posed by the question and therefore feels no compunction about answering it. At present, however, our interpretation is but a guess among guesses and much more work needs to be done on this problem of how young people reconcile reason with dogma.

Answers to Question 1 (Recurrent Religious Experiences)

The answers to the question "When do you feel closest to God?" suggested six types of recurrent religious experiences. These experiences together with illustrative examples are presented below.

Table 1
Per Cent of Boys, Girls, Honor, and Average Students
Replying to Three Religious Questions

Question	B (N = 67)	G (N = 77)	H (N = 36)	A (N = 108)	T (N = 144)
				Group	
1*	92	91	94	91	92
2†	73	79	86	73	76
3‡	16	10	0	20	15
X^2		2.69ns.		8.05**	

* "When do you feel closest to God?"
† "Have you ever had a particular experience of feeling especially close to God?"
‡ "Why does God permit war, murder, and disease?"
** Significant at the .05 level.

Church Experiences. The most frequent type of experience for the group as a whole was associated with the Church or Synagogue.

"In Church every Sunday is probably the time when I feel closest to God. On Holy Days of Obligation I sometimes feel inspired and go to Church about 6 A.M."

Solitary Experiences. Next in frequency to Church experiences were those which occurred when the adolescent was alone.

"I think the time when I feel closest to God is at night when my brothers and sisters are sleeping and the house is quiet. Everything is so peaceful and I have time to think about all the wonderful things He has given us. ... I fall asleep recalling these things and thanking God for them."

Anxiety and Fear Experiences. A number of adolescents wrote they felt closest to God when there was some real or imagined threat to their family or themselves.

"The time when I feel closest to God is when I think my life is in danger."

"I feel close to God when someone I love is in danger."

Worry Experiences. Still another group of students felt closest to God when they were worried about problems or personal difficulties.

"God is close to me most of the time, but especially when I am in trouble or have a real problem."

Prayer Experiences. For some adolescents feeling closest to God came at times of prayer.

"I feel closest to God lots of times, but closest when I am praying 'cause when I am praying, I am praying to Him."

Moral Action Experiences. Although experiences of this type were seldom reported they were distinctive enough to be classed alone.

"I feel closest to God whenever I do anything really wrong or get into bad trouble."

"I feel closest to God whenever I do something for someone else. I don't need any reward: the feeling I get is all I need."

The per cent of adolescents reporting each of these types of experience is given in Table 2. As Table 2 indicates, there were significant differences both between the boys and the girls and between the Honor and the Average Groups in the frequency with which particular experiences were reported. For the denominational groups (not shown in Table 2) the only difference was that nearly all of the Catholic group reported feeling closest to God when in Church.

As Table 2 shows, the differences between the boys and the girls were primarily in the categories of solitary, fear-anxiety, and moral action experiences. It is possible to interpret these boy-girl differences at many levels.

One could, for example, relate them to the (Freudian) dynamic complexes which presumably differentiate boys and girls or to the constitutional or temperamental differences between the sexes. In our discussion, however, we will focus on the different cultural expectations encountered by boys and girls in our society. This in no way denies the applicability of additional interpretations, for it is a psychological truism that human behavior is always multi-determined. At this point in our knowledge, however, an explanation in terms of cultural expectations seems closest to the data and to involve the fewest assumptions about human nature.

In American middle-class society the expectations for boys and girls with respect to religion are not the same. Girls are expected to be more pious and God-fearing, whereas boys are supposed to be rebellious and "full of the devil." This expectation is presented in many different ways from nursery rhymes in which girls are supposed to be made of "sugar 'n' spice and everything nice" and boys to be made of "snakes, snails, and puppy dog tails," to movies and TV dramas in which the mother drags a reluctant father off to Church. The result of these cultural expectations is that, other things being equal, women do tend to be more religious than men as Allport, Gillespie and Young[7] have shown. In addition James[8] has pointed out that the most intense religious experiences occur in solitude. Taken together the tendency for women to be more religious than men and for more intense religious experiences to occur in solitude may account, at least in part, for the finding that more girls than boys report having religious experiences when alone.

Likewise the tendency for more girls than boys to report religious experiences when anxious or afraid is also in keeping with cultural expectations. Girls but not boys in our society are expected to frighten easily and to readily admit such feelings. (The standard joke about girls running at the sight of a mouse reflects this expectation. The same response would be unheard of in a boy.) Finally the tendency for more boys than girls to report religious experiences associated with moral actions can also be given a cultural interpretation. Boys, but not girls, are expected to show their dominance through aggressive (and often troublesome) action but are also supposed to show their chivalry through polite and considerate behavior. It is not surprising, therefore, that a boy who has proved his manhood through performing a troublesome or gentlemanly act is willing to admit a religious experience in connection with it.

These interpretations regarding the role of cultural expectations in the differential religious experience for boys and girls are in keeping with what

[7] G. W. Allport, J. M. Gillespie, and J. Young, "The Religion of the Post-War College Student," *J. Psychol.*, XXV (1948), pp. 3–33.
[8] James, *op. cit.*

we know from cultural anthropology. Mead,[9] for example, has shown that, depending upon cultural expectations and training, boys can become aggressive or passive, active or inert, and that the same holds true for girls. In short, if religiosity is regarded as a trait of personality then we are saying that it is a trait which is, in part, culturally determined.

Turning now to the differences between the Honor and the Average Group, these occur primarily in the categories of Church, solitary, and fear-anxiety experiences. These differences seem best explained by the personality traits associated with high and with average intelligence. Children of high intelligence are usually more curious, more independent and more abstract thinkers than their average age-mates. Consequently they should be able to conceive the Deity more broadly than their average fellows and should also be more resistant than their peers to relating to Him in a conforming situation such as a Church service. These two conditions, then, the ability to conceive God more broadly (and thus in a greater variety of situations) and the resistance to conformity (which is necessarily present in a Church service) could explain why more Honor than Average Group students reported feeling closest to God when alone and why the reverse was true for feeling closest to God when in Church. Likewise, the greater self-confidence associated with high intelligence could account for the finding that less Honor than Average Group students reported feeling closest to God when anxious or afraid.

The last difference to be discussed is that found between the denominational groups. Significantly more Catholic than Protestant or Jewish children reported religious experiences while in Church. This result is in keeping with the teachings of Catholicism which holds that the Church is the necessary intermediary between the individual and the Deity. One would therefore expect Catholic children to feel closest to God when in Church and this, of course, is what we found.

Answers to Question 2 (Acute Religious Experience)

With the exception of 11 students, whose statements about the circumstances of feeling especially close to God were the same as their statements about the occurrences of feeling closest to Him, the adolescents who answered the second question described experiences other than those given in answer to Question 1. The compositions describing the occurrence of feeling "especially close to God" suggested five more varieties of religious experience. These acute experiences, together with illustrative descriptions, are described below.

[9] Margaret Mead, "The Childhood Genesis of Sex Differences in Behavior," *Discussions in Child Development*, III, ed. J. M. Tanner and Barbel Inhelder (New York: International Univer. Press, 1958).

Table 2

**Per Cent of Boys, Girls, Honor, and Average Group Students
Who Acknowledged Feeling Close to God
for 6 Varieties of Such Experience**

Experience	B ($N = 62$)	G ($N = 70$)	H ($N = 35$)	Group A ($N = 98$)	T ($N = 132$)
Church	50	42	35	49	45
Solitary	8	26	38	10	17
Fear and Anxiety	10	17	6	17	14
Worry	13	11	12	12	12
Prayer	11	3	6	7	7
Moral Action	8	1	3	5	5
X^2		14.40*		16.06†	

* Significant at the .05 level.
† Significant at the .01 level.

Appreciation Experiences. The most frequent experience of being especially close to God occurred when either the student or someone close to him barely escaped death or injury.

"As my mother started to make a left turn, a car coming parallel to the turn collided with us. It just seemed to happen in a second. One minute everything was all right and the next I didn't know what happened. As it was, the car was a total wreck. I was sitting in the front seat and if the other car hit one inch from where it did I would have been killed. To me this did not happen out of coincidence but out of the will of God."

Meditation Experiences. Next in frequency were those experiences involving moments of quiet philosophic rumination sometimes accompanied by a heightened awareness of self and surroundings.

"I had gone into the woods as I often did, but for some reason I felt more alone. I began to think of what had brought me back to camp that year and my motives and how right and wrong they were. The way in which I answered my own questions seemed to go deeper than my own personal thoughts . . . I felt He had been a guiding influence in my decision."

Lamentation Experiences. A number of students described religious experiences following the death of a loved one. The following is a particularly poignant example of such an experience.

"The experience at which I felt closest to God was when my family and I were in Maine in a cottage on the lake. One night I heard a horrible voice calling for help and found out that my mother and father and uncle were in the middle of the lake drowning. Later I heard that my uncle and father were all right but that my mother was trapped in the air pocket underneath the over-turned boat. That's when I felt closest to God. I asked Him to save her but I guess He wanted her and He took her."

Initiation Experiences. Experiences of this kind were reported by adolescents who wrote that they felt closest to God when participating in a religious (usually initiation) ceremony.

"I felt closest to God when I took my first Holy Communion."

"I think the day of my Bas Mitzvah I felt closest to God. During the ceremony, when I became an adult according to Jewish law, I felt a holiness and closeness to God which I never felt before."

Revelation Experiences. Although few in number, these experiences were distinctive because in each one the young person had the feeling of actually speaking to or perceiving the Deity.

"I feel my greatest experience was one day while walking up a hill on a slippery day. While walking I slipped and fell down. I got up but slipped and fell down again. This time I used the Lord's name in vain. Still lying on the ground, I looked up and saw the outline of a saint or God. After watching the image fade away, I heard a voice say, 'There is no place in Heaven for sinners' . . . I don't know what really happened and probably never will."

The per cent of subjects who reported each type of experience is given in Table 3. As shown in Table 3, there were no significant differences either between the boys and girls or between the Honor and Average Groups with respect to experiences associated with feeling especially close to God. For the denominational groups, not shown in Table 2, there were differences. Both the Catholic and the Jewish children, but not the Protestant children, reported feeling especially close to God when participating in religious rituals.

It is necessary to attempt an explanation of the fact that differences between boys and girls and between Honor and Average students were found for recurrent but not for acute varieties of religious experience. This fact, it seems to us, derives from the opposed characteristics of these two types of experience. It will be recalled that recurrent types of experience are those which are consciously chosen by the individual to strengthen and to maintain a relationship. The choices an individual makes, however, are determined by the traits which form his personality. This may explain why boys and girls, Honor and Average students who differ in their personality traits, also differ in their choice of Church, solitude, prayer, etc. for strengthening and maintaining their spiritual relationships.

The matter is quite different when we look at acute types of religious experience which serve to test a relationship. Such testing, whether between man and man or between man and God is, with the possible exception of initiation and meditation experiences, seldom consciously chosen. This is not to say that personality plays no role in such experiences, for it is obvious that different individuals will respond quite differently to, say, a death in the family or a near-fatal accident. But in acute types of experience the *occasion* for the response is independent of conscious volition and dependent upon chance. Since before the laws of chance all individuals—regardless of their personality differences—are equal, there was no reason to expect that boys or girls, Honor or Average Group students should have more near fatal accidents, deaths in their family, or other occasions for acute religious experience. The fact that no differences were found between these groups with respect to the frequency with which they reported occurrences of acute religious experience is in keeping with the view that such occurrences are largely the result of chance. Put differently, one might say that the occasions for recurrent religious experiences are largely a matter of *subjective choice,* whereas the occasions for acute types of experience are largely a matter of *objective chance.*

Although we have emphasized the differences between recurrent and acute occurrences of religious experience, we do not wish to imply that these differences are in any way absolute, for there are many in-between cases. The occurrence of initiation experiences, for example, is not a matter of chance but of design. It is classed as an acute occurrence because the experience is not, at least initially, the personal choice of the individual but of the religion to which he belongs and is proscribed for all members of the religion regardless of their sex or intelligence. All Catholics are expected to take their first Holy Communion and all Jews are expected to have a Bar or Bas Mitzvah. The fact that there is no comparable ceremony in the Protestant Church may account for the fact that only Catholic and Jewish children reported occurrences of initiation experiences. In the case of initiation experiences, then, they are determined in part by a conscious design which is built into the religion and in part by the chance that a child will be born into that religion.

Meditation experiences provide another example of an in-between case. Occurrences for meditation experiences are consciously chosen insofar as the individual seeks out an opportunity to commune with God. But they are determined by chance to the degree that the individual cannot choose when he will be "overcome" with a heightened sense of self-awareness and feeling of well-being. We have chosen to classify meditation experiences as acute because the feeling of communion with God may come on at times when it is not sought and may not appear when it is. But the fact remains that meditation is frequently successful when it is consciously sought and this would render it more like a recurrent occasion for religious experience.

The distinction between recurrent and acute occurrences of religious experience thus suffers from the defects of any classification. Whenever we classify, there is a tendency to accentuate differences between classes and disregard their similarities. In our classification the same holds true. There may be, for example, more similarity between the recurrent experience associated with being alone and the acute experience associated with meditation than between any two recurrent or acute experiences. Meditation and being alone are nevertheless classed as different because of the degree of conscious choice involved. Classification is thus arbitrary but also necessary in the initial stage of inquiry for it serves to focus thought and to direct investigation. For the present, the distinction between recurrent and acute occurrences of religious feeling seems the most meaningful and straightforward way to organize our data but future research may suggest a more adequate criterion for differentiating among the varieties of religious experience.

Table 3
Per Cent of Boys, Girls, Honor, and Average Group Students Who Acknowledged Feeling Especially Close to God for 5 Varieties of Such Experience

			Group		
Experience	B	G	H	A	T
	($N = 49$)	($N = 61$)	($N = 30$)	($N = 80$)	($N = 110$)
Appreciation	35	38	34	38	36
Meditation	23	20	23	20	20
Initiation	10	18	23	11	15
Lamentation	14	13	10	15	14
Revelation	6	3	3	5	5
X^3		2.31ns.		3.38ns.	

NOTE: Per cents do not total to 100 because 12 per cent of the boys and 8 per cent of the girls reported the same type of experience when they felt especially close to God as they did when they felt closest to Him. These replies were not included in Table 3.

Answers to Question 3

The explanations given by the 22 students who attempted to explain why God permits war, murder, and disease were quite varied but did fall into two broad categories: the practical and the theological. Representative statements under each category are given below.

Practical explanations:

"God can't watch everybody at the same time."

"Teach us something, what drives man."

"The world is becoming overpopulated and employment scarcer."

"In a perfect world there would be nothing to strive for or to overcome."

Theological explanations:

"Evil is a temptation, it is a test of faith."

"God wants the deceased in Heaven."

"God created man and the universe and then left them to go on their own."

"There is no way to understand God's purpose but there is a reason why some people die."

"God can influence only those who believe in Him."

Reliability of Experience Classifications

Each of the compositions was read first by D. E., who then classified them according to experience type. Copies of the compositions, together with a description of the experience types, were then given to our research assistant,[10] who classified the paragraphs independently. Agreement between the classifications of the research assistant and D. E. was 91 per cent for answers to Question 1, and 90 per cent for answers to Question 2. Differences between the two readers were resolved in conference.

DISCUSSION

The results of the present study revealed six types of recurrent (strengthening and maintaining) and five types of acute (testing) religious experiences. In addition, the results showed that there were significant differences between boys and girls in the frequency with which they reported particular types of recurrent but not acute religious experiences. Finally, evidence was obtained that there were differences between Protestant, Catholic, and Jewish children in the frequency with which they reported both recurrent and acute types of experience. After presenting our findings we attempted to interpret them from the point of view of cultural and denominational expectations and individual differences in personality. It remains to take up in the present section the possible objections to our results and interpretations.

Perhaps the most fundamental objection to our study centers about the sincerity of the adolescent compositions we obtained. Isn't it likely that the answers young people gave to such questions as "When do you feel closest to God?" were dictated by what they thought the teacher expected, and motivated by the desire to win her approval? That is, were the students who answered our questions more concerned with putting themselves in a good light than in giving an accurate account of their religious experience? The best answer to this question comes from the experience of others who have used such compositions in their work. In their study of the personal docu-

[10] We wish to express our thanks to Mr. Gerald Beck, our research assistant, for his careful reading and classifying of the protocols.

ments of American university students, Gillespie and Allport[11] noted a "high degree of frankness, individuality and straightforward reporting. There seems to be little reticence, little posing, little striving for literary effects." Another author, Strang,[12] was so confident of the sincerity of adolescent literary productions that she based her book upon themes written by young people. As for the compositions obtained in the present study, the examples cited earlier reflect the same qualities which Allport and Gillespie noted in the writing of older adolescents. By and large, our compositions were free of the flowery and ostentatious language associated with the desire to impress and it seems reasonable to assume that they were sincere expressions of religious experience.

Granted that the compositions have a reasonable claim to validity, the results might still be objected to on the ground that they were obtained from a single age group. Might it not be the case that the varieties of religious experience change with age, or at least that their relative frequency of occurrence varies at different age levels? Fortunately there is evidence with which to answer both of these questions. In the course of several investigations into the development of denominational conceptions (Elkind),[13] it was possible to ask children at different age levels and of different denominations the question "When do you feel closest to God?" Although the results of this questioning have not yet been published, they indicate that the types of religious experience described in the present paper were reported at all age levels from 5 to 14. There was also evidence, however, that the relative frequency with which different types of experience were reported changed with age. This latter finding is in keeping with what has been reported by other investigators. For example: Beekman,[14] Pixley and Beekman,[15] and Allport, *et al.*,[16] have shown that for high school seniors and university students prayer is one of the most important types of religious experience. For the ninth grade youngsters in our study, however, prayer was one of the least mentioned types of experience. It seems likely, therefore, that while the *varieties* of religious experience may remain the

[11] J. M. Gillespie and G. W. Allport, *Youth Outlook on the Future, a Cross-National Study* (New York: Doubleday and Company, Inc., 1955), p. 13.

[12] Ruth Strang, *The Adolescent Views Himself* (New York: McGraw-Hill Book Co., 1957).

[13] D. Elkind, "The Child's Conception of His Religious Denomination I: The Jewish Child," *J. Genet. Psychol.*, XCIX (1961), pp. 209–225; D. Elkind, "The Child's Conception of His Religious Denomination II: The Catholic Child," *J. Genet. Psychol.* (in press); D. Elkind, "The Child's Conception of His Religious Denomination III: The Protestant Child," *J. Genet Psychol.* (in press).

[14] Emma Beekman, "What High School Seniors Think of Religion," *Religious Education*, XLII (1947), pp. 333–337.

[15] Emma Pixley and Emma Beekman, "The Faith of Youth as Shown by a Survey of Public Schools in Los Angeles," *Religious Education*, XLIV (1949), pp. 336–342.

[16] Allport, Gillespie, and Young, *op. cit.*

same at all age levels, the *frequency* with which particular types of experience occur will vary considerably from childhood to adolescence.

A final objection must be taken up and this is directed not to the results or to the subjects but to our interpretations. Is it not true that the interpretations made regarding the significance of cultural and denominational expectations and individual differences are hypotheses which require further verification and not established truths? With this objection we are in wholehearted agreement. None of the explanations put forward in this paper were intended as final pronouncements on the subject but rather as guides for future research. For example, the notion that sex role expectations affect the frequency with which particular types of religious experience occur will have to be checked with different cultural groups in which sex role expectations are quite unlike those which obtain for the white, middle class Americans of our study. Likewise, the notion that denominational differences affect religious experience will have to be checked by studying children from a wider range of religious groups or from clearly demarcated sects within any one denomination. Finally, the idea that brighter children experience personal religion in less conforming ways than their peers will have to be tested with a larger number of students and at different age levels. In short, we regard none of the interpretations given in the present paper as adequate without further empirical support.

It is perhaps appropriate at this point, after having exercised the necessary scientific cautions, to express a personal opinion. We came away from the reading and re-reading of the compositions with the conviction that the majority of the young people who participated in the investigation regarded personal religious experience as a significant part of their lives. In a way this is amazing because these very same young people are resistant to attending Church, Sunday School, and formal Church activities in general. This fact points up the value of James'[17] distinction between personal and institutional religion. Personal religion, the individual apprehension of the Divine, apparently remains an important force in the adolescent's life during the very period in which institutional religion is losing its hold on his interest and participation. This split between allegiance to personal and institutional religion may be a phenomenon of adolescence since it is generally not seen in children. It is possible that just as the adolescent rebels against the authority of his parents, yet continues to need and rely upon their love and guidance, so he may also rebel against the authority and the dogma of the Church yet continue to feel the need for a religious orientation in his life. Put differently, the adolescent's rebellion against the Church may destroy his religious belief without injury to his religious faith.

[17] James, *op. cit.*

SUMMARY

One hundred and forty-four ninth grade students wrote compositions regarding their recurrent (strengthening and maintaining) and their acute (testing) religious experiences. The results indicated 6 types of recurrent and 5 types of acute experience. It was also found that there were differences between boys and girls and between Honor and Average Group students in the frequency with which they reported particular types of recurrent, but not acute, religious awareness. Differences were also found between Protestant, Catholic, and Jewish children in the frequency of their reported recurrent and acute experiences. These results were interpreted from the point of view of cultural and denominational expectations and from that of personality differences. In addition, an attempt was made to answer possible objections to the sincerity of the compositions, the limited age group, and the interpretations of results. The paper concluded with some general impressions regarding the role of religious experience in adolescence.

The Development of Ethnic Attitudes in Adolescence[*]

W. Cody Wilson

Attitudes toward ethnic groups develop just as inevitably as attitudes toward beauty and athletics; presumably they are a product of interlocking historical, sociocultural, and personality factors. Ethnic attitudes may exert considerable, directive influence upon social behavior, and there exists widespread belief that by adolescence these attitudes become "crystallized." In the following paper, Wilson investigates the stability, variability, and consistency of ethnic attitudes during adolescence. Although a review of the findings of other studies "reveals no simple consistent pattern of attitude development in adolescence," Wilson's own findings confirm the notion that the content of ethnic attitudes becomes stable in adolescence; moreover, development of this stability appears to begin early in adolescence.

Social scientists today agree that social attitudes are rooted in experience —are learned.[1] They do not agree, however, about the process of development of attitudes toward ethnic groups, especially during the period of adolescence. For example, Harding and his associates[2] declare, "By the age of 14 ethnic attitudes have become crystallized in the vast majority of children. . . ." But Allport[3] suggests, to the contrary, that adolescence is a period of integrating and organizing ethnic attitudes to form coherent units within the adult personality.

[1] G. W. Allport, *The Nature of Prejudice* (Cambridge: Addison-Wesley, 1954); J. Harding, B. Kutner, J. Proshansky and I. Chein, "Prejudice and Ethnic Relations," *Handbook of Social Psychology,* ed., G. Lindzey (Cambridge: Addison-Wesley, 1954), Chap. 27.
[2] Harding, *et al., op. cit.,* p. 1036.
[3] Allport, *op. cit.,* p. 312.

[*] A revision by the author of "The Development of Ethnic Attitudes in Adolescence," *Child Development*, XXXIV (March, 1963). Reprinted by permission of the author and the Society for Research in Child Development.

The present paper seeks to clarify the issue; it will review briefly the existing pertinent empirical literature, present several developmental trends inferred from the literature, and present new empirical data testing hypotheses derived from these inferred trends.

THE LITERATURE

The most often cited investigation of the development of ethnic attitudes is that of Horowitz;[4] he used three different instruments in the study of attitudes toward Negroes of boys at various school levels from kindergarten to eighth grade. Each instrument yielded a different result: with one test, there was no change in prejudice with age; with a second test, there was an increase in prejudice with age until about age 12 when the level or prejudice became stable; and with the third test there was a slight but statistically significant tendency for prejudice to increase with age throughout the range tested. The intercorrelations among the tests increased with advance in age.

Minard[5] investigated both attitudes and perceived norms for behavior among secondary school pupils. He administered a questionnaire describing a number of behavioral situations involving several ethnic groups to over 1,000 children in junior and senior high school. The subjects were asked both what ought to be done (or what is right), and how they themselves would feel or act. The level of prejudice as indicated by what the pupils thought ought to be done (or was right) decreased from grade seven to grade ten, with no changes after that. But the level of prejudice as indicated by how the pupils themselves would feel or act was fairly constant at grades seven, eight, and nine, but thereafter increased steadily through grade twelve. The junior high school pupils and the senior high school pupils were not from the same communities, however, and this fact poses some difficulties for interpretation.

Zeligs[6] reported a longitudinal study of 12 adolescents who were investigated at ages 12, 15, and 18 years of age. She concludes that there is little change in racial tolerance during the six year period from 12 to 18.

Meltzer[7] found that the preference order for several nationalities was quite stable over the interval from grade five through grade eight.

[4] E. L. Horowitz, "Development of Attitude Toward Negroes," *Archiv. Psychol.*, (1936), No. 194.
[5] R. D. Minard, "Race Attitudes of Iowa Children," *Univ. Iowa Stud. Char.*, IV (1931), No. 2.
[6] Rose Zeligs, "Tracing Racial Attitudes Through Adolescence," *Socio. Soc. Res.*, XXIII (1938), pp. 45–54.
[7] H. Meltzer, "The Development of Children's Nationality Preferences, Concepts, and Attitudes," *J. Psychol.*, XI (1941), pp. 343–358.

Blake and Dennis[8] studied differences among children in the fourth through eleventh grades in the degree to which they attributed various traits to Negroes rather than whites. Their sample included all the children in these grades in a consolidated public school in the south—a total of 324 subjects. The children were asked to compare Negroes and whites with regard to 60 traits and to tell whether the trait was more characteristic of Negroes or whites. The most relevant result was that there was more agreement—greater consensus—among the older children as to whether Negroes or whites were more characterized by a trait. The degree of consensus steadily increased from the fourth through the eleventh grades. These data are consistent with the author's interpretation that there is increased accuracy in the perception of adult norms—in this case stereotypes of Negroes—with increased age during the adolescent years.

Radke and Sutherland[9] used a different technique in investigating ethnic attitudes among secondary school children. They asked the children to write essay responses to the questions, "What do you think Negroes are like?" and "What do you think Jews are like?" The responses were then categorized into several mutually exclusive classes. All the children in grades five through 12—a total of 275 children—in a small midwestern town answered the questions. The proportion of children describing Negroes as bad and inferior increased with grade level and the proportion describing Negroes with a positive tone decreased. The proportion of children describing Jews as bad also increased with grade level and the proportion describing Jews with positive terms decreased. The investigators also found that the proportion of children rejecting both Negroes and Jews increased with grade level. There was a tendency for conflicting descriptions (characterizing Jews and Negroes as being both good and bad) to be most prevalent within the middle grade levels.

Gough, Harris, Martin, and Edwards[10] in an introduction to a study of children's ethnic attitudes say, ". . . If ethnic attitudes are characterized by such a closely knit and fundamental structure in the adult, then it would seem reasonable to suppose that their genesis and early development should be found in the childhood and adolescent years." Unfortunately, they do not offer any empirical data related to this contention.

Frenkel-Brunswik and Havel[11] also say in the introduction to another

[8] R. Blake and W. Dennis, "The Development of Stereotypes Concerning the Negro," *J. Abnorm. Soc. Psychol.*, XXXVIII (1943), pp. 525–531.

[9] Marion Radke and Jean Sutherland, "Children's Concepts and Attitudes About Minority and Majority American Groups," *J. Educ. Psychol.*, XL (1949), pp. 449–468.

[10] H. G. Gough, D. B. Harris, W. E. Martin and M. Edwards, "Children's Ethnic Attitudes: I. Relationship to Certain Personality Factors," *Child. Develpm.*, XXI (1950), pp. 83–91.

[11] Else Frenkel-Brunswik and J. Havel, "Prejudice in the Interviews of Children: I. Attitudes toward Minority Groups," *J. Gen. Psychol.*, LXXXII (1953), pp. 91–136.

study of children's ethnic attitudes, "Children's attitudes, being less structured and less consistent than those of adults . . . ," but again they present no data relevant to the assertion.

Livson and Nichols[12] note that the inter-item correlations of the California E, F, and PEC scales were considerably lower for two groups of adolescents than for adults. They suggest the possibility that differences in age may be the important factor underlying the differences in organization of attitudes.

The above review of the literature on the development of ethnic attitudes reveals no single consistent pattern of attitude development in adolescence. Certainly it does not support the assertion of Harding, *et al.*, that ethnic attitudes are crystallized by the age of 14 years. Rather, several trends are manifested.

1. There is a tendency for level of prejudice to increase with age through adolescence.[13]

2. There is a tendency for level of prejudice to be stable over the later ages of adolescence.[14]

3. There is a tendency for perceived norms to become stabilized at some time in adolescence.[15]

4. There is a tendency toward an increase in the degree of consistency among an individual's responses to a given ethnic group during adolescence.[16]

The first two, seemingly contradictory, tendencies may be reconciled by assuming that the two tendencies represent projections of two segments of a growth curve. The data are consistent with the general model of a negatively accelerated growth curve for prejudice in childhood and adolescence; the level of prejudice increases with age, but at a progressively declining rate until it levels off and stabilizes at the adult level. One study may fit one segment of the model growth curve and another study a different segment, even though they cover the same age interval, because they use different measures of ethnic attitudes and different subjects. Different aspects of attitude may exhibit the same shaped growth curve but reach the same stage of development at different times. Different groups may manifest similarly shaped growth curves, yet one group may develop earlier than the others.

The third tendency found in the literature suggests that there is a

[12] N. Livson and T. F. Nichols, "Assessment of the Generalizability of the E, F, and PEC Scales," *Psychol. Reports,* III (1957), pp. 413–420.

[13] Cf. Blake and Dennis, *op. cit.;* Horowitz, *op. cit.;* Minard, *op. cit.;* Radke and Sutherland, *op. cit.*

[14] Cf. Horowitz, *op. cit.;* Meltzer, *op. cit.;* Minard, *op. cit.;* Zeligs, *op. cit.*

[15] Cf. Blake and Dennis, *op. cit.;* Minard, *op. cit.*

[16] Cf. Frenkel-Brunswik and Havel, *op. cit.;* Gough, *et al., op. cit.;* Horowitz, *op. cit.;* Livson and Nichols, *op. cit.;* Radke and Sutherland, *op. cit.*

second growth curve related to the development of ethnic attitudes; not only is there a process of learning behavior, but there is also a process of learning what kinds of behavior are expected or appropriate—norms for behavior. It seems very probable that the stabilization of an individual's attitude must await the accurate perception of adult norms for behavior; then the content of his responses toward a class of objects is brought into some sort of relative conformity to the norm.

The fourth tendency found in the literature indicates that there is a third growth curve associated with the development of attitudes. After an individual has acquired his culture's repertoire of responses and has learned its norms for behavior, he must organize the responses that he accepts as appropriate for himself and integrate them into a self-consistent pattern.

One may infer from the foregoing discussion three processes involved in the development of attitudes: the learning of specific responses, the perceiving of and conforming to societal norms, and the organizing and integrating of already acquired responses. The identification of these three processes provides an organization for most of the previously unconnected observations reported in the literature.

These three processes are, however, after the fact explanations; and the "facts" themselves are often not well established. The data relating to perceptions of norms is very tenuous, and the phenomenon of increased consistency of response is mostly conjecture. The following cross-sectional investigation was designed for the purpose of testing the generalizations derived from the existing empirical literature.

HYPOTHESES

The first of the inferred processes involved in the development of ethnic attitudes is the learning of specific responses. The individual learns specific responses toward members of ethnic groups until he has accumulated his society's general store of cultural facts in regard to the ethnic group. The general model for such cumulative growth is a negatively accelerated curve. In other areas, for example in the measuring of intelligence, the acquisition of the general store of cultural facts begins to level off in middle adolescence. Therefore, Hypothesis One is: the mean level of an ethnic attitude for age groups becomes stable with increased age in adolescence.

The second inferred process in the development of ethnic attitudes is the perceiving of and conforming to societal norms. If members of a group are conforming to a norm, the group's responses in the area of the norm will become less varied. Hence, Hypothesis Two follows: the variance of the level of attitude for age groups decreases with age in adolescence.

The third process inferred above is the organizing and integrating of already acquired responses. Increased organization and integration of an attitude would result in a greater degree of consistency among the responses mediated by the attitude. Thus, Hypothesis Three is: the degree of consistency among responses that are mediated by an attitude increases with age in adolescence.

SUBJECTS

The subjects were all of the male students in attendance in the public secondary school in a single suburban community near Boston, Massachusetts on the two days in which testing was conducted. A total of 821 boys participated; 539 were present both days of testing; 136 were present on the first day but absent on the second, and 146 were absent on the first day but present on the second.

The total represents approximately 95% of the male students in these schools. No relevant bias appears to be in the sample; those pupils who were absent on one day did not differ in any relevant characteristics from those who were present on both days. There are no parochial secondary schools in the community, and, since the school has a local reputation for educational excellence, few students go to private secondary schools. Thus the sample contains practically all of the population defined as the male residents of secondary school age in the given community.

The community has been described informally by social scientists who reside in it as being an upwardly mobile upper middle class community. In addition to the older Yankee stock there is also a sizable upper middle class population of Italian extraction and a smaller minority of lower middle class of Italian and Irish extraction. There is only one Negro family with secondary school age children in the community, and a few Jewish families.

PROCEDURE

The data were collected by means of two self-administered questionnaires containing the attitude scales described below, a number of other scales, filler items, and explicit directions. The questionnaires were administered by teachers in the two 40 minute school periods approximately one week apart.

The time allotment and the level of difficulty were such that at least 95% of the seventh grade pupils were able to complete the questionnaire. Brief follow-up interviews by the investigator indicated that even the seventh grade pupils were able to follow the directions with a minimum of difficulty and that the language was within the grasp of the seventh grader. One item contained a word that a large number of the younger pupils did not understand, and was discarded.

MEASURES

Each subject reported his age to the nearest birthday.

The level of the subjects' ethnic attitudes was measured by the following five scales prepared especially for the present study.

1. The Behavior toward Negroes Scale is a 15 item Thurstone-type scale with non-cumulative or "point" items. A low score indicates a favorable attitude toward Negroes. Each item presents a one sentence description of a situation and a sentence description of a possible behavior in that situation. The style of the items originated with Rosander.[17] The respondent is asked to indicate the likelihood that he would engage in that action in that circumstance. An example of the items in the scale is, "Suppose that you see a white girl whom you know walk down the street with a Negro boy: I would stop and talk with them."

2. The Negro Social Distance Scale is an 11 item Thurstone-type scale with cumulative items. A low score indicates a favorable attitude toward Negroes. Each items consists of the stem, "I would not mind" followed by a phrase indicating a Negro in a social relationship to the respondent. The respondent is asked to indicate the extent of his agreement or disagreement with the item. An example is, "I would not mind a Negro eating at my table in a cafeteria."

3. The Opinion of Negroes Scale is a 14 item Thurstone-type scale using "point" items. A low score indicates a favorable attitude toward Negroes. Each item is a simple evaluative declarative sentence about Negroes. The respondent is asked to indicate the extent of his agreement or disagreement with the sentence. An example is, "The more I know about Negroes the better I like them."

4. The Opinion of Jews Scale is a 13 item scale similar in all respects to the Opinion of Negroes Scale.

5. The Opinion of Southerners Scale is a 14 item scale similar in all respects to the Opinion of Negroes Scale.

The above five scales were prepared especially for the present study to insure that the vocabulary level was appropriate for the age range to be studied. The scale-values of the items were derived from the judgments of 25 adults using the successive intervals technique, and were checked by the judgments of another 20 adults. For each of the scales Kendall's "W,"[18] a measure of the amount of consensus among judges concerning the position of each item in the attitude scale, was greater than .90 for the 25 judges.

[17] A. C. Rosander, "An Attitude Scale Based upon Behavior Situations," *J. Soc. Psychol.,* VIII (1937), pp. 3–15.
[18] M. G. Kendall, *Rank Correlation Methods* (London: Griffen, 1948)

Two measures of consistency of attitude were used. The first, a group measure, is the correlation between scores on equivalent halves of a scale for a group of subjects. The second, an individual measure of attitude consistency, is derived from the same base as Guttman's coefficient of reproducibility in scalogram analysis—the number of "errors" in "response pattern." Such a measure of consistency can be used with any scale comprised of ordered items.

ANALYSIS

The hypotheses are stated in terms of differences among means, variances, and correlation coefficients for several groups. The following techniques were used in the statistical analysis.

The analysis of variance was used to test for differences among several group means. Assumptions of analysis of variance were not met by some of the sets of data, but empirical investigations[19] have demonstrated that it is relatively insensitive to departures from these assumptions, and since there is no practical alternative, it was used.

Bartlett's test for the homogeneity of variances[20] was used to test hypotheses about difference among several sample variances.

A technique proposed by Johnson and Jackson[21] for testing differences among several (more than two) correlation coefficients was used to test hypotheses when reliability of scales was the relevant measure. A correction for lack of heterogeneity suggested by McNemar[22] was employed before using the test of differences among several correlation coefficients; all correlation coefficients were transformed to what they would have been with a common variance for all samples.

RESULTS

Hypothesis One stated that: the mean level of a social attitude for age groups becomes stable with increased age in adolescence.

Level here refers to the score on the attitude scales, to the degree of favorableness, acceptance, or approach toward the class of objects that is the referent of the attitude. A low score represents a favorable attitude and a high score represents an unfavorable attitude.

[19] P. O. Johnson and R. W. B. Jackson, *Modern Statistical Methods* (Chicago: Rand McNally, 1959); E. F. Lindquist, *Design and Analysis of Experiments in Psychology and Education* (Boston: Houghton Mifflin, 1953).

[20] Q. McNemar, *Psychological Statistics* (New York: John Wiley, 1955).

[21] Johnson and Jackson, *op. cit.*, p. 358.

[22] McNemar, *op. cit.*, p. 149.

Table 1
Mean Level of Attitude by Age for Five Scales

Scale	Age 13–14 N = 317*	15–16 N = 218*	17–18 N = 150*	Analysis of Variance (df = 2, 682) F	P
Opinion of Jews	31.4	31.7	29.9	1.38	>.05
Opinion of Negroes	32.7	32.5	31.7	.92	>.05
Behavior toward Negroes	18.4	20.5	18.7	2.72	>.05
Negro Social Distance	22.4	26.2	25.3	2.55	>.05
Opinion of Southerners	31.7	33.4	33.7	5.19	<.01

* The N's for the Opinion of Negroes Scale were 288, 194, and 193. This scale was in a questionnaire administered on a different day from the one containing the other scales.

Hypothesis One is not strictly confirmed by the data presented in Table 1. For four scales, the one for Jews and the three for Negroes, there are no significant differences in mean attitude scores for the ages studied. Significant differences in mean attitude scores do occur within the age range studied for the Opinion of Southerners Scale; but level of attitude is stable from age 15 to age 18. The data in Table 1 support a revised version of Hypothesis One: the mean level of an attitude for age groups is stable in later adolescence. It becomes stable in late childhood or early adolescence. Stability of level of attitude develops later with regard to Southerners than with regard to the other groups.

The boys who were the subjects in the present study were not, in general, prejudiced toward the ethnic groups that were the objects of the attitude scale. The mean level of attitude on all the scales is very near the neutral point.

Hypothesis Two stated that: the variance of the level of attitude for age groups decreases with age in adolescence. Hypothesis Two is confirmed by the data presented in Table 2.

Significant differences among the variances for the several age groups are found for each of the five scales. For all five scales the variance of the attitude for the 17–18 year olds is less than the variance for the 15–16 year olds; and for four of the five scales (Opinion of Southerners is the exception), the variance of attitude scores for the 17–18 year old group is smallest of all the age groups. The older group of adolescents' attitudes are more similar among themselves than are the attitudes of the younger adolescents. It is as if the attitudes are converging around a norm. The increase in variance in middle adolescence that was not predicated will be discussed below.

Table 2
Variance of Attitude Scores by Age for Five Scales

Scale	Age 13–14 N = 317*	15–16 N = 218*	17–18 N = 150*	Bartlett's Test V (2df)	P
Opinion of Jews	118.8	141.6	90.3	7.59	<.05
Opinion of Negroes	53.3	60.8	41.0	84.81	<.001
Behavior toward Negroes	96.0	148.8	79.2	20.97	<.001
Negro Social Distance	501.8	519.8	357.2	7.99	<.02
Opinion of Southerners	34.8	81.0	54.8	236.3	<.001

* The N's for the Opinion of Negroes Scale were 288, 194, and 193. This scale was in the questionnaire and was administered on a different day from the one containing the other scales.

Hypothesis Three stated that: the degree of consistency among responses that are mediated by an attitude increases with age in adolescence.

Data relevant to Hypothesis Three are in Tables 3 and 4. The mean number of errors in response pattern decreases significantly with age for the Opinion of Jews and the Opinion of Negroes scales, but not for the other three. The reliability of the Opinion of Jews and the Opinion of Negroes scales increases significantly with age, but there are no significant differences with age for the other scales.

The data only partially confirm Hypothesis Three: the consistency of the Opinion of Jews and Opinion of Negroes attitudes, as measured by both scale reliability and errors in response pattern, increases with age from

Table 3
Mean Errors in Response Pattern by Age for Five Scales

Scale	Age 13–14 N = 317*	15–16 N = 218*	17–18 N = 150*	Analysis of Variance (df = 2, 682) F	P
Opinion of Jews	1.14	1.00	.94	3.90	<.05
Opinion of Negroes	.97	.81	.65	7.35	<.001
Behavior toward Negroes	.99	1.10	1.10	.70	>.05
Negro Social Distance	.89	.94	.96	.20	>.05
Opinion of Southerners	.71	.76	.89	1.97	>.05

* The N's for the Opinion of Negroes Scale were 288, 194, and 193. This scale was in a questionnaire administered on a different day from the one containing the other scales.

Table 4
Scale Reliability* by Age for Five Scales

Scale	Age 13–14 $N = 317$†	15–16 $N = 218$†	17–18 $N = 150$†	Test for Differences $X^2(2df)$	P
Opinion of Jews	.59	.67	.74	7.97	<.05
Opinion of Negroes	.47	.56	.76	26.66	<.001
Behavior toward Negroes	.57	.55	.55	.16	>.05
Negro Social Distance	.59	.57	.68	3.02	>.05
Opinion of Southerners	.33	.46	.38	3.32	>.05

* Correlation coefficient between odd and even halves of each scale corrected for lack of heterogeneity.

† The N's for the Opinion of Negroes Scale were 288, 194, and 193. This scale was in a questionnaire administered on a different day from the one containing the other scales.

age 13 to age 18. No increase in consistency of the three other scales accompanied increased age, however.

DISCUSSION

The three hypotheses investigated in this study were explicit statements of trends inferrable from the existing empirical literature. Their confirmation brings a degree of order into previously isolated facts.

The data presented in Table 1 and relevant to Hypothesis One demonstrate three tendencies reported in the literature: the tendency for the content of ethnic attitudes to be stable in adolescence; the tendency for this stability of content to develop in early adolescence; and the tendency for the different attitudes to develop on different schedules. The Opinion of Jews, Opinion of Negroes, and Behavior toward Negroes scales were all three stable, in terms of mean level of attitude, throughout the age range studied—ages 13 through 18. The Negro Social Distance and the Opinion of Southerners scales reached a stable level in later adolescence, but were still in the process of developing to that level in early adolescence.

Three possible explanations of the differential rates of development occur to the writer. First, more personal relationships may develop more slowly than impersonal ones, particularly where contact with the social object has been negligible; the Negro Social Distance Scale involves more personal relationships than do the other scales. Secondly, finer differentiations may develop more slowly than gross ones; the items on the Negro Social Distance Scale are closer together on the evaluative continuum than are the items of the other scales. Thirdly, attitudes toward more salient classes of social objects may develop earlier than do attitudes toward less salient objects; it seems reasonable to assume that "Southerners" is a less salient class of social objects than are "Negroes" and "Jews," for these subjects. "Southerners" probably become a more salient class when individuals begin to read newspapers fairly regularly and are exposed to news stories about discrimination and school desegregation in the South. This is likely to happen increasingly during adolescence.

Data similar to those presented in Table 2 and relevant to Hypothesis Two have not previously been reported in the literature, although Hypothesis Two can be inferred from previous empirical data. One may observe a second trend in Table 2, in addition to the phenomenon of a decrease in variance of attitude scores in late adolescence that was predicted by Hypothesis Two: that is, that the variance of scores is greatest in the middle of the adolescent age period. The most obvious explanation lies in the fact of differential rate of development. In the middle years of the age range encompassed by adolescence will be found the greatest variation in stages of development. Early in the age range most individuals will be at the beginning of adolescent development, a few in the middle, practically none at the end of adolescent development. Late in the age range most individuals will be toward the end of adolescent development, a few in the middle, but practically none at the beginning. But in the middle of the age range will be found large numbers of individuals at each stage of development. To the extent that content of attitude is a function of the stage of development, then variation in attitude scores may be expected to be greatest in the middle of the age range spanned by adolescence.

Data similar to those presented in Tables 3 and 4 and relevant to Hypothesis Three have not previously been reported in the literature, although Hypothesis Three has been anticipated several times. The data do not completely confirm Hypothesis Three—that consistency of attitude increases with age in adolescence; the predicted phenomena occurred with only two of the five scales: Opinion of Jews and Opinion of Negroes. With two other scales, Behavior toward Negroes and Negro Social Distance, consistency of attitude remained rather stable over the age range investigated. The Opinion of Southerners Scale manifested a nonsignificant tendency to decrease in consistency over the age range from 13 through 18 years. These phenomena pose a problem for interpretation.

One interpretation is that there is no real relation between consistency of attitude and age; the results for the two scales that did show such a relationship were simply Type 1 statistical errors which occur one time in twenty when the .05 level of significance is used as a statistical criterion. This interpretation does not fit well with either the previous research findings or other findings of the present study.

Another interpretation is that the age range studied was too restricted to manifest the phenomena predicted; if older age groups had been included in the study, the phenomena would have been observed in the other three scales. This interpretation invokes an explanation that also seemed to be demanded by the data reported in Table 1; namely, differential rate of development for different scales. Indeed the scales that did not manifest increased consistency with age were the same scales that were slowest in stabilizing in terms of level of attitude—that is, the scales that sampled more personal relationships, that required the finer discriminations, or that referred to a less salient class of objects. Attitudes tested by scales with these characteristics seemingly develop later than do other attitudes.

A second explanation may be offered within the framework of the latter interpretation—that age is not the relevant underlying variable that affects consistency; rather, another variable, that is correlated with age within the adolescent period, underlies consistency. If the correlation between age and the underlying variable is not too high over the restricted age range, then the observed phenomenon—no strong relationship between consistency and age—would be expected.

The two explanations, that there are differential development schedules for different attitudes and that a variable other than, but correlated with, age underlies consistency, are not in opposition to each other. Both factors may very well be operating.

SUMMARY

Three processes involved in the development of ethnic attitudes during adolescence are inferred from existing empirical literature. Hypotheses about adolescent attitudes are derived from them: (1) the level of ethnic attitudes becomes stable in adolescence, (2) the variance of ethnic attitudes decreases with age in adolescence, and (3) attitudes become increasingly consistent in adolescence. A cross sectional study of 821 secondary school boys from a single community partially supported each of the hypotheses.

Child-Rearing Practices and Moral Development: Generalizations from Empirical Research*

MARTIN L. HOFFMAN

Except for an occasional research report or theoretical treatise, research on conscience development and moral behavior was virtually neglected in the first half of the twentieth century. During the past ten years, however, a spate of research papers on conscience has appeared. Stemming primarily from theoretical bedrock provided by the dissimilar contributions of Freud and Piaget, various theories of identification and developmental stages have been proposed and several tests of hypotheses predicting relationships between such antecedents as childrearing practices or age and development of moral behavior have been conducted. Conscience has been mapped out in terms of ability to make moral judgments, guilt, defenses against guilt, resistance to temptation, pressures to deviate, etc. But now and then in any field of scientific endeavor a chronicler is needed; fortunately Hoffman fulfills such a function in the paper included here. In a thorough review of recent research on moral behavior, he organizes "the research findings on parental practices and the child's moral development so as to point up tentative generalizations, gaps, and inconsistencies which can be used as guides in further research."

In complex areas such as that of morality and its antecedents no single research can supply the answers to all important questions. Each study can do no more than shed light on a small facet of the problem, especially in the early stages of research when measuring instruments and experimental procedures are cumbersome and inefficient. Progress therefore requires many research efforts, along with systematic attempts to assess methods and integrate results. This paper is such an attempt. Its purpose is to pull

* From *Child Development*, XXXIV (June, 1963), abridged. Reprinted by permission of the author and the Society for Research in Child Development.

together the research findings on parental practices and the child's moral development so as to point up tentative generalizations, gaps, and inconsistencies which can be used as guides in further research. The studies examined are those which were designed primarily to investigate parental antecedents of moral variables and which meet current methodological standards. The focus is substantive although methodological points are made where necessary in interpreting contradictory findings and suggesting directions for further research.

THEORETICAL FOUNDATIONS OF THE RESEARCH

Most of our theoretical knowledge about moral development derives from the works of Piaget and Freud. Piaget and his followers have focussed on the cognitive aspects of the child's moral orientation and their empirical investigations have centered on the child's concepts of justice, his attitudes toward rules, and toward violations of moral norms.[1] In these studies the child's moral perspective has been probed with great depth and a number of valuable concepts bearing on the cognitive aspects of morality have been contributed to the field, e.g., moral realism, immanent justice, and the role of cognitive processes in moral growth. Although considerable importance is assigned to decreased adult constraint and increased interaction with peers, the main interest of these investigators is to establish developmental sequences which are more or less universal, fixed, and intrinsic to the organism, rather than to study individual differences and the antecedent role of the parent. The one exception, a study of the effects of parental restriction on the child's moral judgment,[2] produced inconclusive results.

Psychoanalytic theory, on the other hand, is concerned primarily with the emotional and motivational aspects of personality structure. And although this theory too was initially intended as a universal explanation of the processes underlying the formation of conscience rather than a source of hypotheses about individual differences, it has provided the main inspiration and the overall direction for most of the research on the role of parental practices in shaping and determining moral character.

Although Freud did not organize the theory into a coherent whole, its concepts are unveiled in scattered references throughout the literature and it may be reconstructed briefly as follows: The young child is inevitably subjected to many frustrations, some of which are due to parental control

---

[1] See, J. Piaget, *The Moral Judgment of the Child* (Glencoe, Ill.: Free Press, 1948); E. Lerner, *Constraint Areas and the Moral Judgment of Children* (Menasha, Wis.: Banta, 1937); L. Kohlberg, "The Development of Modes of Moral Thinking and Choice in the Years 10 to 16" (unpublished Doctoral dissertation, University of Chicago, 1958).

[2] D. MacRae, Jr., "A Test of Piaget's Theories of Moral Development," *J. Abnorm. Soc. Psychol.*, XLIX (1954), pp. 14–18.

and some of which have nothing directly to do with the parent, e.g., illness and other physical discomforts. All of these frustrations contribute to the development of hostility toward the parent. The child's anxiety over counter aggression by the parent or over the anticipated loss of the parent's love leads him to repress his hostility, incorporate the parent's prohibitions, and generally model his behavior after that of the parent. Among the important parental characteristics adopted by the child is the capacity to punish himself when he violates a prohibition or is tempted to do so—turning inward, in the course of doing this, the hostility which was originally directed toward the parent. This self-punishment is experienced as guilt feelings which are dreaded because of their intensity and their resemblance to the earlier fears of punishment or abandonment by the parent. The child, therefore, tries to avoid guilt by acting always in accordance with the incorporated parental prohibitions and erecting various mechanisms of defense against the conscious awareness of impulses to act contrary to the prohibitions.

This theory is thus far unchallenged as a comprehensive account of the role of family dynamics in the moral development of the child. Although many researchers in the field disagree with some of its details, most have accepted its basic premise: that sometime in early childhood the individual begins to model his behavior after that of the parent; and through this process of identification codes of conduct such as moral standards and values which are originally externally enforced, become part of the child's own set of standards.

Because of the complexity of the theory no investigator has attempted to test it in its entirety. Instead, each study has focussed on one or another of its concepts—such as identification or guilt—often modifying it somewhat in line with other theoretical approaches, e.g., reinforcement learning theory.

IDENTIFICATION

The psychoanalytic concept that has received the most attention from theorists and researchers is identification. Two general types of identification are discussed in the literature. In one—referred to as identification with the aggressor or defensive identification—the child, treated punitively by the parent but fearful of further punishment if he fights backs, avoids the conflict and gains further parental approval by taking on the characteristics and point of view of the parent. Although Freud considered this type of identification to be central to the development of a conscience, especially in the male, it is now often thought of as a more or less temporary mechanism or one which leads to an aggressive, hostile outlook toward the world rather than a process which underlies the development of an inner conscience.[3] The other type, referred to as developmental or anaclitic identification,[4] is based on the child's anxiety over the loss of the parent's love. To get rid of this anxiety and assure himself of the parent's continued love, the child strives to become like the parent—to incorporate everything about him including his moral standards and values. This type of identification, seen by Freud as especially characteristic of females, is assumed by most present-day writers to underlie the development of an inner conscience.

Numerous attempts have been made in recent years to clarify these concepts[5] and to place them within broader theoretical frameworks.[6] In each case the concepts are modified somewhat in line with the author's theoretical preference, resulting in a variety of subtly different notions that have guided the empirical research on identification. With each investigator stressing one or another aspect, e.g., motivation to emulate the parent, actual similarity between parent and child, or similarity as perceived by the child, the measures used have been many and varied and there has been little overlap between those used in the different studies.

In a study of five-year-old boys[7] the manipulation of the father doll in a structured doll play situation was used as an index of father identification, and was found to relate positively to the father's warmth and affection toward the boy. The data on the father's behavior were obtained from interviews with the mother. Further evidence that paternal warmth contributes to the boy's identification with the father comes from a study of high school juniors and seniors[8] in which an "actual similarity" measure of identification was used—the extent to which the boys responded to personality and atti-

[3] Anna Freud, *The Ego and the Mechanisms of Defense* (New York: International Univer. Press, 1946).

[4] U. Bronfenbrenner, "Freudian Theories of Identification and Their Derivatives," *Child Develpm.*, XXXI (1960), pp. 15–40.

[5] See, A. J. Brodbeck, "Learning Theory and Identification: IV. Oedipal Motivation as a Determinant of Conscience Development," *J. Genet. Psychol.*, LXXXIV (1954), pp. 219–227; Bronfenbrenner, *op. cit.;* Edith Jacobson, "Contributions to the Metapsychology of Psychotic Identification," *J. Amer. Psychoanal. Ass.*, II (1954), pp. 239–262; O. H. Mowrer, *Learning Theory and Personality Dynamics* (New York: Ronald, 1950); R. N. Sanford, "The Dynamics of Identification," *Psychol. Rev.*, LXII (1955), pp. 106–118; S. M. Stoke, "An Inquiry into the Concept of Identification," *J. Genet. Psychol.*, LXXVI (1950), pp. 163–189.

[6] J. Kagan, "The Concept of Identification," *Psychol. Rev.*, LXV (1958), pp. 296–305; J. P. Seward, "Learning Theory and Identification," *J. Genet. Psychol.*, LXXXIV (1954), pp. 201–210; P. Slater, "Toward a Dualistic Theory of Identification," *Merrill-Palmer Quart.*, VII (1961), pp. 113–126; J. W. M. Whiting, "Social Structure and Child Rearing: A Theory of Identification" (unpublished paper, presented at Tulane University as part of the Mona Bronsman Sheckman Lectures in Social Psychiatry, March 17–19, 1960).

[7] Pauline Sears, "Child Rearing Factors Related to the Playing of Sex-typed Roles," *Amer. Psychologist*, VIII (1953), p. 431 (abstract).

[8] D. E. Payne and P. H. Mussen, "Parent-child Relations and Father Identification Among Adolescent Boys," *J. Abnorm. Soc. Psychol.*, LII (1956), pp. 358–362.

tude tests the same way their fathers did. Here a positive relationship was obtained between identification and the perception of the father as warm, helpful, and kind—as revealed by the boy's completion of a number of stories dealing with family interaction, e.g., one in which an adolescent boy wants to use the family car.[9] The results of these two studies are generally taken as support for the anaclitic view of identification. Although they demonstrate that identification relates to *receiving* parental love—rather than being *threatened with its loss,* as the anaclitic view would predict— it seems reasonable to assume that discipline by a loving father is more apt to elicit anxiety over love-withdrawal than discipline by a non-loving one.

Seemingly contradictory findings were obtained in another study, using high school senior boys as subjects.[10] This study was guided by the Freudian notion that the boy, motivated by fears and anxieties related to hostility toward his father, shifts his identification from the mother to the father during the Oedipal phase of development. Identification with the father was measured in terms of the similarity between the boy's responses on a vocational interest blank and the responses he thought his father would make. In accordance with the theory, identification was found to relate positively to intensity of castration anxiety, as measured by the Blacky Test—a projective device using dogs to represent family figures. On the assumption that castration anxiety in boys signifies the fear of a physically punitive father, this finding is viewed as providing some empirical support for the notion of identification with an aggressive parent rather than with a loving one.

Thus, although the aggressive and anaclitic conceptions of identification dynamics are quite different, each has some empirical support. It is difficult to assess which receives the greater support, since the identification measures used in these studies differ widely and we do not know which are more valid. While these measures leave much to be desired[11] they all have a certain amount of face validity since they tap aspects of behavior which are manifestly close to the concept of parent identification. Thus, two deal directly with the similarity—real or perceived—between the child and his own parent.[12, 13] The third is less direct and makes the assumption that taking

---

[9] In this study father identification also related to the perception of the mother as warm, helpful and kind; but not as strongly as for the father.

[10] E. L. Cava and H. Raush, "Identification and the Adolescent Boy's Perception of His Father," *J. Abnorm. Soc. Psychol.,* XLVII (1952), pp. 855–856.

[11] U. Bronfenbrenner, "The Study of Identification Through Interpersonal Perception," *Person Perception and Interpersonal Behavior,* ed., R. Tagiuri and L. Petrullo (Stanford, Cal.: Stanford University Press, 1958), pp. 110–130.

[12] It should be noted that identification is largely unconscious according to psychoanalytic theory. From this standpoint, actual similarity may be preferable to perceived similarity as a measure since it may include characteristics shared with the parent of which the child is not aware. One the other hand, actual similarity measures are limited in that similar institutional influences which impinge on both the parent and child very likely account for a good part of their resemblance. (T. M.

the father role projectively reflects identification with the father, and not merely with adult males in general or with an abstract conception of the paternal role. But the subjects in this study seem young enough to justify this assumption.

The other studies of the antecedents of identification generally support the view that love rather than punitiveness is the significant parent variable, but the evidence provided is limited since the identification measures used are highly indirect and therefore of questionable validity. These measures deal with personality characteristics such as sex-role typing[14] and conscience[15] which are presumed on theoretical grounds to be consequents of parent identification and therefore adequate as measures of identification. However, they may also result from other developmental processes including identification with persons other than the same-sexed parent.

A possible explanation for the support given both the aggressive and anaclitic conceptions is that the significant antecedent of father identification is the father's *salience* in the child's experience, which can be heightened by *either* affection or punitiveness. Another possible explanation, suggested by the predominantly lower class sample in the study finding father identification related to punitiveness,[16] is that identification may have different bases in different segments of the population. Identification with the aggressor may more often be the underlying process in the lower class setting with its more traditional orientation toward obedience and more frequent use of physical discipline.[17] In the more psychologically oriented

---

Newcomb and G. Svehla, "Intra-family Relationships in Attitude," *Sociometry,* I [1937], pp. 180–205).

[13] Bronfenbrenner, *op. cit.,* has criticized measures like these on the grounds that they may be tapping no more than the child's similarity with adults of the same sex. To support this point he cites findings by Helper and Lazowick that children show little or no more similarity to their same sexed parent than to adults of the same sex selected at random. Helper's measures deal with the relation between the child's ideal for himself and the parent's ideal for the child, and Lazowick's, with the "semantic similarity" existing between parent and child. Although these measures differ from those under discussion, it is possible that further investigation will show the latter to be subject to the same limitation.

[14] See, Wanda S. Bronson, "Dimensions of Ego and Infantile Identification," *J. Per.,* XXVII (1959), pp. 532–545; P. Mussen and L. Distler, "Masculinity, Identification, and Father-son Relationships," *J. Abnorm. Soc. Psychol.,* LIX (1959), pp. 350–356; H. Levin and R. R. Sears, "Identification with Parents as a Determinant of Doll Play Aggression," *Child Develpm.,* XXVII (1956), pp. 135–153.

[15] R. R. Sears, Eleanor E. Maccoby, and H. Levin, *Patterns of Child Rearing* (Evanston: Row-Peterson, 1957).

[16] Cava and Rausch, *op. cit.*

[17] Beverly B. Allinsmith, "Expressive Styles: II. Directness with which Anger is Expressed," *Inner Conflict and Defense,* ed., D. R. Miller and G. E. Swanson (New York: Holt, 1960) pp. 315–336; J. Aronfreed, "The Nature, Variety, and Social Patterning of Moral Responses to Transgression," *J. Abnorm. Soc. Psychol.,* LXIII (1961), pp. 223–241; U. Bronfenbrenner, "Socialization and Social Class Through Time and Space," *Readings in Social Psychology,* ed., Eleanor E. Maccoby, T. M.

middle class, on the other hand, the parental pattern may be more conducive to anaclitic identification.

These explanations are conjectural and further work on the antecedents of identification is needed. With no evidence for the superiority of any particular approach to the measurement of identification investigators might consider using a battery. Each test would tap a different aspect of identification and subjects would be scored on how consistently they identified. The practices used by the parents of subjects who consistently identify, identify primarily with aggressive and power-oriented characteristics, and consistently do not identify could then be compared. Such a procedure might provide the necessary data for generalizing with confidence about the optimum antecedents of each type of identification. It might also provide appropriate criterion groups for validating more practical measures of identification.

Knowing the antecedents of identification, however, would still leave us a long way from our goal of understanding the dynamics of conscience formation. For one thing, there is no empirical support for the implicit assumption made by some researchers that identification is total, i.e., that the child strives to emulate the parent in all respects. It is therefore theoretically possible for a highly motivated child to adopt certain valued parental characteristics like mechanical skills, social prestige, sense of humor, and power; but not others, values and moral standards included. Even assuming identification in the moral realm, the child's moral structure would still be unknown unless the particular parental standards internalized could be ascertained. Another reason for not inferring conscience from parent identification is that parents' consciences vary in strength and in content. The child who identifies with his parent is not necessarily more moral than one who identifies with a teacher, minister, or older sibling. The general problem of the relationship between the process of identification and what aspect of the parent model is internalized is highlighted by the finding, reported by McCord and McCord,[18] that boys whose fathers are criminals are less apt to become criminals if accepted by their fathers than if rejected by them. Apparently paternal acceptance may operate against identification when the parent model is opposed to the norms of the larger society.

Perhaps the precise role of parent identification in moral development would be clarified by developing measures of the child's identification with the parent's moral standards; and using these in conjunction with inde-

---

Newcomb and E. L. Hartley (New York: Holt, 1958), pp. 400–425; M. L. Hoffman, "Power Assertion by the Parent and Its Impact on the Child," *Child Development*, XXXI (1960), pp. 129–143; M. L. Kohn, "Social Class and the Exercise of Parental Authority," *Amer. Sociol. Rev.*, XXIV (1959), pp. 352–366.

[18] Joan McCord and W. McCord, "The Effect of Parental Role Model on Criminality," *J. Social Issues*, XIV (1958), pp. 66–75.

pendent indices of what the parent's moral standards actually are. These measures might then be studied in relation to the child's identification in other areas than the moral, and in relation to parental practices.

REACTIONS TO TRANSGRESSION

A more profitable approach to the role of the parent in the child's moral growth is to drop, tentatively, the assumption that identification is the intervening process and study the various manifestations of conscience more directly. The focus of our research efforts would then become the parent's role in developing a child whose motives are generally to behave in a morally acceptable way; who when under pressure from external forces or inner desires to violate a moral standard, can generally exercise the controls necessary to resist these pressures; who when he does submit to temptation or accidentally violates a standard, can generally be expected to recognize the wrong, be aware of his own responsibility, experience an appropriate amount of guilt or remorse, and attempt to make reparations where possible. Further, to react in all these ways not due to fear of external consequences but due to an inner moral sense.

Some work along these lines has already been done, mainly on the child's reactions after committing a transgression. Allinsmith[19] designed a study to test the hypothesis derived from psychoanalytic theory that harsh treatment in infancy creates excessive aggression, which must later be turned inward by the child in the course of identifying with the parent; and which therefore leads eventually to experiencing severe guilt upon violating a prohibition. The prediction was that early weaning and harsh toilet training, data on which were obtained in interviews with the mothers, would relate to severe guilt reactions by the child in later life. His subjects were junior high school boys whose guilt severity was assessed with a projective story completion technique. The subject completed a number of stories each one having a central figure who violates a commonly held moral standard, e.g., disobeys his mother, steals, or has hostile thoughts about an authority figure. The assumption underlying this technique is that the child tends to identify with the central figure of the story and to express his own characteristic guilt reaction pattern in his completions, without being aware that his own reactions are the focus of study. The stories are so phrased that the infraction can neither be detected nor attributed to the central figure unless he gives himself up or inadvertently gives himself away. Therefore, responses in which the central figure confesses, makes reparation, or feels remorse can be assumed to reflect an inner sense of guilt rather than fear of external consequences.

[19] W. Allinsmith, "The Learning of Moral Standards," *Inner Conflict and Defense,* ed., D. R. Swanson and G. R. Swanson (New York: Holt, 1960), pp. 141–176.

Allinsmith's findings provide evidence for the effect of early infant experience on later guilt severity. But the direction of the findings varies depending on which particular transgression—that is, which story—is being considered. Thus, the severity of guilt over hostile thoughts relates in a curvilinear fashion to severe weaning and severe toilet training—the more severe practices in each case relating to moderate guilt and the less severe practices, to high and low guilt. The stealing and disobedience findings were more clear-cut and linear but in the opposite direction from that predicted: severe infant training related *negatively* to guilt severity. In the main, then, Allinsmith's findings suggest that severe infant practices are associated with low or moderate guilt. This is at variance with the findings reported in a study by Heinicke[20] using five-year-old boys as subjects, and a cross-cultural study by Whiting and Child.[21] Heinicke used as a measure of guilt the children's responses to interview questions dealing with their conceptions of right and wrong and how they feel and act when they have done something wrong. He found severe weaning to relate to high guilt. Whiting and Child's approach was to study a large number of cultures and relate their predominant child-rearing patterns to a cultural index of guilt severity: the prevalence in the culture of self recrimination as a response to illness. The assumption underlying this measure was that blaming oneself for being ill is a reflection of guilt. They found, like Heinicke, that severe weaning related positively to the severity of guilt. For toilet training, neither study gave a consistent trend.

There are many possible reasons for the discrepancy between the Allinsmith and Heinicke findings. The measures of guilt were different. The ages of the subjects varied, which meant among other things that the parents in the Allinsmith study had to recall the practices used twelve years earlier, while those in the Heinicke study only had to think back about four years. And, although both investigators used the same index of toilet training severity, which considered both the age of onset and the duration of training, their measures of weaning severity differed. Allinsmith used the age of completion, whereas Heinicke's measure considered both age of completion and duration. With no further empirical evidence to draw upon, we cannot determine which measures are better or draw any firm conclusions about how infant training relates to later guilt severity. Nor can we be sure that the true antecedent variable is the particular infant practice reported by the parent or some other related aspect of infancy and early childhood. The Whiting and Child findings are of little help in interpreting the overall results since we cannot even be sure of their relevance to the parent-child relationship. For

---

[20] C. M. Heinicke, "Some Antecedents and Correlates of Guilt and Fear in Young Boys," (unpublished Doctoral dissertation, Harvard University, 1953).

[21] J. W. M. Whiting and I. L. Child, *Child Training and Personality: A Cross-Cultural Study* (New Haven: Yale University Press, 1953).

one thing, cultural influences other than the assumed socialization processes might account for the relationship obtained between discipline and guilt. This possibility is increased by the fact that the guilt measure was not based on child data. Even if it were, however, a general methodological problem would still apply: relationships obtained with groups as the unit of analysis are not necessarily the same as those obtained with individuals as the unit.[22, 23] There is some empirical evidence on this point: Hollenberg[24] and Faigin[25] found a lack of agreement between relationships obtained cross-culturally and those obtained with parents and children within the same culture.

The above studies as a group, then, seem to provide empirical support for the general hypothesis that early experiences can have a bearing on the child's later moral response. Just what kind of bearing, however, remains a matter for further study.

The Allinsmith and Heinicke studies also investigated the relationship between the parent's current discipline practices and the child's guilt severity. Allinsmith distinguished between two broad types of discipline: corporal discipline which includes spanking, whipping, slapping, and beating the child; and psychological discipline which includes manipulaton of the child by shaming, appeals to pride and guilt, and expressions of disappointment. His hypothesis that psychological discipline would contribute to guilt severity especially around aggression, was derived from the theory that in disciplining the child psychologically the parent provides a model of self-restraint about aggression and about the manner in which to express disap-

[22] See, J. R. Hills, "Within-Groups Correlations and Their Correction for Attenuation," *Psychol. Bull.,* LIV (1957), pp. 131–134; Patricia L. Kendall and P. F. Lazarsfeld, "The Relation between Individual and Group Characteristics," *The Language of Social Research,* ed., P. F. Lazarsfeld and M. Rosenberg (Glencoe, Ill.: Free Press, 1955), pp. 290–297.

[23] This point also applies to social class findings. Knowing, for example, that in the lower class the parents use more physical discipline and the children are more openly aggressive than in the middle class tells us nothing about how physical discipline and aggressiveness relate in either class.

A related criticism can also be made of relationships obtained between parent and child variables even within culturally homogeneous samples. That is, such relationships might be accounted for by other aspects of home life than the ones studied. But in this case we would at least be sure the parent and child variables were related. To find the true antecedent variables may ultimately require studies which include the entire range of parental behaviors—reduced perhaps by factor analysis to a relatively small number of independent influences. Until such studies are done, our inferences must be based on the amount of agreement among different investigators —the approach used in this paper.

[24] Eleanor Hollenberg, "Child Training Among the Zeepi with Special Reference to the Internalization of Moral Values" (unpublished Doctoral dissertation, Harvard University, 1952).

[25] H. Faigin, "Child Rearing in the Rimrock Community with Special Reference to the Development of Guilt" (unpublished Doctoral dissertation, Harvard University, 1952).

proval; thus contributing to the child's tendency to inhibit and feel guilty about his own hostile tendencies. Further, in psychological discipline the punishment is not likely to be gotten over and done with and the parent's anger is apt to smolder unexpressed and thus convey strong disapproval, thereby increasing the child's anxiety about displeasing the parent. The parent who favors corporal punishment, on the other hand, was viewed as providing a model of aggression and as condoning it implicitly, if not explicitly; and also as providing the child with a suitable target for the direct expression of aggression. Allinsmith found no relationship between the two discipline categories and the child's guilt; but in a later study,[26] using a more homogeneous middle class college sample, he found that male students who recalled both parents (especially their mothers) as having used mainly psychological discipline, obtained higher guilt-over-aggression scores on a story completion measure than those whose parents used corporal punishment. The female subjects only showed a slight tendency in the same direction but, as the authors point out, this may be due to the fact that the story-beginning used was designed for boys and had a masculine theme. Heinicke found a similar pattern with his five-year-olds. The frequent use of praise and the infrequent use of physical punishment and isolation related to high guilt. Heinicke also found that the parent's expression of affection toward the child is positively related to the child's guilt.

Further evidence for the relationship between psychological discipline and guilt severity comes from the Whiting and Child cross-cultural study (with due regard for the precautions mentioned earlier that are necessary in interpreting these findings). They found a positive relationship between their cultural index of guilt and the prevalence in a culture of "love-oriented" techniques of discipline. These techniques overlap considerably with those fitting Allinsmith's "psychological" category. However, whereas Allinsmith views these techniques as providing a model of restraint, Whiting and Child's theory is that they contribute to guilt by keeping the child oriented toward the goal of affection and at the same time arousing uncertainty as to the attainment of this goal. Examples are rewarding by praise, punishing by isolation, and punishing by the withdrawal of love.

Sears, Maccoby, and Levin[27] found similar results with kindergarten children, using as a measure of conscience another aspect of the child's behavior following a transgression: whether he characteristically confesses, hides, or lies—as reported by the parent. This index related positively to the mother's reported use of love-oriented techniques and negatively to the

[26] W. Allinsmith and T. C. Greening, "Guilt over Anger as Predicted from Parental Discipline: A Study of Superego Development," *Amer. Psychol.*, X (1955), 320 (abstract).
[27] Sears, Maccoby and Levin, *op. cit.*

use of object-oriented techniques (tangible rewards and incentives; physical punishment; deprivation of privileges as punishment). But the love-oriented discipline pattern was found to relate to the child's conscience only in conjunction with the frequent expression of love and affection. That is, mothers who were both warm and used love-oriented techniques produced children who tended to confess to their deviations rather than hide or deny them. The author's explanation for this finding is that the effectiveness of love withdrawal depends somewhat upon the amount of love that is being taken away. That is, the child who generally experiences a warmly affectionate relationship with his parents is more affected by the threat that this relationship will be broken than the child who has never enjoyed such parental warmth. In response to the pressure to devise habitual means of insuring the continuation of the parent's love, the child adopts as his own the parent's restrictions and ideals.

Aronfreed[28] investigated still another aspect of the child's post-transgression behavior; whether it is motivated by internal or external forces. He studied sixth grade children, using a projective story completion technique. In each story-beginning the central figure commits an act of aggression, the stories varying with respect to the person toward whom the aggression is directed and in the type of aggression expressed. The story completions were coded according to whether the central figure, without any reliance on outside forces or events, accepts responsibility for his action and actively seeks to correct the situation, for example, by making reparation or modifying his future behavior in the direction of social acceptability; or whether the events following the transgression are dominated by external concerns, mainly in the form of accident and other unpleasant fortuitous happenings. Data on parent discipline were obtained by interviewing the mothers about how they handled aggression in the child. The discipline techniques reported were classified as "induction" techniques or "sensitization" techniques. The "induction" category is similar to Allinsmith's "psychological" one, but in his theory about the effects of this type of discipline Aronfreed focusses not so much on its relevance for the kind of behavior model presented the child, as Allinsmith does, but more directly on its capacity to arouse unpleasant feeling reactions in the child about his misbehavior; reactions which are seen as being independent of external threat. Certain induction techniques (asking the child why he behaved as he did, insisting that he correct the damage he has done, or refraining from punishment when he takes the moral initiative) are also seen as encouraging the child to accept responsibility for his actions. And others, especially the use of explanations or reasoning, are viewed as "utilizing a verbal and cognitive medium of exchange that can provide the child with his own resources for evaluating his behavior." The "sensitization" category resembles Allin-

28 Aronfreed, op. cit.

smith's "corporal" techniques but also includes attempts to control the child through direct verbal assault (yelling, shouting, bawling-out, etc.). These techniques are viewed as attempting only to extinguish or control the child's unacceptable behavior and as tending "not to be translated into a set of independent moral functions because they emphasize only the painful external consequences of the child's transgression and the importance of external threats or demands in carrying out moral actions." Aronfreed found, as he hypothesized, that the use of induction techniques is positively related to a high degree of internally motivated self-corrective action in the child stories and with the absence of punishment from external forces. Mothers who used more extinction techniques, on the other hand, had children whose moral actions were more passive or externally motivated and whose stories contained more external punishment.

Hoffman and Saltzstein[29] obtained similar results with seventh grade children. The children were asked to make moral judgments about norm violations (e.g., stealing, lying, violating a trust) committed under different conditions and to give the reasons for their judgments. Their responses were classified as expressing an internalized standard or merely the fear of detection and punishment by external authorities. The data on parental practices were obtained from the children's responses to highly structured objective items bearing on the parent's current disciplinary pattern in several types of situations, expressions of affection toward the child, and participation in child-centered activities. The results were that the more internalized boys as compared to those who were more externally oriented reported that both parents were more permissive in their discipline; that their mothers less often used techniques which openly asserted their power over the child (this category included the use of force, threat of force or deprivation, or direct commands, and therefore resembles Allinsmith's "corporal" and Aronfreed's "extinction" categories); that their mothers more often used techniques indicating the painful consequences of the child's act for the parents; and that their mothers were more affectionate. The only significant findings for girls were that the internalized girls less often reported their mothers as threatening to have the father discipline them and more often reported their fathers as using rational appeals in their discipline. The internalized subjects of both sexes also gave more consistently severe guilt responses than the externals on a story completion measure. Thus, although the above findings are more directly relevant to the child's conscious moral orientation, they also have a bearing on his reactions to transgression.

Despite the diversity of theoretical approaches, measuring instruments,

[29] M. L. Hoffman and H. D. Saltzstein, "Parent Practices and the Child's Moral Orientation," Interim research report presented at the American Psychological Association (Chicago, September, 1960).

and moral content areas involved in the studies discussed in this section, their results have a common core of agreement that is encouraging. The relatively frequent use of discipline which attempts to change the child's behavior by inducing internal forces toward compliance appears to foster the development of an internalized moral orientation, especially as reflected in the child's reactions to his own transgressions. The use of coercive measures that openly confront the child with the parent's power, on the other hand, apparently contributes to a moral orientation based on the fear of authority.

Further, the studies in this group that include data on parental affection[30] suggest that this variable, too, contributes to internalization. Putting all of this together, we may tentatively conclude that an internalized moral orientation is fostered by an affectionate relationship between the parent and child, in combination with the use of discipline techniques which utilize this relationship by appealing to the child's personal and social motives.

RESISTANCE TO PRESSURES TO DEVIATE

Perhaps a more important index of conscience than the child's reaction to transgressing is the degree to which he behaves in accordance with his standards and avoids transgressing in the first place. The ability to resist pressures to deviate from one's standards may be a better test of their strength and integration with the personality than the experiencing of guilt after having transgressed. Pressures to deviate may be external (e.g., peer-group pressures) or internal (e.g., desires for objects which are themselves forbidden or which require prohibited action for their attainment). Some research has been done on parental antecedents of the child's response to external pressures[31] but not where the pressures were opposed to the child's values and standards. The latter is an important aspect of the larger social problem of how the individual learns to resolve conflicts between inner- and other-directed pressures.[32] There is need for empirical research on this problem, for example, on the antecedents of the moral strength or courage necessary to resist social pressures to deviate from one's internalized standards; and, more generally, the antecedents of how one copes with conflict between moral norms internalized in the home and opposing pressure from peers.[33]

[30] Heinicke, *op. cit.;* Sears, Maccoby, and Levin, *op. cit.;* Hoffman and Saltzstein, *op. cit.*

[31] M. L. Hoffman, "Some Psychodynamic Factors in Compulsive Conformity," *J. Abnorm. Soc. Psychol.,* XLVIII (1953), pp. 383–393; P. Mussen and J. Kagan, "Group Conformity and Perception of Parents," *Child Development,* XXIX (1958), pp. 57–60.

[32] D. Riesman, R. Denney and M. Glaser, *The Lonely Crowd* (New York: Doubleday Anchor, 1953).

[33] There is empirical evidence that, at least in communities not characterized by

Although external pressures against moral standards have been neglected in research, considerable work has been done on resistance to inner temptation. In the Allinsmith study already cited, two additional story-beginnings were included, one dealing with theft and the other with disobedience, in which the hero has not yet transgressed but is tempted to do so. The subject's resistance-to-temptation score was determined by whether or not in his story completions the hero transgressed. In one of the several parental background variables investigated, the use of explained requests rather than arbitrary demands was found to be positively associated with the resistance-to-temptation scores obtained for both stories. In an earlier study Mac-Kinnon[34] used a more direct behavioral index of resistance to temptation. His subjects, all college students, took a written test under conditions of no tangible reward. Cheaters were detected without their knowledge by observations through a one-way screen. Data on early parental practices were obtained from questionnaires filled out by the student. The findings showed a positive relationship between physical punishment and cheating; and between psychological punishment—defined as techniques which indicate that the child has fallen short of some ideal in some way, or hurt the parent and therefore that they love or approve of him less—and not cheating. Although these results are broadly consistent with Allinsmith's findings, the latter's own measures of psychological and corporal discipline did not relate to resistance to temptation.

Further confusion as to the antecedents of resistance to temptation is apparent when we examine the results of the three most recent studies in this area. Two used preschool age children[35] and the other, eleven to twelve year olds.[36] All three used the child's behavior in an experimental test situ-

---

rapid social change, peer pressures tend to reinforce parentally inculcated norms rather than oppose them (R. F. Peck and R. J. Havighurst, *The Psychology of Character Development* [New York: John Wiley, 1960]) and that most adolescents favor parental advice over peer advice (H. H. Remmers and D. H. Radler, *The American Teenager* [New York: Bobbs-Merrill Co., 1957]). Still, in a national sample one-third of the boys and one-sixth of the girls replied to the question "When do you think a (boy) (girl) might break a rule?" by stating that they might do so under the influence of the group (Elizabeth Douvan, *A Study of Adolescent Boys* [Ann Arbor: Institute for Social Research, The University of Michigan, 1955]; Elizabeth Douvan and C. Kaye, *Adolescent Girls* [Ann Arbor: Institute for Social Research, The University of Michigan, 1956]).

34 D. W. MacKinnon, "Violation of Prohibitions," *Exploration in Personality,* ed., H. W. Murray (New York: Oxford University Press, 1938), pp. 491–501.

35 R. V. Burton, Eleanor E. Maccoby and W. Allinsmith, "Antecedents of Resistance to Temptation in Four-year-old Children," *Child Development,* XXXII (1961), pp. 689–710; R. R. Sears, L. Rau and R. Alpert, "Identification and Child Training: The Development of Conscience," Interim Research Report presented at the American Psychological Association (Chicago, September, 1960).

36 R. E. Grinder, "Behavior in a Temptation Situation and Its Relation to Certain Aspects of Socialization" (unpublished Doctoral dissertation, Harvard University, 1960).

ation as the index of his ability to resist temptation. The test consisted of placing the child in a situation in which he was tempted to violate the rules of the game in order to win a prize, and then leaving him to play alone. Although the child thought no one was watching him, his reactions were observed through a one-way-screen, as in the MacKinnon study; and he was assigned scores indicating whether or not and to what degree he cheated or resisted the temptation to do so. All three studies used parent interviews consisting of a large number of structured and unstructured items and there is considerable overlap in the items used. Despite the similarities in conceptual approach, the way in which resistance to temptation was measured, and the parent interview items used, the findings in the three studies have little in common. Each investigator found several parent variables to relate to the child's ability to resist temptation, but there was little agreement among them as to which of the many parent variables used were the ones which related significantly to the child measure. Further, in those few cases in which the parent variables relating significantly to the child's resistance to temptation were similar, the direction of the relationships were as likely to be discrepant as not. Here are two examples: Burton and Grinder found the severity with which the child was weaned to relate positively to resistance to temptation, but Sears *et al.* found the same variable to relate negatively—the findings being statistically significant in all three cases; and whereas the general pattern of the Grinder and the Sears *et al.* findings was for resistance to temptation to relate to verbal rather than physical means of control, the Burton findings tended to be in the opposite direction. Finally, none of these three studies replicated MacKinnon's findings of a positive relationship between psychological discipline and not cheating, although all three had obtained psychological and physical discipline scores roughly comparable to those used by MacKinnon.

Such discrepant results among studies using similar methodologies cannot be ignored in our efforts to pull together and find meaning in the research in this area. A possible explanation for the inconsistencies lies in the choice of a situation involving success and failure in a task as the behavioral index of resistance to temptation. Such a measure is open to the damaging influence of unequal motivation to do well on the task, i.e., the temptation to cheat may not be the same for all subjects. Not cheating for some, for example, may signify disinterest in the prize or perhaps low achievement strivings in general rather than a strong conscience. Some of the investigators (especially Grinder) indicate awareness of this problem and attempt in one way or another to take cognizance of it in interpreting their findings. But none of the studies actually control the child's general needs for achievement or his desire for the particular prize.

Although the studies of resistance to temptation were undertaken with the expectation that its parental antecedents would roughly approximate those obtained for guilt, we have seen that this did not turn out to be the case. The expectation of a generally positive relationship between the two variables is based on the notion that a person with a strong conscience generally tends to resist temptation; and that when he does transgress for some reason, he experiences relatively severe guilt. Or, adhering more closely to the psychoanalytic formulation, that the person capable of experiencing severe guilt resists temptations in order to avoid guilt. Correspondingly, the person with little guilt potential—or one with smoothly functioning defenses against guilt—has little reason to resist temptation.

The assumption of a positive relationship between resistance to temptation and guilt is thrown into question not only by the lack of empirical evidence for their having common parental antecedents, but more directly by the fact that they have not been found to relate to each other with any consistency. Thus, while MacKinnon,[37] Grinder,[38] and Sears, *et al.*,[39] report low positive relationships between resistance to temptation and guilt (for girls, Sears, *et al.*, find a slight negative relationship), Allinsmith[40] and Maccoby[41] report no relationship and Burton,[42] a negative one. The lack of a clear cut relationship suggests that the motivation to avoid guilt is insufficient for resisting temptation and that other personality and situational variables should be considered. For example, a person might become so highly involved in striving for highly desired objectives that though he wishes to avoid guilt, he actually fails to anticipate it and acts accordingly. This is especially likely in the young child who is too immature cognitively to discriminate relevant cues and anticipate consequences. Or the person might be fully aware of the consequences at all times, yet lack the ego controls necessary to resist gratifying the impulse or need in question. Another possibility is that he might both foresee the consequences and have the necessary controls, yet be quite willing to tolerate considerable guilt in order to attain his objectives. Finally, a guilt-prone individual might violate a standard because of an unconscious wish for punishment. Simply because a person has strong moral concerns then, does not necessarily mean he will *behave* morally; whether he resists or submits to temptation is a function of a complex balance of forces between his achievement needs and specific goal strivings, guilt and other aspects of his moral structure, his system of ego controls, and various aspects of the immediate situation. Conversely, resistance to temptation need not necessarily imply guilt but might be done in the service of a

---

37 MacKinnon, *op. cit.*
38 Grinder, *op. cit.*
39 Sears, Rau and Alpert, *op. cit.*
40 Allinsmith, *op. cit.*
41 Eleanor E. Maccoby, "The Generality of Moral Behavior," *Amer. Psychologist,* XIV (1959), p. 358 (Abstract).
42 Burton, Maccoby and Allinsmith, *op. cit.*

value or ideal, e.g., masculine self control, which—like guilt—competes with the gratification of the impulse in question.

Such considerations highlight the complexities of doing empirical research on resistance to temptation. Very likely the closer our concepts approach the level of overt behavior which is subject to conscious volitional controls, the more multidetermined they become; and the more difficult it becomes empirically to institute the various methodological controls that are necessary for establishing specific antecedent-consequent relationships. Internal states like guilt, on the other hand, may be more unitary and less subject to such complexities. This line of argument may explain why the studies dealing with guilt and guilt-related reactions to transgressions reviewed above have a great deal of agreement despite the diversity of approaches used; while the resistance-to-temptation studies, which used similar concepts and methods, have little agreement. It may also account in part for the low relationships obtained in the classical studies by Hartshorne and May[43] between different manifestations of morality, since these investigators used mainly overt behavioral indices and did not control for such variables as motivation and fear.

Several suggestions for further research on resistance to temptation seem to follow from this discussion. First, every effort should be made not only to control on motivation but, more specifically, to make certain that all the subjects are highly motivated. To measure resistance to temptation adequately obviously requires that there be temptation. Otherwise we could only be sure, at best, of measuring the absence of cheating or of whatever unacceptable behaviors were under study. Studies of resistance to pressure from peers might for the same reason need to control on the subject's needs for affiliation and fears of rejection as well as his needs to continue behaving in the manner opposed by the group.[44] Secondly, resistance to temptation scores should probably be based on a battery of measures dealing with different kinds of moral standards. This might pose new problems, e.g., the ethics of inducing children, even in the service of science, to commit acts more strongly prohibited in our culture than cheating, such as stealing and physical violence. This may be why a relatively harmless (and from the experimenter's standpoint, passive) test situation has been used in all the experimental studies of resistance to temptation. Perhaps compromise solutions can be found, e.g., using a complex index based on a carefully controlled experimental cheating situation, in conjunction with a projective measure dealing with temptation in areas more difficult to study in the

[43] H. Hartshorne and M. May, *Studies in Character* (3 vols.; New York: Macmillan, 1929).

[44] The literature on sex differences in our culture suggests that for boys controls on needs for achievement might be especially important and that for girls, controls on needs for affiliation.

laboratory. From a large sample children who consistently resist temptation on both the experimental and projective measures might then be compared with those who consistently do not resist. Thirdly, since the relationship between resistance to temptation and guilt is variable and apparently unpredictable, it must be assumed in any given sample that the resistance to temptation measure may be confounded with guilt. Studies having the theoretical goal of isolating out the specific antecedents of resistance to temptation per se may, therefore, have to control on guilt, e.g., by comparing children who are high on both guilt and resistance to temptation with those who are high on guilt but low on resistance to temptation.

SOCIALIZATION: PEER AND SCHOOL INFLUENCES

Popularity Among Adolescents in Western Australia and in the United States of America*

D. K. WHEELER

Doubtless popularity and prestige among peers have enormous influence upon every adolescent's sense of well-being. Popularity may affect an adolescent's choice of friends, extracurricular activities, and vocational goals. In the paper presented below, Wheeler explores the nature of popularity during adolescence by attempting to answer several specific questions. For example: "In adolescence, do characteristics associated with popularity differ at different ages?" and "Do the characteristics of popular boys differ from characteristics of popular girls?" His data show that "developmental and sex differences in characteristics associated with popularity appear to be neither large nor important. . . . Popularity with the opposite sex requires much the same behavior as popularity with one's own sex." He concludes that popularity depends rather upon fundamental "core" values common to both sexes than upon sex and developmental differences.

One of the most important developmental tasks of the adolescent is to establish more mature relationships with age mates of both sexes, a task which is closely related to the individual's social adjustment. While many factors can contribute to the popularity of an adolescent, we suggest that certain personality traits, physical skills, and physical characteristics are most important. We propose to compare the factors that make for popularity in the United States with factors that make for popularity in Western Australia and explore some of the questions raised by the comparison.

Almost every textbook on adolescence published in the past fifteen years has quoted Tryon[1] and Kuhlen and Lee.[2] We shall, therefore, only outline

[1] Caroline M. Tryon, "Evaluations of Adolescent Personality by Adolescents,"

* From the *School Review*, LXIX (1961), pp. 67–81. Reprinted by permission of the author and the University of Chicago Press.

the research of these authors. Tryon, who worked with about 160 boys and 160 girls in urban California, found the traits of the popular twelve-year-old boy quite different from the traits of the popular twelve-year-old girl. Popular pre-adolescent boys were active and competent in group games; enthusiasm, good humor, good looks, happiness, friendliness, and daring— all seemed important in determining status. Although the trait group "restless, talkative, attention-seeking" was less important than the others mentioned, it had some significance. According to Tryon, nearly all the twelve-year-olds studied would rather have been considered untidy, bossy, vigorous, and noisy than neat and submissive. By fifteen, the pattern had changed. Cheerfulness and humor, physical competence, courage, and self-assertion were still important, but more emphasis was placed on personal attractiveness and ease in mixed social situations. The boisterous hyper-activity significant earlier was now regarded as childish.

The popular twelve-year-old girl exhibited behavior that was more con-forming to adult demands. She presented a neat, attractive appearance; she had a friendly, demure manner; and she showed quiet good humor. For the fifteen-year-old girl the criteria approached those of the ideal boy of that age—extraversion, good sportsmanship, social poise, humor, and gaiety.

Kuhlen and Lee studied six groups of children from villages and rural areas in central New York: 100 boys and 136 girls in Grade 6, 120 boys and 120 girls in Grade 9, and 124 boys and 136 girls in Grade 12. These researchers compared the personality characteristics of the most popular 25 per cent with those of the least popular 25 per cent in each of these six groups. For students of both sexes and all grades, the traits that made for popularity were cheerfulness, friendliness, enthusiasm, enjoying jokes, and initiating games and activities.

The difference between the results reported by these researchers and those reported by Tryon points to the need for investigating more repre-sentative samples, particularly of eleven- and twelve-year-olds. Further, both researches used the "Guess Who" technique. Because in this technique the investigator determines what traits or trait groups are presented to the student, there is a danger that he may include irrelevant traits or omit relevant ones. For this reason, in our own study we preferred to use ques-tions that gave adolescents a chance to mention characteristics they thought important, though it must be admitted that such questions are difficult to score quantitatively.

Monogr. Soc. Res. Child Develpm., IV, No. 4 (Washington: National Research Council, 1939); Caroline M. Tryon, "The Adolescent Peer Culture," *Adolescence*, The Forty-third Yearbook of the National Society for the Study of Education, Part I (Chicago: University of Chicago Press, 1944).

    [2] R. G. Kuhlen and Beatrice J. Lee, "Personality Characteristics and Social Ac-ceptability in Adolescence," *J. Educ. Psychol.*, XXXIV (1943), pp. 321–340.

The Western Australian Adolescent Survey from which our data are drawn covered a representative sample of some eight hundred adolescents from all types of secondary schools throughout the state. Most of our information came from answers to the instructions: "Without mentioning names, describe briefly a very popular boy or girl in your class." Responses were checked against responses to additional questions: "Without mentioning names, describe briefly a very *un*popular girl or boy in your class." "What sort of girl do you admire most?" "What sort of boy do you admire most?" Each student had already filled in one Pressey XO type list concerned with the sort of person of the same sex he or she liked or admired, and another list for the sort of person of the opposite sex he or she admired. We are reporting here only our major conclusions, using the .02 level of significance for differences.

As any observer of the Australian scene can testify, athletic skill or sporting ability is a means to popularity among adolescents as well as adults. The students made some mention of other skills useful in keeping a group amused, but these were unimportant compared with sporting ability, which was a characteristic of popular boys and girls at all ages.

Under the heading of sociality we included manners, conversational ability, and social relationships. Good behavior, or manners, and conversational abilities seemed relatively unimportant in popularity. Perhaps, however, these tended to be included in good social relationships, which were important, in that popular classmates got on well with others, were willing to participate, and had social poise.

Another important group of traits we called *altocentric,* defined positively as kind, generous, helpful, sympathetic, and negatively as not a bully, a snob, or a "skite" (a conceited person). There was a non-significant trend for these traits to become more important with age, but all we can suggest from the evidence is that warmth and kindness are as likely to make a boy or girl popular at thirteen as at seventeen.

While these three trait groups—sporting ability, sociality, altocentric— showed no significant differences between the sexes or age groups, the traits that follow did show sex differences or developmental trends.

Certain physical attributes were associated with popularity. At all ages, from a quarter to a half of the adolescents described as popular were depicted as tall, well built, and engaging in physical activity. Also characteristic of the socially acceptable were good looks, cleanliness, and grooming (tidiness). The last two appeared more important at the youngest age for both boys and girls. Perhaps older adolescents take these qualities for granted, or perhaps school authorities tacitly impose a minimum standard. Whatever the reason, the importance attached to these qualities diminished with age.

One important group of traits we designated as *euphoric*—defined by such replies as cheerful, witty, jolly, carefree. These traits ranked fairly high at most levels but seemed more important to the oldest girls. Cheerfulness and good humor were significantly greater determinants of popularity for seventeen-year-old girls than for seventeen-year-old boys.

It is significant that cognitive abilities ("has brains" or "good at schoolwork") were not so important to the adolescent as to his teacher. They were a factor in popularity—ranking fifth for the boys in frequency of mention and sixth for the girls—but not to the same extent as the other attributes mentioned.

In Western Australia, then, the half-dozen traits or trait groups associated with adolescent popularity are sporting ability, sociality, good physical appearance, altocentric and euphoric personality traits, and cognitive abilities. In general, girls have to meet much the same pattern of expectations as boys, except that there is not quite the same emphasis on sporting ability. From the protocols of these eight hundred students we can form a picture of a popular adolescent—Noel—in a high school in Western Australia. Noel is above average in height, well built, neither too fat nor too skinny, has regular features, and an attractive face that some might call good-looking. This well-developed teen-ager is neat, tidy, clean, and dresses in clothes suitable to the occasion. Noel takes part in a number of sporting activities with success, which seems natural enough for a person of physical energy and vigor.

Everyone in the class agrees that this adolescent is kind and considerate, sympathetic and good-hearted, friendly and approachable. When Noel was younger, vivacity and humor were commented on more, but now kindliness and warmth of personality seem to be more appreciated. A few think that occasionally there is a touch of conceit in Noel's manner, but no one suggests the descriptions "skite" or "bossy." While some classmates mention Noel's attractive personality, there is little suggestion that it might be described as a strong one, and few comment on leadership qualities. Perhaps these qualities are present. If so, they are exercised so skilfully and so unobtrusively that age mates are not led to mention them. It is the light and amusing side of Noel's nature, the cheerfulness and the fun, that come in for most comment in phrases such as "the life of the party" and in a few references to social skills such as "sings well" or "is a good pianist." Relationships with classmates are very good, probably because of Noel's lack of snobbishness, social poise, and willingness to take part in group activities.

Other students say that Noel is "reasonably brainy" and a good student, but it can be seen that the intelligence mentioned is not too far above the average of the group, nor does Noel boast of intellectual attainments or spend too much time on study. Relationships with individual teachers and the staff as a whole appear to be harmonious.

Friends may stress Noel's honesty and good character, but other class-mates appear to take these traits for granted, since they are not often mentioned, except for an occasional reference to the fact that Noel does not smoke or swear or tell dirty jokes.

This adolescent's chief interest is sports, though dancing and modern music also appeal. Noel does not seem to be interested in reading, cultural activities, politics, religion, or intellectual pursuits—or at least does not show interest in these subjects when with the group. Noel may be a good conversationalist, but few classmates mention this social skill.

In this sketch of a popular adolescent, personal pronouns which would indicate Noel's sex have been deliberately omitted. The name Noel, which might be a girl's or a boy's, was also chosen deliberately to emphasize the fact that the traits associated with popularity in boys are very similar to those associated with popularity in girls.

In making cross-cultural comparisons we shall consider first the factors that make for popularity in boys at each age level in the United States and in Western Australia. Next we shall compare traits of popular girls. Finally we shall explore the more general questions of developmental trends and sex differences.

Data in Table 1 show traits and trait groups in order of importance. We have eliminated the trait *popular* from the New York lists. To say that the 25 per cent most popular students in a grade or age group are described as *popular* does not offer much information. Two points should be re-membered about these data. Tryon's findings differ considerably from those of Kuhlen and Lee, and there are considerable age differences between the youngest groups in Western Australia and in the United States.

The data in the table and in the other studies mentioned show fairly clearly that for boys approaching adolescence or just past the threshold of adolescence, friendliness, cheerfulness, enthusiasm, and humor play an important part in popularity. Participation and competence in games and sporting activities also rank high. Good looks ranks lower on our list, but it must be noted that good physical build (which may include what thirteen-year-olds call *good looks*) is third on our list. Tryon found that restlessness, fighting, and fearlessness were concomitants of popularity at about age twelve,[3] but our results showed daring as the only trait in this group that was mentioned with any frequency. As to whether untidiness, bossiness, and fighting are characteristic of the popular twelve-year-old boy, and the American studies do not agree on this point,[4] we can report for our sample only that they are associated with unpopularity. If we neglect such dis-crepancies, which may be due to subcultural variation, we find that the characteristics associated with popularity are similar in both countries.

---

[3] *Ibid.*
[4] Tryon, "The Adolescent Peer Culture," *op. cit.;* Kuhlen and Lee, *op. cit.*

Table 1
Trait or Trait Groups Associated with Adolescent Popularity Among Boys and Girls in the United States and in Western Australia, Listed in Order of Importance

| | BOYS | | GIRLS | |
	New York*	Western Australia	New York*	Western Australia
Grade	Grade 6	First-year high school	Grade 6	First-year high school
Mean age	11.9	13.5	11.6	13.4
Number of students	25†	152	29†	148
Traits	Cheerful	Sporting abilities	Friendly	Sociality
	Enthusiastic	Euphoric traits	Enthusiastic	Euphoric traits
	Friendly	Build and activity	Good looking	Sporting abilities
	Good looking	Sociality	Initiates games and activities	Cognitive abilities
	Enjoys joke on self	Sportsmanship	Enjoys joke on self	Build and activity
	Active in games	Grooming		Altocentric traits
		Altocentric traits		Good looks
		Cognitive abilities		
Grade	Grade 9	Third-year high school	Grade 9	Third-year high school
Mean age	14.7	15.4	14.3	15.3
Number of students	30†	142	30†	152
Traits	Enthusiastic	Build and activity	Cheerful	Euphoric traits
	Friendly	Sporting abilities	Friendly	Sociality
	Willing to take a chance	Sociality	Enthusiastic	Altocentric traits
	Cheerful	Euphoric traits	Initiates games and activities	Good looks
	Initiates games and activities	Cognitive abilities	Neat and clean	Sporting abilities
	Active in games	Altocentric traits		Build and activity
	Likes opposite sex	Good looks		
Grade	Grade 12	Fifth-year high school	Grade 12	Fifth-year high school
Mean age	17.4	17.3	17.3	17.2
Number of students	26†	115	29†	75
Traits	Friendly	Sporting abilities	Friendly	Euphoric traits
	Initiates games	Build and activity	Enthusiastic	Sociality
	Enthusiastic	Sociality	Sociable	Build and activity
	Cheerful	Altocentric traits	Enjoys jokes	Altocentric traits
	Enjoys joke on self	Cognitive abilities	Enjoys joke on self	Sporting abilities
	Likes opposite sex	Euphoric traits		Cognitive abilities

* Adapted from Kuhlen and Lee, op. cit. Tables 3 and 4.
† This group represents the top quarter in popularity.

302

Popular fifteen-year-old boys seem alike in both countries. In California, personal attractiveness, social assertion and ease, cheerfulness, and good humor were highly rated. In New York, activity, friendliness, good looks and grooming, cheerfulness, and good humor were associated with popularity. In Western Australia, good physical build, sporting ability, ease in social relations, the euphoric traits (cheerful, enthusiastic, good humor), and cognitive abilities were important. With our boys there was less emphasis on self-assertion and more prestige attached to sporting and cognitive abilities.

Among seventeen-year-olds likenesses outweigh differences. Kuhlen's popular twelfth-grade boy is the active, socially aggressive extravert, cheerful, enthusiastic, friendly, with some stress on social sensitivity. His counterpart in Western Australia is active in sports and games, cheerful, enthusiastic, and friendly, of an outgoing sociable nature, with "brains" or good at schoolwork. Possibly the greater stress on cognitive abilities is due to the fact that the proportion of seventeen-year-olds still at school is smaller in Western Australia than in New York.

It is evident in Table 1, in which traits and trait groups are listed in order of importance, that the Western Australian results for girls are more like the New York results than the California results. The popular twelve-year-old girl depicted by Kuhlen and Lee shows friendliness, humor, enthusiasm, good looks, neatness, initiative, and activity, and appears rather less demure and docile than Tryon would suggest. In Western Australia, the popular thirteen-year-old is friendly, sociable, cheerful, enthusiastic, and good-humored. She shows initiative and activity in sports and games. She is well built, good-looking, clean, and tidy. She also has "brains" or is good at schoolwork, and here there is a difference between the two countries. It should be pointed out, however, that the "Guess Who" statements used in both American investigations made no reference to "brains," or being good at schoolwork, so that it was not possible for American adolescents to indicate whether this trait was a concomitant of popularity.

"By the age of fifteen," says Tryon, "many of the criteria for the idealized boy, such as extraversion, activity and good sportsmanship are highly acceptable for the girl."[5] Competence and poise in social activities, humor, and gaiety were also characteristic. This description is like Kuhlen and Lee's picture of the fourteen-year-old girl as cheerful, friendly, sociable, enthusiastic, neat, and initiating games and activities. It can be seen, too, that the description differs little from the Western Australian picture, where the emphasis is on cheerfulness and good humor, friendliness and social ease, good build and good looks, kindness and consideration, intelligence or success at schoolwork, and participation in games and activities. Again the major difference is the reference to cognitive abilities.

[5] Tryon, "Evaluations of Adolescent Personality by Adolescents," *op. cit.,* p. 77.

For the oldest American girls, the acceptable characteristics are much the same as for the younger ones and closely parallel the trait groups associated with popularity in Western Australia. Our sample places more emphasis on sporting and cognitive abilities and on build and activity, but friendliness, enthusiasm, good humor, and social sensitivity are common characteristics. In both countries, apparently, extraversion makes for acceptance, but in Western Australia extraversion must not be allied with bossiness or aggressiveness.

In a consideration of developmental changes, Tryon's work suggests that there is a good deal of continuity in boys' values from preadolescence to adolescence, while a much more radical change must occur in girls' values between the ages of twelve and fifteen. The New York study offers little corroborative evidence for the latter view, for there the traits most significantly related to popularity remained the same over the six-year period, though there was a tendency for the importance of good looks and games activity to diminish while the importance of being sociable and enjoying a joke increased. Such changes among girls can be paralleled in Western Australia, though there were few of statistical significance. Between the first and the third years of secondary school, sporting ability became less important, while over the five years the value attached to neatness and tidiness declined. There was obviously unanimity among the Western Australian girls about the traits associated with popularity. Ranking the traits in order of mention by each of the three girls' groups gives a Kendall coefficient of concordance (W) of .91.

In both countries there is no great developmental change in the characteristics associated with popular boys. According to Tryon, there is some decline in the value attached to aggressive defiant behavior and an increase in the importance attached to social qualities and personal appearance between the ages of twelve and fifteen. In contrast, Kuhlen and Lee state that, from a consideration of those traits that show greatest differentiation between popular and unpopular persons for both sexes and in all grades, it is apparent that the highly accepted person is cheerful and happy, enthusiastic, friendly, enjoys jokes, and initiates games and activities. Similarity in relative importance of various traits in all grades is obvious, these researchers say. In Western Australia, except for a decline with increasing age in the number of boys who mentioned good sportsmanship and cleanliness and grooming, there was the same agreement among the boys as among the girls $(W = .91)$. The dwindling importance of neatness and cleanliness with increasing age is also found in the New York boys, though not in the New York girls.

When we consider sex differences, we see that the New York study does not reproduce the California picture of the popular twelve-year-old boy and girl as distinct types, the boy noisy, energetic, unkempt, rather defiant of adults, though friendly and cheerful; the girl, amenable, demure, tidy, friendly, and cheerful. Instead, four of the five traits most closely associated with popularity were common to both boys and girls; similarly traits having lowest (or negative) association with acceptability were common to both sexes. As we have already indicated, this lack of differences in ratings of traits by boys and girls may be noted in the Western Australian samples. If there is any difference, it is that girls of thirteen tend to describe a popular classmate in terms of general attractiveness of personality, while boys place more emphasis on sporting ability. It seems that sheer energy and vigor are not admired for themselves, but only when channeled into sporting activities where girls as well as boys can earn prestige.

At fifteen it seems that the likenesses between the sexes are greater than the differences. Tryon remarks that many of the criteria for the idealized boy are highly acceptable for the girl, though she maintains that male prestige is still in large measure determined by physical skill, aggressiveness, and fearlessness. We are uncertain whether Tryon equates prestige with popularity, but she often describes popular adolescents as leaders— as children who are friendly, enthusiastic, happy, humorous, and daring. These traits are similar to those Kuhlen and Lee found in popular adolescents of both sexes. In our results we found that significantly more popular boys than girls were described as well built, good sports, and strong in moral character. These last two traits, however, contributed little to popularity: for the traits that did contribute to popularity (sporting ability, sociality, good humor, kindness, and good looks) there were no significant sex differences, except that more girls than boys mentioned altocentric traits. One clearly marked cultural difference emerges: in Western Australia at this age, neither boys nor girls consider aggressiveness a factor in popularity.

At the end of the secondary years, of the five traits most significant in popularity, three—friendly, enthusiastic, enjoys joke on self—are common to both sexes in the United States sample. Cheerfulness and initiating games and activities are the other two traits most associated with popular boys, while the remaining two for girls are sociability and enjoying jokes. In Western Australia, though characteristics associated with popularity do not show much sex difference, sporting abilities seem more important to the boys and euphoric personality traits to the girls.

For Western Australian adolescents, who were as representative a sample of the total adolescent population still in school as we could make it, we must report that we found little or no basic difference in the traits associated with popularity, either over the period of adolescence or between the sexes. What differences we observed have been pointed out, but they are all minor or concerned with the relative importance of much the same traits at different periods. The high coefficients of concordance for boys and girls have been mentioned; putting traits in order of mention for all sex and age groups, we find $W = .82$.

Our results raise the question as to whether there are major differences in the characteristics associated with popularity in adolescents, either sex differences or developmental trends. American textbook writers commonly say there are and cite the two United States studies we have discussed here. We think that this generalization is based on insufficient data and that differences have been studied and emphasized at the expense of essential similarities. Tryon suggested that her California group should not be taken as descriptive of children and adolescents throughout the United States, but this suggestion is often forgotten. The nature of her sample may explain why her findings differ from those of Kuhlen and Lee, particularly for the youngest girls. While it is possible to agree with Kuhlen and Lee that the importance of various characteristics may change during adolescence, there is not sufficient evidence that such changes have the significance often attached to them. More important is their statement that "Similarity in relative importance of various traits at Grades VI and XII (also for Grade IX, though not shown) is obvious."[6]

Our results dispose us to put forward the view that there will inevitably be minor differences in the order of characteristics associated with popularity in the United States and in Western Australia, as well as in various adolescent subcultures in either country. Nevertheless, we suggest that the characteristics of popular adolescents in the two countries comprise a solid core of physical and personality attributes. That is, in the two cultures and probably in most subcultures within them, there is widespread agreement about desirable personality traits. Some weight is lent to this view by the work of Jennings[7] and Dimock,[8] who, in such widely divergent environments as a training school for delinquent girls and a summer camp for boys, found that personality traits most associated with popularity were cooperation, helpfulness, courtesy and consideration, initiative, self-control, and unselfishness. We suggest that the core of characteristics associated with adolescent popularity is compounded of an attractive appearance, the euphoric and altocentric traits, participation in sporting and other activities, and some degree of cognitive ability shown in or out of school.

If we favor a suggestion that characteristics making for popularity in adolescent groups in both countries are reflections of characteristics approved by the culture at large, obviously there are important educational implications that cannot be spelled out here. Two points should be noted, however. Research of the type reported here can refer only to the mean

6 Kuhlen and Lee, *op. cit.*, 335.
7 Helen M. Jennings, *Leadership and Isolation* (New York: Longmans, Green and Co., 1943).
8 H. S. Dimock, *Rediscovering the Adolescent* (New York: Association Press, 1937).

prestige value of characteristics of groups of adolescents (whether these groups be representative or quite atypical) and not to the factors that account for popularity in this or that group. Nor do we suggest that boys and girls must learn the same role, but only that the characteristics that are associated with popularity in adolescents are those which make for good interpersonal and intragroup interaction. These characteristics will be much alike in societies that speak the same language and share many of the same values.

There has been a tendency to consider the works of Tryon and Kuhlen and Lee as complementary. Actually their conclusions show differences that must be resolved. Perhaps some United States investigator will explore the problem with a representative sample of adolescents, for the research considered here offers ambiguous or contradictory answers to the following questions:

In adolescence, do characteristics associated with popularity differ at different ages?

Do the characteristics of popular boys differ from characteristics of popular girls?

Do girls need to change more than boys to maintain status during the adolescent years?

Is there sufficient evidence to say that, in order to be popular with girls, boys must also be popular with their own sex, while girls who are popular with boys are not necessarily popular with girls?

To what extent are the characteristics associated with popularity among adolescents also associated with popularity among adults?

In general, writers on adolescence have answered yes to the first four questions and have not considered the fifth to any extent. Ausubel,[9] Fleming,[10] Horrocks,[11] Hurlock,[12] and Kuhlen[13] have stressed developmental differences. Most of them, too, have stressed sex differences and in general have agreed with Tryon's views. For example, Ausubel has said that girls, unlike boys, "have no core value—such as athletic prowess—which persists in the peer culture as a significant determinant of status." Yet he has also said: "The pattern of personality characteristics admired in persons of the opposite sex also shows considerable sex agreement during adolescence." The last statement agrees with our own findings; the first does not.

[9] D. P. Ausubel, *Theory and Problems of Adolescent Development* (New York: Grune and Stratton, 1954), pp. 363–364.

[10] C. M. Fleming, *Adolescence* (London: Routledge and Kegan Paul, 1948), pp. 144–147.

[11] J. E. Horrocks, *The Psychology of Adolescence* (Boston: Houghton Mifflin Co., 1951), pp. 119–120.

[12] Elizabeth Hurlock, *Adolescent Development* (New York: McGraw-Hill Book Co., 1949), p. 202.

[13] R. G. Kuhlen, *The Psychology of Adolescent Development* (New York: Harper and Bros., 1952), pp. 333–338.

Ausubel also notes "the general correspondence of preadolescent and adolescent evaluations of personality traits to those of adults." Cole appears to agree with our position, on the developmental side at least, when she says: "There are some changes from early to late adolescence in the traits that are admired, although the chief difference lies in emphasis rather than in selection of characteristics."[14] Obviously further work must be done if we are to get definitive answers to the questions posed.

For Western Australian adolescents who are still in school we are prepared to speak with some certainty. Developmental and sex differences in characteristics associated with popularity appear to be neither large nor important. Expectations for boys and girls are much the same and consonant with adult expectations as far as we can judge them. Popularity with the opposite sex requires much the same behavior as popularity with one's own sex. Western Australian girls, we would say, certainly have a persistent core value—just as the boys have—for athletic prowess is not the sole determinant of status, which depends on the physical attributes and skills and personality traits we delineated in our picture of Noel. While we do not wish to generalize beyond our data, we believe, from our analysis of the evidence reported here, that the core values associated with adolescent popularity in Western Australia are the same values associated with popularity in the United States. We have found in American textbooks so much emphasis on sex and developmental differences that we wish to stress these core values.

[14] Luella Cole, *Psychology of Adolescence* (New York: Rinehart and Co., 1948), p. 227.

Status in the Informal Group: Influence and Influencibility at Differing Age Levels* [1]

O. J. HARVEY AND
JEANNE RUTHERFORD

In the following study concerned with patterns of influence in small informal groups at different age levels, 405 students from the third, sixth, ninth, and eleventh grades are divided into small groups by age in order to investigate: "(a) the differential influence of the highest and lowest status member on the opinions of other group members; (b) the relationship of an individual's status in the group to his own influencibility; and (c) the relationship between status or effective initiative and popularity at different ages." Although one might predict that the effect of status would be less critical in childhood than in adolescence, Harvey and Rutherford's findings demonstrate unexpectedly a reversal between the sixth and ninth grades, viz., status affects degree of influence in the sixth but not in the ninth grade. As one might expect, however, low-status group members appear to be more susceptible to influence than those of high status, and popularity and status appear to be very highly correlated at all the grade levels.

The importance of status in the informal group as a factor that relates both to one's influencibility and influence of others has been recognized by several writers concerned with related issues. Yet very little experimental effort

[1] This study was initiated under a research grant from the Institute for Research and Training in the Social Sciences, Vanderbilt University. It was completed under support of the Group Psychology Branch, Office of Naval Research, Contract Nonr 2149(02). Our thanks are extended to the above for their support and to the officials and teachers of the Davidson County school system who permitted the study to be carried out among their students. Reproduction of this study in whole or part is permitted for any purpose of the United States Government.

---

* From *Child Development*, XXXI (1960), pp. 377–385. Reprinted by permission of the authors and the Society for Research in Child Development.

has been expended toward delineating the effects of specific status positions within the group hierarchy; and even greater is the paucity of effort aimed at establishing the chronological age levels at which status evolves as a major determinant of patterns of influence in the small group. This study sought to investigate the reciprocal relationships of status in the informal group to influence and influencibility as a function of the chronological ages of the group members. Information was also gathered on the adjunctive question of the relationship between status and popularity at differing age levels.

Both empirical and experimental bases exist for the prediction of greater influence on other members by the leader and other higher ranking members,[2] at least at the adult or near-adult level. The picture concerning the weight of status in influencibility by other members is, however, more complex and less clear. Logical bases exist that would be compatible with the greatest conformity or influencibility of the occupant of almost any status position within the group. For example, one of the key determinants of a member's influencibility by the deviant judgments of other group members is his striving to gain and maintain status within his reference group.[3] The higher a member's motivation to attain these status ends, and hence the greater his dependency on the group for satisfaction of this motive, the greater should be his susceptibility to influence from other members, particularly from the higher status members.

The hypothesis that motivation is a simple function of the distance from the goal, as well as the possibility of expulsion from the group with loss of his lowly position, would favor greatest striving and conformity on the part of the lowest status man. And yet the very remoteness of the lowest status man from the top position might result in his being less motivated to try to move up the status ladder and consequently in his being less susceptible to influence by discrepant judgments of other members, especially if his position were a secure one.

The second ranking person could prove to be the member on whom the goal of the top position exercises greatest motivational pull. Studies relating to goal gradient, level of aspiration, and class mobility seem to be consistent with this possibility, as well as are the findings of Dittes and Kelley.[4] These authors found the highest incidence of conformity to group evaluations in both private and group surveillance situations to occur among those indi-

[2] C. I. Hovland, I. Janis and H. H. Kelley, *Communication and Persuasion* (New Haven: Yale University Press, 1953); F. M. Thrasher, *The Gang* (Chicago: University of Chicago Press, 1927); W. F. Whyte, *Street Corner Society* (Chicago: University of Chicago Press, 1943).

[3] G. M. Hochbaum, "The Relation Between Group Members' Self Confidence and Their Reactions to Group Pressures to Conformity," *Amer. Sociol. Rev.*, XIX (1954), pp. 678–687.

[4] J. E. Dittes and H. H. Kelley, "Effects of Different Conditions of Acceptance upon Conformity to Group Norms," *J. Abnorm. Soc. Psychol.*, LIII (1956), pp. 100–107.

viduals who had been led to believe that their degree of acceptance by the other members was average, which in this case was next to the highest of the four degrees of induced acceptance.

The leader or highest ranking member's behavior should be less affected by the striving for the top position than that of the lowest or next to highest status member by virtue of his having attained that goal. The attainment of the top position, however, exposes the leader to pressures from a new source, that of maintaining the leadership status. If his position were a secure one, the leader could afford perhaps to deviate further from the behavior of the other members;[5] but, if insecure in his position, the leader might be the most susceptible to group pressures because of the greater psychological distance he could fall if displaced from the apex of the hierarchy.

Important procedural differences in the present study add further to the uncertainty of the relationship that should be expected here between status and influencibility. The "issue" of this study was, purposely, a non-involving one, being related neither to a group norm nor to strong personal attitudes of the participants. Moreover, the method of inducing influence deviated from the more typical approaches. The discrepant evaluation instead of being presented as *majority opinion,* as is more usual, was in this study introduced as emanating from *single* individuals, those of highest and lowest status within the subject's own informal group.

Any effect of status in influencing others or resisting their influence assumes a certain level of social development of the participants. The age at which status and role relations become important determinants of behavior is undoubtedly quite early in childhood. Yet these social relations seem to remain for several years in a state of flux, moving toward greater stability with the approach to adulthood. Thus, for example, the weight of status in the influence patterns within the informal group should be less at the third than the eleventh grade, the extreme age levels included in this study.

Despite its being an old question, still little is known of the relationship between status and popularity when viewed developmentally. The extent of the relationship should at all age levels be expected to vary somewhat with the demands of the particular situation, which in turn would give rise to the degree of differentiation between effective initiative and friendship. The degree of differentiation between friendship and leadership characteristics could become so marked that one's choice of a friend would bear little relationship to his choice of a leader. The condition conducive to such a situation would probably be one where great value is attached to job proficiency, such as in military combat. On the other hand, such a minimal distinction could be made between friendship and leadership qualities that

---

[5] Hochbaum, *op. cit.;* H. H. Kelley, "Communication in experimentally created hierarchies," *Hum. Relat.,* IV (1951), pp. 39–56.

a perfect correlation would obtain between one's standing on these two dimensions. This latter possibility would be more likely among younger, undifferentiating children and in situations where task proficiency is not so highly valued.

METHOD

Test Materials

The materials consisted of two sociometric questionnaires, enlarged reproductions of five pairs of pictures from the Meier Art Judgment Test (MAJT) and small answer booklets in which the subjects indicated their picture preferences subsequent to the "communication."

The sociometric questionnaires were used to obtain measures of status and popularity at the different age levels. The requisite of making the criterion questions relevant to activities characteristic of a given age necessitated the construction of separate questionnaires for the lower (third and sixth grades) and the higher (ninth and eleventh grades) age levels. Questions aimed at popularity and leadership were included in both questionnaires, the difference being that the specific situations to which the questions related were different for the higher and lower age groups. The criteria for leadership related to the initiation and direction of group activities in various specific situations, while the popularity questions were meant to ascertain personal liking for individual members.

The MAJT presents to the individual pairs of pictures in booklet form, the intrapair similarity of which ranges from high to almost identity. The task of the subject is to indicate his preference for one of the pictures in the pair. For this study five pairs of pictures were selected, four of which were used as camouflage for the attempts at influencing preferences for the *remaining pair,* which served as the *critical stimulus* or the *opinion issue* of this study. In choosing the critical stimulus, the aim was to select a pair of pictures sufficiently similar to preclude strong preference for one over the other, but not so similar as to destroy the reliability of preferences under noninfluence choice situations. Incidence of change in preference on the critical pair of pictures provided the measure of effectiveness of the influence attempts. Enlarged reproductions of all the pictures were made so they could be seen clearly by all students, thereby allowing the "test" to be used in a group situation which was necessary for this study.

Procedure

The experiment was carried out in two sessions, each in natural classroom settings. In the first session sociometric measures of popularity and status were obtained, and subjects indicated their preferences for the critical stimulus (which was presented as a sample of the art test to follow a week later). In the second, the influence session, subjects were informed of the first session preferences of the highest and lowest status individuals in their own informal group after which they again recorded their preference for the critical stimulus along with their choices for the noncritical pictures.

The influence attempt was made to appear as a logical sequence in the administration of the art test. The first step in the second session was passing out to each subject a specially prepared answer booklet on which his (her) name had been written earlier by the experimenters. In this pre-assigned booklet was contained the communication intended for that specific recipient. This message was conveyed in the simple note that "——— chose left," "———chose right," penned by the experimenters on the bottom of the "sample" page, the page on which the preference for the critical stimulus following the influence attempt was to be recorded. The names of the highest and lowest ranking members in the subject's own informal group were always inserted in the two blanks. The first session choices of the highest and lowest status members were thus always presented as opposites. When the highest status member, or leader, was represented as having agreed with the subject in his initial preference, the lowest status individual was depicted as having chosen the opposite picture, and vice versa.

Two experimental conditions were thus provided: highest status disagree–lowest status agree (*HSD-LSA*) and lowest status disagree–highest status agree (*LSD-HSA*). Subjects within each of the 12 classes were divided approximately equally among these two experimental conditions and a control group in which subjects received no information concerning preferences of others. It was thought that the simultaneous exposure of the individual to contradictory influences would provide a more valid index of the differential influence of the highest and lowest status members. It was this assumption that gave rise to the selection of the particular stimulus ("issue") used in this study, one dictating dichotomous responses and thus allowing for two sources plausibly to be represented as maintaining opposite stands.

Presentation of the communication was rationalized to the subjects as being intended to give them an idea of the choices of some other class members on the sample picture. To allay suspicion within the control group, it was pointed out that only in some of the answer booklets, selected by chance, had the information on others' preferences been included. This explanation preceded the subjects' turning to the "sample" page on which was written the communication. The critical ("sample") picture was then presented, and, after recording their postcommunication choices on it, subjects were then "tested" with the four pairs of noncritical pictures. All pairs of pictures, critical and camouflage, were shown for 10 seconds. Subjects indicated their preferences by checking on the appropriate page of the answer booklet in front of the letter "L" or "R" for the left or right picture of the pair. The pictures of each pair were clearly labeled "L" or "R" to prevent positional error in recording of choices.

To reduce the danger of their suspecting the true purpose of the study, Ss were not permitted to talk nor to compare notes during the experiment. All Ss appeared to accept the study as a test of art ability in line with its announced rationale.

Subjects

Pre- and postcommunication measures, along with sociometric data, were obtained from 405 Ss. This number was comprised of students from three third grade, two sixth grade, three ninth grade, and four eleventh grade classes. The total number of Ss from the third grade was 102, from the sixth grade 57, from the ninth grade 77, and from the eleventh grade 169. For all grades and classes combined, 149 Ss served in the HSD-LSA experimental condition, 132 in the LSD-HSA condition, and 124 in the control group.

RESULTS AND DISCUSSION

This study was concerned primarily with three questions: (a) the differential influence of highest and lowest status members of an informal group on the opinions of the other group members at different developmental stages; (b) relationship of an individual's status in the group to his own influencibility; and (c) relationship of popularity to status and effective initiative at different age levels. The measure of opinion change was the incidence of reversal of choices on the critical pair of pictures.

Comparative Effectiveness of High and Low Status
Sources at Different Ages

In Table 1 is presented a comparison of the frequency of change in the experimental and control conditions for the total sample and for each of the four grade levels.

The total incidence of change in the HSD-LSA condition across age levels was clearly greater than in the LSD-HSA condition ($\chi^2 = 21.76$, $p < .001$, 1 df). The number of changers in the HSD-LSA condition was also significantly greater than in the control group ($\chi^2 = 7.72$, $p < .01$, 1 df), while in the LSD-HSA situation the frequency of preference shifts was significantly fewer than in the control group ($\chi^2 = 4.18$, $p < .05$, 1 df). Thus, the over-all net effect of simultaneous contradiction by the leader and support by the lowest status man was a tendency to shift toward the choice of the leader. And, conversely, support by the leader coincident with disagreement by the lowest ranking person tended to reinforce the individual's initial preference.

At the third grade level the difference in the number of changers between the two experimental conditions was not significant, nor was the incidence of change in either of these conditions significantly different from change in the control group.

Table 1
Proportion and Percentage of Individuals Changing Preference in the Experimental and Control Conditions

	HSD-LSA N = 149		LSD-HSA N = 132		CONTROL N = 124	
Grade	*Proportion*	*%*	*Proportion*	*%*	*Proportion*	*%*
3rd	9/35	25.7	7/37	18.9	8/30	26.7
6th	11/23	47.8	3/20	15	5/14	35.7
9th	4/26	15.4	3/24	12.5	3/27	11.1
11th	30/65	46.1	3/51	5.9	10/53	18.8
Grand Total	54/149	36.2	16/132	12.0	26/124	21

Among the sixth graders, however, significantly more subjects changed their preference in the HSD-LSA than in the LSD-HSA condition ($\chi^2 = 5.24, p < .05$, 1 *df*). While differing significantly from each other, frequency of change in neither of these conditions differed significantly from that in the control group.

The number of subjects among the ninth graders who changed their preferences was, unexpectedly, very similar to that at the third grade level, there being no significant difference between source effects in a comparison of the experimental groups with each other and against the control group.

But status of the source reappeared as an important variable at the eleventh grade. Here a significant difference did occur in the incidence of change between the two experimental groups ($\chi^2 = 23.12, p < .01$, 1 *df*), and each experimental group differed significantly from the control group (χ^2 for HSD-LSA = 9.70, $p < .01$, 1 *df;* and χ^2 for LSD-HSA = 4.03, $p < .05$, 1 *df*).

The unexpected similarity of change behavior of the ninth graders to that of the third graders could be due to two general factors: less general susceptibility to peer influences of the ninth graders as a consequence of their developmental stage or to a less well defined group formation among them. The latter possibility would appear the more probable, however, since most of the subjects at the sixth and eleventh grade levels had been in school and in the same classes together for several years, a condition favoring evolvement of more stabilized status and role positions. Many of the ninth graders, on the other hand, were in school and class together for the first time, having entered high school from different elementary schools only five months before.

It should be pointed out that this explanation is not directly deducible from the sociometric results. From these, the group delineation among the ninth graders appeared as clear as that among the other grade levels. Yet this could well be an artifact of the sociometric measurement, stemming from the instructions to the subjects to limit their choices to members of the present classes. This limited choice situation could easily have led to an individual's ranking high another person who in reality had far less psychological significance for him than order of the choice might suggest.

Sex and Influencibility

From the results in Table 2, it can be seen that the tendency toward greater effectiveness of the high status source is more pronounced among the girls than among the boys from the third through the ninth grades. This picture is reversed, however, in the eleventh grade, the influence of the high status member being greater here for the boys than for the girls. These differences between sexes in frequency of change were not significant at any grade level, but the shift at the eleventh grade level to greater influence among the boys was significant ($\chi^2 = 31.19$, $p < .001$, 6 df).

Table 2
Sex Differences in Preference Changes in Experimental and Control Conditions

	HSD-LSA		LSD-HSA		CONTROL	
	MALE $N = 76$	FEMALE $N = 73$	MALE $N = 59$	FEMALE $N = 73$	MALE $N = 57$	FEMALE $N = 67$
Grade	Prop. %	Prop. %	Prop. %	Prop. %	Prop. %	Prop. %
3rd	3/20 15	5/15 33.2	6/18 33.3	1/19 5.3	4/18 22.2	3/12 25
6th	3/10 30	8/13 61.5	2/9 22.2	1/11 9.9	2/6 33.3	3/8 37.5
9th	1/8 12.5	4/18 22.2	2/7 28.6	1/17 5.9	1/12 8.3	3/15 20
11th	21/38 55.3	9/27 33.3	1/25 4.0	2/26 7.7	5/21 23.8	6/32 18.8
Total	28/76 36.8	26/73 35.6	11/59 18.6	5/73 6.8	12/57 21	15/67 22.4

Popularity and Status in Susceptibility to Influence

It was felt that the wide variation in group definitiveness and age levels among the informal groups utilized in this study would render rather meaningless attempts at relating specific status and popularity positions to conformity. Accordingly, subjects were divided only into upper and lower halves on the status and popularity dimensions, and the difference in frequency of preference change between these two segments was ascertained. Only subjects in the HSD-LSA condition were included in this analysis due to the low frequency of change in the LSD-HSA condition.

Using the median test, popularity was found not to relate to influencibility. Status, on the other hand, was related negatively to susceptibility to influence, with significantly more changers being found among the lower than the higher status subjects ($\chi^2 = 3.93$, $p < .05$, 1 df).

Relationship Between Status and Popularity

This measure was obtained by a correlation between the total scores derived from the popularity and leadership criteria in the sociometric questionnaires. Responses to three questions in each of the areas of popularity and status were included. Total scores were derived by weighting received choices in the reverse order of the preference. Weights for first, second, third, fourth, fifth, and above order of choices were 5, 4, 3, 2, and 1, respectively. The sum of all the choices received by an individual multiplied by the appropriate weights represented his total score in popularity or status.

The degree of correlation between status and popularity was, respectively, for the third, sixth, ninth, and eleventh grade levels: .74, .82, .78, and .79, all significant at less than the .001 level. The differences between these values are not significant for any grade levels. It would appear from this that by the time individuals reach the age of the third graders they differentiate between their friends and leaders in relation to every day life activities to the same general extent as do the older adolescents.

SUMMARY

This study was concerned primarily with three questions having to do with patterns of influence in the small informal groups at differing age levels: (a) the differential influence of the highest and lowest status member on the opinions of other group members; (b) the relationship of an individual's status in the group to his own influencibility; and (c) the relationship between status or effective initiative and popularity at different ages.

The subject first indicated his preference for one of two pictures taken from the Meier Art Judgment Test. After a communication, he again indicated his choice of the picture, along with his preference on four other pairs of noncritical pictures. The communication always presented the highest and lowest status members as having chosen opposite pictures of the critical pair. This meant that in one experimental condition (HSD-LSA) the leader was presented as having disagreed with the subject's earlier choice while the low status man was depicted as having agreed. In the other condition (LSD-HSA) the lowest status man was represented as having disagreed and the highest status man as having agreed with the subject's precommunication choice.

A total of 405 students from the third, sixth, ninth, and eleventh grades served as subjects in the two experimental and control conditions.

The number of individuals changing their preference in the HSD-LSA condition across age levels was significantly greater than in the LSD-HSA and control groups, while the incidence of changers in the LSD-HSA was significantly less than in the control group. The over-all net effect of simultaneous contradiction by the leader and support by the lowest status man was a tendency to shift toward the leader. And, conversely, support by the leader coincident with disagreement by the lowest status members tended to reinforce the individual's initial preference.

At the third and ninth grade levels status of the sources did not significantly affect preference changes. Among the sixth and eleventh graders, however, significantly more subjects changed their preferences in the HSD-LSA than in the LSD-HSA condition. And at the eleventh grade the number of changers in both experimental conditions differed significantly from the control group with more changes for the HSD-LSA condition and fewer changes in the LSD-HSA condition.

Popularity did not relate to influencibility; status related negatively, but only at the .05 level.

The degree of correlation between status and popularity, as derived from sociometric questionnaires, was, respectively, for the third, sixth, ninth, and eleventh graders: .74, .82, .78, and .79, with no significant differences among any of these values.

The Development of Moral Values in Children—Pre-Adolescent Gangs and the Moral Development of Children*

A. R. CRANE

The following study is based upon 326 boys' and 54 girls' pre-adolescent gangs in both Australia and England. The author's findings indicate that girls' gangs generally engaged in socially approved activities, while on one or more occasions all the boys' gangs conducted some form of socially disapproved behavior. Nevertheless, in his analysis of the functions that gangs play in the moral and social development of children and adolescents, Crane contends that belonging to a gang is not necessarily an indication of future delinquent behavior. "On the contrary, gang membership can be an important bridge between the kinship-based status conferred on the child by the family and the achievement-based status conferred by society at large."

I. INTRODUCTION

In this article the word gang will be used to indicate a primary group of children having a defined membership and a strong awareness of belonging to that group. The gang may be distinguished from the peer group or the play group in that it is more closely knit, usually smaller and has a stronger sense of in-group and out-group.

The literature on, and research into, gangs of pre-adolescents is scanty indeed, whereas there is an over-abundance of material on adolescent gangs. This latter field of inquiry was largely inspired by Thrasher's[1] now classic report on the street gangs of Chicago. One unfortunate result of this

---

[1] F. M. Thrasher, The Gang (Chicago: University of Chicago Press, 1927).

* From the British Journal of Educational Psychology, XXVIII (1958), pp. 201–208. Reprinted by permission of the author and the British Psychological Society.

situation is that the conclusions of Thrasher concerning the etiology, morphology, sociology and psychology of adolescent gangs have been applied also to gangs of pre-adolescents. For example, it is often stated that such gangs are found almost exclusively in subnormal or unsatisfying environments[2] and a recent publication goes so far as to use "gang" as a synonym for "a group of juvenile delinquents."[3]

Prior to Thrasher's overshadowing report, Puffer[4] (the Principal of an Industrial School for Boys at Boston) had expressed the opinion that "the predatory activities of the gang do, in no small measure, tend to cure themselves" and Furfey had pointed out that pre-adolescence was "a period of profound change which finds the boy an individual and leaves him a member of a social whole. The boy learns civics from his teacher, but democracy from his gang."[5] However, the same writer admitted four years later, in 1930, that "the average gang of the average boy is an unexplored territory from the scientific view point."[6] This is still largely true. The only empirical investigations that have yet been carried out in this field are those by Wolman[7] in Israel, and by the present writer[8] in Australia and England. These investigations show that pre-adolescent gangs do not conform to the pattern of the adolescent gangs described by Thrasher.

Even though there has been a dearth of actual data on pre-adolescent gangs, there has been a developing interest in pre-adolescence since Redl's[9] article in 1944. In 1951 came Blair and Burton's[10] book on the pre-adolescent and in 1955 Havighurst's *Human Development and Education*.[11] All these were serious and significant attempts to provide a theoretical framework by means of which the behaviour of pre-adolescents might be better understood.

[2] G. E. Outland, "Informal Groupings of Children," *Sociological Foundations of Education,* ed., E. Roucek (New York: Crowell, 1942), p. 131.

[3] S. N. Eisenstadt, *From Generation to Generation* (London: Routledge and Kegan Paul, 1956), p. 97.

[4] J. A. Puffer, *The Boy and His Gang* (New York: Houghton Mifflin, 1912).

[5] P. H. Furfey, *The Gang Age* (New York: Macmillan, 1926), p. 132.

[6] P. H. Furfey, *The Growing Boy* (New York: Macmillan, 1930), p. 99.

[7] B. Wolman, "Spontaneous Groups of Children and Adolescents," *J. Soc. Psychol.,* XXXIV (1951), pp. 171–182.

[8] A. R. Crane, "A Note on Pre-Adolescent Gangs," *Australian J. Psychol.,* III (1951), pp. 43–46; A. R. Crane, "Pre-Adolescent Gangs—a Topological Interpretation," *J. Genet. Psychol.,* LXXXI (1952), pp. 113–123; A. R. Crane, "Pre-Adolescent Gangs—a Socio-psychological Interpretation," *J. Genet. Psychol.,* LXXXVI (1955), pp. 275–279.

[9] F. Redl, "Pre-Adolescents—What Makes Them Tick?" *Child Study* (Winter, 1943–44), pp. 44–48.

[10] A. W. Blair and W. H. Burton, *Growth and Development of the Pre-Adolescent* (New York: Appleton-Century, 1951).

[11] R. J. Havighurst, *Human Development and Education* (New York: Longmans-Green, 1953).

The aim of this article is to summarise data which have been collected on pre-adolescent gangs and to draw some conclusions as to the part played by these groups in the social and moral development of children.

II. THE DATA

This report is based upon information gained over the years since 1948 from students attending the Teachers' College at Armidale, in Northern New South Wales, Australia, and from students at a Training College in the Midlands of England during 1954–55.

The method of collecting the data was simple to the point of naïveté. The students were asked to indicate whether or not they had been a member of a gang during their junior school days. If they had, they were asked to supply information under the following headings: the number in the gang, sex and age of the members, the name of the gang, a description of any initiation ceremony, secret codes, languages, signals or badges which might have been used, where the gang met and the activities of the gang once it had convened.

It is freely admitted that to rely on data collected in this way has many dangers. Respondents were between the ages of 16 and 20 and, therefore, had to call on memories of events that had occurred some six or seven years previously. However, it turned out that in most cases these memories were still vivid. Several times I was shown actual mementoes of their gang days—an initiation scar on a forearm where a lighted cigarette had been held, a crumbling piece of paper with the key to the gang code written on it, and, in one case, a tattoo that had been made using a hot needle and charcoal.

A further reason for placing considerable reliance upon the reports was the fact that they were remarkably consistent. A clear pattern of the pre-adolescent gang soon emerged, a pattern which has remained constant over the years during which information has been collected and which applied equally to the English and the Australian data.

Another possible source of criticism is that no attempt was made to collect information from a random sample of young people in the 16 to 20 age group. Only prospective teachers were used, and, as will be shown later, these came predominantly from lower-middle and working-class homes.

Some nine-tenths of the men who were asked and some two-fifths of the women reported that they had belonged to at least one gang between their eighth and their fourteenth year. This proportion remained the same whether the persons reporting were living in the city or in the country during those years. It was also constant for both the English and the Australian students.

It is clear that pre-adolescent gangs are not confined to subnormal environments, nor to those where recreational outlets were lacking. As a matter of fact, some rural natural features which had recreational possibilities were often the centre around which the gang was formed. Secluded pools, densely foliaged trees, caves and quarries seemed positively to invite a gang to form to exploit them.

The detailed data about the gangs were based on information about 326 separate gangs reported by the men and 54 reported by the women. Of the boys' gangs 272 were made up of boys only, 32 were boys with one girl and 22 included an approximately equal number of boys and girls. The girls' gangs were exclusively for girls.

The boys' gangs were strongly antagonistic to girls as a rule and very often any member caught so much as talking to a girl was disciplined by some punishment. At times, the supreme penalty of expulsion from the gang was applied. In every case where one girl was a member of a boys' gang, there was some special reason for her being accepted: she was the sister of the leader and had discovered some of the secrets which she threatened to "tell" unless allowed to join the gang. It might have been that the solitary girl had shown special prowess in activities valued by the gang—running, climbing, "doing dares," etc. In one case the girl's family owned the disused cow-shed where the gang met. Wherever a girl was accepted as a member of the gang, she was treated as a boy and to all intents the gang was a boys' gang.

The groups made up of roughly equal numbers of boys and girls were, as a rule, short-lived and in most cases were classified as gangs with some hesitation. They were on the borderline between gangs and play groups. There was certainly no suggestion that sex played any part in their activities as it often does in mixed adolescent gangs.

The ages of gang members ranged from 8 to 13 years with a median at 11. Most of the gangs went out of existence as the members approached adolescence. This is another reason why it is wrong to treat these groups as though they were adolescent gangs in embryo.

The numbers in the gang ranged from 3 to 12 with a median at 7. It appeared that gangs with more than 7 or 8 members were unstable and often broke into two gangs, sometimes through internal dissension, but at other times by agreement. It was considered "more fun" that way, since competitions, contests and other rivalry situations could be arranged without endangering group solidarity.

Just under three-fifths of the boys' and slightly over one-quarter of the girls' gangs had special names. These usually had a geographical ("North Hill Gang") or a personal ("Mac's Boys") reference. Others gave themselves more imaginative titles such as "The Red Hand Club," "The Hooded Raiders," "The Skull and Bones Gang." This last gang mentioned had a leader who was addressed as "Skull" and the members had titles "First Bone," "Second Bone," and so on in order of precedence. The most junior member was "Little Toe."

Group identity and group cohesion of some three-quarters of the boys' gangs and about one-third of the girls' gangs were further strengthened by an initiation ceremony through which all candidates for membership were required to pass. The form of the ceremony varied. It might be an ordeal by pain or fear such as being thrown into a clump of blackberries or being required to crawl through a stormwater channel infested with rats. It might be a demonstration of prowess in some activity valued by the gang. Examples were riding a bicycle across the brick parapet of a railway bridge and swimming 50 yards whilst carrying two bricks. In a few cases the ceremony involved the initiate's committing an act of aggression, such as throwing a stone on a house roof. In Australian country towns most houses are roofed with corrugated iron. A stone landing on this creates a din inside the house but does no real damage to the roof.

With the girls' gangs the initiation ceremony was usually less demanding and less complicated. The form it most usually took was the demonstration of skill in a game or the formal signing of a document—at times, in one's own blood.

The places where the gangs met had in common the fact that they were outside adult supervision: in a pit or quarry, in the loft of a barn, in a special hideout in the bush. Whereas the boys met well away from home, the girls showed a preference for such places as "in the cellar," "at the end of the school yard," or "down the bottom of the garden."

Perhaps the most interesting features of pre-adolescent gangs are the activities in which they engage. In analysing the reports, activities were classified under five headings:

1. *Predatory Activities.* These included such things as raiding orchards, pulling down fences, lighting fires, teasing girls and attacking boys who did not belong to the gang. Four-fifths of the boys' and one-fifth of the girls' gangs were concerned in some kind of predatory behaviour.

2. *Disapproved Social Activities.* Here were included smoking, "telling yarns" and swearing—usually in a competitive way. Two-fifths of all gangs had such activities in their agenda.

3. *Approved Social Activities.* Examples were collecting money for charity, writing and acting plays and practising various hobbies. Only 3 of the 326 boys' gangs reported any such activity whereas over half of the girls' gangs did.

4. *Sport.* This included hiking, playing competitive games, swimming

(with the boys, more often than not, in the nude). About half of all gangs reported engaging in this type of activity.

5. *Sex*. Six of the boys' gangs included some sex exploration and activity. However, this was by no means the main occupation.

A striking fact emerges when gang activities are divided into the two categories of socially approved (i.e., by parents and teachers) and socially disapproved or "delinquent." Every one of the boys' gangs included some socially disapproved activity in its agenda. Two of the reporters, for example, stated, "We did anything that it was not considered right for boys to do." All the boys' gangs were at times "delinquent."

Girls, on the other hand, were more concerned with socially approved activities and with playing games. Scandal-mongering was the most common disapproved activity reported. It has, therefore, been correctly pointed out by Lewis that "from an early age they (i.e., girls' groups) give more time to discussion . . . much of the girls' adventure is verbalised rather than enacted, consisting of communal daydreams and recapitulation of stories heard and read."[12]

From these data some important facts emerge:

(a) Gangs of pre-adolescents are not exclusively the product of subnormal or borderline environments where approved recreational outlets are few.

(b) Amongst the male population from which information was obtained, ganging was a very common phenomenon during pre-adolescence. It would, however, be dangerous to conclude from this that the phenomenon is equally well represented amongst all pre-adolescents. The group represented here was made up solely of teachers in training who came from predominantly lower-middle and working class backgrounds (10 per cent of the fathers were in the professional and managerial group, 70 per cent in the clerical, skilled trades, retail business and farming group, 13 per cent were in the semi-skilled trade, shop assistant group and 7 per cent in the unskilled workers and labourer group). The present data tell us nothing about the situation as it applies to upper middle or upper class boys.

(c) It is a fact that boys' gangs were characteristically occupied in much socially disapproved activity. Yet none of the ex-members had come under the notice of the police. They would not have been accepted into a teachers' college if they had.

It is clear that predatory activities are not confined to children who are, in Hollingworth's words when speaking about gangs, "represented by the delinquent classes."[13] In most cases the behaviour is a passing phase—a

12 E. Lewis, "The Function of Group Play during Middle Childhood in Developing the Ego Complex," *Brit. J. Med. Psychol.*, XXVII (1954), p. 16.
13 L. S. Hollingworth, *The Psychology of Adolescence* (London: King, 1930), p. 215.

fact which is becoming recognised amongst such students of delinquency as Ferguson[14] and Mays.[15] Edelstone, for example, refers to it as "benign delinquency."[16]

III. DISCUSSION

The questions that will now occupy us are, what part do gangs play in the moral and social development of children? Have they any influence on the establishment of value systems and the making of value judgments?

In approaching answers to questions such as these it will be necessary first to say something in general about age groups in a culture such as ours.

Eisenstadt[17] maintains that our society is "achievement orientated" whereas the family is "kinship orientated." For example, within the family circle children are treated, and status is accorded to them, mainly on the basis of who they are: son, eldest daughter, representative of a worthy family name, and so on. This is an example of what Talcott Parsons[18] has termed "ascriptive" status, that is, the status accorded an individual on the basis of who he is or of his being a member of a given group or category of people.

On the other hand, when the child begins to attend school and later when he enters adult society the way he is treated and the status he is accorded will depend more on what he has achieved than on who he happens to be.

It is also a fact that the roles enacted by the parents (especially the father) in the family circle differ considerably in their value orientations from the way they play their roles in other aspects of their life as adults. Many boys in our culture, for example, see their father in only a few aspects of his adult male role, and these usually are not those aspects which appear most important to the growing boy. The occupational, recreational and sexual roles of their fathers are all but a closed book to many boys. Much of the father's life is lived in secret so far as his children are concerned. On the basis of experimental evidence, Schoeppe came to the same conclusion, viz.: "One may conclude that for the male identification is an overwhelmingly important factor, more difficult to accomplish and a task fraught with more hazards than for the female. Girls seem to be forced by the culture to grow up more by evolution, while boys do it by revolution."[19]

[14] T. Ferguson, *The Young Delinquent in His Social Setting* (Oxford: Oxford University Press, 1952).

[15] J. B. Mays, *Growing Up in the City* (Liverpool: University of Liverpool Press, 1954).

[16] H. Edelstone, *The Earliest Stages of Delinquency* (Edinburgh: Livingstone, 1952), p. 116.

[17] Eisenstadt, *op. cit.*

[18] T. Parsons, *The Social System* (Glencoe, Ill.: Free Press, 1951).

[19] A. Schoeppe, "Sex Differences in Adolescent Socialisation," *J. Soc. Psychol.*, XXXVIII (1953), p. 179.

To some extent at least the family is segregated from the other institutional spheres of adult society. There is, therefore, a discontinuity between the system of values presented to children (especially to boys) in the family and the system in operation in non-familial spheres.

It is not necessarily from their parents at all that boys begin to learn the real values which activate adult male behaviour. This information comes "pediarchically"[20] through the peer group and reticulates down from age level to age level. In this way, rather than from the family or the school, a boy learns what as a man he is "supposed to know." James, in his study of "Plainville" states: "In league to prevent his learning this (i.e., the actual adult male behaviour pattern) are his mother and other women, his school teachers, all genteel and respectable forms, stated ideals and rituals in the community and usually the spoken word of his father. In league to teach him, all the older boys and men, gossip, actual observance of social behaviour and often the tacit connivance of his father."[21]

The father is often an unsatisfactory mediator of adult male culture. With the girl the situation is somewhat different. The adult female role is played more openly before the eyes of girls who see more of their mother than boys see of their father. One would expect, then, that the mother would be a more satisfactory mediator for her daughters than the father is for his sons. Havighurst puts the matter this way: "He (i.e., the boy) cannot accept the same sort of support from his family that it gave him earlier; his world now extends far beyond the family and even more important, he has grown out of his old relationships."[22]

If we accept this as a true statement of the position, one implication is that the family by itself is not an adequate instrument for the socialisation of children and for teaching them the norms and value systems that will gain them acceptance and secure status in society outside the home. In societies where this gap exists, age-homogeneous groups arise during the transition period between kinship relations and those regulated by achievement. In his gang life the universe of the boys is redefined in terms of the society into which he will enter rather than in terms of the family which he is already beginning to leave.

In modern societies there have developed three types of age groups: the school, adult sponsored groups (e.g., Boy Scouts) and spontaneous groups of children. The school as an institution concentrates its time on activities calculated to prepare the children for some future status. These "prepara-

[20] This word has been adopted from W. Watson who was, so far as I know, the first to use it in an article on "Society and Children's Play" in the *Scottish Education Journal*, XXXV (Feb. 22, 1952).

[21] A. Kardiner, *The Psychological Frontiers of Society* (New York: Columbia University Press, 1945), p. 324.

[22] Havighurst, *op. cit.*, 44.

tory" activities, so far as the children are concerned, often do not constitute ends in themselves and do not provide adequate outlets for those needs which arise during the period of transition from the family.

The status conferred by gang membership is both ascriptive (e.g., "I am a Secret Seven") and achievement based (e.g., I have successfully measured up to the initiation requirements). Gang membership during this period of transition supplements the security previously gained solely within the family.

In the gang the scope of activities projects beyond those of family, and, as we have seen, are often opposed to it and to the school as well. A change in the individual's mode of assessing himself is involved. The gang member takes on a new identity which is often the first step towards coming to grips with the achievement based values of adulthood. This new identity for a time is inseparably connected with the gang. The motivation towards gang-valued activities is, therefore, very strong and quite often overcomes motivation towards family-valued and school-valued activities.

The group life, as well as providing a means of extending the child's social sphere, serves as a good basis for education in new techniques. It also involves new restrictions and patterns of obedience. These, however, are felt to be different from those imposed within the family, the school or any other adult controlled group.

Part of the essence of the behaviour of boys' gangs is that it is a testing of the adult-imposed barriers upon his behaviour. These barriers have not yet been accepted into the value system of the pre-adolescent, so when adults are absent, these barriers no longer exist and the boy is free from imposed standards of how he "should" behave. However, gangs have norms and a value system of their own and to these the member must conform if he is to keep his membership. Norms of hardihood, of achievement along certain group-valued lines, of "taking it," of gang loyalty, and so on, are almost universal. The important fact is that the child enters the gang voluntarily and the rules, norms and codes of behaviour have either been freely determined by the gang members themselves or at the very least, have been fully accepted by the members. In voluntarily accepting restrictions the child begins to become a truly moral being. This is essentially the same as Piaget's position. "The adult's command, in spite of the nimbus which surrounds it, will always remain 'stuck on' as it were to a mind whose structure is of a different order."[23] Piaget goes on to argue that authority cannot be the source of morality. Morality begins when co-operation between equals leads to voluntary restraint on the behaviour of each one. To Piaget, solidarity amongst equals appeared as the source of all morality.

[23] J. Piaget, *The Moral Judgment of the Child* (London: Kegan Paul, 1932), p. 174.

Much the same position is represented by G. H. Mead, whom many look upon as the father of modern social psychology: "In so far as the child does take the attitude of the other and allows that attitude of the other to determine the thing he is going to do with reference to a common end, he is becoming an organic member of society."[24]

If we accept the position that membership of a pre-adolescent gang helps towards the development of morality, how can this be maintained in the face of the fact that, so far as boys are concerned, they are occupied in anti-social behaviour during a part of the time spent with the gang? Rather than being a training ground of morality, might it not be, in Talcott Parsons' words, "the growing point of the delinquent sub-culture?"[25]

In answer to this apparent paradox, it might be said that as the idea of "status by achievement" becomes more and more clearly accepted by the growing boy, so does the importance of the age group subside and activities which will orientate him towards achieving status in the wider society will absorb his energies and his time. When this happens the attraction which the gang holds for its members is weakened and they look upon gang activities as childish and somewhat "infra dig."

The data presented here show that all of those who reported had left the gang by the age of 14. Presumably, by this time they had become ego-involved in status-earning "achievement" type activities at school. This is very likely to be the case with the population from which information was collected for this study. As mentioned above, the reports came predominantly from upwardly-mobile lower middle and working class students. The fact that they had been accepted as trainee teachers indicated that they had dealt quite successfully with the "preparatory" activities with which their secondary school courses had been almost exclusively concerned. They had shown that they could cope with the achievement demands of society as symbolised by the school.

This raises the question of what happens to members of pre-adolescent gangs who find that they cannot cope with these demands. Do they continue to seek status on an "ascriptive" basis through gang membership? The work of Thrasher,[26] Whyte[27] and Cohen[28] in America, and the work of Ferguson[29] and Mays[30] in Britain, would indicate that this might well be so. In

24 G. H. Mead, *Mind, Self and Society* (Chicago: University of Chicago Press, 1934), p. 160.
25 T. Parsons and R. F. Bales, *Family-socialisation and Interaction Process* (London: Routledge and Kegan Paul, 1956), p. 116.
26 Thrasher, *op. cit.*
27 W. F. Whyte, *Street Corner Society* (Chicago: University of Chicago Press, 1949).
28 A. K. Cohen, *Delinquent Boys—The Culture of the Gang* (London: Routledge and Kegan Paul, 1956).
29 Ferguson, *op. cit.*
30 Mays, *op. cit.*

addition, two descriptive studies of adult-sponsored youth groups, one by Paneth[31] and one by Berger-Hamerschlag[32] all point in the same direction. They emphasise the importance of the youth's failure to cope with the achievement-orientated values inherent in our culture. Such pre-adolescents as these are the ones most likely to become members of adolescent gangs which are in some way deviant within the culture, for example, the "Teddy Boys" of England, the "Bodgies" of Australia and the "Street Corner Society" of America. All these are examples of Topping's[33] "Pseudo-social boy"—the boy socialised within the boundaries of a deviant group.

31 M. Paneth, *Branch Street* (London: Allen and Unwin, 1944).

32 M. Berger-Hamerschlag, *Journey into a Fog* (London: Gollancz, 1955).

33 R. Topping, "Treatment of the Pseudo-social Boy," *Amer. J. Orthopsychiatry,* XIII (1943), pp. 353–360.

Relationships Between Social Need Strivings and the Development of Heterosexual Affiliations[*][1]

WILLIAM J. MEYER

Earlier studies have shown, on the one hand, that children perceive same-sex rather than opposite-sex peers as being better able to satisfy their social needs, and on the other, that adolescents are relatively more likely to choose opposite-sex peers. Hence, it has been assumed generally that an increase in heterosexual affiliations occurs with age. The findings presented in the following study, however, contradict this generalization. After administering the Syracuse Scales of Social Relations to 387 pupils from grades five through twelve, Meyer concludes on the basis of his data that "same-sex social interactions are perceived by preadolescent and adolescent children as more reinforcing than social interactions with the opposite sex."

The purpose of this investigation was to examine the developmental relationships believed to exist between two social-psychological needs and the social relations structure existing between boys and girls during preadolescence and adolescence. The data to be reported concern boys' and girls' perceptions of the degree to which their same-sex and opposite-sex classmates afford satisfaction of two relatively specific social-psychological needs. Several investigators have reported developmental trends with respect to heterosexual affiliations.[2] Generally these studies have shown a

---

[1] This study is an abridged version of a doctoral dissertation submitted to the Psychology Department of Syracuse University. The writer wishes to express his gratitude to George G. Thompson, Chairman of the doctoral committee, and its members, especially Eric F. Gardner and Raymond G. Kuhlen.

[2] M. E. Bonney, "Choosing Between the Sexes on a Sociometric Instrument," *J. Soc. Psychol.*, XXXIX (1954), pp. 99–114; Helen A. Koch, "A Study of Some Fac-

---

[*] From the *Journal of Abnormal and Social Psychology*, LIX (1959), pp. 51–57. Reprinted by permission of the author and the American Psychological Association.

decrease in the frequency of opposite-sex choices until grade six and then an increase in such choices. These findings, derived from sociometric tests, suggest that for both sexes the relative ability of the opposite sex to satisfy social needs increases considerably after pubescence. Such an interpretation of these data is somewhat complicated by the fact that the subjects in these studies were required to make choices on the basis of several discrete social situations from which their sociometric scores were computed. This procedure precludes a precise interpretation in terms of the satisfaction of their social needs. Several other important statistical considerations further limit the interpretive value of these studies.[3]

The present study is based on the assumption that a person is attracted to those group members who are perceived as having a high potential for satisfying one of his social-psychological needs. Rotter[4] has postulated that a person acquires expectancies "that a particular reinforcement will occur as a function of a specific behavior on his part in a specific situation or situations." The probability that he will seek interactions with another individual in a particular social situation can be ascertained from a knowledge of his previous reinforcements with all the individuals in his group. If the behavior of the group members has been reinforcing, the probability that he will be attracted to them in similar social situations is increased.

Several inferences may be drawn from the foregoing assumptions as they relate to the development of "sex-typed" behavior. Research on this topic indicates that sex appropriate responses to specific social stimuli are well integrated by the sixth year of life.[5] Boys are typically described as outgoing, restless, and mischievous, whereas girls are described as docile, quiet, and conforming. Tuddenham[6] has shown that preschool children are aware of these sex differences in behavior. Radke[7] and Sears, Maccoby, and Levin[8] have shown that parental attitudes towards the limits of acceptable

---

tors Conditioning Social Distance between the Sexes," *J. Soc. Psychol.,* XX (1944), pp. 79–107.

[3] E. F. Gardner and G. G. Thompson, *Social Relations and Morale in Small Groups* (New York: Appleton-Century-Crofts, 1956); G. Lindzey and E. F. Borgatta, "Sociometric Measurement," *Handbook of Social Psychology,* ed., G. Lindzey (Cambridge, Mass.: Addison-Wesley, 1954).

[4] J. Rotter, *Social Learning and Clinical Psychology* (New York: Prentice-Hall, 1954).

[5] L. A. Hattwick, "Sex Differences in Behavior of Nursery School Children," *Child Development,* VIII (1937), pp. 343–355; Jean MacFarlane, H. P. Honzik and M. H. Davis, "Reputation Differences Among Young School Children," *J. Educ. Psychol.,* XXVIII (1937), pp. 161–175; R. D. Tuddenham, "Studies in Reputation: I. Sex and Grade Differences in School Children's Evaluations of Their Peers. II. The Diagnosis of Social Adjustment," *Psychol. Monogr.,* LXVI, No. 1 (1952).

[6] Tuddenham, *op. cit.*

[7] M. Radke, *The Relation of Parental Authority to Children's Behavior and Attitudes* (Minneapolis: University of Minnesota Press, 1946).

[8] R. R. Sears, Eleanor E. Maccoby and H. Levin, *Patterns of Child Rearing* (Evanston: Row, Peterson, 1957).

behavior differ for the behavior of sons and daughters and that parents are more demanding and restrictive with their daughters than with their sons. These studies suggest that there are sex differences in the development of psychological needs, an assertion that has received general support in the research literature.[9] In addition, these studies suggest that each sex acquires the behavior that is most need-satisfying to its members, and that sex-appropriate social behavior is more clearly defined for girls than for boys.

In this study two relatively specific social needs were investigated for their influence on the development of heterosexual affiliations. The needs of playmirth and succorance were selected because of their relative independence of each other, their relevance to children, and the existence of sex differences in appropriate social behavior for their reduction.[10] Since the research literature indicates that sex differences exist not only in need strength but also in the behavior required for need reduction, it is anticipated that subjects of each sex will perceive others of the same sex as having a higher potential for satisfying their social need strivings. This sex differential is expected to be maintained throughout the age range included in this study. In addition to the foregoing tentative hypothesis, data relevant to boys' and girls' perceptions of the opposite sex will be examined. One might speculate that since males are allowed more freedom in their social relationships they acquire certain positive expectancies regarding female behavior, which will be reflected in their giving higher opposite-sex sociometric scores.

METHOD

The Sociometric Instrument

Gardner and Thompson have published a series of rating scales that overcome some of the psychometric and psychological deficiencies of the traditional sociometric instrument. Underlying these scales is the assumption that the social desirability of a group depends upon the ability of the group members to satisfy specific social-psychological needs. The problem of comparability of social ratings within groups and between groups is resolved by requiring all Ss to construct a psychological frame of reference by identifying certain anchor points along a broad psychological continuum. The near equal-interval scaling of this continuum is established from a composite of individual ratings by a factionation procedure.

[9] A. Edwards, *Manual for the Personal Preference Schedule* (New York: Psychological Corp., 1954); C. J. Klett, "Performance of High School Students on the Edwards Personal Preference Schedule," *J. Consult. Psychol.,* XXI (1957), pp. 68–72.

[10] The definition of these needs follows that of H. A. Murray, *Explorations in Personality: A Clinical and Experimental Study of Fifty Men of College Age* (New York: Oxford University Press, 1938).

Each group member is asked to consider a specified hypothetical social situation. He is then required to think of the *one* person out of all the individuals he has ever known, including members of his group, who would be the very best individual to have as a partner for the particular activity. To aid the *S*s in forming a concept of the *best* individual, a normal distribution curve is provided, with five equal appearing intervals, set off with sufficient space to write in the appropriate names. The *S*s place the name of the best individual in the box marked *most*. A similar procedure is followed for the *least* liked individual. The preferred-most and preferred-least positions define a psychological continuum common to the members within the group and also common to two or more groups. The next step requires the *S*s to bisect this continuum into four equal segments by first identifying a *median* individual, and then the individuals who are half-way between the *least* and *median* positions and the *median* and *most* positions. The names, placed at equal intervals along the base line, yield an eight-point scale ranging from slightly above the *least* position to slightly below the *most* position. Ratings of individual group members are made in terms of this reference population by means of a series of forced-choice comparisons.

Separate scales were prepared for each of the two social-psychological needs. To determine the heterosexual social structure for succorance needs, the following hypothetical situation was presented to the *S*s: "Sometimes you get into trouble and feel unhappy. It might be that you have been blamed for something you didn't do. Think about some time when you were very unhappy and would have liked to talk over your trouble with some kind and sympathetic person." The heterosexual social structure for the playmirth need was assessed by means of the following hypothetical situation: "Suppose you want to have a party. You especially want to invite someone who is always doing things to make people have a good time and have lots of fun." Ten graduate students, making judgments from a large number of such statements, were in unanimous agreement that these statements represent the needs for succorance and playmirth.

The individual ratings of the group members were recorded on a matrix. An average rating *made* by each individual of his classmates was computed by summing across each row of the matrix for each individual and dividing by *N*-1 to obtain the mean. The average rating *received* by each individual from his classmates was computed by summing down each column of the matrix for each individual and dividing by *N*-1.

Subjects

A total of 387 pupils, 212 girls and 175 boys, in Grades 5 through 12 in a rural community in central New York State were administered the scales. The majority of these children were from lower-middle income homes. The distributions of sex, age, and intelligence are not unlike those expected in the average public school. The influence of selection due to school dropouts at the upper grade levels was minimal, since somewhat less than 15% had left school for reasons other than transfer.

Procedure

Test booklets with lists of names appropriate for each classroom were distributed. Four graduate students who were thoroughly familiar with the testing procedures administered the scales. The entire sample was tested on the same day at he end of the sixth month of the school year. The four examiners introduced the test to the pupils as part of a cooperative research study in their school. The average total testing time was approximately 40 minutes. Student cooperation was excellent.

Reliability indices were computed using two sixth-grade classrooms. Since the stability of sociometric scores has been shown to increase with age, it was not considered necessary to determine reliability beyond Grade 6.[11] Both the need-playmirth and need-succorance scales were readministered two weeks after the initial testing period. Separate indices were determined for ratings given and received. The mean reliability for the ratings made on the need-succorance scales is .76; and for the ratings received, .91. For the ratings made and received on need-playmirth, the corresponding values are .69 and .84.

RESULTS

The hypothesis that a person's perceptions of his own sex are more positive than his perceptions of the opposite sex was tested by comparing the mean ratings made by each sex of their own sex, with the mean ratings made of the opposite sex.[12] Similar analyses were made for both need situations. Since these comparisons involve the same rater making both judgments, the *t* test for matched pairs was used to determine statistical significance.[13] The results of these analyses are summarized in Table 1. As anticipated, the same-sex social ratings are generally higher regardless of the rater's sex. There are no reversals at any of the grade levels for the need-succorance situation though there are two reversals for playmirth. These results lend support to the hypothesis that for each sex, persons of the same sex are best able to reduce social needs. They further suggest that sex differences in ability to satisfy social-need strivings are more clear-cut for succorance than for playmirth behavior.

To test for the presence of a developmental trend in the differences between same-sex and opposite-sex ratings, an analysis of variance of the difference scores was carried out. The null hypothesis concerns the variance between grades. As shown in Table 2, three of the four analyses fail to show a significant effect. The generally nonsignificant between-grades effect can be interpreted as meaning that there is little change in boys' and

[11] J. E. Horrocks and G. G. Thompson, "A Study of the Friendship Fluctuations of Rural Boys and Girls," *J. Genet. Psychol.*, LXIX (1946), pp. 189–198.

[12] The *mean* made and received same-sex and opposite-sex ratings are redundant. To facilitate communication the data reported in this paper are all in terms of ratings made, i.e., a mean rating made by boys of girls.

[13] Helen Walker and J. Lev, *Statistical Inference* (New York: Holt, 1953).

girls' perceptions of their opposite-sex classmates' ability to satisfy their social needs. For the playmirth situation, however, the data indicate that girls perceive their male classmates as becoming increasingly more capable of satisfying their needs. The sex difference in the developmental trends for the playmirth situation suggests that beginning around Grade 7, girls shift in their perceptions of boys as social companions, though they maintain a greater preference for girls. Boys do not show a similar shift at any grade level.

Table 1

Matched *t* Tests Between Mean Same-Sex Ratings Minus Mean Opposite-Sex Ratings for Each Social-Need Situation

Grade Placement	B × B / B × G	*t*	G × G / G × B	*t*	B × B / B × G	*t*	G × G / G × B	*t*
			Need Succorance				*Need Playmirth*	
5	3.80		4.17		3.80		4.42	
		2.19*		4.50†		−.37		5.48†
	3.43		2.77		3.88		2.99	
6	3.84		3.95		4.75		4.24	
		1.67		7.90†		2.08*		6.49†
	3.38		2.42		4.06		2.71	
7	3.51		3.56		3.93		3.92	
		2.70*		7.92†		3.03†		6.59†
	2.76		2.35		3.16		2.57	
8	2.95		3.42		3.63		3.76	
		.81		4.69†		.17		4.74†
	2.80		2.38		3.59		2.84	
9	3.18		3.48		3.74		3.47	
		6.01†		4.88†		4.15†		.87
	2.36		2.24		3.06		3.28	
10	3.56		2.78		3.83		3.09	
		1.89		3.75†		2.35*		−1.18
	3.04		2.15		2.94		3.37	
11	2.86		3.14		3.46		3.57	
		3.66†		5.27†		2.10		3.60†
	2.01		1.90		2.86		2.66	
12	3.27		3.10		3.60		3.43	
		2.28*		5.26†		.86		2.76*
	2.68		2.35		3.34		2.84	

* *p* < .05.
† *p* < .01.

Another approach to analyzing the data involves a comparison of differences when the sex of the *rater* is different but the sex of the recipient is the same. Since this analysis involves comparisons between independent raters, it was not necessary to analyze difference scores. The analysis of variance is based on the procedure appropriate to categories with unequal *N*s, as described in Walker and Lev.[14] The effect of sex of rater was statistically significant in all four analyses (Table 3). This result further supports the hypothesis that same-sex social interactions are more reinforcing than opposite-sex interactions. The statistically significant differences between grades are a somewhat more complex issue and will be discussed below. The interaction terms for the need succorance (B $\times$ B$-$G $\times$ B) and

Table 2
Analysis of Variance of Difference Scores for Each Sex Comparison and for Each Social Situation

Source of Variance	Need Succorance $D_{B \times B - B \times G}$			Need Succorance $D_{G \times G - G \times B}$			Need Playmirth $D_{B \times B - B \times G}$			Need Playmirth $D_{G \times G - G \times B}$		
	df	MS	F	df	MS	F	df	MS	F	df	MS	F
Grade	7	1.36	1.48	7	2.51	2.34*	7	3.07	2.06	7	11.04	7.61†
Within	167	.92		204	1.07		167	1.49		204	1.45	

* $p < .05$.
† $p < .01$.

Table 3
Analysis of Variance of Mean Same-Sex Ratings as Contrasted with Mean Opposite-Sex Ratings for Each Social Situation

Source of Variance	df	Need Succorance B $\times$ B$-$G $\times$ B		Need Succorance G $\times$ G$-$B $\times$ G		Need Playmirth B $\times$ B$-$G $\times$ B		Need Playmirth G $\times$ G$-$B $\times$ G	
		MS	F	MS	F	MS	F	MS	F
Grade	7	3.49	3.79	7.45	7.02†	2.16	2.40*	5.81	5.81†
Sex	1	102.43	111.33†	36.30	34.24†	77.32	85.91†	13.33	13.33†
S $\times$ G	7	.92	1.00	2.20	2.07*	3.20	3.56†	.76	.76
Within	370	.92		1.06		.90		1.00	

* $p < .05$.
† $p < .01$.

need-playmirth (G $\times$ G$-$B $\times$ G) social situations are statistically significant. Inspection of the appropriate means for the playmirth analysis (see Table 1) indicates that the interaction can be attributed to a positive change in the opposite-sex social ratings of the girls after the seventh grade. After Grade 6, girls perceive the boys as increasing in their ability to satisfy

[14] *Ibid.*

playmirth needs, whereas the boys perceive their same-sex classmates as maintaining their same relative ability. A similar trend is not apparent for the opposite-sex ratings of the boys. The significant interaction term for the need-succorance situation (G × G−B × G) appears to be a function of both a decrease in same-sex ratings and an increase in cross-sex ratings.

A more sensitive test of this latter generalization is achieved by an analysis of the opposite-sex ratings (B × G−G × B) for each need situation, as shown in Table 4. The significant interaction for playmirth can be interpreted as meaning that the differences between boys' and girls' perceptions of the opposite sex decrease with increasing grade placement. Figure 1 shows that the decrease in the difference scores can be attributed to the increasingly higher ratings of the girls after Grade 7 in contrast to the relatively constant opposite-sex rating made by the boys. The nonsignificant interaction term for the succorance situation can be interpreted as meaning that the same relative distance between the sexes is maintained over the eight grades studied.

The analyses presented in Table 4 are also relevant to the hypothesis that boys' perceptions of girls are more positive than girls' perceptions of boys. For each need situation the opposite-sex ratings of the boys are significantly higher than the similar ratings of the girls. These results suggest that boys perceive their female classmates as being better able to satisfy their succorance and playmirth needs than the girls perceive them in terms of the same social needs.

DISCUSSION

This study supports the hypothesis that same-sex social interactions are perceived by preadolescent and adolescent children as more reinforcing than social interactions with the opposite sex. The hypothesis that the dif-

Table 4
Analysis of Variance of Mean Opposite-Sex Ratings Made by
Each Sex on Each Social-Need Situation

Source of Variance	df	Need Playmirth B × G−G × B		Need Succorance B × G−G × B	
		MS	F	MS	F
Grade	7	2.32	2.67*	5.36	6.30†
Sex	1	18.44	21.19†	21.11	24.83†
S × G	7	3.90	4.48†	1.17	1.38
Within	370	.87		.85	

* $p < .05$.
† $p < .01$.

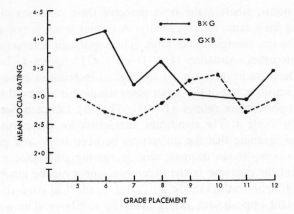

**Figure 1. Mean opposite-sex ratings of boys and girls
on the need-playmirth social situation.**

ference between boys' and girls' perceptions of their own sex and opposite
sex remains constant was upheld in the succorance-need ratings of both
sexes. The hypothesis was again upheld in the boys' ratings of their own
sex and opposite sex for the playmirth situation. However, the girls' ratings
in the playmirth situation showed that after Grade 7, girls perceived boys
as increasingly more capable of satisfying their playmirth needs although
they still prefer female companions.

There are very few comparable studies of the development of heterosexual affiliations. Harris and Tseng,[15] in a study that is particularly relevant, found that same-sex attitudes for both boys and girls were more
favorable than opposite-sex attitudes at all grades. The percentage of
favorable attitudes expressed by boys towards girls was found to decrease
slightly from three to twelve, though they are generally higher at all grades
than the attitudes of girls towards the opposite sex. The percentage of
favorable attitudes expressed by girls of boys was found to decrease until
Grade 6, then increase until Grade 9, after which they remain constant.
From Grade 8 on the degree of favorable attitudes expressed towards the
opposite sex for both boys and girls is essentially equal. The similarity of
these trends to those for the opposite-sex ratings on the playmirth situation
is striking.

These studies appear to support the view that early sex-typed behavior is
maintained throughout the preadolescent and adolescent years. The negative expectancies attached to the behavior of opposite-sex peers acquired

[15] D. B. Harris and S. C. Tseng, "Children's Attitudes Toward Peers and Parents
as Revealed by Sentence Completions," *Child Development,* XXVIII (1957), pp.
401–411.

during the preschool years are maintained because the attitudes and behavior of the opposite sex are not reinforcing. Early expectancies concerning the social behavior of same-sex peers are generally reinforced and appear to maintain themselves throughout the school years and, possibly, into adulthood. The only divergence from this pattern occurs for the girls who display definite changes in their attitudes and perceptions of boys. These changes are probably related to the onset of pubescence and to the concomitant changes in the definition of acceptable female behavior; i.e., after pubescence girls are not only permitted to have social interactions with boys, but they are probably encouraged to do so. At least during the adolescent years girls perceive boys as being as capable of satisfying their playmirth needs as the boys perceive the girls. We might speculate that this state of affairs leads to a measure of social harmony between the sexes which has not existed since the very earliest preschool years.

The over-all decrease in mean ratings from Grades 5 through 12 warrants comment. A trend analysis, reported elsewhere,[16] of the mean ratings for each need situation reveals in almost all cases a significant decelerating trend with increasing grade placement. The interpretation of these grade trends is complex. The most reasonable of several plausible interpretations can be developed from an examination of the reference population used by the Ss. It will be recalled that all Ss were required to define a reference continuum using "all people you have ever known" as the basic population. For the younger Ss it seems reasonable to believe that a large proportion of all their acquaintances would include their classmates, whereas in the upper grades, classmates constitute a relatively small proportion of all acquaintances. If such an hypothesis is plausible then the observed decreases in mean sociometric ratings probably reflects the social attractiveness of people outside of school for the older Ss and explains in part the concomitant decrease in the perceived ability of classmates to satisfy social needs.

The importance of the reference population in the use of these scales cannot be overemphasized. Though the writer can bring no direct evidence to bear on the foregoing interpretation, there is evidence to support a similar interpretation of the significantly lower average ratings made in the need-succorance social situation. Examination of the individuals used by the Ss in defining the *most* position on the reference continuum for each social situation shows that the majority of the Ss selected an adult for the most preferred position on the succorance scale and a peer on the playmirth scale. When called upon to rate their peers in terms of the former frame of reference it seems unlikely that many classmates would approach the

---

[16] W. J. Meyer, "Relationships Between Social Need Affiliations" (unpublished Doctoral dissertation, Syracuse University, 1957).

most preferred category. However, when called upon to rate their class-mates in terms of the latter frame of reference, there is a greater likelihood of higher ratings.

The conclusions drawn from this study are limited to a rural community and to the social needs of playmirth and succorance. It seems likely that in a more urban community the greater social sophistication of the pupils would have led to different trends. Judgmental situations derived from different social needs and the use of a different reference population would have similarly revealed different relationships from those here described. The influence of these variables on the development of hetero-sexual affiliations merits further research.

SUMMARY

The purpose of this investigation was to examine the influence of two social-psychological needs on the development of heterosexual affiliations. The Syracuse Scales of Social Relations were administered to 387 pupils from Grades 5 through 12. Analysis of the differences between same-sex and opposite-sex ratings indicated that the same-sex ratings were significantly higher for the succorance-need situation and, to a lesser degree, the playmirth situation. Contrasting developmental trends between the two need situations and between the sexes were reported. The girls' ratings of the boys on the playmirth situation changed to a positive direction after Grade 7. This shift was not evident for the boys nor was it evident for either sex on the succorance-need situation. The data were interpreted as supporting the notion that early sex-typed behavior is maintained throughout the school years by means of a system of social reinforcements.

Predicting Leadership Ratings from High School Activities*[1]

John D. Krumboltz,
Raymond E. Christal, and
Joe H. Ward, Jr.

It is generally taken as axiomatic that an adolescent who participates in high school activities gains valuable experiences for post–high school leadership roles. Although this reasonable assumption has been extant for a long time, only recently has it received substantial support. For example, in the following study the high school extracurricular activities of preflight cadets were correlated with their leadership potential, as rated by their flight comrades, and the results confirm that high school activities in general predict later leadership ratings. Krumboltz, Christal, and Ward show, moreover, that "certain types of activities tended to have differential predictive power for people from large and small high schools."

Can a self-report questionnaire about high school activity participation be used to predict later leadership peer ratings? A recent review of the literature,[2] concerning the relationship of high school activities to leadership criteria revealed no conclusive evidence one way or the other. There was some evidence that college activities were predictive of future

[1] This report is based on work done under ARDC Project No. 7719, Task No. 17009, in support of the research and development program of the Personnel Laboratory, Wright Air Development Center, Lackland Air Force Base, Texas. Additional support was received from an All-University Research Grant from Michigan State University.

[2] J. D. Krumboltz, "The Relation of Extra-curricular Participation to Leadership Criteria," *Personal Guid. J.*, XXXV (1957), pp. 307–314 (ASTIA Document No. 134202).

* From the *Journal of Educational Psychology*, L (1959), pp. 105–110, slightly abridged. Reprinted by permission of the authors and the American Psychological Association.

leadership success, but the studies dealing with high school activities were of such a nature that no valid conclusions could be drawn. More recently, a study[3] at the Air Force Academy revealed correlations ranging from .21 to .28 between high school activity participation and leadership ratings. The present study was designed to determine whether high school activity participation can be used to predict future leadership ratings within the aviation cadet population. It is an attempt to verify the findings of the Air Force Academy study using a different population. However, the present study differs in three respects. First, a special inventory form was developed by which the examinee records his high school activity participation on an IBM Mark Sense card. Secondly, data for individuals from large and small high schools were analyzed separately. Finally, individual items were selected and combined by an iterative multiple regression technique to produce the highest possible relationship with the criterion.

The establishment of any positive relationship between high school activity participation and leadership criteria does not, of course, necessarily indicate a cause and effect relationship. If a successful prediction can be made, this fact has important implications in a selection program whether or not leadership ability may have resulted from the training received in high school activities.

Sample

The total sample consisted of 956 aviation cadets in preflight training at Lackland Air Force Base, Texas. Of these, 857 graduated from preflight training, while 99 were eliminated for a variety of reasons. Since students from smaller high schools generally have available a fewer number of high school activities (although perhaps more opportunity to participate in those activities which are available), students from large and small schools were analyzed separately. Each cadet was asked to indicate approximately how many persons there were in his graduating class including midyear and summer session graduation. If he reported 99 or less, he was arbitrarily considered to be from a "small" high school. If he reported 100 or more, he was arbitrarily considered to be from a "large" high school.

Six aviation cadet classes were involved in this study. The first three, Classes V-15, A-16, and B-17, who entered training in June and July of 1956, were grouped together and are hereinafter referred to as Group A. The three classes who entered training in July and August immediately after Group A, Classes C-18, D-19, and E-20, are hereinafter referred to as Group B.

[3] J. D. Krumboltz and R. E. Christal, "Predictive Validities for First-year Criteria at the Air Force Academy," *USAF Personnel Train. Res. Cent. Res. Rep.* (1957), No. 57–95 (ASTIA Document No. 134218).

Thus, four subsamples were formed out of the 857 graduates for analysis purposes:

1. Small high school, Group A, $N = 162$;
2. Small high school, Group B, $N = 135$;
3. Large high school, Group A, $N = 306$;
4. Large high school, Group B, $N = 254$.

The High School Activities Inventory

The High School Activities Inventory was devised to measure the extent and nature of each individual's participation in his high school's extra-curricular (or co-curricular) activity program. Since extracurricular programs vary considerably in different parts of the country and among different high schools in the same geographical region, it was necessary to devise a questionnaire that could be interpreted equally well by anyone attending high school anywhere in the United States or its territories. Fortunately, it was possible to obtain the records of applicants to the Air Force Academy Class of 1959. Each applicant had written out a list of all his extracurricular activities. These lists were then consolidated into a master list of 226 separate activities. The activities ranged from polo to chess and many of them were listed by only one individual. By combining very specific activities into more general categories and by eliminating rare types of activities, it was possible to reduce the list to a more manageable 44 activities which were included in the final inventory. Actually there were 70 items since the extent of one's participation was often included as a separate item under one given activity. For example, participating in football and winning a letter in football were two separate items.

Each item takes the form of asking how many years an individual participated in a given activity or how many years he received a certain honor. The initial instructions directed the examinees to consider only the last three years of their high school career in answering how many years they participated. Thus, there were only four possible answers to each item: 0, 1, 2, and 3. In this way individuals who attended four-year high schools had no "time" advantage over individuals who attended three-year high schools.

It was considered possible that some cadets might try to exaggerate the extent of their extracurricular participation although there was no reason why they should. To discourage this possibility each cadet was asked to list the names and locations of the high schools he attended, the names of the high school principals, and the names of three teachers at each high school who could verify his activities. Although no attempt was made to follow up this information, it was believed that the possibility of verifying a cadet's responses made it less likely that he would exaggerate them.

Responses and identifying data were recorded on mark sense cards (IBM 850259MS-O). A list of 20 of the 70 items may be found in Table 1 in summarized form. For the most part each item is self-explanatory if it is understood that each activity in Table 1 is preceded by "How many years did you participate in . . ." or "How many years did you receive this honor. . . ."

To determine how well the inventory covered the wide variety of possible activities the first 200 cadets to answer the inventory were asked to write on the back of the inventory any activities in which they had participated but which were not covered in the inventory. A total of 105 comments were received including two or more comments from some cadets. Eighty-five of the comments were judged to be irrelevant for a variety of reasons, while 20 were considered as legitimate criticisms of omissions in the inventory. The irrelevant comments concerned activities the questionnaire was not designed to cover such as intramural athletics, high school fraternities, scholastic awards, and church activities. Other irrelevant comments included very specific honors or activities which could not be classified, activities that had already been covered in the inventory directly or indirectly, and excuses for little or no participation. The main area of activity that was omitted by the inventory concerned school service activities. Four persons listed the visual aid department, five were managers of athletic teams, seven served on various school committees, and four listed other miscellaneous school activities.

Criterion

Leadership peer ratings were collected on the aviation cadet sample twice during their preflight training. Each man in a flight was asked to rank-order each other man in his flight on the basis of his leadership potential. The first time was after the first four weeks of training, and the second time was after the first ten weeks of training. Cadets were rank-ordered on the basis of the pooled rankings within each flight, and the rank orders were then converted to T scores. The stability of these rankings over a six-week interval is indicated by correlations for the six classes ranging from .40 to .82 with a median r of about .68.

A number of studies[4] have demonstrated the reliability and validity of

[4] E. P. Hollander, "The Reliability of Peer Nominations under Various Conditions of Administration," *J. Appl. Psychol.*, XLI (1957), pp. 85–90; D. K. Trites and S. B. Sells, "Combat Performance: Measurement and Prediction," *J. Appl. Psychol.*, XLI (1957), pp. 121–130; Personnel Research Section, U. S. Dept. of the Army, "Follow-up Validation of Predictor Instruments for West Point Classes of 1944, 1945, and 1946 against 1948 Ratings on DA AGO Form 67–1," *USA TAGO Personnel Res. Br. Tech. Res. Rep.* (1949), No. 811; Personnel Research Section, U.S. Dept. of the Army, "Studies of the Performance of Officers in Combat: I. Relationship of

peer ratings as an intermediate criterion of future leadership behavior. The results of these and other studies have been briefly discussed elsewhere.[5] It may be concluded from these studies that leadership peer ratings have a substantial relationship to future leadership ratings collected in an on-the-job situation.

*   *   *

RESULTS AND DISCUSSION*

The correlations of each of 20 items with the criterion for each of the four samples are reported in Table 1.[6] Asterisks beside a correlation indicate that the item was weighted into the multiple regression equation for that sample. The 20 items appearing in Table 1 were selected from among those judged to be of most interest and yielding the most substantial relationships with the criterion.

Positive correlations were consistently obtained for most of the major sports and for athletic honors. In small high schools being assistant editor on the school newspaper received negative weight, while being a member of the debate team received positive weight. In large high schools being president or vice-president of the class was consistently and positively related to high leadership ratings, while such consistent relationships were not found for the small high school samples. Being a member or officer in student government was positively related to the criterion in large high schools but not in small high schools.

Many items that one might reasonably expect to be positively related to leadership ratings showed no relationship whatsoever. For example, all of the following were unrelated to the criterion: being a delegate to Boys' State; being president of a career interest club, a hobby or interest club, a language club, or a science club; and being editor of the school newspaper or yearbook. The reasons for this are a matter for conjecture. Perhaps individuals with relatively low leadership ability go into such activities. Being president or editor in a group of nonleaders would then give no indication

---

West Point Measures to Later Combat Effectiveness," *USA TAGO Personnel Res. Br. Tech. Res. Rep.* (1952), No. 969.

[5] Hollander, *op. cit.*; J. D. Krumboltz, "Physical Proficiency as a Predictor of Leadership," *USAF Personnel Train. Res. Cent. Res. Rep.* (1957), No. 57–60. (ASTIA Document No. 126391).

[6] A four-page table for all 70 items and including the extent of participation by eliminees as well as graduates has been deposited with the American Documentation Institute, Order Document No. 5955 from ADI Auxiliary Publications Project, Photoduplication Service, Library of Congress, Washington 25, D. C. remitting in advance $1.25 for microfilm or $1.25 for photocopies. Make checks payable to Chief, Photoduplication Service, Library of Congress.

---

* [Ed.] A discussion of the statistical techniques used in analyzing the data has been omitted.

Table 1

Relationship of High School Activity Items to the Leadership Criterion

| Item No. | Activity | Correlation with Criterion in | | | | Mean No. of Years per Man (N = 857) |
| | | Small HS | | Large HS | | |
		A (N = 162)	B (N = 135)	A (N = 306)	B (N = 254)	
1	Football	.18*	.18	.14*	.19	.80
3	Basketball	.04	.29*	.13	.25*	.56
7	Track	.18	.12	.07	-.02	.46
13	Tennis	.05	-.08	.11*	.00	.11
15	Swimming	.04	.20*	.02	.06	.11
19	Other sport	-.16*	-.02	.03	-.01	.24
23	Newspaper assistant editor	-.15*	-.04*	-.13	.14	.09
25	Newspaper photographer	-.07	-.07	-.17*	.02	.04
34	Debate team	.14*	.18*	.11	-.03	.10
36	Chorus or glee club	.07	.05	-.01	.18*	.52
41	Science club member	-.08	-.23*	-.08	.04	.31
44	Language club member	.00	.16*	.00	.12*	.22
47	Hobby or interest club member	-.15	-.17*	-.04	-.09*	.49
57	Student government president	-.06	.11	.11	.20*	.06
58	Student government: other officer	-.12*	-.07	.08	.14	.14
59	Student government: member	-.03	.09*	.15	.11	.34
63	President of class	-.02	.06	.16	.23*	.14
64	Vice-president of class	.09	.20	.18*	.14	.12
65	Secretary of class	.03	.12	.15*	-.06	.07
69	Outstanding student award	.13*	-.01	-.04	.00	.13

* Items weighted into multiple regression equations.

346

of one's leadership status in a larger more representative group. Perhaps leadership is specific to the situation.

By summing each individual's responses to items 1–20 and 70, an Athletic Activity Score was computed for each individual. Similarly the summation of each cadet's responses to items 21–69 provided his Nonathletic Activity Score. The sum of these two scores was the Total Activity Score. Table 2 reports the zero order correlations of each score with the criterion

Table 2
Zero Order Correlations of Activity Scores with the
Leadership Criterion

Sample	N	r_{ac}	r_{nc}	r_{an}	r_{tc}	Athletic Score Mean	SD	Nonathletic Score Mean	SD
		\multicolumn{4}{c}{Correlations*}				
1. SA	162	.10	−.05	.24†	.02	6.3	6.3	10.8	7.3
2. SB	135	.29†	.02	.28†	.18	5.7	5.2	9.2	6.1
3. LA	306	.18†	.06	.27†	.12	3.2	3.8	7.6	6.5
4. LB	254	.23†	.18†	.42†	.24†	3.6	4.2	6.7	5.5

* Subscripts represent the following variables: a, Athletic Activity Score; n, Non-athletic Activity Score; t, Total Activity Score; and c, the leadership criterion.
† Significant at the .01 level.

and the correlations of the Athletic and Nonathletic Activity Scores for each sample. The correlations of the Athletic Activity Score with the criterion ranged from .10 to .29 and were consistently higher than the correlations of the Nonathletic Activity Score with the criterion which ranged from −.05 to .18.

The multiple regression equations derived from each sample yielded spuriously high multiple Rs ranging from .36 to .62. When the regression equations derived from each sample were cross-validated on each other sample, the results shown in Table 3 were obtained. It is of special interest to note the cross-validities of the small high school samples on each other and the cross-validities of the large high school samples on each other. Multiple Rs shrank from .47 to .17 and from .62 to .19 in the small high school samples. In the large high school samples the multiple Rs shrank from .36 to .19 and from .42 to .14.

SUMMARY AND CONCLUSIONS

The purpose of this study was to determine whether a self-report questionnaire about high school activity participation can be used to predict later leadership peer ratings. An inventory on high school activity participation was administered to a total of 956 aviation cadets undergoing preflight

Table 3
Validities of Regression Equations in Each Sample

Weights Derived from Sample	N	Validated on Sample				Criterion	
		1	2	3	4	Mean	SD
1. SA	162		*.19*	.11	.03	100.7	16.1
2. SB	135	*.17*		.19	.12	98.7	15.8
3. LA	306	.16	.21		*.14*	100.1	14.5
4. LB	254	.11	.29	*.19*		100.1	15.5

training at Lackland Air Force Base. The criterion consisted of the summation of T-scored leadership peer ratings collected after the fourth and after the tenth week of training. The data were analyzed by computing zero order and multiple correlations between the predictor items and the criterion.

The analysis revealed consistently low but positive correlations between inventory scores and the criterion. The multiple regression equations derived from each subsample yielded multiple Rs which shrank upon cross-validation on comparable samples to values which ranged from .14 to .19 with a median of .18. Three of the four zero order correlations between the Athletic Activity Index and the criterion were significantly different from zero at the .01 level. Only one of the four correlations between the Nonathletic Activity Index and the criterion reached significance.

On the basis of these results the following conclusions were reached:

1. A self-report inventory on extracurricular participation succeeded in predicting leadership ratings of aviation cadets better than chance, but considerable error still remained in such predictions. The low positive correlations do not, of course, necessarily mean that training received in high school activities produced increased leadership ability since those choosing to take part in high school activities might very well have been above average in leadership ability originally.

2. Although certain types of activities tended to have differential predictive power for people from large and small high schools, in general activities in large and small high schools were about equally predictive of the criterion.

3. Athletic participation and honors were more predictive of future leadership than nonathletic participation and honors.

4. The iterative multiple regression technique did not produce a more valid composite than the simpler zero order correlation technique in this study.

A Study of Socialization Patterns at the High School Level*

MARY COVER JONES

When an adolescent enters into the extracurricular activities of his high school, he exposes himself to an array of social reinforcements. If he finds the pattern of social interaction rewarding, he may gain valuable lessons in conducting himself with his peers and for preparing himself to become an adult. In the following study, perhaps the only one of its kind, Mary Cover Jones draws upon the data of the Adolescent Growth Study, University of California, to make group and individual comparisons between high-participating and non-participating youth on the basis of physical, intellectual, and social attributes. She asks: "What are the major differences between those students who manifestly identified with the purpose of the school to promote peer group interaction through extra-curricular activities, and those who were unresponsive to this socializing influence?" In addition to providing a thorough analysis of the factors that differentiated the adolescents, Jones also takes a look at her subjects fifteen years after they finished high school and describes how they have fared.

A. PROBLEM

The school and the peer group as socializing agents are interdependent. With the growth of mass education in our culture and the use of education as a social ladder, schools have become more and more aware of the importance of this interaction as a motivating force in learning. One evidence of this is the increasing value placed upon extracurricular functions as part of the school program. The collaboration of the school and the peer group in promoting activities common to their social goals is a powerful and pervasive force in the high school student's daily life. Some students respond to

* From the *Journal of Genetic Psychology*, XCIII (1958), pp. 87–111. Reprinted by permission of the author and the Journal Press.

this socializing pressure and identify with its purposes. Others resist or escape its influence in varying degrees.

Can we specify some of the factors—pertaining perhaps to intelligence, physical maturity, social class status, or social attitudes—which may make individuals psychologically more or less accessible to the molding influences of the school through its program of social participation? What criteria can we use to determine which students are responding to, which evading, the efforts at socialization?

B. PROCEDURE

In an attempt to answer some of these questions, the present study contrasts two groups of high school students (members of the Adolescent Growth Study of the Institute of Child Welfare) who fall at opposed extremes of a sample distributed on the basis of frequency of mention in the daily newspaper of the high school which they attended for three years. The analysis may be looked upon as selecting individuals according to the rôles which they play in one area of their social living, that of contributing to group life in high school.[1] On the one hand we have the students who identified themselves with the purposes and plans of this large amorphous population (the student body), and who were successful in demonstrating this identification to the faculty and to their peers. On the other hand, there are those students who received no public recognition (in the school news organ) because they lacked either the ability or the inclination to be drawn into activities which were a matter of common interest. They were so little identified with the school subculture as to ignore or deny the pressures inherent in its value systems.

The newspaper which served as the basis of selection for these two opposed groups was the daily publication of a co-educational, public senior high school in a large western city. The school also served as a teacher training center for student teachers from the education department of a state university and was one of the coöperating schools in a nation wide educational research program.[2] The administrative and teaching staff enunciated and fostered the concept of the school as a broadly functioning institution: "In contrast to the traditional emphasis upon preparation for living, University High School holds that adolescents are living here and now and that it is the school's business to help them to live successfully"[3]

[1] "It's easy to classify people by skin color, sex, or age; it's relatively easy to classify them by the number of dollars they earn in a year. Very little grouping of human beings is done in terms of the roles they reveal in their own immediate social world." (G. Murphy, "The Relationships of Culture and Personality," *Culture and Personality,* ed., S. S. Sargent and M. Smith [New York: Viking Fund, 1949], p. 23.)

[2] M. Brown, *et al.,* "The University High School Study of Adolescents; Basic Philosophy," *Univ. High Sch. J.,* XVII (1938), pp. 67–69.

[3] *Ibid.,* 68–69.

The school had prestige as an educational and social institution; it tended to attract able students of superior home backgrounds (largely upper middle class) from all areas of the city and from neighboring communities.[4] It was also the neighborhood school for a large proportion of those who attended. For many of the latter, with an admixture of lower middle class families, it was simply the school most conveniently located for them.

Whether or not the students had selected the school because of its status as an educational institution they were early and often reminded of its unique atmosphere. Because this school served as a pilot for educational policy and research, it was articulate in defining its tenets and active in motivating staff and students toward a recognized goal.[5] One approach to its educational aims was through enlisting the peer group in extensive activities of the sort usually classed as extracurricular. That this aspect of school life was lively and successful is attested by the fact that at the time of one report, 86 per cent of the student body engaged in some form of extra-class school activity.[6]

The daily newspaper (one of the extracurricular activities) was devoted to the reporting of school affairs exclusively. It therefore served much as an official "house organ," reflecting the interests, activities, and values of the student group. It instructed its readers as to where and when they could buy tickets for events, what to see in exhibit cases, how to sign up for try-outs, what elective and appointive positions were available, and, in general, what the extracurricular program offered and who was prominent in school affairs. Editorials, signed articles which reviewed events or evaluated activities, and letters to the editor were also included.

Occasionally a student received recognition for an achievement or honor attained under other than school auspices such as appearance on a radio program or selection as a delegate to a Scout conference. Those who were never mentioned in even such a passing manner as "credit goes to the following students who have been associated with office mimeographing . . ." or "among those who also tried out for parts were . . ." must, in general, have found school a narrower and less socially molding experience than those who participated in school life to an extent which brought frequent recognition. Participation in extracurricular activities was the accepted and approved pattern and a certain amount of pressure was exerted through the

[4] About 20 per cent of the student body were from outside of the school district and represented those families which sought admittance to the school because of its educational and social advantages. None of this 20 per cent (a relatively high status group from the neighboring university city) were included in the study.

[5] In a published discussion of the school's basic philosophy this statement (Brown, *et al., op. cit.,* 67) was made: "Fortunately because this philosophy was clearly formulated . . . the school was established upon a system of enduring values and was developing according to a well-defined but continuously evolving plan."

[6] M. Brown, *Leadership Among High School Pupils* (New York: Columbia University Press, 1933).

daily paper to foster this kind of behavior. "Girls' League President Asks for Girls' Support of Afternoon Teas" . . . "Dean of Girls Asks Members of League to Support Vocational Talks" . . . Such headlines as these appeared frequently in the daily newssheets.

Five hundred and forty issues (covering a three-year period) were read and all mentions tabulated for the 122 study members who attended this high school throughout the 10th, 11th, and 12th grades. The total number of mentions for different individuals ranged from zero to 112. The zero category included 9 boys and 9 girls, and these were selected as representing the "low prominence" or "no-mention" group. In selecting a group at the high-mention extreme, consideration was given to the differing significance of items; it was decided that a weighted score (based on prestige) would provide a more defensible basis for determining prominence than would a raw frequency score. Table 1 illustrates the categories into which the items were classified, and the assigned weights, on an estimated prestige scale.

The weighting of news items was derived from the composite judgment of staff members who were intimately acquainted with the school. This introduces a subjective factor which was uncontrolled by the use of formal scaling methods. However, in selecting for further study the 12 cases of each sex who were in the top 20 per cent of the distribution of weighted scores, it was found that all but one of each sex would also have been chosen if the raw frequencies had been used.

The resulting selection includes not only the student body leaders, but a wide variety of persons in other social rôles who used their talents or energies in behalf of their high school associates.[7]

Indeed, followers, the so-called "middle" leaders, or "second level" as well as top leaders, are represented in this group since, as the discussion will show, some students by dint of zealously carrying out the committee work prescribed by an executive officer (chairman, editor, president, etc.) were frequently recognized in this middle leader or follower capacity. There were also those who caught the public attention because of their special talents or energetic services which were not necessarily associated with leadership ability. In the adult community, persons who espouse causes, get out the vote, start fads, or win decisions, vary greatly in talents though all may frequently get their names in the paper.

Differences in purposes and abilities which led to greater or less success in their participating or non-participating rôles will be discussed in the presentation of the records of individual students. But group comparisons will be considered first. The question was raised earlier: What are the major

[7] "The high school with its athletics, clubs, sororities and fraternities, dances and parties, and other 'extracurricular activities' is a fairly complete social cosmos in itself." (R. S. Lynd and H. M. Lynd, *Middletown* [New York: Harcourt-Brace, 1929], p. 211).

Table 1
Descriptive Categories for Classifying Names Mentioned

Category	Example	Assigned weight
I. *School leadership*		
A. Student body president.	I. *"Karl Envick,* new student-body president, gives welcome to new pupils."	15
B. Chairman of major committees or school groups.	"So congratulations to *Sheila Harmon* for putting on a swell Follies. . . ."	12
C. Member of major committee or council, student body officer, president or chairman of minor committee.	" 'I want to welcome all L-10 boys to this school,' stated *Bob Rank,* Boys' League Prexy."	8
D. Class officer, chairman of a temporary committee.	"The committee chairmen for the senior luncheon are as follows: *Marie Anderson,* decorations, *Ruth Roberts,* publicity. . . ."	6
E. Member of a minor or temporary committee, also mentioned.	"The clean-up committee this term included *Art Dawson, Roscoe Benson.* . . ."	3
II. *Athletics*		
A. Athletic star, state-wide recognition.	*"Sid Murphy,* 6 feet 5 inches, all-around athlete, receives scholarship to Harmon University."	10
B. Special contribution.	*"Bill Hewitt,* veteran of last year's team, shows extreme promise on this year's gridiron. . . ."	7
C. Team member.	"Tomorrow's line-up against Polytechnic will probably be . . ."	
III. *Intellectual Leadership*		
A. Editor of the daily paper.	*"John King,* L-12, has been chosen editor of the 'Daily U-N-I' for the fall term."	6

Table 1 (cont.)

Category	Example	Assigned weight
B. Important signed contribution, editor of other minor school publications, staff position.	"East Bay writer picks San Carlos School to win grid Race. *Rod Brown*, sports writer for paper, picks winning teams. . . ."	5
C. Member of group contributing.	"A protest against middy regulations . . . signed, *Lillian Marvis, Beatrice Vanetti*, etc."	4
IV. *Arts, Drama, Music, Dance*		
A. Outstanding talent displayed.	"*Glen Marks* wins summer scholarship to Franklin College of Arts and Crafts."	5
B. Special contribution, performance.	"*Ann Mason, Clair Wilson* and *Gladys Carson* won first place on Bennie Walker's Amateur Hour of April 18."	4
C. Also played, accompanied group among those trying out.	"A group of students from the voice class including *Katherine Boyd* . . . will sing on tomorrow's assembly program."	3
V. *Interest Clubs*		
A. President.	"*Wes Rogers*, president of the Pet Club announced that a puppy would be raffled off at the School Fair next Friday."	2
B. Member.	"The French Club attended the Campus Theater to see "Dark Eyes" last Saturday. Among those who attended were *Lillian Mansfield* and . . ."	1

Table 1 (cont.)

Category	Example	Assigned weight
VI. *Miscellaneous*		
A. Extraordinary, unusual, outstanding event.	"And the King of the Carnival is none other than our own *Karl Envick*."	10
B. Special mention of interest.	*"Bernard Thomas* again displays his private gun collection. . . ."	7
C. Member of group mentioned.	"Credit goes to the following students who have been associated with office mimeographing, *Marion Vallejo, Charlotte Smith*. . . ."	2

differences between those students who manifestly identified with the purposes of the school to promote peer group interaction through extracurricular activities, and those who were unresponsive to this socializing influence? The hypotheses relevant to this question are implicit in the following selection of data categories:

Table 2 lists the variables used in comparing the members of the two extreme groups.

C. RESULTS

1. Skeletal Age

Chronological age was not a differentiating factor. Skeletal age, however, was relatively advanced among the high-mention boys and among the low-

Table 2
Variables Used for Group Comparisons

1. Chronological Age.
2. Skeletal Age.
3. Total strength scores (right hand grip, left hand grip, thrust and pull with dynamometer).[8]
4. Mental Age and *IQ*.
5. Adjustment Inventory Scores (U. C. Inventory I) Total score, and sub-

[8] H. E. Jones, *Motor Performance and Growth* (Berkeley: Univer. of Calif. Publ. Child Develpm., 1949).

scores for Family, Social and School Adjustment, Fears, Inferiority Feelings, Physical Symptoms, Generalized Tensions.[9]

6. U. C. Interest Test Scores. (Athletic, Social, Mechanical-Scientific, Intellectual Interests).[10]
7. Attitudes Tests (Selected Items).[11]
8. Reputation Measures: U. C. Reputation Test. Ratings by classmates of appearance, leadership, bossiness, talkativeness, restlessness, attention getting, daring, sense of humor, popularity, enthusiasm, friendliness, happiness, activity.[12]
9. Ratings of behavior in social situations by staff members.[13]
10. Ratings on home and neighborhood. (Census Tract Data and Home Ratings.)
11. Drive Ratings: Autonomy, Social Ties, Achievement, Recognition, Aggression, Succorance, Control, Abasement, Escape.[14]

mention girls (Table 3). For the total group of 56 boys of the Adolescent Study attending this school, a correlation[15] of .42 was found between skeletal age over *CA* at 15 years, and rank order of mention, with a significance level of .005. For 52 girls the corresponding correlation was −. 42 (significance level .005).

Table 3
Skeletal Age at 15 Years

	Boys		Girls	
	N	Mean	N	Mean
High-mention group	12	16.43	12	15.43
Low-mention group	9	15.46	9	15.97
Significance of difference		.02		.10

Other reports from the Adolescent Study indicate that in this middle period of adolescence early-maturing tended to be a factor of advantage for the boys in our group and a disadvantage for the girls.[16] This is to be explained partly on the basis of the timing of individual development in rela-

[9] C. McC. Tryon, *U. C. Inventory 1, Social and Emotional Adjustment* (Berkeley: Univer. of Calif. Press, 1939).

[10] M. C. Jones, *The Interest Record* (Berkeley: Univer. of Calif. Press, 1944).

[11] N. Anastasiou, "A Study of Prejudice in an Adolescent Group" (unpublished paper on file; Berkeley: Institute of Child Welfare, Univer. of Calif., 1950).

[12] C. McC. Tryon, "Evaluation of Adolescent Personality by Adolescents," *Monogr. Soc. Res. Child Develpm.*, IV, No. 4 (1939).

[13] F. B. Newman, "The Adolescent in Social Groups; Studies in the Observation of Personality," *Appl. Psychol. Monogr.*, XIX (1946).

[14] E. Frenkel-Brunswik, "Motivation and Behavior," *Genet. Psychol. Monogr.*, XXVI (1942), pp. 121–265.

[15] Pearson Product-Moment.

[16] H. E. Jones, "Adolescence in Our Society," *The Family in a Democratic Society*

tion to the group norms. Girls who in general are early-maturing in relation to boys, as well as to other girls, find it a disadvantage to be at the extreme in this respect. They are conspicuously large in relation to other girls in their classroom and decidedly so in relation to boys of their own age. For adolescent girls in our culture this is not an admired characteristic. Boys, on the other hand, find that early maturity puts them on a par with the majority of the girls in their peer group in size and in the accompanying changes of interests.

The relationship between maturity level and recognition status in high school is shown in the accompanying four figures. Figure 1 illustrates the findings in regard to boys. Although only 20 per cent of our total population of 90 boys were accelerated more than one year in skeletal age, they con-

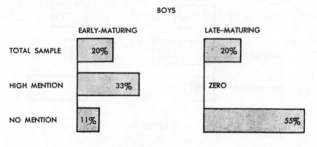

Figure 1.

stitute 33 per cent of those having great "newsworthiness."[17] None of the late-maturing boys appeared in this prestige hierarchy. Among the no-mentions, five times as many were late- as early-maturing (55 vs. 11 per cent).

Figure 2 shows corresponding data with regard to girls. A reversal of prestige position, in relation to maturity level, is clearly shown. Early-maturing girls fall more frequently in the no-mention group, while the late-maturing dominate the high mentions to the extent of about twice their expected quota.

Figures 3 and 4 provide cross-comparisons for boys and girls.

2. Behavior Ratings

It is not surprising that the two contrasted groups of this study were differentiated most clearly by estimations of their social behavior characteristics as displayed in group situations. It was the recognition of social

(New York: Columbia University Press, 1949), pp. 70–84; M. C. Jones and N. Bayley, "Physical Maturing Among Boys as Related to Behavior," *J. Educ. Psychol.*, XLI (1950), pp. 129–148.

[17] Jones and Bayley, *op. cit.*

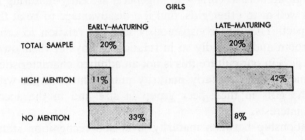

Figure 2.

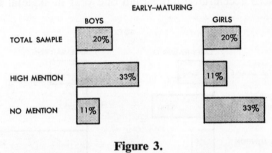

Figure 3.

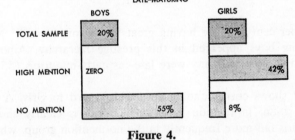

Figure 4.

behavior in connection with school activities which determined their news-print value. Those who came frequently to the attention of classmates through prominence in extracurricular activities and those who escaped such notice, practiced behavior patterns and social rôles which distinguished between them in other situations as well.

With no knowledge of information based on the school paper, staff members who observed these adolescents on playgrounds, in school halls, club meetings, informal and formal social gatherings, school excursions and the like, ascribed certain traits to members of one of the extreme groups significantly more often than to the other.[18] Both boys and girls in the promi-

18 Newman, *op. cit.*

nently mentioned group were more frequently rated by adults as making a good impression on the basis of appearance and grooming (differences significant at the .02 level). Other descriptions based on adult ratings differentiated the girls' groups significantly (at the .05 level) in regard to their expressive behavior.[19] The frequently mentioned girls were considered to be more talkative, active, peppy, animated, and eager. Boys showed a tendency in the same direction but the difference was not significant. Other reports from the Adolescent Study have suggested that expressiveness, as defined here, is socially approved to a greater extent for girls than it is for boys.[20]

Girls and boys in the frequent-mention group were rated as buoyant (relaxed, cheerful), poised (assured, confident), and as having prestige (others seek his approval, expect him to take the lead; has a marked effect on the group). Table 4 and Figure 5 present these findings. The data are in terms of standard scores, in which 50 represents the average for the total group, and the *SD* is 10. Although boys and girls show differences in the same direction on each characteristic, the high- and low-mention groups are more clearly differentiated among the girls.

Table 4
Observers' Ratings: Standard Scores: Means

	Boys			Girls		
	High	Low	Sig. diff.*	High	Low	Sig. diff.*
Expressiveness	52	47		58	43	.05
Buoyancy	53	45		59	43	.05
Poise	58	48	.10	67	43	.001
Prestige	54	46		60	40	.01
Appearance	60	45	.02	64	45	.02

* Wilcoxan Rank Test

3. Reputation Measures

It may of course be expected that students who are centers of influence in extracurricular activities will have reputations with classmates, as well as with adults, quite different from those acquired by the non-participating. This was revealed by the Reputation Test, a "Guess Who" rating technique

[19] The description of expressiveness is as follows: Very self-expressive; overtly active practically all of the time including verbalization, gross movement, aggressive contact with physical environment; eager, animated facial expression and bodily movements. The other end of the scale was described in these words: Extremely unexpressive, very little overt movement; silent; stationary, indifferent attitude; idle; stolid, listless expression. (Newman, *op. cit.*)

[20] H. E. Jones, "Adolescence in Our Society," *op. cit.,* 78.

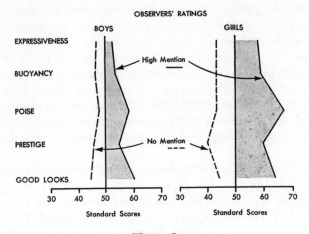

Figure 5.

administered in the classroom.[21] Those whose names were entered in the school paper most frequently were also judged to be well above the average in all prestige traits. The frequently-mentioned boys, for example, averaged approximately 2 *SD* above the group mean in class estimates of popularity ("here is someone that everybody likes, others are glad to have him around"); friendliness ("very friendly, has a lot of friends, is nice to everybody"), and humor. Among boys, the no-mention group tended to be overlooked in classmate nominations, rather than to have explicitly unfavorable reputations.

As will be shown in the later discussion of individual cases, lack of mention in the school paper did not serve to select a group considered by their classmates as "queer" or as having markedly distasteful qualities, although negative scores were relatively frequent in the case of the no-mention girls. Table 5 and Figures 6 and 7 present the data for reputation traits.

4. Drive Ratings

Toward the end of their high school careers, all of the study members were rated on a series of motivational traits based on Murray's needs. The ratings were made, independently, by staff members most competent for this assignment because of their intimate association with the group over a period of 4 to 7 years.[22]

Both among boys and girls, members of the high-mention group were judged to have relatively strong drives (a low rating on the 5-point scale indicates a strong drive). The differences were significant, however, only among boys in the need or desire for recognition (drive to excite praise and

21 Tryon, "Evaluation of Adolescent Personality by Adolescents," *op. cit.*
22 The nine drives are presented in Table 2, Item 11.

Table 5
Reputation Measures: Standard Scores: Means

	Boys			*Girls*		
	High	Low	Sig. diff.	High	Low	Sig. diff.
Popular	69.20	50.62	.02	69.83	53.59	.001
Friendly	68.83	44.63	.02	72.25	46.67	.02
Leader	65.00	48.00	.02	58.17	33.56	.02
Daring	65.00	49.00	.001	61.33	42.33	
Enthusiastic	59.83	54.00		69.16	52.33	.10
Talkative	50.16	47.16		56.83	39.67	<.02
Humor	71.00	53.25	<.02	54.00	36.00	<.10
Good looking	64.25	50.88		65.75	44.11	.02

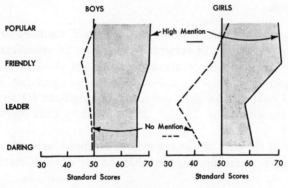

Figure 6.

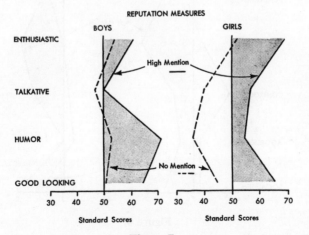

Figure 7.

commendation) and for control (to control one's environment, by suggestion, persuasion or command). The comparative data are shown in Table 6 and Figure 8.

Table 6
Drive Ratings: 5-Point Scale: Means

| | Boys | | | Girls | | |
	High	Low	Sig. diff.	High	Low	Sig. diff.
Achievement	2.3	2.9		2.5	2.8	
Recognition	1.9	3.2	.02	2.1	3.0	.10
Control	2.6	3.8	.01	2.3	3.1	.10
Aggression	2.8	3.1		3.0	3.2	
Social ties	2.4	3.1		2.2	2.6	

5. Intelligence

The foregoing has dealt with the areas in which the most striking differences in the two groups of subjects were found. Of considerable interest, however, are the findings concerning measures on which no differences occur. Differences in intelligence test scores were not significant. For the total group of 57 boys and 54 girls, the correlation between *IQ* and number of newspaper mentions was .22 and .25 respectively (not significant at the .05 level).

A review of the kind of ego rewards which individuals achieve from extensive social participation suggests that the use of intellectual ability was

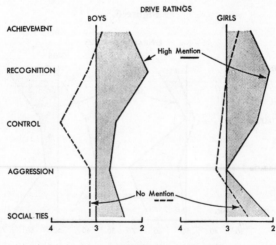

Figure 8.

only one among many possibilities. Several athletes, a cartoonist, a band-leader, a contralto singer, were among those who contributed, conspicu-ously, to the richness of school life though their intelligence scores were no greater than average.

On the other hand, some students with superior mental endowment were motivated to use this asset in more task-oriented and less social areas. There were four girls and four boys in this sample with *IQ*'s above 120 who were never mentioned in the "Daily." Here were potential resource persons who did not use their capabilities in the interest of high school extracurricular participation and leadership. Three of the four girls in this high *IQ* cate-gory who were non-participants were early-maturing. We have suggested that these girls tend not to fit into the school peer culture readily and it is not surprising that they failed to join in extracurricular activities. Three of the four boys in this same low prestige classification were late-maturing, a factor which has also been reported to be a disadvantage to social accept-ance in adolescence. Maturity level is one of the more obvious in a matrix of complicated factors which we would need to understand in order to ex-plain why these intellectually able individuals did not yield to the pressures to conform to the preferred socialization pattern.

6. Physical Abilities

Since in this particular peer subculture athletic skill in girls had little status value, we would not expect and did not find any relationship between physical ability and frequency of mention for the girls' groups. Among boys, a previous study of this sample of adolescents has shown that the muscular build which goes with strength and athletic ability is associated with class-mate and adult ratings of "good looks."[23] Though "good-looking" was de-scriptive of those with high mention, the relationship found between strength indices (see Table 2, Item 3) and prominence in the school activities pro-gram was not significantly discriminating for boys. Several boys in the high-mention group were well-known athletes, but others (such as the sports writer on the school paper) had poor physical ability and attained recogni-tion through other channels. Several boys in the no-mention group were relatively high in their strength indices, but never chose to join a team or to exhibit their physical abilities competitively.

7. Socio-Economic Status

Social status was found to exert only a small influence upon high school recognition, in terms of the criterion used in this study. There were to be sure certain prestige positions which tended to be filled by students of high

[23] Jones and Bayley, *op. cit.*

social status.[24] However, these were not the top ranking officers, and participation in school activities attracted students from all social classes. Correlations of .16 for boys (58 cases) and .17 for girls (54 cases) were found between socio-economic status and frequency of mention. As in the comparisons of extreme groups, these were not significant at the .05 level. Perhaps the implication to be drawn is that the "common man" class of students tend to use the school as an educational medium for practicing leadership and participation rôle (upward mobile activities). Those of a higher social stratum are learning these rôles to some extent in the greater variety of social settings (outside school) which are available to them. Although prominence in school affairs gave a coveted mark of distinction regardless of social status, it is also possible that other prestige groups with which the students of higher socio-economic level identified themselves tended to divide their loyalties, so that less effort was expended in student body activities. Perhaps typical of these students is one boy whose attitude is illustrative:

Reese, from an upper-class home, reported enthusiastically to his mother during his first week in High School: "There are four ways to make a name for yourself at Uni: One is in student body activities, another is in scholarship, a third is in the social life, and fourth in athletics. I have a good chance to get out in front in all of them." After a year during which time he had joined an out-of-school social club drawing members from several high schools, this same boy remarked: "If you belong to a good club it doesn't matter much which high school you go to—you meet the best guys from all of the schools in your club and would feel at home in any school." This boy's school loyalty had been supplanted by loyalty to his social club. Success in school and in extracurricular activities were weaker goals and ceased to command his best efforts.

In the geographic area of this study, schools and community agencies which offered resources for group participation were increasingly aware of the competition of invitational social clubs. Their problem was to offer equally satisfying social opportunities and goals, and to help the young people who came under their jurisdiction to coördinate and integrate their loyalties toward the various groups in which they functioned.

8. Attitudes

As has been indicated, members of the prominently mentioned group were frequently rated by classmates on the reputation test as outstandingly friendly. This seems to corroborate the impression of an over-all democratic atmosphere in the school and "a chance for anyone to become president."

---

[24] Measures used were ratings of home and neighborhood, census tract data, and use of community welfare agencies. At the time of this report (the depression era), the families of the children who were most active in school affairs used public service agencies as frequently as those who did not participate.

This should not imply, however, that the awareness of social distances did not exist. The following note by a staff member illustrates how some students felt about their reception into Senior High School. *"Jack* (a member of the frequently mentioned group) now in the 11th grade is less of a leader than he was in Junior High and he resents this. He bears a definite grudge against 'the hill students' and especially against the girls whom he describes as 'proud and snobbish.' "* (Later he succeeded in marrying one of them.) Our attitude tests did not indicate significant differences between the groups in prejudice toward outgroups or in ethnocentric tendency.[25]

9. Self-Concepts

Did these students have self-concepts which differed for the two groups? Data available for quantitative analysis of self-estimates were the self-report inventory, an interest check list, and attitudes measures (see Table 2). None of these yielded significant differences between the two groups. There was a slight tendency for girls who did not participate to report family problems and for boys who did not function in school events to mention more physical symptoms and to express greater dissatisfaction with school. Girls who did engage in school activities frequently tended to indicate more interests of an intellectual nature than did those who were isolated from the school extracurricular program.

Although there is a tendency to ascribe favorable qualities to leaders and others in prominent positions, being successful in these rôles is not primarily a matter of being well-adjusted, happy, or self-accepting. Nor did the successful students so reveal themselves. On the one hand, those who endorsed the socialization pattern would, presumably, experience ego satisfaction in achieving their goals. On the other hand, tension-producing conflicts would be involved for some, in learning the behavior expected of them in their selected rôles. Adults who rated these boys and girls did not describe the high-mention group as particularly social or good-natured. Nor did they attribute to them the kind of drives which are associated with a need for warm social ties or self-reliance. In describing their goal-seeking behavior, the staff differentiated between achievement needs "to increase self-regard by successful exercise of talent and ability" and a desire for recognition—"to excite praise, command respect, prestige, social approval." The participating group were considered to exhibit the latter in a greater degree (see Chart 8). Individuals who rated high on the drive for achievement may have tended more toward "inner-directedness," while those with high scores on need for recognition may be thought of as "other-directed," depending upon the approval of peers to define success for them.[26]

[25] Anastasiou, *op. cit.*

[26] D. Riesman, N. Glazer, and R. Denney, *The Lonely Crowd* (New Haven: Yale Univer. Press, 1950).

10. Rôle Patterns: Individual Descriptions

As has been indicated earlier, newspaper publicity accrues to or is sought by persons who provide a wide variety of community functions and portray numerous social rôles. For this study three types of rôles have been roughly designated as among those shown by the most frequently mentioned group. The individuals who function in these rôles may appropriately be described as "the leaders," "the performers" and "the willing workers." An individual may combine these rôles in greater or less degree and with varying success.

Leaders were those who won elective offices and carried out the tasks of student body government. There were three boys and one girl in our sample who qualified in this category.

Karl, student body president, represents those who have rather generalized leadership ability and have accepted the prevailing cultural goals. These individuals usually hold student body offices and count their followers in large numbers. They have accepted the dictate "to amount to something" and "to be somebody." Karl was an only child from a lower middle class, Protestant, first generation Northern European family. Parental goals for their son were those typically ascribed to adults who seek acceptance and improvement of status in the middle class culture: assumption of responsibility, conformity to accepted social codes, and individual achievement. With other outstanding leaders among Karl's peers, such factors as the stress of family position or the example of older siblings may have weighed more heavily in furnishing motivation for performing leadership rôles. For Karl, his family expectations were to be accomplished through the prescribed channels of home, school, church, youth groups. His mental and physical endowments (he was "college material," well-built, and early maturing) gave promise of his being able to achieve these goals. It was said that Karl's "impressive physical development did not allow him to relax into easy mediocrity" (he was the tallest boy in the study). At home there was a tendency to protect Karl because of his early growth spurt and conspicuous physique. He did not enter serious athletic competition until the late high school years. But at school, from the earliest grades he was selected by teachers and principals for leadership rôles. Before the end of his elementary school years, he was recognized as a leader among his peers.

In general, Karl's personal-social characteristics exemplify those which distinguished the student body leaders as a group, described by teachers and staff members in such terms as these: "not obviously dominating but directing," . . . "officiating in a paternal way," . . . "carrying the load of the conversation with adults."

More than the average student, Karl and his kind are willing to make approaches to young people outside their accustomed circles; to do the unpopular chore. "Voluntarily assumes positions in the game which no one else wants," was noted of one boy in this group. Of others it was noted:

"Treats the boys tolerantly" . . . "speaks cordially to everyone as she goes down the hall" . . . "went to the physical exam with 'Dutch' " (an isolate) . . . "spoke with girls who were being ignored by her friends."

In spite of the appearance of buoyancy, none of these student body leaders escaped a certain appearance of striving. Occasionally the notation "worried" appears. More frequently such phrases as the following are used: "Takes responsibility seriously" . . . "definitely strives for leadership position" . . . "popular as a leader but has to work for prestige."

On the self-report inventory, these young people did not describe themselves in such a way as to indicate high self-acceptance. Admission of fears, physical symptoms, tensions, and feelings of inferiority suggest that at least some of the striving for status is motivated by compensatory feelings. It also implies the ability to internalize emotional behavior and to tolerate anxiety.[27][28] We might catalogue these leaders as standard bearers; they had assumed responsibility for carrying on—mid snow and ice if necessary —the standards which their high school peers recognize and accept as those approved by the adult culture as well as their own peer subculture.

A second group of students receiving high mention in the school paper are "the performers." They rely upon "talent" to reach their goals. The athletes would come first in this category but it also included the musicians, cartoonists, dramatists, and writers. The personal approach played a less important rôle in their functioning and they actually varied widely in their social appeal. An athlete hero who also had social facility might be elected to leadership positions. One such student, *Bill,* was elected class president.[29] On the other hand among the "performers" was one boy who received a very low score for "friendliness" on classmate ratings. He won his laurels by his clever, though often biting, cartoons. One of the girls with "talent" was described by adult observers: "Paula has a somewhat snobbish manner which does not attract friends but does suggest an air of assurance, which is effective in some social situations."

A few in this talent group had aimed at the top social-prestige hierarchy (primarily represented by membership in invitational social clubs) and with reluctance had lowered their sights to suit their talents and social status. "Nancy (successful in dramatic rôles) had a great deal to say about how discouraging it was to have the 'hill bunch' run the school." Among these students, as with the standard bearers, there is evidence of anxiety to attain recognition: "There has always seemed to be some underlying irritability that keeps Jane in action" . . . "Tony seems ridden by his ambition to be

---

[27] H. E. Jones, "The Study of Patterns of Emotional Expression," *Feelings and Emotions,* ed., M. L. Reymert (New York: McGraw-Hill, 1950), pp. 161–169.
[28] It will be recalled that no significant differences were found between the two groups in adjustment scores.
[29] Karl became an outstanding athlete also in his senior year, which contributed to his prestige. However, it was not the basis on which his status was primarily built.

a popular band leader." . . . "John was apologetic about not having enough time to work with his committee."

Tony, the band leader, represents the group who won recognition through their entertainment value. While Karl, student body president, was mentioned in every category of school activities except that of "The Arts," Tony participated exclusively in the area of his talent. He received publicity only in relation to his band. Some of the forces at work in motivating Tony are suggested from data in our files. Tony was among those students in whom the desire to be well liked was positively reflected in his behavior and furnished one of the strong forces urging him toward his goal. Another emotional impetus was his love of music, a symbol of his father-identification. A third may have been what he meant by "ambition," a physiologically high irritability which at times was drained off in nervous mannerisms, at other times consumed his energy, and threatened his health.

"To be a band leader," Tony said, "you have to have personality—to be able to talk to people and sell your band, unless you are a terrifically outstanding musician." Was Tony saying that he had to sell himself because he was not "terrific?" "And," said he, "you have to have ambition—you can't just have musicianship and personality; you have to *work.*"

Prosaically a fourth factor which helped to mold Tony's choice of expressive medium was circumstance. When opportunity knocked—Tony was ready. The factors associated with Tony's choice of activity may best be reported beginning with the counselor's summary of Tony at the end of junior high school.

Tony belongs to an ambitious and cultured Greek-American family. His father is a musician. For the first two years in Junior High School he was a quiet, tense, conscientious boy anxious to do what he could to get along well in school and with the peer group. He was accepted but not particularly popular. He was so anxious to be well-liked and to please everybody that he was really too submissive, both to adults and to his own classmates. He was asked to fill in at a few parties when he was in the H8 and at the beginning of the H9, but he was among the least popular as far as the girls were concerned. Then the orchestra was started, sponsored by the study staff.

Tony became the center of and the leader of seven boys in this group. Everyone liked him as soon as he stopped being too anxious to please and acted more like the other boys. The dance orchestra became *his* orchestra. Bill began to pal around with him. It was when Bill was at the height of his popularity with both boys and girls. Tony rode to popularity with him, as Bill had certainly selected him for his best friend. Tony became less quiet, not so overly conscientious and anxious to please, more natural—though still a bit excitable and tense with his newly found musical and social life. With the opening of the H9 semester he had climbed to a position among the most popular boys, both among other boys and with the opposite sex. The girls who like him now, like him, I think, for his prestige as a dance orchestra leader. Several are honoring him with their pursuit. But, as he puts it, he doesn't want to get in love again. (An earlier episode claimed his emotions and was unrequited.) He is very much absorbed in music, learning the trombone which his family, at a great sacrifice, managed to buy for him.

In the 9th grade Tony started the college preparatory course and will barely finish his Latin. Algebra he finds extremely difficult. This year's work has made him decide not to count on going to college and law school. He plans now to take a business course and keep on with his music. This change does not bother him as it would have a year ago when he was straining to get ahead academically and socially.

Thus Tony was well on his way socially when he entered high school, and became one of those frequently mentioned in the "Daily." Tony's need for social ties was evident, but others in this group with "talent" were not similarly motivated. *Walt* who wrote for the school paper and had the highest *IQ* in the group had a turn in his social fortunes which was practically the reverse of Tony's. From a grade school youngster with satisfactory friendships, Walt became more and more of a problem to himself in the adolescent years and by his grouchy, sullen, and arrogant behavior alienated his former good friends. His mother commented, "He's a know-it-all, and he argues everlastingly." The psychologist who administered the Stanford-Binet test wrote: "Walt interpreted the second proverb: 'You must not cast pearls before swine' as 'Don't waste your.talents on things that don't deserve it.' This epitomizes his attitude. He did not want to appear to be taking the trouble to think out correct answers, to be the least bit concerned about the results, or to give the examiner the satisfaction of having him consider the task of any importance."

Walt's week-end diary written in the 12th grade described work at the newspaper office, going to a "show" alone, developing and printing pictures, alone. Although unhappy and socially isolated from his age group, Walt presumably gained satisfaction from the recognition gained through the exercise of his talent. And his classmates accorded him a measure of honor and fame on the basis of his ability and in spite of his condescending and critical attitudes.

Still a third category proved to be useful in classifying some of the high-prestige individuals: The "willing workers" or "middle leaders" . . . those students who are committee members *ad infinitum*—or who occasionally head small subcommittees where they are delegated to carry out a part of a larger project (such as a function at the Class Day Activities) but are practically never elected to major appointments. Such a girl was *Ruth,* a late-maturing, middle class girl of superior ability, who wrote in her 12th grade autobiography: "I had always admired certain girls who seemed to know how to run things at school or who had fun helping on committees. It was not until the 11th grade that I had my first chance and served on the poster committee." From this time on until graduation, Ruth was an indefatigable committee member.

The "willing workers" were less colorful as well as less stimulating than their more dominant classmates. Nevertheless they were imbued with the importance of participating in the high school social life. Wrote one of these:

A girl in high school should enter school activities of all kinds in order to have a well rounded social pattern. She should, if possible, be a leader, be on committees and join organizations. Popularity plays its part in a modern girl's life. We all like to be popular and the best way is by getting in and doing things to make ourselves known. People come to know us by the activities we participate in and the clubs we belong to, that's why it's a good idea to enter all social affairs.

By dint of efficient or energetic participation these "workers" created a demand for their services, and were frequently appointed to committees; a fact duly reported in the school newspaper.

This high school was exceptional in the opportunities available to young people to practice leadership and engage in peer group social activities. It was stated earlier that nearly 90 per cent of the student body engaged in some school-connected activity. What then of the adjustment of the young people whose share in the school life was so meager as to bring no recognition?

For several who were in a "negative phase," failure to accept the high school pattern was merely an extension of a generalized rejective attitude. This is illustrated for example by *Florence* who was a "sturm und drang" adolescent, and a glum, sober, self-imposed isolate. An observer recorded: "She dislikes the University visit (part of the study program) because it imposes social adjustments which she is unable to make. . . . Today she had to go to the physical examination with Amy, a bad arrangement since Amy, though not as able a student as Florence, is poised, gracious, friendly —qualities which Florence would love to have but at the same time despises herself for wanting." In college Florence developed an absorbing interest in a professional career and married a man with similar ambitions. She is now a wife and mother as well as as a professional partner with her husband. Her life seems rich and satisfying. But as a high school student she rejected the avenues of communication open to her through the school and peer group. At one time she remarked that her friendship with her older sister was more convenient than trying to make and keep friends outside the family. After high school she admitted that she had wanted to join clubs and go out for activities but blamed her sister for not taking the lead in this. Thus did she excuse her non-social existence. (Her self-report inventory revealed her tendency to project.) Florence is one of several in the study group who reacted to difficulties in their adolescent years by behaving negativistically toward others. Some individuals like Florence handled their adolescent adjustment problems by negativism or withdrawal. As adults they may now find satisfactions in professional achievement or in family living. Their social contacts are primarily with fellow workers or the family group.

Angela, another non-participating student, was a shy but bright, eager, responsive person. Observers noted: "Angela takes a docile rôle. . . ." "She is unobtrusively interested in all that the others are doing or saying" . . . "she is pleased at small attentions" . . . "others seem to like Angela well enough but pay little attention, and she seems to expect none" . . . "no one chose her for a partner" . . . "likes to be with others but does not seek recognition, nor has she enough stimulus value to be actively accepted or avoided." Angela was a motherless child, below par in health and physical vigor, tolerated rather than loved in a foster home. Like Angela, several others in the non-mention group were retiring. The heavy hand of repression had early placed its stamp upon them.

Although only five girls in the study have not married to date, Angela and two others of these are from this non-mentioned group.

Among the non-participating boys, *Eugene* was an early-maturing, tall, lanky, blond boy with a pale, rather homely, sad face. His health had not been good and he tended to complain of aches and pains. The youngest of a family of five and the only boy, his parents, older than the average of parents for high school boys, subscribed to the adage "Satan finds some mischief still for idle hands to do." The family had a financial struggle and Eugene had been deprived of money to spend on adequate clothes even when he earned the money himself. His parents kept Eugene busy with housework and carefully scrutinized his private and social life. Was it lack of enterprise or of security (characteristics of his high school days) which was suggested in this statement from his autobiography? "I am still living in the same house in which I was born and hope to keep on living in it as long as it stands."

In the 11th grade this comment was written by an adult: "For the last two years Eugene has not been mentioned by anyone as a best friend." The sense of isolation from a group of contemporaries is revealed in a composition written by him.

"The dog that shared six very enjoyable years with me died but a few weeks ago after being poisoned by some person still unknown. He was small but showed more affection than any human that I have ever known, or shall probably ever know." This was Eugene—who never got his name in the paper in the three years of high school career.

Vincent started adolescence handicapped in physique, family background, and intellectual ability. He received few mentions either favorable or unfavorable on the reputation test. His early maturing, however, brought new strength and power to his physique, helped him to face his situation in junior high school and to accept his limitations. As a high school student now stable and more assured, he was described as "quiet, almost sedate . . . seems like an uncle to the other boys. . . . He joins their games but as an adult who tolerates play, rather than as a boy who craves it . . . reserved yet friendly . . . listened quietly to others . . . rarely spoke . . . relaxed and self-contained." His responses on a self-report inventory were consistently on the well-adjusted side. His vocational aim, accepted as practical at a relatively early age, was to become a truck driver like his father. He has realized this ambition and is now working for the same company as his father. Although observed to be very shy with girls in high school, he is now married and a family man. There is little evidence that lack of recognition while in school has had serious detrimental effects.

11. Discussion

What has happened to the active high-mention group 15 years out of high school? Some had four years in college. In this situation, similar to high school in its emphasis on campus activities, the pattern of participation continued. This was more true of the girls than of the boys. The latter, especially those in professional schools, were taking studies more seriously and so had less time for extracurricular activities. Seventy-five per cent of the high-mention group went to college as compared with 55 per cent of the no-mention group. (Forty-five per cent of the total study group went to college.)

The armed services provided another screening situation for the two groups. Sixty per cent of the frequently mentioned boys became officers, and only one member of the no-mention group. The only woman officer from the group of girls was in the high-mention category.

Fifteen years after high school, in a follow-up study, the boy who was remembered by his associates most frequently (from a high school photograph) was the band leader, Tony. Next was his best friend, Bill the athlete-leader. Karl, the outstanding student-body leader was third. Some post–high school events probably influenced this order. Tony is still the leader of his own band which keeps him before the public. At one time, Bill received local mention in the papers for a war history involving injuries. But there was also a colorfulness about the first two which was somewhat lacking in Karl's appeal. Tony was warm, urgently in need of acceptance. Bill was the adolescent hero, in build, looks, masculinity, athletic ability— even in the possession of temperamental qualities which stamped him as human. Karl was admired, respected, trusted, perhaps not so well loved.

If a rank of the individuals in the study group on the basis of prestige were to be made at the present time, there would be some decided shifts. One young man who can now properly be described as a celebrity was below average in number of mentions in high school.

The high-mention group furnishes more individuals who have achieved status in jobs or community, but in the no-mention group at least a third of the girls and a fourth of the boys have attained a degree of recognition comparable with any in the group who were so much more conspicuous in high school. The pattern of social interaction represented by participation in extracurricular high school activities provided many adolescents with social rôles which they found intrinsically congenial and likewise useful as a step toward other kinds of satisfying interpersonal relationships.

Some students who were not ready or able to practice this approved social behavior in high school felt insecure and unappreciated. Some found more personally appropriate avenues of communication through task-oriented activities, family, church, or community sponsored social activities or through small intimate friendship groups. In general, the patterns of social participation whether through leadership, entertainment, or service tended to persist into college and adult life. However, this varied with the opportunities available and the values placed upon such rôles in the individual adult's immediate environment.

At present a few young people are active in labor or church organizations. Among the married young women, leadership abilities are in some cases being used effectively by cooperative nursery schools.

All of the girls who were frequently mentioned in the high school paper are married and living with their husbands.[30] A few are now exhibiting more active public roles and receiving more acclaim than they did as high school students. At present the more intimate interpersonal relationships of family life and the exigencies of a vocation are claiming the attention of these young adults who are now in their thirties.

In general, opportunities to lead and influence of the kind available in high school are relatively lacking to these individuals as young adults. Perhaps we should put it another way and say that such opportunities are luxuries which they cannot afford. For the most part, neither their working nor their leisure hours are organized so that they have anything comparable with the number of interpersonal contacts which were customary in high school.

[30] At this time 96 per cent of the girls and 90 per cent of the boys in this study were married. Nineteen per cent of the married girls and 6 per cent of the married boys have been divorced.

Residential Segregation of Social Classes and Aspirations of High School Boys*

ALAN B. WILSON

In the paper presented below, Wilson considers the impact of the school society upon adolescents' educational aspirations, occupational goals, and political party preferences. Specifically he asks: "Are the sons of manual workers more likely to adhere to middle-class values and have high educational aspirations if they attend a predominantly middle-class school, and, conversely, are the aspirations of the sons of professionals more modest if they attend a predominantly working-class school?" In controlling family status and parental educational level, Wilson demonstrates that the social climate of the school does in fact play an important function in influencing adolescents' aspirations.

Consistent and strong evidence has been accumulated showing that members of different socio-economic strata, as groups, adhere to differing values which reinforce their respective statuses.[1] Members of the working class tend to devalue education and to aspire to modest but secure occupations and income levels. Through familial socialization and divergent perceptions of their opportunities these aspirations are transmitted to the younger genera-

---

[1] See, e.g., H. H. Hyman, "The Value Systems of Different Classes: a Social Psychological Contribution to the Analysis of Stratification," R. Bendix and S. M. Lipset, editors, *Class, Status and Power*, Glencoe, Ill.: Free Press, 1953, pp. 426–442; J. A. Kahl, "Educational and Occupational Aspirations of 'Common Man' Boys," *Harvard Educational Review*, 23 (Summer, 1953), pp. 186–203; W. H. Sewell, A. O. Haller, and M. A. Straus, "Social Status and Educational and Occupational Aspiration," *American Sociological Review*, 22 (February, 1957), pp. 67–73.

---

* From *American Sociological Review*, XXIV (1959), pp. 836–845. Reprinted by permission of the author and the American Sociological Association. The research reported herein was performed pursuant to a contract with the United States Office of Education, Department of Health, Education, and Welfare. The writer is indebted to T. Bentley Edwards, director of this research program, for permission to analyze and report this aspect of the problem; and to Seymour M. Lipset, Martin Trow, and T. Bentley Edwards, for their suggestions and criticisms.

tion. The social inheritance of such values and attitudes tends to inhibit social mobility.

Many investigations have shown the relevance of individual personality characteristics to aspirations. These aspects of personality have been linked in turn to such variations in the familial socialization of children as direct exhortation and positive valuation of education and status, early independence training, the level of adult-child contact indicated by the size of family or the child's position in the order of siblings, and matriarchal *versus* patriarchal authority structure within the family.[2] Since the familial characteristics which are conducive to a high level of aspirations are more typical of the middle class than of the working class, these variates can be viewed, at least in part, as intervening between the parent's social class and his children's aspirations.

While the association between youths' educational and occupational aspirations and their parents' class position is strong, regardless of what dimension of social stratification is employed, there is considerable variation in aspirations among youths within a single class. This study is concerned with a related matter: the derivation of values from the immediate social milieu—the climate of the school society.

A variety of experimental and descriptive investigations have demonstrated the influence of social context upon judgments, attitudes, and aspirations.[3] Berenda, using the technique developed by Solomon Asch, found that when a child is confronted with classmates giving unanimous, incorrect judgments, only seven per cent of the younger children (ages 7 to 10) and 20 per cent of the older children (ages 10 to 13) remained independent.[4] A series of studies have shown the homogenization of certain social and political attitudes at college.[5] Herbert Hyman also has suggested that a current reference group, such as one's current co-workers, may provide a systematic factor accounting for differences in values among individuals with common class-origins.[6]

Because of the sifting of like social types into specific zones within an urbanized area, school districting tends to segregate youths of different

[2] See especially, S. M. Lipset and R. Bendix, *Social Mobility and Industrial Society,* Berkeley: University of California Press, 1959, Chapter 9.

[3] See, e.g., R. K. Merton, *Social Theory and Social Structure,* Glencoe, Ill.: Free Press, 1957, Chapters 8 and 9; E. Katz and P. F. Lazarsfeld, *Personal Influence,* Glencoe, Ill.: Free Press, 1955, *passim.*

[4] R. W. Berenda, *The Influence of the Group on the Judgment of Peers,* New York: King's Crown, 1950; the technique is presented in S. E. Asch, *Social Psychology,* New York: Prentice-Hall, 1952, pp. 450–501.

[5] T. H. Newcomb, "Attitude Development as a Function of Reference Groups: the Bennington Study," in E. E. Maccoby, T. H. Newcomb, and E. L. Hartley, editors, *Readings in Social Psychology,* New York: Henry Holt, 1958, pp. 265–275. Several studies are summarized by P. E. Jacob, *Changing Values in College,* New Haven: Hazen Foundation, 1957.

[6] Hyman, *op. cit.,* pp. 441–442.

social strata. Consequently school populations have modally different attitudes toward educational achievement and aspirations for a college education. The proposition that the aspirations of the bulk of the students in a high school district provide a significant normative reference influencing the educational aspirations of boys from varying strata is investigated in this paper by comparing the aspirations of students with similar social origins who attend schools characterized by different climates of aspiration. Concretely, are the sons of manual workers more likely to adhere to middle-class values and have high educational aspirations if they attend a predominantly middle-class school, and, conversely, are the aspirations of the sons of professionals more modest if they attend a predominantly working-class school?

PROCEDURE

The data for this study are provided by a survey of students' interests as related to their success in school and their decisions about educational and occupational specialization. This survey gathered information on students in thirteen high schools in and around the San Francisco-Oakland Bay area.[7] Five of these schools, located in cities and places outside the urbanized area, are excluded from the present analysis; and the study is confined to boys, since the educational and occupational aspirations of girls are more homogeneous and are conditioned by different factors.

A high degree of concordance ($W = .92$) is found among the several rank orders of occupational and educational stratification obtained from the census data describing the populations from which the student bodies were recruited, and the data from the observed sample of students at the seven public schools.[8] The entire population of a private boys' school, the students of which are not recruited from continuous tracts, was sampled. The sample distributions obtained clearly place this school in the first rank (group A) in Table 1. The schools are grouped, for this study, on the basis of these rank orders, as well as congruent distinctions not reflected in the statistics —impressions of the school "atmospheres" obtained while observing students in the classrooms, halls, and playgrounds. Because of the high con-

[7] The schools were selected purposively from those accessible which had been stratified on the basis of census data. Confidence in the findings depends upon their internal consistency and their congruence with the body of parallel research and relevant theory. Ultimately, the generalizability of the study must depend upon replication with other populations rather than statistical inference to a population of schools which, necessarily, would also be arbitrarily limited by their accessibility.

[8] The census data use different classifications, based upon a wider population (not limited to the parents of high school boys), and were gathered at an earlier date than the sample data. The concordance of ranks rather than the correlation of actual percentages is all that is pertinent, in any event, to confirm the appropriateness of the ordering and grouping of schools.

cordance between the various dimensions of stratification, the grouping would be the same whichever combination one might choose to emphasize.[9]

Detailed contrasts between the three groups of schools (designated *A, B,* and *C,* respectively) in the distribution of several dimensions of stratification are shown in Table 2. The distributions show the gross correlation between these various dimensions of stratification, and reflect the extent of segregation between strata due to school districting along lines of social concentration. While only 10 per cent of the students in the group *A* schools are children of manual workers, one-half of the boys in the group *C* schools are manual workers' sons; and while 65 per cent of the fathers in the group *A* schools have at least some college education, only 14 per cent of the fathers of students at the group *C* schools have any college training. Other comparisons show similar contrasts. (It is interesting to note that the families of the students in the group *A* schools have resided in California longer than those in the group *C* schools. This reflects the predominantly working-class origins of the recent large-scale immigration into California and the upward mobility of the established urban residents.)

FINDINGS

It was found, as anticipated, that there is a great divergence between the schools in the proportions of students aspiring to a college education.[10] Eighty per cent of the students in the *A* schools, 57 per cent in the *B* schools, and only 38 per cent in the *C* schools want to go to college. (See the bottom row of Table 3.) This difference is due to a great extent, of course, to attributes of the parents who serve as reference individuals for the students. This is seen by making vertical comparisons in Table 3: many more children of professionals have collegiate aspirations than children of manual workers in each school group. But *within* occupational strata, reading across

[9] The grouping of schools on the basis of occupational and educational dimensions of stratification, and the subsequent pooling of a predominantly Catholic with a predominantly Negro school as working-class schools might be unjustified if religion and race were independently associated with the dependent variable, i.e., educational aspirations. Altogether, 58 per cent of the Protestants and only 47 per cent of the Catholics in the sample aspire to go to college. But within educational and occupational strata the difference between Protestants and Catholics is small and unsystematic, while within each religious group the differences between occupational and educational strata are large. For example, among the children of professionals with at least some college education, 87 per cent of both Protestants and Catholics wish to go to college; among the children of manual workers who are high school graduates, 44 per cent of the Protestants and 46 per cent of the Catholics so wish; 34 per cent of the Protestants and 28 per cent of the Catholics whose fathers are manual workers who have not finished high school, want to go to college.

Similarly, the overall differences in educational aspirations between Negroes and Whites are "explained" by the predominantly working-class and low educational status of the Negroes.

[10] Educational aspirations were inferred from the following question:

[*Cont. on p. 379*]

Table 1

Census and Sample Distributions of Educational and Occupational Variates by Schools

Schools	Median Years of Schooling	1950 Census		College Graduates		Fathers' Occupation	
		Pro-fessional	Laborers	Fathers	Mothers	Pro-fessional	Manual
Group A: Upper white collar							
1. Private boys' school	*	*	*	65%	53%	30%	6%
2. Residential	13.3	26%	2%	51	35	22	2
3. Sub-urban	12.3	13	8	28	23	14	22
Group B: Lower white collar							
4. Metropolitan	12.0	13	5	27	21	8	32
5. Metropolitan	11.1	11	9	21	17	13	38
Group C: Industrial							
6. Predominantly Catholic	10.7	5	10	11	5	1	53
7. Heterogeneous	9.6	4	12	2	2	4	56
8. Predominantly Negro	8.7	2	32	9	7	6	72

The High School Sample spans the College Graduates and Fathers' Occupation columns.

* The private school's population is drawn from scattered tracts.

Table 2
Distributions of Selected Variates by School Groups

Variate Category	School Group A	B	C
Fathers' occupation			
Professional	22%	8%	2%
White collar	42	29	25
Self employed	17	20	8
Manual	10	30	49
Not available	9	12	15
Fathers' education			
Some college or more	65	35	14
High school graduate	20	29	26
Some high school or less	14	32	54
Not available	2	3	6
Mothers' education			
Some college or more	56	31	12
High school graduate	34	41	39
Some high school or less	9	25	45
Not available	1	3	4
Residence in California			
Over 25 years	58	48	32
Race			
White	98	78	66
Religion			
Catholic	21	27	38
Number of cases	(418)	(480)	(457)

[10 *Cont.*]

After I graduate from high school (and, if necessary, serve in the military forces)—

1. ....I plan to get a job right away
2. ....I plan to be a housewife
3. ....I plan to go to a technical or trade school
4. ....I plan to go to a junior college
5. ....I plan to go first to a junior college, and then to a four-year college or university
6. ....I plan to go directly to a four-year college or university
7. ....I have other plans

. . . .
(What are they?)

Responses 5 and 6 were considered as indicating an aspiration to go to college. Since there are several free junior colleges in the area which are open to all high school graduates regardless of past scholarship, poor students can and often do use them as a means of remedying their academic deficiencies. Any student who *wants* to go to college can *plan* to do so, unless, of course, he does not believe he is capable of

[*Cont. on p. 380*]

the table, we see that attributes of the reference group—the norms of the school society—symmetrically modify attitudes: while 93 per cent of the sons of professionals in the group *A* schools want to go to college, less than two-thirds of the sons of professionals in the group *C* schools wish to do so; whereas only one-third of the sons of manual workers wish to go to college if they attend a predominantly working-class school, more than one-half of such sons so wish in the middle-class schools. This isotropic relationship provides *prima facie* confirmation of the cumulative effects of the primary and contextual variates—the boys' own class origins and the dominant class character of the high schools' student body.

Table 3
Percentages Aspiring to Go to College by School Groups and Fathers' Occupations

	School Group		
Fathers' occupation	*A*	*B*	*C*
Professional	93%	77%	64%
	(92)	(39)	(11)
White collar	79	59	46
	(174)	(138)	(111)
Self employed	79	66	35
	(68)	(90)	(37)
Manual	59	44	33
	(39)	(140)	(221)
Weighted mean of per cents	80	57	38
Total	(373)*	(407)*	(380)*

* The total number of cases on which these percentages are based is less than the totals shown in Table 2 because cases for which data were unavailable for either the control or dependent variates are not shown. Variation in the total number of cases in the succeeding tables is for the same reason unless otherwise noted.

It is possible, however, that these differences between schools reflect uncontrolled systematic variation in the attributes of the parents. Within each of these broad occupational strata there is considerable variation of occupational status, income, education, habits of consumption, and the like, each of which makes a cumulative impact upon values. The more successful and better educated professionals tend to move to more exclusive residential areas, send their children to private schools, or both; among the "white

[10 *Cont.*]
improving and, therefore, has no intention of trying. A student might value higher education without aspiring to attain a higher education. However, differences in school achievement do not account for the differences between schools in aspirations. (See Tables 11 and 12.)

collar" occupations more prosperous executives reside in the group *A* school district, clerks in the group *C* districts, and so on. Differences of this kind between schools within roughly defined occupational strata are shown in Table 4.

Table 4
Percentages Within Each Occupational Category with High Status Jobs and High Education by School Groups

Occupational Stratum *Sub-stratum and* *Education*	School Group		
	A	*B*	*C*
Professional			
"Free" (self employed)	59%	55%	27%
Some college or more	96	98	73
Number of cases	(92)	(40)	(11)
White collar			
"Executive"	42	14	3
Some college or more	65	47	20
Number of cases	(177)	(141)	(113)
Self employed			
Merchants (e.g., retail)	51	41	30
Some college or more	62	36	14
Number of cases	(71)	(95)	(38)
Manual			
Skilled	60	52	43
Some college or more	21	14	9
Number of cases	(40)	(144)	(225)

If the apparent effects of the school climate were in fact due to such uncontrolled variation along several dimensions of familial status, then one would expect the differences between the aspirations of the students at the different schools to diminish as the control categories are progressively refined—that is, as the students are compared within more homogeneous background categories. The refinement of any one or a few dimensions of stratification will result in groups which one may reasonably assume are also somewhat more homogeneous with respect to uncontrolled correlated dimensions.

This question is considered in Table 5, which is designed to show the impact of school norms upon students from more homogeneous occupational strata. This table is not, of course, "independent" of Table 3, which can be reproduced by recombining the sub-strata shown in Table 5. But it indicates that the refinement—the homogenization, so to speak—of the control categories, does not systematically modify the effect of the school society upon aspirations. For example, three-fourths of the children of self-employed artisans and skilled manual workers aspire to go to college at the group *A* schools, while considerably fewer than one-half of them do so at the group *C* schools.[11]

Table 5
Percentages Within Occupational Sub-Strata Aspiring to Go to College by School Groups

	School Group		
Fathers' Occupation	*A*	*B*	*C*
"Free" professional	94%	67%	. . .
	(54)	(21)	(3)
Salaried professional	92	89	. . .
	(38)	(18)	(8)
Executive	88	79	. . .
	(75)	(19)	(3)
Upper white collar	79	59	55
	(68)	(64)	(40)
Lower white collar	55	53	40
	(31)	(55)	(68)
Self employed: merchants	88	77	18
	(33)	(35)	(11)
Self employed: artisans	73	60	44
	(33)	(53)	(25)
Manual: skilled	75	46	40
	(24)	(74)	(93)
Manual: semi- and unskilled	33	42	29
	(15)	(66)	(128)

The education of the parents is likewise known to have a strong independent effect upon students' aspirations. Fathers' and mothers' educations are controlled in Tables 6 and 7, respectively. The effect of the school society upon aspirations is still found to be operative and strong when holding constant the influence of either parent's education. A comparison of these two tables does not substantiate the notion that the mother's education is more influential than the father's upon the high school boy's educational aspirations. Hyman suggests the importance of the woman's role in the transmission of educational values on the basis of the fact that youths and adult women both *recommended* college more frequently than adult men.[12] Perhaps women directly exhort educational values more frequently,

[11] The largest irregularities—the sons of merchants at the group *C* schools, and the sons of semi- and un-skilled manual workers at the group *A* schools—are based upon very few cases.
[12] Hyman, *op. cit.*, pp. 431–432.

Table 6
Percentages Aspiring to Go to College by School Groups and Fathers' Education

	School Group		
Fathers' Education	A	B	C
College graduate	88%	73%	73%
	(207)	(109)	(30)
Some college	79	68	58
	(61)	(56)	(33)
High school graduate	74	51	35
	(81)	(138)	(115)
Some high school	63	39	30
	(32)	(74)	(109)
Grammar school or less	32	29	33
	(22)	(76)	(131)

independently of their own educational background. But these data do not suggest that the mother's role is more significant than the father's with respect to the more subtle and indirect effects of the parents' own education.

Looking more closely at the effect on educational aspirations of the interaction between the education of the two parents, it can be seen, in Table 8, that each makes an independent and cumulative impact of about the same degree. The only asymmetrical effect lies in the extreme combinations: if the father has not completed high school it makes little difference whether the mother has gone to college or not, but it makes considerable difference whether or not the father has gone to college even though the mother has

Table 7
Percentages Aspiring to Go to College by School Groups and Mothers' Education

	School Group		
Mothers' Education	A	B	C
College graduate	87%	77%	67%
	(64)	(88)	(24)
Some college	87	54	53
	(67)	(57)	(30)
High school graduate	74	54	35
	(140)	(191)	(170)
Some high school	50	35	39
	(20)	(69)	(120)
Grammar school or less	44	34	24
	(16)	(47)	(83)

Table 8
Percentages Aspiring to Go to College by Fathers'
and Mothers' Education

Fathers' Education	Mothers' Education			
	Col.	H.S.	Less than H.S.	Total*
Some college or more	85%	72%	53%	79%
	(309)	(149)	(36)	(495)
High school graduate	71	50	37	51
	(65)	(191)	(75)	(334)
Some high school or less	40	38	31	35
	(50)	(154)	(239)	(445)
Total*	77	53	35	56
	(430)	(501)	(355)	(1311)

* Marginal totals include those cases for which information is unavailable on the respective control variates.

not completed high school. Since these extreme combinations are the rarest, however, their effects are the least reliable.

The possibilities of holding several variates constant simultaneously are limited in tabular analysis, due to the rapid reduction of the number of cases which can be matched. The homogenization of categories is carried as far as is feasible within the limitations of the size of our sample in Table 10. In this table the educational and occupational attributes of the parents are simultaneously held constant while comparisons are made between the educational aspirations of students in different groups of schools. While the reduced numbers of cases make these percentages less reliable, of the nine comparisons available,[13] seven clearly substantiate the hypothesis, while the two reversals are small. The average percentile differences between adjacent schools are as great within these homogeneous groups as in the coarser groupings of Tables 3, 6, and 7, where the fathers' occupations and parents' education are controlled separately. The only comparison available for all three school groups is among the sons of manual workers both of whose parents have a high school education. Among these boys, 60 per cent in the A school, 54 per cent in the B schools and 32 per cent in the C schools seek to go to college.

ACHIEVEMENT AND EDUCATIONAL VALUES

Educational values and achievement interact and reinforce one another. On the one hand, those who devalue education are poorly motivated to achieve; on the other, those who have been poor achievers will defen-

[13] Percentages are shown in Table 10 for each classification where there are ten or more cases in two school groups on which to base a comparison. The empty cells and categories not shown have fewer than ten cases.

sively devalue education, and perhaps realistically, modify their educational aspirations. A much higher proportion of students in the middle-class schools obtain "A's" and "B's" than do those in the working-class schools. In addition to the influence of the family and school norms upon achievement, with which hitherto we have been concerned, there is the possibility that teachers grade more liberally at the middle-class schools—either for entirely extraneous reasons or, more plausibly, because the parents' expectations and the students' aspirations place pressure on them to raise the grading curve.

Table 9
Percentages Attaining High ("A" or "B") Median Grades by School Groups and Fathers' Occupations

	School Group		
Fathers' Occupation	*A*	*B*	*C*
Professional	66%	50%	18%
	(91)	(40)	(11)
White collar	50	28	18
	(176)	(138)	(111)
Self employed	51	35	11
	(71)	(95)	(37)
Manual	35	13	11
	(40)	(141)	(221)
Weighted mean of per cents	52	27	13
	(378)	(414)	(380)

If the latter interpretation is sound, then the students who are high achievers at the group *C* schools will be higher achievers, on an absolute basis, than those at the group *A* schools. But, holding grades constant and reading across the rows in Table 11, we see that even under these conditions more students receiving the same grade in the middle-class schools want to go to college.[14] Virtually all of those who receive "A's" at the group *A* schools want to go to college, but only three-fourths of the "A" students at the group *C* schools want to go to college.[15]

Using IQ scores as an index of achievement which is standardized across school lines, and thus eliminating the possibility of systematic differences between school grading policies, we see in Table 12 that high achievers are less likely to wish to go to college if they attend a working-class school

---

[14] The number of cases on which these percentages are based reflects the fact, shown in Table 9, that far fewer students do receive "A's" at the group *C* schools.

[15] Note that the aspirations of the students who receive high grades at the group *B* schools resemble those of the students of the group *A* schools, while those who get low grades have aspirations similar to those students at the group *C* schools. This suggests the possibility of two dominant norms in the intermediate schools providing alternative normative references.

Table 10
Percentages Aspiring to Go to College by School Groups Within Educational and Occupational Strata

FATHERS' EDUCATION / Fathers' Occupation	MOTHERS' EDUCATION							
	College Graduate		High School Graduate			Less than High School		
	School Group		School Group			School Group		
	A	B	A	B	C	A	B	C
College graduate								
Professional	92% (52)	78% (18)						
Upper white collar	86 (57)	94 (17)	83% (24)	62% (13)				
High school graduate								
Upper white collar			85 (20)	65 (20)				
Lower white collar				50 (10)	20% (15)			
Manual			60 (10)	54 (26)	32 (25)		32% (25)	35% (48)
Less than high school								
Lower white collar				60 (10)	27 (15)			
Manual							36 (45)	26 (86)

386

Table 11
Percentages Aspiring to Go to College
by School Groups and Grades

	School Group		
Median Academic Grade	*A*	*B*	*C*
"A"	98%	96%	78%
	(60)	(24)	(9)
"B"	90	89	72
	(152)	(90)	(46)
"C"	72	55	41
	(145)	(207)	(184)
"D"	43	21	25
	(47)	(120)	(169)

and, conversely, that low achievers are more apt to want to go to college if they attend a middle-class school.[16] Almost all of the students with IQ scores over 120 at the group *A* schools hope to go to college, whereas only one-third of those with such scores at the group *C* schools want to do so. Those who adhere to the interpretation of intelligence test scores as more or less valid measures of innate capacity will see the "waste" of talent implicit in the horizontal contrasts in Table 12, from the stance of the prevalent concern with the conservation of talent.

Comparing the effect of the school climate upon grades and upon educational aspirations in Tables 9 and 3, we can see that the devaluation of

Table 12
Percentages Aspiring to Go to College
by School Groups and IQ Scores

	School Group		
IQ Score	*A*	*B*	*C*
120+	96%	83%	33%
	(100)	(81)	(18)
110–119	93	72	51
	(128)	(108)	(53)
100–109	76	52	41
	(87)	(89)	(82)
90–99	47	24	35
	(30)	(63)	(68)
89–	25	29	25
	(12)	(69)	(111)

[16] This relationship disappears among those with IQ's below 89—that is, those for whom collegiate aspirations are unrealistic.

education in the working-class schools affects academic achievement as much as it is reflected in educational aspirations. In fact, it adversely affects the achievement of the sons of professional and white-collar workers more than it does their aspirations.

TANGENTIAL CONFIRMATION

The imputation of the variation in educational aspirations and behavior between schools to the "moral force" of the normative values within the school society is of course inferential.[17] This interpretation has been argued, up to this point, by holding constant other factors known to affect educational attitudes and attributing the residual difference to the hypothetical factor. The hypothesis, moreover, is theoretically congruent with a considerable accumulation of research on small groups, studies of peer-group influences, and of the differential effects of contrasting community structures: it has been shown that the perception of the opportunity for upward mobility by lower-strata youth is facilitated by the economic and occupational heterogeneity of the community.[18] Yet, if Occam's razor is to be scrupulously applied against the contextual hypothesis, it might be argued that, however homogeneous the students' familial backgrounds may be in terms of all available external indices, those working-class families living in predominantly middle-class districts are showing "anticipatory socialization" in their values and are inculcating them in their children.

While the latter interpretation is reasonable, it is not so persuasive to argue the corollary that middle-class families would act to depress the aspirations of their children if they live in a predominantly working-class neighborhood. ". . . inherent in the very existence of a stratification order, of higher and lower valuations of social positions, is the motivation to move up in the social structure if one's position is low, or to retain one's position if it is high."[19] It is plausible to assume that middle-class youth, even when living in a predominantly working-class neighborhood, will be stimulated by their families toward educational diligence and to aspire to high-status occupations. The fact that the aspiration of these children is depressed when they attend a working-class school is more compelling evidence for the effect of the school milieu and peer-group norms than is the fact of the upward mobility of working-class youths in middle-class schools.

It has been reported frequently that students from middle-class families are generally over-selected for peer-group leadership positions. But "in order to become a *leader* . . . one must share prevailing opinions and atti-

17 This requires no apology—the step from data to a theoretical proposition is always inferential. One does not *see* a cause.
18 Lipset and Bendix, *Social Mobility* . . . , *op. cit.*, pp. 220–224.
19 *Ibid.*, p. 203.

tudes."[20] This view has led to a presumption of the universality of upward aspirations. It was found in the present study, however, that one-half of those who had held peer-group offices in the group *C* schools were children of manual workers, while only eight per cent of those in the group *A* schools were the sons of manual workers (see Table 13). The distribution of peer-group offices among occupational strata is very close to that of the student bodies at large at each school group (as can be seen by comparing Table 13 with the first distribution in Table 2). But, consequently, the leaders who reflect, express, and mold the attitudes of the school society reinforce and extend the pre-existing differences in group characteristics.

Table 13
Distribution of Peer-Group Offices Among
Occupational Strata by Schools

		School Group	
Father's Occupation	*A*	*B*	*C*
Professional	25%	9%	3%
White collar	49	38	40
Self employed	18	29	7
Manual	8	24	50
Number of cases*	154	160	92

* Percentages are based on the number of students who have held some peer-group office—either within the school, such as team captain, student council member or class president, or outside of school, as an officer of "De Molay," "Teen-age Club," or similar group.

THE IMPACT OF SCHOOL NORMS UPON OTHER VALUES

Sociologists concerned with inter-generational mobility and the formation of social attitudes might well direct more attention to the investigation of contextual variables—attributes of membership groups which serve as references during the adolescent period of socialization—particularly to the society of the school. While the importance of both the family and the peer-group in the development of the economic and political values of the adolescent have been pointed out, most investigation has concentrated upon the influence of the family.[21] That the influence of the school climate is not

[20] Katz and Lazarsfeld, *op. cit.,* p. 52.
[21] Richard Centers, "Children of the New Deal: Social Stratification and Adolescent Attitudes," in *Class, Status and Power, op. cit.,* pp. 359–370; S. M. Lipset *et al.,* "The Psychology of Voting: An Analysis of Political Behavior," in G. Lindzey, editor, *Handbook of Social Psychology,* Cambridge: Addison-Wesley, Vol. II, pp. 1124–1175.

confined to education aspirations is shown by brief explorations, presented in Tables 14 and 15, into the differences between schools in occupational aspirations and in political preferences. These tables provide *prima facie* evidence, comparable to that of Table 3, suggesting that the dominant climate of opinion within a school makes a significant impact upon students' occupational goals and their political party preferences.

Table 14
Percentages Aspiring to Professional Occupations by School Groups and Fathers' Occupations

Fathers' Occupation	School Group		
	A	B	C
Professional	78%	60%	60%
	(81)	(35)	(10)
White collar	61	37	35
	(160)	(120)	(31)
Self employed	44	47	23
	(62)	(79)	(106)
Manual	44	31	27
	(36)	(121)	(198)
Weighted mean of per cents	60	39	30
	(339)	(355)	(345)

Table 15
Percentages Expressing Preference for the Republican Party by School Groups and Fathers' Occupations

Fathers' Occupation	School Group		
	A	B	C
Professional	81%	71%	33%
	(73)	(31)	(9)
White collar	72	64	36
	(120)	(98)	(72)
Self employed	80	62	39
	(56)	(68)	(23)
Manual	50	32	24
	(26)	(107)	(161)
Weighted mean of per cents	74	53	29
	(275)*	(304)*	(265)*

* Percentages are based on the number of students expressing preference for the Republican or Democratic party, omitting those who indicated "other," "none," or failed to respond.

CONCLUSION

Whether the modification of attitudes by the normative climate of the school society persists or a reversion toward familial norms in later life takes place cannot be determined on the basis of static comparisons. But certainly the student's high school achievement and his decision for or against college entrance have irreversible consequences in channeling him into the stream of economic and social life, and in biasing the probability of future intimate contact with countervailing reference groups.

The Supreme Court has found that, even though the "tangible" provisions of schools are the same, schools segregated along racial lines are inherently unequal. The "sense of inferiority affects the motivation of the child to learn." The *de facto* segregation brought about by concentrations of social classes in cities results in schools with unequal moral climates which likewise affect the motivation of the child, not necessarily by inculcating a sense of inferiority, but rather by providing a different ethos in which to perceive values.

Psychological Health and Classroom Functioning: A Study of Dissatisfaction with School Among Adolescents*[1]

PHILIP W. JACKSON AND
JACOB W. GETZELS

School achievement is generally assumed to be a prime factor in youth's satisfaction or dissatisfaction with high school. The data of Jackson and Getzels, however, place the authority of this venerable notion in jeopardy. "Contrary to popular expectations the 'satisfied' and 'dissatisfied' students did not differ from each other in either general intellectual ability or in scholastic achievement." The researchers assert that "dissatisfaction with school appears to be part of a larger picture of psychological discontent rather than a direct reflection of inefficient functioning in the classroom."

The problem of dissatisfaction with school among children is of theoretical and practical significance to both psychologists and educators. At the theoretical level dissatisfaction with school becomes part of a broader area of inquiry which aims at an understanding of the individual's functioning in an institutional setting and which includes studies of staff morale, role conflict, productivity, and the like. At a practical level the question of why children like or dislike school is directly related to the immediate problems of school dropouts, grouping procedures, planning for the gifted child, and the like.

As might be expected, a social phenomenon as important as dissatisfaction with school is not without its explanatory hypothesis. Some of these spring from empirical findings, while others appear to be part of our cul-

[1] This study was supported by a research grant from the United States Office of Education. The present report is an expanded version of a paper read at the American Psychological Association meeting, Cincinnati, Ohio, September 1959.

* From the *Journal of Abnormal and Social Psychology*, L (1959), pp. 295–300. Reprinted by permission of the authors and the American Psychological Association.

tural ethos. Educational studies that point to an empirical linkage between school failure and school dropouts, and industrial studies that demonstrate a relationship between low morale and decreased output, lead one to suspect that reduced effectiveness in school (i.e., low scholastic achievement) would be a natural concomitant of dissatisfaction with the institution. Thus one would expect to find heightened dissatisfaction among students who have low ability or who are unable for one reason or another to deal adequately with scholastic material.

More recently it has been suggested (although never adequately demonstrated) that many successful students with high ability are dissatisfied with their school experiences; the term "boredom" is often linked with the term "gifted child" in current expositions by educators. The boredom problem among "gifted" combined with the failure experiences of the low ability child suggests that the greatest number of dissatisfied students is to be found among extreme ability groups. Those who are low in ability and achievement would be expected to show dissatisfaction because of the numerous frustrations they experience in the classroom. Those who are high in ability and achievement would be expected to show dissatisfaction because of the relative lack of stimulation which they experience in the classroom.

Both of these explanations (or, more accurately, hypotheses) contain the implication that dissatisfaction with an institution arises out of the individual's interaction with that institution. An alternative explanation might be that the individual brings a set toward satisfaction or dissatisfaction *to* the institution—that it is a reflection of a more pervasive personal orientation and that success or failure experiences within the institution have a limited influence upon it. This hypothesis obviously places more emphasis than do the earlier ones upon psychological variables, as opposed to environmental variables, in understanding dissatisfaction with school. The research described here was designed to test the relative merit of these alternative views.

PROBLEM

The purpose of this investigation is to examine the differences in psychological functioning and classroom effectiveness between two groups of adolescents—those who are satisfied with their recent school experiences and those who are dissatisfied.

SUBJECTS AND PROCEDURE

The *S*s of this investigation were two groups of adolescents identified from among 531 students enrolled in a Midwestern private school. These students were divided into five class groups ranging from the prefreshmen to the senior year of high school. In this institution a single grade, the pre-freshmen, is substituted for the usual seventh and eighth grades. The instrument used to select the experimental groups, called the Student Opinion Poll, was a 60-item opinionnaire designed to elicit responses concerning general satisfaction or dissatisfaction with various aspects of school—viz., the teachers, the curriculum, the student body, and classroom procedures. The following are sample items, one in each of the four areas.

3. While there are some differences among them, most teachers in this school are:
   a. Very inspiring
   b. Quite inspiring
   c. Somewhat inspiring
   d. Not inspiring
16. Most of the subjects taught in the school are:
   a. Interesting and challenging
   b. Somewhat above average in interest
   c. Somewhat below average in interest
   d. Dull and routine
14. From the standpoint of intellectual ability, students in this school are:
   a. Too bright—it is difficult to keep up with them
   b. Just bright enough
   c. Not bright enough—they do not provide enough intellectual stimulation
5. The freedom to contribute something in class without being called upon by the teacher is:
   a. Discouraged more than it should be—students do not have enough opportunity to have their say
   b. Encouraged more than it should be—students seem to be rewarded just for speaking even when they have little to say
   c. Handled about right

The instrument was scored by giving one point each time the S chose the "most satisfied" response to a multiple-choice item. Thus, the possible range of scores was from 0 to 60. For the total school population the mean score on the Student Opinion Poll was 37.30; the standard deviation was 9.57. The experimental groups were chosen as follows:

Group I—the "dissatisfied" group—consisted of all students whose score on the opinionnaire was at least one and a half standard deviations *below* the mean of the entire student body. This group contained 27 boys and 20 girls.

Group II—the "satisfied" group—consisted of all students whose score on the opinionnaire was at least one and a half standard deviations *above* the mean of the entire student body. This group contained 25 boys and 20 girls.

The experimental groups were compared on the following variables:

1. *Individual intelligence tests.* In most cases this was the Binet. A small number of children were given the Henmon-Nelson, the scores of which were converted by regression equation into equivalent Binet scores.

2. *Standardized verbal achievement test.* The Cooperative Reading Test was used. Prefreshmen and freshmen were given Test C_1, Form Y; older students were given C_2, Form T.

3. *Standardized numerical achievement tests.* Because of differences in the curricula of the various grade groups it was not possible to administer the same test of numerical achievement to all Ss. The following tests were given according to grade placement:

Prefreshman—Iowa Everypupil Arithmetic Test, Advanced Form O.
Freshmen—Snader General Mathematics Test.
Sophomores—Cooperative Elementary Algebra Test, Form T.
Juniors—Cooperative Intermediate Algebra Test.
Seniors—Cooperative Geometry Test, Form 2.

4. *California Personality Test.* Two forms of this instrument were used. The intermediate form was given to prefreshmen; the secondary form was given to all of the older groups. Two subscores were obtained, "personal adjustment" and "social adjustment."

5. *Direct Sentence Completion Test.* Ss were asked to complete 27 sentences of the type: "When I saw I was going to fail I . . . ," or, "I think my father is . . ." Each sentence was given a plus or minus score depending upon the presence or absence of morbid fantasy, defeatism, overt aggression, and the like. The total score was the summation of the individual sentence scores.

6. *Indirect Sentence Completion Test.* This instrument was identical with the Direct Sentence Completion Test except that proper names were inserted for the pronoun "I," thus changing it from a "self-report" to a "projective" instrument. Boys' names were used in the male form of the instrument and girls' names in the female form. The instrument was presented as a "thinking speed" test. To reinforce this notion Ss were asked to raise their hands when they were finished and the elapsed time was written on their test booklet. This instrument was administered approximately two weeks prior to the administration of the Direct Sentence Completion Test.

7. *Group Rorschach.* Cards III, IV, IX, and X were projected on a screen. For each picture the S was presented with 10 responses and was asked to choose the three which he thought to be most appropriate. Each list of 10 contained four "pathological" responses. The S's score was the number of non-pathologic responses among his 12 choices. This group technique follows that described by Harrower-Erikson and Steiner.[2]

8. *Teacher ratings.* Each student was given three ratings by his present teachers. These ratings included: (*a*) his general desirability as a student; (*b*) his ability to become involved in learning activities; and (*c*) his possession of

[2] M. R. Harrower-Erikson and M. E. Steiner, *Large Scale Rorschach Techniques* (Springfield, Ill.: Charles C. Thomas, 1945).

leadership qualities. Teachers were required to place all of their students on a five-point scale so that Categories 1 and 5 each contained one-twelfth of the students; Categories 2 and 4 each contained one-fourth of the students; and Category 3 contained one-third of the students. The values 5, 8, 10, 12, and 15 were assigned to the categories and were used in quantifying the ratings.

9. *Adjective Check List*. From a list of 24 adjectives each student was asked to choose the 6 which best described his characteristic feelings while attending classes in particular school subjects. The list contained 12 "positive" (e.g., confident, happy, eager, relaxed) and 12 "negative" adjectives (e.g., bored, restless, misunderstood, angry). The use of the negative adjectives by the experimental groups was analyzed both quantitatively and qualitatively.

RESULTS

With the exception of the adjective check list the results of all comparisons are shown in Table 1. Contrary to popular expectations the "satisfied" and "dissatisfied" students did *not* differ from each other in either general intellectual ability or in scholastic achievement. Those differences which did appear were linked to psychological rather than scholastic variables. More specifically, each of the test instruments designed to assess psychological health or "adjustment" was effective in distinguishing "satisfied" from "dissatisfied" students within one or both sex groups.

For both sexes the experimental groups were differentiated by their scores on the California Test of Personality. The experimental groups of boys were further differentiated by their responses to the Indirect Sentence Completion Test. For girls additional differences appeared in their responses to the Direct Sentence Completion Test and the Group Rorschach.

On all of these test variables the "satisfied" group attained the "better" score—i.e., the score signifying a more adequate level of psychological functioning. It is also worthy of note that whenever a significant difference appeared, the mean score of the total student population fell between the mean scores of the experimental groups. Thus, the variables that differentiate the experimental groups tend also to distinguish them from the total population of students.

In addition to showing differences on psychological health variables, "satisfied" and "dissatisfied" boys were perceived differently by their teachers. On all three of the teachers' ratings the "satisfied" boys received more favorable judgments than did "dissatisfied" boys. The fact that this result does not appear to be true for girls lends support to the popular expectation that boys are more likely to express their negative feelings publicly than are girls. This hypothesis receives some confirmation from the results of the adjective check list which are described below.

In Table 2 are shown the number of *S*s who chose negative adjectives when asked to describe their typical classroom feelings. As they are arranged in Table 2 the adjectives reflect the rankings of four judges who were asked to rank the words on the degree to which they involved an implicit or explicit criticism of others. The 12 adjectives were typed on separate cards and were accompanied by the following directions:

On the following cards are a number of negative adjectives which a person might use to describe himself. Rank these adjectives on the degree to which they involve an implicit or explicit criticism of others. For each adjective ask the question: If a person used this adjective to *describe himself* would he also be implicitly or explicitly criticizing others? Give a rank of 1 to the adjective which would be *least* critical of others and a rank of 12 to the adjective which would be *most* critical of others.

Four psychologists served as judges. The average rank order correlation among the four sets of judgments was .84. The adjectives are presented in Table 2 according to the ranked sum-of-ranks of the judges. The adjective "inadequate" was judged as being most free of criticism of others, while the adjective "restrained" was judged as involving the greatest amount of criticism of others.

As might be expected, the use of negative adjectives was far more frequent among dissatisfied students than among satisfied students. Four adjectives seemed to discriminate equally well between the experimental groups for both sexes; these were: "bored," "angry," "restrained," and "dull."

An examination of Table 2 also suggests the existence of sex differences in the students' description of their typical classroom feelings. Remembering the classificatory scheme by which the adjectives are ranked in Table 2, it appears that dissatisfied girls are somewhat less likely than dissatisfied boys to use negative adjectives involving implicit criticism of others. Dissatisfied boys, on the other hand, are less likely than dissatisfied girls to be distinguished from their satisfied counterparts by the use of adjectives *not* involving implicit criticism of others. If one thinks of criticism directed toward others within Rosenzweig's schema of "intropunitiveness" and "extrapunitiveness,"[3] then the observed sex differences may be conceptualized by saying that dissatisfied girls are more *intropunitive* than satisfied girls; dissatisfied boys are more *extrapunitive* than satisfied boys.

This difference in the direction of aggression may provide a context for the obtained differences in teacher ratings discussed earlier. If the dissatisfied boy is more likely than his female counterpart to lay the blame for his dissatisfaction upon others in his environment, particularly school authorities, it is reasonable to expect that he would be viewed as somewhat less

[3] H. A. Murray, *Explorations in Personality* (New York: Oxford University Press, 1938).

Table 1
Mean Scores, Standard Deviations, and t Statistics for Satisfied and Dissatisfied Adolescents on Dependent Variables‡

| | Boys | | | | | | Girls | | | | | |
| | Dissatisfied (N = 27) | | Satisfied (N = 25) | | | Dissatisfied (N = 20) | | Satisfied (N = 20) | | |
	$\bar{x}$	s	$\bar{x}$	s	t	$\bar{x}$	s	$\bar{x}$	s	t
IQ	134.85	14.58	136.44	14.59	ns	128.45	15.06	128.00	11.45	ns
Verbal Achievement	49.96	8.69	50.68	7.87	ns	50.63	9.11	52.28	6.76	ns
Numerical Achievement	50.35	9.75	52.17	10.52	ns	47.78	8.61	48.50	10.26	ns
Calif. Personal Adjust.	45.58	9.82	53.40	7.63	3.18†	47.90	13.03	54.76	9.25	1.86*
Calif. Social Adjust.	44.85	11.37	51.84	8.93	2.45†	47.00	13.15	55.76	7.89	2.50†
Direct Sentence Comp.	46.93	10.58	49.25	10.02	ns	46.65	12.01	54.00	5.73	2.53†
Indirect Sentence Comp.	47.19	9.61	51.29	6.95	1.75*	49.60	10.35	53.47	7.97	ns
Group Rorschach	48.35	10.66	47.44	10.30	ns	47.35	11.35	54.16	8.32	2.15†
Teacher Rating I:										
Desirability as a student	8.94	1.83	10.35	1.70	2.85†	9.84	1.91	10.05	1.59	ns
Teacher Rating II:										
Leadership qualities	9.01	2.08	10.13	1.96	2.00*	9.91	2.37	10.04	1.24	ns
Teacher Rating III:										
Involvement in learning	9.09	2.14	10.23	1.69	2.14†	9.67	2.32	10.33	2.11	ns

* Significant at the .05 level.
† Significant at the .01 level.
‡ With the exception of IQ, all scores were based upon parameters of the total student body from which the experimental groups were drawn. The scores of all tests were transformed to T scores with a mean of 50 and a standard deviation of 10. For the total population the teacher ratings have a mean of 10 and a standard deviation of 2. The mean IQs for the total school population are: boys, 132, and girls, 128.

Table 2
Number of Subjects Choosing Negative Adjectives When Asked to Describe Typical Classroom Feelings

Adjective	Boys			Girls		
	Dis-satisfied ($N = 27$)	Satisfied ($N = 25$)	Chi Square	Dis-satisfied ($N = 20$)	Satisfied ($N = 20$)	Chi Square
Inadequate	19	16	ns	17	7	10.42†
Ignorant	19	13	ns	15	3	14.54†
Dull	25	16	6.36*	16	9	5.60*
Bored	24	13	8.61†	20	13	8.48†
Restless	20	15	ns	19	9	11.90†
Uncertain	20	21	ns	17	13	ns
Angry	15	4	8.76†	13	4	8.29†
Unnoticed	19	5	13.25†	7	4	ns
Unhelped	18	8	6.24*	9	6	ns
Misunderstood	16	5	8.31†	5	2	ns
Rejected	12	3	6.66†	4	0	ns
Restrained	17	2	16.91†	9	3	4.29*

* Significant at the .05 level.
† Significant at the .01 level.

than completely desirable by the classroom teacher. The dissatisfied girl, on the other hand, seems more willing to direct her negative feelings inward, thus avoiding the additional risk of counter-aggression by school authorities or by other adults.

DISCUSSION

Two major conclusions are suggested by the findings of this study. First, dissatisfaction with school appears to be part of a larger picture of psychological discontent rather than a direct reflection of inefficient functioning in the classroom. It is almost as if dissatisfaction were a product of a pervasive perceptual set that colors the student's view of himself and his world. Second, it appears that the "dynamics" of dissatisfaction operate differently for boys and girls. Boys seem to project the causes of their discontent upon the world around them so that adults are seen as rejecting and lacking in understanding. This tendency to blame adults may be one reason why these boys are seen as less attractive by teachers than are satisfied boys. Girls, on the other hand, are more likely to be self-critical, turning blame for their dissatisfaction inward. Feelings of inadequacy, ignorance, and restlessness more sharply differentiate satisfied and dissatisfied girls than is the case with boys. This tendency to be intropunitive may partially explain why teacher ratings fail to distinguish between our two experimental groups of girls.

The atypicality of the sample population used in this research places a number of limitations upon the inferential statements which can be made on the basis of these findings. Fortunately, however, the major portion of the investigation has recently been replicated using seventh and eighth grade lower-class Negro adolescents as Ss.[4] The findings of the latter study are essentially the same as those reported here. Again the psychological rather than the intellectual or scholastic variables discriminated between satisfied and dissatisfied students. The findings with respect to the use of negative adjectives were not as clear-cut but, again, every intropunitive adjective was used more frequently by dissatisfied girls as compared with dissatisfied boys, while the latter exceeded the girls in their use of extra-punitive adjectives.

It should be noted that even the most satisfied students made some use of negative adjectives when asked to describe their typical feelings in the classroom. Also, the average member of the satisfied group expressed some dissatisfaction on one-sixth of the questions in the Student Opinion Poll. These two observations should serve as ample cautions against the danger of interpreting any sign of dissatisfaction with school as symptomatic of deeper psychological difficulties. Apparently, some degree of dissatisfaction is the rule rather than the exception. Nonetheless, the responses of the extremely disgruntled group of students leaves little doubt that dissatisfaction with school, like beauty, is frequently in the eye of the beholder.

SUMMARY

This investigation examines the differences in psychological functioning and classroom effectiveness between two groups of adolescents—those who are satisfied with their recent school experiences and those who are dissatisfied. The major findings point to: (*a*) the relevance of psychological health data rather than scholastic achievement data in understanding dissatisfaction with school; (*b*) the importance of differentiating the attitudes of dissatisfied girls from those of dissatisfied boys, the former being characterized by feelings of personal inadequacy, the latter by feelings critical of school authorities. Rosenzweig's concepts of intropunitiveness and extrapunitiveness are applied to these findings and a relevant theoretical framework is proposed.

4 R. J. Spillman, "Psychological and Scholastic Correlates of Dissatisfactions with School among Adolescents" (unpublished Master's thesis, University of Chicago, 1959).

High School Antecedents of Young Adult Achievement*[1]

ROBERT D. HESS

Adolescence is viewed traditionally as a period of transition, bridging the developmental chasm between childhood and adulthood. Of the various aspects of adolescence that have been investigated, the adolescent's passage into adult social roles and responsibilities has been accorded relatively little attention. Yet as Hess suggests, in the following paper, late adolescence and early adulthood may be "a more critical period of development than is adolescence." His findings show that successful performance in the early twenties, as evaluated by occupational commitment, psychological health, and social accomplishment and skill is "more closely related to events and experiences that occur after high school than to high school behavior." Furthermore, his "data indicate the fluid and unstable nature of adolescent behavior patterns," and provide substantive, empirical support for the notion "that the processes of identity that make for stable adult behavior and personality continue well past high school."

In American society the late teens and early twenties span a period of critical psychosocial career development in the life of the typical young person. In a sense the post–high school years give the adolescent his first opportunity to make his own decisions in major life areas. Until this time he has undergone a long period of more or less compulsory socialization in two of the central institutions of the society—the family and the public school.

[1] The study upon which this paper is based was directed by Professor Allison Davis and the author. It was supported by a grant (HEW SAE 8138) from the Cooperative Research Bureau of the United States Office of Education and by grants-in-aid from the Social Science Research Committee of the University of Chicago. We wish to acknowledge the assistance of Mr. Jack Forman in the preparation of material for this paper.

* This paper was prepared especially for this volume. It is an expanded version of a paper that was presented at the annual meetings of the American Educational Research Association, Atlantic City, February 1962.

In this transition period the structuring of his behavior is less compelling, and he is in a position to exercise some impact upon the events and situations which will eventually determine the nature and direction of his career.

The fluid and formative character of adolescence has been described by many writers, but there is little theory or information about the processes which bring to an end the diffuse features of this stage of development. There has been a tendency to see adolescence as a period of preparation and rehearsal for adult roles and an implicit assumption that such experimentation *per se* is a good thing which will accrue positive carry-over to adult behavior. The reinforcing impact of the peer group has been given particularly high value; the advantages of intensive and extensive social experience with peers of both sexes has seldom been questioned.

Late adolescence, however, is a time for transition from one age grade to another in our society and there is a need for more thorough study of the steps by which this transition is completed. This is especially important in view of the fact that the society does not establish a formal, well-defined set of experiences which lead the pre-adult into the roles and behavior he will be called upon to demonstrate as an equal member of the adult community. An equally important problem is the extent of the influence of adolescent and childhood experience upon the ease with which the transition to adulthood can be accomplished and upon adult achievement and behavior. The question we posed in our research was this: do the relative experience and success of teenagers in either the academic or social areas during high school hold a systematic relationship to subsequent performance as young adults?

This report deals with the time of transition from the viewpoint of educational and developmental psychology. It is based upon a follow-up study of a high school senior class and is concerned with analysis of data gathered at two points in time, rather than a sequence of longitudinal data. It involves three major dimensions of behavior: achievement in work, integration into the social aspects of the community, and the development of internal areas of experience—self-evaluation, satisfaction with accomplishments, and identity. The emphasis in this report will center upon the achievement-success variables of the project and upon the relationships between school performance and later performance measures.

DESIGN OF THE PROJECT

This project began in 1952 with a study of 351 metropolitan high school seniors. The high school was located in a stable community and drew from both white-collar and working-class families. There were few professional families in the district and almost no students from slum areas.

The design of the project rests upon the analysis of relationships between behavior observed or reported in two points in time: the high school senior year when the subjects were approximately 17 or 18 years of age, and eight years later when the members of the class were in their mid-twenties. Several obvious advantages would have accrued from access to data at some point between these two ages, but data were not available to us on a systematic basis.

The High School Study: Definition of Variables

The information gathered in the high school phase, and the measures derived from the original data sources may be grouped into three broad areas of behavior.

A. Measures of Academic Talent and Achievement.

1. A composite measure of scholastic ability, based upon administrations of two standard group intelligence tests.
2. Grade point average, based upon performance in academic subjects during the junior and senior years in high school.
3. Rank in class, based upon the school's records of performance in all subjects over the four-year high school period.
4. Disparity score, derived from a comparison of the subject's relative standing on the composite measure of scholastic ability and grade point average.

B. Measures of Social Facility and Participation.   Information gathered in this area was intended to afford an estimate of the degree of participation, rather than the nature of interpersonal relationships. The measures used were:

1. Membership in formally-approved clubs and organizations within the context of the high school's official activities.
2. Membership in informal social clubs at school not recognized or approved by the school administration. These clubs were organized in the sense that they elected officers, held regular meetings, were known to the student body, and followed a set of regulations developed by the members.
3. Mutual choice friends in the senior class. Social activities were indicated by responses to a questionnaire which included sociometric-type items.
4. Membership in formal organizations outside of high school. This measure indicated the number of adult-sponsored (church youth groups, YMCA, etc.) associations in which the subject held membership.
5. Membership in informal groups and clubs outside of school. The

distinction between participation in cliques and memberships in informal clubs was sometimes difficult to make. The criteria adopted were that an informal club was one with administrative structure (president, etc.), that held regular meetings, had a name, and was not sponsored or supervised by an adult or adult organization.

6. Teachers' ratings on social ability of the high school class. The ratings indicated the teacher's opinion of the social adeptness and success of the student. Teachers' ratings were averaged for each subject to obtain a perceived sociability score.

7. Popularity votes by peers. The questionnaire administered to the high school class asked each senior to list the names of his classmates who were "the most outstanding" members of the class.

C. **Information on Attitudes and Other Internal States.** Our initial testing schedule included a group-administered Murray Thematic Apperception Test, an Incomplete Sentences Test, and a number of questions which probed the student's motivation for post-high school achievement and his feelings about his high school experience.

In addition to the data included in these major categories, information was obtained from the sample on a number of variables dealing with family background and with parental attitudes toward future education and career choice.

The Follow-Up Study

The follow-up study was planned as a basis for examining the high school antecedents of adult performance. The central thrust of the adult phase of the project was the attempt to discover and understand the social, emotional, and psychological factors in adolescents of high-school age which indicated the likelihood of later achievement or failure by these persons in adult roles and responsibilities.

With this broad objective in mind we decided to contact as many of the original class as possible. However, the total amount of data to be obtained from each subject was so great that a decision was made to obtain certain minimal information from the majority of the class and extensive information from a small proportion of the class. This proportion was selected to represent the total senior class in several important respects.

One of the central problems in designing the instruments of the follow-up study was the attempt to obtain data in areas of behavior comparable to behavior measured in the initial study. It was decided that information should be gathered in the three broad areas already indicated—work-achievement, social, and psychological—even though the instrument and questions used would not be identical. The character of the follow-up study was, by necessity, based on individual interview contacts. While some of our data were obtained by mailed questionnaires, the larger part of the data on which this report is based was elicited in face-to-face interview situations, a methodological consideration that should be kept in mind in evaluating the results.

The Follow-Up Study: Definition of Variables

On the basis of staff conferences and preliminary interviewing, a guided questionnaire was prepared to include multiple-choice as well as open-end questions. In addition to the interview, the data-gathering session included administration of a semantic differential and a TAT. The types of information obtained from each subject of the intensive sample may be summarized in categories roughly comparable to those of the earlier phase of the project.

A. **Measures of Work Achievement and Social Prestige.** The information gathered in this area of behavior was intended to reflect accomplishments in the area of success as defined in the society—the acquisition of prestige in the community and the development of earning power. The specific measures involved were: level of occupation, defined in terms of a scale of occupational prestige based upon the categories used by Warner and modified for use in a metropolitan region by McCall;[2] income; social mobility, defined as social status of subject relative to social status of father when the subject was in high school.

B. **Measures of Social Participation and Involvement in the Community.** These measures attempted to assess both informal and formal social activity on these specific points: membership in formal institutions of the community (i.e. church, lodge, civic, and other service organizations); membership in informal social clubs (i.e. organizations of primarily social nature, including sports); range and number of informal social activities; frequency and type of interaction with friends; and interaction with family of origin.

C. **Measures of Psychosocial Responses and Adaptation to Young Adulthood.** Our techniques for gathering data relating to internal states ranged from projective devices to direct questions asking for self-evaluation and satisfaction with achievement. In addition each subject was rated by the interviewer on several scales. The methods used were: self-report, each subject rating himself on satisfaction with his achievement in three

[2] W. Lloyd Warner, Marchia Meeker, and Kenneth Eells, *Social Class in America* (Chicago: Science Research Associates, Inc., 1949). Bevode McCall, Report Number Three on the Chicago Tribune Sample Census, February 15, 1956, Appendix I: Methodological and Operational Considerations in the Application of the Index of Status Characteristics to the Metropolitan Community, unpublished manuscript.

areas—work, social activities, and family; evaluation of self-concept based upon semantic differential rating scales; projective material elicited by the Thematic Apperception Technique; and interview ratings. Based upon the interview with each subject, the interviewer rated the respondent on a scale that indicated the extent to which the subject had completed the transition from adolescence to young adulthood.

The central purpose of the rating was to indicate the degree to which the individual under consideration had assumed the responsibilities of adult life in this society. Three formal criteria were selected as most nearly representing the basic and minimal expectations of adults in this country: an occupation, as represented by a steady job or career (including housewife); marriage as a representation of sexual identity; and residence apart from parent's home as representing responsibility for one's own way of life and readiness to establish a family. The interviewer exercised judgment in applying these criteria so that an unmarried person who had clearly taken on adult roles and responsibilities was not necessarily rated lower than maximum. A school teacher, for example, who was pursuing a professional career might receive a rating as high as a woman who had taken on the roles of wife and mother.

Method of Analysis

The relationships between high school achievement and young adult performance were examined by several procedures. The results of this analysis are presented in a report now in preparation for the Cooperative Research Bureau of the Office of Education. The most general summary of the findings relevant to the topic of this paper is, first, that there is a great deal of variability and change between the adolescent and young adult patterns of behavior; and second, the area showing greatest consistency and predictive power was scholastic performance in high school.

Because of the prominence of high school scholastic achievement as an indication of later success, this report will be confined to the analysis of four criterion groups based upon achievement during high school and young adulthood. High and low achievement in high school was defined on the basis of grades, taking the upper and lower 30 per cent as the cut-off points. High achievement in young adulthood was defined by any one of three criteria: level of occupation, social mobility of at least one social class step, and salary. Low achievement was defined by level of occupation, downward mobility, and salary. No individual qualified for the high group if he were low in any one of the three criteria; no individual qualified for the low group if he were high in any one of the three criteria.

Combining criteria at both high school and young adult levels resulted in the following achievement groups:

High-high Group: subjects who were relatively high academic achievers in high school and who were in relatively high occupational levels or were socially mobile eight years later

High-low Group: subjects who were high achievers in high school but low in occupational achievement

Low-high Group: subjects who were low achievers in high school and high in occupational achievement

Low-low Group: subjects who were low in achievement at both points in time

Of the original 351 subjects, 51 males and 69 females fell into one or another of these four groups (Table 1). The four groups were aligned in several ways for purpose of comparison on each variable to be considered. For example, those who were high in school performance were compared with those who were low, irrespective of young adult performance; those high in young adult performance were compared with those low in young adult performance, irrespective of high school performance; those high in young adulthood but low in high school performance were compared with those high in both, and so forth. All possible comparisons were made in which differences in the variables under consideration could have been attributed to either high school or young adult performance.

RESULTS

Using achievement as the dependent variable, we will present data bearing on the relationship between patterns of achieving behavior and other areas of performance at the high school and young adult periods. While this strategy focuses upon a fairly specific type of performance and is thus somewhat limited in scope, it also provides a method for a gross examination of the consistency of behavior in several other sectors.

Relationship of Achievement Grouping to Adolescent Behavior

Scholastic Ability and Performance. As indicated above, the absolute level of high school grades was the most potent indicator of later success, particularly for males. This pattern raised a question about the extent to which such achievement, at both high school and adult levels, is a function of mental ability, as measured by tests, and how much it is a consequence of industry. In our data the relationship between intelligence and grades was significant at typical levels ($r = .56$) and so differences of ability among the four achievement groupings were apparent. However, intelligence did not distinguish among the post–high school achievement groups to the same degree. In part, this change was accounted for by the relative achievement of females (as measured by husband's occupation in the follow-up stage) which tended to decline more than did that of males.[3]

A similar pattern was found for the tendency to over- or under-achieve (*disparity scores*) as measured by the discrepancy between grades and IQ. High school performance in all groupings was related to disparity scores, but these scores were not predictive of occupational success. (See Table 2.)

As was expected, the amount of post–high school education differed greatly among the groups, as the data in Table 3 show. Those who did well scholastically in high school more often went on to college and went farther in higher education than did low school achievers.

Social Class Background, Social Skills, and Activities.   The typical relationship between social class background and school achievement did not appear in our data, possibly because of the relatively homogeneous nature of this senior class and because of the self-selective motivational factors which kept those young people in high school while many of their peers from unskilled and semi-skilled occupational levels had already dropped out. At any rate, neither the ISC nor occupational level of the students' fathers differentiated among any of the four groups in any combination.

Social participation seems to have slight association with both high school performance and success in young adulthood. The high-high group was consistently high on all social variables (with one exception) and the low-lows were low. Table 4 presents the patterns of social activity by achievement groupings. Although the difference between groups on any given measure was relatively small, it is significant that all the differences were in the same direction; i.e., the high-highs were more socially active than the low-lows, with the high-lows being intermediate in most cases.[4]

While differences in social behavior between the extreme achievement groups may be considered significant, that is, not merely random fluctuation, the relationship between high school social skills and young adult performance was not great. A study of the 20 socially most popular and prominent members of the senior class showed that this group did not maintain a relative advantage or success in either social or other areas of young adult performance when compared with a matched group of socially non-prominant peers.

Personality and Family Data.   Although the subjects' level of occupa-

---

[3] There were a number of differences between males and females in the relationship between high school and young adult performance. For example, the correlation between occupational level and disparity scores in high school was positive and significant for males (.27) but not for females (.11); the correlation between grades and occupation was .54 for males in the total sample on which we had data but only .39 for females.

[4] The consistency that appeared from one measure to another was not a result of a high relationship among them. The actual correlation among these variables for the total group were very low.

tional aspiration (as reported in the high school phase of the study) was associated with academic success, such aspiration held no relation to actual occupational success later. Similarly, those whose parents held high occupational aspirations for them did well in high school but did not necessarily show occupational achievement as adults. Neither fathers' nor mothers' attitudes toward college attendance of our subjects or actual level of parental education bore any relationship to the subject's success either in high school or after.

From the Thematic Apperception Test given the subjects, a measure (ego functioning) was designed to indicate the individual's ability to perceive reality accurately, to recognize the salient features in his environment, and to organize and integrate experience meaningfully. Another measure (ego complexity) evaluated the subjects' sensitivity to external events and surroundings, to ego expansion (as opposed to constriction) rather than the more integrative aspects of ego functioning.

These measures, which have been shown to distinguish well-adjusted from poorly-adjusted groups in a clinical situation,[5] are only slightly associated with academic behavior in high school or achievement in young adulthood. There is a significant association between "ego functioning" in high school, as measured by this technique, and the TAT, but this trend is reversed at the later period. Indeed, there was very little relationship for individual subjects between these psychological indicators at adolescence and scores eight years later. The most significant pattern in these indices was the tendency for the scores of males to be higher at young adulthood than at adolescence and the scores of females to be somewhat lower.

Relationship of Achievement Groupings to Young Adult Performance

Since the selection of the groups was based upon occupational level at the follow-up stage and upon social mobility as indicated by the attainment of an occupational level higher than that of the father, the analysis of performance at the follow-up stage is restricted to social variables and measures of personality.

Achievement groupings and integration into the social life of the community. In the area of sociability and social activities, no association was found between the achievement groupings and popularity, as measured by the number of friends the subject claimed to have. However, those who performed relatively well as young adults more frequently held memberships in formal associations. Reports of informal associations showed no such relation.

[5] R. H. Dana, "Cross-validation of Objective TAT Behavior," *Journal of Consulting Psychology,* XX (1956), 33–37; and R. H. Dana, "Proposal for Objective Scoring of TAT Behavior," *Perceptual and Motor Skills,* IX (1959), 27–43.

Another measure of informal sociability was obtained by inquiring about the number of social activities engaged in per week. This variable was used to measure current activities, whereas the prior indices attempted to gauge membership in organizations without evaluating frequency of activity in these organizations. However, frequency of social activities showed no significant associations with achievement. Also, total number of intra-familial social activities per week and a composite of family and non-family interaction showed no significant differences among the achievement groups.

A summary of the level of social activities of the several achievement groupings is shown in Table 5. Again, the differences between the groups do not generally attain statistical significance, but the pattern of difference is relatively consistent over the several measures.

Achievement groupings and personality measures. The measures that we obtained on the nature of internal status of satisfaction, self-concept, and ego functioning as estimated from the TAT response did not show high association with achievement at the adult level. Ego functioning and ego complexity, as discussed earlier, were derived from a second administration of the TAT. Neither of these showed any relation to the achievement groups.

Another measure dealt with an assessment of psychosocial growth. The interviewers rated each subject on "role acceptance," a rating designed to reflect the extent to which the subject had made the transition from adolescence to adulthood. The basis for this rating was an assessment of the individual's willingness to assume the responsibilities of adulthood. When compared on this measure of psychosocial transition, those subjects who performed well in school were rated relatively higher as young adults than those who did not do well in high school. In addition, subjects who achieved, by our criteria, in young adulthood were also rated higher on this measure. The effect of post–high school experience is indicated by the fact that of our two groups who did poorly in high school, those who achieved in young adulthood were rated higher on this area of psychosocial achievement. (See Table 6.)

SUMMARY AND IMPLICATIONS
OF THE FINDINGS

Our data bear upon theories of psychosocial development in several ways. While this report has centered upon results obtained from comparison of extreme categories comprising only one third of the total class, there is sufficient consistency in the findings to justify several general conclusions about the relevance of high school experience for the young adult performance of our group. The utilization of extreme groups probably overestimates the trends that appear. Because of this problem in the use of high and low achievement groupings as a basis for generalizations, this summary treats the data presented here in light of other data available on the entire group which has not yet been reported.

The trend that is most clearly supported by our data is that academic achievement in high school is significantly associated with work-related variables in young adulthood. This pattern applies both to occupational level and the tendency to be socially mobile, i.e., to attain a higher social status than one's father. Achievement in the work arena is not simply a matter of intellect; indeed, grade average shows a higher association with occupation than do mental test scores. The predictive power of school academic achievement is particularly evident for males; for females the relationship is not so strong. This is an interesting finding in view of the fact that in our group, as in many others, girls tend to get higher grades than boys and to over-achieve more than do males. Thus, high school grades, which are generally not highly valued by males, are apparently very important for later success but are not so indicative of success for girls, who value grades and exert more effort than boys to achieve in the classroom. That is, the high school seems to be a more compatible climate for females than for males but its effect upon later success is to the advantage of boys.

In contrast to the apparent impact of academic achievement is the low relationship that exists between social experience and skill in high school and work achievement in young adulthood. Also, on the basis of data from the total group there seems to be little tendency for adolescents who were socially adept and active in high school to be unusually socially active as young adults. Nor is there an appreciable gain from high school social participation behaviors estimated by ratings of role acceptance or by the several measures of psychological behavior.

This lack of measurable benefit from social experience is of particular interest in view of the emphasis placed upon social interaction and popularity by adolescents, parents, and the schools. The close study of the socially-prominent high school seniors confirmed the trends apparent in other parts of the data. While it is recognized that we are not dealing with extremes of social ineptness or social isolation, it nonetheless appears that the impact of an active social schedule in high school does not necessarily result in long term gains. Some of the high school wallflowers are now leading very active social lives, and some of the sociometric queens of the prom now have little social interaction outside their immediate family.

The ease of the transition from adolescence to young adulthood and the degree to which this has been accomplished by the middle twenties is apparently not greatly affected by high school social experience and only slightly associated with academic achievement. The rating on role acceptance does distinguish between the achievement groupings at the young adult level because of the overlapping of the ratings and achievement. However, the correlation between high school grades and the young adult ratings for the entire interview sample was slightly positive for girls, slightly negative for boys with a combined correlation of .01. There seems to be only slight reason to regard success in social and academic areas of high school experience as particularly helpful in preparing adolescents for the transition to young adulthood. The variety of experience after graduation and the sequence of events which follow upon graduation seem to be more influential in the nature of the transition process.

It seems likely that adult performance is more closely related to events and experiences that occur after high school than to high school behavior. This is especially true of occupational commitment and other identity measures. Occupational commitment, for example, is related to occupational level, to salary, to social activities, and, of course, to expressed satisfaction with work. It is not significantly related to any high school variable. The interviews given us by our group illustrate vividly the importance of post-high school events. There seems to be a moratorium during high school, a waiting for things to happen that is abruptly broken by graduation. Although the experiences that break the relatively stable high school pattern are extremely varied and may be difficult to study systematically, they appear to be exceedingly influential upon later experiences and achievement.

These trends in our data indicate the fluid and unstable nature of adolescent behavior patterns. They suggest that the processes of identity that make for stable adult behavior and personality continue well past high school. The tendency of our results points toward late adolescence and the early twenties as perhaps a more critical period of development than is adolescence. They emphasize the need for concentrated research and theoretical attention to the transition between pre-adult and adult stages of development and the effects of this stage upon subsequent performance.

Table 1
Distribution of Achievement Groups by Sex
(Percentages)

Group	N	Males	Females
High-High	41	44	56
High-Low	17	06	94
Low-High	21	52	48
Low-Low	41	54	46

Table 2
Over- and Under-Achievement in High School
and Achievement Groupings
(Percentages)

Group	N*	Over-achievers	Under-achievers
High-High	41	56	44
High-Low	17	82	18
Low-High	20	25	75
Low-Low	38	34	66

* Slight difference in *N* from table to table indicates lack of information on the specific variable.

Table 3
Educational Attainment by Achievement Groups
(Percentages)

Group	N	High School Only	Some College	College Graduate
High-High	41	15	22	63
High-Low	18	61	22	11
Low-High	21	52	29	19
Low-Low	39	67	28	08

Table 4*
High School Activity by Achievement Groups
(Percentages classified as *high*)

Variable	High-High	High-Low + Low-High	Low-Low
Teacher's rating (apparent sociability)	86	57	37
Mutual choice friends	59	33	33
Formal school associations	66	47	40
Formal outside school associations	56	45	33
Popularity	46	39	44
Informal school associations	59	70	50
Informal outside school associations	29	30	33

* Using the sign test to examine the significance of the patterns of response, the following two-tailed probabilities were found: the difference between high-high and low-low is less than .05; between high-high vs. high-low and low-high, not significant; and between high-low and low-high vs. low-low, not significant.

Applying the Wilcoxin Matched-Pairs Ranked Sign Test to the high-low + low-high vs. low-low difference gives a two-tailed probability of less than .02.

Table 5
Young Adult Social Activities by Achievement Groups
(Percentages classified as *high*)

Variable	High-High	High-Low + Low-High	Low-Low
Formal associations	77	48	32
Social Index I	45	35	27
Social Index II*	59	30	45
Social Index III†	81	59	55
Number of friends	59	39	41
Non-family social activities	59	61	22
Expressed satisfaction with people	50	36	23

* Summary of organizational membership and number of friends.
† This variable represents the total number of social activities participated in per week.

Table 6
Role Acceptance Ratings and Achievement Groupings
(Percentages)

Group	N*	Low	High
High-High	26	12	88
High-Low	14	07	93
Low-High	13	23	77
Low-Low	23	52	48

* Not all of the achievement groups were interviewed; these ratings were made only on the basis of interview contact.

PHYSICAL AND INTELLECTUAL GROWTH DURING ADOLESCENCE: RELATIONSHIPS BETWEEN MATURATIONAL AND SOCIETAL FACTORS

The Course of Children's Growth*

J. M. TANNER

The spurt in physical growth that occurs during adolescence is one of the more reliable phenomenon of this period. Although its magnitude and duration varies from one youth to another, every adolescent experiences a degree of suddenness in his growth. In the paper included here, Tanner describes the nature of the adolescent growth spurt, the order in which parts of the body develop, the changes in body size, shape, and athletic ability that occur, and the development of the reproductive system. As the next three papers in this volume profess, the relations between changes in physical growth and personality dynamics are intimate and pervasive.

THE GROWTH CURVE OF HEIGHT

In Fig. 1 is shown the growth curve in height of a single boy, measured every six months from birth to 18 years. Above is plotted the height attained at successive ages; below, the increments in height from one age to the next. If we think of growth as a form of motion, and the passage of a child along his growth curve as similar to the passage of a train between stations, then the upper curve is one of distance achieved, and the lower curve one of velocity. The velocity, or rate of growth, naturally reflects the child's situation at any given time better than does the distance achieved, which depends largely on how much the child has grown in all the preceding years. Accordingly it is usually more important to concentrate on the velocity rather than on the distance curve. In some circumstances the acceleration may reflect physiological events even better than the velocity; thus at adolescence it seems likely that the great increase in secretions from the endocrine glands is manifested most clearly in an acceleration of growth. In general, however, nothing more complex than velocity curves will be considered here.

* From J. M. Tanner, *Education and Physical Growth* (London: University of London Press Ltd., 1961), pp. 14–19, 22–34. Copyright, 1961, by J. M. Tanner. Reprinted by permission of the author and the University of London Press.

The record of Fig. 1 is the oldest published study of the growth of a child; it was made during the years 1759 to 1777 by Count Philibert de Montbeillard upon his son, and published by Buffon in a supplement to the *Histoire Naturelle*. It shows as well as any more modern data that in gen-

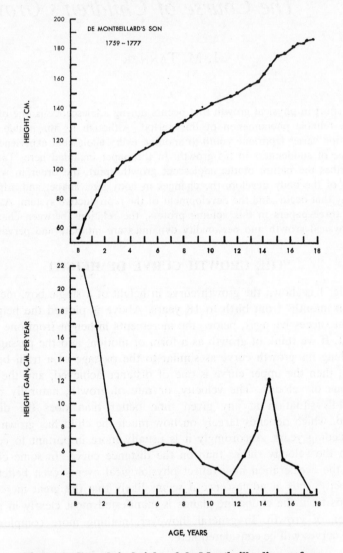

Figure 1. Growth in height of de Montbeillard's son from birth to 18 years, 1759–77. Above, distance curve, height attained at each age; below, velocity curve, increments in height from year to year. Data from Scammon, 1927, *Amer. J. Phys. Anthrop.* (From Tanner, *Growth at Adolescence*, Blackwell Sci. Publ.: Oxford.)

eral the velocity of growth in height decreases from birth (and actually from as early as the fourth intrauterine month) onwards, but that this decrease is interrupted shortly before the end of the growth period. At this time, from 13 to 15 in this particular boy, there is a marked acceleration of growth, called the *adolescent growth spurt*. From birth up to 4 or 5 the rate of growth declines rapidly, but the decline, or deceleration, gets gradually less, so that in some children the velocity is practically constant from 5 or 6 up to the beginning of the adolescent spurt.[1]

As the points of Fig. 1 show, growth is an exceedingly regular process. Contrary to opinions still sometimes met, it does *not* proceed in fits and starts. The more carefully the measurements are taken, with, for example, precautions to minimize the decrease in height that occurs during the working day for postural reasons, the more regular does the succession of points on the graph become. In a series of children each measured for seven years or more by the same measurer, my colleagues and I have found that at least over the age range 3 to 10 the deviations of the actual points from a very simple mathematical curve

$$\text{Height} = a + bt + c \log, t, \quad \text{(where } t \text{ is age)}$$

[1] A slight increase in velocity of height growth from about 6 to 8 years, providing a second wave on the general velocity curve, has been sometimes thought to occur and has been called the juvenile or mid-growth spurt. I can find no satisfactory evidence of its presence in the individual records covering the period 3 to 13 that are known to me.

Some teachers have acquired the quite erroneous notion that growth occurs in a series of alternating periods of "stretching up" (increased velocity in height) and "filling out" (increased velocity in breadth). The idea seems to have originated in 1896 in a paper by Winfield Hall, an American school doctor, who measured, very carefully, some 2,400 boys aged 9 to 23. The study was cross-sectional, with between 100 and 300 in each yearly age group. Medians were calculated but no standard deviations. The 13-year-old value for height was rather higher than might have been expected. Though to the modern eye its deviation is well within the limits of sampling error, Hall took it at face value and thus obtained a large 12–13 increment, small 13–14 increment and large 14–15 increment, this last being the adolescent spurt proper. In circumferences of the joints this did not occur, the curves being fairly regular. Hence, when the values were expressed as percentages of the 9-year-old value, the distance curves for height and for circumferences crossed at 12–13, 13–14 and 14–15. Hall thereupon formulated (in italics) a Law of Growth "When the vertical dimension of the human body is undergoing an acceleration in its rate of growth the horizontal dimensions undergo a retardation and vice versa." The idea was taken up and generalized to the whole period of growth by the German anthropologist C. H. Stratz, who in many articles wrote of a first *Streckung* at 5 to 7 and a second at 8 to 10. The data on which these opinions were based were quite insufficient to support them, but somehow they got into textbooks, where in some instances they have remained safely cocooned till the present day, despite the severest attempts to dislodge them by people such as Schiotz (see C. Schiotz, "Physical Development of Children and Young People during the Age of 7 to 18–20 Years. An Investigation of 28,700 Pupils of Public [Elementary] and Higher [Secondary] Schools in Christiania," *Videnskapsselskapets Skr. I. Mat.-Naturv. Klasse*, No. 4 [1923]), whose measurements of children were adequate in number, taken longitudinally (see below), and interpreted with statistical sense.

were seldom more than 6 mm., or ¼ in., and were on average equally above and below the curve at all ages (see Fig. 2). There is no evidence for "stages" in height growth except for the spurt associated with adolescence. Perhaps the increments of growth at the cellular level are discontinuous, and proceed by starts and stops; but at the level of bodily measurements, even of single bones measured by X-rays, one can only discern complete continuity, with a velocity that gradually varies from one age to another.

The adolescent spurt is a constant phenomenon, and occurs in all children, though it varies in intensity and duration from one child to another. In boys it takes place, on the average, from 12½ to 15, and in girls about two years earlier, from 10½ to approximately 13. The peak height velocity reached averages about 4 inches per year in boys and a little less in girls; this is the rate at which the child was growing at about 2 years old. The sex difference can be seen in Fig. 3, which shows the velocity curves for a group

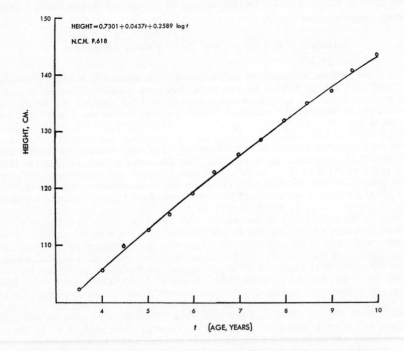

Figure 2. Curve of form $y = a + bt + c \log t$ fitted to stature measurements taken on a girl by R. H. Whitehouse every six months from age 3½ to 10. Data from Harpenden Growth Study. (From W. J. Israelsohn, "Description and Modes of Analysis of Human Growth," *Human Growth*, ed. J. M. Tanner, Sym. Soc. Hum. Biol. [London: Pergamon, 1960], vol. 3.)

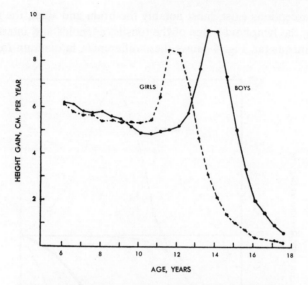

Figure 3. Adolescent spurt in height growth for girls and boys. The curves are from subjects who have their peak velocities during the modal years 12–13 for girls, and 14–15 for boys. Actual mean increments, each plotted at centre of its half-year period. Data from Shuttleworth, 1939, Tables 23 and 32. (From Tanner, *Growth at Adolescence,* Blackwell Sci. Publ.: Oxford.)

of boys who have their peak between 14 and 15 and a group of girls with their peak between 12 and 13. The earlier occurrence of the spurt in girls is the reason why girls are bigger than boys from about 10½ to 13 years. Boys are larger than girls by only 1–3 per cent in most body measurements before puberty, so that the girls' adolescent spurt soon carries them ahead of the boys. The boys catch up and pass the girls when their greater and probably more sustained adolescent spurt begins to take effect, and they finish some 10 per cent larger in most dimensions. Thus the adult difference in size between men and women is to a large extent the result of the difference in timing and magnitude of the adolescent spurt.

*   *   *

GROWTH CURVES OF DIFFERENT TISSUES AND DIFFERENT PARTS OF THE BODY

Most measurements of the body show a generally similar growth curve to the curve of height given in Fig. 1. The great majority of skeletal and muscular dimensions, whether of length or breadth, grow in this manner.

But some exceptions exist, most notably the brain and skull, the reproductive organs, the lymphoid tissue of the tonsils, adenoids and intestines, and the subcutaneous fat. Fig. 4 shows these differences in diagram form, using

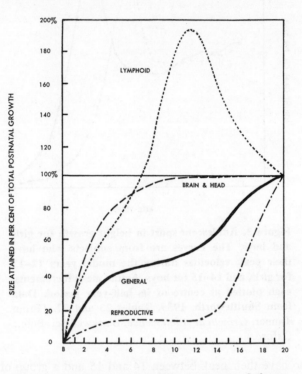

Figure 4. Growth curves of different parts and tissues of the body, showing the four chief types. All the curves are of size attained (in per cent of the total gain from birth to maturity) and plotted so that size at age 20 is 100 on the vertical scale. Redrawn from Scammon, 1930, "The Measurement of Man," Univ. Minn. Press. (From Tanner, *Growth at Adolescence*, Blackwell Sci. Publ.: Oxford.)

Lymphoid type: thymus, lymph nodes, intestinal lymph masses.

Brain and head type: brain and its parts, dura, spinal cord, optic apparatus, head dimensions.

General type: body as a whole, external dimensions (except head), respiratory and digestive organs, kidneys, aortic and pulmonary trunks, musculature, blood volume.

Reproductive type: testis, ovary, epididymis, prostate, seminal vesicles, Fallopian tubes.

size attained, or distance curves. Height follows the "general" curve. The reproductive organs, internal and external, follow a curve which is not, perhaps, very different in principle, but strikingly so in effect. Their pre-pubescent growth is very slow, and their growth at adolescence very rapid; they are less sensitive than the skeleton to one set of hormones and more sensitive to another.

The brain and skull, together with the eyes and ears, develop earlier than any other part of the body and have thus a characteristic postnatal curve . . . by 1 year old the brain has attained about 60 per cent of its adult weight, and by 5 years about 90 per cent. Probably it has no ado-lescent spurt, although a slight spurt does occur in the measurements of head length and breadth due to thickening of the skull bones. The face, unlike the portion of the skull encasing the brain, follows a path closer to the general skeletal curve, with a considerable adolescent spurt in most measurements. The jawbone, for example, has only completed 75 per cent of its growth in length before adolescence in boys.

The eye seems probably to have a slight adolescent acceleration in growth, though no data are accurate enough to make the matter certain. Very likely it is this that is responsible for the increase in frequency of short-sightedness in children at the time of puberty. Though the degree of myopia increases continuously from at least age 6 to maturity, a particu-larly rapid rate of change occurs at about 11 to 12 in girls and 13 to 14 in boys, and this would be expected if there was a rather greater spurt in the axial dimension of the eye than in its vertical dimension.

The lymphoid tissue has quite a different curve from the rest: it reaches its maximum value by the beginning of adolescence and thereafter actually decreases in amount, largely under the influence of the sex hormones. Ac-cordingly, children with troublesomely large, but otherwise normal, tonsils and adenoids may generally be expected to lose their snuffles when ado-lescence starts.

The subcutaneous fat undergoes a slightly more complicated evolution. Its thickness can be measured either by X-rays, or more simply at certain sites by picking up a fold of skin and fat between the thumb and forefinger and measuring the thickness of the fold with a special, constant-pressure, caliper. In Fig. 5 the distance curves for two measurements of subcutaneous fat are shown, one taken at the back of the upper arm (triceps), the other at the back of the chest, just below the bottom of the shoulder blade (sub-scapular). The data come from different sources at each of the three age ranges, and this has been indicated by leaving the three sections separate. The thickness of subcutaneous fat increases from birth to reach a peak at nine months or a year, and thereafter decreases, rapidly at first and then more slowly, until about 6 to 8 years, depending on the individual child.

At that time the width of fat begins to increase again. In the trunk fat (sub-scapular measurement) this increase continues up to maturity in both boys and girls. The limb fat (triceps measurement) follows this same pattern in girls, but in boys it thins out at the time of the adolescent spurt in height.

The curves for muscle and bone widths follow the general height curve. Because weight represents a mixture of these various components of the body its curve of growth is somewhat different from those discussed above, and often less informative. Though to some extent useful in following the health of a child, weight has severe limitations; an increase may be due to bone or muscle or merely to fat. A boy may cease growth in height and muscle and put on fat instead (as happens in certain clinical circumstances when large doses of cortisone are given) and his weight curve may continue to look perfectly normal. Even failure to gain weight or actual loss of weight in an older child may signify little except a better attention to diet and exercise, whereas failure to gain height or muscle would call for immediate investigation. For these reasons regular measurements of height and weight in the schools should be supplemented by measurements of subcutaneous fat by skinfolds, and muscular dimensions by circumference of upper arm and calf corrected for the covering subcutaneous fat.

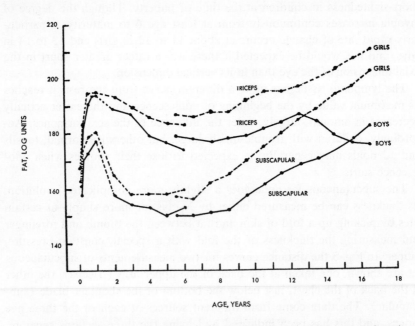

Figure 5. Amount of subcutaneous fat on the back of the arm (triceps) and on the chest (subscapular) from birth to age 16. Distance curves; measurements by skin-fold calipers, reported as logs of readings less 1.8 mm. (From Tanner, *Growth at Adolescence*, Blackwell Sci. Publ.: Oxford.)

GROWTH AND DEVELOPMENT AT ADOLESCENCE

Practically all skeletal and muscular dimensions take part in the adolescent spurt. There is a fairly regular order in which the dimensions accelerate; leg length as a rule reaches its peak first, followed a few months later by the body breadths and a year later by trunk length. Most of the spurt in height is due to trunk growth rather than growth of the legs. The muscles appear to have their spurt a little after the last skeletal peak.

At adolescence a marked increase in athletic ability occurs, particularly in boys. The heart, just like any other muscle, grows more rapidly, as can be seen from Fig. 6. The strength of the muscles also increases sharply, especially in boys. The results of two strength tests given to a group of girls and boys every six months throughout adolescence are plotted (as distance curves) in Fig. 7. Arm pull refers to the movement of pulling apart clasped hands held up in front of the chest, the hands each grasping a dynamometer handle; arm thrust refers to the reverse movement, of pushing the hands together. Each individual test represents the best of three trials made in competition against a classmate of similar ability, and against the individual's own figure of six months before. Only with such precautions can reliable maximal values be obtained. There is a consider-

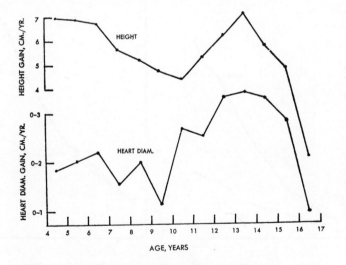

Figure 6. Velocity curves of transverse diameter of the heart, measured by X-ray, for 71 boys. Mixed longitudinal data, reported cross-sectionally. Height curves of same boys given above for comparison. Data from Maresh, 1948. (From Tanner, *Growth at Adolescence*, Blackwell Sci. Publ.: Oxford.)

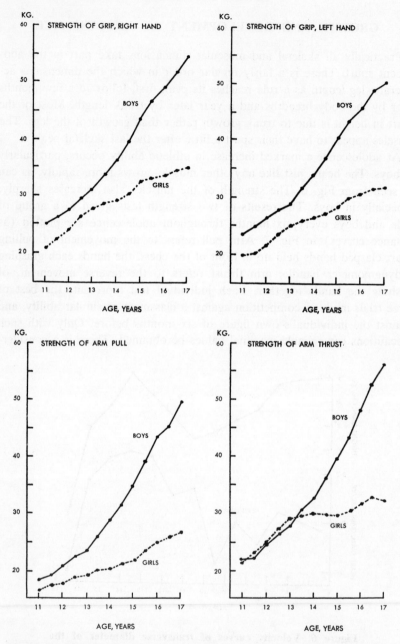

Figure 7. Strength of hand grip, arm pull and arm thrust from age 11 to 17. Mixed longitudinal data, 65–93 boys and 66–93 girls in each age group. Data from Jones, 1949, Tables 15–22. (From Tanner, *Growth at Adolescence*, Blackwell Sci. Publ.: Oxford.)

able adolescent spurt visible in all four of the boys' curves from about age 13 to 16 (the curves turn more sharply upwards), and a less definite spurt from about 12 to 13½ in the girls' hand-grip curves. There is no sex difference before puberty in strength of arm thrust and little in arm pull (the same is true of calf and thigh muscle strengths). The boys' later superiority arises partly from their greater adolescent growth in muscular bulk, and partly because the male sex hormone secreted then for the first time acts on muscle to produce more strength per cross-sectional area.

In hand-grip a more considerable sex difference appears to be present as early as age 11. This is a reflection of the greater development, even before puberty, of the male forearm. It is often forgotten that a number of sex differences, besides those of the reproductive organs, antedate puberty, and are not the result of the endocrine gland secretions of adolescence. At birth boys have longer and thicker forearms, relative to upper arms, legs and other parts of the body, and the sex difference increases steadily throughout the whole growing period. (This is not peculiar to man, but occurs in several species of apes and monkeys as well.) Another difference which is already present at birth is the relatively greater length of the second finger in comparison to the fourth in girls. Whether any similar sex differences occur in the brain is not known, but the possibility of them clearly exists.

Not only the muscles increase in size and strength at adolescence; the vital capacity of the lungs, that is, the amount of air they will hold on maximum inspiration less the amount retained after maximal expiration, also shows a pronounced increase in boys. The number of red blood cells, and hence the amount of hemoglobin in the blood, also rises sharply in boys but not in girls, as shown in Fig. 8. Thus the amount of oxygen which can be carried from the lungs to the tissues increases.

It is as a direct result of these anatomical and physiological changes that athletic ability increases so much in boys at adolescence. The popular notion of a boy "outgrowing his strength" at this time has little scientific support. It is true that the peak velocity of strengh increase occurs a year or so after the peak velocity of most of the skeletal measurements, so that a short period exists when the adolescent, having completed his skeletal, and probably also muscular, growth, still does not have the strength of a young adult of the same body size and shape. But this is a temporary phase; considered absolutely, power, athletic skill and physical endurance all increase progressively and rapidly throughout adolescence. It is certainly not true that the changes accompanying adolescence even temporarily enfeeble, through any mechanism except a psychological one.

Though the main change at puberty is in body size, there is also a considerable change in body shape. The shape change differs in the two sexes, so that boys acquire the wide shoulders and muscular neck of the man, and girls the relatively wide hips of the woman. Before puberty it is usually impossible to distinguish whether a particular child is a boy or girl from its body proportions or amounts of bone, muscle and fat alone (despite the few small but perhaps important differences mentioned above). After puberty it is easy to do so in the great majority of cases.

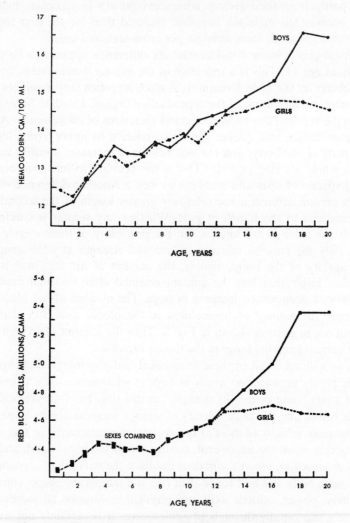

Figure 8. Change in blood hemoglobin and number of circulating red blood cells during childhood, showing the development of the sex difference at adolescence. Distance curves. Mixed longitudinal data reported cross-sectionally. Redrawn from Mugrage and Andresen, 1936, 1938, "Amer. J. Dis. Child." (From Tanner, *Growth at Adolescence*, Blackwell Sci. Publ.: Oxford.)

ENDOCRINOLOGY OF GROWTH

Thus at adolescence there is a great and sudden increase in body size and strength and a change in many physiological functions besides the reproductive ones. These changes all take place in a co-ordinated manner and a child who is early in respect of one feature is early in respect of all. The changes are mostly more marked in boys than girls, and take place approximately two years later in boys than in girls.

The immediate cause of all these changes is the secretion into the blood stream (and hence the contact with all tissues) of hormones from the ovaries, testes and adrenal glands. However, ovaries, testes and the particular functional part of the adrenal which secretes androgenic (i.e., male-determining) hormones have first to be stimulated to grow and function by other hormones. These come from the pituitary gland, which lies just underneath the base of the brain in approximately the geometrical center of the head. The pituitary itself, however, awaits the receipt of a chemical stimulus before manufacturing and releasing these trophic hormones, and this stimulus comes from a particular small area in the basal part of the brain known as the hypothalamus. What causes the hypothalamus to initiate all these events we do not know; it seems to be normally under some form of restraint emanating from its anterior portion. There is a hereditary disorder, manifested only in boys, in which this restraint is partially lacking and a precocious puberty occurs any time from 4 years onwards. When this happens all the events of puberty take place normally, including the production of sperm. In girls a similar, though not hereditary, condition occurs occasionally and the youngest known mother, who had a child by Cæsarian section at age 5, was an example of this. In these cases no other untoward effects take place; the children otherwise are quite healthy. In certain progressive diseases of the brain, however, the restraint on the hypothalamus may be destroyed and precocious puberty may also occur then.

Evidently certain maturational changes have to take place in the restraining anterior hypothalamus before it releases its grip and lets the mechanism begin; but we are totally ignorant of their nature. Starvation retards puberty, which simply waits for the body to reach its usual prepubertal size, irrespective of the passage of time. Maturation of the hypothalamus occurs at a certain sequence in a chain of events and not, fundamentally, at a certain chronological age. We shall return to this very important point again in the next two chapters.

The factors controlling growth before adolescence are imperfectly understood, but it is clear that another pituitary hormone, called growth hormone, controls to a great extent the speed of growth. Its absence causes the type of dwarf who has approximately normal body proportions. Thus the pre-adolescent phase of growth has been called the growth-hormone phase, and the adolescent the steroid-hormone phase (since the hormones concerned then belong to a class of compounds called by this name). Several other hormones, notably that secreted by the thyroid gland, have to be maintained within normal limits for growth to occur normally; but they do not act directly to regulate growth rate. Presumably because of the different hormonal control there is a considerable degree of independence between growth before, and growth at, adolescence.

DEVELOPMENT OF THE REPRODUCTIVE SYSTEM

The adolescent spurt in skeletal and muscular dimensions is closely related to the great development of the reproductive system which takes place at that time. The sequence of events for the average boy and girl is shown diagrammatically in Figs. 9 and 10. This sequence is not exactly the same for every boy and girl, but it varies much less than the time at which the events occur.

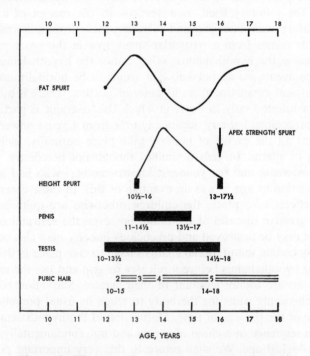

Figure 9. Diagram of sequence of events at adolescence in boys. An average boy is represented: the range of ages within which each event charted may begin and end is given by the figure (appropriate to 1955) placed directly below its start and finish. (From Tanner, *Growth at Adolescence*, Blackwell Sci. Publ.: Oxford.)

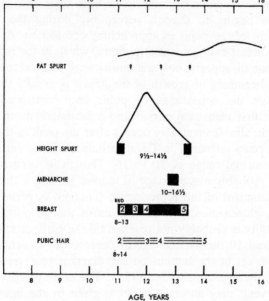

Figure 10. Diagram of sequence of events at adolescence in girls. An average girl is represented: the range of ages within which some of the events may occur is given by the figures (appropriate to 1955) placed directly below them. (From Tanner, *Growth at Adolescence*, Blackwell Sci. Publ.: Oxford.)

The first sign of impending puberty in boys is usually an acceleration of the growth of testes and scrotum (beginning of bar marked "testis" in Fig. 9). Slight growth of the pubic hair may begin at about the same time, but proceeds slowly until the advent of the general spurt. The accelerations in height and in penis growth begin about a year after the testicular acceleration, when the cells of the testis have grown and begun to secrete male sex hormone. Axillary hair usually first appears about two years after the beginning of pubic hair growth, though the relationship is sufficiently variable so that a very few children's axillary hair actually appears first. Facial hair in boys begins to grow at about the same time as axillary hair. There is first an increase in length and pigmentation of hairs at the corners of the upper lip, then a spread of this to complete the moustache, then the appearance of hair on the upper part of the cheeks and just below the lower lip, and finally along the sides and border of the chin. This last development seldom occurs until genital and pubic hair development is far advanced.

The enlargement of the larynx occurs a little after the spurt in height and the voice begins to deepen perceptibly during the period when the development of the penis is approaching completion. A few boys undergo a slight breast enlargement at puberty, which in the majority is temporary, and soon disappears; only a minority need medical treatment.

In girls the beginning of growth of the breast is usually the first sign of puberty, though the appearance of pubic hair sometimes precedes it. Menarche, the first menstrual period and a landmark much used by students of growth, almost invariably occurs after the peak of the height spurt is passed. It occurs currently in Great Britain at an average age of 13.1 years, with a normal range of 10 to 16. Though its occurrence marks a definitive and probably mature stage of uterine growth, it does not usually signify the attainment of full reproductive function. A period of infertility of a year or eighteen months follows in most, though not all, cases; and maximum fertility is probably not reached till the early or middle twenties.

In Figs. 9 and 10 the average age of occurrence of each event is given by the scale of age at the bottom on the diagram (e.g. menarche a little after 13 years, the figures being for 1955). The *range* of ages within which some of the events may normally occur is given by the figures placed directly below the event (e.g. for menarche 10–16½). A glance will suffice to show how very large these ranges are. One boy, for example, may complete his penis growth at 13½, while another has not even started at 14½. An early-maturing boy may have finished his entire adolescence before a late-maturing boy *of the same chronological* age has even begun his first enlargement of the testes.

Development of Sexual Behavior in Human Beings*

CLELLAN S. FORD AND
FRANK A. BEACH

The sexual expressions of human beings extend in scope far beyond "genital and pelvic reflexes." To a large extent, the social sanctions within a society determine the forms and variations of sexual behavior that are allowable. In a world-wide survey of cultural practices, Ford and Beach classify societies whose adult attitudes toward sexual expression range from extremely restrictive to highly permissive. Their analyses suggest that "the social code pertaining to sexual behavior of children and un-married adolescents in the United States is clearly a restrictive one." For students who desire a cross-cultural perspective of the development of sexual behavior in human beings, the next selection provides an excellent frame of reference.

It has been explained that the attainment of sexual maturity is a gradual process and that the various organs and organ systems involved in repro-duction become functional at different stages in the life of the individual. We have further noted that in many societies the individual's entrance into adolescence receives public recognition in the form of puberty ceremonials. But up to this point very little has been said about sexual behavior per se. The nervous and muscular mechanisms involved in sexual arousal and its overt expression can properly be classified as very important elements in the interrelated system of physiological factors that must become mature before reproduction can occur.

* From C. S. Ford and F. A. Beach, *Patterns of Sexual Behavior* (New York: Harper & Brothers, 1951), pp. 178–192. Copyright, 1951, by C. S. Ford and F. A. Beach. Reprinted by permission of the authors and Harper & Brothers.

Reflexive Components

Some of these mechanisms for behavior are reflexive, whereas others develop only as a result of practice and learning. For example, the human male does not have to learn how to fill his penis with blood so that it becomes erect and rigid, but he may have to learn how to copulate; the conditions under which an adult man experiences erection undoubtedly are influenced by his life experiences. There are decided differences between various animal species as regards the extent to which mating responses depend upon or are modified by learning and conditioning.

It is possible to analyze separately the several reflexes and more complex reactions that normally appear simultaneously or sequentially in the sexual act of adult males and females. When this is done it becomes obvious that different segments of the total response mature at different rates. In the human male, for example, complete genital erection is possible from the day of birth, and baby boys frequently show this reaction under the influence of bladder distention or in response to manipulation of the phallus. The power of ejaculation, in contrast, is not acquired until puberty, and the production of normal sperm is delayed until even later in life.

In grown men orgasm and ejaculation usually occur together, but they are not necessarily mutually dependent. As a matter of fact, it is reported that sexual climax or orgasm can be produced in very young human infants of either sex. Kinsey, Pomeroy, and Martin state that male infants less than one year of age respond to manipulation of the genitals by making thrusting movements with the pelvic muscles; and if the stimulation is continued the baby's movements become more rapid and vigorous and culminate in a general spasm quite similar to that which characterizes climax in most adults.

The evidence therefore suggests that the neuromuscular system of the human animal is capable at birth of mediating at least two of the basic reflexive patterns that will later be woven into the complete sexual act. But adult patterns of sexual behavior consist of a great deal more than genital and pelvic reflexes. What other mechanisms are involved, how do they develop, and when do they become mature.? How are the simple, inherited reflexes elaborated into the much more complex and variable forms of sexual expression that characterize adults in different societies? A fully satisfactory answer to these questions could be obtained only by studying the sexual play of many children of varying ages in a large number of different cultural settings. Unfortunately, however, the amount of such activity that occurs and the ease with which the observer can obtain information concerning it are controlled to a large extent by the attitudes of adults. And these attitudes vary to a great extent from one society to the next.

Restrictive Societies

In a minority of the societies concerning which we have adequate information adults attempt to deny young children any form of sexual expression.[1] As will be explained later, this is the prevailing attitude in American society, although there is considerable variance between actual behavior and the idealized standards of the moral code.

The severity of restrictions and punishments associated with sexual transgressions in childhood varies from one restrictive society to another. Among the Apinaye, for example, boys and girls are warned from infancy not to masturbate and a severe thrashing awaits the child suspected of such behavior. In Africa, Ashanti boys are told by their fathers at an early age not to masturbate or engage in any sexual play. In New Guinea, Kwoma boys are constantly warned not to finger their genitals; if a woman sees a boy with an erection she will beat his penis with a stick, and boys soon learn to refrain from touching their genitals even while urinating. Kwoma girls also are told not to finger their genitals but are not punished for so doing. The Cuna specifically forbid their children to engage in either homosexual or heterosexual play; and youngsters among the Chiricahua are whipped if they are detected playing sex games.

Most of these restrictive societies maintain a public conspiracy against the acquisition of any sexual knowledge by children. Adults avoid mentioning matters of sexual significance in their presence, and make every attempt to keep them in total ignorance of the reproductive process. Among the natives of the western Carolines sex is never discussed before children, especially girls. Cuna children remain ignorant of sexual matters (as far as adult instruction is concerned) until the last stages of the marriage ceremony. They are not even allowed to watch animals give birth. Chagga children are told that babies come out of the forest.

In a number of these societies particular pains are taken to prevent young children from accidentally observing sexual behavior. In some instances, as among the Murngin of Australia, boys are removed from the dwelling to the boys' house or bachelors' hut when they are four or five years old; this is done for the specific purpose of preventing them from witnessing sexual behavior at home. The Kwoma husband and wife are always careful to wait until the children are asleep before indulging in sexual intercourse.

Such adult attitudes toward childhood sexuality may prevent youngsters from engaging in sexual practices in the presence of their elders, but whether they successfully suppress sexual activity in secret is another matter. There is evidence that in some of these societies children do engage in a certain amount of sexual behavior despite strong adult disapproval. In Haiti little

[1] Abelam, Apinaye, Ashanti, Chagga, Chiricahua, Cuna, Dahomeans, Haitians, Kwoma, Manus, Murngin, Penobscot, Rengma, Trukese.

boys and girls privately experiment in sexual activity from early childhood until puberty. Manus children masturbate, but always in solitude and surrounded by shame. When they are alone in the bush Kwoma boys scrape the penis with nettles. And on Truk, children play at intercourse at an early age, although their parents will beat them if they are caught. In Trukese society children do sometimes observe their elders engaging in sexual activities at night. Apinaye boys and girls masturbate frequently even though such play is punished whenever it happens to be observed, and despite the fact that at a ceremony which is conducted when they are half grown their genitalia are examined and the children are flogged if there appears to be evidence of masturbation. In the case of boys, this "evidence" is described "as retractibility of the prepuce." But the validity of such criteria is questionable. Actually, there are no known physical stigmata that constitute reliable evidence of habitual masturbation as far as the male is concerned. R. L. Dickinson has long held that prolonged habits of feminine masturbation involving vulvar traction and friction leave permanent signs in the form of lengthened and corrugated labia. However, Dickinson's thesis is not accepted by all authorities, and in any event it applies to mature women and not to "half-grown" girls.

Some peoples make a sharp distinction between socially immature and mature persons with respect to permissible sexual activity. These societies take the attitude that sexual intercourse before adulthood must be avoided; but once the person is mature by their standards, considerable freedom in sexual matters may be allowed.[2] For the most part these peoples seem particularly concerned with the prepubescent girl, believing that intercourse before the menarche may be injurious to her. Girls of the east central Carolines are strictly forbidden intercourse before puberty, but after that they enjoy almost complete sexual freedom. After menarche, Ao girls begin to sleep in dormitories where they indulge in intercourse with partners of their choice. Among the Siriono intercourse before puberty is forbidden, but premarital affairs are customary once the girl has menstruated. The Chukchee believe that intercourse will harm a girl until her breasts are fully developed or until she begins to menstruate. However, immature girls often engage in coitus despite this belief. In this society it is considered proper for a girl to carry on serious love affairs between the time of the first menstruation and marriage. The Ashanti are convinced that sexual intercourse with a girl who has not undergone the puberty ceremony is so harmful to the community that the offense is punishable by death for both partners. Premarital intercourse is also forbidden to the postpubescent Ashanti girl, but this rule is not nearly so strictly enforced.

[2] Ao (girls), Ashanti (girls), Choroti (girls), Chukchee (girls), Haitians (boys), Jukun (girls), Lamba (girls), Mataco (girls), Seniang, Siriono (girls), Swazi, Toba (girls), Tupinamba (girls).

In most of the African societies in our sample[3] boys are strictly forbidden to have intercourse before undergoing the puberty ceremony or initiation rite. The Chagga boy, for example, cannot have intercourse until he has been circumcised and properly initiated into adult status. If caught in the act the boy and his partner are laid one on the other and staked to the ground. After circumcision all Chagga boys have intercourse with a barren woman and subsequently they sally forth to seek other sex partners. Until marriage they are instructed to practice either interfemoral intercourse or coitus interruptus unless the girl places a pad in the vagina to avoid conception. A comparable attitude is taken by the Jivaro of Ecuador, who strictly forbid boys to engage in intimate relationships with girls until they have gone through an initiation ceremony at puberty.

In other societies the prohibitions against sexual intercourse continue unabated or, in some instances, are intensified after puberty and remain in force until marriage or at least until betrothal. The methods used to prevent premarital sexual activity during adolescence include segregation of the sexes, strict chaperonage of girls, and threats of severe disgrace or physical punishment. The extreme pains to which adults in these societies are forced to go in order to control the sexual behavior of young people is an eloquent expression of the strength of the tendency on the part of older children and adolescents to engage in such activity. There are indeed very few societies in which any method of control appears to be completely effective in preventing heterosexual intercourse among young unmarried couples.

Perhaps the most nearly successful method of controlling the sexual activity of young people is to separate the sexes and keep the girls under constant surveillance. Among the Abipone, for example, boys and girls were strictly segregated at all times and premarital chastity is said to have been universal. A similar situation exists among the Arapaho, Cheyenne, Papago, and Wapisiana, all of whom keep the sexes strictly apart from childhood. Boys and girls never play together, and until marriage young men and women never associate in the absence of chaperones. The only completely effective prevention of premarital relations has been devised by the Wapisiana. They define cohabitation as marriage, and thus rule out the possibility of intercourse between two unmarried people. At the same time, of course, they eliminate the problem of the unmarried mother.

In most of the societies that practice segregation and chaperonage to control the sexual behavior of adolescents, boys are less carefully watched than girls; and, in some cases at least, it appears that youths are able to circumvent the barriers, with the result that sexual intercourse before marriage not infrequently occurs. For example, among the Hopi a strong attempt is made to keep boys and girls apart from the age of ten until marriage; the girls are kept at home and are accompanied by an older woman

[3] Chagga, Masai, Pedi, Swazi, Thonga (inferred), Wolof.

whenever they go out. Girls are expected to be chaste until marriage. Boys, however, are not similarly restricted, and, whenever possible, they defeat the chaperonage system by crawling into the girl's house stealthily at night or by holding clandestine prearranged meetings. The Hopi place all the blame for illegitimate pregnancy squarely upon the girl who is involved. Her friends ignore her and her family scolds her, but the lover is not regarded as at fault and is neither forced nor expected to marry her.

A similar situation exists among the Kiwai Papuans of New Guinea. There, girls are carefully chaperoned by their parents and usually kept in ignorance of love-making for some time. The boy, however, is not similarly restricted and will take the initiative in attempting to get around the rules. The young pair have to be very clever to meet; they usually are able to do so only at night. The girl may slip out of the house after her parents are asleep or the boy may sneak into her house through the floor. And apparently, despite every effort on the part of adults, many couples find it possible to carry on love affairs in secret.

Threats of the most severe disgrace and punishment do not appear to be completely effective in preventing young people from engaging in sexual activity before marriage. In the Gilberts, for example, great emphasis is placed on a girl's chastity before marriage. If a girl is seduced and it becomes public knowledge, both parties are put to death. Nevertheless, the evidence indicates that many transgressions take place in secret. In only a few societies—namely, the Vedda, Keraki, Chiricahua, and Sanpoil—is the burden of guilt placed upon the boy. Among the Vedda, for example, if a man were seen even talking to an unmarried girl her relatives would kill him. In most of these restrictive societies, however, the threats of disgrace and punishment are specifically directed toward misbehavior on the part of the girl.

The attempts of adults to restrict the sexual behavior of adolescents seem, in many of these societies, to be intended primarily as a means of insuring the virginity of the unmarried girl. Some peoples attempt to determine whether or not a girl has remained chaste by conducting a crude examination of her sexual organs. The hymen or "maidenhead" is a tab of tissue which, in most virgins, partially obstructs the entrance of the vagina. Very often this structure is nicked or stretched when the vagina is sufficiently penetrated for the first time, and a certain amount of blood may be lost. However, the size and thickness of the hymen vary from individual to individual. As a result, some fully virginal girls may bleed very little if at all during the first intercourse, whereas in other women a great deal of stretching is necessary before the obstruction offered by this tissue is completely removed.

Despite the actual unreliability of their tests, some societies use the occurrence of bleeding in response to vaginal penetration as an important index to chastity. Among the Kurd, for example, when the bridegroom has intercourse with the bride the nuptial cloth is examined for blood. If a girl is shown to have been a virgin, the cloth is paraded on a stick through the village and the bride price is then paid. If, however, the bridegroom finds himself disappointed, the girl is heaped with abuse, given back to her parents, and in some instances subjected to further public disgrace. Yungar girls are "deflowered" a week before marriage by two old women. If, at this time, examination fails to indicate chastity severe penalties are meted out to the girl, including starvation, mutilation, torture, and even death.

American Society

The social code pertaining to sexual behavior of children and unmarried adolescents in the United States is clearly a restrictive one. In this country, constant pressure is exerted, ideally at least, to prevent any form of sexual behavior until it is legalized and can occur in the bonds of matrimony. In this society, as in many others, there is a tendency toward a double standard in respect to premarital sexual behavior. More pressure is brought to bear upon unmarried girls than upon boys. In actual practice, furthermore, the burden of protecting young persons from indulging in sexual activity falls somewhat more heavily upon the parents of American girls than upon the parents of boys. This tendency toward a double sex standard is also reflected in attitudes toward extramarital sexual activity. As has been shown, a double sex standard during late childhood and adolescence is characteristic of many societies, but not of human beings in general. There are societies in which there is little if any difference in the premarital sexual restrictions placed upon girls and boys, and in a few societies the more severe restrictions confine the male rather than the female.

Kinsey and his associates have shown in statistical fashion what has generally been recognized for many years, namely, that in spite of the attitudes of adults, children in our society frequently indulge in many forms of sexual activity. Although the strictness with which the moral code is enforced varies considerably from one social class to another, a more or less concerted attempt to prevent children from indulging in any form of sex play continues well into adolescence and up to the time of marriage. And, as we have noted, most other societies that discourage infantile and childhood sex play also attempt to control premarital experimentation in sexual matters on the part of adolescents or young adults.

Although this attitude is characteristic in America, the strength of condemnation varies somewhat from one social group to another. However, regardless of the prohibitions against it, premarital sexual behavior does occur in a fairly large proportion of the population. It does not necessarily involve actual copulation. Landis and his co-workers report that 59 per cent of the married women whom they questioned had indulged in extensive heterosexual play without coitus prior to marriage. Forty-two per cent of the unmarried women in this study admitted the occurrence of sex play.

According to Kinsey, Pomeroy, and Martin, more than 60 per cent of American males engage in petting before they are twenty years old. By the age of twenty-five, approximately one-third of the male population has achieved orgasm in this fashion. Men from the higher educational levels are likely to confine their adolescent activity to noncoital techniques, whereas individuals from the lower socio-educational strata tend to proceed more or less directly to coitus and indulge in a minimum of petting.

As far as actual copulation is concerned, Kinsey and his collaborators report that it was attempted during or before adolescence by 22 per cent of the American boys they interviewed. The first experiment usually takes place between the ages of 10 and 14. By the time he is 12 years old approximately one boy in every four or five has at least tried to copulate with a girl or woman. More than 10 per cent of these youths experience their first ejaculation in connection with heterosexual intercourse. Considering all the men interviewed in Kinsey's study, it becomes apparent that more than two-thirds of them had at least one premarital experience involving copulation. The incidence of such behavior varies with the individual's socio-educational level, being least frequent in college-educated groups, and nearly universal among men who have no more than an eighth-grade education.

Terman found that approximately one-half of 760 American husbands whom he studied admitted premarital intercourse with the women they later married. Seven per cent of this group said they had copulated with at least one other woman prior to marriage, and 26 per cent mentioned intercourse with five or more women before marriage. Only 13.3 per cent of the 777 wives represented in Terman's sample admitted premarital relations with the husband, and much smaller percentages listed intercourse with other males before marriage. The lack of agreement between accounts given by husbands and wives probably reflects chiefly a different degree of resistance to confessing premarital freedom. Terman was particularly impressed with differences between older and younger married couples as regards premarital behavior. He noted that the proportion of men and women who were virgins at marriage had steadily decreased between the approximate dates of 1910 and the early 1930's. *"If the drop should continue at the average rate shown for those born since 1890* virginity at marriage will be close to the vanishing point for males born after 1930 and for females born after 1940. It is more likely that the rate of change will become somewhat retarded as the zero point is approached and that an occasional virgin will come to the marriage bed for a few decades beyond the dates indicated by the curves. It will be of no small interest to see how long the cultural ideal of virgin marriage will survive as a moral code after its observance has passed into history." (L. M. Terman, *Psychological Factors in Marital Happiness* [New York: McGraw-Hill Book Co., 1938], p. 323).

Semirestrictive Societies

There is no clear-cut dividing line between restrictive and semirestrictive societies; and often, as we have pointed out, the sexual codes that adults attempt to enforce on immature members of the group differ according to the young person's sex or age. There are, however, many societies[4] in which the adult attitudes toward sex play in children or toward premarital affairs in adolescents are characterized by formal prohibitions that are apparently not very serious and in fact are not enforced. In such cases sexual experimentation may take place in secrecy without incurring punishment, even though the parents know perfectly well what is going on. The Alorese formally object to any form of sex play on the part of older children. But overt homosexual and heterosexual practices on the part of boys and girls occur, and children playing together in field houses imitate the sexual intercourse of their parents. Unless this is brought flagrantly to the attention of the adults they do nothing about it.

Among the Andamanese premarital promiscuity is common and the parents do not object as long as the love affairs are kept secret. Parents object to such activities in theory, but unless they are practiced openly no punishment is involved. Should a girl become pregnant, however, the parents of the couple usually arrange for them to be married. The Huichol uphold an ideal of premarital chastity for both sexes, but in practice this is rarely realized. If an adolescent couple is caught in sexual intimacy both individuals are beaten and they are forced to marry; but parents do not keep close surveillance over the activities of young people, and the latter have many opportunities to slip off into the bush in the evening during feasts and dances.

In some societies the only recognized sign of sexual transgression on the part of young people is premarital pregnancy. Among such peoples it appears that intercourse frequently takes place between unmarried couples, but numerous devices and techniques are employed either to prevent conception or to abort an unwanted fetus. In a number of African societies it is customary for adolescent boys to practice interfemoral intercourse or coitus

---

[4] Alorese (older children), Andamanese, Aranda (girls), Azande, Bena, Chagga (girls), Colorado (girls), Cree, Creek, Crow (girls), Dusun (girls), Flathead, Ganda (girls), Havasupai, Huichol, Kickapoo, Kiowa, Apache, Kiwai, Klamath, Kurtatchi (girls), Kutchin, Kutenai, Kwoma, Lango, Mailu, Mandan, Mangarevans (now), Manus, Mbundu, Menomini, Omaha, Orokaiva (girls), Papago, Pedi (girls), Purari (girls), Ramkokamekra, Reddi, Rengma (girls), Seminole, Sinkaietk (girls), Tinguian, Tokelauans, Venda, Wappo, Yagua, Yako, Zulu (older children).

interruptus to avoid impregnating the girl. Contraceptive measures used by young people in these societies include placing a pad of absorbent material in the vagina, washing the passage after intercourse, and orally ingesting certain medicines believed to insure temporary sterility. Should these fail to prevent conception the girl may resort to an abortion.

Permissive Societies

Adults in a large number of societies take a completely tolerant and permissive attitude toward sex expression in childhood.[5] Under such conditions youngsters engage in a certain amount of sexual play in public. The fingering of the child's own genitals follows exploratory movements of the hands which contact the various parts of the body. If adults do not attempt to discourage such behavior, fingering the genitals becomes an established habit of occasional occurrence. As the child grows old enough to walk about and play with others, he tends to extend the range and to increase the variety of sexual activities. Handling the genitals of others of the same or opposite sex occurs frequently under conditions of free sex play. Additional forms of sexual activity on the part of young children sometimes include oral-genital contacts and attempted copulation with a sex partner.

In a few permissive societies adults participate actively in the sexual stimulation of infants and young children. Hopi and Siriono parents masturbate their youngsters frequently. And in these societies self-masturbation passes practically unnoticed during early childhood, adults taking a tolerant and permissive attitude toward all sexual behavior at least until the age of puberty. Among the Kazak, adults who are playing with small children, especially boys, excite the young one's genitals by rubbing and playing with them. In this society autogenital stimulation on the part of young children is accepted as a normal practice. Mothers in Alorese society occasionally fondle the genitals of their infant while nursing it. During early childhood Alorese boys masturbate freely and occasionally they imitate intercourse with a little girl. As the children grow older, however, sexual activity is frowned upon and during late childhood such behavior is forbidden to both boy and girl. Actually, however, they continue their sexual behavior, but in secret.

Among the Pukapukans of Polynesia where parents simply ignore the sexual activities of young children, boys and girls masturbate freely and openly in public. Among the Nama Hottentot no secret is made of autogenital stimulation in early childhood. Young Trobriand children engage in

---

[5] Alorese, Chewa, Copper Eskimo, Crow (boys), Easter Islanders, Hopi, Ifugao, Ila, Kazak, Kwakiutl, Lepcha, Lesu, Mangarevans (formerly), Maori, Marquesans, Marshallese, Masai, Nama, Ojibwa, Palauans, Ponapeans, Pukapukans, Samoans, Seniang, Siriono, Tikopia, Trobrianders, Walapai, Wogeo, Yapese, Yaruro, Zulu.

a variety of sexual activities. In the absence of adult control, typical forms of amusement for Trobriand girls and boys include manual and oral stimulation of the genitals and simulated coitus. Young Seniang children publicly simulate adult copulation without being reproved; older boys masturbate freely and play sexual games with little girls, but the boys are warned not to copulate on the grounds that this behavior would weaken them. Lesu children playing on the beach give imitations of adult sexual intercourse, and adults in this society regard this to be a natural and normal game. On Tikopia small boys induce erections in themselves through manual manipulation, and this is ignored or at most mildly reproved by adults. Little girls also may masturbate in this society without being punished for such behavior.

Most of the societies that permit children free sex play (and some that are semirestrictive) also allow them opportunity to observe adult sexual behavior and to participate in discussions of sexual matters.[6] Among the Alorese sex knowledge is completely accessible to young children and by the age of five they are well informed on all details of the entire reproductive act. All members of the Pukapukan household sleep in the same room under one mosquito net; and although some parents wait until they think the children are asleep, there are frequent opportunities for youngsters to observe adult sexual activities and sexual matters are often talked about. Lesu children are free to observe adults copulate, with the specific exception that they may not watch their own mothers having intercourse. On Ponape children are given careful instruction in sexual intercourse from the fourth or fifth year. Trukese children receive no formal tutelage, but they learn a great deal by watching adults at night and by asking their elders about sexual matters. Among the Wogeo sexual matters are freely discussed by adults in the presence of children. In this society, however, parents take some precautions against their own children observing them in intercourse.

In the societies where they are permitted to do so, children gradually increase their sexual activities both as they approach puberty and during adolescence. There are, indeed, some societies in which enforcement of the prevailing incest regulations is the only major restriction on sexual activity among adolescents.[7] As in the case of very young children, their sex play first includes autogenital stimulation and mutual masturbation with the

---

[6] Alorese, Copper Eskimo, Cree, Dusun, Easter Islanders, Flathead, Ganda, Hopi, Ifugao, Lesu, Marquesans, Ojibwa, Ponapeans, Pukapukans Samoans, Tikopia, Tinguian, Trobrianders, Trukese, Wogeo, Yapese.

[7] Ainu, Aymara, Balinese, Barama, Chewa, Copper Eskimo, Crow (boys), Dobuans, Easter Islanders, Futunans, Gilyak, Goajiro, Gond, Ofugao, Ila, Lapps, Lepcha, Lesu, Macusi, Mangarevans (formerly), Maori, Marquesans, Marshallese, Mongols, Nandi, Naskapi, Natchez, Nauruans (commoners), Palauans, Palaung, Ponapeans, Pukapukans, Seniang, Siriono (boys), Taos, Tarahumara, Thonga (girls), Toda, Tongans (boys), Trobrianders, Trukese, Tuareg, Walapai, Wogeo, Yakut, Yapese, Yaruro, Yukaghir.

same and opposite sex, but with increasing age it is characterized more and more by attempts at heterosexual copulation. By the time of puberty in most of these societies expressions of sexuality on the part of older children consist predominantly of the accepted adult form of heterosexual intercourse, the pattern which they will continue to follow throughout their sexually active years of life.

Among the Chewa of Africa parents believe that unless children begin to exercise themselves sexually early in life they will never beget offspring. Older children build little huts some distance from the village, and there, with the complete approval of their parents, boys and girls play at being husband and wife. Such trial matings may extend well into adolescence, with periodic exchanges of partners until marriage occurs. The Ifugao head-hunters of the Philippines maintain a similar attitude toward the sex play of older children and adolescents. In this society unmarried individuals live in separate dormitories from early childhood. It is customary for each boy to sleep with a girl every night. The only check on promiscuity is that imposed by the girls themselves. Usually a girl is unwilling to form too prolonged an attachment to one boy until she is ready to be married. Boys are urged by their fathers to begin sexual activities early, and a man may shame his son if the latter is backward in this respect. Even after puberty there seem to be relatively few instances of conception resulting from this free sexual activity. Pregnancies do occasionally occur, however, and in that event one of the girl's lovers must marry her.

The Lepcha of India believe that girls will not mature without benefit of sexual intercourse. Early sex play among boys and girls characteristically involves many forms of mutual masturbation and usually ends in attempted copulation. By the time they are eleven or twelve years old, most girls regularly engage in full intercourse. Older men occasionally copulate with girls as young as eight years of age. Instead of being regarded as a criminal offense, such behavior is considered amusing by the Lepcha. Sexual life begins in earnest among the Trobrianders at six to eight years for girls, ten to twelve for boys. Both sexes receive explicit instruction from older companions whom they imitate in sex activities. Sex play includes masturbation, oral stimulation of the genitals of the same and opposite sex, and heterosexual copulation. At any time a couple may retire to the bush, the bachelor's hut, an isolated yam house, or any other convenient place and there engage in prolonged sexual play with full approval of their parents. No marriage is consummated in Trobriand society without a protracted preliminary period of sexual intimacy during which both sincerity of affection and sexual compatibility are tested. Premarital pregnancy is said to be rare in this society, despite postpuberal sexual intercourse over a period of three years or more before marriage. This experience has led the Trobrianders to doubt a causal relationship between coitus and conception. Instead they consider supernatural influences to be far more significant in causing a child to be conceived.

In this instance, as in other cases of frequent but infertile coitus among postpubescent males and females, the phenomenon of adolescent sterility would appear to be particularly pertinent. It may well be that although they have passed the menarche, the girls involved in this activity are not yet ovulating, or at least are incapable of carrying a fetus to term. Any such interpretation must remain speculative, however, until there is more satisfactory proof for the absence of any form of contraception.

An interesting attitude toward the sexual activity of adolescents is taken by the Ila-speaking peoples of Africa. Childhood is regarded as a time of preparation for adult life and mature sexual functions. At harvest time each girl is given a house to which she takes a boy of her choice, and there they play as man and wife. It is reported that there are no virgins among these people after the age of ten. On Easter Island children from the age of six on imitate the sexual behavior of adults without censure; and young people among the Maori play together at being husband and wife at night in the bush. Full copulation frequently occurs before puberty. Lesu adults regard as natural the attempts at intercourse in which children engage, and they give full approval to free sexual activity on the part of adolescents.

The Behavior-Inferred Motivations of
Late- and Early-Maturing Boys*

PAUL HENRY MUSSEN AND
MARY COVER JONES

The intensity and variability of physical growth during adolescence is such that at any specific age from approximately eleven to eighteen some youth are nearly mature whereas others are relatively immature in respect to their ultimate physical stature. Research at the Institute of Child Welfare, University of California, regarding the effects of early- and late-maturing upon personality dynamics of boys has shown that early-maturing boys, among other advantages, enjoy greater esteem from peers and adults, substantially more athletic prowess, and considerably enhanced heterosexual status. By and large over-all psychological adjustment has appeared to be more satisfactory in the early- rather than the late-maturing boys. In the study presented below, the behavior of 34 physically accelerated and retarded boys was rated in a wide variety of situations on the basis of nine drives, and the findings lend "further support to the general hypothesis that the late-maturing adolescent is more likely to be personally and socially maladjusted than his early-maturing peer."

A number of studies indicate that the adolescent's physical status, mediated by the sociopsychological environment, may exert profound and lasting influences on his personality.[1] In our culture, physically retarded adolescent boys are in a disadvantageous competitive position in athletic activities and are likely to be regarded and treated as immature by both adults and peers.[2]

[1] M. C. Jones, "The Later Careers of Boys Who Were Early- or Late-Maturing," *Child Develpm.*, XXVIII (1957), pp. 113–128; M. C. Jones and N. Bayley, "Physical Maturing among Boys as Related to Behavior," *J. Educ. Psychol.*, XLI (1950), pp. 129–148; P. H. Mussen and M. C. Jones, "Self-conceptions, Motivations, and Interpersonal Attitudes of Late- and Early-maturing Boys," *Child Development*, XXVIII (1957), pp. 243–256.

[2] Jones and Bayley, *op. cit.*

* From *Child Development*, XXIX (1958), pp. 61–67. Reprinted by permission of the authors and the Society for Research in Child Development.

Hence, they are more likely than their physically accelerated peers to be personally and socially maladjusted during adolescence. Analysis of the TAT responses of early- and late-maturing boys about 17 years of age, subjects in the Adolescent Growth Study,[3] revealed that significantly more of the latter group had negative self-concepts, profound feelings of rejection by others, strong affiliative needs (especially for heterosexual affiliation), prolonged dependency needs, and rebellious attitudes toward parents. The psychological picture of the physically accelerated boys, on the other hand, seemed to be much more favorable. As a group, they appeared to have acquired more self-confidence, were less dependent and in need of help, and were more capable of playing an adult male role in interpersonal relations. Contrary to what had been predicted, the two groups did not differ in needs for achievement and recognition, and there was some evidence that early-maturers had stronger aggressive needs than late-maturers.[4]

The motives reflected in fantasy productions are presumably covert and not readily apparent in ordinary manifest behavior. It has been demonstrated that, in many cases, manifest behavior and fantasy may be independent or even negatively related.[5] Hence, inferences about motivation based on the individual's overt behavior may be quite different from those made on the basis of his fantasy productions.

In the present study, we shall examine the *behavior*-inferred ratings of motivation assigned to early- and late-maturing boys. Under Else Frenkel-Brunswik's direction, almost all subjects in the Adolescent Growth Study were rated on nine drives about a year after they had graduated from high school.[6] The strength of each drive was inferred from behavior observed in a wide variety of situations. " 'Intuitive' judgments about motivational tendencies were obtained in the form of standardized ratings from a number of judges well acquainted with the adolescents."[7]

The nine drives, selected from Murray's list of needs, were briefly described as follows:

1. *Drive for Autonomy. Striving for independence and freedom;* desire to be free from social ties, to shake off influence, coercion, and restraint; relatively little care for conventions and group ideology; tendency to act as one pleases.

[3] H. E. Jones, "Observational Methods in the Study of Individual Development," *J. Consult. Psychol.,* IV (1940), pp. 234–238; H. E. Jones, *Development in Adolescence* (New York: Appleton-Century, 1943).

[4] Mussen and Jones, *op. cit.*

[5] P. H. Mussen and H. K. Naylor, "The Relationship Between Overt and Fantasy Aggression," *J. Abnorm. Soc. Psychol.,* XLIX (1954), pp. 235–240; R. N. Sanford, N. M. Adkins, R. B. Miller, E. A Cobb, *et al,* "Physique, Personality, and Scholarship: a Cooperative Study of School Children," *Monogr. Soc. Res. Child Develpm.,* VIII, No. 1 (1943).

[6] Else Frenkel-Brunswik, "Motivation and Behavior," *Genet. Psychol. Monogr.,* XXVI (1942), pp. 121–265.

[7] *Ibid.,* 134.

2. *Drive for Social Ties, Social Acceptance. Desire to be generally well-liked;* to conform to custom, to join groups, to live sociably, to be accepted by a group in any form, to make contacts.

3. *Drive for Achievement. Desire to attain a high standard of objective accomplishments;* to increase self-regard by successful exercise of talent, to select hard tasks; high aspiration level. (Rating scale starts from "no desire to accomplish something outstanding" and ends with "excessive demands on himself.")

4. *Drive for Recognition. Desire to excite praise and commendation, to demand respect, social approval and prestige, honors and fame.*

5. *Drive for Abasement. Tendency to self-depreciation, self-blame or belittlement;* to submit passively to external forces, to accept injury, blame, criticism, punishment; tendency to become resigned to fate, to admit inferiority and defeat, to confess, to seek punishment and misfortune; masochistic tendency.

6. *Drive for Aggression. Desire to deprive others* by belittling, attacking, ridiculing, depreciating.

7. *Drive for Succorance. Desire for support from outside;* from people, institutions, or supernatural agencies.

8. *Drive for Control (Dominance). Desire to control one's human environment,* by suggestion, by persuasion or command.

9. *Drive for Escape. Tendency to escape all unpleasant situations;* to avoid blame, hardship, etc., to project own failures on others or on circumstances; to gain immediate pleasure with inability to postpone pleasure; use of fantasy, etc.[8]

"The rating scale was used as a means of summarizing what the judges 'privately' think, or what their hypothesis was, about each subject, or what they otherwise would have used only in writing up an interpretative case study of individuals whom they observed over a long period of time."[9] "Though ultimately referred to observed behavior, reference to the underlying motivations was established as the result of a complex process of inference utilizing more subtle indirect cues together with gross features of behavior."[10]

Since the drive ratings were found to be significantly correlated with many ratings of social responses and personality traits, Frenkel-Brunswik concluded that they "helped to organize the . . . data on overt behavior observed in social situations."[11] "One drive variable [may circumscribe] a family of alternative [behavioral] manifestations unrelated to each other. The meaning of the drive concept emerges in terms of families of divergent manifestations held together dynamically or genotypically, though often not phenotypically."[12]

[8] *Ibid.*, 141–142.
[9] *Ibid.*, 144.
[10] *Ibid.*, 261.
[11] *Ibid.*
[12] *Ibid.*, 262.

In view of the interrelationships discovered, it may be assumed that these drive ratings refer to "a level of personality which stands behind the surface of overtly displayed social techniques,"[13] but which is probably not generally as remote from behavior as drives reflected in responses to projective tests. Comparison of late- and early-maturers' motivational ratings may, therefore, provide additional information about the factors underlying behavioral differences between the two groups. The objective meanings of these ratings may be derived from examination of the variables significantly correlated with them.

SUBJECTS AND PROCEDURE

The 34 subjects of this study, part of a normal sample of 90 boys who were members of the Adolescent Growth Study[14] were drawn from the two extremes of a distribution of rate of physical maturing. Sixteen of them had been among the most consistently accelerated throughout the adolescent period; the other 18 had been among the most consistently retarded.[15]

Three members of the Adolescent Growth Study staff who were well acquainted with the subjects over a period of years served as judges. They independently rated each subject on each of the nine drives listed above. In making the ratings, the judges were asked "to forget about manifest behavior and to group the children according to assumed motivation rather than according to similarities of displayed techniques."[16]

Each drive was rated on a five-point scale, a rating of one representing the highest degree, a rating of five representing almost complete absence of the drive in question. In the present study, the three judges' ratings on each drive were averaged to obtain the individual's motivational rating.[17]

RESULTS

Frequency distributions of the ratings of all subjects were made for all the drives. Each distribution was then dichotomized at the point which most nearly enabled the placing of half of the 34 subjects above, and half of

13 *Ibid.*, 144.

14 Jones, "Observational Methods in the Study of Individual Development," *op. cit.;* Jones, *Development in Adolescence, op. cit.*

15 The present sample includes all those subjects among the 19 most consistently accelerated and 19 most consistently retarded boys in the Adolescent Growth Study who were assigned motivational ratings. Twenty-nine of them were also in Jones and Bayley's group and 31 in Mussen and Jones' (Jones and Bayley, *op. cit.;* Mussen and Jones, *op. cit.*).

16 Frenkel-Brunswik, *op. cit.*, 139.

17 The interrater agreements on the nine drive ratings assigned to all the subjects of the Adolescent Growth Study are fully reported by Frenkel-Brunswik. The average reliabilities, corrected by means of the Spearman-Brown formula, were between .70 and .80, with the exceptions of those for Autonomy and Succorance which were .55 and .63 respectively (*ibid.*, 100).

them below, the dividing point. Subjects having scores above this point were considered *high* in this particular drive; those with scores below this point were considered *low* in it. Chi square tests were used to ascertain whether or not high ratings in certain drives were more characteristic of one group (late- or early-maturers) than of the other.

Table 1 shows the number of late- and early-maturers with high ratings in each of the drives, the chi square values obtained, and the levels of significance.

Table 1
Number of Early- and Late-Maturers Assigned High
Drive Ratings

| | NUMBER RATED HIGH | | | |
| | Early-Maturers | Late-Maturers | | |
Drive	($N = 16$)	($N = 18$)	Chi Square	p
1. Autonomy	7	10	.47	ns
2. Social Ties	6	13	4.37	.02–.05
3. Achievement	10	9	.53	ns
4. Recognition	7	9	.15	ns
5. Abasement	9	8	.47	ns
6. Aggression	5	12	4.27	.02–.05
7. Succorance	5	9	1.30	ns
8. Control	9	9	.13	ns
9. Escape	9	11	.09	ns

As the table shows, the two groups were significantly different in two of the nine drives. A greater proportion of late- than of early-maturing boys were rated high in *Drive for Social Ties; Social Acceptance* and *Drive for Aggression.*

While these drives overlap to some extent, they are by no means identical. The correlation between them, based on the entire Adolescent Growth Study male population, was .48.[18] It should be noted, however, that the early- and late-maturing groups did *not* differ significantly in other drives (*Drives for Recognition, Control, and Escape*) that were even more highly correlated with *Drive for Aggression* and/or *Drive for Social Ties* in the entire sample of adolescent boys.[19]

It is of course possible that the independent (physical status) and dependent (motivational ratings) variables were not completely independent, i.e., that in evaluating underlying drives the judges were influenced by their own impressions of the subject's rate of physical maturation. However, it

[18] Frenkel-Brunswik, *op. cit.*
[19] *Ibid.*

seems unlikely that this factor had any significant effects, since the judges were specifically instructed to rate "assumed motivations" rather than more superficial characteristics. Moreover, if the judges had been considerably influenced by the subjects' rates of maturation, the two groups might be expected to differ significantly on more than two of the nine drive ratings.

DISCUSSION

The finding that late-maturers appear to have relatively high motivation for social affiliation and social acceptance is entirely consistent with Jones and Bayley's data which showed that observers rated these boys as higher in sociability, social initiative and eagerness.[20] Moreover, the TAT protocols of the late-maturers revealed that these boys have strong needs for affiliation, particularly with the opposite sex.[21]

On the basis of evidence reported in earlier studies, it has been hypothesized that the late-maturers' emphasis on social activity and their social initiative and participation are largely of an attention-getting, compensatory nature.[22] Examination of the overt social behavior and personality trait variables correlated with *Drive for Social Acceptance* lends support to this hypothesis. For example, high ratings in this drive tended to be associated with high ratings in *energy output, interest in opposite sex, social participation, social self-confidence, social stimulus value, popularity, self-assertiveness* (bossiness), *exuberance, orientation toward the opposite sex*.[23][24] These are characteristics which indicate expressiveness, energy, eagerness and sociability, a constellation labelled "overt social activity" by Frenkel-Brunswik. At the same time, however, high *Drive for Social Ties* was associated with many traits considered to be indicative of emotional maladjustment: *attention-seeking, affectation, dependence on approval, excitedness, tenseness, impulsiveness,* and *exploitiveness*.[25] Hence, it may be inferred that, while late-maturers often reveal high motivation for social affiliation and a great deal of social activity, their social techniques are often childish and affected. Moreover, their high social drives may be based on general insecurity (reflected in *tenseness* and *impulsiveness*) and basic feelings of dependency (indicated by *dependence on others* and *exploitiveness*). The last conclusion is consistent with the finding that the TAT protocols of late-maturers revealed strong underlying dependency needs.[26]

---

[20] Jones and Bayley, *op. cit.*
[21] Mussen and Jones, *op. cit.*
[22] Jones and Bayley, *op. cit.;* Mussen and Jones, *op. cit.*
[23] The correlations between the drive ratings and social behavior are fully reported in Frenkel-Brunswik's monograph (Frenkel-Brunswik, *op. cit.,* pp. 186–187).
[24] Frenkel-Brunswik, *op. cit.*
[25] *Ibid.*
[26] Mussen and Jones, *op. cit.*

The relatively high aggressive motivation ratings assigned to the late-maturers may also be attributed, at least in part, to their basic insecurities, feelings of rejection, and intense dependency needs. Frenkel-Brunswik's data showed that *Drive for Aggression* had considerably higher correlations with emotionally maladjusted behavior than with "overt social activity." Among the manifestations of the latter, only four (*energy output, interest in opposite sex, social participation,* and *social self-confidence*) were significantly correlated with *Drive for Aggression*. On the other hand, 10 indicators of emotional maladjustment (*attention-seeking, affectation, dependence on approval, excitedness, tenseness, impulsiveness, frequent mood swings, selfishness, irresponsibility,* and *exploitiveness*) were associated with high ratings in aggressive motivation. Apparently, the personal and social maladjustments of the late-maturers are often reflected in overt behavior which trained observers are likely to interpret as stemming from strong underlying aggressive motivations.

This finding is particularly interesting in view of the fact that late-maturers had relatively *low* fantasy (TAT) aggression scores, while the early-maturers had *high* scores in this variable.[27] The present data do not enable us to specify the determinants of this discrepancy between behavior-inferred aggressive ratings and TAT aggression scores. Some of it may be due to the middle-class status of most of our subjects. It has been suggested that in this social class cultural prohibitions prevent the overt gratification of aggressive needs and thereby increase their intensity in the individual's fantasies.[28] If this is true, it may be hypothesized that the early-maturers, having identified with a mature male role, have incorporated these prohibitions and are less likely to behave aggressively. As a result, they are more likely to express their aggressive motivations in fantasy. On the other hand, the late-maturers, being defiant of authority[29] may not accept the middle-class standards of behavior so readily. Consequently, they may express aggression more freely and overtly and, therefore, may reveal less aggressive motivation in their fantasy productions.

It may be concluded that these group differences in motivational ratings add further support to the general hypothesis that the late-maturing adolescent is more likely to be personally and socially maladjusted than his early-maturing peer. Apparently in our culture, the physically retarded boy is more likely to encounter a sociopsychological environment which may have adverse effects on his personality development. The early-maturer's experiences, on the other hand, seem to be more conducive to good psychological adjustment.

27 *Ibid.*
28 Mussen and Naylor, *op. cit.;* Sanford *et al., op. cit.*
29 Mussen and Jones, *op. cit.*

SUMMARY

In this investigation, observers' ratings of 18 late-maturing and 16 early-maturing adolescent boys on nine drives were compared. The results showed that high drives for social acceptance and for aggression are more characteristic of the physically retarded than of the physically accelerated.

The meaning of group differences in these ratings may be clarified by examination of the social behavior and personality correlates of the two drives. These suggest that the late-maturer's high social drives may stem from feelings of insecurity and dependence and are often manifested in childish, affected, attention-getting social techniques. Moreover, high aggressive drives tended to be associated with social behavior and personality characteristics indicative of social and emotional maladjustment. Thus, among the physically retarded, the strength of these drives may be partially attributable to underlying feelings of inadequacy, rejection, and dependence.

In general, the data of this investigation support the findings of earlier studies which showed that, among boys, physical retardation may have adverse effects on personality. Physical acceleration, on the other hand, may be conducive to better social and psychological adjustment.

Self-Conceptions, Motivations, and Interpersonal Attitudes of Early- and Late-Maturing Girls* [1]

MARY COVER JONES AND
PAUL HENRY MUSSEN

Even though the preceding paper reports that early-maturing in physical growth affords important social advantages for boys, the converse would be expected for girls. Early physical acceleration in an adolescent girl's growth may make her more conspicuous, tall, and stocky, and none of these attributes are assets by contemporary standards of feminine pulchritude. Hence, Jones and Mussen predicted, in the following study of attitudes toward the self and rate of physical maturation, that "early-maturing girls would reveal negative self-feeling and less satisfactory interpersonal attitudes." Contrary to their expectations, early-maturing girls appear to have "more favorable self-concepts" than late-maturing girls. Therefore, the differences between the early- and late-maturing girls are in the same rather than the opposite direction as early- and late-maturing boys. The researchers interpret their findings as indicating "that late-maturing adolescents of both sexes are characterized by less adequate self-concepts, slightly poorer parent-child relationships, and some tendency for stronger dependency needs."

"The changing body and the changing self" is a phrase associated with adolescent development.[2] It suggests that the shaping into mature form of the childhood body pattern is accompanied by new self-concepts. These

[1] The TAT data for this study were obtained by Harold E. Jones in connection with a test program at the Institute of Child Welfare.

[2] C. B. Zachry, *Emotion and Conduct in Adolescence* (New York: Appleton-Century, 1940).

* From *Child Development*, XXIX (1958), pp. 491–501. Reprinted by permission of the authors and the Society for Research in Child Development.

altered attitudes toward the self reflect at least in part the youth's response to his physical metamorphosis.

What "growing-up" connotes for the individual adolescent depends upon a complex of psychobiological factors. One of the most important of these is rate of physical maturation. Adolescent growth may be relatively regular and even, or it may be uneven or abrupt. The timing of puberty, in relation to social norms of the peer group, may present problems of special importance for some adolescents.

Previous reports of systematic comparisons between the behavior and personality characteristics of early- and late-maturing adolescents have indicated that acceleration in growth tends to carry social advantages for boys[3] but disadvantages for girls.[4] At their peak of growth, early maturing girls are not only taller than their girl classmates but are actually taller than most of the boys in their class.[5] They are conspicuously large at a time when physical size is not an asset for girls in our culture. Many girls consider tallness to be a physical stigma.[6] At the end of adolescence the early-maturing are no longer taller than their age-mates, but in body proportion they tend to have a broad and stocky build,[7] less attractive (in terms of current feminine standards) than the more slender physique of the late-maturing.

Among boys, ascendance in size and musculature is an asset because of our cultural values and the functional advantages of such a build for athletic prowess. This more favorable status is indicated in observational records for early-maturing boys. Staff members rated them as physically more attractive and better-groomed than the late-maturing, and in social situations they were more poised and matter-of-fact, and less attention-seeking.[8]

In contrast, both classmates[9] and adult observers[10] saw the early-maturing girls as relatively submissive, listless or indifferent in social situa-

---

[3] M. C. Jones and N. Bayley, "Physical Maturing Among Boys as Related to Behavior," *J. Educ. Psychol.,* XLI (1950), pp. 129–148; P. H. Mussen and M. C. Jones, "Self-conceptions, Motivations, and Interpersonal Attitudes of Late- and Early-maturing Boys," *Child Development,* XXVIII (1957), pp. 243–256.

[4] H. E. Jones, "Adolescence in Our Society," *The Family in a Democratic Society: Anniversary Papers of the Community Service Society of New York* (New York: Columbia University Press, 1949), pp. 70–82.

[5] F. K. Shuttleworth, "The Physical and Mental Growth of Girls and Boys Age 6 to 19 in Relation to Age at Maximum Growth," *Monogr. Soc. Res. Child Develpm.,* IV (1939).

[6] H. R. Stolz and L. M. Stolz, "Adolescent Problems Related to Somatic Variations," *Yearb. Nat. Soc. Stud. Educ.,* XLIII, Part I (1944), pp. 80–99.

[7] F. K. Shuttleworth, "Sexual Maturation and the Physical Growth of Girls Age 6 to 19," *Monogr. Soc. Res. Child Development,* II (1937).

[8] Jones and Bayley, *op. cit.*

[9] C. M. Tryon, "Evaluations of Adolescent Personality by Adolescents," *Monogr. Soc. Res. Child Develpm.,* IV (1939).

[10] F. B. Newman, "The Adolescent in Social Groups," *Appl. Psychol. Monogr.,* IX (1946).

tions, and lacking in poise.[11] Such girls have little influence upon the group and seldom attain a high degree of popularity, prestige or leadership.[12]

The girls in the slower-maturing classification were seen as relatively more outgoing and more assured. They were eager, animated, peppy, and talkative. This behavior seems to be acceptable among girls since those who exhibit it are also described as confident and having leadership abilities.[13] While the same characteristics of expressiveness are attributed to slow-growing boys, it is associated in their case more specifically (and especially in later adolescence) with show-off behavior, affectation, and tenseness.[14]

In accounting for these sex differences in the response to early or late puberty, we may note that although early-maturing boys have physical advantages over other boys and are socially in step with girls, the girl who develops earlier than her classmates may be temporarily isolated. H. E. Jones has expressed this as follows:

> The early-maturing girl quite naturally has interests in boys and in social usages and activities more mature than those of her chronological age group. But the males of her own age are unreceptive, for while she is physiologically a year or two out of step with the girls in her class, she is three or four years out of step with the boys—a vast and terrifying degree of developmental distance.[15]

A study of responses to the Thematic Apperception Test, given to members of the Adolescent Growth Study when they were seniors in high school, yielded a somewhat unfavorable psychological picture for the late-maturing boys. Compared with their early-maturing peers, they showed greater evidence of negative self-concepts, prolonged dependency needs, feelings of rejection by others, rebellious attitudes toward parents, and strong affiliative needs. These findings were in agreement with evidence from other sources.[16]

A similar TAT comparison of early- and late-maturing girls should be expected to show results different from those obtained for boys. Thus, it might be expected that early-maturing girls would reveal negative self-feeling and less satisfactory interpersonal attitudes.

[11] H. E. Jones, "Adolescence in Our Society," *op. cit.*
[12] M. C. Jones, "A Study of Socialization at the High School Level," *J. Genet. Psychol.*, XCIII (1958), pp. 87–111.
[13] H. E. Jones, "Adolescence in Our Society," *op. cit.*
[14] H. E. Jones, *Development in Adolescence* (New York: Appleton-Century, 1943); Jones and Bayley, *op. cit.*
[15] H. E. Jones, "Adolescence in Our Society," *op. cit.*, 78.
[16] Mussen and Jones, *op. cit.*

PROCEDURE

The present study, paralleling that for boys, was designed to investigate the relationship between maturational status and self-conceptions, motivations, and interpersonal attitudes in a normal public school sample of girls.[17] Personality assessment was made on the basis of their responses to the Thematic Apperception Test (TAT).

The 34 17-year-old girls of this investigation constitute approximately the 20 per cent at each extreme of the total sample of the Adolescent Growth Study, selected on the basis of their physical maturity status as determined by X-rays of the wrists and hands.[18] Sixteen had been among the most consistently accelerated over a four-year period during adolescence; the other 18 were among the most consistently retarded. All of the subjects took the TAT at around age 17 when they were seniors in high school.

The TAT consisted of 18 pictures: nine from the Murray set which is now standard (cards 1, 5, 6, 7BM, 10, 11, 14, 15, 17); five pictures from the set generally used in 1938 when these data were collected (a man and woman seated on a park bench; a bearded old man writing in an open book; a thin, sullen, young man standing behind a well-dressed older man; a tea table and two chairs; an abstract drawing of two bearded men); and four cards not in the Murray series (a madonna and child, the nave of a large church, a dramatic view of mountains, a boy gazing at a cross which is wreathed in clouds).

The tests were administered individually. Each card was projected on a screen while the subject told a story which was recorded verbatim. Standard instructions were given for the Murray cards, and subjects were asked to describe the feelings elicited by the other four pictures. Most of the stories were brief.

The scoring scheme involved counting the relevant needs, press, and descriptions of the heroes of the stories, the assumption being that the storyteller has identified with the hero; the hero's needs are the same as the girl's; the press that impinge upon the hero are the ones that affect the girl telling the story. A total of 20 needs, press, and descriptive categories, each defined as specifically as possible, was developed in the analysis of the protocols. A score for each subject for each TAT category was derived by counting the number of stories in which it appeared. Table 1 presents a list of the categories used, together with definitions of these categories.

To test the reliability of this analysis, one of the authors (PM) and

[17] H. E. Jones, "Observational Methods in the Study of Individual Development," *J. Consult. Psychol.,* IV (1940), pp. 234–238.

[18] N. Bayley, "Size and Body Build of Adolescents in Relation to Rate of Skeletal Maturing," *Child Develpm.,* XIV (1943), pp. 51–89.

another psychologist[19] independently scored 15 complete protocols (300 stories). The percentage of interrater agreement was 90, computed by the usual formula (number of agreements divided by number of agreements plus number of disagreements).

In order to eliminate bias, the scoring used in the present study was done "blind," that is, independently of knowledge of the subject's maturational status.

RESULTS

Frequency distributions of the scores of all subjects were made for all the TAT variables. Each distribution was then dichotomized at the point which most nearly enabled the placing of half of the 34 subjects above, and half of them below, the dividing point. Subjects having scores above this point were considered high in this particular variable; those with scores below this point were considered low in this variable.

Table 1 lists the TAT variables together with the number of late- and early-maturers with high scores in each variable. The exact probabilities of obtaining these distributions of high and low scores in the two groups (or all other possible more extreme sets), calculated in accordance with Fisher's method,[20] are given in the fourth column. The last column gives the levels of significance of the differences between early- and late-maturing boys on these same variables, previously reported by the authors.[21]

As may be seen from Table 1, early- and late-maturing boys differed from each other on many more characteristics than the two groups of girls did. The boys' groups were significantly different from each other, at the 5 per cent level or better, in six of the 20 variables scored, while the early- and late-maturing girls differ significantly in only two of the variables (*negative characteristics* and *n Recognition*). It should be noted, however, that the *direction* of the differences tended to be the same, rather than reversed, in the two sets of data. For example, the following similarities may be noted:

1. In this list of characteristics a significantly greater proportion of late-maturing girls than of early-maturing girls have high scores on *negative characteristics*. This finding is similar to that found in the comparison of early- and late-maturing boys. For girls, it is contrary to expectation.

2. The differences between early- and late-maturing girls in respect to *p Dominance* and *p Rejection* are similar to those for early- and late-maturing boys in these variables. These may be interpreted to indicate slightly poorer parent-child relationships among the late-maturing.

[19] We are indebted to Dr. Virginia B. Ware for her participation in this aspect of the study.
[20] R. A. Fisher, *Statistical Methods for Research Workers* (7th ed.; Edinburgh: Oliver and Boyd, 1938).
[21] Mussen and Jones, *op. cit.*

3. The early- and late-maturing boys differ significantly on *n Autonomy 1,* suggesting a greater tendency for the late-maturing to avoid or defy authority. The differences are in the same direction for girls, but are not significant.

4. Similar results for boys and girls in *n Succorance* may be interpreted as showing some tendency for stronger dependency needs in the late-maturing.

5. Similar results for boys and girls in *p Nurturance* (significant in one variable for boys) may also be interpreted as indirect indications of stronger dependency needs in the late-maturing.

The chief differences between the sexes are as follows:

1. With respect to *n Aggression* more early- than late-maturing girls show "argumentative aggression," but the two groups of girls do not differ in physical aggression. On the other hand, more early-maturing than late-maturing boys show high degrees of both kinds of aggression.

2. On one category of *n Affiliation* (involving romantic love) higher proportions of high scores are shown for early-maturing girls as contrasted with their late-maturing peers. The differences between the early-maturing and the late-maturing boys are in the opposite direction for this category.

3. The variables *n Achievement* and *n Recognition* do not differentiate the two groups of boys. Among girls scores are higher for the late-maturing, very significantly so in the case of *n Recognition.*

4. *Denial of feeling* does not differentiate early- and late-maturing girls but tends to yield higher scores for early-maturing boys.

DISCUSSION

The failure of the TAT data to support observational findings, especially with reference to the variable, negative characteristics, might be accounted for in a number of ways. Some writers report that in many cases thematic fantasies and manifest behavior operate independently and are even negatively related.[22] If we assume this to be the case for our subjects, no further explanation would be needed. But there is also evidence from the literature that, for some groups, TAT findings and overt behavior may be congruent.[23] Our data on boys are in line with this assumption, since, according to observational ratings, late-maturing boys tend to be socially disadvantaged, and, according to the TAT, personally more maladjusted.

The findings for girls are quite different, however. The early-maturing received more unfavorable ratings from both peers and adult observers on

[22] P. H. Mussen and H. K. Naylor, "The Relationship Between Overt and Fantasy Aggression," *J. Abnorm. Soc. Psychol.,* XLIX (1954), pp. 235–240.

[23] R. Harrison, "The Thematic Apperception Test," in "Personality Development in Adolescent Girls," L. K. Frank, *et al., Monogr. Soc. Res. Child Develpm.,* XVI (1951), pp. 60–88.

Table 1
Number of Early- and Late-Maturers Scoring High in TAT Variables

TAT Variable (with Definition)	High Early-Maturers	High Late-Maturers	p	p (boys)
Negative Characteristics—H is described in negative terms (e.g., imbecile, weakling, fanatic)	3	13	.002	.01
p Dominance 1—H forced by parents to do something he doesn't want to	2	7	.08	.09
p Dominance 2—H prevented by parents from doing something he wants to	3	6	—	—
p Dominance 3—Total instances of H's being forced by parents to do something and/or prevented from doing something	4	10	.07	.11
p Rejection—H rejected, scorned, or disapproved by parents or authorities	3	7	.21	.03
n Aggression 1—H is aggressive in physical, asocial way	8	9	—	.02*
n Aggression 2—H is mad at someone, argues	12	14	—	.10*
n Aggression 3—Total of all H's aggressive actions	5	8	—	.10*
n Autonomy 1—H leaves home	8	10	—	.20
n Autonomy 2—H disobeys or defies parents	4	5	—	.11
n Autonomy 3—Total of instances in which hero leaves and/or defies his parents	5	7	—	.02
n Affiliation 1—H establishes good relations with his parents	9	8	—	—
n Affiliation 2—H falls in love, has a romance, marries	11	7	.08	.05*
n Affiliation 3—Total instances in which H establishes and/or maintains friendly relations	7	6	—	.11*
n Succorance—H feels helpless, seeks aid or sympathy	5	10	.16	.06
p Nurturance 1—H is helped, encouraged, or given something by parents	5	7	—	.18

Table 1 (cont.)

TAT Variable (with Definition)	High Early-Maturers	High Late-Maturers	p	p (boys)
p Nurturance 2—H is helped, encouraged, or given something by someone else (not parents)	5	10	.16	.02
n Achievement—H attempts to attain a high goal or do something creditable	7	13	.09	—
n Recognition—H seeks fame and/or high prestige status	3	12	.01	—
Denial of Feeling—S states that picture elicits no thoughts or feelings	10	9	—	.06

* Differences are in the opposite direction for boys as compared with girls.

many characteristics. But in the TAT they appear to be somewhat better adjusted than their late-maturing peers. This discrepancy between observers' ratings and the picture derived from the personality tests may stem partly from the fact that the reported observational records represented an average of repeated ratings taken over a period of time (from 11 to 17 years) while the TAT stories were collected at the end of this period.

Girls who enter puberty early would be expected to have more difficulties in personal-social relations when they are out of phase with their group. However, after the peer group "catches up," these difficulties would be reduced. By the end of senior high school maturational discrepancies, and social distance due to this factor, would be less marked. It is also possible that even a slight improvement in status would bolster morale and be reflected in a projective technique designed to register attitudes and self-concepts.

There is some slight evidence of a trend toward improved social status for the early-maturing in observational ratings over the seven-year period. Twenty-five items concerned with appearance, emotional tone, social participation, responsiveness, and assurance were used in the comparison. Three of these reflected an improved status at the twelfth grade level for early-maturing girls.[24] In two of these, "laughing" vs. "sober" and "sociable" vs. "unsociable," the accelerated girls, while still rated lower than the late-maturing, had improved sufficiently so that the differences between the two groups were no longer significant. But for one important characteristic, "popular" vs. "unpopular," the average ratings for the accelerated girls were now actually slightly higher than for the late-maturing, though the differences were not significant. This last year at high school was the

[24] E. G. Everett, "Behavioral Characteristics of Early- and Late-maturing Girls" (unpublished Master's thesis, Univer. of California, 1943).

only period when the early-maturing girls were rated by observers as above average in popularity.

It is conceivable that other improvements in social relationships were undetected because of the "halo effect" which, in spite of precautions, may have influenced observers who had rated these same adolescents in earlier years. It is not unlikely that if these girls of more mature status had been observed in social groups of their own choosing (presumably outside of school) the behavior picture might have been more favorable.

It may be noted that over the seven-year period the observational records received little corroboration from a self-report inventory.[25] Although differences were not consistent in all categories, the early-maturing girls tended to score more favorably than the slow-maturing on "total adjustment," and also on family adjustment and feelings of personal adequacy. These data from the self-report inventory seem to be generally consistent with the findings from the TAT.

However, we may note that in both the inventory and the TAT the early-maturing girls appear in a somewhat better light than in their reputation scores or in ratings by adult observers. In some individual cases a favorable self-report score should not be taken at face value, in view of the tendency for some individuals to cover up or deny their deficiencies.

The only other variable which yields a significant difference between the maturity groups in the category *n Recognition,* late-maturing girls manifesting a greater desire for personal recognition. The results for *n Achievement,* though not showing significant differences, tend to support these findings. Other data for this group of girls would lead us to expect this relationship between maturity status and desire for recognition. Late-maturing girls were rated by adult observers as attaining higher prestige, showing more leadership, and having greater stimulus value than their early-maturing peers.[26] They were also mentioned more frequently in the high school daily paper over a three-year period and were elected to more offices in extracurricular activities.[27] The late-maturing girls' leadership abilities, their greater social participation, and their apparent social success may have been more closely related to desires for recognition and achievement in the social sphere than to a need for affiliation.[28]

It should be noted that, among boys, *n Achievement* and *n Recognition* were not significantly associated with rate of physical maturation. Perhaps this is due to the fact that for boys in our culture the pressures to strive for achievement and personal recognition are powerful and pervasive; hence, the boy's physical status may have little influence on his acquisition

25 C. M. Tryon, *U.C. Adjustment Inventory I: Social and Emotional Adjustment* (Berkeley: Univer. of California Press, 1939).
26 H. E. Jones, "Adolescence in Our Society," *op. cit.*
27 M. C. Jones, "A Study of Socialization at the High School Level," *op. cit.*
28 *Ibid.*

of strong achievement and recognition needs. Since these cultural pressures are undoubtedly less severe for girls, the strength of these personal needs may be more influenced by such factors as rate of physical maturation.

As we have pointed out in an earlier article,[29] the relationship between physical status and psychological characteristics in boys is by no means simple. The evidence of the present study indicates that this relationship is even more complex in the case of girls. While the TAT analysis reported in this study suggests that early-maturing girls have fewer negative self-concepts and fewer needs for personal recognition, the results must be interpreted very cautiously. Since only two variables were found to be significantly related to physical status, it is obvious that many psychological and social factors are more important than rate of maturing in determining girls' self-concepts and personality characteristics. Furthermore, these data, considered together with the data from earlier studies on girls,[30] suggest that the rate of maturation may affect overt behavior and covert characteristics in different—sometimes seemingly contradictory—ways.

It is also possible that, at least for girls, early- or late-maturing means different things at different stages of adolescent development. It has been proposed that since girls who enter puberty early are out of step physically with both the boys and girls in their classrooms, they tend to be socially handicapped during early adolescence. We have assumed that this would carry emotional hazards, and evidence is available from observational data and reputation measures to indicate that this is the case.[31]

However, the accelerated girl may gain assurance from knowing that she is on the way toward a goal which is a common task for all adolescents, that of being an adult. By the end of high school, many girls in this group were beginning to feel that they had made satisfactory progress toward this goal. If, in addition to this, she can cope with the problems of this period without too much stress, her self-esteem and feelings of adequacy may be enhanced. A resulting improvement in self-concepts may be reflected in the relative infrequency of negative characteristics in TAT stories.

In conclusion, it is evident that each individual's unique personality structure is determined by a complex of interacting variables, including rate of maturation. Comments made by these subjects as young adults indicate that they were aware of a variety of surface phenomena which affected their adolescent adjustment:

"High school is not a pleasant memory. I felt remote from my mother. If I could have talked to her, it would have helped" (a slow-maturer).

"I wasn't very happy in adolescence. My father was out of work. I felt in-

[29] Mussen and Jones, *op. cit.*
[30] H. E. Jones, "Adolescence in Our Society," *op. cit.*; M. C. Jones, "A Study of Socialization at the High School Level," *op. cit.*
[31] H. E. Jones, "Adolescence in Our Society," *op. cit.*

ferior outside my own circle of friends—I always aimed to please" (a very popular late-maturing girl).

"I was slightly rattle-brained" (a popular late-maturing girl).

"I didn't have much fun in high school. I look forward to more happiness now than I did when I was in high school. I was an ugly duckling" (a slow-maturer who ascribed many negative characteristics to the hero).

"I seemed to be separated from friends in high school. I'm more outgoing now, less cautious and fearful" (accelerated girl).

"I was overweight and sensitive about it—now I take things more for granted" (accelerated girl).

"I had a feeling of being different when growing up" (accelerated).

"I felt stupid in school" (accelerated girl).

"I was very lacking in self-confidence in high school" (accelerated girl).

"I'm more optimistic now. I didn't know many people in high school. I would make an effort to get on with people if I had it to do over again" (accelerated).

Feelings of inadequacy and isolation are expressed by these girls and they are attributed to lack of mental ability, financial difficulties, separation from parents, poor social status, overweight, and unattractiveness. They are about equally common among those whose maturational status was at one extreme or the other.

It is obvious that the findings for this specific group of girls need to be particularized for each individual. These results might be modified also for girls in another geographical area or social level or in another generation. It is possible that school and community programs may be able to de-emphasize maturational status by providing an easier access to mixed social groups through classroom, extra-curricular, and recreational activities which cut across age classifications.

SUMMARY

The present study was designed to investigate the relationship between maturational status and TAT scores for a group of physically-accelerated as contrasted with a group of slow-developing girls from a normal class-room sample. The TAT protocols of 34 17-year-old girls—16 who had been consistently accelerated and 18 who had been consistently retarded—were analyzed according to a scoring scheme involving 20 needs, press, and descriptive categories.

The scores of early- and late-maturing in each of the categories were compared. Earlier reports[32] had indicated that girls who reach puberty early are likely to be socially disadvantaged, at least until the rest of their age group "catch up" with them. It was assumed that this social disadvan-

32 *Ibid.;* M. C. Jones, "A Study of Socialization at the High School Level," *op. cit.*

tage would be reflected in the TAT protocols and that differences between the two maturity groups in self-concepts, attitudes, and motivations would be found. Analysis of the data of the present study found few striking differences between the two groups of girls. However, early-maturing girls had significantly lower scores on the category *negative characteristics,* indicating more favorable self-concepts. This finding is contrary to what might have been expected on the basis of observational ratings by adults and reputational ratings by classmates. On the other hand, the TAT results are in line with scores (total adjustment, self-adequacy, family adjustment) on a self-report inventory.

Late-maturing girls have significantly higher scores on *n Recognition,* which is corroborated by data from other sources.

When the differences between early- and late-maturing girls are compared with the differences between early- and late-maturing boys,[33] they are found to be in the same direction more often than in the opposite. These findings are interpreted to indicate that late-maturing adolescents of both sexes are characterized by less adequate self-concepts, slightly poorer parent-child relationships, and some tendency for stronger dependency needs.

It has been emphasized that complex psychological and cultural factors as well as maturational status contribute to personality development and that the pattern of these influences varies for each individual.

[33] Mussen and Jones, *op. cit.*

Implications of Preadolescent and Early Adolescent Cognitive Development for Secondary-School Teaching *

DAVID P. AUSUBEL

Between childhood and adolescence, thinking processes become less bound to experiences of concrete reality and more dependent upon comprehension of abstractions and manipulation of hypothetical relationships. The man who has done more than any other to chart this transition in cognitive development is Jean Piaget, and, broadly speaking, he has mapped the change as being from a "concrete" to an "abstract" stage of thinking. In the following paper, Ausubel discusses the implications of these stages for teaching at the secondary level. His analyses suggests that the secondary school student is ready "for a new type of verbal expository teaching that uses concrete-empirical experience primarily for *illustrative* purposes." Ausubel's discussion warrants the serious attention of students and teachers who are interested in the changes in cognitive behavior that are associated with the adolescent period.

From the standpoint of the secondary school teacher, the most significant development in cognitive functioning that occurs during the preadolescent and early adolescent years is the gradual transition from a predominantly concrete to a predominantly abstract mode of understanding and manipulating complex relational propositions. This developmental shift, in turn, has far-reaching implications for teaching methods and curricular practices in the secondary school.

---

* From *The High School Journal*, XLV (1962), pp. 268–275. Reprinted by permission of the author and the publisher.

THE TRANSITION FROM CONCRETE TO ABSTRACT
COGNITIVE FUNCTIONING[1]

The elementary school child is by no means dependent on *immediate* concrete-empirical experience in understanding and manipulating simple abstractions or ideas about objects and phenomena. It is true, of course, that the emergence of such ideas must always be preceded by an adequate background of direct, nonverbal experience with the empirical data from which they are abstracted. But once their meaning becomes firmly established as a result of this background of past experience, the child can meaningfully comprehend and use them without any *current* reference to concrete-empirical data.

The meaningful understanding or manipulation of relationships between abstractions or of *ideas about ideas,* on the other hand, is quite another matter. In this kind of operation the elementary school pupil is still dependent upon current or recently prior concrete-empirical experience: when such experience is not available, he finds abstract relational propositions unrelatable to cognitive structure and hence devoid of meaning. This dependence upon concrete-empirical props self-evidently limits his ability meaningfully to grasp and manipulate relationships between abstractions, since he can only acquire those understandings and perform those logical operations which do not go beyond the concrete and particularized representation of reality implicit in his use of props. Thus, where complex relational propositions are involved, he is largely restricted to a subverbal, concrete, or intuitive level of cognitive functioning, a level that falls far short of the clarity, precision, explicitness, and generality, associated with the more advanced abstract stage of intellectual development.

Beginning in the junior high school period, however, children become increasingly less dependent upon the availability of concrete-empirical experience in meaningfully relating complex abstract propositions to cognitive structure. Eventually, after sufficient gradual change in this direction, a qualitatively new capacity emerges: the intellectually mature individual becomes capable of understanding and manipulating relationships between abstractions, *directly,* that is, without any reference whatsoever to concrete, empirical reality. He can now transcend the previously achieved level of subverbal, intuitive thought and understanding, and can come to grips in more general terms with all possible or hypothetical relations between abstract ideas.

[1] The following description of this transitional stage of cognitive development is a modified version and somewhat idiosyncratic interpretation of the account given in B. Inhelder and J. Piaget, *The Growth of Logical Thinking from Childhood to Adolescence* (New York: Basic Books, 1958).

Determinants of Change

It is hypothesized that the combined influence of three concomitant and mutually supportive developmental trends accounts for the transition from concrete to abstract cognitive functioning. In the first place, the developing individual gradually acquires a working vocabulary of transactional or mediating terms that makes possible the more efficient juxtaposition and combination of different relatable abstractions into potentially meaningful propositions. Second, he can relate these latter propositions more readily to cognitive structure, and hence render them more meaningful, in view of the growing fund of higher-order concepts and principles encompassed by and made available within that structure. Finally, it seems reasonable to suppose that after many years of practice in meaningfully understanding and manipulating relationships between abstractions with the aid of concrete-empirical props, he gradually develops greater facility in performing these operations, so that eventually (after acquiring the necessary transactional and higher-order concepts) he can perform the same operations just as effectively without relying on props.

How Valid Are These Stages?

Many American psychologists and educators have been sharply critical of Piaget's designation of concrete and abstract stages of cognitive development. They argue that the transition between these stages occurs gradually rather than abruptly or discontinuously; that variability exists both between different cultures and within a given culture with respect to the age at which the transition takes place; that fluctuations occur over time in the level of cognitive functioning manifested by a given child; that the transition to the abstract stage occurs at different ages both for different subject-matter fields, and for component subareas within a particular field; and that environmental as well as endogenous factors have a demonstrable influence on the rate of cognitive development. But although much more rigorous empirical data than have been presented to date are required to substantiate Piaget's conclusions with respect to the existence of these two *particular* stages of cognitive development, the aforementioned criticisms reflect many gratuitous and unwarranted assumptions regarding the criteria that *any* designated stage of development must meet. Actually, developmental stages imply nothing more than identifiable, qualitatively distinctive sequential phases in an orderly progression of development; and from the standpoint of this definition, all of the above cited arguments disputing the legitimacy of Piaget's concrete and abstract stages seem quite irrelevant.

Thus a new stage of development can occur gradually as well as abruptly, particularly when the factors that bring it into being are operative over many years and are cumulative in their impact. It should also be self-evident that the designation of an age level for the appearance of a given stage of cognitive development is solely for purposes of convenience, and does not necessarily imply that changes in question are reflective of "internal ripening" and hence take place invariably at this age. The precise age at which the transition does occur obviously varies from one culture and individual to another, in accordance with intercultural and idiosyncratic differences in such factors as experience, education, intelligence, and personality. Nor should it be considered remarkable that, in as much as transitions to new stages do not occur instantaneously, fluctuations between stages are common until the newly emerging stage is consolidated. Finally, because of intrinsic differences in level of subject-matter difficulty, and because of intra- and inter-individual differences in ability profiles and experiential background, it is hardly surprising that the transition from concrete to abstract cognitive functioning does not occur simultaneously in all subject-matter areas and subareas.

General and Specific Aspects of the Transition

It is apparent, therefore, that the transition from concrete to abstract cognitive functioning takes place specifically in each separate subject-matter area, and invariably presupposes a certain necessary amount of sophistication in each of the areas involved. In the more general sense of the term, however, it is possible to designate the individual's *overall* developmental status as "concrete" or "abstract" on the basis of an estimate of his characteristic or predominant mode of cognitive functioning. This distinction is important for two reasons: First, the individual necessarily continues to undergo the same transition from concrete to abstract cognitive functioning in each *new* subject-matter area he encounters—even *after* he reaches the abstract stage of development on an overall basis. However, once he attains this latter general stage, the transition to abstract cognitive functioning in unfamiliar new subject-matter fields takes place much more readily and presupposes less specific subject-matter sophistication.

Thus, even though an individual characteristically functions at the abstract level of cognitive development, when he is first introduced to a wholly unfamiliar subject-matter field he tends initially to function at a concrete, intuitive level. But since he is able to draw on various transferable elements of his more *general* ability to function abstractly, he passes through the concrete stage of functioning in this particular subject-matter area much more rapidly than would be the case were he still generally in the concrete stage of cognitive development. These facilitating transferable elements presumably include transactional terms, higher-order concepts, and successful experience in *directly* understanding and manipulating relationships between abstractions (*i.e.*, without the benefit of props), which, although acquired in specific subject-matter contexts, are generally applicable to other learning situations.

IMPLICATIONS FOR SECONDARY SCHOOL TEACHING

Once the developing individual reaches the abstract stage of cognitive functioning he becomes in large measure an abstract verbal learner. He now forms most new concepts and learns most new propositions by *directly* apprehending verbally or symbolically stated relationships between previously learned abstractions. To do so meaningfully, he need no longer refer to first-hand, nonrepresentational experience, nor actually perform any of the abstracting or generalizing operations on the underlying empirical data. With his developmental dependence on concrete-empirical props removed, the only condition necessary for the meaningful understanding and manipulation of higher-order concepts and relational propositions is that their substantive import be nonarbitrarily relatable to his particular cognitive structure, and that he adopt a set to learn them in this fashion. Hence, on developmental grounds, he is ready at the secondary school level for a new type of verbal expository teaching that uses concrete-empirical experience primarily for *illustrative* purposes, *i.e.*, to clarify or dramatize truly abstract meanings rather than to generate intuitive meanings.

Didactic Verbal Exposition

Since a largely verbal type of expository teaching is both more economical in terms of time cost, and also makes possible a qualitatively superior kind of abstract meaningful understanding, one might reasonably ask why the secondary school has not placed greater emphasis on more abstract and verbal techniques of effecting meaningful verbal learning. In the first place, by unwarrantedly extrapolating childhood learning conditions to adolescence and adult life, the Progressive Education movement fostered widespread acceptance of the proposition that all verbal concepts and generalizations are *necessarily* nothing more than rotely memorized glib verbalisms unless they both reflect current or recently prior concrete experience and are products of independent problem-solving or discovery. This belief led, in turn, to summary rejection of verbal exposition, and to paradoxical endorsement of such inherently rote problem-solving and discovery practices as the teaching of "type problems," the wholly mechanical manipulation of mathematical symbols, and the performance of cookbook laboratory experiments.

Second, the tendency among educational psychologists uncritically to extrapolate findings from laboratory studies of nonverbal or verbal rote learning to meaningful verbal learning in the classroom, reinforced the educator's perception of verbal learning as necessarily rote in character, and further encouraged him to repudiate expository verbal teaching. Lastly, the failure of educational psychologists to investigate the nature and conditions of meaningful verbal learning and retention, delayed the discovery of more effective techniques of verbal exposition, as well as helped perpetuate the use of traditional rote techniques. Only within the last few years have curriculum specialists and educational psychologists concerned themselves with substantive and programmatic aspects of the problem of facilitating the meaningful acquisition and retention of viable bodies of knowledge.

Discovery and Problem-Solving Techniques

Occasional use of inductive discovery techniques for teaching subject-matter content is didactically defensible when pupils are in the *concrete* stage of cognitive development. It is true, of course, that only the availability of concrete-empirical experience is necessary to generate the semi-abstract or intuitive level of meaningfulness characteristic of this stage of cognitive development. Hence, either simple verbal exposition, using concrete-empirical props, or a semi-autonomous type of discovery, accelerated by the judicious use of prompts and hints, is adequate enough for teaching simple and relatively familiar new ideas. But when the learning task is more difficult and unfamiliar, autonomous discovery probably enhances intuitive meaningfulness by intensifying and personalizing both the concreteness of experience and the actual operations of abstracting and generalizing from empirical data. In these circumstances also, the time-cost disadvantage of discovery learning is relatively less serious, since the time-consuming concrete-empirical aspects of learning must take place anyway, and since a large volume of subject-matter cannot be covered in any case during the elementary school period.

When students reach the *abstract* stage of cognitive development, however, it is obvious that the time-cost disadvantage of discovery techniques is much more serious. Furthermore, in as much as expository verbal teaching can directly induce a level of abstract understanding that is qualitatively superior to the intuitive level in terms of generality, clarity, precision and explicitness, there is no longer any point in attempting to enhance intuitive meaningfulness.

Virtually the same argument applies to the use of deductive problem-solving techniques in the secondary school as a means of furthering intuitive understanding of subject-matter content. Earlier use for this purpose is justifiable in some instances, because these techniques, although time-consuming, undoubtedly enhance the generality of intuitive insight by applying it deductively to the solution of relevant problems. But again, both time-cost considerations and the possibility of directly achieving through expository teaching a much more highly generalized level of abstract understanding, renders continued use at the abstract stage of cognitive development pedagogically unsound.

It would be very misleading, however, to assert that secondary school and even older students can *never* profit either from the use of concrete-empirical props to generate intuitive meanings, or from the use of inductive discovery and deductive problem-solving techniques to enhance such meanings. As previously suggested, generally mature students tend to function at a relatively concrete level when confronted with a particular new subject-matter area in which they are as yet totally unsophisticated. But since abstract cognitive functioning in this new area is achieved with the attainment of a minimal degree of subject-matter sophistication, these special auxiliary techniques should only be employed for the aforementioned purposes during the early stages of instruction. Continued use for other purposes, however (*i.e.,* to illustrate abstract meanings, to improve problem-solving skills, to foster appreciation of scientific method, or to test verbal understanding) is quite another matter.

Volume and Depth of Subject-Matter

The transition from concrete to abstract cognitive functioning enables the secondary school student to master a much greater volume of subject-matter knowledge. To begin with, the logistics of the learning situation become more favorable. His ability to understand abstract relational propositions directly (*i.e.,* to dispense with the time-consuming operations of using both concrete-empirical props and discovery and problem-solving experience to generate and enhance intuitive insights) permits the teacher to present much more subject-matter in the same period of time. In addition, his qualitatively higher level of abstract understanding makes possible a more efficient means of organizing and integrating the materials that are presented. Because his higher-order concepts and relational propositions are no longer intuitive, but are meaningfully formulated in truly abstract and general terms, they become clearer, more stable, more precise, and sufficiently inclusive to subsume a wider array of differentiated facts and subconcepts.

In view of these latter developments and of the greater differentiation of his abilities and interests, the secondary school student is prepared to cope with a greater depth as well as with a greater volume of subject-matter. He is ready for more intensive and differentiated coverage of smaller areas of knowledge as opposed to more global and superficial coverage of larger areas. "Depth" in this context, however, implies greater substantive density of knowledge rather than greater degree of autonomy in discovering the principles and obtaining the information to be learned. If the secondary school student is required to discover most principles autonomously, to obtain most subject-matter content from primary sources, and to design his own experiments, he only has time to acquire methodological sophistication. In terms of *substantive* depth, he has simply moved from previously superficial coverage of broad areas to comparably superficial coverage of more circumscribed areas. The aim of secondary school and undergraduate education is not to produce substantively ignorant junior scholars and scientists, but to produce students who are knowledgeable both in breadth and depth of subject-matter.

Quantity Conceptions in Junior and Senior High School Students[*][1]

David Elkind

In the following study, several hundred youths, ranging from 12 to 17 years in age, were tested to ascertain if they had developed abstract concepts of mass, weight, and volume. The findings show that "87 per cent had abstract conceptions of mass and weight, but only 47 per cent had an abstract conception of volume." The data also demonstrate that for each age level boys were more likely than girls to have the abstract conception of volume. Elkind reports his results within the framework of Jean Piaget's formulations, and his discussion provides an excellent analysis of the ways in which age, sex, and IQ relate to the development of quantity concepts during adolescence. Furthermore, Elkind interprets the adolescent's conceptualization of social roles as having a marked influence upon cognitive activity, and asserts that "the adoption of adult roles beginning at ages 11 to 12 results in an attenuation and selectivity of inductive conceptualizing that must be taken into account before generalizing about the cognitive development of adolescents."

In Piaget's[2] experiments dealing with the development of quantity conceptions in children, he found that abstract responses to mass, weight, and volume appeared in a regular sequence that was related to age. Abstract responses to mass appeared (i.e., in 75 per cent of the subjects tested) by ages 7 to 8, abstract responses to weight appeared at ages 9 to 10, and abstract responses to volume by ages 11 to 12. A systematic replication of one of Piaget's experiments[3] confirmed Piaget's ages for mass and weight

---

[1] This investigation was supported (in part) by a PHS Small Grant M-3466 from the Department of Health, Education, and Welfare, U.S. Public Health Service; the author was then at Wheaton College.

[2] J. Piaget, *The Child's Conception of Number,* First published in Switzerland, 1941 (London: Kegan Paul, 1952).

[3] D. Elkind, "Children's Discovery of the Conservation of Mass, Weight and Volume: Piaget Replication Study II," *J. Genet. Psychol.* (in press).

---

[*] From *Child Development,* XXXII (1961), pp. 551–560. Reprinted by permission of the author and the Society for Research in Child Development.

but failed to confirm his age for volume which was conceived abstractly by only 27 per cent of 11- to 12-year-old American children. The present study seeks to extend the replication to 12- to 18-year groups and to determine the influence of age, sex, and IQ on the attainment of abstract conceptions of quantity in adolescents.

According to Piaget, the criterion of an abstract conception of quantity is the child's judgment of its conservation, its sameness despite perceptual change. For example, in one of Piaget's experiments he showed his subjects two identical clay balls, one of which was subsequently rolled into a "sausage." Those children who judged the mass, weight, or volume of the "sausage" as conserved (the same) demonstrated an abstract conception of quantity. The same technique and criterion were used in the present study.

METHOD

Subjects

Four hundred and sixty-nine junior and senior high school students attending the Norton High School in Norton, Massachusetts, were tested.[4] The majority of children came from lower-middle class families. The mean age and IQ for boys and girls at each grade level are given in Table 1.

Tests and Procedure

The tests for conservation were given as group[5] tests, and the students wrote their answers in blue books. Materials for all tests were the same: two identical clay balls (1½ inches in diameter) and a small scale. The tests were always given in the following order.

1. Test for the Conservation of Mass. E began by explaining that the two balls were identical in every way, that there were no tricks in the experiment, and that he was simply repeating an experiment originally performed with elementary school pupils. Several students were asked to verify by means of the scale that the two balls weighed the same. E asked any student who still had doubts to voice them. Questions raised permitted E to explain further that the balls were made of the same kind of clay and that "same amount" meant to the degree of accuracy permitted by the scale and did not mean absolute equivalence.

Once the students agreed that the balls were the same, E asked: (a) "Do

---

[4] The writer is indebted to Mr. Henri A. Yelle, Principal of the Norton High School, and to the teachers and students whose friendly cooperation made the study possible.

[5] In Piaget's experiments and in the first replication with elementary school children, the tests were administered individually. (J. Piaget and B. Inhelder, *Le Developpement des Quantités chez l'enfant* [Neuchatel and Paris: Delachaux and Niestle, 1941]; Elkind, *op. cit.*)

the balls both contain the same amount of clay?" (identity question); (b) "Suppose I made one of the balls into a sausage, would the two pieces of clay still contain the same amount of clay?" (prediction question). E then actually rolled one of the balls into a sausage and asked: (c) "Do they both contain the same amount of clay now?" (judgment question); (d) "Explain your answers" (explanation question).

2. **Test for the Conservation of Weight.** E rolled the "sausage" back into a ball and then repeated the whole procedure described above save for the use of "weight" instead of "amount."

3. **Test for the Conservation of Volume.** E again rolled the "sausage" back into a ball and repeated the procedures for mass and weight, except that the terms "volume" and "same room or space" were substituted for the previously used quantity concepts.

Controls

Objections were raised by Baldwin[6] against Dennis'[7] finding of animism in college students. The brunt of these objections was that verbal misunderstandings and verbal ambiguities made interpretation hazardous. In the present study a number of controls were introduced to minimize the verbal misunderstanding and ambiguity: (a) the preliminary procedures of weighing the balls and of answering questions regarding the experiment tended to reduce misunderstandings; (b) the four types of question asked for each concept—identity, prediction, judgment, and explanation—gave some measure of the reliability of responses; (c) finally, as a special check on the conservation of volume test (which proved most difficult for children in the original and replication study), students were asked what would happen if the ball and the sausage were put into identical glasses filled equally high with water.

Scoring

A test was considered passed only if the subject correctly identified, predicted, judged, and explained the conservation of a quantity.

RESULTS

Controls

The control tests indicated that students who failed the conservation tests did so because of inadequate conceptions and not because of verbal misunderstanding.

[6] A. L. Baldwin, *Behavior and Development in Childhood* (Dryden, 1955).
[7] W. Dennis, "Animistic Thinking among College and University Students," *Sci. Mon.*, LXXVI (1953), pp. 247–250.

All of the students who failed the volume test agreed (answered "Yes" to the identity question) that initially the balls were the same in volume. But they predicted, judged, and explained that the volume of the clay changed with the change in its shape. This was true for the same students who on the previous pages had written that mass and weight were conserved because either: (a) nothing was added or taken away; or (b) changing the shape did not change the amount; or (c) what the sausage lost in width it gained in length and therefore was the same as the ball.[8] Thus, the students clearly understood the conservation questions with regard to mass and weight, but failed to generalize their judgments, predictions, and explanations to the conservation of volume which they treated as an entirely different problem. Kay (16–5) wrote, for example, that mass and weight were conserved because nothing was added or taken away but to the volume question she wrote, "The molecules may be more compressed in one object (the ball) than in the other (the sausage); although it (the sausage) has the same number of molecules and the same weight, its volume is not the same."

The question about the water levels, introduced as a control, revealed a fact significant in itself. Over two thirds (70 per cent) of the students said that the water levels would rise because of the weight (often described as impact or pressure) of the submerged objects. Gla (15–4) "The water with the ball will rise more because the impact (*sic*) of the ball is greater because it is more condensed and it will rise more."

Such examples could be multiplied, but even these are sufficient to show that students who failed to judge volume conservation did so, not because of verbal misunderstanding, but rather because they failed, in Piaget's terms, to dissociate their subjective sensorimotor conceptions (impact, compression) of weight and volume from their objective (molecules), logico-mathematical conceptions.

Percentage of Subjects Judging Conservation

Of the 469 junior and senior high school students tested, 87 per cent had abstract conceptions of mass and weight, but only 47 per cent had an abstract conception of volume. A test of the difference between the three percentages gave an χ^2 of 254.2 which is significant beyond the .001 level. Table 1 shows that, according to the usual 75 per cent criterion for placing a test at a given year level, the volume test is too difficult for all but the oldest age group. This result, like that of the first replication, fails to confirm Piaget's age (years 11 to 12) for the abstract conception of volume.

---

[8] These are the same three explanations given by the elementary school children.

Table 1
Percentage and Mean IQ of Students, Classed by Sex and Age, Having Abstract Conceptions of Quantity

Sex	N	Mean Age	Mean IQ	QUANTITY CONCEPTION Mass	Weight	Volume
M	56	12.6	94.6	79	71	38
F	66	12.6	99.2	79	86	26
M	46	13.6	89.6	78	74	43
F	48	13.6	100.9	90	92	29
M	28	14.6	99.6	93	96	68
F	45	14.6	107.9	93	93	40
M	31	15.5	95.3	97	90	58
F	41	15.7	101.9	98	93	39
M	29	16.4	100.0	83	90	72
F	43	16.6	107.9	86	86	58
M	14	17.7	109.9	100	100	79
F	12	17.7	103.3	100	95	68

TOTALS

Sex	N	Mean Age	Mean IQ	Mass	Weight	Volume
M	204	15.1	96.5	85	83	54
F	265	15.1	104.3	89	90	40
M & F	469	15.1	100.4	87	87	47

Variables Influencing Volume Conservation

Age. As shown in Table 1, there was a regular increase with age in the percentage of students who had abstract volume conception.

Sex. Table 1 shows that for each age level the percentage of boys was consistently higher than the percentage of girls who had an abstract conception of volume. For the two groups as a whole the difference gave an χ^2 of 7.9 which is significant at the .01 level.

IQ. The point biserial coefficient for the correlation of IQ (Kuhlmann-Anderson) with passing the volume test was .31 significant beyond the .01 level. This finding agrees with the results of other studies[9] which have also shown a low but positive correlation of IQ with measures of conceptual development.

[9] J. M. Deutsche, "The Development of Children's Concepts of Causal Relations," *Univer. Minn. Inst. Child Welf. Monogr.*, No. 13 (1937); D. Elkind, "The Development of Quantitative Thinking: a Systematic Replication of Piaget's Studies," *J. Genet. Psychol.*, XCVIII (1961), pp. 37–46; Elkind, "Children's Discovery of the Conservation of Mass, Weight, and Volume: Piaget Replication Study II," *op. cit.*

DISCUSSION

The results of the present study raise two interrelated questions: (a) Why do significantly more students attain abstract conceptions of mass and weight than attain the abstract conception of volume? (b) In what respect are age, sex, and IQ related to volume conservation? Both questions can be answered within the framework of Piaget's genetic psychology.

In the course of more than 40 years of continuous research on mental development Piaget has evolved a genetic theory of intelligence, adaptive thinking and action. He derives, in a necessary sequence of age-related stages, the abstract intelligence of adults from the sensorimotor coordinations of infants. It is a nature theory in the sense that the stages—sensorimotor (0 to 2 years); preoperational (2 to 7 years); concrete operational (7 to 11 years); formal operational (11 to 15 years)—are assumed to reflect maturational changes in the forms of thinking. It is also a nature theory in the sense that the gradual attainment of particular conceptions is assumed to reflect the influence of physical and social environment on the contents of thought.

Unlike reinforcement learning theorists, Piaget holds that there is no real separation between drives and cognitive structures: "À tous les niveaux, les intérêts et les besoins qui son intervenus dans ces apprentissages étaient eux mêmes solidaires des structures déjà construdes ou en voie de construction."[10] For Piaget the appearance of new structures gives rise to new drives to exercise those structures. Such exercise is self-reinforcing through the production of function pleasure. In the course of being exercised, novel stimulation leads to the differentiation of new structures which in turn give rise to new drives in a continuous progression.

The attempt by the organism to use the stimulation of the environment to develop and conserve its structures, Piaget speaks of as assimilation. The modification of structures due to environmental influence, he speaks of as accommodation. Any particular cognitive system attains its final stage of development when assimilation and accommodation are in equilibrium. The two processes are in equilibrium when novel stimulation can be used by the system without either disrupting its activity or necessitating a structural differentiation. According to Piaget, the attainment of the equilibrium stage is the underlying dynamic of all intellectual growth.

Applied to quantity conceptions, Piaget's theory holds that the child is ready[11] for attaining the abstract volume conception at ages of 11 to 12. The child is ready in the maturational sense because the conceptualization

[10] P. Greco and J. Piaget, *Apprentissage et Connaissance* (Paris: Presses Universitaires de France, 1959), p. 30.

[11] This is not Piaget's term but economically describes the child's state.

of volume requires only concrete operations (internalized actions) which are present in most children by the age of seven.[12] The child is also ready in the experiential sense that he has had sufficient object contacts to form abstract conceptions of mass and weight which are the structural prerequisites for the attainment of the volume conception.[13] On the basis of his findings Piaget[14] assumed that this operational and structural readiness was sufficient for the attainment of the volume conception by a majority of 11- to 12-year-old children. His theory, on the contrary, suggests that a majority of young people should not, as in the present study they did not, attain an abstract conception of volume.

Piaget's theory proposes two kinds of events which when taken in combination can account for the results of this investigation. According to Piaget, the age at which a young person is ready to attain the volume conception is also the age at which he is developing formal mental operations. Whereas concrete operations (7 to 11 years) are concerned with classifying, relating, and quantifying the immediate environment, formal operations are concerned with constructing systems and theories. Put simply, concrete operations are concerned with immediate reality, formal operations with possibility.[15]

Because of the unity of operations and drives, the appearance of formal operations means the appearance of new interests and horizons:[16] "The adolescent is no longer content to live in the interindividual relations offered by his immediate surroundings or to use his intelligence to solve problems of the moment."[17] The result of the new interests and motivations arising from formal operations is necessarily an attenuation in the drive for conceptualizing the immediate physical environment. This attenuation of drive for inductive conceptualizing therefore decreases the possibility of children spontaneously discovering the conservation of volume.

[12] Elkind, "The Development of Quantitative Thinking: a Systematic Replication of Piaget's Studies," op. cit.; Elkind, "Children's Discovery of the Conservation of Mass, Weight, and Volume: Piaget's Replication Study II," op. cit.; Piaget, op. cit.; Piaget and Inhelder, op. cit.

[13] Elkind, "Children's Discovery of the Conservation of Mass, Weight, and Volume: Piaget Replication Study II," op. cit.; Piaget and Inhelder, op. cit.

[14] Piaget and Inhelder, op. cit.

[15] J. Piaget and B. Inhelder, The Growth of Logical Thinking from Childhood to Adolescence (Basic Books, 1958).

[16] This may be one of the reasons for the well established decline of interest in school at about the same age. (A. T. Jersild and R. J. Tasch, Children's Interest [Bureau of Publications, Teachers College, Columbia Univer., 1949]; L. Monash, "Why Children Like or Dislike School," Understanding the Child, XVI [1947], pp. 67–70; S. Tenenbaum, "Attitudes of Elementary School Children to School, Teachers and Classmates," J. Appl. Psychol., XXVIII [1944], pp. 134–141.) Perhaps, the school curriculum does not take sufficient account of the early adolescent's need for hypothetical propositions.

[17] Piaget and Inhelder, The Growth of Logical Thinking from Childhood to Adolescence, op. cit., 341.

Intimately bound up with the appearance of formal operations is a second event which affects the early adolescent's conceptualizing activity. This second event is the adoption, beginning around ages 11 to 12, of adult roles. In Piaget's view, roles are systems of values and ideals which serve to control and direct the individual's behavior. Roles are adopted only in early adolescence because ideals and values are possibilities, not realities, and therefore can only be constructed by means of formal operations.

Prior to the adoption of adult roles, conceptualization was directed by the activity of concrete mental operations and the problems posed in structuring the physical environment. With the appearance of formal operations and adult roles at ages 11 to 12, these come to play the leading part in the direction of conceptualizing activity.

With social roles directing cognitive activity, the adolescents' conceptualizing becomes much more selective than it was during childhood. Unlike the relatively constant physical environment which poses similar problems for all youngsters, the diversity of social roles makes for enormous variety of concept formations among adolescents. For example, the young person who wishes to become a scientist will meet a different set of experiences— and hence conceptual problems—than will another young man whose aim is to be a mechanic. And, in general, adolescents will attain different conceptions according to the kinds of experiences and conceptual problems their particular roles provide. Accordingly, those adolescents who attain the volume conception, despite the attenuation of motivation, would have adopted roles conducive to the formation of quantity conceptions.

These two events—(a) the attenuation of interests and motivations for quantity conceptualizing due to the development of formal operations and (b) the increased selectivity, at the same age, of conceptualizing due to the adoption of diverse social roles—can explain why so many young people who spontaneously discovered the conservation of mass and weight nevertheless failed to discover the conservation of volume. It remains to determine whether this conclusion is consistent with the relations of age, sex, and IQ to volume conservation.

Age. The increase with age in the percentage of students having abstract volume conceptions is misleading because the number of students who dropped out of school also increased with age (Table 1).[18] The groups in the higher grades were therefore a much more select sample than were the groups in the lower grades. What the relation of age and volume conservation shown in Table 1 really means is that those young people who remain

18 School records showed that the *N* for the 7th grade was average for the initial size of the groups at the older age levels. The difference between the number of 7th graders and the number of the higher grades indicates the number of dropouts at each grade level.

in school are more likely than those who leave school to have attained an abstract conception of volume.

This finding is in agreement with the hypothesis that individual differences in social roles lead to selective conceptual learning. Students who stay in school are more likely than those who leave to have adopted professional or academic occupational roles. It seems reasonable to assume that the motivations and interests associated with the adoption of such roles would be more likely than nonacademic or nonprofessional roles to lead individuals into situations requiring the conceptualization of quantity.

Sex. The consistently higher percentage of boys than girls having an abstract volume conception can hardly be attributed to innate differences in conceptual ability between the sexes. For one thing, the mean IQ of girls is higher than that of boys at each age level. Secondly, there is no difference between sexes with respect to the attainment of mass and weight conceptions. It seems very unlikely that there is an ability specifically for the attainment of the volume conception. Finally, Hurd[19] has shown that even when girls are far behind boys in their knowledge of physics they are almost completely able to catch up with additional training. For all these reasons differences in conceptualizing ability between sexes seems an improbable explanation for the difference in their performance.

The performance differences between boys and girls are consistent with hypothesis presented earlier. The roles adopted by the American girl differ considerably from the roles adopted by the boy.[20] Girls are supposed to be more interested in social relations than boys and to find mathematics and physics incomprehensible.[21] Boys, on the other hand, are supposedly awkward in social situations and intuitively adept at science and mechanics. Many more boys than girls have experiences in measuring and building things, and most boys and few girls get scientific and mechanical books and toys as gifts. This difference in experiences and opportunity for developing quantity conceptions could account for the fact that more boys than girls attain an abstract conception of volume.

IQ. Individual differences in social roles could also explain the low but positive correlation of IQ with volume conservation. The IQ is neither a necessary nor a sufficient condition for the adoption during adolescence of any particular occupational role. Children with high IQs may never adopt a professional or academic ideal, while youngsters with low IQs may set their hearts on being doctors or lawyers. With the adoption of the ap-

[19] A. W. Hurd, "Sex Differences in Achievement in Physical Science," *J. Educ. Psychol.*, XXV (1934), p. 70.

[20] D. Ausubel, *Ego Development and the Personality Disorders* (Grune and Stratton, 1952).

[21] For example, one girl who had an IQ of 140 but failed the volume test told me her father did not believe in women getting too much education.

propriate role, even adolescents with MAs of 8 or 9 could attain the volume conception since it can be formed with the mental operations present in the average seven-year-old. One would, therefore, not expect a one-to-one correlation between volume conservation and IQ.

Nevertheless, brighter children would choose professional or academic roles more frequently than children with less ability. There would then be a tendency for bright children, more frequently than dull children, to attain the abstract conception of volume. This tendency would be reflected in a low but positive correlation of volume conservation and IQ in agreement with the correlation obtained in the present study.

In sum, the results of this investigation suggest that the appearance of formal operations and the adoption of adult roles beginning at ages 11 to 12 results in an attenuation and selectivity of inductive conceptualizing that must be taken into account before generalizing about the cognitive development of adolescents.

SUMMARY

Four hundred and sixty-nine junior and senior high school students were tested for their conceptions of mass, weight, and volume. Results showed: (a) of the students tested, 87 per cent had attained abstract conceptions of mass and weight, but only 47 per cent had attained an abstract conception of volume; (b) the percentage of students having an abstract volume conception increased significantly between the ages of 12 and 18; (c) a significantly higher percentage of boys than girls attained an abstract conception of volume; (d) there was a low but positive correlation of IQ with attainment of the volume conception.

The results of the study were interpreted within the framework of Piaget's genetic theory of intelligence. According to this theory, the operational and structural readiness for the attainment of the volume conception appears just at the onset of formal operations and the adoption of adult roles. These two events produce an attenuation of interest and opportunities for spontaneously attaining quantity conceptions whose formation is now dependent upon the particular role the young person adopts. This conclusion was found to be consistent with the relations of age, sex, and IQ to the attainment of an abstract conception of volume.

Factors That Aid and Hinder Creativity[*][1]

J. P. GUILFORD

In comparison with adults, adolescents enjoy greater physical health, stamina, and athletic prowess, yet in respect to cognitive talents they are neither more nor less endowed. It is during adolescence, however, that cognitive aptitudes most rapidly develop, and teachers at the secondary level are inevitably involved in facilitating the development of cognitive skills.

One of the more highly esteemed cognitive abilities in the contemporary, technological societies is creativity. And in the following paper, Guilford, who has been investigating creative aspects of personality for several years, discusses "the basic facts concerning the nature of creative thinking and of the more creative persons." As Guilford observes, "when we know what kind of skill is to be developed, we have a more clearly defined goal toward which to work." His paper is recommended reading for students and teachers who are seeking descriptions of creative behaviors, data about "basic traits and creativity," and information regarding the relationships of IQ, temperament, and motivational qualities to creative performance.

In the part of our current *Zeitgeist* pertaining to psychology and education, no word has had a more dramatic rise in popularity than "creativity." After generally ignoring the subject, psychologists have come to realize their backwardness in knowledge of this subject. Employers have been asking for more inventive scientists, engineers, and managers. Special courses on how to think creatively have been springing up by the score. Special institutes are being held on the subject. Teachers and educators are asking how

[1] Adapted from an address presented at the Creative Education Institute at San Jose State College, June 21, 1961.

* From *Teachers College Record*, LXIII (1962), pp. 380–392. Reprinted by permission of the author and the publisher.

they can make courses more stimulating and how they can arouse more productive thinking on the part of students.

The interest is international, as well it might be. The whole world faces two very critical problems—how to feed its exploding population and how to keep the peace. It has been estimated that in the next 20 years we shall need three times the number of scientists and engineers we now have, and they shall have to exercise all the ingenuity of which they are capable. We are reminded by the scriptures, however, that man does not live by bread alone. There is, I think, a very noticeable surgence of interest in the arts in all their forms. We wish to walk in beauty as well as in peace, freedom, and dignity. There is also good reason to desire increased creativity to achieve aesthetic goals.

INVESTIGATION OF CREATIVITY

My topic suggests that I give most consideration to the abilities and other traits of individuals that make some of them creative and some not. Knowing these traits should help us to recognize which persons are likely to have the potentialities of becoming creatively productive. The same knowledge should help us in taking steps that should increase creative output in ourselves and in others, and other steps that may remove obstacles in the way of creative productivity. Our primary concern, then, will be the basic facts concerning the nature of creative thinking and of the more creative persons, with reference to the application of this information.

Serious investigation of creativity by psychologists began only in recent years. For centuries the common idea had been that only the exceedingly rare person is genuinely creative and that creativity is a divine gift. As such, it was not to be investigated, or at best, there was little hope of understanding it. Even after Darwin came upon the scene, when creativity came to be regarded as some kind of rare, hereditary blessing, there was still little incentive to attempt to understand it because there was thought to be little that one could do about it. In addition to being very rare, the highly creative person's behavior is sometimes eccentric. This has sometimes branded him as being abnormal and even pathological. Mental pathology was similarly avoided as a subject of study by scientific investigators for a long time.

Creativity became an object of scientific study primarily because of the general interest in individual differences. This approach recognizes that individuals differ psychologically in traits or attributes that can be conceived as continua or dimensions—that there can be varying degrees of a quality possessed by different individuals. This concept was eventually applied to creativity, but in serious ways only about a dozen years ago. This new way of looking at the matter permitted us to think that not only a few peculiarly gifted persons but individuals in general possess some degree of the same creative trait or traits.

This conception has opened the door to many kinds of research. We need no longer study creativity by catching the rare persons who are recognized as having creativity to high degree; a multitude of subjects is now available to investigators. We can discover the various aspects of the phenomenon called "creativity." We can find out the conditions under which creative performance occurs or does not occur.

As in the case of all psychological characteristics that make up personality, we may be forced to recognize that heredity establishes limits of development for an individual. But there is considerable faith among educators that rarely does an individual realize full development in any respect and that there is generally considerable room for improvement. This faith should also be applied to the creative aspects of personality.

BASIC TRAITS AND CREATIVITY

There are a number of approaches to the investigation of the traits or characteristics in which creative individuals are most likely to excel. Some investigators appear to regard the phenomenon of creativity as a single dimension of personality. It is my view that the creative disposition is made up of many components and that its composition depends upon where you find it. Practically all investigators recognize that there are many potentially contributing conditions.

When the problem is approached from the standpoint of individual differences, the most natural scientific technique to apply is that of factor analysis. This is the approach that my associates and I have taken almost exclusively in the Aptitudes Project at the University of Southern California.

According to our original hypotheses,[2] we expected to find the more creative individuals to think with greater fluency, with more flexibility, and with greater originality. The tests designed to measure fluency present very simple tasks, and the quantity of output determines the scores. When told to produce a list of items of information of a certain kind, how many responses can the examinee give in a limited time? Quality does not count, but, of course, the responses must be appropriate.

Flexibility in thinking means a *change* of some kind—a change in the meaning, interpretation, or use of something, a change in understanding of the task, a change of strategy in doing the task, or a change in direction of thinking, which may mean a new interpretation of the goal.

[2] J. P. Guilford, "Creativity," *Amer. Psychologist*, V (1950), pp. 444–454.

There has been some debate concerning the meaning of "originality." In our research and in that of others, originality means the production of unusual, far-fetched, remote, or clever responses. But there are some who say that an idea is not original or novel unless no human being has ever thought of it earlier. This conception is worthless to the scientist because there is no way of knowing that an idea has never existed before. It is somewhat better to say that a novel idea is a new one so far as the particular individual who has it is concerned. But unless we know the individual's past history of thinking, we cannot be sure of meeting this criterion either.

Fortunately, we can resort to empirical signs of novelty in terms of the statistical infrequency of a response among members of a certain population that is culturally relatively homogeneous. This gives us some workable operations for applying the criterion of unusualness. The index of unusualness can therefore be purely objective. As for the far-fetched or remote associations and the clever responses, we have as yet no way to avoid some degree of subjectivity of judgment in assessing test performance to obtain an index of originality.

Another somewhat popular criterion of an original idea is that it is socially useful. Those who deal with practical affairs may be appropriately concerned about this aspect of produced ideas. But such a criterion involves us in values in a way that science cannot deal with directly; hence, the criterion of social usefulness can be quickly dismissed by the psychologist. This does not mean that as a person he is unconcerned about social usefulness. It does mean that as a scientist he cannot afford to be so concerned and so restricted.

FLUENCY FACTORS

We shall now give closer attention to the various factors of fluency, flexibility, and originality. It turns out that in verbal tests alone there are three differentiated fluency factors.[3] Ideational fluency has to do with the rate of generation of a quantity of ideas. The idea produced may be as simple as a single word, as complex as the title for a picture or a story, or as phrases and short sentences that convey unitary thoughts. In a test, we may ask the examinee to list all the things he can think of that are solid, flexible, and colored. He may respond with *cloth, leaf, rose petal, hair, skin, leather,* etc. Any response that fulfills the specifications is accepted and counts toward the total score. In other tests, we may ask the examinee to list the consequences of a certain action or event, the various uses of an

[3] J. P. Guilford and P. R. Christensen, "A Factor-analytic Study of Verbal Fluency," *Rep. Psychol. Lab.*, No. 17 (Los Angeles: University of Southern Calif., 1957).

object, or some appropriate titles for a given story. In all such tests, there are strict time limits.

It is easy to see where an operation such as that in tests of ideational fluency fit into problem solving of many kinds. Perhaps a problem situation, when interpreted in a certain way, calls for an object with a certain set of specifications in order to solve it. Once these specifications are realized, the person who can list pertinent possibilities most rapidly could, other things being equal, solve the problem most quickly.

Many a problem calls for a running through of the likely possibilities during the earlier stage of interpreting or structuring it as well as during the stage of finding solutions. This process also probably depends in some degree upon ideational fluency. Of course it is not necessary to run through *all* the logical possibilities in solving a problem. One can ignore the less promising ones. This point will be touched upon later.

Another kind of fluency is called "associational fluency." It pertains to the completion of relationships, in distinction from the factor of ideational fluency, which involves giving ideas that fit a class. As a test of associational fluency, we may ask the examinee to list all the words he can think of that mean the opposite, or nearly the opposite, of the word "good." He may respond with *bad, poor, sinful, defective, awful, terrible,* and so on. This ability is most obviously of use to the creative writer, who wants to find quickly a variety of verbal expressions without having to resort to a thesaurus.

The factor of associational fluency may have more general utility—for example, whenever we apply thinking by analogy as our strategy in solving problems. Thinking of a correlate is the completion of an analogy. Many solutions to new problems are achieved by the practice of thinking by analogy. The success of certain kinds of engineers in their work has been predicted to a small extent by means of a test of associational fluency as found by Saunders (1956).[4]

A third kind of fluency is called "expressional fluency." It has to do with the facile construction of sentences. We ask the examinee to write as many four-word sentences as he can, all different, with no word used more than once. We may give the initial letters of the four words, the same four being specified for each sentence—for example, "W____ c____ e____ n____." To this task, he may reply "We can eat nuts." "Willie comes every night," "Wholesome carrots elevate nations," "Weary cats evade nothing," and so on. You will probably not be surprised when I tell you that in a ninth-grade sample, the girls obtained a higher mean score than the boys.

We do not know yet how much generality to attach to this factor, whether it is limited to tasks such as the writing of sentences or whether it

---

[4] C. W. Taylor (ed.) *Research Conference on the Identification of Creative Scientific Talent* (Salt Lake City, Utah: University of Utah Press, 1956, 1958, 1959).

is so broad as to pertain to organizing ideas into systems. If it is as broad as the latter suggestion, it should be of considerable consequence, perhaps in something as important as the trial-and-error development of a scientific theory. The factor has been found significantly related to ratings by psychologists of the creative performances of military officers.[5]

FLEXIBILITY FACTORS

One type of flexibility we first recognized as "spontaneous flexibility" because the tests that measure it do not even suggest that the examinee be flexible.[6] Without his knowing it, he can make a good score if he varies his *kinds* of responses. If we tell the examinee to list all the uses he can think of for a common brick, the total number of uses listed is a good score for his status on the factor of ideational fluency. But we also score his performance in terms of the number of times he changes *category* of uses. For example, the person who responds with *build a house, build a school, build a factory*, etc., does not change his class of uses. Another person who responds with *make a paper weight, drive a nail, make baseball bases, throw at a cat, grind up for red powder, make a tombstone for a bird*, etc., changes class with each new response. He shows much more flexibility.

The person who makes a low spontaneous-flexibility score is rigid in the sense that he perseverates within one or a very few classes. As there are several kinds of flexibility in thinking, so there are several kinds of rigidity. When someone tells you that a certain person is rigid, beware of overgeneralization of the term. We do not find in normal (nonpathological) people a very general trait of rigidity vs. flexibility. We find several. This does not say that there are no individuals who are rigid in just about every respect, but the general rule is that they may be rigid in some respects and not in others, at least so far as thinking is concerned.

A new hypothesis may be considered in connection with the factor of spontaneous flexibility. Some advisers on how to think creatively suggest that in starting to solve a new problem, we keep our thinking at a rather high level of abstraction. We think of it first in very general terms. Thus, the person who goes from class to class in the Brick Uses test is operating within the frame of reference of a much broader class within which there are subclasses. A higher level of abstraction may mean thinking in terms of broader classes. This has the effect of broadening the scope of the scanning process in searching for information. Going from one class to another in

[5] From an unpublished study conducted jointly by the Aptitudes Project at the University of Southern California and the Institute for Personality Assessment and Research, University of California, Berkeley.

[6] J. W. Frick, J. P. Guilford, P. R. Christensen, and P. R. Merrifield, "A Factor-analytic Study of Flexibility in Thinking," *Educ. Psychol. Measmt.*, XIX (1959), pp. 469–496.

the Brick Uses test also means considering all the properties of a brick—its weight, its color, its texture, and so on. These are abstractions all lying within the class of the total nature of a brick. This is reminiscent of a stock method of practicing creative thinking, a method known as "attribute listing" and advocated by Crawford.[7]

A second kind of flexibility has been called *"adaptive* flexibility" for the reason that in tests in which it was first found, the examinee, to succeed, must make changes of some kind—changes in interpretation of the task, in approach or strategy, or in possible solutions. Our current interpretation of the factor of originality is that it is adaptive flexibility in dealing with verbal information.

We have a kind of test, called Plot Titles, in which the examinee is told a very short story and that he is to suggest as many appropriate titles for the story as he can. One of the stories is about a wife who is unable to speak until a specialist performs the appropriate surgery. Then her husband is driven to distraction by her incessant talking until another surgeon eliminates his hearing, when peace is restored in the family.

The number of commonplace titles given to the story may be used as a score for ideational fluency. Such titles include,

A man and his wife
Never satisfied
Medicine triumphs
A man's decisions
Talking and hearing

The number of responses rated as "clever" serves as a score for originality. Such titles are exemplified by

The deaf man and the dumb woman
Happiness through deafness
Operation—peace of mind
Yack, yack, hack

Several other types of tests serve to indicate individual differences in the factor of originality.

ELABORATION

In the course of our investigations of abilities involved in planning,[8] we found another kind of ability we have called "elaboration." In one test, given the bare outlines of a plan, the examinee is asked to produce the de-

[7] R. P. Crawford, *Techniques of Creative Thinking* (New York: Hawthorne Books, 1952).

[8] R. M. Berger, J. P. Guilford, and P. R. Christensen, "A Factor-analytic Study of Planning Abilities," *Psychol. Monogr.,* LXXI, Whole No. 435 (1957).

tailed steps needed to make the plan work. The more details he adds, the better is his score. We believe that the unique feature of this ability is that in tests for it, one item of information leads to another as a kind of extension or completion. In more technical language, we say that the examinee is producing a *variety of implications*.

It was eventually recognized that the abilities of fluency, flexibility (including originality), and elaboration are similar in that the tests of them call for a variety of answers. There is no right or fully determined answer in connection with the information given in the item. There are now parallel tests in which each item *does* have one right answer because it is fully determined by the information given or because there is one conventionally accepted answer. A distinction has therefore been made between *divergent* thinking and *convergent* thinking to represent the two classes of abilities. The abilities of which I have been speaking thus far belong in the divergent-thinking category. Because the individual has to generate his answer or answers, starting from given information, in both categories of abilities, we speak of divergent-*production* factors vs. convergent-*production* factors, respectively.

QUANTITY vs. QUALITY

Several questions arise concerning the relationship of quantity and quality of production. One debated and investigated hypothesis is that "quantity breeds quality." This hypothesis holds that if a person produces a greater total number of ideas, he also produces a greater number of high-quality ideas in a limited time. Another view is that a mental set for quantity is inefficient because if a person spends his time producing a lot of low-quality responses, he cannot produce so many good ones.

There is another aspect of this controversy. When a person is set to give "good" answers, he is applying judgment or evaluation as he goes along. On the one hand, it is believed that an evaluative or critical attitude is generally inhibiting to the flow of ideas, good and poor alike. On the other hand, it is believed that the application of evaluation as one proceeds has a selective effect, holding back the low-quality responses and letting the high-quality responses come through.

The well-known brainstorming technique, attributed to Alex Osborn[9] and employed by many others, conforms to the first of these two schools of thought. One of its chief claimed virtues is that the separation of production and evaluation—in other words, suspended judgment—is better procedure. As originally applied, of course, brainstorming has other features, which include thinking in small groups rather than thinking by individuals in seclusion.

[9] A. F. Osborn, *Applied Imagination* (New York: Scribner's, 1953).

The experimental results bearing upon the issue of suspended judgment are somewhat mixed. Meadow *et al.*[10] report that with suspended judgment, the production of "good" answers was a little more than doubled. The problems were to suggest unusual uses for a wire coat hanger and for a broom. The criteria for "good" responses were "unique" and "useful."

In our Aptitudes Project,[11] we gave the Plot Titles test with and without the specific instruction to give clever titles. It was expected that the instruction for clever titles would entail more evaluation. The effects of this instruction were shown by a reduction in the number of low-quality responses, an increase in the number of high-quality responses, and a higher average rating of degree of cleverness.

Hyman[12] found that his subjects generated 68% more responses under quantity instructions, but that this increase in "good" responses, where "good" meant uncommon and of "high quality," failed to keep pace with the total output. Hyman is probably right when he concludes that quantity may breed quality for some types of problems but not for others. It is also probably true that the *kind* of evaluative attitude applied by the thinker has much to do with the quantity and quality of responses he produces.

Divergent thinking is a matter of scanning one's stored information to find answers to satisfy a special search model. Evaluation comes into the picture in determining whether or not the produced information fits the search model. Relaxed evaluation would permit a broadening of the base of the search, whereas an evaluative attitude with some degree of strictness should narrow the search. In doing so, however, it may lead more efficiently to good answers. This should depend upon the clarity and accuracy of the search model. If the thinker has a good search model, the application of evaluation while he thinks should be helpful.

But if evaluation is of a more vague kind, such as that involving a fear of being unconventional, a fear of thinking socially unacceptable thoughts, or a fear of being wrong, it should be definitely better to suspend judgments based on such criteria. Evaluation incident to an overly strong desire for a quick solution would also be handicapping. But evaluation for the sake of efficient scanning, where there is good strategy in the scanning process, should be beneficial.

Hyman[13] has found that a general critical attitude can have rather broad transfer effects in solving problems. A group of engineers, in Hyman's ex-

---

[10] A. Meadow, S. J. Parnes, and H. Reese, "Influence of Brainstorming Instructions and Problem Sequence on a Creative Problem Solving Test," *J. Appl. Psychol.,* XLIII (1959), pp. 413–416.

[11] P. R. Christensen, J. P. Guilford, and R. C. Wilson, "Relations of Creative Responses to Working Time and Instructions," *J. Exp. Psychol.,* LIII (1957), pp. 82–88.

[12] H. Hyman, *Some Experiments in Creativity* (New York: General Electric, Relations Services, 1960).

[13] *Ibid.*

periment, read some previously given solutions to a certain practical problem under the instruction to list all the good points that they could see in those solutions. A second group was instructed to list all the faults they could see in the same solutions. Later, in solving the same problem and in solving a new one, the uncritical readers suggested solutions of their own that were rated higher on the average than those of the critical group. Thus, very general critical attitudes must be taken into account.

GROUP vs. INDIVIDUAL THINKING

The question of group thinking vs. individual thinking has received a great deal of attention. The virtue claimed for group thinking in brainstorming is that one person stimulates another. In support of this hypothesis, Osborn[14] reports that about a third of the ideas produced in group brainstorming are of the "hitch-hiking" type. In such a case, one person's idea is based upon another person's idea.

There are results which do not support his hypothesis, however. Taylor et al.[15] found a larger number of unrepeated ideas produced by individuals working alone than by those working in groups, where both kinds of thinkers were working under the condition of suspended judgment. Taylor points out that the group condition may have the effect of channeling thinking in similar directions, reducing the variety and therefore the quantity of unrepeated ideas.

Perhaps neither the group nor the isolation condition is best under all circumstances or for all individuals. It is quite possible that both can be applied to advantage. The preference of the thinker should have something to do with the choice of condition. A great deal is made of the point that the highly creative person is an independent thinker and that his creation may be a highly personal thing. Torrance (1959)[16] found that the more highly creative child (as indicated by his test scores) in a small group often works by himself or is somehow induced by the others to do so.

Whatever the outcome of brainstorming sessions in particular instances, experiments show that courses on creative thinking that are heavily weighted with brainstorming exercises seem to leave the students with beneficial results, and these results have some degree of permanence.[17]

[14] A. F. Osborn, *Development of Creative Education* (Buffalo, N.Y.: Creative Education Foundation, 1961).

[15] D. W. Taylor, P. C. Berry, and C. H. Block, "Does Group Participation When Using Brainstorming Facilitate or Inhibit Creative Thinking?" *Admin. Sci. Quart.*, III (1958), pp. 23–47.

[16] Taylor, *op. cit.*

[17] A. Meadow and S. J. Parnes, "Evaluation of Training in Creative Problem Solving," *J. Appl. Psychol.*, XLIII (1959), pp. 189–194; S. J. Parnes and A. Meadow, "Evaluation of Persistence of Effects Produced by a Creative Problem Solving Course," *Psychol. Reports*, VII (1960), pp. 357–361.

How much of the improvement to attribute to the brainstorming technique and to which aspects of it the improvement should be attributed are open questions.

CONTEXT OF CREATION

From the discussion thus far, one may conclude that creative performances are to be identified psychologically as a small number of divergent-production operations. Two different qualifications must be introduced. One exception is that two of the factors that we in the Aptitudes Project regarded from the first as being pertinent to creative thinking fall outside the divergent-production group. The other exception is that I have not yet told the whole story regarding the divergent-production factors. I shall make good on the latter omission first.

I have repeatedly stated that the tests on the factors thus far described are *verbal* tests. They pertain to verbally stated information. There are other kinds of information, and the question comes up whether the same person is usually equally creative in handling different kinds of information, material, or content. From our analytical results, we can say that it can happen, but we should rarely expect the same person to be equally capable of creativity in science, in the arts, mathematics, administration, and musical composition. Highly creative individuals in many of these different areas may have outstanding qualities in common, but psychological study indicates that they also have some marked differences.

In the area of divergent-production abilities alone, we find that individuals may be uneven in handling verbal vs. concrete vs. symbolic material. Symbolic material is the kind with which the mathematician deals —numbers and letters. Fluency, flexibility, and elaboration in dealing with concrete (perceived) material are probably of greater importance to the inventor of gadgets, the painter, and the composer, whereas the same kinds of abilities for dealing with verbal material or content are more important for the creative writer and the scientist. In other words, there are parallel abilities for dealing with concrete (or figural) material, symbolic material, and verbally meaningful (or semantic) material.

One of our earlier hypotheses[18] was that the unusually creative person has a high degree of sensitivity to problems. One person notices something wrong or in need of improvement, whereas another fails to observe defects, deficiencies, or errors. The observation of imperfections starts the creative person on his way to creative production. The observation of inadequacy of solutions also keeps the creative thinker at work on his problem.[19]

[18] Guilford, *op. cit.*
[19] P. R. Merrifield, J. P. Guilford, P. R. Christensen, and J. W. Frick, "A Factor-analytical Study of Problem-solving Abilities," *Rep. Psychol. Lab.*, No. 22 (Los Angeles: Univer. Southern California, 1960).

Factor analysis has consistently upheld this hypothesis by finding an ability common to a variety of tests calling for the noticing of defects and deficiencies in such things as common household appliances, social customs, or in solutions to problems. Such an ability, however, seems to fit better in the general category of evaluative factors than it does in that of divergent production.

Not being satisfied with things as they are is a matter of evaluation. We hear a great deal about the "divine discontent" of the creative person. It is said that Thomas A. Edison frequently admonished his workers with the comment, "There must be a better way. Go and find it." The uncreative, in contrast, are often willing to settle for half-way measures and tolerably successful solutions to problems.

Another of our initial hypotheses was that many an invention or new idea is the revision of something that is already known. But the revision is not an obvious one. It takes quite a change in the meaning, interpretation, or use of an object to achieve such an innovation. One of our tests, designed for such an ability, asks which of five objects or their parts could be most reasonably adapted to be used to start a fire when there are available the following items: a fountain pen, an onion, a pocket watch, a light bulb, and a bowling ball. The accepted answer is "pocket watch," since the cover of the watch face could be used as a condensing lens. Since this and other such tests call for one best answer, this factor falls logically in the convergent-production category. The feature that makes a contribution to creativity is that a *transformation* must occur; objects must be redefined. Individuals who are clever at improvising seem to show this kind of ability.

There are other abilities outside the divergent-production category that make some contribution to creative performances in their own ways. We have seen that one of the evaluative abilities—sensitivity to problems—has a function in getting the creative thinker started. Other evaluative abilities should have their uses, whether judgment is suspended or not, in determining whether the products of thinking are good, useful, suitable, adequate, or desirable. If the creator is to finish his job, he will eventually appraise his product, and he will revise it if he feels that revision is called for.

COGNITION AND MEMORY

Thus far I have spoken of three major categories of intellectual factors —abilities of divergent production, convergent production, and evaluation. There are two other major categories—cognitive abilities and memory abilities—all distinguished from those in the first-mentioned categories and from each other. Cognitive abilities have to do with discovery, recognition, or comprehension of information in various forms. Memory abilities have to do with storage or retention of information.

Many people, including some teachers, have for some reason disparaged memory and memory abilities. Some of them, who emphasize the importance of thinking, seem wrongly to believe that good thinking and good memory are incompatible qualities, perhaps even negatively correlated. Actually, good memory contributes to good thinking.

It is not a good, well-stocked memory, as such, that is bad, for even the most creative people have given due credit to stored information. It is the way in which storage is achieved and organized that makes the difference between the graduate who is sometimes described as "merely a walking encyclopedia" and the graduate who has a usable and fruitful fund of information. Memory abilities thus make their indirect but important contribution to creative performance.

The question often arises concerning the relation of creativity to intelligence. In connection with this question, the usual conception of "intelligence" is that which is measured by such tests as the Stanford Binet, the Wechsler scales, or the California Test of Mental Maturity.

In discussing abilities related to creativity, I have referred to them as intellectual factors. It is very doubtful whether these abilities, particularly those in the divergent-production category, are represented to any appreciable degree in standard IQ tests. IQ tests were designed to predict success in school learning, particularly in reading, arithmetic, and the subject-matter or informational courses. But we now know that there are many other kinds of intellectual abilities.

Studies of groups of research scientists and engineers[20] show that such groups have high average scores on IQ tests. They would need to have higher-than-average IQs to have passed all their academic hurdles, most of them including the PhD. But only a fraction of these are outstanding for creative performance. But within groups of scientists and engineers, the correlation found between IQ-test scores and creative performance is usually rather low. This is due in part to the restriction of range of IQ within such groups. The evidence seems to indicate that although the qualities in traditional IQ intelligence may be of some help to the creative scientist or engineer, they are by no means sufficient.

The low correlation between creativity and IQ is also found at younger age groups. In high school students, Getzels and Jackson (1959)[21] found that if the highest 20% of the subjects on IQ were selected as "gifted," 70% of those who stood in the highest 20% in terms of divergent-thinking tests would have been missed. Torrance (1959)[22] has reported a similar

[20] D. W. Taylor, "Thinking and Creativity," *Ann. N.Y. Acad. Sci.,* XCI (1960), pp. 108–127.
[21] Taylor, *Research Conference on the Identification of Creative Scientific Talent, op. cit.*
[22] *Ibid.*

finding in the elementary grades. In both instances, it was reported that the teachers knew their high-IQ students better and liked them better. The high-creative without high IQs were often regarded as nuisances, and they were somewhat estranged from other students. Those with both high IQ *and* high creativity were recognized as having unusual but sound ideas, to be good in planning and improvising, and effective in getting attention (1959).[23, 24]

NON-APTITUDE TRAITS

The assessment of traits of temperament, interest, and attitude in connection with creativity has been approached in various ways. One approach has been to find the most outstandingly creative individuals in different professional groups, such as architects, writers, and scientists, and to assess them quite thoroughly by methods that are available. If a creative group differs systematically from the general population or, better, some group outside the profession but matched with it for age, sex, and educational level, it is concluded that this creative group stands apart or is distinguished by the personality trait or traits in question.

There are obvious dangers in drawing conclusions from studies of this kind, unless an appropriate control group has been used. When it is found that creative architects, scientists, mathematicians, and writers alike tend to score highest on theoretical and esthetic interest on the Allport-Vernon-Lindzey *Study of Values,* this may occur just because any high-IQ group would do the same.[25] When it is found that the creative males tend to score relatively in the direction of femininity on the masculinity-femininity scale of the *Minnesota Multiphasic Personality Inventory* scale, we remember that Terman and Miles[26] found that as members of the two sexes are more intelligent and better educated, they respond more alike to test items on masculinity vs. femininity. Nor should it be surprising that the creative groups just mentioned should tend to score high on the Strong *Vocational Interest Blank* scales for architect, psychologist, and author-journalist.

A somewhat better approach is to obtain two samples from the same profession, composed of highly creative and less creative individuals, respectively. The groups can then be compared with respect to various assessed qualities. Sometimes the groups are distinguished on the basis of

[23] *Ibid.*

[24] For systematic treatments of a unified theory of intelligence see J. P. Guilford, "Three Faces of Intellect," *Amer. Psychologist,* XIV (1959), pp. 469–479; J. P. Guilford and P. R. Merrifield, "The Structure of Intellect Model: Its Uses and Implications," *Rep. Psychol. Lab.,* No. 24 (Los Angeles: University of Southern California, 1960).

[25] D. MacKinnon, "What Do We Mean by Talent and How Do We Use It?" *The Search for Talent* (New York: College Entrance Board, 1960).

[26] L. M. Terman and Catherine C. Miles, *Sex and Personality* (New York: McGraw-Hill, 1936).

judgments by their teachers.[27] In still other studies, subjects of mixed occupations but similar in IQ and educational level have been tested with measures of creative aptitude and of non-aptitude traits.[28]

NON-APTITUDE DIFFERENCES

We have had to recognize that creative occupational groups share parallel but different exceptional abilities. We should expect the various groups to show some non-aptitude qualities in common and also to show some differences. One difference, for example, has been noted between creative students of art and of science. The more creative art student has been reported to be more of an observer than a participant in what is going on.[29] The more creative science student is reported to be more of a participant than the less creative student.[30] Such observations should prevent our generalizing conclusions obtained from one creative group to all other creative groups.

There are many ways in which creative people of many groups are alike, however. There is general agreement that the highly creative person, particularly the original person, is self-confident. Which comes first, originality or self-confidence? It is a little like the old hen-and-the-egg problem. Probably, it works both ways: Originality yields success and hence self-confidence, and self-confidence leads the individual to attempt to solve problems where others would give up. In some instances, self-confidence goes over into conceit, as we have all been aware. Sometimes this is fed by the adulations of admirers. Sometimes it may suggest an underlying hypersensitivity to criticism.

Along with self-confidence, there is usually self-assurance or social boldness. The creative person is especially confident about his own judgment and his own evaluations of his work. He is often described as an independent thinker, which includes having an independent set of values. If he thinks his product is good, he discounts the criticisms of others and may disparage their judgments.

Not only is he more or less independent of other people's judgments, he may be self-sufficient in that he can take people or he can let them alone. He is likely to find ideas more important than people, though he is not necessarily a social recluse. These qualities do not add to his popularity with others, so he is in danger of becoming estranged from his parents, his

27 J. E. Drevdahl, "Factors of Importance for Creativity," *J. Clin. Psychol.* XII (1956), pp. 21–26; E. F. Hammer, *Creativity* (New York: Random House, 1961).

28 J. P. Guilford, P. R. Christensen, J. W. Frick, and P. R. Merrifield, "The Relations of Creative-thinking Aptitudes to Non-aptitude Personality Traits," *Rep. Psychol. Lab.*, No. 20 (Los Angeles: Univer. Southern California, 1957).

29 Hammer, *op. cit.*

30 D. S. Garwood, "Some Personality Factors Related to Creativity in Young Scientists" (unpublished Doctoral dissertation, Claremont Graduate School, 1961).

teachers, and his peers. Contributing to this state of affairs also is a lack of mutual understanding. The creative child and his associates may need special counseling to help smooth over some roughness in interpersonal relationships. This can be done without curbing development along creative lines.

We have found that young men who stand high in one or more kinds of fluency are likely to be somewhat impulsive, cheerful, and relaxed. Those who score high in tests of originality tend to have strong esthetic interests, and they like to indulge in divergent thinking. They do not feel much need for meticulousness or for discipline. Somewhat surprisingly, they show no particular dislike for conventional or socially approved behavior, nor do they show signs of neuroticism.

One of the striking traits found by Getzels and Jackson (1959)[31] among high school students who stand high in divergent-thinking tests is a strong sense of humor. This is shown particularly in the kinds of stories they tell in response to pictures. For example, one picture showed a young man working at his desk at six-thirty in the morning. A bright but less creative student wrote the following kind of story: "This young man is very ambitious to get ahead. He comes early every morning to impress his boss so he will be promoted." A more creative student told the following kind of story: "This picture is the office of a firm that manufactures breakfast cereals. It has just found a formula to produce a new kind of cereal that will bend, sag, and sway. The man is a private eye employed by a rival firm to obtain the formula. He thinks he has found it and copies it. It turns out to be the wrong formula, and the competitor's factory blows up."

Such stories usually involve some novel twist or transformation, such as the expression regarding the cereal that will "bend, sag, and sway." Many stories derive their humor from such a source. The person who makes up such stories is exhibiting verbal or semantic transformations, which is a sign that he has a fair degree of the factor of originality. Since this is a semantic ability, and since Getzels and Jackson's tests were verbal, we may well question whether the affiliation of humor and the ability to produce transformations extends to other kinds of content, figural or symbolic. It is probably true, however, that creative painters, composers, and mathematicians also experience a certain amount of enjoyment, if not amusement, in playfulness with their own kinds of materials.

FINAL SUGGESTIONS

Although the temperament and motivational qualities can help us somewhat in identifying potentially creative people, no one of them is a dependable sign, nor would all of them collectively be sufficient. Neither do

[31] Taylor, *Research Conference on the Identification of Creative Scientific Talent,* op. cit.

these qualities help us very much in understanding the nature of the creative processes. On the whole, we have less chance of changing individuals with respect to these qualities in order to increase their creativity, except for changing certain attitudes.

Our chief hope, then, of either identifying the more creative persons or enhancing their creative performances lies with the aptitude factors. If we regard the intellectual factors as distinct but somewhat generalized thinking skills, this statement seems more reasonable. We develop skills by practicing them. The question, then, is one of what kinds of practice can best be applied and under what conditions.

An understanding of the nature of the skills is one of the most important steps either for the teacher or the student. When we know what kind of skill is to be developed, we have a more clearly defined goal toward which to work. Torrance (1959)[32] reports that even after 20 minutes of instruction on the nature of divergent-thinking processes, grade-school children showed a clearly observable improvement in performing tasks of this type.

Although special courses on creative thinking have proved beneficial, our whole educational system can be of greater help by giving more attention to this subject. There is abundant opportunity to teach almost any subject in ways that call for productive thinking rather than rote memory. Even the multiplication tables can be taught in ways that give the pupil insight into properties of the number system.

In some experimental courses at the University of Illinois in which mathematics is taught from the lower grades on by what is called a "discovery" method, instead of telling the child the axioms and other principles of mathematics, the teacher lets him discover them for himself by exposing him to appropriate examples. Also at the University of Illinois, science is being taught to children by a discovery method. Some natural phenomenon is demonstrated without explanations to the class, perhaps in motion-picture form. From then on, it is a matter of the students' asking questions, with minimum information being given by the teacher, until the student develops his own satisfactory hypothesis.

Education in this country has unfortunately been too much dominated by the learning theory based upon the stimulus-response model of Thorndike, Hull, and Skinner. People, after all, are not rats (with a few exceptions), and they are not pigeons (with similar exceptions). Let us make full use of the human brains that have been granted to us. Let us apply a psychology that recognizes the full range of human intellectual qualities. We must make more complete use of our most precious national resource— the intellectual abilities of our people, including their creative potentialities.

32 *Ibid.*

Conditions Productive of
Superior Children*

ROBERT J. HAVIGHURST

Although modern investigators would be the first to admit that the task of identifying the factors associated with the development of intellectual superiority is still unfinished, most would agree with Havighurst, who believes "that production of mentally superior people is more a matter of social engineering than of discovery and exploitation of a rare natural resource." In the paper presented below, the author first discusses the influences of social class, urbanization, and family background upon mental superiority. He then suggests several steps that might be taken to increase the supply of mentally superior children. For example, he proposes that we increase cultural opportunities among families of lower social status, support counseling and guidance services, and be more explicit and articulate in our concern that parents develop in their children motivations for intellectual achievement. Furthermore, as perhaps "the most potent means of increasing the numbers of mentally superior children," Havighurst holds that teachers must teach in a fashion that stimulates highly creative, intellectual accomplishments.

Children become mentally superior through a combination of being born with superior potential and being raised in a superior environment. Nobody knows the relative importance of these two factors. Certainly, biological intelligence is too low in some children to permit them to develop even average mental ability. Probably a severe environmental handicap can prevent the potentially most able child from showing more than average mental ability.

It seems probable that our society actually discovers and develops no more than perhaps half its potential intellectual talent. Some evidence for this statement lies in the fact that former immigrant groups, which at one

---

* From *Teachers College Record,* LXII (1961), pp. 524–531. Reprinted by permission of the author and the publisher.

time did the heavy labor of America, at first produced very few mentally superior children; but after a sojourn in this country of two or three generations, they have produced large numbers of mentally superior people. They did this through bettering the environment in which they reared their children. The same process is now going on in the underprivileged groups of today—the Negroes, the Puerto Ricans, the rural southern whites—as they secure better economic conditions and then create a more favorable environment for the mental development of their children.

There is some validity to a view of the production of mentally superior people as a *processing* of human material. Some of this material is of better biological quality than other parts of it, but it all depends heavily on social processing for the quality of the final product.

In this paper we shall deliberately ignore the biological element in the production of mentally superior children and consider only the cultivation of mental superiority through the family, the school, and the community. We shall try to answer the question: What kind of social environment produces mentally superior children most efficiently, and how can we expand this environment and make it more effective?

SOCIAL CLASS AND CITIES

Mentally superior children come in relatively high proportions from upper and upper-middle class families and in relatively lower proportions from lower working class families. This fact has been affirmed in dozens of studies of the relations between IQ and socio-economic status.

Some idea of the relative efficiencies of the various social classes in processing their children for mental ability is given in Table 1, which comes from a study of all the children in the sixth grade of the public schools of a medium-sized midwestern city. The upper and upper-middle classes, combined, produced 1.8 times as many children in the upper quarter of the IQ distribution as they would if all social classes had been equally efficient at this, and only .4 times as many children in the lowest quarter. The lower working class showed a reversal of these efficiency ratios.

If all four socio-economic groups had been as efficient as the upper and upper-middle class groups in providing children with IQ's in the top quarter (above about 110), there would have been 180 children with IQ's over 110 in this community for every 100 such children today. In other words, the numbers of mentally superior children would have been almost doubled, and the intelligence level of the child population would have been lifted enormously.

Similar conclusions arise from a study of high school seniors in a city of 500,000. Roughly 5 per cent of the seniors were selected by a systematic

Table 1
Efficiencies of the Various Social Classes in Producing Children in the Top and Bottom Quarters of IQ Distribution
(Sixth Grade in River City)

		Efficiency Ratio* in Producing Children in	
Social Class	Percentage Distribution of Children	Top Quarter	Bottom Quarter
Upper and Upper Middle	10	1.8	.4
Lower Middle	27	1.5	.6
Upper Lower	39	.8	1.1
Lower Lower	24	.4	1.6

* These ratios indicate the relative efficiencies of the various social classes. If all classes were equally efficient in producing children of a given quartile in IQ, the ratios would all be 1.

screening program as being "academically superior." As can be seen in Table 2, the various high schools contributed to this total in rough proportion to the socio-economic status of the parents. The school with highest socio-economic status contributed 19 per cent of its seniors to the select group. Within this group, 92 per cent of the fathers were high school graduates; 65 per cent were college graduates. The three schools with lowest socio-economic status contributed 1.5 per cent of their seniors to the select group. Less than 40 per cent of the fathers of the superior students in these three schools were high school graduates. If all schools had contributed as

Table 2
Efficiencies of Schools of Various Socio-Economic Levels in Producing Academically Superior High School Seniors
(Data from an American city of 500,000 population)

	High School						
	A	B	C	D	E	FGH	Total
No. of graduates	412	392	325	71	400	1,203	2,803
No. of superior students in graduating class	77	45	30	5	17	20	194
Per cent of superior students	19	12	9	7	4	1.5	5.1
Rank in Socio-economic status	1	2	3	4	5	7	
No. of superior students if A ratio prevailed	77	74	62	14	76	229	532

efficiently as School A to the production of superior students, there would have been 532 instead of 194, or almost three times as many. Probably the reason this proportion is higher than the proportion reported in Table 1 is that Table 1 refers to sixth graders, Table 2 to twelfth graders. The cultural advantages of the higher status children probably cumulated between the sixth and twelfth grades to give them even greater superiority over their less privileged agemates.

Granted the assumption we are making in this paper—that mental superiority is largely a product of social environment—the mental level of the population would be raised very greatly if we could give all children the kinds of social environment which upper middle class children have today.

Mentally superior children also tend to come from urban and suburban communities, rather than from rural communities. This is not as pronounced an effect as the social class effect, but it seems to indicate that the urban-suburban environment is more stimulating mentally than the rural environment.

Within the families lower on the socio-economic scale, there is enough production of mentally superior youth to indicate that socio-economic status alone is not what makes the difference between a good and poor environment for mental growth. It is probably certain cultural and motivational deprivations that often go with low socio-economic status that reduce the efficiency of lower status families. Whenever a very bright boy or girl is discovered in a family of low economic status, it turns out that this family has unusual characteristics which give the youth an advantage. These characteristics may consist of thrift and ambition or of an interest on the part of the mother or father in literature, art, or science.

Summing up the argument thus far, it seems that boys and girls who are mentally superior have become so because of (1) a home and school environment which stimulated them to learn and to enjoy learning; (2) parents and other significant persons who set examples of interest and attainment in education which the children unconsciously imitated, and (3) early family training which produced a desire for achievement in the child. When these influences act upon a child with average or better biological equipment for learning, the child will become mentally superior. They are sometimes found in unexpected places.

For instance, Paul is a very good student in high school. His mother has worked as a waitress for years, since her husband deserted her, to support herself and Paul. She placed Paul in a boys' home sponsored by a church, and he has lived there from the age of 8 until his present age of 18. He says, "My father and mother never went to college. I thought I'd like to do better in life than they did." At the boys' home, the superintendent and the teachers were demanding but warm. Under them, Paul performed well in the elementary school until time for senior high, when he went to the local public school. Here he had some difficulty at first. He says, "English was about my worst subject. The teacher helped me though, and I improved a lot. I consider her an important person in my life." A careers unit in civics helped him to decide on engineering or mathematics, and he will go to college with scholarship help. Two of his closest friends have college plans. The superintendent of the home has urged him to go. "He told me to go to college. He said I was a good student, and I ought to go to college."

DIVERGENT THINKERS

Among the mentally superior part of the population some people are creative and some are not. Much attention has been paid recently to the quality or qualities of creativity on the assumptions that our society needs not only intellectually facile people but, more especially, creative people, and that a high IQ does not guarantee creativity.

Guilford and others have made a distinction between "convergent thinking" and "divergent thinking." The person with "convergent" intellectual ability is retentive and docile. He tends to seek the single, predetermined "correct" answer to an intellectual problem. On the other hand, the "divergent" thinker is constructive and creative. He tends to seek the novel, experimental, and multiple answer to an intellectual problem.

Guilford has devised a number of tests of creative intelligence which have only a low positive correlation with the usual intelligence tests. Getzels and Jackson,[1] using these tests, picked out a group of high school pupils who were high in IQ (average 150) but not especially high in creative thinking for comparison with a group high in creative thinking but lower in IQ (average 127). The two groups did equally well in achievement tests, but the high intelligence, non-creative group were preferred by their teachers as the kind of students they liked to have in their classes. The high creative group, in freely-written stories, showed more humor, more unexpected endings, more incongruities, and generally a freer play of fantasy. Similarly, Cattell and Drevdahl[2] compared outstanding research scientists with outstanding teachers and administrators in the same fields on the 16 P.F. Personality Inventory. They found the researchers to be more self-sufficient and schizothymic (introverted), to have a greater drive for mastery, and to entertain more radical ideas.

[1] J. W. Getzels and P. W. Jackson, "The Highly Creative and the Highly Intelligent Adolescent," *Third University of Utah Research Conference on the Identification of Creative Scientific Talent* (University of Utah Press, 1959), pp. 46–57.

[2] R. B. Cattell and J. E. Drevdahl, "A Comparison of the Personality Profile (16 P.F.) of Eminent Researchers with that of Eminent Teachers and Administrators, and of the General Population," *British J. Psychol.,* XLVI (1955), pp. 248–261.

We know relatively little, as yet, about creative people and even less about what makes them creative. If it proves to be true that some or all of the qualities of creativity can be taught, this will become another goal in the society's processing of mentally superior children.

THE UNDERACHIEVERS

In the study of intellectually superior children, attention has been called to a substantial group whose educational performance falls below what might reasonably be expected from their performance on intelligence tests. These mentally superior underachievers are people with biological or environmental superiority who have not put their superiority to use in school. They may be regarded as products of an inadequate processing in the home, the community, or the school. This conclusion emerges from a number of recent studies of bright underachievers.

Thus, Terman and Oden, in their study of adults whom they had followed from childhood as gifted children,[3] compared the 150 men in their sample who had been most successful in their occupations with the 150 least successful men. As children, these men had all had IQ's of 135 or higher. The more successful group had had an average IQ of 155 in 1922, while the less successful had had an average of 150. However, there were considerable differences in other respects between the two groups. Ninety per cent of the more successful had been graduated from college, compared with 37 per cent of the less successful. Fifty per cent of the fathers of the more successful group were college graduates, compared with only 16 per cent of the fathers of the less successful. In occupation, 38 per cent of the fathers of the more successful were professional men, compared with 19 per cent of the fathers of the less successful.

Terman concludes, "Where all are so intelligent, it follows necessarily that differences in success must be due largely to non-intellectual factors"; and "Everything considered, there is nothing in which the (more successful and less successful) groups present a greater contrast than in drive to achieve and in all-round social adjustment. . . . At any rate, we have seen that intellect and achievement are far from perfectly correlated."

Most of the studies of underachievement have been made on boys rather than girls, because bright boys are underachievers in school much more frequently than girls are. The many studies have produced substantially similar results and point to underachievement as a form of personal and social maladjustment. In one or another of these studies, the following characteristics of underachieving able students appear:

[3] L. M. Terman and Melita Oden, *The Gifted Child Grows Up* (Stanford, Cal.: Stanford University Press, 1947).

1. They see themselves as inadequate persons.
2. They have lower aspirations than achievers.
3. They do not like school as well as achievers do.
4. They do not enjoy learning from books.
5. They have lower popularity and leadership status in the eyes of their age-mates.
6. They tend to come from homes that are broken or emotionally inadequate in other ways.
7. They tend to come from homes of low socio-economic status.
8. Their vocational goals are not as clearly defined as those of achievers.
9. Their study habits are not as good as those of achievers.
10. They have narrower interests than those of achievers.
11. They have poorer personal adjustment than that of achievers.

Haggard,[4] comparing high with low achieving high IQ children, found that the high achievers had better mental health. In particular, the high achievers in arithmetic, "had by far the best-developed and healthiest egos, both in relation to their own emotions and mental processes and in their greater maturity in dealing with the outside world of people and things." Haggard concluded, "Our findings indicate that the best way to produce clear thinking is to help children develop into anxiety-free, emotionally healthy individuals who are also trained to master a variety of intellectual tasks."

Much of the same conclusion is expressed by Gowan[5] after reviewing a number of studies of underachievement. He says, "To summarize, achievement is an indication that the individual has successfully transferred a large enough portion of his basic libidinal drives to areas of cultural accomplishment so that he derives a significant portion of his gratification from them."

Although the general proposition seems justified that high IQ underachievers are people with inadequate socialization and poor personal-social adjustment, there are two major exceptions to this generalization. One exception refers to a group of high IQ boys with a limited horizon. They are well-adjusted within a small world which does not require more than average school achievement and does not require a college education. Take Kenny, for example. With an IQ of 145, Kenny found school work easy and more or less coasted through his studies, doing enough work to get fairly good grades, but falling down somewhat in high school, where he graduated at about the middle of his class. Kenny's parents were earnest people, good church members, with little formal education. They did not read very much and had no intellectual interests. They were satisfied with

[4] E. A. Haggard, "Socialization, Personality, and Academic Achievement in Gifted Children," *School Rev.,* LXV (1957), pp. 388–414.

[5] J. C. Gowan, "Factors of Achievement in High School and College," *J. Counsel. Psychol.,* VII (1960), pp. 91–95.

Kenny's report cards and pleased that he was going further in school than they had gone. They were especially pleased with Kenny's interest in earning money. He always had several jobs waiting for him and showed great enterprise as a salesman. During his later years in high school, he worked in a shoe store where his employer was so pleased with his work that he offered Kenny a full-time job and a chance to buy into his business when he was graduated from high school. This seemed good to Kenny, and he is now getting along well as junior partner in the store.

The other exception refers to a rather large group of girls with high intelligence who achieve very well up to the end of high school, when their grades fall off and they show little or no interest in going to college. These girls either get married as soon as they finish high school or they take a job in an office or a shop for a few years until they marry. Girls do not generally show as underachievers because their school grades are pretty well maintained until the end of high school. But they would be called underachievers if underachievement were defined as failure to go as far in education as one's abilities would justify.

With this broad definition of underachievement, one can say that the gifted underachievers have not been effectively processed by the society for maximal or optimal educational achievement for one or more of the following reasons:

Inadequate home environment leaves them personally maladjusted and unable to use their intellectual ability.

Inadequate home environment limits their horizon and fails to stimulate them to use education for vocational achievement, although they are personally well adjusted.

Inadequate home environment fails to instill in them a deep drive or need for achievement.

School and home together fail to instill in them an intrinsic love of learning.

The social role of wife and mother is seen by some girls as more important than that of student; and the home, school, and community have caused them to see a conflict between marriage and a home, on the one hand, and continued educational achievement on the other.

INCREASING THE SUPPLY

Holding to our tentative assumption that production of mentally superior people is more a matter of social engineering than of discovery and exploitation of a rare natural resource, we may essay an answer to the question of how to increase the supply of mentally superior children who are well motivated to achieve in school and college.

First, it must be remembered that our culturally deprived families, both in the big cities and in isolated rural areas, have always in the past im-

proved themselves as producers of superior children when they had economic opportunity. The same process of improvement is evident today
among working class Negroes, Puerto Ricans, and white emigrants from
the rural South. It is to these groups that we may look for an increased
supply of able youngsters, and the rate of increase is likely to be considerably facilitated by increasing their degree of economic opportunity and en-
riching their cultural environment. This point is a central one for those
social policies related to our long-range needs for manpower and for school
programs aimed at the underprivileged and academically impoverished.
Within the schools, there is a grave need for greater attention to rewards
for achievement within these groups, for a keener recognition of developing
intellectual effort, and for a greater responsiveness to embryonic academic
motives.

Second, counseling and guidance services could usefully focus on increasing educational motivation among superior pupils. The well adjusted child
with limited horizons, like Kenny, represents a kind of national loss. If
education is concerned with the actualizing of individual potentialities, then
special attention to youngsters of this kind is more than warranted. A
sound argument can be made for the school counselor's devoting more of
his time to this sort of developmental enterprise than to the remediation of
"problem cases" and to the support of the pathological, the delinquent, and
the dull. Both kinds of service are desirable and necessary, of course; but
we may have overemphasized the guidance worker's obligation to the edu-
cationally handicapped to the serious neglect, both in training and in on-
the-job functionings of his potentialities for working productively with the
superior child with low academic motivation.

Third, studies of the unconscious drive for achievement, like those by
McClelland[6] and Rosen,[7] indicate that the early training of boys in the
home has a great deal to do with their motivation to use their mental ability
for school achievement. Closer collaboration between school and home,
especially with lower class parent groups, can be helpful here. Even more,
an explicit and articulate concern with the development of intellectual motivations in the earliest school years could possibly harvest a more widespread drive for academic achievement and a deeper channeling of intellectual capacities into school work and the kinds of goals that our schools
and colleges represent. It is not so much that boys lack a need to achieve,
but they often find little reward in harnessing their motives to the activities
of the conventional classroom or school.

Fourth, the demonstration that intellectually superior and "creative"

[6] D. C. McClelland, J. Atkinson, R. Clark, and E. Lowell, *The Achievement Motive* (New York: Appleton-Century-Crofts, 1953).

[7] B. C. Rosen and R. D'Andrade, "The Psycho-social Origins of Achievement
Motivation," *Sociometry*, XXII (1959), pp. 185–218.

abilities are not the same thing suggests that we could profitably expand our search for the gifted to include the "divergent thinker." More clarity and precision in our methods of identifying creative youngsters with above-average but not extremely high IQ's, and more imagination and effort in our attention to such children might yield a happy increment in the numbers of those able to think inventively about important problems. This approach requires, of course, that we reward the innovator, the person with new and deviant ways of dealing with the world; and while this requirement is one to which we all pay lip service, it is one that is likely to entail trouble and inconvenience if it is realistically met. That the trouble and inconvenience will be worth the result is highly probable, but the result hardly alters, although it may more than justify, the cost.

Finally, the most potent means of increasing the numbers of mentally superior children that lies at hand for teachers is to teach so that learning is made more attractive to children. This alone will cause children to increase their own mental abilities. For example, the experiment in Manhattanville Junior High School and the George Washington Senior High School in New York City is having this effect.[8] Boys and girls from culturally deprived families are getting an enriched program, combined with guidance and attempts to improve the home environment. This program has kept pupils in school longer, and there has been a measurable increase in IQ points for these children as they have progressed from the sixth to the ninth grades.

[8] Board of Education of the City of New York, "Demonstration Guidance Project: Junior High School 43 Manhattan and George Washington High School," *Third Annu. Progr. Rep.* (1958–59).

Creative and Academic Performance Among Talented Adolescents* [1,2]

JOHN L. HOLLAND

What are highly talented adolescents like? What do teachers think of them? What is their family background? In the following study based exclusively upon talented adolescents, ratings of scientific accomplishments, artistic achievements, and high school grades were correlated with 72 aptitude, personality, and family background variables. "The results suggest that creative performance at the high school level occurs more frequently among students who are independent, intellectual, expressive, asocial, consciously original, and who have high aspirations for future achievement. Students who are persevering, sociable, responsible, and whose parents hold somewhat authoritarian attitudes and values, are more frequently academic achievers." The findings also suggest that "the traditional predictors of scholastic aptitude are of little or no value for predicting creativity" among students of superior scholastic aptitude.

The need to understand the nature of academic achievement and creative behavior is pressing; such knowledge is vital for the proper development of educational practice, the administration of scholarship and fellowship programs, and the fostering of talented behavior generally. Unless attempts to encourage the development of creative talent rest on valid assumptions about the nature of academic and creative behavior, such efforts will have little useful influence.

The present study is one of several investigations planned to explore the

[1] This study was partially supported by research grants from the National Science Foundation and the Old Dominion Foundation.

[2] I am indebted to the following staff members for their skillful assistance in all phases of this project: Virginia Chalmers, Laura Kent, Donald Thistlethwaite, and Elizabeth van Laer.

* From the *Journal of Educational Psychology*, LII (1961), pp. 136–147. Reprinted by permission of the author and the American Psychological Association.

511

nature of academic achievement and creative behavior in adolescents and young adults.[3] The earlier studies were concerned primarily with academic performance. This study tests a large number of hypotheses about variables which are often assumed to be associated with both academic and creative achievement—aptitude scores, self and teacher ratings, originality measures, parental attitudes and values, vocational interests and aspirations, and background information. Most of the variables were used to test a limited number of hypotheses; a few were included for exploratory purposes. The hypotheses about the nature of the academic achiever were derived in part from an extensive literature which suggests that the student who gets good grades in high school is bright, persistent, conforming, self-controlled, responsible, serious, and rated high by his teachers.[4] Drews and Teahan[5] indicate that the academic achiever tends to have a somewhat authoritarian mother. Several recent reports[6] imply also that good grades in high school and college may be either unrelated to, or negatively correlated with, potential for creative performance. Taken together, these findings have somewhat consistent implications about the academic achiever and his parents' attitudes and values. The hypotheses derived from the literature and tested here are summarized as follows.

1. Outstanding academic achievement—High School Rank (HSR)—will be positively associated with high scores on the Scholastic Aptitude Test (Math and Verbal factors) (SAT-M and SAT-V), and on the Mastery, Deferred Gratification, and Control scales; with high Self-Ratings of Drive to Achieve and Perseverance; with high Teacher Ratings of Maturity, Popularity, and Social Leadership; with Fathers' Values of Good Student; and with mothers' authoritarian attitudes as measured by the Parental Attitude Research Inventory (PARI).

2. Outstanding academic achievement will be associated with low scores on measures of creativity and originality (Differential Reaction Schedule,

[3] J. L. Holland, "The Prediction of College Grades from the California Psychological Inventory and the Scholastic Aptitude Test," *J. Educ. Psychol.*, L (1959), pp. 135–142; J. L. Holland, "Some Limitations of Teacher Ratings as Predictors of Creativity," *J. Educ. Psychol.*, L (1959), pp. 219–223; J. L. Holland, "The Prediction of College Grades from Personality and Aptitude Variables," *J. Educ. Psychol.*, LI (1960), pp. 245–254.

[4] Adma D'Heurle, Jeanne C. Mellinger, and E. A. Haggard, "Personality, Intellectual, and Achievement Patterns in Gifted Children," *Psychol. Monogr.*, LXXIII, Whole No. 483 (1959); H. G. Gough, "What Determines the Academic Achievement of High School Students?" *J. Educ. Res.*, XLVI (1953), pp. 321–331; Holland, "The Prediction of College Grades from the California Psychological Inventory and the Scholastic Aptitude Test," *op. cit.*; Holland, "Some Limitations of Teacher Ratings as Predictors of Creativity," *op. cit.*

[5] Elizabeth M. Drews and J. E. Teahan, "Parental Attitudes and Academic Achievement," *J. Clin. Psychol.*, XIII (1957), pp. 328–332.

[6] Holland, "The Prediction of College Grades from Personality and Aptitude Variables," *op. cit.*; D. W. MacKinnon, "What Do We Mean by Talent and How Do We Test for It?" *The Search for Talent: College Admissions 7* (New York: College Entrance Examination Board, 1959).

Complexity-Simplicity, Independence of Judgment, and Barron Originality scales) and with low self-evaluations.

The hypotheses about the nature of the creative student were drawn principally from the work of Barron,[7] Gough,[8] and MacKinnon,[9] which depicts the creative person as independent, complex in outlook, curious, self-assured, intellectual, interested in science and art, and generally effective. This characterization implies also a more permissive parental background which encourages independence and the exploration of self and environment. The hypotheses derived from this literature are summarized as follows:

1. Creative performance (winning public competitions which demand creativity) will be positively associated with high scores on measures of creativity and originality (Differential Reaction Schedule, Complexity-Simplicity, Independence of Judgment, and Barron Originality scales), and on the Initiative and Self-Assurance scales; with high Self-Ratings of Originality, Independence, and Perseverance; with Fathers' Values of Curious and Independent; and with mothers' nonauthoritarian attitudes.

2. Creative performance will have no correlation, or negative correlations, with good high school grades; with high Self-Ratings of Popularity; with high Teacher Ratings; and with Fathers' Values of Dependable, Good Student, Happy and Well-Adjusted, and Popular.

METHOD

Student and Parent Sample

The student and parent samples were obtained from a one-sixth random sample of National Merit Finalists (approximately 9,868 high-scoring students by state from an initial pool of 478,991 high school juniors), who were polled and tested by mail. An 84% return was obtained, but incomplete information reduced the sample to 59%, 649 boys and 345 girls, and their parents. The average aptitude level of these samples on the SAT were: For boys, SAT-V and SAT-M, 658.4 and 697.9 with SDs of 56.8 and 62.2, respectively. For girls, the SAT-V and SAT-M means are 659.2 and 635.4 with SDs of 60.6 and 70.3

Academic and Creative Performance

The criterion of academic performance was high school grades (HSR) during the first 3 years of high school. The criteria of creative performance were derived from a checklist of accomplishments assumed to require creative or

---

[7] F. Barron, "Complexity-simplicity as a Personality Dimension," *J. Abnorm. Soc. Psychol.,* XLVIII (1953), pp. 163–172; F. Barron, "Some Correlates of Independence of Judgment," *J. Pers.,* XXI (1953), pp. 287–297.

[8] H. G. Gough, "Imagination: Undeveloped Resource," paper read at Proceedings of the first conference on research and development in personnel management, Los Angeles, Calif., 1957.

[9] MacKinnon, *op. cit.*

original behavior. Creative performance is defined as a performance which is accorded public recognition through awards, prizes, or publication, and which may therefore be assumed to have exceptional cultural value. Because of the difficulty in arriving at a generally acceptable definition of "creativity," these criteria should perhaps be regarded as either "notable scientific or artistic performance," although we will refer to the criterion as "creative" performance hereafter to enhance readability. With this definition as a guide, a list of 20 achievements at the high school level was derived by reviewing the secondary school achievements of Finalists from previous years. Items were divided by content into two scales: Creative Science (5 items) and Creative Arts (11 items). (Four of the original 20 items were omitted because they appeared to be inadequate signs of creative behavior.) The items on the two scales are shown below. Students were asked to check those which applied to them.

CREATIVE SCIENCE SCALE

1. Gave an original paper at a scientific meeting sponsored by a professional society.
2. Won a prize or award in a scientific talent search.
3. Constructed scientific apparatus on own initiative.
4. Invented a patentable device.
5. Had scientific paper published in a science journal.

Item 3 does not meet the criteria of "public recognition" and "unusualness," but in order to lengthen the scale, it was included as a low-level sign of creative performance. Similarly, Item 4 depends on the student's judgment, and may or may not be an accomplishment which has received public recognition.

CREATIVE ARTS SCALE

1. Won one or more speech contests.
2. Had poems, stories, or articles published in a *public* newspaper or magazine (not school paper) or in a state or national high school anthology.
3. Won a prize or award in an art competition (sculpture, ceramics, painting, etc.).
4. Received the highest rating in a state music contest.
5. Received one of the highest ratings in a national music contest.
6. Composed music which has been given at least one public performance.
7. Arranged music for public performance.
8. Had minor roles in plays (not high school or church-sponsored).
9. Had leads in high school or church-sponsored plays.
10. Won literary award or prize for creative writing.
11. Had cartoon published in public newspaper or magazine, etc. (not high school paper).

For boys, the estimated reliabilities (Kuder-Richardson Formula 20) of the Arts and Science scales, respectively, are .36 and .55. For girls, the reliabilities are .38 and .37. These low reliabilities may be attributed to the brevity of the scales; they limit the level of correlation between the predictors and these criteria. The Arts and Science scales correlate with one another .15 and .09 for boys and girls, respectively.

Predictors

Students and parents were sent the following inventories and scales. Students filled out:

1. The Gough[10] Differential Reaction Schedule (DRS), an inventory which was designed to predict originality and which contains the following scales: Intellectual Competence, Inquiringness, Cognitive Flexibility, Esthetic Sensitivity, Sense of Destiny, Total Score (sum of all scores), and Potential Success (PIV), an index of general drive and ambition derived from a variety of Institute of Personality Assessment and Research (IPAR) studies of achievement and personal effectiveness.

2. The Complexity-Simplicity, Independence of Judgment, and Originality scales from Barron's[11] Inventory of Personal Philosophy. Only 54 of the 150 items in the Originality scale were used. The Complexity-Simplicity scale consists of items from the original 900-item IPAR inventory, selected for their significant correlations with scores on the Barron-Welsh Art Scale in five different samples, four groups of college students and one of military officers. The successive sample method was used for item selection; on cross-validation the final scale correlated .7 with the Figure Preference scale. The Originality scale was developed out of an MMPI-CPI pool by correlating each item with a composite score on four measures of originality (Guilford's Unusual Uses, Consequences, and Plot Titles; and the IPAR Word Rearrangement test) in a sample of 343 military officers. It was cross-validated by correlating it with a composite of the three Guilford tests in a sample of 150 undergraduates at the University of California.[12]

3. The Mastery scale, an 18-item scale derived from three items on Strodtbeck's Value Scale.[13]

4. The Deferred Gratification scale, formerly called the Play scale, from the National Merit Student Survey.[14]

[10] H. G. Gough, Researchers' Summary for the Differential Reaction Schedule (Univer. Calif., 1957). (Ditto.)

[11] F. Barron, *Inventory of Personal Philosophy* (Institute of Personality Assessment and Research, Berkeley, Calif.: University California Press, 1952).

[12] Frank Barron, personal communication, June 1960.

[13] F. L. Strodtbeck, "Family Interaction, Values, and Achievement," *Talent and Society*, eds. D. C. McClelland, A. L. Baldwin, U. Bronfenbrenner, and F. L. Strodtbeck (New York: Van Nostrand, 1958), Chap. 4.

[14] Holland, "The Prediction of College Grades from Personality and Aptitude Variables," *op. cit.*

5. The Vocational Preference Inventory (VPI), a short revision of the Holland Vocational Preference Inventory.[15]

6. The Ghiselli Self-Description Inventory. Since the correlations between weighted and unweighted scale scores for the Initiative, Self-Assurance, and Occupational Level scales ranged from .89 to .96, the items of these scales were scored with unit weights rather than being weighted differentially.

7. Self-ratings on a four-point scale and a Self-Evaluation score based on the number of times a student rates himself above average on 20 traits.

8. The Creative Activities scale (CAS), a list of hobbies and activities assumed to demand original behavior. Teacher Ratings of Citizenship, Popularity, and Social Leadership were also available for each student, as well as SAT scores, level of degree sought, Birth Order, and a Breadth of Interest score based on the number of activities and interests checked from a list of 47 items.

Mothers filled out the PARI,[16] and 16 of the 23 five-item scales were used. Fathers gave information on family background and ranked nine goals and traits in the order in which they considered them valuable for their children to possess.

RESULTS

Correlational Analysis.   The 75 predictors and criteria were intercorrelated (product-moment) and the complete 75 × 75 matrices for boys and girls, along with the means and standard deviations, have been deposited with the ADI.[17] Tables 1 and 2 show only the correlations between the three criteria of academic and creative performance and the 72 predictive variables. The influence of intelligence has been partialed out, using the SAT-M score as an estimate of intelligence for all three criteria, since the math score has higher correlations with the three criteria than does the verbal score. Generally, SAT-M has low correlations with the predictors. The largest absolute difference between corrected and uncorrected r's was only .05.

For boys, a review of the correlations at the 1% level reveals that the three kinds of performance (scientific, artistic, and academic) are associated with somewhat different variables, generally in expected directions.

15 J. L. Holland, "A Personality Inventory Employing Occupational Titles," *J. Appl. Psychol.,* XLII (1958), pp. 336–342.

16 E. S. Schaefer and R. Q. Bell, "Development of a Parental Attitude Research Instrument," *Child Development,* XXIX (1958), pp. 339–361.

17 The following tables have been deposited with the American Documentation Institute: Tables A and B, Correlational matrices for boys and girls; Tables C and D, Means and standard deviations for boys and girls on 75 variables; and Tables E and F, Daydreams about future occupations for students who are high and low in academic and creative performance. Order Document No. 6611 from ADI Auxiliary Publications Project, Photoduplication Service, Library of Congress; Washington 25, D.C., remitting in advance $1.75 for microfilm or $2.50 for photocopies. Make checks payable to: Chief, Photoduplication Service, Library of Congress.

The boy with a high score on the Creative Science Scale also has many artistic achievements (3) and Creative Activities (8), plans to get an advanced degree (71), is a first-born or an only child (74), and has high scores on the Independence of Judgment (17), Mastery (19), Deferred Gratification (20), Initiative (23), Physical Activity (28), and Intellectuality (29) scales and low scores on the Responsibility (30) and Status (36) scales. He rates himself high on Originality (37), Independence (40), and Perseverance (42). Fathers of boys high on scientific performance regard curiosity (48) as a valuable trait for their sons to have; mothers of these boys tend to be agreeable (supposedly comfortable in their role as mothers) rather than irritable (59).

The boy with a high score on the Creative Arts Scale engages in many Creative Activities (8), plans to get an advanced degree (71), and has high scores on the Esthetic Sensitivity (12), Sense of Destiny (13), DRS (Total Score) (14), Breadth of Interest (21), Self-Evaluation (22), Self-Assurance (24), Occupational Level (25), Response Bias (Acquiescence) (26), Responsibility (30), Verbal Activity (32), Emotionality (33), Control (34), and Status (36) scales, and low scores on SAT-M (5). He rates himself high on Originality (37), Drive to Achieve (39), Independence (40), Self-Confidence (41), and Perseverance (42). Mothers of these boys are slightly more accepting of the homemaking role than are mothers of students with low artistic performance (62).

The variables related to academic performance are somewhat different from those related to creative performance. Academic performance (HSR) is negatively correlated with high scores on the Complexity-Simplicity (16), Independence of Judgment (17), and Barron Originality (18) scales and positively correlated with high scores on the Mastery (19), Deferred Gratification (20), Self-Evaluation (22), Self-Assurance (24), Control (34), and Status (36) scales. Boys with high grades rate themselves high on Popularity (38), Drive to Achieve (39), Self-Confidence (41), and Perseverance (42). Their teachers rate them high on Citizenship (43), Popularity (44), and Social Leadership (45). Fathers of these students want their sons to be Good Students (50) and are less concerned with their being Independent and Self-Reliant (52). Mothers tend to be authoritarian (at the 1% level), Avoidance of Communication (65); at the 5% level, Seclusion of Mother (56), Martyrdom (57), Suppression of Aggression (61), and Acceleration of Development (70).

The findings for girls, shown in Table 2, are similar to those for boys. The girl with a high score on the Creative Science Scale tends to engage in many Creative Activities (8), plans to get an advanced degree (71), has low scores on the Intellectual Competence scale (9) and high scores on the Mastery (19), Breadth of Interest (21) scales. She rates herself high on

Table 1
Correlations between Three Criteria of Academic and Creative Performance and 72 Aptitude, Personality, and Background Variables for Boys
($N = 649$)

Variable	Creative Performance		High School Grades	Variable	Creative Performance		High School Grades
	Scientific	Artistic			Scientific	Artistic	
1. HSR	00	08	—	39. Drive to Achieve	08°	22†	28†
2. Scientific Performance	—	15	00	40. Independence	15†	20†	06
3. Artistic Performance	15†	—	08	41. Self-Confidence	10°	23†	13†
4. SAT-V	02	—09°	—04	42. Perseverance	11†	15†	27†
5. SAT-M	04	—19†	09°				
6. Humanities Comprehension	—01	03	02	Teacher Ratings			
7. Scientific Comprehension	06	02	04	43. Citizenship	00	09°	26†
8. Creative Activities (NMSS)	36†	37†	—03	44. Popularity	01	05	17†
				45. Social Leadership	00	10°	19†
Gough DRS							
9. Intellectual Competence	—03	02	—01	Father's Values and Goals			
10. Inquiringness	00	02	02	46. Defend Self	—01	00	—02
11. Cognitive Flexibility	02	01	—09°	47. Ambitious	06	00	05
12. Esthetic Sensitivity	01	12†	01	48. Curious	11†	—08°	—09°
13. Sense of Destiny	03	23†	—04	49. Dependable	—10°	—02	02
14. Total Score (Above 5)	03	15†	—03	50. Good Student	—02	06	16†
15. Potential Success (PIV)	01	04	01	51. Happy, Well-Adjusted	—02	01	—06
				52. Independent, Self-Reliant	—02	04	—12†
Originality-Personality				53. Popular	—01	01	09°
16. Complexity-Simplicity	07	07	—14†	54. Self-Controlled	—01	00	—06
17. Independence of Judgment	10°	03	—11†				
18. Barron Originality	07	08°	—12†	PARI			
19. Mastery	11†	10°	13†	55. Fostering Dependency	—01	—06	05
20. Deferred Gratification	11†	06	11†	56. Seclusion of Mother	01	—02	10°
21. Breadth of Interest	09°	23†	00	57. Martyrdom	03	—03	09°
22. Self-Evaluation	01	23†	24†	58. Strictness	—07	03	03
				59. Irritability	—11†	—05	—02
Ghiselli				60. Excluding Outside Influences	03	—06	06
23. Initiative	11†	07	—02	61. Suppression of Aggression	07	—04	08°
24. Self-Assurance	09°	12†	11†	62. Rejection of Home-making Role	—02	—11†	02
25. Occupational Level	01	11†	—07	63. Equalitarianism	—05	03	02
				64. Approval of Activity	00	—07	06
VPI				65. Avoidance of Communication	05	03	12†
26. Response Bias	—02	13†	05	66. Suppression of Sex	03	—04	05
27. Infrequency	—07	—01	03	67. Ascendency of Mother	—05	—09°	05
28. Physical Activity	18†	—04	02	68. Intrusiveness	10°	03	05
29. Intellectuality	23†	03	07	69. Comradeship and Sharing	—07	—02	06
30. Responsibility	—17†	20†	05	70. Acceleration of Development	07	—03	10°
31. Conformity	—07	01	06				
32. Verbal Activity	—10°	11†	00	Miscellaneous			
33. Emotionality	—05	31†	02	71. Degree (level) Sought	15†	13†	04
34. Control	—02	12†	15†	72. Father's Educational Level	05	05	—08°
35. Masculinity-Femininity	10°	—05	03	73. Mother's Educational Level	—02	03	—10°
36. Status	—18†	18†	12†	74. Birth Order (first born)	09°	—04	01
Self-Ratings				75. School Size	—02	—04	03
37. Originality	15†	27†	—01				
38. Popularity	—05	10°	12†				

° Significant at the .05 level.
† Significant at the .01 level.

Table 2
Correlations between Three Criteria of Academic and Creative Performance and 72 Aptitude, Personality, and Background Variables for Girls
$(N = 345)$

Variable	Creative Performance Scientific	Creative Performance Artistic	High School Grades
. High School Grades	00	—09	—
. Scientific Performance	—	09	—03
. Artistic Performance	09	—	—09
. SAT-V	07	01	08
. SAT-M	13°	—12°	24†
. Humanities Comprehension	03	05	07
. Scientific Comprehension	11°	—01	05
. Creative Activities (NMSS)	23†	36†	—19†
...ugh DRS			
. Intellectual Competence	—14†	—02	—01
. Inquiringness	00	02	—03
. Cognitive Flexibility	00	09	—12°
. Esthetic Sensitivity	06	06	—01
. Sense of Destiny	03	23†	—04
. Total Score (Above 5)	—01	14†	—08
. Potential Success (PIV)	—04	00	00
...iginality-Personality			
. Complexity-Simplicity	02	06	—14†
. Independence of Judgment	06	02	—11°
. Barron Originality	07	10	—05
. Mastery	19†	02	08
. Deferred Gratification	11°	03	14†
. Breadth of Interest	18†	24†	—09
. Self-Evaluation	08	19†	13°
...iselli			
. Initiative	—03	07	03
. Self-Assurance	03	00	15†
. Occupational Level	01	10	01
...PI			
. Response Bias	00	05	09
. Infrequency	—05	—06	06
. Physical Activity	08	—04	—03
. Intellectuality	11°	—07	—06
. Responsibility	02	06	06
. Conformity	—03	—07	02
. Verbal Activity	—06	06	11°
. Emotionality	—02	10	07
. Control	04	—01	14†
. Masculinity-Femininity	06	06	—02
. Status	—02	02	16†
...f-Ratings			
. Originality	13°	32†	—03
. Popularity	—01	10	04

Variable	Creative Performance Scientific	Creative Performance Artistic	High School Grades
39. Drive to Achieve	15†	13°	18†
40. Independence	07	12°	—04
41. Self-Confidence	05	11°	12°
42. Perseverance	13°	13°	22†
Teacher Ratings			
43. Citizenship	05	—04	30†
44. Popularity	—02	—04	23†
45. Social Leadership	01	04	23†
Father's Values and Goals			
46. Defend Self	08	00	00
47. Ambitious	13°	05	04
48. Curious	06	03	—16†
49. Dependable	—15†	—02	16†
50. Good Student	11°	08	—01
51. Happy, Well-Adjusted	—13°	00	—02
52. Independent, Self-Reliant	00	—09	—01
53. Popular	—11°	—04	00
54. Self-Controlled	—05	—01	02
PARI			
55. Fostering Dependency	—02	—10	04
56. Seclusion of Mother	—03	02	15†
57. Martyrdom	—06	—05	08
58. Strictness	03	—01	07
59. Irritability	—08	—07	03
60. Exluding Outside Influences	—01	—10	11°
61. Suppression of Aggression	—06	—06	16†
62. Rejection of Homemaking Role	—06	—05	06
63. Equalitarianism	—04	—06	01
64. Approval of Activity	—01	—06	13°
65. Avoidance of Communication	00	—07	13°
66. Suppression of Sex	—05	—06	10
67. Ascendency of Mother	—01	—13°	05
68. Intrusiveness	—09	—03	05
69. Comradeship and Sharing	—08	—13°	00
70. Acceleration of Development	04	—01	15†
Miscellaneous			
71. Degree (level) Sought	19†	09	—03
72. Father's Educational Level	06	10	—08
73. Mother's Educational Level	01	13°	00
74. Birth Order (first born)	—08	—02	—01
75. School Size	—03	—05	02

° Significant at the .05 level.
† Significant at the .01 level.

519

Drive to Achieve (39). Her father ranks being Dependable (49) low on the list of goals and traits which he values for his children.

The girl with a high score on the Creative Arts Scale has high scores on the Creative Activities (8), Sense of Destiny (13), DRS (Total Score) (14), and Breadth of Interest (21) scales; has a positive Self-Evaluation (22), and rates herself high on Originality (37).

Academic performance is negatively correlated with high scores on the Creative Activities (8) and Complexity-Simplicity (16) scales and positively correlated with high scores on SAT-M (5) and the Deferred Gratification (20), Control (34), Status (36), and Self-Assurance (24) scales; with high Self-Ratings of Drive to Achieve (39) and Perseverance (42), and high Teacher Ratings of Citizenship (43), Popularity (44), and Social Leadership (45). Fathers of girls who get high grades value being Dependable (49) and do not value being Curious (48). Mothers of these girls are characterized by the PARI as "authoritarian"—Seclusion of Mother (56), Suppression of Aggression (61), Acceleration of Development (70).

The differences between creative and academic performance for the 72 variables replicate the trends found for boys. Academic performance appears to be the function of a personal syndrome characterized by perseverance, self-control, good behavior (good citizenship), and rigidity; this personality pattern is related to parental attitudes which seem conducive to such a pattern. Creative performance, on the other hand, seems to be the outcome of a conscious conception of being original, active participation in creative hobbies, and reinforcement by parents who possess values and attitudes which appear to be conducive to such performance.

Free Response Analysis. As a part of the assessment, students were asked about their vocational choice, the factors which influenced this choice, and their images and daydreams about their future occupations. Their free responses to the question, "What do you daydream about when you think of your future occupation?" were coded, using 10 coding categories developed from a sample of 200 students and tested for reliability on a sample of 160 students. Two raters, coding independently, obtained 75% agreement. Tables E and F* compare the responses of students high on creative performance with those of students low on creative performance, and of students high on academic performance with students low on academic performance.

According to Table E, boys with outstanding scientific performance daydream of "high achievement and creative accomplishment"; for this scoring category, the percentage difference between high and low science scores is significant at the .01 level. The same trend is observable in the Arts scale, though the percentage difference is not significant at the .05 level. The responses of students above the median on HSR do not differ significantly from those of students below the median.

* [Ed.] See footnote 17.

Girls with outstanding scientific achievement daydream more about work activities than about helping others ($p < .001$), whereas girls with low achievement are less concerned with work and more interested in helping others ($p < .05$). Again, the comparisons of girls high and low on academic achievement do not reveal significant differences.

These results, which support some of the correlational findings, imply that academic achievement involves somewhat different motives than creative performance; good grades in high school appear to be a function of socialization (citizenship and popularity) and perseverance, whereas creative performance is a function of conscious concern with high accomplishment, independence, and originality.

Getzel's Analysis. In a recent study of elementary school children, Torrance[18] following Getzel's classification of students as "high IQ" or "high creative," reports that the most intelligent students (top 20%) are not necessarily the most creative (top 20%): only about 30% of the students were in both groups.

The present study supports Torrance's findings. Eight tables were obtained for the present study by relating SAT-V and SAT-M to the scientific and artistic checklist scores for each sex. Within each table, distributions of creative performance scores were formed for approximately the top 20% of students on the SAT and the top 20% of students on creative performance. The percentages of overlap between these two contrasting student groups ranged from 1–6.5% of the total samples for the eight tables and deviate only slightly from an expected overlap of 4%. The larger deviations were in the direction expected from the correlations in Tables 1 and 2. These results are consistent with the negligible correlations between aptitude and outstanding creative achievement shown in Tables 1 and 2. We may conclude, then, that in a group of exceptionally bright students, intelligence has little or no relationship to creative performance in arts and science or to academic achievement.

These results may in part be a function of the regression of creativity on aptitude; students are selected initially for their high aptitude, and then the relationships between aptitude and creativity are studied within this narrow range of aptitude. These low relationships are, only in part, a function of the narrow range on aptitude, however. In Tables A and B of the ADI material SAT-V and SAT-M correlate as much as .64 and .57 with the Humanities and Scientific Comprehension scores of the National Merit Scholastic Scholarship Test (an achievement test given about one year before the SAT was administered). Even these correlations are probably underesti-

[18] E. P. Torrance, "Explorations in Creative Thinking in the Early School Years: A Progress Report," *The Third Univer. of Utah Research Conference on the Identification of Creative Scientific Talent* (Salt Lake City: University of Utah Press, 1959), pp. 58–71.

mates, due to the artificial restriction of range imposed on the NMSQT by its use as a selection device for this sample. The latter findings suggest that the SAT does discriminate efficiently and reliably within this narrow range of talent so that higher relationships between aptitude and creative as well as academic performance were possible.

DISCUSSION

The results of the present study are probably conservative. The distribution of scores for all criteria are at least moderately skewed and all scales have relatively low reliability; moreover, the range of scores on the remaining predictor variables, including background variables, is restricted. Therefore, the correlational results are probably underestimated. Since the students in the sample are all exceptionally talented, the correlations between originality measures and scholastic aptitude are reduced. Whether or not the observed relationships can be generalized to more representative student populations is questionable.

The correspondences between the present study and related studies are numerous. The originality scales developed by Barron (Independence of Judgment, Complexity-Simplicity, and Originality) and by Gough (DRS) have been frequently correlated with criteria of creative performance and our results are generally consistent with earlier reports.[19] Although the relationships obtained in this study are generally low, it is surprising that the Barron and Gough scales correlate at all, since they were constructed for adult samples and used different criteria of creative behavior.

The CAS has promising validity since it is the best single correlate of creative performance (r's range from .23–.37 for the CAS against the Arts and Science criteria for both sexes), and since its highest correlations are with a set of variables which lend support to this interpretation. For boys, the variables having the largest correlations with the CAS are, in descending order (.37–.15): Breadth of Interest, Self-Ratings of Originality and Independence, Emotionality, Self-Ratings of self-control, Total DRS Score, Complexity-Simplicity, level of degree sought, and Barron Originality. For girls, the largest correlates of the CAS are (.43– –.16): Breadth of Interest, Self-Ratings of Originality and Independence, Barron Originality, Complexity-Simplicity, Sense of Destiny, Self-Evaluation, and mother's education. The Fostering Dependency and Ascendency of Mother scales of the PARI correlate negatively with the CAS (–.16 and –.17, respectively).

The assumed validity of the CAS may be overestimated, since 4 or 5 of the 32 scale items involve activities which are preparatory to or associated

[19] Barron, "Complexity-Simplicity as a Personality Dimension," *op. cit.;* Barron, "Some Correlates of Independence of Judgment," *op. cit.;* Gough, *Researchers' Summary for the Differential Reaction Schedule, op. cit.*

with the accomplishments listed in the Creative Science and Arts Scales. The correlates of the CAS listed above imply some validity independent of the CAS's correlations with the performance scales, however.

The CAS was suggested by the Chorness and Nottelmann study[20] in which it was found that a set of extracurricular hobbies had significant correlations (.27–.45) with four or five Guilford factor composites when intelligence is partialed out. The item overlap, if any, between the Chorness creative hobbies and the CAS is not known.

The unexpected concurrent validity of the Self-Ratings is of special interest; of all the variables used, the Self-Ratings show most clearly that academic and creative performers conceive of themselves as different from other people. It is of interest too that high Self-Ratings of Perseverance and Self-Confidence—two of the three most discriminating traits for Terman's high and low achievers—are correlated here with both creative and academic performance.[21]

The findings for the Intellectuality and Emotionality scales of the VPI appear to replicate several studies[22] in which vocational interests in science and the arts were found to be associated with rated creative performance and high scores on tests of creative behavior. Since the Intellectuality scale has its highest significant correlations with the Self-Sufficiency, Schizothymia, and Masculinity scales of the 16 PF, the present results are consistent with the characterization of the creative person as independent, asocial, and masculine. Similarly, the Emotionality scale of the VPI is correlated most highly with femininity, instability, and introversion (16 PF).[23]

Generally, the results seem to support many other hypotheses about the nature of the creative person, but an attempt to relate all of the specific findings to the voluminous theorizing about creativity would be a gargantuan task. Briefly, those hypotheses which regard the creative person as independent, intellectual, expressive, asocial, consciously original, and open to experience gain some support.[24] The creative student not only has an identifiable personal disposition, but also he has relationships with teachers and parents which are in accordance with our expectations. His parents appear to be more permissive and more nurturant of his ideas and impulses so

[20] M. H. Chorness and D. N. Nottelmann, "The Prediction of Creativity among Air Force Civilian Employees," *USAF Personnel Train. Res. Cent. Res. Rep.* (1957), No. AFPTRC-TN57-36.

[21] L. M. Terman and Melita H. Oden, *Genetic Studies of Genius: IV. The Gifted Child Grows Up* (Stanford: Stanford University Press, 1947).

[22] MacKinnon, *op. cit.*

[23] J. L. Holland, "The Relation of the Vocational Preference Inventory to the Sixteen Personality Factor Questionnaire," *J. Appl. Psychol.*, XLIV (1960), pp. 291–296.

[24] C. W. Taylor (ed.), *The First, Second, and Third University of Utah Research Conferences on the Identification of Creative Scientific Talent* (Salt Lake City: University of Utah Press, 1955, 1957, 1959).

that communication with the self and the world is stimulated. It is not surprising, then, that such students appear to come in conflict with teachers who demand conforming, controlled, nonexploratory behavior.

Perhaps the most unequivocal finding in the present study is that, for samples of students of superior scholastic aptitude, creative performance is generally unrelated to scholastic achievement and scholastic aptitude. Since the traditional predictors of scholastic aptitude are of little or no value for predicting creativity, it seems clear that scholarship programs, colleges, and other agencies, if they are concerned primarily with rewarding students or selecting employees who have potential for creative performance, need to make a more active effort to devise predictors of creative potential. In fact, attempts to build better scholastic aptitude tests may even be detrimental, since they may lead to a greater dependence on instruments which are of limited value and thus delay unnecessarily the development of efficient predictors of creative performance.

The finding that teachers generally rate students with good grades higher than those with lower grades, together with the results of an earlier study[25] which indicates that teachers give lower ratings to students with more potential for creativity (as measured by the 16 PF) than to students with less potential, suggests that school personnel value the good grade-getter more than the creative student. Recently, Jex[26] found that school principals rate teachers with high scores on an ingenuity test lower than teachers with low test scores. Taken together, these results reinforce a common belief that some of our traditional education may be stultifying rather than nurturant and fructifying.

SUMMARY

The relationships between three criteria of academic and creative performance and 72 personal, demographic, and parental variables were studied in a sample of talented adolescents. The results suggest that creative performance at the high school level occurs more frequently among students who are independent, intellectual, expressive, asocial, consciously original, and who have high aspirations for future achievement. Students who are persevering, sociable, responsible, and whose parents hold somewhat authoritarian attitudes and values, are more frequently academic achievers. The negligible relationships found between academic aptitude and creative performance at a high aptitude level suggest that we need to use nonintellectual criteria in the selection of students for scholarships and fellowships.

[25] Holland, "Some Limitations of Teacher Ratings as Predictors of Creativity," op. cit.

[26] F. B. Jex and R. M. Merrill, "An Evaluation of the First Academic-year Institute, University of Utah, 1957–58," Univer. Utah Res. Monogr. Educ., I, No. 2 (1958).